You know when you think about writing a book, you think it is overwhelming. But, actually, you break it down into tiny little tasks any moron could do.
ANNIE DILLARD

I have rewritten—often several times—every word I have ever published. My pencils outlast their erasers.   VLADIMIR NABOKOV

Read, read, read. Read everything—trash, classics, good and bad, and see how they do it. Just like a carpenter who works as an apprentice and studies the master.   WILLIAM FAULKNER

A writer is a person for whom writing is more difficult than it is for other people.   THOMAS MANN

I am never as clear about any matter as when I have just finished writing about it.   JAMES VAN ALLEN

... Nothing is more satisfying than to write a good sentence. It is no fun to write lumpishly, dully, in prose the reader must plod through like wet sand. But it is a pleasure to achieve, if one can, a clear running prose that is simple yet full of surprises. This does not just happen. It requires skill, hard work, a good ear, and continued practice. ...   BARBARA TUCHMAN

The St. Martin's Guide to Writing

Short Second Edition

THE ST. MARTIN'S

RISE B. AXELROD

University of California, Riverside

CHARLES R. COOPER

University of California, San Diego

GUIDE TO WRITING

SHORT SECOND EDITION

ST. MARTIN'S PRESS
New York

Editor: Nancy Perry
Developmental Editor: Marilyn Moller
Project Editors: Anne McCoy, Denise Quirk
Production Supervisor: Chris Pearson
Text Design: Betty Binns Graphics/Betty Binns
Cover Design: Darby Downey

For information, write St. Martin's Press, Inc.
175 Fifth Avenue, New York, NY 10010
ISBN: 0-312-00284-X

ACKNOWLEDGMENTS

Agee, James. "The Treasure of the Sierra Madre" by James Agee reprinted by permission of Grosset & Dunlap from AGEE ON FILM, Vol. 1 by James Agee, copyright © 1958 by The James Agee Trust, copyright renewed © 1986 by Teresa, Andrea, and John Agee.

Angelou, Maya. From I KNOW WHY THE CAGED BIRD SINGS by Maya Angelou. Copyright © 1969 by Maya Angelou. Reprinted by permission of Random House, Inc.

Asimov, Isaac. © 1986, The Los Angeles Times Syndicate. Reprinted by permission.

Baker, Russell. From GROWING UP by Russell Baker. Copyright © 1982 by Russell Baker. Reprinted by permission of Congdon & Weed, Inc.

Bly, Carol. "To Unteach Greed" from LETTERS FROM THE COUNTRY by Carol Bly. Copyright © 1977 by Carol Bly. Reprinted by permission of Harper & Row, Publishers, Inc.

Brooks, Cleanth, Jr. and Robert Penn Warren. Cleanth Brooks/Robert Penn Warren, UNDERSTANDING FICTION, 2/e, © 1959, pp. 189–191. Reprinted by permission of Prentice-Hall, Inc., Englewood Cliffs, New Jersey.

California State Department of Education excerpt. Reprinted, by permission, from the HANDBOOK FOR PLANNING AN EFFECTIVE LITERATURE PROGRAM, copyright 1987, California State Department of Education. The complete book is available for $3 from Publications Sales, California State Department of Education, P.O. Box 271, Sacramento, CA 95802-0271.

Dillard, Annie. Specified excerpts (approximately 500 words in toto) from TEACHING A STONE TO TALK: Expeditions and Encounters by Annie Dillard. Copyright © 1982 by Annie Dillard. Reprinted by permission of Harper & Row, Publishers, Inc.

Ehrlich, Gretel. From "Rules of the Game: Rodeo" in THE SOLACE OF OPEN SPACES by Gretel Ehrlich. Copyright © 1985 by Gretel Ehrlich. Reprinted by permission of Viking Penguin Inc.

Ellerbee, Linda. Reprinted by permission of The Putnam Publishing Group from "AND SO IT GOES" ADVENTURES IN TELEVISION by Linda Ellerbee. Copyright © 1986 by Linda Ellerbee.

Fuchs, Victor. Excerpted by permission of the publishers from HOW WE LIVE by Victor Fuchs, Cambridge, Mass.: Harvard University Press, Copyright © 1983 by The President and Fellows of Harvard College.

Goss, Kristin A. "Taking a Stand Against Sexism," from The Harvard Crimson, March 5, 1986. Reprinted by permission of The Harvard Crimson.

Gould, Stephen Jay. Excerpts reprinted from EVER SINCE DARWIN, REFLECTIONS IN NATURAL HISTORY, by Stephen Jay Gould, by permission of W. W. Norton & Company, Inc. Copyright © 1977 by Stephen Jay Gould. Copyright © 1973, 1974, 1975, 1976 by The American Museum of Natural History.

Greer, Jane. "Paradise Enow: A Midwestern Perspective." Reprinted with permission from the February 1987 Chronicles: A Magazine of American Culture. Copyright © by The Rockford Institute.

Hemingway, Ernest. Excerpted from DEATH IN THE AFTERNOON. Copyright 1932 Charles Scribner's Sons; copyright renewed © 1960 Ernest Hemingway. Reprinted with the permission of Charles Scribner's Sons, an imprint of Macmillan Publishing Company.

Acknowledgments and copyrights are continued at the back of the book on page 597, which constitutes an extension of the copyright page.

To the Instructor

When we first wrote the *St. Martin's Guide to Writing,* we tried to take the best that has been thought and said in the field of rhetoric and composition and turn it to practical use. We saw the *Guide* as continuing the classical tradition of treating rhetoric very seriously indeed, not just as a matter of producing correct prose but as one of thinking, reading, and writing intelligently. To the best insights from that tradition, we added what we believed to be the most promising developments in the "New Rhetoric."

We have been tremendously gratified by the enthusiastic reception that the first edition has received from instructors and students. For this second edition, we have enlarged coverage of some topics, but our basic goal remains unchanged: to help students discover, develop, and present their ideas. We aim to teach them to manage the writing process, to think critically and use evidence wisely. We seek to give them an understanding of rhetoric of many different situations. We hope to inspire them with the desire to discover ideas and influence readers and we want to acquaint them with the tools to write clearly and gracefully.

A comprehensive rhetoric with readings, the *St. Martin's Guide,* Short Second Edition, introduces students to the major forms of nonfiction writing: personal sketches, profiles, reports, position papers, proposals, evaluations, causal analyses, and literary interpretations. Part One provides several models of each kind of writing (both professional and student) along with detailed commentary and carefully sequenced guides to help students understand the constraints and possibilities of each kind of writing they attempt. The guides include specially designed invention activities as well as advice for drafting, critiquing a draft, revising, and editing. Purpose and audience are central issues in all these chapters. Each chapter ends with a section called "A Writer at Work," which shows one stage of the writing process from a student essay in that chapter.

Part Two looks at a wide range of essential writers' strategies: invention and revision; paragraphing and coherence; logic and reasoning; and the familiar modes of presenting information, like narrating, defining, and classifying. Examples and exercises are almost all taken from contemporary nonfiction, and many exercises deal with reading selections appearing in Part

One. This cross-referencing between Parts One and Two facilitates teaching writing strategies in the context of purpose and audience.

Part Three covers research strategies. These chapters discuss both field and library research and include thorough guidelines for using and documenting sources, with detailed examples of the two prominent documentation styles, those of the Modern Language Association and the American Psychological Association. The part concludes with a sample student research paper.

Part Four treats a special kind of academic writing: essay examinations. Here we show students how to analyze different kinds of exam questions and offer strategies for writing answers. The chapter is illustrated with actual questions from courses throughout the disciplines, plus two sample student essays.

Noteworthy features   The *St. Martin's Guide to Writing* has several features that distinguish it from other college rhetorics. Chief among these are the practical guides to writing, the particularization of invention, the integration of modes and aims, and the integration of reading and writing.

Practical Guides to Writing. We do not merely talk about the composing process; rather, we offer practical, flexible guides that will lead students through the entire process, from invention through revision and self-evaluation. Thus, this book is more than just a rhetoric that students will refer to occasionally. It is a guidebook that will help them to write. Commonsensical and easy to follow, these writing guides teach students to assess a rhetorical situation, identify the kinds of information they will need, ask probing questions and find answers, and organize their writing to achieve their purpose most effectively.

Particularization of Invention. Like most other current rhetorics, we offer a full catalogue of general invention heuristics. But because we recognize how hard it is for students to know when and how to use these tools, we have designed specific invention strategies for each writing guide in Part One. By particularizing invention, the *St. Martin's Guide* helps students discover the pertinent questions to ask in any writing situation. Moreover, we try to promote a certain recursiveness in the composing process by encouraging students to continue generating and testing their ideas as well as analyzing and synthesizing information at *all* stages of planning, drafting, and revising—to put off closure until they have explored the full possibilities of their topic.

Integration of Modes and Aims. The *St. Martin's Guide* treats the traditional modes of writing from two perspectives: as forms to be mastered, and as writing strategies to be used to achieve particular purposes. Unlike many current rhetorics, we do not distinguish writing by its modes but rather by its aims. Hence, while we focus on craft in our discussion of the modes in Part Two, we emphasize the integration of modes with aims through exercises analyzing how the modes are used strategically in the essays in Part One.

Systematic Integration of Reading and Writing. Because we see a close relationship between the abilities to read critically and to write intelligently, the *St. Martin's Guide* combines reading instruction with writing instruction. Each chapter in Part One introduces one kind of discourse, which students are led to consider both as readers and as writers. Readings are followed by questions that make students aware of how they as readers respond and at the same time help them understand the decisions writers make. Students are then challenged to apply these insights to their own writing as they imagine their prospective readers, set goals, and write and revise their drafts.

New to this edition As the acknowledgments further on indicate, we had the benefit of much helpful advice from instructors across the land who had used the first edition. They helped us to see what worked well and what needed improvement, and they provided many valuable suggestions for specific changes and additions.

First among the additions is much *greater coverage of argumentation.* To the four argument chapters in the first edition, we have added two new chapters. Chapter 6, on the position paper, introduces the basic concepts of arguing a claim. Chapter 19 teaches argumentation strategies—making claims, using evidence, refuting counterarguments—as well as avoiding logical fallacies.

Chapter 11 provides a catalogue of invention strategies (found in Chapter 18 in the first edition) and a new, *specially designed plan for revising.* The plan presents a three-part process of rereading, re-envisioning, and rewriting, to help students gain critical distance, use the comments of other readers, clarify their purpose, and understand the needs and expectations of their readers.

Each of the Part One chapters now includes a new section on the purpose and audience common to that type of writing. In addition, the commentaries and questions following each reading directly address purpose and audience, to help students understand the way they affect the writer's decisions about the selection, organization, and presentation of information.

We have tried also to show *clearer connections between Parts One and Two.* The first edition had many cross-references from Part Two to Part One, but few in the reverse. To help instructors bring material from Part Two into discussion of the readings in Part One, we have tried to strengthen the connections between the parts. Commentaries following the readings in Part One now introduce the major concepts in Part Two, and discussion of the basic features for each type of writing in Part One includes extensive cross-referencing to relevant Part Two chapters.

Also new to this edition is *advice on computer word processing*. Although student writing, it can help students manage the process, and, therefore, make them more willing both to write and revise. In Chapter 1 we attempt to familiarize students with this technology and to show them how to use it as they would any other writing tool.

As a rhetoric and reader, the *St. Martin's Guide* may be used in courses with diverse emphases. Courses focusing on the writing process, for example, might rely most heavily on the writing guides and the "Writer at Work" sections of Part One, whereas writing workshops might be centered on the guides' invention activities and shared critical readings of student drafts. Courses in writing centered in readings, on the other hand, have thirty-five complete pieces and more than a hundred passages to consider. For courses requiring attention to usage, punctuation, and mechanics, the *St. Martin's Guide* is also available with a brief handbook included.

Detailed course plans for these and other courses, as well as commentary, teaching suggestions, and additional student essays, can be found in the Instructor's Resource Manual. Whatever approach is taken, we hope our book will provide an exciting and innovative course of study for your students.

ACKNOWLEDGMENTS

We owe a great deal to others. The history of rhetoric reaches back to Greece in the fifth century B.C., and among our predecessors are teachers and scholars—Aristotle, Quintilian, and Cicero in classical times; Erasmus from the early Renaissance; the eighteenth-century Scottsmen George Campbell and Hugh Blair; and Henry Day, the author of the most distinguished American rhetoric of the nineteenth century—who believed that rhetoric instruction was of great intellectual, social, and ethical importance. They considered rhetoric to be a study of thinking, speaking, and writing intelligently and responsibly. From this humanistic tradition comes our belief that students must learn to write well to realize their potential as thinkers, and as citizens.

And we owe a great deal to our contemporaries. Any list of debts will necessarily be incomplete, but we would be remiss in failing to acknowledge how much we have learned from Arthur Applebee, Walter Beale, James Berlin, Rexford Brown, Kenneth Burke, James Britton, Wallace Chafe, Francis Christensen, Robert Connors, Robert de Beaugrande, Peter Elbow, Jane Emig, Jeanne Fahnestock, Linda Flower, Toby Fulwiler, Sidney Greenbaum, Joseph Grimes, Anne Gere, M.A.K. Halliday, Ruqaiya Hasan, John Hayes,

George Hillocks, James Kinneavy, William Labov, Richard Larson, Richard Lloyd-Jones, Elaine Maimon, Ann Matsuhashi, John Mellon, James Moffett, Donald Murray, Lee Odell, Anthony Petrosky, Sir Randolph Quirk, Tristine Ranier, Richard Rieke, D. Gordon Rohman, Mike Rose, John Schultz, Marie Secor, Mina Shaughnessy, Malcolm Sillars, Frank Smith, William Strong, Barbara Tomlinson, Stephen Toulmin, Tuen van Dijk, John Warnock, Eliot Wigginton, Joseph Williams, Ross Winterowd, Richard Young, and Robert Zoellner.

We must also acknowledge immeasurable lessons learned from all the writers, professional and student alike, whose works we read in search of selections and examples for this text. The clarity and grace found in much current nonfiction prose have repeatedly astounded us. To all the writers represented in this text we owe a great debt—together, they have set a high standard indeed for all writers. Our aim has been not to contradict their practice by anything we recommend to students in this book.

With this second edition, our debt is even greater to the staff, instructors, and students in the Third College Writing Program at the University of California at San Diego. Since 1979 this book has been developed very gradually in courses there, with instructors and students helping us to discover what worked and what did not. We appreciate their candor and support. The first edition has served as the main text in this program, and we are indebted to all of the thirty or so instructors who have used it and provided helpful criticism and advice. Special and notable contributions have been made by James Degan, Kate Gardner, Keith Grant-Davie, Kristin Hawkinson, Karen Hollis, Du-Hyoung Kang, Gesa Kirsch, Mary Jane Lind, Michael A. Pemberton, Evelyn Torres, and Pamela Wright. Once again, we owe an enormous debt to Phyllis Campbell and Rebekah Kessab, who have continued to eliminate the sort of administrative fuss and bother that discourages teachers and writers. And we would like to express special thanks to our students, for generous and willing feedback.

Many instructors across the nation helped us to improve the book by responding to a questionnaire about the first edition. We appreciate the valuable comments and suggestions of Bert Barry, St. Louis Community College at Meramec; Donald Billiar, Union County College; Robert Branda, Rock Valley College; Jo A. Chern, University of Wisconsin at Green Bay; Bonnie Davis, St. Louis Community College at Meramec; Trish Geddes, Cyruss College; Matthew Green, St. Louis Community College at Meramec; Mary Helen Halloran, University of Wisconsin at Milwaukee; Arthur Lorentzen, South Seattle Community College; Anne McEvoy, Catonsville Community College; G. Douglas Meyers, University of Texas at El Paso; Mary Minock, University of Michigan; Lois Powers, Fullerton College; Leora Schermerhorn, Seminole Community College; Carole Schneebeck, Cyruss College; Lonnie L. Willis, Boise State University; and Ben Wilson, Greensboro College.

We would also like to thank our reviewers, whose expertise helped us to make this a better book. We could not have done without the generous and valuable contributions of Marvin Diogenes, San Diego State University; Jennifer Ginn, North Carolina State University at Greensboro; Cheryl Hofstetter-Towns, Colby Community College; Barry Kroll, Indiana University; Eileen Lundy, University of Texas at San Antonio; David Mair, University of Oklahoma; Mary McGann, University of Rhode Island; Mildred Parker, Texas Women's University; Nancy Sommers, Harvard University; Whitney Vanderwerff, Elon College, North Carolina; Joan Worley, University of California at Santa Barbara; and Richard Zbaracki, Iowa State University.

We want to express our most sincere appreciation to the staff at St. Martin's Press, whose patience and hard work have made this book possible. We are especially indebted to Nancy Perry, who never lost faith; to Marilyn Moller, who usually understood what we were trying to do better than we did ourselves; to Anne McCoy and Denise Quirk, for their editing skill; and particularly to Mark Gallaher, whose contributions enabled us to complete this second edition.

Finally, we wish to thank our families: Rise Axelrod's husband, Steven; son, Jeremiah; and her loving and beloved parents, Edna and Alexander Borenstein; and Charles Cooper's wife, Mary Anne; daughters, Susanna and Laura; and son, Vincent.

A Brief Contents

PART THREE

Research Strategies

PART FOUR

Writing under Pressure

Contents

6

22   The Research Paper: Using and Acknowledging Sources   550

PART FOUR

Writing Under Pressure

23   Essay Examinations   576

The St. Martin's Guide to Writing

Short Second Edition

Introduction

Why is writing important? Does it always take time and hard work? Can computer word processing make it any easier? Is good writing worth the effort? If you have just opened this book and are about to begin a writing course, you may be asking yourself questions like these. If so, read on. This book has some of the answers.

Writing makes a special contribution to the way people think. When we write, we compose meanings. We put together facts and ideas and make something new, whether in a letter home, in a college essay, or in a report at work. When we write, we create an intricate web of meaning in which sentences have special relationships to each other. Some sentences are general and some specific; some expand a point and others qualify it; some define and others illustrate. These sentences, moreover, are connected in a still larger set of relationships, with every sentence related in some way to every other. By controlling these complex relationships, writers forge new meanings.

Writing also contributes uniquely to the way we learn. When we take notes during lectures or as we read, writing enables us to sort out the information and to highlight what is important. Taking notes helps us to remember what we are learning and yields a written record that we can review later for tests or essays. Outlining or summarizing new information provides an overview of the subject and also fosters close analysis of it. Annotating as we read by underlining and making marginal comments involves us in conversation—even debate—with the author. Thus, writing makes us more effective learners and critical thinkers.

But writing makes another important contribution to learning. Because it is always a composing of new meaning, writing helps us to find and establish our own networks of information and ideas. It allows us to bring together and connect new and old ideas. Writing enables us to clarify and deepen our understanding of a new concept and to find ways to relate it to other ideas within a discipline. Thus, writing tests, clarifies, and extends understanding.

Writing does still more: it contributes to personal development. As we write we become more potent thinkers and active learners, and we come eventually to a better understanding of ourselves through the recording, clarifying, and organizing of our personal experiences and our innermost thoughts.

Besides contributing to the way we think and learn, writing helps us connect to others, to communicate. The impulse to write can be as urgent as the need to converse with someone sitting across the table in a restaurant or to respond to a provocative comment in a classroom discussion. Sometimes we want readers to know what we know; we want to share something new. Sometimes we want to influence our readers' decisions, actions, or beliefs. We may even want to irritate or outrage readers. Or we may want to amuse or flatter them. Writing allows us to overcome our isolation and to communicate in all of these ways.

Good writing makes a special contribution to success in college and on the job. Students who write confidently and well learn more and earn better grades, for a student's writing is often the only basis an instructor has for an evaluation. Your first job may not require you to write, but later advancement often depends on skill in writing letters, memos, reports, and proposals. The United States is now an "information" society, one in which the ability to organize and synthesize information and to write intelligently and effectively is even more important than it was in the past. The ability to write will continue to be a decisive factor in the careers of larger and larger numbers of people every year. But for many college students, writing is more of an obstacle than an opportunity. Because writing seems difficult and threatening, they approach it reluctantly, even with fear. Knowing *how* writing works, however, can dispel the mystery and reduce the threat.

HOW WRITING WORKS

What is the nature of the writing process? Research and published interviews with writers as well as our own experience as writers reveal a great deal about the process.

Perhaps the most important point to remember is this: writing is not a mystery. To be sure, writing is a complex process and, as such, contains elements of mystery and surprise. But writing is a skill that anyone can learn to manage. Greatness as a writer may be a dream that only a few of us will pursue, but we can all learn to write well enough to handle any writing situation we encounter in college or on the job.

Writing is a process of discovery. Writers rarely begin with a complete understanding of their subject. They gather facts and ideas, start writing, and let the writing lead them to understanding. They know they will be making significant discoveries as they write.

> I don't see writing as a communication of something already discovered, as "truths" already known. Rather, I see writing as a job of experiment. It's like any discovery job; you don't know what's going to happen until you try it.
> William Stafford

No matter that the process of writing can seem messy and meandering, writers learn to trust it. In fact, writers are likely to depend on the act of writing to lead them to new ideas and insights. Writing gives form to thought. When we write something down, we can examine it from one angle and then another, studying its many facets as we would a diamond. Many writers claim they write to discover what they think.

> I write entirely to find out what I'm thinking, what I'm looking at, what I see and what it means.   Joan Didion
> How do I know what I think until I see what I say.   E. M. Forster

Once started, the process of writing continues even when writers are away from their desks. Always alert for ideas, they keep journals and notebooks ready for new thoughts and discoveries. Consciously or unconsciously, they continue to work at their writing.

> I never quite know when I'm not writing.   James Thurber

Seasoned writers accept the fact that writing takes time and hard work.

> I believe in miracles in every area of life *except* writing. Experience has shown me that there are no miracles in writing. The only thing that produces good writing is hard work.   Isaac Bashevis Singer

The hard work in writing comes in thinking things out. Writers may have promising ideas, but until they have written them down and tried to develop them, they cannot know if their ideas make sense and are worthwhile.

> You have to work problems out for yourself on paper. Put the stuff down and read it—to see if it works.   Joyce Cary

The same thing applies to planning. Like the discovery of ideas, plans also need to be refined during the process of writing.

> You are always going back and forth between the outline and the writing, bringing them closer together, or just throwing out the outline and making a new one.   Annie Dillard

Sometimes the hardest part of writing is getting started, just writing that first sentence. It may be reassuring to know what agony this first sentence sometimes causes even highly acclaimed writers.

I suffer always from fear of putting down that first line. It is amazing the terrors, the magics, the prayers, the straightening shyness that assails one. John Steinbeck

Most writers know they will solve problems if they can just get started and keep on going. Consequently, they employ various strategies to keep the writing flowing, particularly during early drafting. Since almost all writers revise their first drafts, they need not worry about getting it right the first time. They know that agonizing indecision is unproductive.

There may be some reason to question the whole idea of fineness and care in writing. Maybe something can get into sloppy writing that would elude careful writing. I'm not terribly careful myself, actually. I write fairly rapidly if I get going. . . . In trying to treat words as chisel strokes, you run the risk of losing the quality of utterance, the rhythm of utterance, the happiness. John Updike

Experienced writers know that strong writing does not always emerge in a first draft. Writers are revisers. "Writing *is* rewriting," Donald Murray insists. Revising can be seen as an opportunity to gain an entirely new perspective on a topic. It can mean moving paragraphs around, rewriting whole sections, or adding substantial new material. It may even mean throwing out the whole draft and starting over.

What makes me happy is rewriting. . . . It's like cleaning house, getting rid of all the junk, getting things in the right order, tightening things up. Ellen Goodman

I have never thought of myself as a good writer. Anyone who wants reassurance of that should read one of my first drafts. But I'm one of the world's great revisers. James Michener

For most writers, frustration in the early period of drafting is natural. So they establish routines and rituals to make the process familiar and comfortable. They set a time to write and find a quiet place away from interruptions.

I prefer to get up very early in the morning and work. Katherine Anne Porter

The desk is in the room, near the bed, with a good light, [I write] midnight till dawn. . . . Jack Kerouac

In spite of the time it takes, the inevitable delays, and the hard work, writers persist because of the great personal fulfillment and pride that writing brings. Many writers write in order to earn a living, but it is not true that they live lives of unrelenting torment. They struggle, but they also celebrate, and they find great satisfaction in the process as well as the result of writing.

Writing for me is a very happy activity—I actually enjoy the time of writing more than publication day. Edward Hoagland

Well, it's a beautiful feeling, even if it's hard work.   Anne Sexton

There is much more to say about how writing works. Most important, writing is something you can master. You can learn about your own writing process and develop new skills to make the process easier to control. You can accept the fact that writing requires planning and rewriting, and give yourself the time you need to draft and revise your essays. You can expand your repertoire of writing strategies and learn what is expected of the particular kinds of writing you need to do. This book will help you to manage your writing process better.

ABOUT THIS BOOK

This book is divided into three major sections:

Part I, Chapters 2 through 10, will guide you in composing several important kinds of nonfiction prose: autobiographies, firsthand biographies, profiles, reports, position papers, proposals, evaluations, causal analyses, and literary interpretations. Each chapter invites you to read carefully the work of published writers and college students and then to write an essay of your own.

Parts II through IV, Chapters 11 through 23, illustrate writing, revising, and research strategies. They also provide guidelines for writing research papers and essay exams, and for using sources.

As you work on the essays in Part I, you will engage in a process of inventing, drafting, and revising. Each chapter in Part I is designed to support your efforts in all these stages of the writing process.

Invention and research The Guide to Writing in each essay chapter in Part I begins with invention activities designed to help you

☐ find a topic
☐ analyze your readers
☐ discover what you already know about the topic
☐ research it further
☐ develop your ideas

These activities involve you in the thinking, planning, problem solving, and writing required for a full exploration of your topic and a promising first draft. Invention—determining your purpose and audience, gathering information, searching your memory, generating ideas, making decisions—is the basic ongoing preoccupation of writers. Invention is necessary to produce any writing of any type or length. Writers cannot choose *whether* to invent. They can only decide *how* to invent. Systematic invention in writing can be especially productive if carried out intensely before you begin drafting.

The invention activities at the beginning of each Guide to Writing ask you to think and write about your topic in systematic ways. They may result in quite a bit of writing. The activities include exploratory writing, the making of lists and charts, the trying out of arguments and explanations, and the stating and clarifying of your purpose or thesis. You may choose to complete all the invention activities, or you may select only a few that seem especially appropriate to your topic. Even if you do all the activities, you will usually not need more than two hours to complete them. The easiest and most productive way to complete the invention activities is to do only one or two each day for several days, thus allowing your mind the longest possible time to do its work on your topic. Completing all the activities gives you the advantage of fully exploring your topic before you attempt a draft.

But there are other ways to use the invention activities. You might feel so confident about your topic and so certain about what you want to achieve that you will attempt a complete draft immediately. During or after the completion of the draft, you might become aware of problems, which the invention activities could help you solve. Even if you do not see problems in your first draft, reviewing the invention activities would help you see possibilities you have overlooked.

The invention activities may also be useful when you revise. As a result of your own evaluation of your draft or comments from your instructor or classmates, you may discover problems that must be solved. The invention activities will help you to solve the problems in your draft. They can help you make small changes or major reorganizations; they can even be useful for drafting entirely new sections.

The invention activities, then, may help you at several stages in the writing of an essay: during initial exploration, while drafting, and during revising. The special advantage of the invention activities in each essay assignment chapter is that they let you go right to work inventing solutions to the problems of a particular kind of writing. Whatever your topic may be, the activities will help ensure full, rich, focused invention.

Chapter 11: Invention and Revision provides a catalog of general invention strategies. Unlike the focused invention activities in the guides to writing, each strategy in the invention catalog may be used to generate many different kinds of writing. Because the catalog strategies are so adaptable, they are valuable tools to have in your repertoire and complement the more specialized invention activities offered in Chapters 2–10.

Planning and drafting

Once a period of intense invention is completed, you should review what you have learned about your topic and start to plan your essay. After thinking about your goals and making a tentative outline, you will be ready to draft. Drafting challenges you to put your ideas in order. Invention continues during drafting: You will make further discoveries about your topic as you work. Drafting does, however, require you to shift your focus from generating new ideas and gathering further information to forging new and meaningful relations among your ideas and information. The Guide to Writing in each chapter offers specific as well as general advice on drafting an essay.

Drafting brings all your information together into a readable essay. This draft is usually called a first draft—the initial effort to find out what you have to say but surely not the only draft you will need. Some call it a rough draft, indicating an essay that is not yet polished or smooth, while others call it a discovery draft, meaning that you are still trying to discover what you want to say and how to say it. It has even been called a zero draft, that is, a draft that does not count yet.

Although this first draft is rough, quick, and full of discoveries, it should be as complete as you can make it. Unless you are writing under the most extreme time pressure, with no chance to make any changes, you should expect to revise this draft, possibly changing it substantially, maybe even starting over with a different focus or new topic. As you begin your first draft, you should try to keep in mind a number of helpful and practical points, many of which have assisted professional writers as they begin drafting:

Choose the best time and place. You can write a draft any time and any place, as you probably already know. You can write in the bathtub or in a restaurant. You can add a sentence while waiting for the bus. Writing gets done under the most surprising conditions. However, drafting is likely to go smoothly if you choose a time and place ideally suited for sustained and thoughtful work. The experience of writers (reported mainly in interviews) suggests that you need a place where you can concentrate for a few hours without repeated interruptions. Writers usually find one place where they write best, and they return to that place whenever they have to write. Try to find such a place for yourself. On a college campus, you may discover the quietest corner of the quietest floor of the library. Or you and your roommate may work out a schedule of quiet times for writing. And—of equal importance—arrange to write at your own best time of day, when you are most relaxed, creative, and productive.

Have your tools at hand. If you are well supplied, you will not have to interrupt your drafting to search for an eraser or a piece of paper. If you draft by hand, have plenty of paper and pencils or pens within reach. Be generous in supplying yourself with tools. Have a big stack of paper. Have a dozen sharpened pencils, an eraser, and a good pencil sharpener close by. If you type, have plenty of typing paper and at least one extra ribbon. Later, for rearranging a draft, you will need scissors and tape (or paste or a stapler). For revising, you will also need a good college dictionary and a dictionary of synonyms.

The word processor is an increasingly common tool for writing. If you own or have access to one, be sure you have a backup disk. Keep a generous amount of paper on hand and an extra wheel and ribbon to ensure dark, readable print. Since you can see only about twenty lines at one time on the screen, you may want to print out parts of your draft so that you can easily reread what you have written before going on to write the next section.

Make revision easy. Write on only one side of the page. Leave wide margins. Write on every other line or triple-space your typing. Laying your draft out on the page this way invites changes, additions, cutting, and rearranging when you revise.

Set reasonable goals. Divide the tasks into manageable bits. Set yourself the goal of writing one section or paragraph at a time. A goal of completing an entire essay may be so intimidating that it keeps you from starting. Just aim for a small part of the essay at a time.

Lower your expectations. Be satisfied with less than perfect writing. Remember, you are working on a draft that you will revise. Approach the draft as an experiment or an exercise, and do not take it too seriously. Try things out. Follow digressions. You can always go back and cross out a sentence or a section. And do not be critical about your writing; save the criticism for later.

Do easy parts first. Do not agonize over the first sentence. Just write. Do not try to write a perfect first sentence or a perfect opening paragraph. If you have trouble with the introduction, write an anecdote or example or assertion first, if that seems easier. If you have a lot of information, start with the part you understand best. If you get stuck at a difficult spot, skip over it and go on to an easier part. Just getting started can be difficult, but doing the simple parts first may ease this difficulty. If you put off getting started, your work will be rushed and late. Your ideas will not grow and change, and you will thus shut off your chances for important new insights about your topic. By starting late, you will increase your fear of writing; but by starting early with an easy part, you will find writing easier and more enjoyable. You will also do your best work.

Guess at words, spelling, facts. If you cannot think of just the right word, or if you have forgotten an important fact, just keep on drafting. You can search out the fact or find the elusive word later. If you cannot remember how to spell a word, guess and keep going. Later, you can look it up in a dictionary. Inexperienced writers lose large amounts of time puzzling over a word or spelling or trying to recall a specific fact. Sometimes they become completely blocked.

Write quickly. If you have reasonable goals, have not set your expectations too high, and are doing the easy parts first, then you should be able to draft quickly. Say what you want to say and move on. Review your notes, make a plan, and then put your notes aside. You can always refer to them later if you need an exact quote or fact. Now and then, of course, you will want to reread what you have written, but do not reread obsessively. Return to drafting new material as soon as possible. Avoid editing or revising during this stage. You need not have everything exactly right in the draft. If you want to delete a phrase or sentence, draw a line through it rather than erasing, in case you want to use the phrase or sentence later. Add new material above the line or in the margins.

Take short breaks—and reward yourself! Drafting can be hard work, and you may need to take a break to refresh yourself. But be careful not to wander off for too long or you may lose momentum. Set small goals and reward yourself regularly. That makes it easier to stay at the task of drafting.

Reading someone else's draft critically

After you have finished drafting your essay, you may want to show it to someone else, to seek advice on how to improve it. Experienced writers very often seek advice from others. A business executive might show the draft of a report to a colleague, while a poet might read a poem-in-progress at a writers' workshop.

To evaluate another's draft, you need to read with a critical eye. You must be both positive and skeptical—positive in that you are trying to identify what is workable and promising in the draft, skeptical in that you are questioning every assumption and decision that has been made.

The Guide to Writing in each chapter in Part I includes a section on reading a draft with a critical eye, which will help you to discover the possibilities and shortcomings in a draft. These guides to critical reading focus on the special requirements of each kind of writing in Part I. Here is some general advice on reading any draft critically.

Make a record of your reading. While conversing with a writer about your impressions of a draft may be pleasurable and useful, you can be most helpful by putting your ideas on paper. When you write down your comments and suggestions—either on the draft or on another piece of paper— you leave a record that can be used later when the writer is ready to revise.

Read first for an overall impression. On first reading, do not be distracted by errors of spelling, punctuation, or word choice. Look at big issues. Look for clear focus, strong direction of movement, forcefulness of argument, novelty and quality of ideas. Then briefly explain to the writer what you think of the draft. What seems particularly good? What problems do you see? If the essay is meant to entertain, note what you found entertaining and why. If it is meant to persuade, indicate what was persuasive and what was not. Let the writer know which ideas need further development or whether something seems to be missing. The purpose of this first reading is to express your initial reaction. It need not be analytical or detailed. All you need to say is how the draft struck you: What you think it was trying to do and how well it did it. Write just a few sentences expressing your initial reaction.

Read again to analyze the draft. Whereas the initial reading considers the whole draft, the second reading focuses on the individual parts. This reading brings to bear what you know about the type of writing and what you already know about the subject. You may question, for example, the appropriateness of a particular argument or type of evidence. Or you may be able to think of a fact or example that contradicts the writer's conclusion.

In reading the draft at this level, you must shift your attention from one aspect of the essay to another. Consider how well the opening paragraphs introduce the essay and prepare the reader to understand and accept it. Attend to subtle shifts in tone as well as more obvious writing strategies. If there is narrative, notice whether it is complete, pointed, and well paced. If there is explanation, decide whether it is clear, organized, and comprehensive. If there is argument, indicate whether it is logical, well supported, and convincing.

As you analyze, you are evaluating as well as describing, but critical reading should not be thought of merely as an occasion for criticizing the draft. A good critical reader helps the writer see how each part works and how all the parts work together. By describing what you see, you help the writer see the draft more objectively, a perspective that is necessary for thoughtful revising.

Offer advice but do not rewrite. As a critical reader, you may be tempted to rewrite the draft—to change a word here, correct an error there, add your ideas everywhere. Resist the impulse. Your role is to read carefully, to point out what you think is or is not working, to make suggestions and ask questions. Leave revising to the writer.

In turn, the writer has a responsibility to listen to your comments but is under no obligation to do as you suggest. Then why go to all the trouble, you might ask. There are at least two reasons, and you can probably think of others. First, when you read someone else's writing critically, you learn more about writing—about the decisions writers make, how a thoughtful reader reads, and the constraints of particular kinds of writing. Second, you play an instrumental role in constructing a text. As a critical reader, you embody for the writer the abstraction called "audience." By sharing your reaction and analysis with the writer, you complete the circuit of communication.

Revising   Even productive invention and smooth drafting rarely result in the essay a writer has imagined. Experienced writers are not surprised or disappointed when this happens, however. They expect to revise a draft—unless an imminent deadline precludes revising. They know that revising will move them closer to the essay they really want to write. As they read their drafts thoughtfully and critically—and perhaps, as well, reflect on critical readings of their drafts from others (see the preceding section)—they see many opportunities for improvement. They may notice misspelled words or garbled sentences; most important, however, they discover ways to delete, move, rephrase, and add material in order to say what they want to say more clearly and thoughtfully.

Chapter 11: Invention and Revision offers a plan for revising that gives specific pointers on using the critical readings you have received in conjunction with your own appraisal of the draft to decide what changes to make. Some general advice on revising follows.

View the draft objectively. In order to know what to revise, you must read your draft objectively, to see what it actually says instead of what you intended it to say. If you have the time, put the draft aside for a day or two. When you read it again, outline or summarize it. Getting another reader to describe the draft can also help you to view it more objectively.

Reconsider your purpose and audience. Ask yourself what you are trying to accomplish with this essay. Does your purpose still seem appropriate for these particular readers? Decide how you could modify it to make the essay more effective. Consider each problem and possible solution in light of your overall writing strategy.

Revise in stages. Do not try to do everything at once. Begin by looking at the whole and then move to an analysis of the parts. Focus initially on identifying problems; consider possible solutions only after you have a general understanding of how the draft fails to achieve its purpose.

Look at big problems first. Identify major problems that keep the draft from achieving its purpose. Does the essay have a clear focus, a strong direction of movement, a consistent and appropriate tone? Is the thesis explicit enough? Is it supported as well as asserted? Are the ideas interesting and developed? Does the essay have all the features that readers will expect?

Focus next on clarity and coherence. Consider the beginning. How well does it prepare readers for the essay? Does it adequately forecast the essay's development and thesis? Look at each section of the essay in turn. Do the paragraphs proceed in a logical order? Are there appropriate transitions to help readers follow from one point to the next? Are generalizations firmly and explicitly connected to specific details, examples, or supporting evidence?

Save stylistic changes and grammatical corrections for last. Do not focus on word choice or sentence structure until you are generally satisfied with what you have written. Then go through the essay carefully considering your style and diction. Focus primarily on key terms to be sure they are appropriate and well defined.

Use a word processor if possible. As the last section of this chapter explains, word processors are very useful tools, particularly during revision. If you use a word processor, be sure to make a backup copy of the essay before you begin revising to ensure that you do not lose parts you want to keep. You may also find it useful to print out the draft so that you can see the complete essay first before you tinker with it on the word processor.

Editing   Once you have finished revising, you then want to edit carefully to make sure that every word, phrase, and sentence is clear and correct. Using language and punctuation correctly is an essential part of good writing. Errors will distract readers and lessen your credibility as a writer.

The essay assignment chapters are designed to encourage you to turn your attention to editing only *after* you have planned and worked out a revision. Too much editing too early in the writing process can limit, even block, invention and drafting. The writing you do for the predrafting invention exercises and the first draft itself should be quick and exploratory. Your main goal is to discover ways to put information together and to find out what you have to say. Worrying obsessively about spelling, punctuation, or precisely the right word at the beginning of the writing process would be the wrong use of your attention and energy.

This book can help you eliminate errors from your revised essays. The comprehensive Handbook in Part V provides the information you need to correct errors you or others find in your writing. You may want to try some of the brief exercises in the Handbook. If you are helping other students edit their work, you may also use the correction symbols printed on the inside back cover of this book. These are keyed to the section of the Handbook where you can learn how to correct particular errors. Your instructor may use these symbols when correcting your writing.

Learning from writing

The final activity in each chapter in Part I gives you an opportunity to reflect on what you learned from the process of writing the essay. You can reread everything you have written from beginning to end and reflect on discoveries you made and problems you solved. You can analyze changes you made when you revised the draft and explain how those changes strengthened the revision. You can decide what was hardest and what was easiest about this particular kind of writing. You can compare your process in writing this essay to the process you used in writing another kind of essay.

These and other reflections can lead you to a deeper understanding of how writing works and why it is important. They can be a valuable record of what you are learning in this course.

EXERCISE 1.1

Make a list of the uses you have made of writing *outside* school in the last four weeks. Then make a second list of the uses you have made of writing in school during the same period. Include everything from lists, notes, and letters to applications, essays, and poems. Include writing you were required to do and writing you chose to do.

What can you conclude about the recent uses you have made of writing? How does your writing outside of school differ from your writing in school? Do you feel the same about all the writing you do? Which do you prefer? Why? Summarize your conclusions.

EXERCISE 1.2

William Styron said that "writing is hell." How would you describe writing? Think of a metaphor (writing is _____) or a simile (writing is like _____) that best expresses your view of writing.

EXERCISE 1.3

Describe your own writing habits. How do you go about writing in the classroom, library, or study hall? What conditions make it easy or hard for you to write? How do you plan and organize? Do you write first drafts slowly or quickly? Do you revise on your own or only at the request of your teacher? What kind of revisions do you usually make?

Do you do things differently when you write at home? Where do you write at home? At what time of day or night? With music? TV? Food? With a pencil or at a typewriter? What is required to get you started? To sustain the writing until you finish?

Do you regularly involve anyone else in your writing? Do you discuss your ideas or show your drafts to friends or parents?

EXERCISE 1.4

Write a brief account of your strengths and weaknesses as a writer. What are your goals for this course? What improvements do you hope to make in your writing?

WRITING WITH A WORD PROCESSOR

A valuable new tool for writers is computer word processing. You need not be a computer whiz or even a good typist to use a word processor, nor do you necessarily have to spend days learning complicated procedures. You may not even have to spend much money, since computers are often available in college libraries or writing centers.

If you feel comfortable with the way you usually write, you may be reluctant to try something new. Now that you are in college, however, this might be an excellent time to change your writing habits. Your college instructors will surely assign more writing than you did in high school, and the papers will be longer and more complex. Also, college instructors usually require that papers be typed and that they be carefully proofread. Word processing offers a new technology that makes writing and revising easier.

Although word processing will not necessarily improve the quality of your writing or guarantee better grades, it may help you manage the writing process more efficiently and confidently. Students who use a word processor tend to write more words and stay at it longer. They are often more willing to try out ideas and experiment with different versions. They write and revise more freely because it is so easy to add and cut as well as move around whole sections of text. In other words, word processing makes the writing process more fluid and natural.

For those with little or no experience with word processing, the following section explains briefly some of the uses of a word processor. Writers have found many different ways of using word processors. Your own experience with one will indicate how you can best take advantage of this new tool.

Some writers use word processors primarily as typewriters. They plan, draft, and revise their essays with pencil and paper, using the word processor only to type and edit the final version. Even this minimal use of the word processor has advantages: typing is quicker than on a typewriter, and small corrections can be made without having to retype the page. For essays that are documented, there are word-processing programs that automatically footnote and compile a list of works cited.

Other writers draft their essays directly on the word processor. If you habitually write longhand, composing as you type might take some getting used to, but it will save time in the long run. In addition, many word-processing programs have notemaking and outlining accessories that enable you to gather and sort information on the computer. You can even take a lightweight laptop computer to the library to enter your notes and sources, thus simplifying the research as well as the writing process.

Word processors are probably most useful for revision. Students are often reluctant to revise their essays heavily because retyping the entire essay takes so much time. With a word processor, however, little retyping is needed.

Moreover, using a word processor allows you to try out different possibilities. You can easily add, delete, substitute, or move a word, phrase, sentence, passage, or multipage section. You can print out different versions of your essay, or if your program has a split-screen capacity, you can display two or more versions on the screen at once.

Many writers follow this general routine: They compose a rough draft on paper, read it and make changes, then type the revised draft into the computer. Next they print out the typed copy and reread it carefully, possibly getting their instructors or other students to read it critically also. Then when they go back to the computer, they can easily add new information, develop their ideas, cut unnecessary words, or rewrite to clarify a point as the need arises. In fact, the mechanics of revising an essay substantially by adding entire new sections or moving around large blocks of text are easy and fun with this tool.

As useful as computers may be, however, it is important to remember that they cannot do the work for us. They can neither compose nor make decisions about revising and editing, although they certainly can make the work easier for us. If you do not have a computer or have access to one, do not feel the least disadvantaged in using this text or in succeeding in this course. No matter what the technology—the quill pen or the computer word processor—writing will always remain essentially the same, an effort to discover what you want to say by trying to say it.

PART ONE

Writing Activities

Remembering Events

☐ A scientist writes a book about a discovery she and several colleagues made, one that revolutionized scientific knowledge in her field. In the chapter describing how the discovery was made, she tells the dramatic story of the race between her research team and a rival group at another university. Her team had nearly solved the problem when they heard a rumor that the other researchers had made a breakthrough. She confesses that she actually broke down and cried, imagining the Nobel Prize being awarded to her rivals. The rumor turned out to be false, and her team did indeed get credit for the discovery. She admits how jealous and frustrated she felt, commenting with self-irony on her feelings. Scientists, she concludes, are only human. They may strive for objectivity and disinterestedness but can never really escape their own egotism.

☐ In her autobiography, a black writer recalls her high school graduation from an all-black school in rural Arkansas in 1940. She writes about how very proud she felt until a white superintendent of schools made a condescending and insulting speech. Describing his speech and the self-hatred it inspired in her, she remembers thinking that she alone was suffering until she heard the restrained applause and recognized the proud defiance in everyone's eyes. Thus the incident, in many ways so grim, actually renewed her sense of racial pride.

☐ Asked to recall a significant early childhood memory for a psychology class, a student writes about a fishing trip he took when he was nine. He reflects that the trip was significant because it was the first he ever took alone with his father and that it heralded a new stage in their relationship. He remembers wanting to go fishing but being afraid that he would do something wrong like getting seasick or losing the rod and disappointing his dad. He relates how they awoke before dawn and drove to the boat, how he soon found his sea legs and learned to bait the hook by himself. He focuses the essay on one particular incident—his attempt to land a big fish. He writes that his first impulse was to panic and try to hand the rod to his father, but his dad insisted that he could handle it. During a struggle that seemed to last an hour but probably took only ten minutes, his dad sat beside him, offering advice and encouragement. Afterward, his dad said how proud he was and took his picture with the fish, a five-pound bass.

☐ For her freshman English class, a student writes about some surprising events that occurred when she was preparing to send her high school newspaper to the printer. She and other staff writers had been working late for two consecutive nights. When the editor expressed irritation at how slowly she was working, she became furious with him. Then when she got home and tried to fall asleep, she had hallucinations that he was actually trying to harm her, that he was in her room approaching her bed. She writes about how astounded she was to realize later that she had hallucinated. In her essay she reflects on the way this experience gave her some understanding about uncontrollable mental events and how it increased her sympathy for other people who experience them.

□ A student in a sociology class studying friendship patterns writes a personal essay about the time in junior high when a girls' gang tried to enlist her. Though she didn't know any of the gang members, she guessed they wanted her because they heard she was taking karate lessons. She describes how frightened she was when they demanded to meet with her after school and then how relieved she felt after they decided she wasn't tough enough. As she writes about this incident, she is able to chuckle at her actions and feelings at the time.

As these writing situations illustrate, people write about events in their lives for different reasons: to tell of their experience, to discover something about themselves, to share the experience and discovery with their readers. The goal of autobiography is to present yourself, to recall an event that will disclose something significant about your life. The way you tell the story allows your readers to learn a little about you as a person and also enables you to learn something about yourself.

The event you choose can be any single experience in your past. It may be brief, lasting only a short time or long, extending over several days. Usually, you will describe the place where the event occurred, and often you will mention other people involved. But the focus will be on you and on what happened.

You may tell it seriously or humorously. But you must tell it honestly. When you write about an event from your past, you must be willing to delve into its significance and to discuss this significance in writing.

In writing about significant remembered events, you need not be limited to documenting the past. Your goal is not historical research; rather, it is to discover a way to present a past event you may only partially recall. The accuracy of your presentation comes from your effort to recreate the mood and to convey the importance of what happened. For you as a writer, this effort can lead to new insights about yourself and to a clarification of your own experience.

For your readers, autobiography leads to reflection on their own lives. We are all interested in other people's lives, in what they have learned from their experiences, in how they have made their way in the world. When you write well about events in your life, you will be providing readers this unusual pleasure and the chance to gain insight into human experience in general. As you read the selections that follow and later read the autobiographical essays of other students, you will experience the delight of reading and writing autobiography.

In writing about past events, you will also learn how to make your writing well paced, vivid, and purposeful. You will learn to select, organize, and narrate incidents to enhance the event's drama;

to describe details of the action, scene, and people to make your description vivid; to invest your language with feeling and to evaluate the event's significance to give your essay meaning.

Storytelling, as you will discover when you attempt to write explanatory and argumentative essays, is an essential strategy in both college and professional writing. Every type of nonfiction prose in this book relies to some extent on narrating. Firsthand biography (Chapter 3) frequently consists of a series of stories about a remembered person. The profile (Chapter 4) is usually organized narratively and like the report (Chapter 5) often relies on anecdotes to particularize and illustrate. The position paper, proposal, evaluation, causal analysis, and literary interpretation (Chapters 6–10) all depend upon various kinds of storytelling to support and develop a thesis. In short, the kind of writing you will practice in this chapter will not only be satisfying in and of itself, but will also prepare you for the other kinds of writing you will need to do in this course as well as later in college and on the job.

The following selections illustrate many possibilities for writing about remembered events. As you read them and consider the questions that follow each selection, you may get ideas for your own writing. You will also learn about the basic features of autobiographical writing and come to understand the various writing strategies autobiographers use to realize their purpose for their particular readers.

READINGS

The first selection comes from Russell Baker's Pulitzer Prize-winning autobiography, *Growing Up* (1982). A nationally syndicated columnist for the *New York Times,* Baker recounts a turning point in his life, an event that occurred toward the end of World War II. The narrative focuses on the test he had to pass to qualify as a Navy pilot. As you read, notice how Baker uses humor to present himself in this difficult situation.

SMOOTH AND EASY
RUSSELL BAKER

For the longest time . . . I flew and flew without ever being in control of any airplane. It was a constant struggle for power between the plane and me, and the plane usually won. I approached every flight like a tenderfoot sent to tame a wild horse. By the time I arrived at the Naval Air Station at Memphis, where Navy pilots took over the instruction, it was obvious my flying career would be soon ended. We flew open-cockpit biplanes—"Yellow Perils," the Navy called them—which forgave almost any mistake. Instructors sat in the front cockpit, students behind. But here the instructors did not ride the controls. These were courageous men. Many were back from the Pacific, and they put their destinies in my hands high over the Mississippi River and came back shaking their heads in sorrow.

"It's just like driving a car, Baker," a young ensign told me the day I nearly 2 killed him trying to sideslip into a farm field where he wanted to land and take a smoke. "You know how it is when you let in the clutch? Real smooth and easy."

I knew nothing about letting in the clutch, but didn't dare say so. "Right," 3 I said. "Smooth and easy."

I got as far as the acrobatic stage. Rolls, loops, Immelman turns. Clouds 4 spinning zanily beneath me, earth and river whirling above. An earnest young Marine pilot took me aside after a typical day of disaster in the sky. "Baker," he said, "it's just like handling a girl's breast. You've got to be gentle."

I didn't dare tell him I'd never handled a girl's breast, either.   5

The inevitable catastrophe came on my check flight at the end of the ac- 6 robatic stage. It was supposed to last an hour, but after twenty minutes in the sky the check pilot said, "All right, let's go in," and gave me a "down," which meant "unfit to fly." I was doomed. I knew it, my buddies knew it. The Navy would forgive a "down" only if you could fly two successful check flights back-to-back with different check pilots. If you couldn't you were out.

I hadn't a prayer of surviving. On Saturday, looking at Monday's flight sched- 7 ule, I saw that I was posted to fly the fatal reexamination with a grizzled pilot named T. L. Smith. It was like reading my own obituary. T. L. Smith was a celebrated perfectionist famous for washing out cadets for the slightest error in the air. His initials, T. L., were said to stand for "Total Loss," which was all anyone who had to fly for him could expect. Friends stopped by my bunk at the barracks to commiserate and tell me it wasn't so bad being kicked out of flying. I'd probably get soft desk duty in some nice Navy town where you could shack up a lot and sleep all day. Two of my best friends, wanting to cheer me up, took me to go into Memphis for a farewell weekend together. Well, it beat sitting on the base all weekend thinking about my Monday rendezvous with Total Loss. Why not a last binge for the condemned?

We took a room at the Peabody Hotel and bought three bottles of bourbon. 8 I'd tasted whiskey only two or three times before and didn't much like it; but now in my gloom it brought a comfort I'd never known. I wanted more of that comfort. My dream was dying. I would plumb the depths of vice in these final hours. The weekend quickly turned into an incoherent jumble of dreamlike episodes. Afterwards I vaguely remembered threatening to punch a fat man in a restaurant, but couldn't remember why. At some point I was among a gang of sailors in a hotel corridor, and I was telling them to stop spraying the hallway with a fire hose. At another I was sitting fully dressed on what seemed to be a piano bench in a hotel room—not at the Peabody—and a strange woman was smiling at me and taking off her brassiere.

This was startling, because no woman had ever taken her brassiere off in 9 front of me before. But where had she come from? What were we doing in this alien room? "I'll bet I know what you want," she said.

"What?" 10

"This," she said, and stepped out of her panties and stretched out flat on 11 her back on the bed. She beckoned. I stood up, then thought better of it and settled to the floor like a collapsing column of sand. I awoke hours later on the floor. She'd gone.

With the hangover I took back to the base Sunday night, I would have 12 welcomed instant execution at the hands of Total Loss Smith, but when I awoke Monday morning the physical agony was over. In its place had come an unnatural, disembodied sensation of great calm. The world was moving much more slowly than its normal pace. In this eerie state of relaxation nothing seemed to matter much, not the terrible Total Loss Smith, not even the end of my flying days.

When we met at the flight line, Total Loss looked just as grim as everybody 13 said he would. It was bitterly cold. We both wore heavy leather flight suits lined with wool, and his face looked tougher than the leather. He seemed old enough to be my father. Wrinkles creased around eyes that had never smiled. Lips as thin as a movie killer's. I introduced myself. His greeting was what I'd expected. "Let's get this over with," he said.

We walked down the flight line, parachutes bouncing against our rumps, 14 not a word said. In the plane—Total Loss in the front seat, me in the back—I connected the speaking tube which enabled him to talk to me but didn't allow me to speak back. Still not a word while I taxied out to the mat, ran through the cockpit checks, and finished by testing the magnetos. If he was trying to petrify me before we got started he was wasting his efforts. In this new state of peace I didn't give a damn whether he talked to me or not.

"Take me up to 5,000 feet and show me some rolls," he growled as I started 15 the takeoff.

The wheels were hardly off the mat before I experienced another eerie sen- 16 sation. It was a feeling of power. For the first time since first stepping into an airplane I felt in complete mastery of the thing. I'd noticed it on takeoff. It had been an excellent takeoff. Without thinking about it, I'd automatically corrected a slight swerve just before becoming airborne. Now as we climbed I was flooded with a sense of confidence. The hangover's residue of relaxation had freed me of the tensions that had always defeated me before. Before, the plane had had a will of its own; now the plane seemed to be part of me, an extension of my hands and feet, obedient to my slightest whim. I leveled it at exactly 5,000 feet and started a slow roll. First, a shallow dive to gain velocity, then push the stick slowly, firmly, all the way over against the thigh, simultaneously putting in hard rudder, and there we are, hanging upside down over the earth and now— keeping it rolling, don't let the nose drop—reverse the controls and feel it roll all the way through until—coming back to straight-and-level now—catch it, wings level with the horizon, and touch the throttle to maintain altitude precisely at 5,000 feet.

"Perfect," said Total Loss. "Do me another one." 17

It hadn't been a fluke. Somewhere between the weekend's bourbon and 18 my arrival at the flight line that morning, I had become a flyer. The second slow roll was as good as the first.

"Show me your snap rolls," Total Loss said. 19

I showed him snap rolls as fine as any instructor had ever shown me. 20

"All right, give me a loop and then a split-S and recover your altitude and show me an Immelman." 21

I looped him through a big graceful arc, leveled out and rolled into the split-S, came out of it climbing, hit the altitude dead on at 5,000 feet, and showed him an Immelman that Eddie Rickenbacker would have envied. 22

"What the hell did you do wrong on your check last week?" he asked. Since I couldn't answer, I shrugged so he could see me in his rearview mirror. 23

"Let me see you try a falling leaf," he said. 24

Even some instructors had trouble doing a falling leaf. The plane had to be brought precisely to its stalling point, then dropped in a series of sickening sideways skids, first to one side, then to the other, like a leaf falling in a breeze, by delicate simultaneous manipulations of stick, rudder pedals, and throttle. I seemed to have done falling leaves all my life. 25

"All right, this is a waste of my time," Total Loss growled. "Let's go in." 26

Back at the flight line, when I'd cut the ignition, he climbed out and tramped back toward the ready room while I waited to sign the plane in. When I got there he was standing at a distance talking to my regular instructor. His talk was being illustrated with hand movements, as pilots' conversations always were, hands executing little loops and rolls in the air. After he did the falling-leaf motion with his hands, he pointed a finger at my instructor's chest, said something I couldn't hear, and trudged off. My instructor, who had flown only with the pre-hangover Baker, was slackjawed when he approached me. 27

"Smith just said you gave him the best check flight he's ever had in his life," he said. "What the hell did you do to him up there?" 28

"I guess I just suddenly learned to fly," I said. I didn't mention the hangover. I didn't want him to know that bourbon was a better teacher than he was. After that I saw T. L. Smith coming and going frequently through the ready room and thought him the finest, most manly looking fellow in the entire corps of instructors, as well as the wisest. 29

Questions for analysis

1. Do you think this essay appeals equally to men and women? If you are a man, do you identify with Baker's wartime experience? If you are a woman, how do you react to the images of women?

2. A conventional motif of life stories—be they fictional or nonfictional—is the rite of passage. For men, this ritual often involves a test of physical prowess. How does Baker play along with—and against—this convention?

3. Paragraphs 1, 2, and 4 contain three images of flying, based on wild horses, cars, and women. How do these images foreshadow the final flight test? What lesson do they suggest the young Baker must learn? What ad-

vantages or disadvantages do you see in Baker's making this point indirectly through images rather than directly through commentary?

4. What role does Total Loss play in Baker's personal drama? Why do you think he compares Total Loss to his father and to a movie killer?

5. Why do you suppose Baker uses so much dialogue, rather than just summarizing what people said? Which bit of dialogue seems especially effective to you?

6. Baker does not tell us the consequences of his success. In fact, he never even mentions his feelings on realizing that he passed the test. Do you feel satisfied with this way of concluding the essay? If yes, why? If not, how could the ending be improved?

7. In what ways does Baker's story of his triumph as a student pilot cause you to reflect on your own experience? Would you be willing to write about a moment of triumph or failure in your own life? Think of a particular moment. In addition to telling your story, what would you want to reveal about yourself?

Commentary   This selection illustrates two important features of autobiographical writing. First, the remembered event is dramatized and made into a suspenseful story. As readers, we want to know how it will turn out for the young Baker. Will he somehow pass the flight check after all? Or, if he fails, will he be able to handle it? Second, as a piece of autobiography, the story includes personal disclosure and suggests how the event was significant in the writer's life. From our reading, we learn something about the writer and also may be led to reflect on significant events in our own lives.

The situation Baker writes about—failing an important test and then getting a chance to redeem himself—has all the elements of an exciting story. It has suspense: will he fail or succeed? And it has a climax: the final flight check. Baker shapes his story by structuring it dramatically around a central conflict—an encounter between himself and the notorious Total Loss. Furthermore, he gives this conflict a psychological dimension. Baker calls it a "struggle for power between the plane and me," but we might see it as an inner struggle for self-mastery or as a rite of manhood.

Good storytelling hinges on tension, the reader's concern for the main character and uncertainty about his future. If the tension slackens, if irrelevant details are introduced or the narrative action meanders pointlessly, readers lose interest. To instill tension in his narrative, Baker uses the narrating strategy called pacing. Pacing, as Chapter 13 explains, refers to the way in which time is portrayed in a narrative by speeding up or slowing down the action. Baker starts his story off with a fast pace, passing quickly over the initial, disastrous acrobatics test and presenting the weekend adventure in a few disjointed images. Only when he reaches the crucial flight check does he slow the pace and use specific narrative action—showing a person's movements or gestures—to provide a close-up of his actions and the plane's re-actions. By making us feel close to the action as if we could actually see Baker's hand pushing the stick against his thigh and feel the pressure of the plane hanging upside down, specific narrative action enhances the sense of immediacy and drama. The pace of the narrative slows, but the dramatic tension heightens. (All these elements of dramatic storytelling—suspense, climax, conflict, tension, and pacing—are discussed further in Chapter 13: Narrating.)

But there is more to writing about remembered events than telling a dramatic story. The narrative also must communicate the autobiographical significance of the experience. By recounting important events in their lives, autobiographers tell us something meaningful about themselves and give us insight into human experience in general. "Smooth and Easy" tells an initiation story. What is being tested is not merely Baker's ability to handle an airplane but also his sense of competence and masculinity.

In writing about this particular event, Baker risks personal disclosure. He reveals how inept and inexperienced he was, letting us see him fail and exposing himself to ridicule. He appears to take neither his failure nor his success seriously, however. He has both in perspective.

Perspective comes with emotional distance, which itself often comes with time. For some events, just a few days will do; for others, emotional distance may not come even after many years. Baker's distance from the event is literally one of time—about forty years. Baker, the autobiographer, is not the same person as Baker, the aspiring pilot. The passage of time gives him the emotional distance to look back with self-irony at this important event in his life. At the time he must have been distraught by his failure; as he reflects upon the experience from his present perspective, however, he can see that it was comical. Not only does he feel sorry for the instructors he endangered, but he also can laugh at himself.

Distance allows Baker to adopt an ironic tone: He regards himself with humor, and his tone encourages us to view him sympathetically rather than critically. In this way, Baker uses tone to influence our response to what could be an embarrassing self-disclosure. Readers tend to trust autobiographers who can write about themselves with humor and irony. As you plan and write about your own remembered experience, consider whether you also can use humor and irony.

Linda Ellerbee, the next author, is a television journalist who has earned recognition from her peers both for the quality of her writing and for her social commentary. Ellerbee obviously takes pride in her writing. In fact, this selection from her autobiography *"And So It Goes"* (1986), makes fun of that pride. Like Baker, Ellerbee steeps her writing in irony, directed at herself and at just about everyone else. Here Ellerbee is highly critical of her own sex, particularly of anchorwomen (pejoratively called "Twinkies") who offer nothing but a pretty face.

As you read this selection in which Ellerbee dramatizes her efforts to get a job as anchorwoman, consider how this attitude influences her feelings about trying out for the job. Like Baker, Ellerbee wants very much to pass the test. Unlike Baker, however, she wants to pass it on her own terms. What is she trying to prove to herself?

THE LOST WEEKEND
LINDA ELLERBEE

I was in Washington, covering the House for NBC News, when it was an- 1 nounced that *Weekend* would stop being a monthly program and become weekly. That was in December, 1977. *Weekend* had aired once a month at 11:30 on Saturday night since 1974. During the rest of the month, *Saturday Night Live* occupied that time slot. Now *Weekend* was moving to prime time, moving to once a week, and seeking a second anchor. Lloyd Dobyns had anchored it alone, but he would need help with the new *Weekend.* I thought I ought to be that help. It was the first time I'd said to myself, "Now there's a job I really want." Could I write well enough for *Weekend,* with its reputation for using the right words, not too many of them, and in the right order, something Lillian Hellman said most people don't do—something almost no television program did?

I thought so and was certain my bosses would think so, too, once they got 2 around to it. After all, hadn't I, in two years at NBC, made clear my reverence for Good Writing, my intention to be a Good Writer? Hadn't I established a reputation as someone who could write a simple declarative sentence, when pressed? Well then, I would just wait for Reuven Frank to come to his senses and come to Washington. That's how sure I was. It was January and two weeks after the announcement that NBC would add a second anchorperson to *Weekend;* it happened exactly as I had predicted, except that Reuven Frank came to Washington to see Jessica Savitch, not me.

When I found out, I called the president of NBC News, Les Crystal, and asked 3 if this meant I wasn't going to be considered for the *Weekend* job? Les said that's what it meant, all right. I was cool. I went to my office and shut the door, but I didn't cry. The Big Boys didn't cry, but they expected girls to cry, and right then I was in no mood to do anything The Big Boys expected of me. I was furious. What I did was grab the saw from the wall where it hung and add another notch to the bookcase, a big notch. Then I decided that while nowhere is it written that anything will be fair, it simply wasn't fair; Jessica Savitch had been at NBC for only a few months, and she was already Senate correspondent and anchor of the Saturday night edition of *Nightly News.* I begrudged her neither of those assignments, but *Weekend* was what *I* wanted, and I didn't give a damn whether I was being a good sport. Then I decided to hell with them. Who wanted to work for Reuven Frank, a man who had been president of NBC News and must have done something horrible because now he was only a producer and all he produced was *Weekend,* a dumb, dumb show. I added a second notch to the bookcase. *Then* I cried.

Three weeks later Reuven Frank came to Washington and asked me to din- 4 ner, a consolation dinner, I figured, and since I didn't want to be consoled or patted on my head or told what a great trooper I was, I opened the dinner table chitchat by asking him how he'd managed to keep a job at NBC News after he'd been fired from his job as president of NBC News? By the time Reuven Frank finished answering my question—and correcting my facts (he had not been fired)—the pasta was gone, along with my resolve to spend the entire evening being openly, genuinely, and perfectly shitty. This white-haired fellow with a face like a Jewish sphinx, Dennis-the-Menace eyes, a shirt that didn't go with his suit, and a tie that went with neither was the smartest person I'd ever met, and the funniest. He still is.

I caved. I asked for the job, at least for a chance at the job. I told him I 5 wanted to work for him badly. Reuven said he hoped not; if I were to work for him he would rather I were good at it—and by the way, working for him was what he'd come to Washington to talk to me about. That was the first of Reuven's gentle attempts to alter my abuse of the language. Getting the message was easy, getting the job took longer.

What about Jessica Savitch? Oh, she was still the odds-on favorite, but Reu- 6 ven had persuaded the president of NBC News to audition at least one more person. It would be fairer that way. (I figured he meant it would *look* fairer that way; I knew the competition was rigged. It was already in the newspapers that Jessica was going to get the job.) Reuven said the president of NBC News had agreed to the audition idea. Here was how it would work. Each of us would be given a copy of a twenty-minute story that had appeared on *Weekend* two years before, but on our copies, all the narration would be erased, all of Dobyns's words gone from the film, leaving only picture, natural sound and pieces of interviews, edited together with holes left for new words. Jessica and I each would write our scripts, record them, and transfer them to the identically cut stories. When that was done, we would fly to New York, sit on the *Weekend* set, introduce our stories, roll our film, then go home and wait. Reuven apologized for the contest aspect of it, which he said he knew was shabby.

Shabby, my ass. Finally I had a chance. In 1963, while I was still at Vanderbilt 7 University, the United Methodist Church decided to send five American college students to spend three months working in its missions in Bolivia. I was taking Latin American history; I wanted to go to Bolivia. There was only one tiny problem. I hadn't been to church since I was thirteen, which was why my mother sent me our church bulletin every week; it was in the church bulletin that I had read about five students getting to go to Bolivia. If church attendance counted, they weren't going to pick me. But then I read that the five students would be selected on the basis of a written essay, and although I'd skipped church, I had not skipped English class. In the essay I explained how, by sending me, they had a chance at saving an extra soul—mine. I learned a lot that summer in Bolivia, but when it was over I still wrote better than I prayed.

Maybe *Weekend* would be another Bolivia, another writing test that would 8 allow me to tap-dance around certain inadequacies—such as the fact that unlike Jessica, I'd had what amounted to *no* experience anchoring. This time, however, the writing test wasn't a Sunday School essay.

When putting together a television news story, the usual practice is to write 9 the words, record them, then go into the editing room and match pictures to them. The pictures are supposed to fit your words. Words first, pictures second. At *Weekend* the pictures came first. That is, the film was shot, the producer arranged the pieces he chose to use in the order he chose to use them, the film editor assembled the pieces, then the reporter wrote and recorded the narration that would complete the story. It is a better way. Changing the words to fit the pictures makes more sense, because once the film is in the house you cannot change the pictures. But it's tougher for reporters; it makes you work harder and think more. It makes you write *to* the pictures and *with* the pictures. I'd never tried this technique or heard of it. Worse, I wasn't going to try it for the first time on some two-minute story; no, I was going to begin with a twenty-minute story.

Jessica and I each had three days. On Friday, we were to bring our stories 10 to New York. I spent hours at a Steenbeck machine, running the film back and forth, stopping and starting, trying to figure out what to say in this 15-½-second gap, that 6-second pause, how to arrange the information I had so that it wove smoothly in and out of interviews, music, and background noise. Consider it, if you like, a sort of super-complicated crossword puzzle. The subject of the story was a twelve-year-old Brooke Shields, and her mother, Teri Shields, but what it really was, was a story about stage moms, a prurient public, and greed. It was inventively produced, shot, and edited, and lacked only something to match in the way of words. The whole time, I felt like a cowboy heading for the shoot-out at high noon.

In order to be alert Friday morning in New York, I planned to take the shuttle 11 from Washington Thursday night. On Thursday morning it began to snow in Washington and to snow even harder in New York. By mid-afternoon I decided not to risk the shuttle and caught a train to New York. Seven hours later the train completed its three-hour trip. I arrived at Penn Station to find a city shut down by the worst blizzard since 1947. Cab? I looked up Seventh Avenue and saw something I'd never seen before and may not again: nothing was moving. Seventh Avenue, New York City, was solid with snow as far as the eye could see. No cabs. No trucks. *No tracks.* Nothing. And nothing to do but pick up my film and suitcase and start walking the twenty-eight blocks to the hotel. It took two hours, and the hotel was so sorry, but when I hadn't shown up earlier, they'd given my room to somebody else: they'd given all their rooms to some-body else, in fact, and perhaps I had a friend nearby? Not one, I assured them, who had a sleigh. Couldn't they call another hotel for me? They could, but I should know it wouldn't do any good. There were no rooms in town. There was a blizzard. Didn't I know?

Kindness is measured by need. The hotel let me sleep in a chair in the lobby. 12 It was two in the morning, and they were so helpful; when the cleaning people woke me at five in the morning, they let me use the hotel employee's toilet to change clothes and wash my face so I could be the well-rested, alert would-be-anchorwoman-gunslinger, primed for the shoot-out, if only my eyes would open.

At nine o'clock, I was at Reuven Frank's door, clutching my film, ready to 13
sit on the *Weekend* set, play it fast and loose and take my best shot. I went
through the door the way Shane did when he came in the saloon, looking for
Jack Palance.

"Reuven, I'm ready." 14

"Good. You've got the job." 15

"I beg your pardon?" 16

Reuven said Jessica had called the day before and said she wasn't going to 17
bring *her* version of the twenty-minute story to New York because she'd thought
it over and she didn't want to work on *Weekend.* She said she already had the
Saturday *Nightly News* anchor spot and the assignment of Senate correspondent; therefore, she thought it only fair that some other reporter have a chance
to anchor *Weekend.* Reuven said they'd tried to call me and tell me, but nobody
knew where I was. Somebody said they thought I was on a train to someplace.

I had the job. I had the job. I had the job by *default.* It bears witness to the 18
competitiveness or outright insanity of journalists that my first reaction to getting
what I wanted was a terrible, fierce anger. Nobody left Gary Cooper standing
in the middle of the street with his gun hanging out, waiting for the other guy
to show up. I mean, I was *ready.* Where the devil was Jessica?

Questions for analysis

1. How do you react to this essay, particularly to the ending? Did you
care whether Ellerbee got the job or not? If you are a woman, do you identify
with her struggle? If you are a man, can you relate to it? Compare your
reactions to Ellerbee and to Baker. Both write about their wish to succeed
and their fear of failure. On the basis of these selections, do you see any
differences in the way men and women view success and failure?

2. In paragraph 10, Ellerbee describes herself in conventionally masculine terms as "a cowboy heading for the shoot-out at high noon." How
appropriate is this self-image in an essay about a woman's aspiration to
succeed in a traditionally male profession? What does it reveal about Ellerbee's values and feelings?

3. How would you describe the central conflict in this essay? What are
the opposing forces? (You might want to refer to the discussion of structure
in Chapter 13: Narrating.)

4. Ellerbee's tone was described earlier as "ironic." Find a passage that
exemplifies this tone. How does Ellerbee's tone influence your reaction to
her personal disclosure? How does her use of irony compare to Baker's?

5. Paragraph 7 interrupts the straightforward chronology of the narrative with a flashback, in which Ellerbee describes an event that occurred years
before the experience she is recounting. (See Sequencing Narrative Action
in Chapter 13 for a discussion of flashbacks.) What purpose, if any, does
this apparent digression serve?

6. How does Ellerbee's story about a job she wanted lead you to reflect on your own experience? Have you ever been challenged to do your best, only to find in the end that your efforts did not matter? Try to recall a specific experience about which you might write. How could you make it interesting for your readers? What would the event reveal about you?

Commentary   Ellerbee, like Baker, invests her narrative with drama and significance, carefully building toward a suspenseful climax—in this case, really an anticlimax. The action centers around two obstacles. First, she must write a script that is better than her competitor's, and then she must triumph over nature and deliver her script to New York.

We have seen the way Baker uses specific narrative action to intensify the pace of his essay. Let us now look at Ellerbee's use of two other pacing techniques: sentence rhythm and dialogue (see Pacing in Chapter 13). By manipulating the rhythm of her prose, she heightens the drama. In paragraph 11, for example, she shifts abruptly from long sentences to short fragments and then back again to long sentences. Varying the sentence rhythm arrests the narrative momentarily and brings the action to a standstill, thereby mimicing the blizzard's effect and underscoring Ellerbee's consternation at being stranded in the middle of Manhattan.

Ellerbee similarly employs dialogue for dramatic effect. This pacing technique is evident in paragraph 4, which portrays her initial encounter with Reuven Frank. In paragraph 5 Ellerbee summarizes the dialogue to capture the quick give-and-take of their tense conversation. Summarizing the dialogue allows Ellerbee to condense the conversation and emphasize its tension. Later in the piece she presents another dialogue. This one, however, she relates directly to emphasize her surprise. As you plan and draft your own autobiographical essay, you will need to decide where the potential points of tension are and which pacing techniques you should use.

Although Ellerbee is writing less than a decade after the event, she, like Baker, has her experience in perspective. Throughout the narrative, she intersperses remembered feelings with remembered actions. In the opening paragraph, for instance, she recalls the circumstances of first learning about the job and admits how eager she was to get it. She goes on to express how uncertain she felt about her ability to write well enough, but then masks her feelings with irony.

Ellerbee's use of irony suggests the conflicting impulses autobiographers often have about disclosing their feelings. On the one hand, they want to reveal how they felt and feel now about the event; that is the reason for writing in the first place. On the other hand, however, they are reluctant to reveal too much. They want to remain in control of their disclosure. They may be afraid of alienating their readers or be reluctant to show their vulnerability. Or they may simply want to present themselves in the best possible light.

In paragraph 3, Ellerbee makes this conflict about self-presentation the focus of her writing by portraying her struggle over expressing her feelings. She apparently felt like crying at the time, but would not allow herself to because she did not want to give her bosses and colleagues—all male—the satisfaction of seeing her behave in a way that was stereotypically female. As she says: "The Big Boys didn't cry, but they expected girls to cry."

Some readers will be disappointed that Ellerbee does not suspend the narrative action at this point to discuss the situation from her present perspective as a social critic and feminist. Instead, she chooses to show rather than tell, to dramatize not to analyze. In addition to presenting the story well, autobiographical writing succeeds by how effectively it conveys the event's significance. Ellerbee may not comment much, but her disclosure of remembered feelings helps us to appreciate how important the event was in her life. Like Ellerbee, you will also have to decide how much to say directly and how much to leave unsaid.

The next selection comes from *Brothers and Keepers* (1984), an autobiography by novelist John Edgar Wideman. Wideman reflects, in this remembered event, about his experience as a college freshman, one of only 10 black students in a class of 1,700. While Baker and Ellerbee view their pasts with ironic detachment, Wideman seems to have little emotional distance from his experience even after 20 years. As you read, consider how Wideman uses his emotional intensity. What do you think is the purpose of his essay? What does he want to convey to us about himself and about ourselves, about our personal and racial identities?

THE ARGUMENT
JOHN EDGAR WIDEMAN

My first year at college when I was living in the dorms a white boy asked 1
me if I liked the blues. Since I figured I *was* the blues I answered, Yeah, sure. We were in Darryl Dawson's room. Darryl and I comprised approximately one-third of the total number of black males in our class. About ten of the seventeen hundred men and women who entered the University of Pennsylvania as freshmen in 1959 were black. After a period of wariness and fencing, mutual embarrassment and resisting the inevitable, I'd buddied up with Darryl, even though he'd attended Putney Prep School in Vermont and spoke with an accent I considered phony. Since the fat white boy in work shirt, motorcycle boots, and dirty jeans was in Darryl's room, I figured maybe the guy was alright in spite of the fact he asked dumb questions. I'd gotten used to answering or ignoring plenty of those in two months on campus. "Yeah, sure," should have closed the topic but the white boy wasn't finished. He said he had a big collection of blues records and that I ought to come by his room sometime with Darryl and dig, man.

Who do you like? Got everybody, man. Leadbelly and Big Bill Broonzy. Light- 2
ning and Lemon and Sonny Boy. You dig Broonzy? Just copped a new side of his.

None of the names meant a thing to me. Maybe I'd heard Leadbelly at a ₃
party at a white girl's house in Shadyside but the other names were a mystery.
What was this sloppy-looking white boy talking about? His blond hair, long and
greasy, was combed back James Dean style. Skin pale and puffy like a Gerber
baby. He wore a smartass, whole-lot-hipper-than-you expression on his face. His
mouth is what did it. Pudgy, soft lips with just a hint of blond fuzz above them,
pursed into a permanent sneer.

He stared at me, waiting for an answer. At home we didn't get in other ₄
people's faces like that. You talked toward a space and the other person had a
choice of entering or not entering, but this guy's blue eyes bored directly into
mine. Waiting, challenging, prepared to send a message to that sneering mouth.
I wanted no part of him, his records, or his questions.

Blues. Well, that's all I listen to. I like different songs at different times. ₅
Midnighters. Drifters got one I like out now.

Not that R-and-B crap on the radio, man. Like the real blues. Down home ₆
country blues. The old guys picking and singing.

Ray Charles. I like Ray Charles. ₇

Hey, that ain't blues. Tell him, Darryl. ₈

Darryl don't need to tell me anything. Been listening to blues all my life. Ray ₉
Charles is great. He's the best there is. How you gon tell me what's good and
not good? It's my music. I've been hearing it all my life.

You're still talking about rock 'n' roll. Rhythm and blues. Most of it's junk. ₁₀
Here today and gone tomorrow crap. I'm talking about authentic blues. Big Bill
Broonzy. The Classics.

When he talked, he twisted his mouth so the words slithered out of one ₁₁
corner of his face; like garbage dumped off one end of a cafeteria tray. He
pulled a cigarette from a pack in his shirt pocket. Lit it without disturbing the
sneer.

Bet you've never even heard Bill Broonzy. ₁₂

Don't need to hear no Broonzy or Toonsy or whoever the fuck he is. I don't ₁₃
give a shit about him nor any of them other old-timey dudes you're talking
about, man. I know what I like and you can call it rhythm and blues or rock 'n'
roll, it's still the best music. It's what I like and don't need nobody telling me
what's good.

What are you getting mad about, man? How can you put down something ₁₄
you know nothing about? Bill Broonzy is the greatest twelve-string guitar player
who ever lived. Everybody knows that. You've never heard a note he's played
but you're setting yourself up as an expert. This is silly. You obviously can't back
up what you're saying. You have a lot to learn about music, my friend.

He's wagging his big head and looking over at Darryl like Darryl's supposed ₁₅
to back his action. You can imagine what's going through my mind. How many
times I've already gone upside his fat jaw. Biff. Bam. My fists were burning. I
could see blood running out both his nostrils. The sneer split at the seams,
smeared all over his chin. Here's this white boy in this white world bad-mouthing
me to one of the few black faces I get to see, messing with the little bit of
understanding I'm beginning to have with Darryl. And worse, trespassing on the

private turf of my music, the black sounds from home I carry round in my head as a saving grace against the pressures of the university.

Talk about uptight. I don't believe that pompous ass could have known, 16 because even I didn't know at that moment, how much he was hurting me. What hurt most was the truth of what he was saying. His whiteness, his arrogance made me mad, but it was truth putting the real hurt on me.

I didn't hit him. I should have but never did. A nice forget-me-knot upside 17 his jaw. I should have but didn't. Not that time. Not him. Smashing his mouth would have been too easy, so I hated him instead. Let anger and shame and humiliation fill me to overflowing so the hate is still there, today, over twenty years later. The dormitory room had pale green walls, a bare wooden floor, contained the skimpy desk and sagging cot allotted to each cubicle in the hall. Darryl's things scattered everywhere. A self-portrait he'd painted stared down from one dirt-speckled wall. The skin of the face in the portrait was wildly mottled, violent bruises of color surrounding haunted jade eyes. Darryl's eyes were green like my brother David's, but I hadn't noticed their color until I dropped by his room one afternoon between classes and Darryl wasn't there and I didn't have anything better to do than sit and wait and study the eyes in his painting. Darryl's room had been a sanctuary but when the white boy started preaching there was no place to hide. Even before he spoke the room had begun to shrink. He sprawled, lounged, an exaggerated casualness announcing how comfortable he felt, how much he belonged. Lord of the manor wherever he happened to plant his boots.

Darryl cooled it. His green eyes didn't choose either of us when we looked 18 toward him for approval. Dawson had to see what a miserable corner I was in. He had to feel that room clamped tight around my neck and the sneer tugging the noose tighter.

A black motorcycle jacket, carved from a lump of coal, studded with silver 19 and rhinestones, was draped over the desk chair. I wanted to stomp it, chop it into little pieces.

Hey, you guys, knock it off. Let's talk about something else. Obviously you 20 have different tastes in music.

Darryl knew damn well that wasn't the problem. Together we might have 21 been able to say the right things. Put the white boy in his place. Recapture some breathing space. But Darryl had his own ghosts to battle. His longing for his blonde, blue-eyed Putney girl friend whose parents had rushed her off to Europe when they learned of her romance with the colored boy who was Putney school president. His ambivalence toward his blackness that would explode one day and hurtle him into the quixotic campaign of the Black Revolutionary Army to secede from the United States. So Darryl cooled it that afternoon in his room and the choked feeling never left my throat. I can feel it now as I write.

Why did that smartass white son of a bitch have so much power over me? 22 Why could he confuse me, turn me inside out, make me doubt myself? Waving just a tiny fragment of truth, he could back me into a corner. Who was I? What was I? Did I really fear the truth about myself that much? Four hundred years of oppression, of lies had empowered him to use the music of my people as a weapon against me. Twenty years ago I hadn't begun to comprehend the larger forces, the ironies, the obscenities that permitted such a reversal to occur. All I had sensed was his power, the raw, crude force mocking me, diminishing me. I should have smacked him. I should have affirmed another piece of the truth he knew about me, the nigger violence.

Questions for analysis

1. How do you react to the violence and rage in this essay? Does it frighten you that Wideman seems to cultivate his fury instead of trying to hide it? Have you ever been as angry as Wideman appears in this essay? Did you allow yourself to be angry or try to stifle your emotions?

2. On the surface, the argument is about the blues, but what is really at stake? Why does Wideman get so angry?

3. Mark the passages in which Wideman describes the white student. What dominant impression of the student do these descriptions convey to you? Why do you think he is unnamed? Compare Wideman's description of his antagonist to Baker's description of Total Loss and Ellerbee's description of Reuven Frank. How do these descriptions serve the authors' purposes?

4. Skim the essay, noting how Wideman describes himself. For example, what do you make of this statement: "I figured I *was* the blues." Compare Wideman's portrayal of himself with Baker's and Ellerbee's self-portrayals. What can you conclude about the way in which writers describe themselves in autobiography?

5. In paragraph 4, Wideman contrasts the white student's way of staring with the avoidance of eye contact that Wideman was used to at home. What other comparisons and contrasts does he make? What does this writing strategy of comparison/contrast allow him to convey about the event's significance? (You will find a discussion of this strategy in Chapter 18: Comparing and Contrasting.)

6. Compare Wideman to Darryl Dawson. In what way could Darryl be considered Wideman's double? How does the information in paragraph 21 about Darryl's past and future contribute to your understanding of Wideman?

7. Autobiographers often write about strong emotions—anger, love, disappointment, frustration, elation. If you were to write about a time in the past when you felt an emotion very strongly, what event would you choose? How would you convey your feelings? What would you want readers to learn about you in particular and about human emotion in general?

Commentary

Wideman's narrative describes a conversation turned confrontation. But on another level it is about anger, personal anger between two particular people as well as racial anger between blacks and whites. To help us understand the event's full significance, Wideman comments on his remembered feelings. He discloses how he felt at the time, acknowledging how little he then understood his feelings. Insight, for him, is primarily retrospective, a matter of hindsight.

Wideman shares his insight by interpreting and evaluating his experience for us. His writing demonstrates some of the ways autobiographers present their reflections. Like Wideman, they may frame the event with reflection, providing a context at the beginning and an interpretation at the end. They also may interject commentary at crucial points in the narrative.

In the opening paragraph, Wideman presents the sociological context. At his school, black students were a minority, only 10 out of a freshman class of 1,700. This objective fact translates into a subjective necessity. He felt impelled to make friends with Darryl Dawson, even though the two were so different, because he needed black friends as allies. His relationship with the white students on campus, he also tells us, was uneasy. They were always asking "dumb questions," which he usually ignored.

In paragraph 15, Wideman interrupts the narrative to explain why the questioning of the white student in Darryl's room was especially threatening:

> Here's this white boy in this white world bad-mouthing me to one of the few black faces I get to see, messing with the little bit of understanding I'm beginning to have with Darryl. And worse, trespassing on the private turf of my music, the black sounds from home I carry round in my head as a saving grace against the pressures of the university.

The three—Wideman, Darryl, and the white student—formed a triangle, not a romantic triangle, certainly, but one that involved jealousy and competition nevertheless. Wideman sensed at the time that he could not count on Darryl. With the wisdom of hindsight, he explains why.

Wideman returns in the last paragraph to the broader cultural context he established at the beginning. The paragraph opens with a series of questions, rhetorical only in part because Wideman does not claim to be able to answer them fully. These questions lead us beyond Wideman's personal story, helping us to generalize from his particular experience. Indeed, autobiography should not only provide insight into one person's life but also teach us about human experience in general. When you choose an event from your own past, consider not only what it might reveal about your life but also what it might suggest more universally.

Born in India and educated in England, George Orwell served for a time in the Indian Imperial Police before returning to Europe to begin a career as a writer. The following autobiographical essay "A Hanging," first published in the collection *Shooting an Elephant and Other Essays*, describes an incident that occurred in the 1920s when Orwell was serving in colonial Burma. Although he is writing nearly a decade later, in 1931, he describes the scene and people in remarkable detail. As you read, ask yourself how this specificity serves his overall purpose.

A HANGING

GEORGE ORWELL

It was in Burma, a sodden morning of the rains. A sickly light, like yellow 1
tinfoil, was slanting over the high walls into the jail yard. We were waiting
outside the condemned cells, a row of sheds fronted with double bars, like small
animal cages. Each cell measured about ten feet by ten and was quite bare
within except for a plank bed and a pot for drinking water. In some of them
brown, silent men were squatting at the inner bars, with their blankets draped
round them. These were the condemned men, due to be hanged within the
next week or two.

One prisoner had been brought out of his cell. He was a Hindu, a puny wisp 2
of a man, with a shaven head and vague liquid eyes. He had a thick, sprouting
moustache, absurdly too big for his body, rather like the moustache of a comic
man on the films. Six tall Indian warders were guarding him and getting him
ready for the gallows. Two of them stood by with rifles and fixed bayonets,
while the others handcuffed him, passed a chain through his handcuffs and
fixed it to their belts, and lashed his arms tight to his sides. They crowded very
close about him, with their hands always on him in a careful, caressing grip, as
though all the while feeling him to make sure he was there. It was like men
handling a fish which is still alive and may jump back into the water. But he
stood quite unresisting, yielding his arms limply to the ropes, as though he hardly
noticed what was happening.

Eight o'clock struck and a bugle call, desolately thin in the wet air, floated 3
from the distant barracks. The superintendent of the jail, who was standing
apart from the rest of us, moodily prodding the gravel with his stick, raised his
head at the sound. He was an army doctor, with a grey toothbrush moustache
and a gruff voice. "For God's sake hurry up, Francis," he said irritably. "The man
ought to have been dead by this time. Aren't you ready yet?"

Francis, the head jailer, a fat Dravidian in a white drill suit and gold spectacles, 4
waved his black hand. "Yes sir, yes sir," he bubbled. "All iss satisfactorily prepared. The hangman iss waiting. We shall proceed."

"Well, quick march, then. The prisoners can't get their breakfast till this job's 5
over."

We set out for the gallows. Two warders marched on either side of the 6
prisoner, with their rifles at the slope; two others marched close against him,
gripping him by arm and shoulder, as though at once pushing and supporting
him. The rest of us, magistrates and the like, followed behind. Suddenly, when
we had gone ten yards, the procession stopped short without any order or
warning. A dreadful thing had happened—a dog, come goodness knows
whence, had appeared in the yard. It came bounding among us with a loud
volley of barks, and leapt round us wagging its whole body, wild with glee at
finding so many human beings together. It was a large woolly dog, half Airedale,
half pariah. For a moment it pranced round us, and then, before anyone could
stop it, it had made a dash for the prisoner and jumping up tried to lick his face.
Everyone stood aghast, too taken aback even to grab at the dog.

"Who let that bloody brute in here?" said the superintendent angrily. "Catch 7
it, someone!"

A warder detached from the escort, charged clumsily after the dog, but it 8 danced and gambolled just out of his reach, taking everything as part of the game. A young Eurasian jailer picked up a handful of gravel and tried to stone the dog away, but it dodged the stones and came after us again. Its yaps echoed from the jail walls. The prisoner, in the grasp of the two warders, looked on incuriously, as though this was another formality of the hanging. It was several minutes before someone managed to catch the dog. Then we put my hand-kerchief through its collar and moved off once more, with the dog still straining and whimpering.

It was about forty yards to the gallows. I watched the bare brown back of 9 the prisoner marching in front of me. He walked clumsily with his bound arms, but quite steadily, with that bobbing gait of the Indian who never straightens his knees. At each step his muscles slid neatly into place, the lock of hair on his scalp danced up and down, his feet printed themselves on the wet gravel. And once, in spite of the men who gripped him by each shoulder, he stepped slightly aside to avoid a puddle on the path.

It is curious, but till that moment I had never realized what it means to 10 destroy a healthy, conscious man. When I saw the prisoner step aside to avoid the puddle I saw the mystery, the unspeakable wrongness, of cutting a life short when it is in full tide. This man was not dying, he was alive just as we are alive. All the organs of his body were working—bowels digesting food, skin renewing itself, nails growing, tissues forming—all toiling away in solemn foolery. His nails would still be growing when he stood on the drop, when he was falling through the air with a tenth-of-a-second to live. His eyes saw the yellow gravel and the grey walls, and his brain still remembered, foresaw, reasoned—reasoned even about puddles. He and we were a party of men walking together, seeing, hear-ing, feeling, understanding the same world; and in two minutes, with a sudden snap, one of us would be gone—one mind less, one world less.

The gallows stood in a small yard, separate from the main grounds of the 11 prison, and overgrown with tall prickly weeds. It was a brick erection like three sides of a shed, with planking on top, and above that two beams and a crossbar with the rope dangling. The hangman, a grey-haired convict in the white uniform of the prison, was waiting beside his machine. He greeted us with a servile crouch as we entered. At a word from Francis the two warders, gripping the prisoner more closely than ever, half led half pushed him to the gallows and helped him clumsily up the ladder. Then the hangman climbed up and fixed the rope around the prisoner's neck.

We stood waiting, five yards away. The warders had formed in a rough circle 12 round the gallows. And then, when the noose was fixed, the prisoner began crying out to his god. It was a high, reiterated cry of "Ram! Ram! Ram! Ram!" not urgent and fearful like a prayer or cry for help, but steady, rhythmical, almost like the tolling of a bell. The dog answered the sound with a whine. The hang-man, still standing on the gallows, produced a small white cotton bag like a flour bag and drew it down over the prisoner's face. But the sound, muffled by the cloth, still persisted, over and over again: "Ram! Ram! Ram! Ram! Ram!"

The hangman climbed down and stood ready, holding the lever. Minutes 13 seemed to pass. The steady, muffled crying from the prisoner went on and on, "Ram! Ram! Ram!" never faltering for an instant. The superintendent, his head on his chest, was slowly poking the ground with his stick; perhaps he was counting the cries, allowing the prisoner a fixed number—fifty, perhaps, or a hundred. Everyone had changed colour. The Indians had gone grey like bad coffee, and one or two of the bayonets were wavering. We looked at the lashed, hooded man on the drop, and listened to his cries—each cry another second of life; the same thought was in all our minds: oh, kill him quickly, get it over, stop that abominable noise!

Suddenly the superintendent made up his mind. Throwing up his head he 14 made a swift motion with his stick. "Chalo!" he shouted almost fiercely.

There was a shaking noise, and then dead silence. The prisoner had vanished, 15 and the rope was twisting on itself. I let go of the dog, and it galloped immediately to the back of the gallows; but when it got there it stopped short, barked, and then retreated into a corner of the yard, where it stood among the weeds, looking timorously out at us. We went round the gallows to inspect the prisoner's body. He was dangling with his toes pointed straight downwards, very slowly revolving, as dead as a stone.

The superintendent reached out with his stick and poked the bare brown 16 body; it oscillated slightly. "*He's* all right," said the superintendent. He backed out from under the gallows, and blew out a deep breath. The moody look had gone out of his face quite suddenly. He glanced at his wrist-watch. "Eight minutes past eight. Well, that's all for this morning, thank God."

The warders unfixed bayonets and marched away. The dog, sobered and 17 conscious of having misbehaved itself, slipped after them. We walked out of the gallows yard, past the condemned cells with their waiting prisoners, into the big central yard of the prison. The convicts, under the command of warders armed with lathis, were already receiving their breakfast. They squatted in long rows, each man holding a tin pannikin, while two warders with buckets marched round ladling out rice; it seemed quite a homely, jolly scene, after the hanging. An enormous relief had come upon us now that the job was done. One felt an impulse to sing, to break into a run, to snigger. All at once everyone began chattering gaily.

The Eurasian boy walking beside me nodded towards the way we had come, 18 with a knowing smile: "Do you know, sir, our friend (he meant the dead man) when he heard his appeal had been dismissed, he pissed on the floor of his cell. From fright. Kindly take one of my cigarettes, sir. Do you not admire my new silver case, sir? From the boxwallah, two rupees eight annas. Classy European style."

Several people laughed—at what, nobody seemed certain. 19

Francis was walking by the superintendent, talking garrulously: "Well, sir, 20 all hass passed off with the utmost satisfactoriness. It was all finished—flick! like that. It iss not always so—oah, no! I have known cases where the doctor wass obliged to go beneath the gallows and pull the prissoner's legs to ensure decease. Most disagreeable!"

"Wriggling about, eh? That's bad," said the superintendent. 21

"Ach, sir, it iss worse when they become refractory! One man, I recall, clung 22 to the bars of hiss cage when we went to take him out. You will scarcely credit, sir, that it took six warders to dislodge him, three pulling at each leg. We reasoned with him. 'My dear fellow,' we said, 'think of all of the pain and trouble you are causing to us!' But no, he would not listen! Ach, he wass very trouble-some!"

I found that I was laughing quite loudly. Everyone was laughing. Even the 23 superintendent grinned in a tolerant way. "You'd better all come out and have a drink," he said quite genially. "I've got a bottle of whiskey in the car. We could do with it."

We went through the big double gates of the prison into the road. "Pulling 24 at his legs!" exclaimed a Burmese magistrate suddenly, and burst into a loud chuckling. We all began laughing again. At that moment Francis' anecdote seemed extraordinarily funny. We all had a drink together, native and European alike, quite amicably. The dead man was a hundred yards away.

Questions for analysis

1. This essay vividly recalls an execution, yet it ends with laughter. Are you shocked, confused, unconcerned, or something else? How do you think Orwell wants you to feel after reading this essay? What makes you think this is his purpose?

2. Beginning with paragraph 16 the mood of the guards and officials changes. Describe the change. How do you interpret it?

3. Except for the reflection in paragraph 10, Orwell tells us about himself mainly by reporting the words and actions of the group he is a part of. What do we learn about Orwell in this essay? What seem to be his moral and political views? How can you tell?

4. Beginning at paragraph 18, the essay is largely dialogue. Look again at the dialogue in paragraphs 18–24. What does it tell us? How does Orwell use this dialogue to disclose the significance of the event?

5. The event seems to be presented in great detail, yet we can assume that Orwell left out much that he remembered. He might also have omitted any mention of the dog; it is easy to imagine the story without it. Why do you think Orwell included the dog and gave it such a prominent place in the essay?

6. Look again at paragraphs 2, 6, 8, 9, and 12 to see how Orwell describes the prisoner and his treatment by the guards. What specific actions and details are described, and what impression do they give of the prisoner? How do they make you feel about him?

7. Have you ever been party to an action that you later regretted? Or have you ever seen or participated in a particularly shocking event? Under what conditions would you be willing to write about such an event? Think about a particular event of this sort. How would you present it? How might you disclose something about yourself in your description of the event?

Commentary   In addition to telling the story dramatically and communicating its significance, autobiographers also vividly describe the scene and people. Vivid description brings the story alive, enabling us to imagine it and to gain pleasure from using our own imagination. Description also carries meaning. The individual images gather together to create a dominant impression that reinforces the story's significance or theme.

The selections by Baker, Ellerbee, and Wideman show how autobiographers often focus their description on one particular person or place. Orwell, on the other hand, gives us a much fuller description of the scene—the prison and gallows—as well as the people—the prisoner, the jailers, and even the dog that interrupts the action temporarily. Studying how Orwell presents people and places and how he invests his description with significance will suggest ways you can use description in your own writing.

To create a vivid image, Orwell uses the describing strategies of naming, detailing, and comparing. These strategies are discussed in Chapter 14: Describing, but the following sentence from paragraph 1 shows how Orwell uses them: "We were waiting outside the condemned cells, a row of sheds fronted with double bars, like small animal cages." Naming allows him to identify the objects in the scene: cells, sheds, bars, cages. Notice that he uses specific nouns for these objects—*sheds,* for example, instead of the more general *buildings* or *structures.* He further specifies by detailing the objects with descriptive adjectives: the cells belong to the *condemned* men, the bars are *double* in number, the cages *small* in size. Finally, by comparing the men's cells to animal cages, he suggests the extent of the prisoners' degradation.

Orwell's description particularizes the scene, and it also helps shape our attitude toward the prison and its inhabitants. He chooses his words purposefully. For example, notice his use of the word *condemned.* It applies to the prisoners who have been condemned to death, but it also applies to the cells themselves. When a building is condemned, it is deemed uninhabitable. By extension, Orwell seems to be describing these sheds as unworthy of human habitation. On yet another level, the phrase *condemned cells* suggests that Orwell condemns the whole enterprise—treating people like animals and taking their lives.

Each description contributes to a dominant impression, a feeling or mood that reflects the significance of the experience. In the opening paragraph, for instance, Orwell pictures the prison as a dreary place where people are reduced to the condition of animals. It is physically as well as spiritually confining. The action that follows suggests that the actors—the prisoner and the officials—lack will and individuality. They seem to be automatons who take no responsibility for their actions. This idea of responsibility pervades the essay. While the prisoner is made to take responsibility for his crime, the officials, including Orwell, refuse to consider their own responsibility. They even deny to themselves the horror of the act they have committed. You, too, can create a dominant impression rich with meaning by carefully planning how you will describe the scene and people for your own remembered event essay. (For a discussion of dominant impression, see Chapter 14: Describing.)

The final next essay was written by Jean Brandt, a college freshman. She tells of an unexpected event on a Christmas shopping trip when she was thirteen. As you read, ask yourself how you would have felt if you were Brandt. Would you have reacted any differently? Would you be willing to write about an experience which might lead readers to judge you negatively?

CALLING HOME

JEAN BRANDT

As we all piled into the car, I knew it was going to be a fabulous day. My grandmother was visiting for the holidays; and she and I, along with my older brother and sister, Louis and Susan, were setting off for a day of last-minute Christmas shopping. On the way to the mall we sang Christmas carols, chattered, and laughed. With Christmas only two days away, we were caught up with holiday spirit. I felt light-headed and full of joy. I loved shopping—especially at Christmas.

The shopping center was swarming with frantic last-minute shoppers like ourselves. We went first to the General Store, my favorite. It carried mostly knickknacks and other useless items, which nobody needs but buys anyway. I was thirteen years old at the time, and things like buttons and calendars and posters would catch my fancy. This day was no different. The object of my desire was a 75-cent Snoopy button. Snoopy was the latest. If you owned anything with the Peanuts on it, you were "in." But since I was supposed to be shopping for gifts for other people and not myself, I couldn't decide what to do. I went in search of my sister for her opinion. I pushed my way through throngs of people to the back of the store where I found Susan. I asked her if she thought I should buy the button. She said it was cute and if I wanted it to go ahead and buy it.

When I got back to the Snoopy section, I took one look at the lines at the cashiers and knew I didn't want to wait thirty minutes to buy an item worth less than one dollar. I walked back to the basket where I found the button and was about to drop it in when suddenly, instead, I took a quick glance around, assured myself no one could see, and slipped the button into the pocket of my sweatshirt. I hesitated for a moment, but once the item was in my pocket, there was no turning back. I had never before stolen anything, but what was done was done. A few seconds later my sister appeared and asked, "So, did you decide to buy the button?"

"No, I guess not." I hoped my voice didn't quaver. As we headed for the entrance, my heart began to race. I just had to get out of that store. Only a few more yards to go and I'd be safe. As we crossed the threshold, I heaved a sigh of relief. I was home free. I thought about how sly I had been and I felt proud of my accomplishment.

An unexpected tap on my shoulder startled me. I whirled around to find a 5
middle-aged man, dressed in street clothes, flashing some type of badge and
politely asking me to empty my pockets. Where did this man come from? How
did he know? I was so sure that no one had seen me! On the verge of panicking,
I told myself that all I had to do was give this man his button back, say I was
sorry, and go on my way. After all, it was only a 75-cent item.

Next thing I knew he was talking about calling the police and having me 6
arrested and thrown in jail, as if he had just nabbed a professional thief instead
of a terrified kid. I couldn't believe what he was saying.

The man led us through the store and into an office, where we waited for 7
the police officers to arrive. Susan had found my grandmother and brother who,
shocked, didn't say a word. The thought of going to jail terrified me. Not more
than ten minutes later, two officers arrived and placed me under arrest. They
handcuffed me and led me out of the store. I had counted on my sister being
allowed to go with me, but I had to face this ordeal all my myself.

As the officers led me through the mall, I sensed a hundred pairs of eyes 8
staring at me. My face flushed and I broke out in a sweat. Now everyone knew
I was a criminal. In their eyes I was a juvenile delinquent, and thank God the
cops were getting me off the streets. The worse part was thinking my grandmother might be having the same thoughts. The humiliation at that moment
was overwhelming. I felt like Hester Prynne being put on public display for
everyone to ridicule.

That short walk through the mall seemed to take hours. But once we reached 9
the squad car, time raced by. I was read my rights and questioned. We were at
the police station within minutes. Everything happened so fast I didn't have a
chance to feel remorse for my crime. Instead, I viewed what was happening to
me as if it were a movie. Being searched, although embarrassing, somehow
seemed to be exciting. All the movies and television programs I had seen were
actually coming to life. This is what it was really like. But why were criminals
always portrayed as frightened and regretful? I was having fun—until I was
allowed my one phone call. I was trembling as I dialed home. I didn't know
what I was going to say to my parents, especially my mother.

"Hi, Dad, this is Jean." 10

"We've been waiting for you to call." 11

"Did Susie tell you what happened?" 12

"Yeah, but we haven't told your mother. I think you should tell her what 13
you did and where you are."

"You mean she doesn't even know where I am?" 14

"No, I want you to explain it to her." 15

There was a pause as he called my mother to the phone. For the first time 16
that night I was close to tears. I wished I had never stolen that stupid pin. I
wanted to give the phone to one of the officers because I was too ashamed to
tell my mother the truth.

"Jean, where are you?" 17

"I'm, umm, in jail." 18

"Why? What for?" 19

"Shoplifting." 20

"Oh no, Jean. Why? Why did you do it?" 21

"I don't know. No reason. I just did it." 22

"I don't understand. You had plenty of money with you." 23

"I know but I just did it. I can't explain why. Mom, I'm sorry." 24

"I'm afraid sorry isn't enough." 25

Long after I got off the phone, sitting in an empty jail cell and waiting for 26 my parents to pick me up, I could still distinctly hear the disappointment and hurt in my mother's voice. I cried. I felt like a terrible human being. I would rather have stayed in jail than confront my mom right then. I dreaded each passing minute that brought our encounter closer. When the officer came to release me, I hesitated, actually not wanting to leave. He led me to the front desk, where I had to sign a form to retrieve my belongings. I saw my parents a few yards away and my heart raced. A large knot formed in my stomach. I fought back the tears.

Not a word was spoken as we walked to the car. Slowly I sank into the back 27 seat anticipating the scolding. Expecting harsh tones, I was relieved to hear almost the opposite from my father.

"I'm not going to punish you and I'll tell you why. Although I think what 28 you did was wrong, I think what the police did was more wrong. There's no excuse for locking a thirteen-year-old behind bars. That doesn't mean I condone what you did, but I think you've been punished enough already."

As I looked from my father's eyes to my mother's, I knew this ordeal was 29 over. Although it would never be forgotten, the incident was not mentioned again.

Questions for analysis   1. How do you react to Brandt's personal disclosure? What seems to be her attitude toward her own behavior? Are you surprised to find a student writing about something so personal in a composition class? What do you think Brandt may have learned about herself from writing about this experience? What do you learn about her or about human experience in general?

2. What makes this story dramatic? How would you describe the basic conflict? What are the opposing forces?

3. Reread this essay, paying particular attention to the way Brandt paces her narrative. Where does she use specific narration, sentence rhythm, and dialogue to heighten the tension? How effective is the pacing? Point to any place where you think the pace slackens and suggest how it might be intensified.

4. Comment on the way Brandt ends the essay, in particular on the contrast she draws between her mother's and her father's reactions. What do Brandt's phone conversation and her feelings afterward reveal about her relationship with her mother? Similarly, what do her father's comments suggest about her relationship with him?

5. Brandt is writing about a traumatic experience that occurred only five years earlier. How much emotional distance from the event does she appear to have? Skim the essay, looking for evidence of distance or the lack of it. For example, how would you classify her admission that she felt proud (paragraph 4) or that she felt like Hester Prynne (paragraph 8)?

6. Like Orwell, Brandt is writing about taking responsibility for one's own actions. How willing does Brandt seem to accept responsibility for what she has done? How does her father's comment at the end give her a way out? Does she take it? Think of a time when you failed to accept responsibility for your actions—failed to apologize for something or failed to do something. What did you learn from your experience that you could put into an essay?

Commentary Brandt shows what happened and recalls how she felt at the time, but she does not let readers know how she feels now, looking back on the experience from her present perspective. She does not try to explain why she stole the Snoopy button in the first place. Nor does she indicate what, if anything, she learned from the experience.

Perhaps the reason her writing lacks insight is that Brandt still does not have sufficient emotional distance to understand the experience. The Writer at Work section that appears at the end of this chapter follows Brandt's progress as she planned, drafted, and revised this essay. It shows how her focus shifted gradually from the act itself to her parents' reactions to it. In the final revision, the confrontation with them takes on an importance equal to the actual arrest. The ambiguity of this ending suggests that Brandt still has not resolved her feelings about responsibility. This ambivalence is represented by the division between her parents. Her mother acts as her moral conscience, making her feel responsible for her actions. In contrast, her father gives her an excuse, making her seem more a victim than a culprit.

Writing about the event helped Brandt sort through her feelings and focus on what is important about her experience. She may not yet fully understand why she acted as she did, but she is able now to acknowledge what she did without embarrassment. Understanding significant experiences often takes time and hard work, and autobiographical essays about such events are frequently unresolved. To write effectively about your past, you do not have to have a pat answer to all your questions. In fact, autobiographical essays that end with a moral tend to disappoint readers because they usually oversimplify complicated human experience.

PURPOSE AND AUDIENCE

Writers have various reasons for writing about their experiences. Reminiscing enables them to relive moments of pleasure and pain, but it also helps them to gain insight, to learn who they are now by examining who they used to be and the forces that shaped them. Reflecting on the past, psychotherapy has shown, can lead to significant self-discovery. Autobiographers know this, and they also know that autobiography, however therapeutic, is public and not private. The autobiographer writes to be read and is therefore as much concerned with self-presentation as with self-discovery. In this way, personal writing resembles persuasive writing because autobiographers want to influence the way readers think of them. They present themselves to their readers in the way they want to be perceived. The rest they keep hidden, although perceptive readers can often read between the lines.

We read autobiography for much the same reason that we write it—communion. There is much to be said about how we live our lives, about the decisions we face, the delights we share, and the fate that awaits us all. Reading autobiography can validate our sense of ourselves, particularly when we see reflected in another's life our own experience. Reading about others' lives can also challenge our complacency and help us appreciate other points of view. Not only can autobiography lead us to greater self-awareness by validating or challenging us, it can also enlarge our sympathies by awakening our humanity. When we read autobiography, we empathize with another's experience and thus break the shell of our own egotism and isolation.

BASIC FEATURES OF ESSAYS ABOUT REMEMBERED EVENTS

As the selections in this chapter illustrate, essays about remembered events share certain basic features. They tell life stories and vividly portray the scenes and people inhabiting them. They invest these stories with autobiographical significance and personal disclosure, and finally, they appeal to the experiences of their readers. Although these essays describe the writers' own experiences, readers can relate to them because they are really concerned with human experience in general.

A well-told story   Writing about remembered events means first of all telling a dramatic story. Whatever else the writer may attempt to do, he or she must shape the experience into a story that is entertaining and memorable. This is done primarily by building suspense. We may expect a surprise or sense disaster, shudder in anticipation of a troubling personal disclosure, or look forward to a humorous turn of events. The important point is that the autobiographer makes us want to know what will happen. We wonder whether Russell Baker will fail his flight test or if Linda Ellerbee will get her job. Sometimes, however, the outcome seems inevitable, as in "A Hanging." In this case, George Orwell makes us curious about what a hanging will be like and how everyone—especially Orwell himself—will react.

Suspense depends on a central conflict. It may be an external conflict or an internal one; often it is a combination of both. John Edgar Wideman, for example, writes about an argument that threatened to explode into violence. The conflict is external, between Wideman and another student. But it also reflects a larger, social conflict between whites and blacks. Moreover, the conflict has an internal, psychological dimension, a struggle within Wideman himself to control his anger. A conflict like this generates a great deal of tension.

Storytellers learn to vary the pace of the narrative in order to create tension and drama. They slow the pace to heighten the tension, as when Baker shifts from general to specific narrative action to give a close-up in the cockpit. They vary their sentence rhythm for dramatic emphasis, as when Ellerbee moves from long sentences to one- and two-word sentence fragments to arrest the action and mimic the blizzard's effect. They use dialogue to convey the immediacy and drama of personal interactions, as when Wideman re-creates the heated argument between himself and the other student. All these pacing techniques contribute to our involvement in the story. One moment, we're distant observers, far from the action; the next, we're thrown right into it, with the participants. (These strategies for presenting a dramatic story are presented in Chapter 13: Narrating.)

Vivid presentation of significant scenes and people

Scenes and people play an important role in most writing about remembered events. As in fiction, the scene provides a setting for the event. Instead of giving a generalized or vague impression, skillful writers re-create the scene and let us hear the people. Vividness and specificity particularize the writing and make it memorable. Carefully selected details create a dominant impression.

By moving in close, writers identify specific objects in the scene: prison cells, handcuffs, rifles, bayonets, dog, cigarette case, and whiskey in Orwell; dormitory room, walls, floor, desk, cot, self-portrait in Wideman. In addition to naming the objects, the writer details them. Orwell characterizes the prison cells as "the condemned cells, a row of sheds fronted with double bars." Wideman specifies the "pale green walls," "bare wooden floor," "skimpy desk and sagging cot." Finally, simile and metaphor make the description evocative. For Orwell, the cells are "like small animal cages"; for Wideman, the other student's presence made the room begin to "shrink." (The describing strategies of naming, detailing, and comparing are discussed further in Chapter 14: Describing.)

For presenting the important people in the events, autobiographers can choose from a variety of strategies, including physical description, action, and dialogue. They can give details of the person's appearance, as Baker does for Total Loss: ". . . his face looked tougher than the leather [of his flight suit]. He seemed old enough to be my father. Wrinkles creased around eyes that had never smiled. Lips as thin as a movie killer's." Another example is Ellerbee's description of Reuven Frank: "This white-haired fellow with a face like a Jewish sphinx, Dennis-the-Menace eyes, a shirt that didn't go with his suit, and a tie that went with neither. . . ." Both these writers give carefully chosen visual details of the person—size, physical features, dress. Notice also how they use imagery to bring the people to life: "lips as thin as a movie killer's," "Dennis-the-Menace eyes."

Writers also show people moving and talking. Orwell not only describes his condemned man, but he shows him walking: "He walked clumsily with his bound arms, but quite steadily, with that bobbing gait of the Indian who never straightens his knees. At each step his muscles slid neatly into place, the lock of hair on his scalp danced up and down, his feet printed themselves on the wet gravel." Dialogue lets us infer what the people are like from what they say. All the readings in this chapter include dialogue. In Ellerbee's essay it is a minor feature. In Orwell's essay, however, the participants' attitudes toward the hanging are revealed mostly by what they say.

A clear indication of the event's significance

In essays about remembered events we expect more than a dramatic story with vivid details of the scene and the people. Since these essays are autobiographical, we also expect to find some kind of self-disclosure. Baker, for example, reveals his incompetence as a flyer and also as a lover. Wideman lets us see the anger he felt as a young man, rage he still has barely under control.

When we present ourselves to others, we usually try to make ourselves look as good as possible. In autobiographical writing, however, this may mean satisfying our readers that we are willing to admit just about anything. Orwell admits moral responsibility for participating in a hanging. Autobiographers admit to jealousy, pride, embarrassment, joy, panic, failure, success. We all know these feelings, of course, which is why we are especially curious about how others handle them.

In addition to disclosing their remembered feelings, writers convey the event's autobiographical significance. Any event can be significant; it just has to have played an important role in the writer's life. Failing the flight test was clearly significant for Baker because it was a turning point in his life. Getting the job on *Weekend* was equally important for Ellerbee because it was her first chance to become an anchorwoman. On the other hand, the argument Wideman describes does not signal any change in his life. The significance of this event comes from the feelings it aroused in him and the larger social forces he sees at work in the encounter. Similarly, Orwell does not tell us how his participation in the hanging changed him, although we sense that it may have.

You could think of the significance of a remembered event as the essay's theme, what it is about. Baker's story is about his coming of age. Ellerbee writes about her need to prove herself. Orwell writes about life and death, and moral responsibility.

Writers communicate the significance of their experience in several ways. They can show us why the event was important or tell us directly. Usually they both show and tell. If we are not made to feel something of what the author felt, then all the telling in the world will not get the message across.

Showing is the heart of an essay about a remembered event. The event must be dramatized if readers are to appreciate its importance and understand the autobiographer's feelings about it. Seeing the important scenes and hearing the people involved help us to imagine what it was really like. Skillful writers know this. They select details and carefully choose their words in order to invest their writing with meaning.

Telling contributes mightily to a reader's understanding. Writers explain what the experience means and why it was important when they reflect upon it from their present perspective. They often embed reflection in the narrative to interpret it for readers. Baker, for instance, cites Navy regulations to indicate why passing the check flight was momentous. Wideman explains that he was furious with the white student not only for coming between him and Darryl but also for invading his turf.

Writers sometimes conclude their narrative by reflecting on the event's significance. The only selection in this chapter to conclude this way is Wideman's. But he is careful not to append these reflections artificially, like a moral tagged on to a fable. He neither simplifies nor moralizes. Instead, Wideman explores his feelings. He asks questions. He tries to place his own experience in a larger historical context. Just as autobiographers strive for honesty in their self-disclosure, they also try to explore the meaning of their experience through their reflections.

An appeal to the reader's experience

Even though writing about remembered events is by definition personal writing, all autobiographers try to connect to their readers' experience. Sometimes they select events their readers will recognize—an argument, for example, or an attempt to get a new job. Occasionally, they choose events that are exotic, but that touch feelings they know will be familiar. You can relate to Baker's frustration and sense of failure, even if you have never tried to learn to fly an airplane, or identify with Brandt's dilemma, even if you have never stolen anything or been arrested.

In reading about the lives of others, we see something of our own lives mirrored back to us. This recognition is what links us to one another. We are curious to know how others live their lives, manage relationships, face defeat, or take responsibility for their actions. This curiosity is not a weakness for gossip, but the strength of empathy.

GUIDE TO WRITING

THE WRITING TASK

Write an essay about a significant event in your life. Choose an event that will be engaging for readers and that will, at the same time, tell them something about you. Tell your story dramatically and vividly, giving a clear indication of its autobiographical significance.

INVENTION

Before drafting an essay about a remembered event you need to remember what happened and to explore its significance. Only then can you write confidently and develop a full and rich draft. Invention is designed to help you choose an appropriate event, test your choice, define its autobiographical significance, recall important details, and then redefine the event's significance.

Choosing an event to write about You may already have an event in mind. Even so, you may want to consider several events in order to make the best possible choice. If you have decided upon an event, however, turn now to Testing Your Choice on the next page.

Listing events. List several events you might write about. Make the list as long as you can. Include different kinds of events: common and unusual, brief ones and longer ones, events close and distant emotionally, events recent and distant in time. The following categories of significant personal events may give you some ideas for your list:

- [ ] Any incident charged with strong emotions such as love, fear, anger, delight, jealousy, embarrassment, guilt, frustration, hurt, pride, happiness, joy
- [ ] Any turning point in your life which challenged or changed the way you feel, think, or act
- [ ] Any "first" such as when you first realized you had a special skill, ambition, or problem; when you first felt rejected or needed; when you first became aware of injustice
- [ ] Any critical moment when you were forced to examine your basic values, attitudes, beliefs, assumptions
- [ ] Any occasion when things did not turn out the way you expected they

would: when you expected to be praised and were criticized, when you were convinced you would fail but succeeded

☐ Any memorably difficult situation: when you had to play an unfamiliar or uncomfortable role, when someone you admired let you down (or you let someone down who was depending on you), when you had to make a tough choice

☐ Any event that shaped you in a particular way, making you perhaps independent, proud, insecure, fearful, courageous, ambitious

Considering your audience and purpose. Deciding on your audience and purpose should help you to narrow your choice of an event. Try to answer these questions before you pick an event from your list of possibilities:

☐ Who will be reading my essay?
☐ What would I feel comfortable disclosing to this audience?
☐ What do I want them to learn about me?
☐ Which of my experiences would connect to their lives?

Look closely at your list and choose an event that you want to share with your readers. Remember that writing about significant remembered events requires a certain honesty and self-reflection. You might find just the right event immediately. Most writers, however, need time to weigh the advantages and disadvantages of several equally attractive possibilities.

Testing your choice   Next you should examine your choice to see whether it is worth writing about and to be sure you will be able to do so. Do this by asking yourself these questions.

☐ As a fragment of my life story, does this event reveal anything important about me or my life?
☐ Do I have enough perspective to disclose my feelings about this event to these particular readers?
☐ Can I shape this event into a dramatic story?
☐ Do I remember enough specific details about the action, scenes, and people to write vividly?

These questions will help you test your choice and you may want to reconsider them as you write your essay. If at any point—inventing, drafting, revising—you decide that you cannot answer these questions affirmatively and confidently, you may want to consider writing about a different event.

Defining the event's autobiographical significance

The invention activities that follow can help you better understand what the event discloses about your life.

Recalling remembered feelings. Try to remember your first response to the event: What were your feelings as it was happening and immediately thereafter? Spend about ten minutes jotting down notes about this initial response, using these questions to stimulate your memory:

☐ What was my first response to the event? What did I think? How did I feel? What did I do?

☐ How did I show my feelings?

☐ What did I want those present to think of me and why?

☐ What did I think of myself at the time?

☐ Did I talk to anyone just after the event? What did I say?

☐ How long did these first feelings last?

☐ What were the immediate consequences of the event for me personally?

Stop a moment to focus your thoughts. In two or three sentences try to articulate what your first response to the event seems to disclose about the event's original importance.

Exploring your present perspective. Next think about your present perspective on the event—your current feelings as well as any thoughts or insights you may have. Write for ten minutes about your present perspective, using these questions to get you started:

☐ How do I now feel about the way I acted at the time of the event? Was my response appropriate? Why, or why not?

☐ Looking back, how do I feel about this event? Do I understand it differently now than I did then?

☐ What do my actions at the time of the event say about the kind of person I was then? In what ways am I different now? How would I respond to the same event if it occurred today?

☐ How would I summarize my current feelings?

☐ Are my feelings settled, or do they still seem to be changing? Am I sure of my feelings about the event or ambivalent?

Now you should focus your thoughts on your current reaction. In two or three sentences explain what your present perspective on the event reveals about its importance in your life.

Recalling specific sensory details

Sensory details are the specific sights, sounds, and smells of the story you want to tell. The following activities will help you recall physical features of the scene and precise sensory details of these features.

Listing important features. Pretend that you are once again at the scene of the event. Make a list of any significant features or objects that you remember. (Exclude people from this list.) If you were planning to write about a water-skiing incident, for example, you might list the skis, rope, boat, plumes of water thrown up by your skis, lake, mountain, other boats, dock, and so on.

Describing important features. Choose at least three items from your list, and write for about five minutes on each one. Try to remember and record specific sensory details: size, shape, color, texture; side view, back view, top view, view from a distance and from up close; sounds and smells. Does it remind you of something else? Would you compare it with anything else?

Recalling other people These activities will help you remember all the significant people in the event—what they looked like, what they did, what you might have said to them.

Listing significant people. List all the people who played more than a casual role in the event. You may have only one or two people to list, or you may have several.

Describing significant people. Choose one or more persons from your list who played a central role in the event. You should select those who may help you to make clear what this event taught you about yourself. Write about each person for around five minutes, describing the person's appearance and actions and stating his or her significance in the event.

Re-creating conversations. Try to reconstruct a conversation between one or more of these persons and yourself. Set it up as a dialogue, as Jean Brandt does (see the Writer at Work section at the end of this chapter).

You may not remember exactly what was said, but you can compose a dialogue that will probably reflect accurately your relationship with that person. Try for a conversational dialogue—no speeches, just a quick, informal exchange of comments. Make an effort to extend the conversation to around ten comments by each person.

Then try to focus your thoughts about the other people by writing a sentence or two about your relationship with these people and the role they played in the event.

Redefining the event's significance Once you have explored both your first response and your present perspective and have recalled details of the scene and people, write a sentence or two restating the significance of the event in your life. Just how is the event important to you? What exactly can you say about yourself by writing about this event?

PLANNING AND DRAFTING

The next activities are designed to help you to use your invention writing, to set goals for drafting the essay, to organize your narrative, and to write a first draft.

Seeing what you have   You have now done a lot of thinking and writing about elements basic to an essay about a remembered event: your feelings, the autobiographical significance, specific sensory details, dialogue. Before you do any further invention or begin planning and drafting, you should reread everything you've written to see what you have. As you read through your invention writings, be on the lookout for surprising details or new insights. Watch for meaningful patterns and relationships. Highlight any such promising material with underscoring or notes in the margin. Guided by the questions that follow, you should now be able to decide whether you have enough material to write an essay and whether you understand the autobiographical significance well enough.

- ☐ Do I understand the autobiographical significance of the event better now than when I first began examining it?
- ☐ Will I be able to make any meaningful statements about my experience? What will they be? Can I find them in the invention writing?
- ☐ Do I have enough descriptive details to recreate the scene and people? What will be the dominant impression of my description?

If you do not see interesting details, connections, and patterns in your invention writing, you may want to write about a different event. An impoverished invention sequence is not likely to yield a good draft. Starting over is no fun, but there is no sense in starting to draft a composition if you do not feel confident about your topic.

If your invention writing looks thin but promising, there are several ways you may be able to fill it out. You might try composing other conversations, recalling additional sensory details, thinking more about your own reactions to the event, elaborating on significant people, describing other people who were involved.

Setting goals   Before starting to draft, you should set goals to guide further invention and planning. Some of these goals concern the piece as a whole, like holding readers' interest with a compelling story, satisfying their curiosity with meaningful self-disclosure, maintaining a good pace in the narrative, or framing the story in a satisfying way. Other goals have to do with smaller issues, like including memorable sensory details, creating vivid images, or making each dialogue sound like real conversation. You will be making dozens of decisions—and solving dozens of problems—as you work your way into a draft; these decisions and solutions are determined by the goals you set.

Following are some questions that can help you set such goals as you plan and draft. Consider all of them thoughtfully before you start drafting. You may also want to return to them as you work, to help keep your main goals in focus.

Your readers and purpose

☐ Will the event be familiar to my readers? How much can I assume they will know about such events? If they know little about such an event, how can I help them understand what happened? If they are familiar with such events, how can I convey the uniqueness of my experience?

☐ How can I help readers to see the significance the event has for me?

☐ How can I get readers to connect to my experience and to reflect on their own lives?

☐ Shall I discuss the personal significance in direct commentary, as Wideman does? Or shall I present it more indirectly, as is done by Orwell and Baker?

☐ How do I want to present myself? What tone should I adopt?

The beginning

☐ How shall I begin? What can I do in my very first sentence that will capture my readers' interest? Shall I begin with a mystery, as Baker does? ("For the longest time . . . I flew and flew without ever being in control of any airplane.") Shall I try a "once upon a time" beginning, like Orwell's? ("It was in Burma, a sodden morning of the rains.") Or shall I begin by having someone say something, or with someone doing something?

☐ What information should I give first? Should I begin with the main event, integrating essential background information as I tell the story? Should I establish the setting and situation right away, as Orwell and Brandt do? Should I first present myself, as Baker does? Or should I provide the complete context for the event, as Ellerbee does?

Telling the story

☐ What are the high points of my narrative and which pacing techniques can I use to emphasize them?

☐ How can I integrate details of the scene, objects, and people smoothly into the narrative?

☐ How can I let actions and conversations carry the narrative?

The ending

☐ How should the essay end? Should I continue the narrative to the end, as Baker and Orwell do? Or should I end as Wideman does, reflecting on the meaning of the experience?

☐ What do I want the ending to accomplish? Do I want to frame the essay by referring to the beginning? Would it be good to jolt the reader with something unexpected?

Outlining the narrative   An autobiographical essay about a remembered event should be first of all a good story. The way you organize this story will depend on what happened, what significance it had for you, who your readers will be, and what impression you want to give them. As you draft and revise, you will discover the most appropriate narrative line for your story. For now, you can plan this narrative line by listing the main incidents in the event. List them in the order in which you think they should be presented in your story. (See Chapter 13: Narrating for information on structuring the narrative.)

Drafting the essay   Before you begin drafting an essay about an event, you may want to review the general advice on drafting in Chapter 1. As you write, try to maintain a focus on what took place in the event you are recounting. Probably you will be telling about the incident chronologically—that is, in the order that it took place. Strive to paint a memorable picture of the scene and of any important people involved. Try also to describe the event in such a way as to say something about yourself and the event's significance in your life. If you feel stuck at any point in drafting the essay, try returning to the writing activities in the Invention section of this chapter.

READING A DRAFT WITH A CRITICAL EYE

The next step is to read over the draft. Whether you are reading your own draft or that of another student, you should make an effort to focus your reading, to read with a critical eye. The commentary that follows offers advice on reading someone else's draft. You might also want to look back to the section on reading someone else's draft critically in Chapter 1 before using this guide.

First general impression

First read the draft straight through to get a quick general impression. Read to enjoy the story and to get a sense of the autobiographical significance of the event. Try to overlook any errors in spelling, punctuation, or usage. After finishing this first reading, tell the writer what you learned about him or her from the draft. What tone do you hear? What does the story tell you about the writer? How would you summarize the autobiographical significance of the essay?

Pointings

One good way to maintain a critical focus as you read the essay is to highlight noteworthy features of the writing with *pointings*. A simple system of lines and brackets, these pointings are quick and easy to do, and they can provide a lot of helpful information for revision. Use pointings in the following way:

☐ Draw a straight line under any words or images that impress you as especially effective: strong verbs, specific details, memorable phrases, striking images.

☐ Draw a wavy line under any words or images that seem flat, stale, or vague. Also put a wavy line under any words or phrases that you consider unnecessary or repetitious.

☐ Look for pairs or groups of sentences that you think should be combined. Put brackets [ ] around these sentences.

☐ Look for sentences that are garbled, overloaded, or awkward. Put parentheses ( ) around these sentences. Put them around any sentence that seems even slightly questionable; don't worry now about whether or not you're certain about your judgment. The writer needs to know that you, as one reader, had even the slightest hesitation about understanding a sentence.

Analysis

To see the possibilities for revision, a writer needs a comprehensive analysis of the main parts and features of the draft—beginning, ending, narrative, scenes and people, action and dialogue, autobiographical disclosure. Following is a list of things to consider in analyzing a draft.

1. Evaluate the beginning. Indicate whether or not the first sentence captured your interest and whether or not the first paragraph made you want to read the essay. Consider whether some other part of the draft might make a better beginning.

2. Evaluate the ending. See if there is any way to improve the ending. Is it too obvious? Does it frame the essay by making some connection with

the beginning? (Framing is not a requirement, but it can be a nice touch.) Consider whether the essay might end better at some earlier point.

3. Consider the completeness of the essay. Point out any places where you have questions about what happened, where you need or would like more information, where you see gaps in the story. Also point to places where you are given more details than you need.

4. Evaluate the pace. Identify the places where you felt the tension build and where it slackened.

5. Say whether you want to know more about the scene and the people or whether you want less because some of the detail seems unnecessary. Point out any especially memorable scenes and people.

6. Look at what the writer says about the experience. Which of these points could be made by showing instead of telling? Does the reflection seem tacked on, like the moral of a fairy tale? Let the writer know if there is any place where you would like more reflection on the event's significance.

7. Dialogue is an effective way of presenting people, of showing what they are like by the way they talk. It is a good way to disclose autobiographical significance as well, because it can show the writer interacting with others. Review the dialogue, pointing out effective passages and suggesting ways to improve any weak passages. Look for places where additional dialogue might improve the draft, where you would like to hear what people said to each other.

8. Now that you have analyzed the draft closely, reconsider the autobiographical significance. Does it seem perceptive? Were you surprised by any of it? Can you see any way to make the disclosure more meaningful?

9. Consider how the essay caused you to reflect on your own life. Was it important to you personally? If so, how? If not, how might it be made more so?

REVISING AND EDITING

Revising may involve strengthening particular sections of your draft, or it may produce a completely rewritten and quite different essay. This section provides guidance in planning your revision. Use it together with Chapter 1, which gives general advice on revising, and Chapter 11, which shows you how to plan your revision.

Revising an essay about an event

Once you have had time to reflect on your draft and perhaps received comments from other students or your instructor, you are ready to revise. The guidance offered here for revising can be used together with the comprehensive plan for revising in Chapter 11. You can, for example, follow the revising plan in Chapter 11 up to the section Read Again To Identify Problems. At that point you should substitute the following specific guidelines for revising an essay about an event for the more general guidelines in Chapter 11.

Revising for autobiographical significance

☐ Reconsider the tone of your essay (tone reveals your attitude toward your subject and your readers). Is your tone ironic or sincere, bemused or serious, mature or childish? Is it consistent throughout the essay, or are there sudden, unexplained shifts in tone?

☐ If you want to establish greater emotional distance, consider whether you should change your tone or add commentary. Try analyzing or evaluating the experience. Put it into a larger perspective. Look at it as if it were someone else's experience. What insight or advice could you offer?

☐ Look to see whether you need to reveal more of yourself. Be certain readers will be able to tell what the event meant to you. Consider ways to reveal more of your feelings through action and dialogue (what you do and say) as well as through explicit commentary. Review your invention notes recalling remembered feelings and exploring your present perspective for insightful reflections and pointed images you might be able to add.

☐ Eliminate any incidents, dialogue, or descriptive details that do not contribute to the autobiographical significance or add drama, tension, or vividness to the story. Before cutting, ask yourself how you can improve what you already have.

Revising for particularity

☐ Evaluate your presentation of scenes and people to see whether additional details or images might enhance their vividness and particularity. Review your invention notes describing important features and people for promising language you might incorporate into your draft. If you need more ideas, you might try one of the all-purpose invention activities like cubing or questioning in Chapter 11: Invention and Revision.

☐ Consider whether you could replace generalized narration with specific narrative action, detailing movements and gestures.

☐ Replace summarized conversation with direct dialogue if the actual language is memorable.

☐ Consider your word choice. Substitute active for passive verbs and concrete for abstract nouns.

Revising for readability

☐ Reconsider your beginning. Decide whether there is a better way to open your essay.

☐ Improve pacing and flow by strengthening connections between sentences and paragraphs.

☐ Reconsider your ending. Decide whether you can end more effectively.

☐ Re-evaluate the whole essay in terms of your readers' needs and interests. Decide whether you have told readers everything they need to know or whether you've given them more than they need to know.

Editing and proofreading As you revise a draft for the final time, you need to edit it carefully. Though you probably corrected obvious errors in the drafting stage, usage and style were not your first priority. Now, however, you must find and correct any errors of mechanics, usage, punctuation, or style. When you have edited the draft and produced the final copy, you must proofread and make corrections before turning your essay in.

LEARNING FROM YOUR OWN WRITING PROCESS

Your instructor may ask you to evaluate what you have learned in writing this autobiographical essay. If so, begin by reviewing quickly the writings and notes you produced during invention and planning. How successful was this part of your writing process? What major discoveries did you make during invention? Were there obstacles in drafting that your invention writings did not help you overcome?

Next, reread your draft, any written analysis of it, and your revision. What did you discover about the event as you were drafting? How did other readers' comments help you improve the draft? What changes did you make between draft and revision? If you had more time, is there anything you would still like to improve? What are you most pleased with in your revision?

A WRITER AT WORK

FROM INVENTION TO DRAFT TO REVISION

This section looks at the writing process that Jean Brandt followed in composing her essay "Calling Home." You will see some of her invention writing and her complete first draft, which you can then compare to the final draft, printed earlier in this chapter.

Invention Brandt's invention produced about nine handwritten pages, but it took her only two hours, spread out over four days. Here is a selection of her invention writings, showing her first attempts to bring the autobiographical significance of the event into focus as she explores her remembered feelings and present perspective. She begins by listing eight possible events to write about. After some reflection, she chooses to write about the time she was arrested for shoplifting. Then she attempts to focus her thoughts about the significance of the event:

> Being arrested for shoplifting was significant because it changed some of my basic attitudes. Since that night I've never again considered stealing anything. This event would reveal how my attitude toward the law and other people has changed from disrespectful to very respectful.

Brandt begins by stating tentatively that the importance of the event was the lesson it taught her. Reading this statement might lead us to expect a moralistic story of how someone learned something the hard way. As we look at the subsequent invention activities and watch the draft develop, however, we will see how her memories of her relations with other people in the incident considerably change this potentially simplistic beginning.

Recalling remembered feelings

> I was scared, humiliated, and confused. I was terrified when I realized what was happening. I can still see the manager and his badge and remember what I felt when I knew who he was. I just couldn't believe it. I didn't want to run. I felt there wasn't anything I could do—I was afraid, embarrassed, worried, mad that it happened. I didn't show my feelings at all. I tried to look very calm on the outside, but inside I was extremely nervous. The nervousness might have come through in my voice a little. I wanted the people around me to think I was tough and that I could handle the situation. I was really disappointed with myself. Getting arrested made me realize how wrong my actions were. I felt very ashamed. Afterward I had to talk to my father about it. I didn't say much of anything except that I was wrong and I was sorry. The immediate consequence was being taken to jail and then later having to call my parents and tell them what happened. I hated to call my parents. That was the hardest part. I remember how much I dreaded that. My mom was really hurt.

Brandt's exploration of her first reaction is quite successful. Naming specific feelings, she focuses on the difference between what she felt and how she acted. She remembers her humiliation at being arrested as well as the terrible moment when she had to tell her parents. As we will see, this concern with her parents' reaction, more than her own humiliation, becomes the most important theme in her essay.

In exploring her first response to the event, Brandt writes quickly, noting down memories as they come to mind. Next, she rereads this first exploration and attempts to state briefly what the incident really reveals about her:

> I think it reveals that I was not a hard-core criminal. I was trying to

live up to Robin Files's (supposedly my best girlfriend) expectations, even though I actually knew that what I was doing was wrong.

After longer pieces of exploratory writing, stopping to focus her thoughts like this helps Brandt see the point of what she has just written. Specifically, it helps her to connect diverse invention writings to her main concern: discovering the autobiographical significance of the event. Thus does she reflect on what her remembered feelings of the event reveal about the kind of person she was at the time: not a hard-core criminal. She identifies a friend, who will disappear from the writing after one brief mention. Next she looks at her present perspective on the event.

Exploring your present perspective

At first I was ashamed to tell anyone that I had been arrested. It was as if I couldn't admit it myself. Now I'm glad it happened, because who knows where I'd be now if I hadn't been caught. I still don't tell many people about it. Never before have I written about it. I think my response was appropriate. If I'd broken down and cried, it wouldn't have helped me any, so it's better that I reacted calmly. My actions and responses show that I was trying to be tough. I thought that that was the way to gain respectability. If I were to get arrested now (of course it wouldn't be for shoplifting) for something, I think I'd react the same way because it doesn't do any good to get emotional. My current feelings are ones of appreciation. I feel lucky because I was set straight early. Now I can look back on it and laugh, but at the same time know how serious it was. I am emotionally distant now because I can view the event objectively rather than subjectively. My feelings are very settled now. I don't get upset when I think about it. I don't feel angry at the manager or the police. I think I was more upset about my parents than about what was happening to me. After the first part of it was over I mainly worried about what my parents would think.

Writing about her present perspective confirms that Brandt has emotional distance from the event. She finds that she can laugh about it even after probing her feelings seriously. Reassessing her reaction at the time, she decides she acted reasonably. She is obviously pleased to recall that she did not lose control. Then, once again, Brandt tries to summarize the autobiographical disclosures she makes about herself in exploring her present perspective on the event.

My present perspective shows that I'm a reasonable person. I can admit when I'm wrong and accept the punishment that was due me. I find that I can be concerned about others even when I'm in trouble.

Finally, at the end of this first set of invention activities, Brandt reflects on what she has written in order to articulate the autobiographical significance of the event.

Redefining the event's autobiographical significance

> The event was important because it entirely changed one aspect of my character. I will be disclosing that I was once a thief, and I think many of my readers will be able to identify with my story, even though they won't admit it.

After this first set of invention activities, completed in about forty-five minutes on two separate days, Brandt is confident she has chosen an event with personal significance. She knows what she will be disclosing about herself and feels comfortable doing it—now that she knows she has sufficient emotional distance. In her brief focusing statements she begins by moralizing ("my attitude . . . changed") and blaming others (Robin Files) but concludes by acknowledging what she did. She is now prepared to disclose it to readers ("I was once a thief"). Also, she has begun to consider her readers: she thinks they will like her story because she suspects many of them will recall doing something illegal and feeling guilty about it, even if they never got caught.

Brandt is now ready to try to recall specific details from the scene of the event and about the other people involved. She writes two dialogues, one with her sister Sue and the other with her father. We include here the dialogue with her sister.

Re-creating conversations

SUE: Jean, why did you do it?

ME: I don't know. I guess I didn't want to wait in that long line. Sue, what am I going to tell Mom and Dad?

SUE: Don't worry about that yet, the detective might not really call the police.

ME: I can't believe I was stupid enough to take it.

SUE: I know. I've been there before. Now when he comes back try crying and act like you're really upset. Tell him how sorry you are and that it was the first time you ever stole something but make sure you cry. It got me off the hook once.

ME: I don't think I can force myself to cry. I'm not really that upset. I don't think the shock's worn off. I'm more worried about Mom.

SUE: Who knows? Maybe she won't have to find out.

ME: God, I hope not. Hey, where's Louie and Grandma? Grandma doesn't know about this, does she?

SUE: No, I sort of told Lou what was going on so he's just taking Grandma around shopping.

ME: Isn't she wondering where we are?

SUE: I told him to tell her we would meet them in an hour at the fountain.

ME: Jesus, how am I ever going to face her? Mom and Dad might possibly understand or at least get over it, but Grandma? This is gonna kill her.

SUE: Don't worry about that right now. Here comes the detective. Now try to look like you're sorry. Try to cry.

This dialogue helps Brandt recall an important conversation with her sister. Dialogues are an especially useful form of invention for they enable writers to remember their feelings and thoughts.

Brandt writes this dialogue quickly, trying to capture the language of excited talk, keeping the exchanges brief. She includes a version of this dialogue in her second draft but excludes it from her revision. The dialogue with her father does not appear in any of her drafts. Even though she eventually decides to feature other completely different conversations, these invention dialogues enable her to evaluate how various conversations would work in her essay.

The first draft   The day after completing the invention writing, Brandt writes her first draft. It takes her about an hour.

Her draft is handwritten and contains few erasures or other changes, indicating that she writes steadily, probably letting the writing lead her where it will. She knows this will not be her only draft.

Before you read the first draft, reread the final draft, "Calling Home," in the Readings section of this chapter. Then as you read the first draft, consider what part it was to play in the total writing process.

It was two days before Christmas and my older sister and brother, my grandmother, and I were rushing around doing last minute shopping. After going to a few stores we decided to go to Lakewood Center shopping mall. It was packed with other frantic shoppers like ourselves from one end to the other. The first store we went to (the first and last for me) was the General Store. The General Store is your typical gift shop. They mainly have the cutesy knick-knacks, posters, frames and that sort. The store is decorated to resemble an old-time western general store but the appearance doesn't quite come off. 1

We were all browsing around and I saw a basket of buttons so I went to see what the different ones were. One of the first ones I noticed was a Snoopy button. I'm not sure what it said on it, something funny I'm sure and besides I was in love with anything Snoopy when I was 13. I took it out of the basket and showed it to my sister and she said "Why don't you buy it?" I thought about it but the lines at the 2 cashiers were outrageous and I didn't think it was worth it for a 75 cent item. Instead I figured just take it and I did. I thought I was so sly about it. I casually slipped it into my jacket pocket and assumed I was home free because no one pounced on me. Everyone was ready to leave this shop so we made our way through the crowds to the entrance.

My grandmother and sister were ahead of my brother and I. They 3 were almost to the entrance of May Co. and we were about 5 to 10 yards behind when I felt this tap on my shoulder. I turned around, already terror struck, and this man was flashing some kind of badge in my face. It happened so fast I didn't know what was going on. Louie finally noticed I wasn't with him and came back for me. Jack explained I was being arrested for shoplifting and if my parents were here then Louie should go find them. Louie ran to get Susie and told her about it but kept it from Grandma. By the time Sue got back to the General Store I was in the back office and Jack was calling the police. I was a little scared but not really. It was sort of exciting. My sister was telling me to try and cry but I couldn't. About 20 minutes later two cops came and handcuffed me, led me through the mall outside to the police car. I was kind of embarrassed when they took me through the mall in front of all those people.

When they got me in the car they began questioning me, while 4 driving me to the police station. Questions just to fill out the report— age, sex, address, color of eyes, etc.

Then when they were finished they began talking about Jack and 5 what a nuisance he was. I gathered that Jack had every single person who shoplifted, no matter what their age, arrested. The police were getting really fed up with it because it was a nuisance for them to have to come way out to the mall for something as petty as that. To hear the police talk about my "crime" that way felt good because it was like what I did wasn't really so bad. It made me feel a bit relieved. When we walked into the station I remember the desk sergeant joking with the arresting officers about "well we got another one of Jack's hardened criminals." Again, I felt my crime lacked any seriousness at all. Next they handcuffed me to a table and questioned me further and then I had to phone my mom. That was the worst. I never was so humiliated in my life. Hearing the disappointment in her voice was worse punishment than the cops could ever give me.

This first draft establishes the main narrative line of events. About a third of it is devoted to the store manager, an emphasis which disappears by the final draft. What is to have prominence in the final draft—Brandt's feelings about telling her parents and her conversations with them—appears here only in a few lines at the very end. But its mention suggests its eventual importance, and we are reminded of its prominence in Brandt's invention writing.

Brandt writes a second draft for another student to read critically. In this draft, she includes dialogues with her sister and with the policemen. She also provides more information about her actions as she considered buying the Snoopy button and then decided to steal it instead. She includes visual details of the manager's office. This second draft is not essentially different in emphasis from the first draft, however, still ending with a long section about the policemen and the police station. The parents are mentioned briefly only at the very end.

The student reader tells Brandt how much he likes her story and admires her autobiographical disclosure. However, he does not encourage her to develop the dramatic possibilities in calling her parents and meeting them afterward. In fact, he encourages her to keep the dialogue with the policemen about the manager and to include what the manager said to the police on the phone in his office.

Brandt's revision shows that she does not take her reader's advice. She reduces the role of the police officers, eliminating any dialogue with them. She greatly expands the role of her parents: the last third of the paper is now focused on her remembered feelings about calling them and seeing them afterward. In dramatic importance the phone call home now equals the arrest. Remembering Brandt's earliest invention writings, we can see that she was headed toward this conclusion all along . . . but she needed invention, three drafts, a critical reading, and about a week to get there.

Remembering People

□ In an article for a sports magazine about the person who most influenced him, a professional football player writes about his high school football coach. In the essay, he admits that his coach held such a powerful influence that he still finds himself doing things to win his approval and admiration, even though he never was able to please him in high school. He relates several anecdotes to show how the coach deliberately tried to humiliate him: challenging him to an arm-wrestling match and laughing at him when he lost, or making him do so many pushups and run so many laps that he actually collapsed in exhaustion.

□ A novelist writes in her autobiography about an aunt who was notorious for lying. She describes some of her aunt's most fantastic lies and the hilarious trouble they caused. Most members of the family found the woman's behavior annoying and embarrassing, but the writer acknowledges having secretly sympathized with her. As she describes her aunt, the writer points out the resemblance between them: not only does she look like her aunt, but she too has a vivid imagination and likes to embellish reality.

□ For his political science class, a college junior writes a term paper about his internship as a campaign worker for an unsuccessful candidate. In one part of the paper he focuses on the candidate, whom he came to know well and to admire. He describes the woman's energy and ambition, her broad understanding of issues and attention to detail. The student writes about the anger and bitterness he felt when she lost and his amazement that the candidate seemed genuinely philosophical about her defeat.

□ Upon learning that her former law professor is to be honored for his service to the community, an attorney decides to write an article about him for her law school alumni magazine. She criticizes him for the hard time he gave her, the first black woman to attend the school, illustrating her point with a few anecdotes. But she also admits that she now realizes that although he often seemed unfair, he prepared her for the competitive world of law better than any of her other teachers did.

3

☐ For a composition class, a student writes about an old friend who had once been like a sister to her. Along with anecdotes demonstrating how very close they were, she composes a dialogue of a conversation they had that she's never forgotten. In it they talked about their hopes for the future, specifically about going away to college together and eventually opening a small business. But the friend got married instead, and they have since grown apart. Reflecting on her friend and on what happened to their friendship, the writer describes the feelings of betrayal she has harbored but realizes that they really are unfair. The friendship just took its natural course.

As these examples suggest, there may be many occasions when writing about a person you have known seems appropriate. Whatever the occasion, your writing must bring the person to life. The person should be carefully described, with distinct physical features and mannerisms, with his or her own characteristic way of thinking and talking, and with a recognizable personal style and sense of values. Whenever you write about someone else, you also make clear your own feelings and attitudes. In expressing your view of another person, you reveal the values and character traits you admire.

As in the examples that begin this chapter, your aim will be not only to portray the person as an individual but also to indicate how the person has been significant in your life. You may, like the football player and the attorney, decide to write about someone who was once in a position of authority over you. Or you may, like the composition student, choose to describe a peer. The person you select may have been a passing acquaintance, like the unsuccessful candidate, or someone you knew for a long time, like the overly imaginative aunt. The possibilities are endless.

Essays about remembered people tap our natural curiosity about other people—what they are like, how they lead their lives, how they relate to others, how they feel. Such essays lead us to reflect on our own lives and on the human condition in general, enabling us to know ourselves better and to empathize with others.

You can more readily understand the focus of this chapter if you consider four familiar ways of writing about people: researched biography, reportage, memoir, and autobiography. In researched biography, the writer relies on published documents. (You may write such a biographical essay in Chapter 5: Reporting Information.) If the biographer's subject is still living or recently deceased, the biographer may also interview people who knew the subject. In reportage, the writer relies on interviews and observations to profile some unusual or interesting person he or she has very likely never met before. (You may write such a profile in Chapter 4: Writing Profiles.) In memoir, the writer presents an important person he or she once knew well. Writers of memoirs are usually people at the end of successful careers who want to record their accomplishments and reflect on unusual and influential people they have encountered. They write from memory and also very often from their own personal journals and correspondence files. Though memoirists may reflect on their own lives, they nearly always keep the focus on others. They write more like historians than like autobiographers. In autobiography, writers explore frankly the personal significance of their relationships with others. Autobiographers write about others in order to learn more about themselves. They reveal as much about themselves as about their subjects.

You can see, then, that this chapter on writing about remembered people pairs with Chapter 2: Remembering Events. Both are autobiographical in that they emphasize the personal significance to the writer of the remembered event or person. Both chapters invite you to take the personal risk of disclosing something about yourself as you tell readers a story about an event or present a person from your past. You will find that contemporary published autobiographies weave together such remembered events and people, along with remembered places, recurring familiar activities, and extended reflection.

READINGS

The first reading is by Maya Angelou, a Renaissance woman who has published poetry as well as a series of autobiographies, and has worked as an actress, singer, dancer, songwriter, editor, and administrator of the Southern Christian Leadership Conference. She has said of her writing: "I speak to the black experience, but I am always talking about the human condition."

Angelou grew up during the 1930s in the small Arkansas town of Stamps. As a child, she lived with her brother Bailey; her grandmother, the "Momma" mentioned in this selection; and her Uncle Willie. Momma and Willie operated a small grocery store. In this section from *I Know Why the Caged Bird Sings* (1970), Angelou shares her childhood memories of her Uncle Willie, writing from her perspective as an adult of 40. As you read, notice how she describes Uncle Willie and selects specific anecdotes to reveal their relationship.

MAYA ANGELOU
UNCLE WILLIE

When Bailey was six and I a year younger, we used to rattle off the times 1 tables with the speed I was later to see Chinese children in San Francisco employ on their abacuses. Our summer-gray pot-bellied stove bloomed rosy red during winter, and became a severe disciplinarian threat if we were so foolish as to indulge in making mistakes.

Uncle Willie used to sit, like a giant black Z (he had been crippled as a child), 2 and hear us testify to the Lafayette County Training Schools' abilities. His face pulled down on the left side, as if a pulley had been attached to his lower teeth, and his left hand was only a mite bigger than Bailey's, but on the second mistake or on the third hesitation his big overgrown right hand would catch one of us behind the collar, and in the same moment would thrust the culprit toward the dull red heater, which throbbed like a devil's toothache. We were never burned, although once I might have been when I was so terrified I tried to jump onto the stove to remove the possibility of its remaining a threat. Like most children, I thought if I could face the worst danger voluntarily, and *triumph*, I would forever have power over it. But in my case of sacrificial effort I was thwarted. Uncle Willie held tight to my dress and I only got close enough to smell the clean dry scent of hot iron. We learned the times tables without understanding their grand principle, simply because we had the capacity and no alternative.

The tragedy of lameness seems so unfair to children that they are embar- 3 rassed in its presence. And they, most recently off nature's mold, sense that they have only narrowly missed being another of her jokes. In relief at the narrow escape, they vent their emotions in impatience and criticism of the unlucky cripple.

Momma related times without end, and without any show of emotion, how 4 Uncle Willie had been dropped when he was three years old by a woman who was minding him. She seemed to hold no rancor against the baby-sitter, nor for her just God who allowed the accident. She felt it necessary to explain over and over again to those who knew the story by heart that he wasn't "born that way."

In our society, where two-legged, two-armed strong Black men were able 5 at best to eke out only the necessities of life, Uncle Willie, with his starched shirts, shined shoes and shelves full of food, was the whipping boy and butt of jokes of the underemployed and underpaid. Fate not only disabled him but laid a double-tiered barrier in his path. He was also proud and sensitive. Therefore he couldn't pretend that he wasn't crippled, nor could he deceive himself that people were not repelled by his defect.

Only once in all the years of trying not to watch him, I saw him pretend to 6 himself and others that he wasn't lame.

Coming home from school one day, I saw a dark car in our front yard. I 7 rushed in to find a strange man and woman (Uncle Willie said later they were schoolteachers from Little Rock) drinking Dr. Pepper in the cool of the Store. I sensed a wrongness around me, like an alarm clock that had gone off without being set.

I knew it couldn't be the strangers. Not frequently, but often enough, trav- 8 elers pulled off the main road to buy tobacco or soft drinks in the only Negro store in Stamps. When I looked at Uncle Willie, I knew what was pulling my mind's coattails. He was standing erect behind the counter, not leaning forward or resting on the small shelf that had been built for him. Erect. His eyes seemed to hold me with a mixture of threats and appeal.

I dutifully greeted the strangers and roamed my eyes around for his walking 9 stick. It was nowhere to be seen. He said, "Uh . . . this this . . . this . . . uh, my niece. She's . . . uh . . . just come from school." Then to the couple—"You know . . . how, uh, children are . . . th-th-these days . . . they play all d-d-day at school and c-c-can't wait to get home and pl-play some more."

The people smiled, very friendly. 10

He added, "Go on out and pl-play, Sister." 11

The lady laughed in a soft Arkansas voice and said, "Well, you know, Mr. 12 Johnson, they say, you're only a child once. Have you children of your own?"

Uncle Willie looked at me with an impatience I hadn't seen in his face even 13 when he took thirty minutes to loop the laces over his high-topped shoes. "I . . . I thought I told you to go . . . go outside and play."

Before I left I saw him lean back on the shelves of Garret Snuff, Prince Albert 14 and Spark Plug chewing tobacco.

"No, ma'am . . . no ch-children and no wife." He tried a laugh. "I have an 15 old m-m-mother and my brother's t-two children to l-look after."

I didn't mind his using us to make himself look good. In fact, I would have 16 pretended to be his daughter if he wanted me to. Not only did I not feel any loyalty to my own father, I figured that if I had been Uncle Willie's child I would have received much better treatment.

The couple left after a few minutes, and from the back of the house I 17 watched the red car scare chickens, raise dust and disappear toward Magnolia.

Uncle Willie was making his way down the long shadowed aisle between 18 the shelves and the counter—hand over hand, like a man climbing out of a dream. I stayed quiet and watched him lurch from one side, bumping to the other, until he reached the coal-oil tank. He put his hand behind that dark recess and took his cane in the strong fist and shifted his weight on the wooden support. He thought he had pulled it off.

I'll never know why it was important to him that the couple (he said later 19 that he'd never seen them before) would take a picture of a whole Mr. Johnson back to Little Rock.

He must have tired of being crippled, as prisoners tire of penitentiary bars 20 and the guilty tire of blame. The high-topped shoes and the cane, his uncontrollable muscles and thick tongue, and the looks he suffered of either contempt or pity had simply worn him out, and for one afternoon, one part of an afternoon, he wanted no part of them.

I understood and felt closer to him at that moment than ever before or since. 21

Questions for analysis

1. What elements of fairness or unfairness do you see in Angelou's portrait of her lame uncle? Recall adults from your childhood who were different in some way. What were your feelings about them? How do you assess those feelings now?

2. In paragraphs 3–6 Angelou reflects on what she calls "the tragedy of lameness." How does she show us the effect of this tragedy on Uncle Willie?

3. Angelou lived with Uncle Willie for years. Here she singles out just

two anecdotes to disclose something about their relationship. One brief anecdote appears toward the end of paragraph 2. Another, much longer anecdote occupies paragraphs 6–18. What does each illustrate about their relationship? What is the relation of the first anecdote to the second?

4. One way autobiographers present people memorably is through specific narrative action—showing a person moving or gesturing or in specific postures. Analyze the long anecdote at the end of the essay (paragraphs 6–18), underlining each instance of specific narrative action. How do the actions contribute to this portrait of Uncle Willie? (You can learn more about specific narrative action in Chapter 13: Narrating.)

5. What role does dialogue play in Angelou's essay? What do we learn about Uncle Willie from what he says and the way he says it? (You can find further information on dialogue in Chapter 13: Narrating.)

6. Angelou informs us about Uncle Willie in both paragraphs 18 and 20, yet the two are quite different. What did she choose to do in each paragraph? How are the two paragraphs related?

7. Consider writing a portrait of an adult who has significantly influenced your life, an adult outside your immediate family. You might write about a grandparent, aunt or uncle, teacher, counselor, or coach. How would you present this person so as to engage readers' interest and disclose the significance of the person in your life? What details would you include? What anecdotes would you relate?

Commentary   We know that Uncle Willie was a very significant person in Angelou's life, yet she never tells us that directly. Instead, she shows us his significance through specific anecdotes, remembered feelings, and reflection. She might have begun the essay by stating her main point, announcing just how Uncle Willie was important to her. She chooses a much more effective and engaging strategy, however: she tells a story about how Uncle Willie forced her and her brother to memorize the multiplication tables. Learning about Uncle Willie's actions and her reactions at the time and reading her brief reflection (at the end of paragraph 2) on these sometimes-terrifying math lessons, we right away begin to understand their relationship.

This was not an easy relationship, but relationships with parents or guardians or mentors rarely are. We have mixed feelings about people we love, even people to whom we owe our lives. Autobiographers explore these mixed feelings frankly. Angelou tells us that Uncle Willie was proud, sensitive, and relatively prosperous. He and Momma provided a home for her and her brother, and he cared about their education. Yet Angelou is not at all sentimental about him. She admits that he sometimes scared her, and that she did not always feel close to him. If she had been his child, she believed, he would have treated her better. Clearly he was not a perfect guardian, and she tells us so.

As Angelou reveals her relationship with Uncle Willie, she also discloses quite a bit about herself. It may take more courage than you at first imagine to tell the world that you were left by your parents in the care of an aging grandmother and uncle. It takes courage to admit, as Angelou seems to in paragraph 3, that her uncle's lameness embarrassed her, that he made her feel impatient and critical. Even though she feared and distrusted her uncle, she could also feel sympathy for him. From these facts we can infer something of what Angelou was like as a child.

We can also infer something of the adult writer she is. She treasures the details of her past and writes honestly about her life. She seems understanding and insightful: for example, she recognizes the pain Uncle Willie's physical disability must have caused him (paragraph 5), and she conjectures astutely about his reasons for deceiving the Little Rock couple about his lameness (paragraph 20). Her tone in the essay (her attitude toward her subject and readers) seems mature and reflective. We know that she does not hate Uncle Willie and that she is no longer embarrassed by him. Her emotional distance from these people that were so important in her life enables her to present them from a balanced perspective.

As a writer, you can learn still more about writing essays about remembered people by considering carefully how Angelou describes Uncle Willie. She describes his posture, face, hands; she mentions his shined high-top shoes, starched shirts, and cane. She describes objects in the scene with the same precision; for example, the stove is "summer-gray" and in winter "rosy red." Uncle Willie leans back on shelves of "Garret Snuff, Prince Albert [smoking tobacco] and Spark Plug chewing tobacco." Coming home from school, Angelou finds not a couple from out of town drinking a bottled drink, but a school teacher couple from Little Rock drinking Dr. Pepper. (These strategies of description are discussed in the sections on Naming and Detailing in Chapter 14: Describing.)

Throughout her essay Angelou relies on inventive similes and metaphors to present people, scene, and feelings. Uncle Willie sits "like a giant black Z" and makes his way down the aisle "like a man climbing out of a dream." When Angelou enters the store, she senses something wrong, "like an alarm clock that had gone off without being set." These comparisons enable Angelou to understand her memories and feelings more fully and to present them to us more concretely. Similes and metaphors are not mere decoration; they are essential. They enable the reader to see and to understand. (Refer to the section on Comparing in Chapter 14: Describing for a discussion of simile and metaphor.)

The next selection comes from Kate Simon's second autobiographical volume, *A Wider World: Portraits in an Adolescence* (1986). Among the many portraits in *A Wider World* of Simon's close men and women friends is this piece about Martha. Though both young women lived in New York City, they met at a summer resort community, which Simon visited with the Bergsons, a family whose children she was caring for. The events take place in the 1930s. As you read, notice how Simon contrasts various people in order to present Martha and herself and to explore their relationship.

MARTHA
KATE SIMON

During my second summer with the Bergsons, when I was fifteen, I had met 1 Martha, probably at one of the entertainments so frequently and ardently staged by the community. I became enmeshed in her. She was Diana, the lithe Diana of the hunt, her movements like the graceful sway of tall reeds; her fingers were long and she joined them in circles and arcs as she spoke, the compelling punctuation of an East Indian dancer. We were the perfect pair, I thought, she dark and vertical, I fair, short, horizontal. She must have been aware of the striking contrast we made, because she wasn't averse—I yearned for it—to walking very close to me, her arm around my shoulder, my arm around her waist. We caught a good number of glances, a few amused, a few censorious because we were being showy in this place that pretended to have no pretenses, because maybe we were attempting to appear to be lesbians, a fashionable stance among those teen-age girls who were avid to read Radclyffe Hall's *Well of Loneliness* (difficult to obtain), of which we heard and spoke a good deal. And there were the titillating shadows on Virginia Woolf and Vita Sackville-West, etched a little too subtly in *Orlando*. And what about Willa Cather and what about the poet H.D.? It was a distinguished company, and a number of intellectually ambitious girls, not prepared to join it, liked to feel linked to its members by dress and gesture, no more.

Martha and I didn't see each other as often as I liked and I never surely knew 2 how important it was for her to see me. We hid potentially emotional words in smart, light commentaries on the stupid world and its stupid people. It was easier to be with and worship her when the summer was over and I could cut classes to meet her downtown at her school and ride the subway with her to her house. I eagerly performed errands for her: a music book in one of the secondhand music stores then on West Fifty-seventh Street or downtown on Fourth Avenue, where I might also pick up a copy of the *Oresteia*, for a classics project in which she was to read Electra. I was willing to do anything for her; the long subway rides to search out music and books were holy ventures, as a devout young solider might march in the Crusades, as the palace slave Charmion might serve Cleopatra.

Although she invited me to her house, I rarely went, preferring to meet her 3 away from the angry glare in her mother's onyx eyes. As she slowly took in my long, worn mouse-gray coat, my black stocking and black sneakers, the golden man's hat, she stripped me of all charm, character, intelligence, of my very being. Behind the tight lips, behind the thick eyebrows and the hair harshly pulled back as if she were trying to tear it off her skull, I could guess the thought that moved through the minds of several mothers I knew: "Dresses like a crazy, not like a girl, not even like a boy; practically homeless, no ties to anyone, obedient to no one. So she works, she says, in a laundry and a library and takes care of a doctor's children. I wouldn't let her touch my children. And she's spoiling my Martha, interfering with her practicing, teaching her to answer me back." I never heard her rebuke but knew this sort of rapaciously possessive parent of a talented child who would carry the family into riches and glory—shades of my father. To fulfill her mother's fantasy Martha must succumb to the unceasing vigilance of the harsh eyes under the aggressive eyebrows and to orders from the sharply defined, almost metallically edged lips. Priding myself on being a rebel, my raison d'être of the time, and working the role for all it was worth, I had expected attention, possibly admiration, or at least acceptance, from a family of avowed Marxists, who should approve of the freedom I had wrested from capitalist convention. Faulty logic or great innocence. Mrs. Alpert's politics had nothing to do with the fact that Martha belonged, all of her, every breath, every cell, every thought and word, to her mother and to her ambitions for her daughter's success in the capitalist world. Her attitude toward her husband was even more chilling than her disdainful manner toward me. I could escape but not the brown man who looked like a pumpernickel loaf and was as simple. He adored his daughter and liked to make little jokes with her, into which Mrs. A. cut with a phrase of contempt: "Stop already with your idiot jokes." Or worse still, called Martha away from her father into the kitchen on one pretext or another, leaving him foolishly suspended in midsentence. I liked him and was sorry for him; I had never seen such a steady attempt to annihilate a person totally. When my mother and father fought they gave each other full size and sound, equal, well-matched adversaries.

Life and love with Martha dwindled to a halt through a progression of causes. 4 Her mother had learned that we had slept together in their country house while she was in the city. Although we lay stiffly holding hands and carefully not touching each other's bodies, Mrs. A. forbade Martha to have anything to do with me. Martha wasn't completely obedient, but she had been invited to work with an amateur chamber group who were more experienced and older than she, and felt the need for more practice; her mother's admonitions not to spend time with an undisciplined sloven folded smoothly into Martha's ambition. I continued, however, to meet her at her school and ride the subway with her. There seemed to be less and less to talk about; she was becoming increasingly laconic and I too discouraged to continue babbling on my own, sensing the futility of being constantly bright and arresting.

When I went early the following summer to live with the Bergsons, I found 5 that Martha had acquired an attractive new friend. She was very blond, delicate, curly, and, compared to my dun shabbiness, dazzlingly chic. She had a cute, feminine name—Bettina, or something like that—and apparently had a clothing allowance that permitted her to wear several striking costumes: from flirtatious headband and hair bow down to her shoes, she was all in one color—a yellow set, a green set, a lavender set, with bag and handkerchief to match. She talked quickly and smiled a good deal and flirted with man, woman, child, dog, cat, and, of course, herself. I was envious and jealous, furious with Martha for taking this froth of bubbles as a serious friend, of paying so much attention to her breezy burbling and, worse, admiring her meticulously matched wardrobe. Bettina refused to notice my presence and never spoke to me, closing a ring around Martha and herself, locking me out. That Martha consented to my being excluded was a terrible blow, not, though, as deadly as I had thought it would be were we ever to be separated. Shocked, bitterly displeased, and yet a little amused, I watched Martha and pert Bettina walk as Martha and I had, an arm embracing a shoulder, an arm embracing a waist, and decided that the effect was posed and fakey, Bettina, so blond and curly, hanging on the straight, flat length of Martha like a parasite vine.

I tried to make Martha's indifference, her heartless perfidy, a dagger to my 6 heart and venom in my veins. Her cruelty was the black swift path to a noose or a leap off a high roof, to the suicide I had promised myself if she ever left me. She *was* leaving me, and I found (though acknowledged reluctantly since it contradicted the view of myself as boundlessly faithful, in spite of love's wounds, to the death) the fact acceptable. What sustenance would Martha get from Bettina? She didn't know Dostoevski from Elsie Dinsmore, nor César Franck from Irving Berlin, but was endlessly informative about where to have yellow shoes dyed pink. And what about Mama, who would certainly not permit the child of her plain-thinking, low-living house to listen long to such decadent frivolity and its little threats; maybe soon even boyfriends. I was—it took some time to admit—growing tired of them, the pumpernickel father who smiled as no one smiled back, the forbidding mother, whom I later recognized as the twin sister of the famous Grant Wood woman, and Martha herself, turning to me, when we met by chance, her mother's disapproving face. There was no farewell speech, no dramatic act of parting, as I had envisioned it, my eloquent, accusing monologue battering at Martha's shamefaced silence. We faded from each other like objects in a fog. I heard considerably later that Cutie had taken her rainbow wardrobe to a boarding school and that Mrs. Alpert and Martha had moved to Philadelphia, possibly to be close to the Curtis Institute, and probably leaving behind—almost absentmindedly—the unimportant father.

Questions for analysis

1. What part have jealousy, betrayal, and anger played in your relationships with same-age friends? Have you caused them in others or felt them yourself? How do you evaluate Simon's resolution of her feelings for Martha?

2. What seems to be the significance of Martha in Simon's life? Like Angelou, Simon does not announce the significance directly. How, then, do you infer it? What clues does Simon provide?

3. Are you surprised that Simon brings up the idea of lesbianism? She could easily have omitted any such reference. What does bringing it up enable Simon to accomplish? What does it risk?

4. Besides portraying Martha, Simon presents brief but vivid portraits of three other people: Martha's mother, Martha's father, and Bettina. Analyze each of these three portraits closely in order to decide how Simon presents each person. What strategies of naming, detailing, and comparing

does Simon employ? (You will find more information on these strategies in Chapter 14: Describing.)

5. When portraying a relationship with a significant person, writers often report both their remembered feelings and insights at the time as well as their present perspective. What specific remembered feelings about Martha does Simon report? What is her present perspective on Martha, her perspective as a writer now in her sixties? What might autobiographers gain by reporting both their remembered and present perspectives on events and people?

6. Like many modern writers, Simon relies on the dash. Skim the essay looking for dashes—they are easy to spot, like those here—and underline the part of the sentence set off with dashes. What role does the material set off by dashes play in the sentence? Does Simon always use the dash for the same purpose or for different purposes?

7. If you were to write about a significant relationship with a person from your childhood or adolescence, whom would you choose? How would you present this person to your readers?

Commentary   Throughout this essay, Simon relies on contrasts to present people and relationships. Simon refers to the "striking contrast" between Martha and herself, and she then demonstrates that contrast by describing their differences. Martha is lithe, graceful, tall, and dark; Simon is short, plump, and fair. These physical differences, which at first seem to intrigue Simon, may foreshadow the differences in style that force Simon and Martha apart. Martha is reserved and laconic, while Simon is eager, devoted, and talkative, for example. Simon also emphasizes the contrasts between herself and Bettina, Martha's new girlfriend of the second summer. Bettina is breezy, unsophisticated, and illiterate, while Simon is serious, knowing, and literate. Bettina is "dazzlingly chic," while Simon offers "dun shabbiness." The contrast is so dramatic that we are convinced that Martha must be truly fickle—as unpredictably changeable in her preferences for friends as anyone we could imagine. Like Simon, you can use concrete contrasts or comparisons when writing about a remembered person. Such pointed comparisons and contrasts strengthen a characterization and reveal aspects of a relationship. (You might want to consult Chapter 18: Comparing and Contrasting for a discussion of this important writers' strategy.)

Another interesting feature of Simon's portrait of Martha is its reliance on generalized recurring activities, rather than specific anecdotes. Unlike Angelou, who centers her portrait of Uncle Willie on two anecdotes, Simon relies on typical activities of her relationship with Martha: walks, home visits, subway rides, errands. Only once or twice does she refer to a specific, one-time event, but she does not develop it into an anecdote with a story, narrative action, and dialogue.

One last feature about Simon's essay worth considering is the abundance of allusions to literary or historical persons or events. Like similes and metaphors, allusions can be richly suggestive. Simon's allusions help us to understand her relationship with Martha and to imagine Martha and her mother. For example, in paragraph 1 Simon compares Martha to Diana, a Roman goddess who never married, was attended by nymphs, and hunted bravely like a man. Statues portray her as tall, trim, and strong. Simon also compares Martha to an East Indian dancer, a dancer trained to use her arms and hands expressively. In paragraph 2, Simon reveals her idealism, dedication, and romanticism by comparing herself to a soldier in the Crusades or to a servant of Cleopatra. In paragraph 6, Simon compares Martha's mother to the thin-lipped, unsmiling woman in Grant Wood's famous painting "American Gothic." As a reader, it is not essential that you recognize every allusion, but if you recognized most of them, you had a better understanding of the people and relationships in Simon's portrait. As a writer, you may want to include allusions in your own writing if they increase the precision and suggestiveness of your description. You should use only those allusions, however, that many—though not necessarily all—of your readers will recognize.

The next selection is from Richard Rodriguez's autobiography, *Hunger of Memory: The Education of Richard Rodriguez* (1982). In it Rodriguez explores his gradual alienation from his parents because of his academic success. As a child attending Catholic schools, he was singled out as a "scholarship boy," a minority or working-class student with special promise. Later, he received degrees from Stanford and Columbia Universities and pursued graduate work at the Warburg Institute and the University of California, Berkeley.

Here Rodriguez portrays his parents in terms of their own educational histories and their aspirations for him. As you read, notice that Rodriguez discloses a good deal about himself while telling us about his parents. What does he disclose about himself and his relationship with his parents?

MY PARENTS
RICHARD RODRIGUEZ

'Your parents must be very proud of you.' People began to say that to me 1 about the time I was in sixth grade. To answer affirmatively, I'd smile. Shyly I'd smile, never betraying my sense of the irony: I was not proud of my mother and father. I was embarrassed by their lack of education. It was not that I ever thought they were stupid, though stupidly I took for granted their enormous native intelligence. Simply, what mattered to me was that they were not like my teachers.

But, 'Why didn't you tell us about the award?' my mother demanded, her 2 frown weakened by pride. At the grammar school ceremony several weeks after, her eyes were brighter than the trophy I'd won. Pushing back the hair from my forehead, she whispered that I had 'shown' the *gringos*. A few minutes later, I heard my father speak to my teacher and felt ashamed of his labored, accented words. Then guilty for the shame. I felt such contrary feelings. (There is no simple roadmap through the heart of the scholarship boy.) My teacher was so soft-spoken and her words were edged sharp and clean. I admired her until it seemed to me that she spoke too carefully. Sensing that she was condescending to them, I became nervous. Resentful. Protective. I tried to move my parents away. 'You both must be very proud of Richard,' the nun said. They responded quickly. (They were proud.) 'We are proud of all our children.' Then this afterthought: 'They sure didn't get their brains from us.' They all laughed. I smiled.

Tightening the irony into a knot was the knowledge that my parents were 3 always behind me. They made success possible. They evened the path. They sent their children to parochial schools because the nuns 'teach better.' They paid a tuition they couldn't afford. They spoke English to us.

For their children my parents wanted chances they never had—an easier 4 way. It saddened my mother to learn that some relatives forced their children to start working right after high school. To *her* children she would say, 'Get all the education you can.' In schooling she recognized the key to job advancement. And with the remark she remembered her past.

As a girl new to America my mother had been awarded a high school 5 diploma by teachers too careless or busy to notice that she hardly spoke English. On her own, she determined to learn how to type. That skill got her jobs typing envelopes in letter shops, and it encouraged in her an optimism about the possibility of advancement. (Each morning when her sisters put on uniforms, she chose a bright-colored dress.) The years of young womanhood passed, and her typing speed increased. She also became an excellent speller of words she mispronounced, 'And I've never been to college,' she'd say, smiling, when her children asked her to spell words they were too lazy to look up in a dictionary.

Typing, however, was dead-end work. Finally frustrating. When her youngest 6 child started high school, my mother got a full-time office job once again. (Her paycheck combined with my father's to make us—in fact—what we had already become in our imagination of ourselves—middle class.) She worked then for the (California) state government in numbered civil service positions secured by examinations. The old ambition of her youth was rekindled. During the lunch hour, she consulted bulletin boards for announcements of openings. One day she saw mention of something called an 'anti-poverty agency.' A typing job. A glamorous job, part of the governor's staff. 'A knowledge of Spanish required.' Without hesitation she applied and became nervous only when the job was suddenly hers.

'Everyone comes to work all dressed up,' she reported at night. And didn't 7 need to say more than that her co-workers wouldn't let her answer the phones. She was only a typist, after all, albeit a very fast typist. And an excellent speller. One morning there was a letter to be sent to a Washington cabinet officer. On the dictating tape, a voice referred to urban guerrillas. My mother typed (the wrong word, correctly): 'gorillas.' The mistake horrified the anti-poverty bureaucrats who shortly after arranged to have her returned to her previous position. She would go no further. So she willed her ambition to her children. 'Get all the education you can; with an education you can do anything.' (With a good education *she* could have done anything.)

When I was in high school, I admitted to my mother that I planned to become 8 a teacher someday. That seemed to please her. But I never tried to explain that it was not the occupation of teaching I yearned for as much as it was something more elusive: I wanted to *be* like my teachers, to possess their knowledge, to assume their authority, their confidence, even to assume a teacher's persona.

In contrast to my mother, my father never verbally encouraged his children's 9 academic success. Nor did he often praise us. My mother had to remind him to 'say something' to one of his children who scored some academic success. But whereas my mother saw in education the opportunity for job advancement, my father recognized that education provided an even more startling possibility: It could enable a person to escape from a life of mere labor.

In Mexico, orphaned when he was eight, my father left school to work as 10 an 'apprentice' for an uncle. Twelve years later, he left Mexico in frustration and arrived in America. He had great expectations then of becoming an engineer. ('Work for my hands and my head.') He knew a Catholic priest who promised to get him money enough to study full time for a high school diploma. But the promises came to nothing. Instead there was a dark succession of warehouse, cannery, and factory jobs. After work he went to night school along with my mother. A year, two passed. Nothing much changed, except that fatigue worked its way into the bone; then everything changed. He didn't talk anymore of becoming an engineer. He stayed outside on the steps of the school while my mother went inside to learn typing and shorthand.

By the time I was born, my father worked at 'clean' jobs. For a time he was 11 a janitor at a fancy department store. ('Easy work; the machines do it all.') Later he became a dental technician. ('Simple.') But by then he was pessimistic about the ultimate meaning of work and the possibility of ever escaping its claims. In some of my earliest memories of him, my father already seems aged by fatigue. (He has never really grown old like my mother.) From boyhood to manhood, I have remembered him in a single image: seated, asleep on the sofa, his head thrown back in a hideous corpselike grin, the evening newspaper spread out before him. 'But look at all you've accomplished,' his best friend said to him once. My father said nothing. Only smiled.

It was my father who laughed when I claimed to be tired by reading and 12 writing. It was he who teased me for having soft hands. (He seemed to sense that some great achievement of leisure was implied by my papers and books.) It was my father who became angry while watching on television some woman at the Miss America contest tell the announcer that she was going to college. ('Majoring in fine arts.') 'College!' he snarled. He despised the trivialization of higher education, the inflated grades and cheapened diplomas, the half education that so often passes as mass education in my generation.

It was my father again who wondered why I didn't display my awards on 13 the wall of my bedroom. He said he liked to go to doctors' offices and see their certificates and degrees on the wall. ('Nice.') My citations from school got left in closets at home. The gleaming figure astride one of my trophies was broken, wingless, after hitting the ground. My medals were placed in a jar of loose change. And when I lost my high school diploma, my father found it as it was about to be thrown out with the trash. Without telling me, he put it away with his own things for safekeeping.

These memories slammed together at the instant of hearing that refrain 14 familiar to all scholarship students: 'Your parents must be very proud. . . . ' Yes, my parents were proud. I knew it. But my parents regarded my progress with more than mere pride. They endured my early precocious behavior—but with what private anger and humiliation? As their children got older and would come home to challenge ideas both of them held, they argued before submitting to the force of logic or superior factual evidence with the disclaimer, 'It's what we were taught in our time to believe.' These discussions ended abruptly, though my mother remembered them on other occasions when she complained that our 'big ideas' were going to our heads. More acute was her complaint that the family wasn't close anymore, like some others she knew. Why weren't we close, 'more in the Mexican style'? Everyone is so private, she added. And she mimicked the yes and no answers she got in reply to her questions. Why didn't we talk more? (My father never asked.) I never said.

Questions for analysis

1. Rodriguez suggests in this selection that education shifts a child's allegiance from the family to the society in general. Is this true in your experience? If so, what are its advantages and disadvantages?

2. Writers sometimes "frame" essays by referring at the end to something at the beginning. How does Rodriguez frame this essay about his parents? What advantages do you see in framing an essay like this?

3. In paragraphs 6, 7, 12, and 13, Rodriguez combines general, recurring incidents with specific, one-time anecdotes. Mark the specific anecdotes with a bracket. What contribution does each make to the essay? Comparing these anecdotes to the two anecdotes in Angelou's essay, what can you conclude about the function of anecdotes in essays about remembered people?

4. Analyze Rodriguez's description of one of his parents. What strategies of naming, detailing, comparing, or sensory description does Rodriguez use to present this parent? Where would you like to see less or more description? (Chapter 14: Describing contains further discussion of these strategies.)

5. Rodriguez sometimes encloses sentences or parts of sentences in parentheses. Skim the essay, underlining parenthetical statements. Then analyze each instance within the context of its surrounding sentences to decide what contribution it makes. What do you think Rodriguez gains or loses from using parentheses so often?

6. In order to see how Rodriguez portrays both of his parents in one essay, make a scratch outline of the essay. (Scratch outlining is illustrated in Chapter 11: Invention and Revision.) Is his treatment of them balanced, or does he emphasize one parent over the other? Why?

7. If you wrote about a parent or guardian, could you do it with perspective, with some emotional distance, and without sentimentality? Consider which anecdotes you might tell to show your readers what your parent or guardian was like.

Commentary   While Angelou and Simon portray just one person, Rodriguez portrays both his mother and his father. Portraying them together enables him to explore the significance of his growing estrangement from his parents during his school years and to disclose his feelings of embarrassment and consequent guilt for being embarrassed. Though he portrays his parents together, Rodriguez does not blur the differences between them. He contrasts his mother and father in order to help us understand their uniqueness and his relationship with each of them. His mother finished high school and took additional courses so that she could get a white-collar job. His father dropped out of school and remained a laborer. His mother saw education as offering job advancement and continually encouraged Rodriguez in school, while his father saw education as a way of escaping physical labor and never verbally encouraged Rodriguez.

One further feature of Rodriguez's portrait deserves comment: his sentences. A special kind of sentence is particularly useful in prose fiction, autobiographies (Chapters 2 and 3), and profiles (Chapter 4), a sentence that adds modifying words and phrases onto a short main clause, with concrete details accumulating phrase by phrase, resulting in a sentence with an unusual pattern and texture (like this one). Here is an example from paragraph 11, with each trailing modifier listed below the main clause:

From boyhood to manhood, I have remembered him in a single image:

  seated, (adjective)
  asleep on the sofa, (adjective plus prepositional phrase)
  · his head thrown back in a hideous corpselike grin, (absolute phrase)
  the evening newspaper spread out before him. (absolute phrase)

In this one sentence, Rodriguez presents a full image of his father asleep on the sofa. The sentence completes a small scene: furniture, objects, person, posture, expression. You can find other examples of this sort of additive or cumulative sentence in the first paragraph of Simon's essay (sentences 3–5). Rodriguez also makes good use of grammatically incomplete sentences. In paragraph 2, he writes: 'Sensing that she [the teacher] was condescending to them [the parents], I became nervous. Resentful. Protective." He might have written, "I became nervous, resentful, and protective," but the fragmentary sentences enable Rodriguez to emphasize significant remembered feelings. Writers choose sentence structures in order to express certain meanings, and any sentence a writer includes must seem appropriate to the writer's purpose and readers. As you write your own essay about a remembered person, consider whether cumulative sentences or short sentence fragments would help you present the person more vividly or express your feelings more emphatically.

In the next selection, a daughter portrays her father, a man for whom she feels strong ambivalence. The essay was written by Jan Gray, a college freshman. Notice, as you read this piece, how Gray uses description to convey her feelings about her father.

FATHER
JAN GRAY

My father's hands are grotesque. He suffers from psoriasis, a chronic skin 1 disease that covers his massive, thick hands with scaly, reddish patches that periodically flake off, sending tiny pieces of dead skin sailing to the ground. In addition, his fingers are permanently stained a dull yellow from years of chain smoking. The thought of those swollen, discolored, scaly hands touching me, whether it be out of love or anger, sends chills up my spine.

By nature, he is a disorderly, unkempt person. The numerous cigarette burns, 2 food stains, and ashes on his clothes show how little he cares about his appearance. He has a dreadful habit of running his hands through his greasy hair and scratching his scalp, causing dandruff to drift downward onto his bulky shoulders. He is grossly overweight, and his pullover shirts never quite cover his protruding paunch. When he eats, he shovels the food into his mouth as if he hasn't eaten for days, bread crumbs and food scraps settling in his untrimmed beard.

Last year, he abruptly left town. Naturally, his apartment was a shambles, 3 and I offered to clean it so that my mother wouldn't have to pay the cleaning fee. I arrived early in the morning anticipating a couple hours of vacuuming and dusting and scrubbing. The minute I opened the door, however, I realized my task was monumental: Old yellowed newspapers and magazines were strewn throughout the living room; moldy and rotten food covered the kitchen counter; cigarette butts and ashes were everywhere. The pungent aroma of stale beer seemed to fill the entire apartment.

As I made my way through the debris toward the bedroom, I tried to deny 4 that the man who lived here was my father. The bedroom was even worse than the front rooms, with cigarette burns in the carpet and empty bottles, dirty dishes, and smelly laundry scattered everywhere. Looking around his bedroom, I recalled an incident that had occurred only a few months before in my bedroom.

I was calling home to tell my mother I would be eating dinner at a girlfriend's 5 house. To my surprise, my father answered the phone. I was taken aback to hear his voice because my parents had been divorced for some time and he was seldom at our house. In fact, I didn't even see him very often.

"Hello?" he answered in his deep, scratchy voice. 6

"Oh, umm, hi Dad. Is Mom home?" 7

"What can I do for you?" he asked, sounding a bit too cheerful. 8

"Well, I just wanted to ask Mom if I could stay for dinner here." 9

"I don't think that's a very good idea, dear." I could sense an abrupt change 10
in the tone of his voice. "Your room is a mess, and if you're not home in ten
minutes to straighten it up, I'll really give you something to clean." Click.

Pedalling home as fast as I could, I had a distinct image of my enraged 11
father. I could see his face redden, his body begin to tremble slightly, and his
hands gesture nervously in the air. Though he was not prone to physical violence
and always appeared calm on the outside, I knew he was really seething inside.
The incessant motion of those hands was all too vivid to me as I neared home.

My heart was racing as I turned the knob to the front door and headed for 12
my bedroom. When I opened my bedroom door, I stopped in horror. The dresser
drawers were pulled out, and clothes were scattered across the floor. Everything
on top of the dresser—a perfume tray, a couple of baskets of hair clips and
earrings, and an assortment of pictures—had been strewn about. The dresser
itself was tilted on its side, supported by the bed frame. As I stepped in and
closed the door behind me, tears welled up in my eyes. I hated my father so
much at that moment. Who the hell did he think he was to waltz into my life
every few months like this?

I was slowly piecing my room together when he knocked on the door. I 13
choked back the tears, wanting to show as little emotion as possible, and quietly
murmured, "Come in." He stood in the doorway, one hand leaning against the
door jamb, a cigarette dangling from the other, flicking ashes on the carpet,
very smug in his handling of the situation.

"I want you to know I did this for your own good. I think it's time you started 14
taking a little responsibility around this house. Now, to show you there are no
hard feelings, I'll help you set the dresser back up."

"No thank you," I said quietly, on the verge of tears again. "I'd rather do it 15
myself. Please, just leave me alone!"

He gave me one last look that seemed to say, "I offered. I'm the good guy. 16
If you refuse, that's your problem." Then he turned and walked away. I was
stunned at how he could be so violent one moment and so nonchalant the next.

As I sat in his bedroom reflecting on what he had done to my room, I felt 17
the utmost disgust for this man. There seemed to be no hope he would break
his filthy habits. I could come in and clean his room, but only he could clean up
the mess he had made of his life. But I felt pity for him, too. After all, he is my
father—am I not supposed to feel some responsibility for him and to love and
honor him?

Questions for analysis   1. Gray opens the essay by describing her father's hands as "grotesque."
Why do you think she focuses on his hands? What impression does this
opening have on you as a reader?

2. What does the anecdote in paragraphs 5–16 convey about her father
and their relationship?

3. How does Gray use dialogue to reveal her father's character? Notice
her father's choice of words and her description of his tone and posture.

4. Notice the parallel between Gray cleaning up her father's apartment and him tearing apart her room. What does this parallel suggest about their relationship?

5. Look again at the descriptions of the disorder in her father's apartment and her own room (paragraphs 3, 4, and 12). How does Gray make these scenes so vivid? What strategies of naming and detailing does she employ? (These strategies are discussed in Chapter 14: Describing.)

6. What seems to you the significance of the description of disorder in her father's apartment and her room? Why does she describe the disorder in such detail? What does it add to your understanding of her relationship with her father?

7. Imagine writing about someone with whom you had a serious conflict. Whom would you write about? How would you present this person? What overall impression of this person and of you would you like your readers to get from this essay?

Commentary   Although description of place often plays a minimal role in essays about
✓   remembered people, it can be an important feature, as it is in this essay. Gray needs to describe her room and her father's apartment to show how destructive her father could be and how out of control his life was. Gray compiles long lists of things she sees, using specific names and sensory details to describe them vividly. She uses a stationary vantage point to orient her readers as she describes the rooms.

PURPOSE AND AUDIENCE

Just how a writer deploys the features common to essays about remembered people depends on the writer's subject, purpose, and readers. Essays about remembered people are as purposeful as arguments, and writers of portraits generally have several purposes in mind. Perhaps the most prominent is better understanding the subject and his or her importance in the writer's life—analyzing and reaching conclusions about a significant personal relationship. Another purpose can be self-presentation, leading readers to see the writer in a particular way. Still another purpose can be entertaining readers with a vivid portrait of an unusual or engaging subject.

Since writing about remembered people is so personal, you might think that writers write only for themselves, but such is not the case. The writer must select and organize details so that readers can easily imagine persons or scenes. Unless readers' imaginations are engaged through vivid details, the portrait will seem to them flat and lifeless. The writer must also shape and pace anecdotes to hold readers' attention. In addition, writers hope that no matter how unusual their subject, readers will recognize in the portrait a significant human relationship and will find themselves reflecting on people who have been important in their own lives.

BASIC FEATURES OF ESSAYS ABOUT REMEMBERED PEOPLE

Successful essays about remembered people have in common certain basic features: they offer a vivid portrait of their subject; they give detailed presentations of anecdotes and scenes; and they reveal the subject's significance to the writer.

A vivid portrait   At the center of an essay about a remembered person is a vivid portrait. Writers rely on dialogue and the full range of descriptive strategies—naming, detailing, comparing—to present a person to their readers. All these features can be seen in the readings in this chapter. They are also illustrated and discussed fully in Chapter 13: Narrating and Chapter 14: Describing.

In presenting Uncle Willie, Maya Angelou names many features of his appearance, singling out his posture, hands, face, and clothing, as well as his pride and sensitivity. Through concrete visual details and comparisons, she helps us imagine Uncle Willie, his face "pulled down on the left side, as if a pulley had been attached to his lower teeth." She also helps us to see Uncle Willie's specific movements, making his way down an aisle "hand over hand, like a man climbing out of a dream."

Kate Simon focuses on Martha's appearance and movements, specifying them through visual details (appearance "dark and vertical," fingers joined in "circles and arcs"), similes, and allusions. Richard Rodriguez portrays his mother through her own schooling, work, values, and intense devotion to education. Her personal style and character emerge, in part, in contrast to her husband. Like Angelou, Jan Gray focuses on specific details. She details her father's hands, gestures, clothing, size, and eating habits. She also presents him through what he says—through dialogue.

To create a portrait, autobiographers also rely on contrasts that accentuate the particular qualities of people in the essay and help us understand the relationships among them. Rodriguez contrasts his parents, their different educational histories, ambitions, and family roles. He also contrasts himself with his parents, tracing his growing estrangement from them as he takes on the language and attitudes of the Anglo culture. Simon sets up vivid contrasts between herself (short, fair, horizontal, devoted, talkative, serious, literate) and Martha (graceful, tall, dark, reserved) and Bettina (breezy, illiterate, unsophisticated). (This important writer's strategy of making comparisons and contrasts is discussed in Chapter 18: Comparing and Contrasting.)

Besides this rich array of strategies for visual presentation of their subjects, autobiographers consistently use dialogue. They let us hear their subjects speak so that we can infer what they are like. All the readings in this chapter include some dialogue. Angelou employs it to present a stuttering Uncle Willie, and Gray gives it prominence in the confrontation with her unpredictable, threatening father. Both Simon and Rodriguez use dialogue only occasionally but tellingly, Simon to reveal Martha's mother's suspicious thoughts and sharp tongue, Rodriguez to present his parents' values. Portraits that center on dramatized anecdotes (Angelou, Gray) are more likely to include dialogue than those that feature recurring activities and extended reflection (Simon, Rodriguez).

A detailed presentation of anecdotes and scenes   In portraying a significant relationship, writers may decide to narrate specific anecdotes and to describe their scenes. Anecdotes—short, pointed stories about specific incidents—reveal the subject's character and dramatize the writer's relationship with him or her. When relating an anecdote, a writer has available all the strategies of sequencing and shaping narrative action discussed at length in Chapter 2: Remembering Events and Chapter 13: Narrating.

Angelou relies on anecdotes to show us what Uncle Willie was like. More than half the portrait is taken up by these anecdotes. In the first, brief one, Uncle Willie stops her just short of burning herself during her recitation of the multiplication table. The second, longer one demonstrates the possibilities of an extended, dramatic anecdote in essays about remembered people. It begins (paragraph 6) with orientation and foreshadowing: "Only once in all the years of trying not to watch him, I saw him pretend to himself and others that he wasn't lame." It ends (paragraph 20) with a framing conjecture about Uncle Willie's feelings abut his lameness and his motives for deceiving the Little Rock couple. (Framing closes an anecdote or portrait by referring at the end to something from the beginning.) Angelou's anecdote includes tension, variation in pacing, specific narrative action, dialogue, and remembered feelings and present perspective. (You can find more information on these strategies in Chapter 13: Narrating.) Angelou also describes parts of the scene in each anecdote. The heater warming the math lesson is a "dull red heater, which throbbed like a devil's toothache." When Uncle Willie pretends he is not lame, Angelou describes his unfamiliar posture and gives us visual details of the store. (You might want to examine Chapter 14: Describing to learn more about these writing strategies.)

Like Angelou, Gray centers her portrait of her father on a single extended anecdote, the time her father trashed her room. There is suspense as she pedals home and enters her bedroom. There is tension as her father opens the door. Their confrontation is physically uneventful and yet emotionally trying for Gray. Gray presents the scene by pointing to the details of her chaotic room and showing us her father leaning against the doorjamb, flicking cigarette ashes.

*A clear indication
of the person's
significance*

Portrait writers choose as their subjects people they consider significant—those who have influenced them, those they have loved or feared, those they have tried to impress or who have impressed them—and they try to make clear exactly what that significance is. You might think of this significance as the *theme* of an essay about a remembered person. From this theme we learn the meaning of the relationship between the writer and subject.

Even when writers state this significance directly, they also convey it through anecdotes, recurring activities, vivid details—or all of these. For example, Simon tells us directly that she became "enmeshed" in Martha, that she was devoted to her; but she also shows us the extent of this devotion through their way of walking together, the errands she ran for Martha, and also through images and allusions. Later, this devotion turns to jealousy and then to acceptance of Martha's ending the relationship. These stages of intensely remembered feelings are all presented vividly, not just asserted. Perhaps the significance of the relationship for Simon, the theme of her essay, is that the fiercest attachments can fade, as she says, "like objects in a fog."

Angelou's relationship with Uncle Willie is highly ambivalent, like Gray's with her father. Portrait writers do not try to force a neat resolution, reducing to love or hate a complex relationship with deep and contradictory feelings. They acknowledge ambivalence and accept it. In many portraits, the significance seems to lie in just this realization about the inevitable complexity of close relationships.

Above all, portrait writers avoid sentimentalizing the relationships, neither damning nor idealizing their subject. Gray comes close to damning her father, but stops just short of it by admitting her feelings of pity and responsibility. Angelou sympathizes with Uncle Willie's shame about his lameness and stuttering, but she does not present him as a one-dimensional, long-suffering saint. Rodriguez admires his parents, but he tells us frankly about their aborted hopes and their resignation.

With emotional distance from their subjects, writers can more easily avoid sentimentality and probe the true significance of the relationship. Emotional distance often comes with the passage of time, but it can also be developed through sustained penetrating reflection. Gray's essay shows her struggle to develop some insight into her relationship with her father. Writing about significant people can actually help you gain emotional distance. We can see this in the Writer at Work section at the end of the chapter in which Gray sorts out some of her feelings and gains some emotional distance from her father. When you choose a person to write about, you will want to consider seriously this issue of emotional distance. It may be both easier and more satisfying to portray someone from earlier in your life, especially if you had strong feelings for this person.

In stating or implying the significance of the relationship, writers of essays about remembered people inevitably disclose something of themselves. They reveal their feelings, values, and attitudes. Angelou, for example, discloses the fear, impatience, and embarrassment she felt for Uncle Willie. Simon discloses both her odd life style and her jealousness and vulnerability. Rodriguez admits that he had "such contrary feelings" for his parents: instead of the pride and gratitude of a dutiful son, he felt shame and guilt.

An appeal to the reader's experience

Although essays about remembered people are expressive and personal, they are still written for particular readers and must engage and hold their interest. Engaging portraits can be written about nearly anyone, but friends, relatives, and family members are especially good choices. All readers have experienced failed friendships, like Simon has, as well as ambivalent relationships with parents or guardians, as Angelou, Rodriguez, and Gray have. Readers are naturally curious to know how others have managed these relationships— and what they have learned from them. Writers who explore relationships fearlessly, report them honestly, and disclose something of themselves will ultimately gain their readers' interest and understanding.

GUIDE TO WRITING

THE WRITING TASK

Write an essay about a person important in your life, someone with whom you have had a significant relationship. Strive to present a vivid portrait of this person, one that will let your readers see his or her character and personal significance to you.

INVENTION

Invention means searching your memory and discovering the possibilities of your subject. The following activities will help you choose a subject for your portrait, define his or her significance for you, characterize your relationship, and describe the person.

Choosing a person to write about

You may already have a person in mind. If so, turn to Testing Your Choice. Even if you do have someone in mind, however, you may first want to consider other people in order to choose the best possible subject for your portrait.

Listing people. Make a list of people you could write about. Make your list as complete as you can, including people you knew for a long time and those you knew briefly, people you knew long ago and those you knew recently, people you knew well and those you knew superficially, people you liked and those you disliked. Following are some categories of significant people that may give you ideas for your list:

- [ ] Anyone who was in a position of authority over you or for whom you felt responsible
- [ ] Anyone who helped you through a hard time or made life difficult for you
- [ ] Anyone whose advice or actions influenced you
- [ ] Anyone who taught you something important about yourself
- [ ] Anyone who ever inspired strong emotions in you—admiration, envy, disapproval, fascination
- [ ] Anyone whose behavior or values led you to question your own behavior or values
- [ ] Anyone who really surprised or disappointed you

Choosing a significant person. Look over your list of possible subjects and choose a person you believe you can describe vividly and whose significance in your life you are eager to explore. It should be a person your readers will want to know about. The relationship you had with this person should still seem important to you, but you should have some perspective on the relationship and understanding of the person's significance in your life.

You may find that your choice is easy to make, or you may have several subjects that seem equally attractive. Make the best decision you can for now. If the subject does not work out, you can try a different subject later.

Stop now to focus your thoughts. In a sentence or two, state your tentative understanding of why the person you have chosen is significant to you.

Testing your choice   After selecting a subject, ask yourself the following questions to determine whether you have chosen someone you will be able to write about vividly and incisively:

- [ ] Will I be able to help readers visualize and understand this person? Do I recall specific anecdotes that will show what this person was like?
- [ ] Will I be able to convey the significance this person holds in my life? Will writing about this person enable me to learn something about myself?
- [ ] Will my portrait of this person lead readers to reflect on their own experience or on human experience generally?

These questions can serve as touchstones for you to consider as you plan and write this essay. If you decide at any point that you cannot answer them affirmatively, you should reconsider your choice.

Defining the person's significance

Now you should consider what significance the person has had in your life. The following activities can help you discover this significance and find a way to share it with your readers.

Recalling remembered feelings and thoughts. Call to mind your earliest memories of the person. Take about ten minutes to put your thoughts in writing, using the following questions to stimulate your memory:

If you have always known this person:

☐ What are my earliest memories of the person?

☐ What was our relationship like at the beginning?

☐ What did we do together? What did we say to each other?

☐ In the early years of our relationship, how was I influenced by the person and how did I influence him or her?

If you met this person at a specific time in your life:

☐ What do I remember about our first meeting—place, time, occasion, particular incidents, other people, words exchanged?

☐ What did I expect him or her to be like?

☐ What was my initial impression?

☐ How did I act? What kind of impression was I trying to make?

☐ Did I talk about the person to anyone? What did I say?

Now stop to focus your thoughts. In a couple of sentences, indicate how important the person was to you early in your relationship.

Exploring your present perspective. Think about how you feel now in reflecting on your relationship with this person. Try to articulate your insights about his or her importance in your life. Take about ten minutes to put your thoughts on paper, using these questions as a guide:

☐ Would I have wanted the person to behave any differently toward me? How?

☐ How do I feel about the way I acted? Would I have behaved any differently had I known then what I know now? What might I have done differently?

☐ Looking back at our relationship, do I understand it any differently now than I did at the time?

☐ What did I want out of the relationship? What were my needs and expectations? How well were these needs satisfied?

☐ Were my feelings toward the person ambivalent? How? Do I still feel the same way? How would I describe my current feelings? Do I have enough emotional distance to write about this person and our relationship?

Now focus your thoughts about your present perspective. In two or three sentences, describe your present perspective on the person.

Recalling key anecdotes and conversations   You should now try to recollect important events and conversations that took place with the person. Putting these in the form of anecdotes and dialogues can help both to reveal the person's character and to dramatize the relationship.

Listing anecdotes. List any anecdotes you might use in presenting the person. Include those that show what the person was like as well as those that suggest what your relationship was like. Make no effort to limit your list at this point—include little things and major events, things that happened often and those that occurred one time only.

Developing an anecdote. Choose one anecdote from the list that you might use in the essay. Writing for no more than ten minutes, tell what happened. Give as much detail as you can remember. Make it dramatic. Tell the story in such a way as to illuminate the person's character and make clear his or her significance to you. Be careful, however, not to explain explicitly what the anecdote shows. Let it speak for itself.

Re-creating conversations. Try to reconstruct one or more conversations you had with the person. Choose significant conversations, ones that reveal something important about the person or the way you spoke to each other. Do more than just write, "John said. . . ." Describe John as he spoke— the tone of his voice, his facial expressions, any gestures or body language. Your goal is to let readers hear what was said *and* see how it was said.

Here, stop to focus your thoughts. Explain in a few sentences what the anecdote and dialogues disclose. Consider what exactly you want them to illustrate about the person. What do you want them to say about you?

Describing the person   Here are two invention activities that should help you recall specific information you can use to describe the person.

Describing the person's appearance. List everything you remember about the person's appearance: distinctive physical features, dress, posture, mannerisms, way of talking, any objects you associate with him or her. The list should be as extensive as possible; make no effort to limit it.

Reread your list and add specific details to particularize the items in your list—color, shape, size, texture, value—anything that might help readers visualize the person. As you think and write more about this person, additional images may come to mind. Simply add them to this list.

Making general statements about the person's character. Reflect on what you know about this person: analyze, judge, explain, evaluate. Try to make some generalizations about him or her.

Put down as many statements as you can about the person's character: values, attitudes, personality, conduct. Include anything you think might help readers understand him or her as a person.

PLANNING AND DRAFTING

This section serves as a bridge between invention and drafting. It can help you see what you have and determine what you need to explore more fully as well as guide you in establishing goals and planning your essay.

Seeing what you have You have now produced a lot of writing focused on the basic features of a portrait: descriptions of the person's appearance and character, disclosure of his or her significance to you, anecdote, dialogue. Before going on to plan and draft your essay, go back and reread what you have already written.

Look for patterns as you read, evidence of growth or deterioration, harmony or tension, consistency or contradiction in the person or in the relationship. See if you make any new discoveries or gain fresh insight. Jot down your ideas in the margins, and underline or star any promising material.

Guided by the following questions, you should now be able to decide whether you have enough material and whether you understand the person's significance well enough.

- ☐ Do I remember specific details about the person? Will I be able to describe him or her vividly?
- ☐ Do I understand how the person was significant to me? Have I been able to state it clearly?
- ☐ Do my anecdotes and dialogues capture the person's character or portray our relationship effectively?

If your invention writing is not full of detail, if it seems superficial, if it has not led you to a clear understanding of the significance the person holds in your life, then you may well have difficulty writing a coherent, developed draft. It may be that the person you have chosen is not a good subject after all. The person may not really be important enough to you personally; conversely, you may not yet have enough emotional distance to write about him or her. As frustrating as it is to start over, it is far better to do so now than later.

If your invention writing looks thin but promising, you may be able to fill it out easily with brief additional writings by returning to the appropriate pages in the guide. You might try thinking more about your relationship with the person, elaborating on your analysis, adding descriptive details, recalling other important anecdotes, reconstructing additional conversations, probing your feelings more deeply.

Setting goals   Before actually beginning to draft, most writers set goals for themselves—things to consider and problems to solve. These can include goals for the whole piece—keeping readers' interest alive, satisfying any curiosity about the person's significance, creating a vivid portrait of that person. Other goals involve smaller issues—selecting rich visual details, creating realistic dialogue, finding fresh images, connecting paragraphs to one another. All these goals—large and small—guide the decisions you will make as you draft and revise.

You have made some decisions already, and you will be making more as you draft. When you reach the revision stage, you will probably find yourself reconsidering some of these decisions. Following are some questions that should help you in setting goals for your essay. These questions relate to your goals for anticipating and satisfying your readers' expectations, beginning and ending your essay effectively, presenting the person vividly, and relating his or her significance. Considering all these questions carefully will help you clarify your purpose and connect to your readers' experience.

Your readers

- ☐ Are my readers likely to know someone like this person? If so, how can I help them imagine this particular person?
- ☐ Will my readers be surprised by this person or by our relationship? Might they disapprove? If so, how can I break through their prejudices to get them to see the person as I do?
- ☐ How can I help readers see the significance this person has for me?
- ☐ How can I get readers to empathize with the person I am portraying? How can I lead them to reflect on their own lives and our common human experience?

The beginning

- ☐ How can the first sentence capture my readers' attention? I could begin as Gray does, with a startling announcement and vivid image ("My father's hands are grotesque."). Or I could open with a quote, as Rodriguez does ("Your parents must be very proud of you.").
- ☐ On what note should I open? Should I first present myself, or should I focus immediately on my subject? How should I modulate my tone—should it be casual, distant, confiding, coy, mournful, angry, sarcastic?
- ☐ Should I provide a context, as Gray does, or jump right into the action, as Angelou does? Should I let readers *see* the person right away? Or should I *tell* them about the person first?

Presenting the person: showing and telling

☐ Which descriptive details best present the person?

☐ What direct statements should I make to characterize the person? What values, attitudes, conduct, character traits should I emphasize?

☐ If I want my readers to understand my relationship with this person, what can I show them in our conversations and experience together?

☐ What insights or feelings do I need to discuss explicitly so my readers will see the person's significance in my life?

☐ What image would best symbolize this person or our relationship?

The ending

☐ What do I want the ending to accomplish? Should it sum things up? Fix an image in readers' minds? Give readers a sense of completion? Open up new possibilities?

☐ How shall I end? With reflection? With a statement of the person's significance? With exploration of my own feelings, as Simon does, or speculation about my subject's feelings, as Angelou does? With an image of the person? With the person's words? With an anecdote?

☐ Shall I frame the essay by having the ending echo the beginning, as Rodriguez does?

Outlining the portrait   After you have set goals to guide your drafting, you might find it useful to make a rough, tentative outline of your essay, indicating an approximate sequence for the main points you will cover. You could make a brief note about how you plan to begin; list in order possible anecdotes, descriptions, conversations, or reflections; and note how you might end. As you draft, do not be alarmed if you find yourself diverging from your outline. You may well be discovering a better way to organize your essay. Once you have drafted several parts, you may want to change their order.

Drafting the essay   Before you begin drafting, review the general advice on drafting in Chapter 1. If you get stuck while drafting, try exploring the problem in writing. You may simply need to recall additional details, or you could be on the verge of an important discovery.

READING A DRAFT WITH A CRITICAL EYE

At this point you should try to have someone else read your draft. The following guidelines will help you analyze the particular features of portrait writing. (Before you begin, you might want to review the general advice on reading another's draft critically in Chapter 1.)

First general impression

Before beginning actual analysis, you should give your general impression of the draft. Read the draft straight through before making any response. Read for enjoyment, ignoring spelling, punctuation, and usage errors for now. Try to imagine the person. Think about his or her significance for the writer. Reflect on your own experience or on human nature generally.

When you have finished this first quick reading, tell the writer your overall impression. Summarize the person's significance as you understand it. If you have any insights about the person or the relationship, share your thoughts.

Pointings

One method of maintaining a critical focus as you read the essay is to highlight noteworthy features of the writing with *pointings*. This simple system of marking a draft with underlining and brackets is quick and easy to do and provides much helpful information about revising the draft. Use pointings in the following way:

☐ Draw a straight line under any words or images that seem especially effective: strong verbs, descriptive details, memorable phrases, striking images.

☐ Draw a wavy line under any words or images that impress you as flat, stale, or vague. Also put a wavy line under any words or phrases that seem unnecessary or repetitious.

☐ Look for pairs or groups of sentences that you think should be combined. Put brackets [ ] around these sentences.

☐ Look for sentences that are garbled, overloaded, or awkward. Put parentheses ( ) around these sentences. Parenthesize any sentence that seems even slightly questionable; don't worry now about whether or not it is actually incorrect. The writer needs to know that you, as one reader, had even the slightest difficulty understanding a sentence.

Analysis

Following are the major points to consider when analyzing a draft of an essay about a remembered person.

1. Strong descriptive writing must be specific and detailed. Note any places where you would like greater specificity or more detail. Point out any descriptions that are particularly effective as well as any that seem to contradict the overall impression the rest of the essay gives about the person.

2. Writers often inform readers about a person's character and conduct by making general statements. Look for vague or unnecessary statements as well as for those that need illustration. Point out any particularly revealing statements, ones that help you understand the person's character or significance. Indicate any statements that seem to be contradicted by the overall impression created by the anecdotes and dialogues. Does the writer rely too

much on telling through general statements rather than on showing through anecdotes, dialogue, and description of the person?

3. Review the anecdotes, alerting the writer to any that seem unnecessary or contradictory. Say if there is anything else you think might be well illustrated by anecdote. Evaluate each anecdote: is it dramatic, and well paced? Can the writer make better use of specific narration (people moving, gesturing, talking)?

4. Review the dialogues. Point out any particularly effective dialogue, for instance, any that helps you to understand the person and to get a feeling for his or her importance to the writer. Indicate also those you find inferior, ones that sound artificial or stilted, that move too slowly, or that seem undramatic.

5. Look again at the beginning. Now that you have thought some about the essay, do you consider the beginning effective? Did it capture your interest and set up the right expectations? Point out any other passages in the essay that you think would make a better beginning, and explain why.

6. Look again at the ending. Is it satisfying? Does it repeat what you already know? Does it oversimplify? If you think the essay could end at an earlier point, indicate where. If you can imagine a better ending—a way to frame the portrait or bring the writer's feelings into perspective—say what it is.

7. Consider again the person's significance. Does the writer sentimentalize the person or the relationship? Is the person's significance stated directly or indirectly? How is it shown?

8. What does the writer disclose about himself or herself? What do you learn about the writer? Why do you think the writer chose this subject?

9. Tell the writer what effect this essay had on you personally. How did it lead you to reflect on your own life or on human nature generally?

REVISING AND EDITING

You are now ready to revise your draft. Review any critical reading notes from classmates or suggestions from your instructor, and rethink what you have written in light of your purpose and goals and your readers' expectations. This section provides guidance in planning your revision.

Revising a portrait The guidance offered here for revising a portrait can be used together with the comprehensive plan for revising in Chapter 11. You may want to turn now to that chapter and follow its revising plan until you reach the section Read Again To Identify Problems. At that point you can substitute for the general guidelines the following specific guidelines for revising a portrait.

Revising to clarify the person's significance in your life

☐ Decide whether you want to disclose anything further about yourself. You might want to report more of your earliest feelings and thoughts about the relationship or add an anecdote that reveals something about you as well as about the person.

☐ Reconsider the person's significance, and strengthen the overall impression you give about it, if necessary.

☐ Eliminate or recast any description, statements, or dialogue that contradicts the overall impression about the person's significance. Refocus the essay if necessary.

☐ Reconsider your tone (tone reveals your attitude toward your subject and readers). Be sure that your tone reflects your feelings about the person and the relationship. Consider whether your essay reads more like an impersonal sketch or historical document than an expressive autobiographical statement. If your tone seems angry or sentimental, consider whether you can increase emotional distance through humor or reflection.

Revising for particularity

☐ Eliminate any statements that tell what you can better show.

☐ Be sure you have enough specific descriptive detail.

☐ Reread dialogues to be sure they show people as they really talk. Eliminate any dialogue that slows the pace or that does not in some way disclose the significance of your subject.

Revising for readability

☐ Reconsider your essay's organization. Rearrange material if necessary so that your readers can more easily see what happened. Help your readers follow the essay easily from section to section.

☐ Reread any anecdotes for dramatic effect. Try varying the pace if they seem dull.

☐ Reconsider your beginning. Ask yourself whether you could improve it with a better anecdote, image, statement, or dialogue.

☐ Reconsider your ending, making sure it accomplishes what you want it to.

Editing and proofreading   As you revise a draft for the last time, you must edit it closely. Though you no doubt corrected obvious errors of usage in the drafting stage, it was not your first priority. Now, however, you must find and correct any errors of mechanics, usage, and punctuation.

After you have edited the draft and produced the final copy, you must proofread it for any careless mistakes. (See the Guide to Editing and Proofreading in the Handbook at the end of this text for help with these important steps.)

If you are asked to write about your experience composing this essay, begin by reviewing everything you have written. Look especially closely at the exploration of the person's significance you did in your invention writing and at any difficulties you encountered finding adequate emotional distance.

Next, discuss the changes you made from draft to revision. What seemed to work in the draft and what needed revising? How did others' analysis of the draft help you to see its problems? What other changes would you make if you had the opportunity? What pleases you most about your essay?

A WRITER AT WORK

REVISING A DRAFT AFTER A CRITICAL READING

In this section we will look at the way Jan Gray's essay about her father evolved from draft to revision. Included here are her first draft and a written critique of it by one of her classmates. Read them, and then turn back to reread her final draft, "Father," printed earlier in this chapter.

The first draft   Gray drafted her essay after spending a couple of hours on the invention and planning activities. She had no difficulty choosing a subject, since she had such strong feelings and vivid memories of her father. She wrote the draft in one sitting and did so quickly, not worrying about punctuation or usage. Though she wrote in pencil, Gray's draft appears here typed with numbered paragraphs and marked up with the pointings from the critical reading.

My father is a large intelligent, overpowering man. He's well-respected in   1
the food-processing trade for his clever but shrewd business tactics but I find
his manipulative qualities a reflection of the maturity that he lacks. For as long
as I can remember he's always had to be in control, decision-maker of the family and what he said was law. There was no compromising with this man and
for that reason I've always feared him.
When I was little and he used to still live with us, everytime he came home   2
from work I avoided him as best I could. If he came in the kitchen I went in
the livingroom and if he came in the livingroom I went upstairs to my bedroom
just to avoid any confrontation.

Family trips were the worst. There was nowhere to go, I was locked up   3
with him in a camper or motel for 1 week, 2 weeks or however long the vacation lasted. I remember one trip in particular. It was the summer after my
12th Birthday and the whole family (5 kids, 2 adults and one dog) were going
to go "out west" for a month. We travelled through Wyoming, North and South
Dakota, Colorado and other neighboring states were on the agenda. My father is
the type who thinks he enjoys these family outings because as a loyal husband
and father that's what he should do. Going to the state parks and the wilderness was more like a business trip than a vacation. He had made the agenda so
no matter what we were to stick to it. That meant at every road sign like Yellowstone Nat'l Park we had to stop, one or more of the kids would get out stand
by the sign and he'd take a picture just so he could say we've been there. Get in
and get out as quick as possible was his motto to cover as much ground in as
little time as he could. I hated having to take those pictures because it seemed
so senseless—who cares about the dumb signs anyway? But dad is a very impatient man and any sign of non conformity was sure to put him in a rage. Not a
physical violence, no, my father never did get violent but you always knew
when he was boiling up inside. I could sense it in the tone of his voice and the
reddish glaze that would cover his eyes. He would always stay very calm yet he
was ready to explode. He never physically hurt anyone of us kids—sure we've
all been spanked before but only when we were younger. Although he con-
strained himself from inflicting harm on people he didn't hold back from dam-
aging objects.

I remember one time I was calling my mother from a girlfriend's house to   4
ask if I could stay over for dinner when my father unexpectedly answered the
phone. "Hello?" he said, in his usually gruffy manner.

"Oh, hi dad. Is Mom around?"   5

"What can I do for you?"   6

"Well, I just wanted to ask her if I could eat dinner over here at Shana's."   7

"I don't think that's a very good idea. Your room is a shambles and if your   8
not home in 10 minutes I'm really going to make a mess for you to clean up."
Click.

I was in shock. I hadn't expected him to be there because at this time my   9
parents were divorced but I knew he was serious so I jumped on my bike and
pedalled home as fast as I could. I know I was there within ten minutes but
apparently he didn't think so. I walked in the front door and headed straight
for my room. When I opened my bedroom door I couldn't believe what I saw.
My dresser drawers were all pulled out and clothes strewn about the room, the
dresser was lying on its side and everything on top of the dresser had been cast
aside in a fit of anger. I closed my door and tears began to well up in my eyes. I
hated him so much at the moment. All those years of fear suddenly turned to
anger and resentment. Who the hell was this man to do this when he didn't
even live in the house anymore? I was slowly piecing my room back together
when he knocked on the door. I choked back the tears because I didn't want

him to know that his little outrage had gotten to me and quietly said, "Come in."

He opened the door and stood in the doorway one arm leaning on the door   10
jamb and a cigarette with ashes falling on the carpet dangling from his other
hand.

"I want you to know I did this for your own good" He said. "I think its time   11
you started taking a little responsibility around this house. Now let me help
you put the dresser back up."

"No thanks. I'd rather do it myself."   12

"Aw, come on. Let's not have any hard feelings now."   13

"Please, I said. I'd rather do it myself so would you please leave me alone." 14
By this time I was shaking and on the verge of breaking out in tears. He gave
me one last look that seemed to say, "I offered, I did the right thing, I'm the
good guy and she refused me so now it's her problem" and he walked out.

I was so upset that he could be so violent one moment and then turn   15
around and patronize me by offering to help clean up what he had done. That
one incident revealed his whole character to me.

My father is a spiteful, manipulative, condescending, malicious man and   16
from that day on I knew I would never understand him or want to.

Gray opens her draft by telling about her father, making a series of direct statements describing his character. She explicitly states her feelings about him. The second paragraph illustrates what we were told in the first. Paragraph 3 also serves as illustration, showing his domination over the family and concluding with a physical description and a suggestion of his potential for violence.

In paragraphs 4 to 15, Gray relates an anecdote. Though long, it is fast paced and dramatic. She uses dialogue to show us her father's character and description to let us visualize the damage he did to her room. The essay ends as it began—with a series of statements and explicit disclosure of the writer's feelings.

A critical reading   A classmate named Tom Schwartz read Gray's draft. He first read the draft once and quickly wrote down his general impression. Following the critical reading guide, Schwartz then reread the draft to analyze its features closely. It took him a little more than half an hour to complete a full written critique of Gray's draft. Following is Schwartz's critique. Each numbered point corresponds to the same step in Reading a Draft with a Critical Eye earlier in this chapter.

FIRST GENERAL IMPRESSION: Your dad sure seems crazy. I can see how he's impossible to live with. Because he's your dad he's naturally significant. You say you hate him and you call him a lot of names. But you also say he thought of himself as a loyal father. Was there anytime he was ok?

1. I can't picture him. What did he look like? I like the description of your messed up room. I'd like even more detail, like what clothes were thrown around and where. Did he break anything when he tipped the dresser? Was the whole room a wreck or just the dresser? Oh yeah, the detail of his cigarette ashes falling on the carpet is great. He's the one who's making the mess, not you.

2. You make a lot of statements. Most need illustration. I don't get it about there being no compromising with him. What do you expect him to do? My dad is pretty strict too. But he doesn't wreck my room. I like his being impatient and violent.

3. I don't get the vacation. Was it a birthday trip? Didn't you go to Yellowstone? Or did you just take pictures of signs? Sounds weird. The room anecdote is the best. It's really dramatic. The dialogue works as a frame I think. He had some nerve offering to help pick up the dresser. How smug and self-satisfied. Patronizing is right. Great anecdote.

4. I already talked about the dialogue. It seems dramatic.

5. The beginning doesn't lead one to expect the room anecdote. The stuff about his business seems out of place. You're writing about your relationship with him not about his business. I don't have any suggestions.

6. The ending may be going too far now that I think of it. Also, even though you say you don't want to understand him, here you are writing about him. Maybe there's more to it than you're admitting. You could end with the paragraph before. The anecdote sure does reveal his character.

7. I just said you might have more feelings than you're admitting. You certainly have every reason to hate him. You say he never really hit you. But he certainly was violent, like you said.

8. I'm not sure why you wrote about your dad. Maybe you just feel strongly about him and need to figure him out. Maybe because he's colorful—unusual, unpredictable, not like other fathers, even divorced ones. I think he was a great choice for an essay. You disclose a lot of unpleasant stuff about your family. You certainly seem honest.

9. I guess it makes me feel lucky my dad and I get along. I don't know what I'd do if he was like your dad. I still wonder if your dad was all that bad. He must have some good sides.

Gray found Schwartz's critique extremely helpful in revising her draft. Reread her revision now to see what she changed; as you will see, many of her changes were suggested by Schwartz.

In writing about what she learned from writing this essay, Gray remarked: "Tom's criticism helped me a lot. He warned me against making too many statements without illustrating them. He said I needed more showing and less telling. He also questioned the vacation anecdote. I guess it didn't have much of a point. And the incident with my room seemed to work so well I decided to add the part about my dad's apartment."

Gray realized that the heart of her essay was in the anecdote about her room. She also saw, from Schwartz's comments, that the opening paragraphs weren't working. Responding to his request for more physical description of her father, Gray returned to the invention activity in which she listed important details about the person's appearance. From this exploration, she came up with the detailed description of her father that now opens the essay. As she was describing her father, she remembered the incident of cleaning his apartment and decided to use the description of his filthy apartment to frame the description of her own ransacked room.

Perhaps Schwartz's greatest contribution, however, was in helping Gray re-examine the real significance her father held in her life. Specifically, Schwartz made her realize that her feelings were more complicated than she let on in her first draft. In writing about what she learned, Gray concluded, "The feelings I wanted to express didn't come across. I had a hard time writing the paper because I held back on a lot of things. I'm pretty ambivalent in my feelings toward my father right now." Gray discovered she could distance herself emotionally and at the same time disclose her feelings by showing her father, his room, and the confrontation over her room. Gray's portrait of her father turned out to be somewhat more sympathetic than her comments about him. She can express her ambivalence—her fury as well as her pity.

Writing Profiles

☐ A college student decides to profile a local radio station for the campus newspaper. In several visits to the station she observes its inner workings and interviews the manager, technicians, and disc jockeys. Her essay shows how the disc jockeys, who make a living by being outrageous, are nonetheless engaged in very routine day-to-day work.

☐ A journalist assigned to write about a Nobel Prize–winning scientist decides to profile a day in her life. He spends a couple of days observing her at home and at work, and interviews colleagues, students, and family, as well as the scientist herself. Her daily life, he learns, is very much like that of other working mothers—a constant effort to balance the demands of her career against the needs of her family. He presents this theme in his essay by alternating details about the scientist's work career with those about her daily life.

☐ A student in an art history class writes a profile of a local artist recently commissioned to paint outdoor murals for the city. The student visits the artist's studio and talks with him about the process of painting murals. The artist invites the student to spend the following day as part of a team of local art students and neighborhood volunteers working on the mural under the artist's direction. This firsthand experience helps the student describe the process of mural painting almost from an insider's point of view.

☐ A student in a sociology class profiles a controversial urban renewal project. She discovers from newspaper reports the names of opponents and supporters of the project, and interviews several of them. Then she visits the site and takes a tour of it with the project manager. Her essay alternates description of the renovation with analysis of the controversy.

☐ **For a writing workshop, a student profiles the library's rare book room. In the essay, he narrates his adventure into this previously uncharted territory. Expecting to find a sedate library with shelf after shelf of leather-bound first editions, he is surprised to find manuscript drafts, letters, diaries, and dog-eared annotated books (including some cheap paperback editions) from famous authors' libraries.**

Magazines and newspapers are filled with profiles. Unlike conventional news stories, which report current events, profiles tell about people, places, and activities in our communities. Some profiles take us behind the scenes of familiar places, giving us a glimpse of their inner workings. Others introduce us to the exotic— peculiar hobbies, unusual professions, bizarre personalities. Still others probe the social, political, and moral significance of our institutions. At the heart of most profiles are vivid details and surprising insights that can capture readers' curiosity.

Profiles share many features with autobiography, such as narrative action, anecdote, description, and dialogue. Strategies you learned in writing about a remembered event (Chapter 2) or person (Chapter 3), therefore, will be useful when you write a profile. Yet profiles differ significantly from autobiography. Whereas autobiography reflects on remembered personal experience, the profile synthesizes and presents newly acquired information. In writing a profile, you practice the field research methods of observing, interviewing, and note-taking commonly used by investigative reporters, anthropologists, and naturalists. You also learn to analyze data and organize it creatively so that it is both informative and interesting to readers. In these ways, the profile provides a bridge from personal writing deriving from memory and reflection to explanatory and argumentative writing based on inquiry and deliberation.

The scope of the profile you write may be large or small, depending on your instructor's advice and your choice of subject. You could attend a single event such as the Rose Bowl parade or a role-playing game convention and write up your observations of the place, people, and activity. Or you might conduct an interview with a person who has an unusual hobby or occupation and write up a profile based on your interview notes. If you have the time to do more extensive research, you might write a full-blown profile based on several observations and interviews with various people. Whatever the scope of your project, the readings that follow will introduce you to the many possibilities of profile writing and the Guide to Writing will help you research and plan your essay.

READINGS

The first selection comes from *The Solace of Open Spaces* (1985), a book about Wyoming by Gretel Ehrlich, a writer and rancher who lives there. Ehrlich observes a classic American event, a rodeo, this one the National Finals in Oklahoma City. If you know rodeo, pause for a moment to remember its competitive events, specifically saddle bronc riding, the opening event in which a cowboy must stay on a wildly bucking horse for eight seconds, holding on to nothing but the reins. Ehrlich will remind you vividly of rodeos you have seen. If you have never been to a rodeo, you will be introduced memorably to one of its major events. As you read, notice how Ehrlich narrates one event on one particular night.

**SADDLE BRONC RIDING
AT THE NATIONAL
FINALS**

GRETEL EHRLICH

Rodeo is the wild child of ranch work and embodies some of what ranching 1
is all about. Horsemanship—not gunslinging—was the pride of western men, and the chivalrous ethics they formulated, known as the western code, became the ground rules for every human game. Two great partnerships are celebrated in this Oklahoma arena: the indispensable one between man and animal that any rancher or cowboy takes on, enduring the joys and punishments of the alliance; and the one between man and man, cowboy and cowboy.

The National Finals run ten nights. Every contestant rides every night, so it 2
is easy to follow their progress and setbacks. One evening we abandoned our rooftop seats and sat behind the chutes to watch the saddle broncs ride. Behind the chutes two cowboys are rubbing rosin—part of their staying power—behind the saddle swells and on their Easter-egg-colored chaps which are pink, blue, and light green with white fringe. Up above, standing on the chute rungs, the stock contractors direct horse traffic: "Velvet Drums" in chute #3, "Angel Sings" in #5, "Rusty" in #1. Rick Smith, Monty Henson, Bobby Berger, Brad Gjermudson, Mel Coleman, and friends climb the chutes. From where I'm sitting, it looks like a field hospital with five separate operating theaters, the cowboys, like surgeons, bent over their patients with sweaty brows and looks of concern. Horses are being haltered; cowboys are measuring out the long, braided reins, saddles are set: one cowboy pulls up on the swells again and again, repositioning his hornless saddle until it sits just right. When the chute boss nods to him and says, "Pull 'em up, boys," the ground crew tightens front and back cinches on the first horse to go, but very slowly so he won't panic in the chute as the cowboy eases himself down over the saddle, not sitting on it, just hovering there. "Okay, you're on." The chute boss nods to him again. Now he sits on the saddle, taking the rein in one hand, holding the top of the chute with the other. He flips the loose bottoms of his chaps over his shins, puts a foot in each stirrup, takes a breath, and nods. The chute gate swings open releasing a flood—

not of water, but of flesh, groans, legs kicking. The horse lunges up and out in the first big jump like a wave breaking whose crest the cowboy rides, "marking out the horse," spurs well above the bronc's shoulders. In that first second under the lights, he finds what will be the rhythm of the ride. Once again he "charges the point," his legs pumping forward, then so far back his heels touch behind the cantle. For a moment he looks as though he were kneeling on air, then he's stretched out again, his whole body taut but released, free hand waving in back of his head like a palm frond, rein-holding hand thrust forward: *"En garde!"* he seems to be saying, but he's airborne; he looks like a wing that has sprouted suddenly from the horse's broad back. Eight seconds. The whistle blows. He's covered the horse. Now two gentlemen dressed in white chaps and satin shirts gallop beside the bucking horse. The cowboy hands the rein to one and grabs the waist of the other—the flank strap on the bronc has been undone, so all three horses move at a run—and the pickup man from whom the cowboy is now dangling slows almost to a stop, letting him slide to his feet on the ground.

Rick Smith from Wyoming rides, looking pale and nervous in his white shirt. 3 He's bucked off and so are the brash Monty "Hawkeye" Henson, and Butch Knowles, and Bud Pauley, but with such grace and aplomb, there is no shame. Bobby Berger, an Oklahoma cowboy, wins the go-round with a score of 83.

By the end of the evening we're tired, but in no way as exhausted as these 4 young men who have ridden night after night. "I've never been so sore and had so much fun in my life," one first-time bull rider exclaims breathlessly. When the performance is over we walk across the street to the chic lobby of a hotel chock full of cowboys. Wives hurry through the crowd with freshly ironed shirts for tomorrow's ride, ropers carry their rope bags with them into the coffee shop, which is now filled with contestants, eating mild midnight suppers of scrambled eggs, their numbers hanging crookedly on their backs, their faces powdered with dust, and looking at this late hour prematurely old.

In the rough stock events such as the one we watched tonight, there is no 5 victory over the horse or bull. The point of the match is not conquest but communion: the rhythm of two beings becoming one. Rodeo is not a sport of opposition; there is no scrimmage line here. No one bears malice—neither the animals, the stock contractors, nor the contestants; no one wants to get hurt. In this match of equal talents, it is only acceptance, surrender, respect, and spiritedness that make for the midair union of cowboy and horse.

Questions for analysis

1. In her final paragraph Ehrlich contrasts sports of communion (acceptance, surrender, respect, spiritedness) with sports of opposition (conquest, victory, scrimmage lines, malice). Classify sports you know well into these two categories. Which sports do you value and why?

2. How has Ehrlich organized this report of her observations at the rodeo? To discover her plan, make a scratch outline of the selection. (Scratch outlining is illustrated in Chapter 11: Invention and Revision.) What advantages or disadvantages do you see in her plan, given her subject and purpose?

3. How many scenes (specific locations) does this selection present? Where does Ehrlich place herself to observe these scenes—and to present them to us? What advantages or disadvantages do you see in her placement or point of view? (For information on point of view, refer to Chapter 14: Describing.)

4. Instead of referring generally to horses and riders, Ehrlich provides specific names in paragraphs 2 and 3. Look closely at these names and decide what you learn from them and whether they are necessary.

5. Mark Twain once wrote: "The difference between the *almost right* word and the *right* word is really a large matter—'tis the difference between the lightning bug and the lightning. After that, of course, that exceedingly important brick, the *exact* word. . . ." Reread Ehrlich's profile, noting any words that seem to you *right* or *exact*. Select two or three of these words and explain why you think Ehrlich chose them.

6. If you were asked to profile an unusual event, activity, or performance, which one would you choose? What would you expect to see and learn there? How could you engage readers in your observations?

Commentary   Ehrlich clearly likes rodeo and admires cowboys, and she hopes we will value them too. She wants us to see one event vividly and to share in her pleasure at experiencing it. But she also has a point to make about rodeos, a point about their larger meaning and significance. She tells us in the opening paragraph that rodeo celebrates the essential ranching partnerships between cowboy and animal and between cowboy and cowboy. In the last paragraph, she asserts that rodeo fosters this partnership—she calls it a "communion." The partnerships all around are a "match of equal talents" in which there is no conquest, opposition, or malice. Everything about the profile reveals or dramatizes this theme; or, from the perspective of Ehrlich's decisions in assembling the profile, the theme controls her selection and organization of scenes and details. Discovering a controlling theme—an angle, interpretation, surprising insight, point, incongruity—will be an important part of your writing process as you work on a profile. You do not need to have a controlling theme in mind when you choose a person, place, or activity to profile. Writers nearly always discover a controlling theme later as they reflect on their observation or interview notes, draft the profile, or discuss with others the possibilities in their draft. Though the theme may emerge late in the process, it is essential. Without it, and without a good understanding of your readers' expectations and knowledge, focusing and organizing your profile and choosing relevant anecdotes or details is difficult if not impossible.

Besides a controlling theme, description and narration are centrally important in profiling people, places, and activities, just as they are in autobiographical writing (Chapters 2 and 3). The more you know about describing and narrating, the more confidently and successfully you can write profiles.

Ehrlich names many objects and people in the chutes, arena, and hotel: rosin, chaps, horses, reins, stirrups, cantle, whistle, pickup man, and more. To help us imagine the scene as she saw it, however, she also provides many details of these objects and people. For example, the cowboys' chaps are "Easter-egg-colored" and, even more specifically, "pink, blue, and light green with white fringe." Reins are "long" and "braided" and saddles are "horn-less." The pickup men wear white chaps and satin shirts. Horses and men have specific names.

Ehrlich also makes very good use of simile, a strategy that helps readers imagine the scene and people. When she says that the horse chutes look like a "field hospital with five separate operating theaters, the cowboys, like sur-geons, bent over their patients with sweaty brows and looks of concern," we understand how serious and professional the cowboys are. Rodeoing requires concentration and commitment. With this apt simile, Ehrlich shows rather than tells us this. Once the action starts, Ehrlich describes a horse bucking "like a wave breaking whose crest the cowboy rides." The bronc-riding cowboy "looks as though he were kneeling on air" or "like a wing that has sprouted suddenly from the horse's broad back." These comparisons surprise and please as well as inform us. They reveal that Ehrlich is watching the bronc riding as though she has never seen it before, trying to see it freshly so that she can report it to us vividly, enabling us to see it as she does. As you write your profile, remember these strategies of naming, de-tailing, and comparing. (You will find more information on them in Chapter 14: Describing.)

In the long second paragraph, Ehrlich relies on narrative strategies to give the story conflict—between the cowboy and the horse—and tension—we are curious to know what will happen to the cowboy as the horse lunges out of the chute. The pace of the narrative seems quick during the early preparations in the chutes but then becomes slow to dramatize the ride. Ehrlich uses specific narrative action to slow the pace and increase the tension and drama. (See Chapter 13: Narrating.) Sentences that present these actions have strong, active verbs: "the ground crew *tightens* front and back cinches," "the chute gate *swings* open," and "the horse *lunges up*." These specific actions along with similes contribute to the image of tense dramatic action.

The next selection, published in *Esquire* in 1983, profiles a team of brain surgeons as they perform a complicated operation. It provides an inside look at something very few of us are likely ever to see—the human brain.

David Noonan, a freelance journalist, started with a sure-fire subject, guaranteed to intrigue readers. He had to handle it with some delicacy, however, so as not to make readers uneasy with overly explicit description or uncomfortable with excessive amounts of technical terminology. Think about your own responses as you read this piece. Are you upset by any of the graphic detail or overwhelmed by the terminology?

INSIDE THE BRAIN

DAVID NOONAN

The patient lies naked and unconscious in the center of the cool, tiled room. 1
His head is shaved, his eyes and nose taped shut. His mouth bulges with the
respirator that is breathing for him. Clear plastic tubes carry anesthetic into him
and urine out of him. Belly up under the bright lights he looks large and helpless,
exposed. He is not dreaming; he is too far under for that. The depth of his
obliviousness is accentuated by the urgent activity going on all around him.
Nurses and technicians move in and out of the room preparing the instruments
of surgery. At his head, two doctors are discussing the approach they will use
in the operation. As they talk they trace possible incisions across his scalp with
their fingers.

It is a Monday morning. Directed by Dr. Stein, Abe Steinberger is going after 2
a large tumor compressing the brainstem, a case that he describes as "a textbook
beauty." It is a rare operation, a suboccipital craniectomy, supracerebellar infratentorial approach. That is, into the back of the head and over the cerebellum,
under the tentorium to the brainstem and the tumor. Stein has done the operation more than fifty times, more than any other surgeon in the United States.

Many neurosurgeons consider brainstem tumors of this type inoperable 3
because of their location and treat them instead with radiation. "It's where
you live," says Steinberger. Breathing, heartbeat, and consciousness itself are
some of the functions connected with this primary part of the brain. Literally
and figuratively, it is the core of the organ, and operating on it is always very
risky. . . .

The human skull was not designed for easy opening. It takes drills and saws 4
and simple force to breach it. It is a formidable container, and its thickness
testifies to the value of its contents. Opening the skull is one of the first things
apprentice brain surgeons get to do on their own. It is sometimes called cabinet
work, and on this case Steinberger is being assisted in the opening by Bob
Solomon.

The patient has been clamped into a sitting position. Before the first incision 5
is made he is rolled under the raised instrument table and he disappears beneath
sterile green drapes and towels. The only part of him left exposed is the back
of his head, which is orange from the sterilizing agent painted on it. Using a
special marker, Steinberger draws the pattern of the opening on the patient's
head in blue. Then the first cut is made into the scalp, and a thin line of bright-
red blood appears.

The operation takes place within what is called the sterile field, a small 6
germfree zone created and vigilantly patrolled by the scrub nurses. The sterile
field extends out and around from the surgical opening and up over the instrument table. Once robed and gloved, the doctors are considered sterile from the
neck to the waist and from the hands up the arms to just below the shoulders.
The time the doctors must spend scrubbing their hands has been cut from ten
minutes to five, but this obsessive routine is still the most striking of the doctor's
preparations. Leaning over the troughlike stainless-steel sink with their masks in
place and their arms lathered to the elbow, the surgeons carefully attend to
each finger with the brush and work their way up each arm. It is the final pause,

the last thing they do before they enter the operating room and go to work. Many at NI are markedly quiet while they scrub; they spend the familiar minutes running through the operation one more time. When they finish and their hands are too clean for anything but surgery they turn off the water with knee controls and back through the OR door, their dripping hands held high before them. They dry off with sterile towels, step into long-sleeved robes, and then plunge their hands down into their thin surgical gloves, which are held for them by the scrub nurse. The gloves snap as the nurse releases them around the doctors' wrists. Unnaturally smooth and defined, the gloved hands of the neurosurgeons are now ready; they can touch the living human brain.

"Drill the hell out of it," Steinberger says to Solomon. The scalp has been 7 retracted and the skull exposed. Solomon presses the large stainless-steel power drill against the bone and hits the trigger. The bit turns slowly, biting into the white skull. Shavings drop from the hole onto the drape and then to the floor. The drill stops automatically when it is through the bone. The hole is about a half inch in diameter. Solomon drills four holes in a diamond pattern. The skull at the back of the head is ridged and bumpy. There is a faint odor of burning bone.

The drilling is graphic and jarring. The drill and the head do not go together; 8 they collide and shock the eye. The tool is too big; its scale and shape are inappropriate to the delicate idea of neurosurgery. It should be hanging on the wall of a garage. After the power drill, a hand drill is used to refine the holes in the skull. It is a sterilized stainless-steel version of a handyman's tool. It is called a perforator, and as Solomon calmly turns it, more shavings hit the floor. Then, using powerful plierlike tools called Leksell rongeurs, the doctors proceed to bite away at the skull, snapping and crunching bone to turn the four small holes into a single opening about three inches in diameter. This is a *craniectomy*; the hole in the skull will always be there, protected by the many layers of scalp muscle at the back of the head. In a *craniotomy* a flap of bone is preserved to cover the opening in the skull.

After the scalp and the skull, the next layer protecting the brain is the dura. 9 A thin, tough, leathery membrane that encases the brain, the dura (derived from the Latin for *hard*) is dark pink, almost red. It is rich with blood vessels and nerves (when you have a headache, it's the dura that aches), and now it can be seen stretching across the expanse of the opening, pulsing lightly. The outline of the cerebellum bulging against the dura is clear. With a crease in the middle, the dura-sheathed cerebellum looks oddly like a tiny pair of buttocks. The resemblance prompts a moment's joking. "Her firm young cerebellum," somebody says. . . .

The dura is carefully opened and sewn back out of the way. An hour and 10 fifteen minutes after the drilling began, the brain is exposed.

The brain exposed. It happens every day on the tenth floor, three, four, and 11 five times a day, day after day, week in and week out, month after month. The brain exposed. Light falls on its gleaming surface for the first time. It beats lightly, steadily. It is pink and gray, the brain, and the cerebellar cortex is covered with tiny blood vessels, in a web. In some openings you can see the curve of the brain, its roundness. It does not look strong, it looks very soft, soft enough to push your finger through. When you see it for the first time you almost expect sparks, tiny sparks arcing across the surface, blinking lights, the crackle of an idea. You stare down at it and it gives nothing back, reveals nothing, gives no hint of how it works. As soon as they see it the doctors begin the search for landmarks. They start talking to each other, describing what they both can see, narrating the anatomy.

In the operating room the eyes bear much of the burden of communication. 12 With their surgical masks and caps in place, the doctors and nurses resort to exaggerated stares and squints and flying eyebrows to emphasize what they are saying. After more than two decades in the operating room, Dr. Stein has developed this talent for nonverbal punctuation to a fine art. His clear blue eyes narrow now in concentration as he listens to Abe explain what he wants to do next. They discuss how to go about retracting the cerebellum. "Okay, Abe," Stein says quietly. "Nice and easy now."

The cerebellum (the word means *little brain*) is one of the most complicated 13 parts of the brain. It is involved in the processing of sensory information of all kinds as well as balance and motor control, but in this case it is simply in the way. With the dura gone the cerebellum bulges out of the back of the head; it can be seen from across the room, protruding into space, striated and strange-looking.

When the cerebellum is retracted, the microscope is rolled into place and 14 the operation really begins. It is a two-man scope, with a cable running to a TV monitor and a videotape machine. Sitting side by side, looking through the scope into the head, Steinberger and Stein go looking for the tumor.

It is a long and tedious process, working your way into the center of the 15 human brain. The joke about the slip of the scalpel that wiped out fifteen years of piano lessons is no joke. Every seen and unseen piece of tissue does something, has some function, though it may well be a mystery to the surgeon. In order to spend hour after hour at the microscope, manipulating their instruments in an area no bigger than the inside of a juice can, neurosurgeons must develop an awesome capacity for sustained concentration.

After two hours of talking their way through the glowing red geography of 16 the inner brain, Stein and Steinberger come upon the tumor. "Holy Toledo, look at that," exclaims Steinberger. The tumor stands out from the tissue around it, purple and mean-looking. It is the end of order in a very small, orderly place. It does not belong. They pause a moment, and Abe gives a quick tour of the opening. "That's tumor, that's the brainstem, and that's the third ventricle," he says. "And that over there, that's memory."

A doctor from the pathology department shows up for a piece of the tumor. 17 It will be analyzed quickly while the operation is under way so the surgeons will know what they are dealing with. The type of tumor plays an important part in decisions about how much to take out, what risks to take in the attempt to get it all. A more detailed tissue analysis will be made later.

It turns out to be a brainstem glioma, an invasive intrinsic tumor actually 18 growing up out of the brainstem. It is malignant. They get a lot of it but it will grow back. With radiation the patient could live fifteen years or even longer, and he will be told so. Abe Steinberger, in fact, will tell him. More than six hours after the first incision, the operation ends.

When the operation is over it is pointed out to Steinberger that he is the 19 same age as the patient. "Really?" he says. "It's funny, I always think of the patients as being older than me."

How they think of the patients is at the center of the residents' approach to 20 neurosurgery. It is a sensitive subject, and they have all given it a lot of thought. They know well the classic preconceived notion of the surgeon as a cold and arrogant technician. "You think like a surgeon" is a medical-school insult. Beyond that, the residents actually know a lot of surgeons, and though they say most of them don't fit the stereotype, they also say that there are some who really do bring it to life.

In many ways the mechanics of surgery itself create a distance between the 21 surgeon and the patient. A man with a tumor is a case, a collection of symptoms. He is transformed into a series of X rays, CAT scans, and angiograms. He becomes his tumor, is even referred to by his affliction. "We've got a beautiful meningioma coming in tomorrow," a doctor will say. Once in the operating room the patient disappears beneath the drapes and is reduced to a small red hole. Though it is truly the ultimate intimacy, neurosurgery can be starkly impersonal.

"The goal of surgery is to get as busy as you can doing good cases and 22 making people *better* by operating on them," says Phil Cogen. "That automatically cuts down the time you spend with patients." Though this frustrates Cogen, who has dreams and nightmares about his patients "all the time," he also knows there is a high emotional price to pay for getting too close. "One of the things you learn to do as a surgeon in any field is disassociate yourself from the person you're operating on. I never looked under the drapes at the patient until my third year in neurosurgery, when it was too late to back out."

While Cogen prides himself on not having a "surgical personality," Abe 23 Steinberger believes that his skills are best put to use in the operating room and doesn't worry too much about the problems of patient relations. "I sympathize with the patients," he says. "I feel very bad when they're sick and I feel great when they're better. But what I want to do is operate. I want to get in there and do it."

Questions for analysis

1. Does it surprise you to hear surgeons talking about "the mechanics of surgery" as if the patient were in for a lube job or a new transmission? Does Noonan seem to be critical of the surgeons' attitude? What might explain their attitude? How do you evaluate it?

2. The closest Noonan comes to explicitly stating the theme of this essay is at the end of paragraph 21: "Though it is truly the ultimate intimacy, neurosurgery can be starkly impersonal." How does he demonstrate this incongruity?

3. The operation actually lasts six hours. To see how Noonan translates clock time into narrative time with its special qualities of pacing, tension, and drama, make a scratch outline of the essay. Where does the pace quicken

and slow? Which events receive the most and least narrative space in the essay? What advantages and disadvantages do you see in Noonan's narrative pacing and structure?

4. Noonan quotes both Dr. Stein and Dr. Steinberger, letting us hear what they say during the operation (paragraphs 3, 7, 12, and 16). What do these quotations add to the essay? How might the essay have been different had Noonan paraphrased rather than quoted?

5. Look at paragraphs 1 and 2. Either one could well have opened the essay. What would have been gained and what would have been lost if Noonan had begun his essay with paragraph 2?

6. The features of an elegant, readable style include active verbs, few -ion nouns or long strings of prepositional phrases, the right words, and no more than necessary, as well as a variety of sentence structures and lengths. Skim Noonan's essay, noting these stylistic features. What seem to be the strengths and weaknesses of his style?

7. If you were asked to profile a highly skilled specialist at work, what specialty would you choose? What kind of information would you need to write such a profile? Where would you get this information?

Commentary   Some profiles, like Noonan's, require the writer to research the subject in order to understand it well. Although most of his information obviously comes from observing and interviewing, he must also have done some background reading to familiarize himself with surgical terminology and procedures.

Just as important as the actual information a writer provides is the way he or she arranges and presents it. Information must be organized in a way appropriate to the audience as well as to the content itself. It must be both accessible to readers and focused on some main point or theme. Noonan focuses on the drama of the operation. He was clearly struck by the incongruity between the intimacy of probing a human brain and the impersonal way it was actually done. Profile writers often use an incongruity—a notable discrepancy or a surprising contradiction, for instance—as the theme of their profile.

Noonan uses narration to structure his profile. Instead of just telling us how brain surgery is done, he shows us the procedures firsthand. He presents us with an actual patient ("belly up under the bright lights"), and takes us through an actual operation—preparing the patient and the surgical instruments, drilling the skull to expose the brain, painstakingly searching through the brain for the tumor.

One way Noonan creates tension and drama is by varying the pace of the narrative, slowing it here and quickening it there, closing in and moving back, telescoping or collapsing time as fits his purpose. Let us take a close look at the craniectomy (paragraphs 7–9) to see how Noonan varies the pace. He begins dramatically by quoting Dr. Solomon ("Drill the hell out of it"), then sets the stage by telling us that the scalp has already been retracted and the skull exposed. With a series of active present-tense verbs and present participles, Noonan re-creates the actual drilling for us. But he only shows us the drilling of one hole; he summarizes the drilling of the other three. He also interrupts the narrative to reflect on his own thoughts and feelings. When he returns to narrating, we see Dr. Solomon calmly turning the perforator as "more shavings hit the floor" and hear the snapping and crunching of bone as an opening is made between the holes.

Noonan not only paces his narrative for dramatic effect, but he also paces the flow of information. Readers are willing to be informed by a profile, but they are not prepared to find information presented as though they were reading a textbook or encyclopedia. By controlling the amount of information he presents, Noonan maintains a brisk pace that keeps his readers informed as well as entertained. He inserts bits of information into the narrative, as in paragraph 8 when he tells us that a hand drill called a perforator is used after the power drill and how a craniotomy differs from a craniectomy. Sometimes the information takes only a minute, subordinated in a clause or a brief sentence. At other times, it takes longer and seems to suspend the narrative altogether, as when he explains the idea of a sterile field and describes the scrubbing-up process in paragraph 6. Defining concisely and explaining clearly are essential to success in writing profiles, as important as in reports (Chapter 5) and persuasive essays (Chapters 6–10). In profiles the information must not divert readers' attention for too long a time from the details of a scene or the drama of an activity. If you decide to profile a technical or little-known specialty, you may want to include concise definitions of terms, tools, and procedures unfamiliar to your readers. (You will find a discussion of strategies of defining in Chapter 16: Defining.)

The next writer, John McPhee, regularly contributes profiles to the *New Yorker* and publishes book-length profiles. This selection profiles J. Anthony Lukas, a Pulitzer Prize–winning author who is also a pinball enthusiast. Video games have replaced pinball machines for the most part, but until the 1970s pinball was king. Its reputation was also somewhat unsavory because of the kinds of activities that went on where public pinball was typically played. Notice as you read how McPhee presents Lukas's philosophy of life as he informs us about pinball.

THE PINBALL PHILOSOPHY

JOHN MCPHEE

New York City, March 1975

J. Anthony Lukas is a world-class pinball player who, between tilts, does 1 some free-lance writing. In our city, he is No. ½. This is to say, he is one of two players who share pinball preeminence—two players whose special skills within the sport are so multiple and varied that they defy comparative analysis. The other star is Tom Buckley, of the *Times*. Pinball people tend to gravitate toward Lukas or Buckley. Lukas is a Lukasite. He respects Buckley, but he sees himself as the whole figure, the number "1." His machine is a Bally. Public pinball has been illegal in New York for many decades, but private ownership is permitted, and Lukas plays, for the most part, at home.

Lukas lives in an old mansion, a city landmark, on West Seventy-sixth Street. 2 The machine is in his living room, under a high, elegant ceiling, near an archway to rooms beyond. Bally is the Rolls-Royce of pinball, he explains as he snaps a ball into action. It rockets into the ellipse at the top of the playfield. It ricochets four times before beginning its descent. Lukas likes a four-bounce hold in the ellipse—to set things up for a long ball. There is something faintly, and perhaps consciously, nefarious about Lukas, who is an aristocratic, olive-skinned, Andalusian sort of man, with deep eyes in dark wells. As the butts of his hands pound the corners of his machine, one can imagine him cheating at polo. "It's a wrist game," he says, tremoring the Bally, helping the steel ball to bounce six times off the top thumper-bumper and, each time, go back up a slot to the ellipse— an awesome economy of fresh beginnings. "Strong wrists are really all you want to use. The term for what I am doing is 'reinforcing.' " His voice, rich and dense, pours out like cigarette smoke filtered through a New England prep school. "There are certain basics to remember," he says. "Above all, don't flail with the flipper. You *carry* the ball in the direction you want it to go. You can almost cradle the ball on the flipper. And always hit the slingshot hard. That's the slingshot there—where the rubber is stretched between bumpers. Reinforce it hard. And never—never—drift toward the free-ball gate." Lukas reinforces the machine just as the ball hits the slingshot. The rebound comes off with blurring speed, striking bumpers, causing gongs to ring and lights to flash. Under his hands, the chrome on the frame has long since worn away.

Lukas points out that one of the beauties of his Bally is that it is asymmetrical. 3 Early pinball machines had symmetrical playfields—symmetrical thumper-bumpers—but in time they became free-form, such as this one, with its field laid out not just for structure but also for surprise. Lukas works in this room—stacks of manuscript on shelves and tables. He has been working for many months on a book that will weigh five pounds. It will be called *Nightmare: The Dark Side of the Nixon Years*—a congenially chosen title, implying that there was a bright side. The pinball machine is Lukas's collaborator. "When a paragraph just won't go," he says, "and I begin to say to myself, 'I can't make this work,' I get up and play the machine. I score in a high range. Then I go back to the typewriter a new man. I have beat the machine. Therefore I can beat the paragraph." He once won a Pulitzer Prize.

The steel ball rolls into the "death channel"—Lukas's term for a long alley 4 down the left side—and drops out of sight off the low end of the playfield, finished.

With another ball, he ignites an aurora on the scoreboard. During the ball's 5 complex, prolonged descent, he continues to set forth the pinball philosophy. "More seriously, the game does give you a sense of controlling things in a way that in life you can't do. And there is risk in it, too. The ball flies into the ellipse, into the playfield—full of opportunities. But there's always the death channel— the run-out slot. There are rewards, prizes, coming off the thumper-bumper. The ball crazily bounces from danger to opportunity and back to danger. You need reassurance in life that in taking risks you will triumph, and pinball gives you that reaffirmation. Life is a risky game, but you can beat it."

Unfortunately, Lukas has a sick flipper. At the low end of the playfield, two 6 flippers guard the run-out slot, but one waggles like a broken wing, pathetic, unable to function, to fling the ball uphill for renewed rewards. The ball, instead, slides by the crippled flipper and drops from view.

Lukas opens the machine. He lifts the entire playfield, which is hinged at the 7 back, and props it up on a steel arm, like the lid of a grand piano. Revealed below is a neat, arresting world that includes spring-loaded hole kickers, contact switches, target switches, slingshot assemblies, the score-motor unit, the electric anti-cheat, three thumper-bumper relays, the top rebound relay, the key-gate assembly ("the key gate will keep you out of the death channel"), the free-ball-gate assembly, and—not least—the one-and-a-quarter-amp slo-blo. To one side, something that resembles a plumb bob hangs suspended within a metal ring. If the bob moves too far out of plumb, it touches the ring. Tilt. The game is dead.

Lukas is not an electrician. All he can do is massage the flipper's switch 8 assembly, which does not respond—not even with a shock. He has about had it with this machine. One cannot collaborate with a sick flipper. The queasy truth comes over him: no pinball, no paragraphs. So he hurries downstairs and into a taxi, telling the driver to go to Tenth Avenue in the low Forties—a pocket of the city known as Coin Row.

En route, Lukas reflects on his long history in the game—New York, Cam- 9 bridge, Paris—and his relationships with specific machines ("they're like wives"). When he was the *Times'* man in the Congo, in the early sixties, the post was considered a position of hardship, so he was periodically sent to Paris for rest and rehabilitation, which he got playing pinball in a Left Bank brasserie. He had perfected his style as an undergraduate at Harvard, sharing a machine at the *Crimson* with David Halberstam ("Halberstam is aggressive at everything he does, and he was very good"). Lukas's father was a Manhattan attorney. Lukas's mother died when he was eight. He grew up, for the most part, in a New England community—Putney, Vermont—where he went to pre-prep and prep school. Putney was "straitlaced," "very high-minded," "a life away from the maelstrom"—potters' wheels, no pinball. Lukas craved "liberation," and devel- oped a yearning for what he imagined as low life, and so did his schoolmate Christopher Lehmann-Haupt. Together, one weekend, they dipped as low as they knew how. They went to New York. And they went to two movies! They went to shooting galleries! They went to a flea circus! They played every coin-operated machine they could find—and they stayed up until after dawn! All this was pretty low, but not low enough, for that was the spring of 1951, and still beyond reach—out there past the fingertips of Tantalus—was pinball, the ban on which had been emphatically reinforced a few years earlier by Fiorello H. LaGuardia, who saw pinball as a gambling device corruptive of the city's youth.

To Lukas, pinball symbolized all the time-wasting and ne'er-do-welling that puritan Putney did not. In result, he mastered the game. He says, "It puts me in touch with a world in which I never lived. I am attracted to pinball for its seediness, its slightly disreputable reputation."

On Coin Row, Lukas knows just where he is going, and without a sidewise 10 glance passes storefronts bearing names like The World of Pinball Amusement ("SALES—REPAIR") and Manhattan Coin Machine ("PARTS—SUPPLIES"). He heads directly for the Mike Munves Corporation, 577 Tenth Avenue, the New York pinball exchange, oldest house (1912) on the row. Inside is Ralph Hotkins, in double-breasted blazer—broker in pinball machines. . . . Lukas greets Hotkins and then runs balls through a few selected machines. Lukas attempts to deal with Hotkins, but Hotkins wants Lukas's machine and a hundred and fifty dollars. Lukas would rather fix his flipper. . . .

Lukas starts for home but, crossing Forty-second Street, decides on pure 11 whim to have a look at Circus Circus, where he has never been. Circus Circus is, after all, just four blocks away. The stroll is pleasant in the afternoon sunlight, to and through Times Square, under the marquees of pornographic movies—*Valley of the Nymphs, The Danish Sandwich, The Organ Trail*. Circus Circus ("GIRLS! GIRLS! GIRLS! Live exotic models") is close to Sixth Avenue and consists, principally, of a front room and a back room. Prices are a quarter a peep in the back room and a quarter to play (two games) in the front. The game room is dim, and Lukas, entering, sees little at first but the flashing scoreboards of five machines. Four of them—a Bally, a Williams, two Gottliebs—flash slowly, reporting inexperienced play, but the fifth, the one in the middle, is exploding with light and sound. The player causing all this is hunched over, concentrating—in his arms and his hands a choreography of talent. Lukas's eyes adjust to the light. Then he reaches for his holster. The man on the hot machine, busy keeping statistics of his practice, is Tom Buckley.

"Tom." 12

"Tone." 13

"How is the machine?" 14

"Better than yours, Tone. You don't realize what a lemon you have." 15

"I love my Bally." 16

"The Bally is the Corvair of pinball machines. I don't even care for the art 17 on the back-glass. Williams and Gottlieb are the best. Bally is nowhere."

Buckley, slightly older than Lukas, has a spectacled and professional look. 18 He wears a double-breasted blazer, a buff turtleneck. He lives on York Avenue now. He came out of Beechhurst, Queens, and learned his pinball in the Army—in Wrightstown, New Jersey; in Kansas City. He was stationed in an office building in Kansas City, and he moved up through the pinball ranks from beginner to virtuoso on a machine in a Katz drugstore.

Lukas and Buckley begin to play. Best of five games. Five balls a game. 19 Alternate shots. The machine is a Williams FunFest, and Buckley points out that it is "classic," because it is symmetrical. Each kick-out well and thumper-bumper is a mirror of another. The slingshots are dual. On this machine, a level of forty thousand points is where the sun sets and the stars come out. Buckley, describing his own style as "guts pinball," has a first-game score of forty-four thousand three hundred and ten. While Lukas plays his fifth ball, Buckley becomes avuncular. "Careful, Tony. You might think you're in an up-post position, but if you let it slide a little you're in a down-post position and you're finished." Buckley's advice is generous indeed. Lukas—forty-eight thousand eight hundred and seventy—wins the first game.

It is Buckley's manner to lean into the machine from three feet out. His whole body, steeply inclined, tics as he reinforces. In the second game, he scores fifty thousand one hundred and sixty. Lukas's address is like a fencer's *en garde*. He stands close to the machine, with one foot projecting under it. His chin is high. Buckley tells him, "You're playing nice, average pinball, Tony." And Lukas's response is fifty-seven thousand nine hundred and fifty points. He leads Buckley, two games to none.

"I'm ashamed," Buckley confesses. And as he leans—palms pounding—into the third game, he reminds himself, "Concentration, Tom. Concentration is everything."

Lukas notes aloud that Buckley is "full of empty rhetoric." But Lukas, in Game 3, fires one ball straight into the death channel and can deliver only thirty-five thousand points. Buckley wins with forty. Perhaps Lukas feels rushed. He prefers to play a more deliberate, cogitative game. At home, between shots, in the middle of a game, he will go to the kitchen for a beer and return to study the situation. Buckley, for his part, seems anxious, and with good reason: one mistake now and it's all over. In the fourth game, Lukas lights up forty-three thousand and fifty points; but Buckley's fifth ball, just before it dies, hits forty-four thousand two hundred and sixty. Games are two all, with one to go. Buckley takes a deep breath, and says, "You're a competitor, Tony. Your flipper action is bad, but you're a real competitor."

Game 5 under way. They are pummelling the machine. They are heavy on the corners but light on the flippers, and the scoreboard is reacting like a storm at sea. With three balls down, both are in the thirty-thousand range. Buckley, going unorthodox, plays his fourth ball with one foot off the floor, and raises his score to forty-five thousand points—more than he scored in winning the two previous games. He smiles. He is on his way in, flaring, with still another ball to play. Now Lukas snaps his fourth ball into the ellipse. It moves down and around the board, hitting slingshots and flippers and rising again and again to high ground to begin additional scoring runs. It hits sunburst caps and hole kickers, swinging targets and bonus gates. Minute upon minute, it stays in play. It will not die.

When the ball finally slips between flippers and off the playfield, Lukas has registered eighty-three thousand two hundred points. And he still has one ball to go.

Buckley turns into a Lukasite. As Lukas plays his fifth ball, Buckley cheers. "Atta way! Atta way, babes!" He goes on cheering until Lukas peaks out at ninety-four thousand one hundred and seventy.

"That was superb. And there's no luck in it," Buckley says. "It's as good a 26
score as I've seen."

Lukas takes a cool final look around Circus Circus. "Buckley has a way of 27
tracking down the secret joys of the city," he says, and then he is gone.

Still shaking his head in wonder, Buckley starts a last, solo game. His arms 28
move mechanically, groovedly, reinforcing. His flipper timing is offhandedly flawless. He scores a hundred thousand two hundred points. But Lukas is out of
sight.

Questions for analysis

1. In paragraph 5 Lukas talks about the need for "reassurance in life that
in taking risks you will triumph." How do you feel about this "pinball
philosophy"? Notice that Lukas's view of competition differs from Ehrlich's.
Their views could be seen as stereotypical: the man likes competition, while
the woman values communion. As a man or woman how do you react to
these views?

2. In paragraphs 2 and 23, underline the specific narrative action of the
ball and the men. What does this narrative technique contribute to the profile? (For information about specific narrative action, refer to Chapter 13:
Narrating.)

3. McPhee defines several words in paragraphs 2–6. What are those
words, and why do you think he bothers to define them? Describe the strategies he uses to define them. (Strategies for defining are illustrated in Chapter
16: Defining.)

4. How does McPhee dramatize the showdown between Lukas and
Buckley (paragraphs 11–28)?

5. What presence does McPhee himself have in this essay? How does he
represent himself? What other roles could he have played? Compare Mc-
Phee's presence here to Ehrlich's presence in her profile and to Noonan's
presence in his.

6. Writers of profiles get much of their material from interviews. Some
of this information they quote, while most of it they present in summary
form. Skim this profile to see how much McPhee relies on quoting. Do any
of the quotations contain information that you think could have been presented as effectively in summary? If so, which quotations? If not, what advantage does quoting seem to have over summarizing?

7. If you were asked to do a profile on someone who has an unusual job
or hobby, whom would you choose? What questions would you ask the
person?

Commentary

Like David Noonan, McPhee uses narrative to organize his essay. McPhee's
strategy is to present Lukas and pinball within the context of an ongoing
narrative of a day in New York. Profile writers very often adopt this strategy,

and you may want to consider it when you write your own profile. As he narrates Lukas's games, the trip downtown, and the showdown with Buckley, McPhee tells us all about Lukas, the game of pinball, and the mechanics of pinball machines. He shifts gracefully from narrating the playing process to describing the inner workings of the machine simply by having Lukas stop play to inspect a broken flipper. In the same way, he uses the cab ride to the repair shop as an occasion to tell us about Lukas's past and the banning of pinball. Both Ehrlich and Noonan focus on activities; people, though important, are not the center of attention. In McPhee's profile, however, while the activity of playing pinball is important, the main focus is on Lukas and his philosophy. Profiles often have this double focus: a person presented in the context of an unusual activity, or an activity profiled by focusing on a key person engaged in the activity.

McPhee gives us a surprising amount of information about his subject. To see how this information is integrated into the narrative, we can divide the profile into three main parts or acts as in a play—the solitary games in Lukas's mansion, the taxi ride to the Times Square area, and the showdown games with Tom Buckley at Circus Circus—and ask what McPhee tells us about Lukas in each part. As Lukas plays his machine at home, we learn that he is a "world-class pinball player," perhaps the best in New York City, as well as a serious writer who has already won a Pulitzer Prize, the most distinguished American award for writers. Knowing that he lives in a landmark mansion, we may infer that he is wealthy. About his appearance, we learn that he is "aristocratic, olive-skinned, Andalusian" and that his voice is "rich and dense." These few details let us imagine a man who is handsome and authoritative.

En route to Times Square we learn that Lukas was a newspaperman who went from a New England prep school to Harvard, and that he has always had an adventurous streak. In the games with Buckley at Circus Circus, we see Lukas in action and overhear his conversation with Buckley. In all these ways—details of place and appearance, commentary, action, and dialogue—McPhee presents Lukas while keeping the narrative of the day and anecdotes about particular games underway. He informs us about both Lukas and pinball as he engages our interest in a narrative that has its exotic and dramatic moments. He relies on all the strategies essential in essays about remembered people and events (Chapters 2 and 3) and many that are useful in reports of information (Chapter 5) as well.

The last selection, written by college freshman Brian Cable, is a profile of a mortuary. Cable treats his subject with both seriousness and humor. He lets readers know his feelings as he presents information about the mortuary and the people working there. Notice in particular the way Cable uses his visit to the mortuary as an occasion to reflect on death.

THE LAST STOP
BRIAN CABLE

Let us endeavor so to live that when we come to die even the undertaker will be sorry.   Mark Twain

Death is a subject largely ignored by the living. We don't discuss it much, 1 not as children (when Grandpa dies, he is said to be "going away"), not as adults, not even as senior citizens. Throughout our lives, death remains intensely private. The death of a loved one can be very painful, partly because of the sense of loss, but also because someone else's mortality reminds us all too vividly of our own.

Thus did I notice more than a few people avert their eyes as they walked 2 past the dusty-pink building that houses the Goodbody Mortuaries. It looked a bit like a church—tall, with gothic arches and stained glass—and somewhat like an apartment complex—low, with many windows stamped out of red brick.

It wasn't at all what I had expected. I thought it would be more like Forest 3 Lawn, serene with lush green lawns and meticulously groomed gardens, a place set apart from the hustle of day-to-day life. Here instead was an odd pink structure set in the middle of a business district. On top of the Goodbody Mortuaries sign was a large electric clock. What the hell, I thought, mortuaries are concerned with time too.

I was apprehensive as I climbed the stone steps to the entrance. I feared 4 rejection or, worse, an invitation to come and stay. The door was massive, yet it swung open easily on well-oiled hinges. "Come in," said the sign. "We're always open." Inside was a cool and quiet reception room. Curtains were drawn against the outside glare, cutting the light down to a soft glow.

I found the funeral director in the main lobby, adjacent to the reception 5 room. Like most people, I had preconceptions about what an undertaker looked like. Mr. Deaver fulfilled my expectations entirely. Tall and thin, he even had beady eyes and a bony face. A low, slanted forehead gave way to a beaked nose. His skin, scrubbed of all color, contrasted sharply with his jet black hair. He was wearing a starched white shirt, grey pants, and black shoes. Indeed, he looked like death on two legs.

He proved an amiable sort, however, and was easy to talk to. As funeral 6 director, Mr. Deaver ("call me Howard") was responsible for a wide range of services. Goodbody Mortuaries, upon notification of someone's death, will remove the remains from the hospital or home. They then prepare the body for viewing, whereupon features distorted by illness or accident are restored to their natural condition. The body is embalmed and then placed in a casket selected by the family of the deceased. Services are held in one of three chapels at the mortuary, and afterward the casket is placed in a "visitation room," where family and friends can pay their last respects. Goodbody also makes arrangements for the purchase of a burial site and transports the body there for burial.

All this information Howard related in a well-practiced, professional manner. 7 It was obvious he was used to explaining the specifics of his profession. We sat alone in the lobby. His desk was bone clean, no pencils or paper, nothing—just a telephone. He did all his paperwork at home; as it turned out, he and his wife lived right upstairs. The phone rang. As he listened, he bit his lips and squeezed his adam's apple somewhat nervously.

"I think we'll be able to get him in by Friday. No, no, the family wants him 8 cremated."

His tone was that of a broker conferring on the Dow Jones. Directly behind 9 him was a sign announcing "Visa and Mastercharge Welcome Here." It was tacked to the wall, right next to a crucifix.

"Some people have the idea that we are bereavement specialists, that we 10 can handle the emotional problems which follow a death: Only a trained therapist can do that. We provide services for the dead, not counseling for the living."

Physical comfort was the one thing they did provide for the living. The lobby 11 was modestly but comfortably furnished. There were several couches, in colors ranging from earth brown to pastel blue, and a coffee table in front of each one. On one table lay some magazines and a vase of flowers. Another supported an aquarium. Paintings of pastoral scenes hung on every wall. The lobby looked more or less like that of an old hotel. Nothing seemed to match, but it had a homey, lived-in look.

"The last time the Goodbodies decorated was in '59, I believe. It still makes 12 people feel welcome."

And so "Goodbody" was not a name made up to attract customers, but 13 the owners' family name. The Goodbody family started the business way back in 1915. Today, they do over five hundred services a year.

"We're in *Ripley's Believe It or Not*, along with another funeral home whose 14 owners' names are Baggit and Sackit," Howard told me, without cracking a smile.

I followed him through an arched doorway into a chapel which smelled 15 musty and old. The only illumination came from sunlight filtered through a stained glass ceiling. Ahead of us lay a casket. I could see that it contained a man dressed in a black suit. Wooden benches ran on either side of an aisle that led to the body. I got no closer. From the red roses across the dead man's chest, it was apparent that services had already been held.

"It was a large service," remarked Howard. "Look at that casket—a beautiful 16 work of craftsmanship."

I guess it was. Death may be the great leveler, but one's coffin quickly 17 reestablishes one's status.

We passed into a bright, fluorescent-lit "display room." Inside were thirty 18 coffins, lids open, patiently awaiting inspection. Like new cars on the showroom floor, they gleamed with high-glossy finishes.

"We have models for every price range." 19

Indeed, there was a wide variety. They came in all colors and various ma- 20 terials. Some were little more than cloth-covered cardboard boxes, other were made of wood, and a few were made of steel, copper, or bronze. Prices started at $400 and averaged about $1,800. Howard motioned toward the center of the room: "The top of the line."

This was a solid bronze casket, its seams electronically welded to resist cor- 21 rosion. Moisture-proof and air-tight, it could be hermetically sealed off from all outside elements. Its handles were plated with 14kt. gold. The price: a cool $5,000.

A proper funeral remains a measure of respect for the deceased. But it is 22 expensive. In the United States the amount spent annually on funerals is about two billion dollars. Among ceremonial expenditures, funerals are second only to weddings. As a result, practices are changing. Howard has been in this business for forty years. He remembers a time when everyone was buried. Nowadays, with burials costing $2,000 a shot, people often opt instead for cremation—as Howard put it, "a cheap, quick, and easy means of disposal." In some areas of the country, the cremation rate is now over 60 percent. Observing this trend, one might wonder whether burials are becoming obsolete. Do burials serve an important role in society?

For Tim, Goodbody's licensed mortician, the answer is very definitely yes. 23 Burials will remain in common practice, according to the slender embalmer with the disarming smile, because they allow family and friends to view the deceased. Painful as it may be, such an experience brings home the finality of death. "Something deep within us demands a confrontation with death," Tim explained. "A last look assures us that the person we loved is, indeed, gone forever."

Apparently, we also need to be assured that the body will be laid to rest in 24 comfort and peace. The average casket, with its inner-spring mattress and pleated satin lining, is surprisingly roomy and luxurious. Perhaps such an air of comfort makes it easier for the family to give up their loved one. In addition, the burial site fixes the deceased in the survivors' memory, like a new address. Cremation provides none of these comforts.

Tim started out as a clerk in a funeral home, but then studied to become a 25 mortician. "It was a profession I could live with," he told me with a sly grin. Mortuary science might be described as a cross between pre-med and cosmetology, with courses in anatomy and embalming as well as in restorative art.

Tim let me see the preparation, or embalming, room, a white-walled cham- 26 ber about the size of an operating room. Against the wall was a large sink with elbow taps and a draining board. In the center of the room stood a table with equipment for preparing the arterial embalming fluid, which consists primarily of formaldehyde, a preservative, and phenol, a disinfectant. This mixture sanitizes and also gives better color to the skin. Facial features can then be "set" to achieve a restful expression. Missing eyes, ears, and even noses can be replaced.

I asked Tim if his job ever depressed him. He bridled at the question: "No, 27 it doesn't depress me at all. I do what I can for people, and take satisfaction in enabling relatives to see their loved ones as they were in life." He said that he felt people were becoming more aware of the public service his profession provides. Grade-school classes now visit funeral homes as often as they do police stations and museums. The mortician is no longer regarded as a minister of death.

Before leaving, I wanted to see a body up close. I thought I could be indif- 28 ferent after all I had seen and heard, but I wasn't sure. Cautiously, I reached out and touched the skin. It felt cold and firm, not unlike clay. As I walked out, I felt glad to have satisfied my curiosity about dead bodies, but all too happy to let someone else handle them.

Questions for analysis   1. Why do you think Cable begins with the quotation by Mark Twain? How does this particular epigraph shape your expectations of the profile? What theme does it suggest?

2. At several points, Cable mentions his own preconceptions about mortuaries. Do you have any similar preconceptions? How does Cable appeal to such preconceptions to draw us into his essay?

3. Cable quotes Howard as saying "We provide services for the dead" (paragraph 10), but later in the essay Tim talks about the service funerals provide for the living (paragraph 23). How does Cable use this contradiction to bring out his theme?

4. Look again at paragraphs 18–21, where Cable describes the various caskets. What impression does this description give? How does it contrast with the preceding scene in the chapel (paragraph 15)?

5. Make a scratch outline to see how Cable organizes his profile. How much space would you estimate he devotes to describing the mortuary, explaining what goes on there, presenting Howard and Tim, reflecting on what he has seen and heard?

6. Look at the first and last paragraphs. How do they work to frame this profile?

7. Think of a place or activity about which you have strong preconceptions. Imagine writing a profile about it. What would you choose to tell about? What preconceptions do you hold? How might you use your preconceptions to capture readers' attention?

Commentary   Cable uses humor in this profile as a way of distancing himself emotionally from a disturbing subject. Although profile writers are not autobiographers, they do often put themselves in their essays as a way of engaging their readers' interest. Cable's profile gives us an inside look at a subject we seldom allow ourselves to think about. By looking at a mortuary through his eyes, we can safely reflect upon our own attitudes toward death and the way society deals with it.

PURPOSE AND AUDIENCE

A profile writer's primary purpose is to inform readers. Whether profiling people (a writer who plays pinball), places (a mortuary), or activities (saddle bronc riding or brain surgery), writers must meet readers' expectations for interesting material presented in a lively and entertaining manner. Unlike an encyclopedia entry on rodeos, a profile embeds its information within a human-interest story. Although a reader might learn as much about saddle bronc riding from Ehrlich's profile as from an encyclopedia entry, reading the profile is sure to be more enjoyable.

Readers of profiles expect to be surprised by such unusual subjects as brain surgery and saddle bronc riding. If the subject is a familiar one, they expect it to be presented from an unusual perspective. When writing your own profile, you will have an immediate advantage if you select an unusual place, activity, or person, one that is almost certain to surprise and intrigue your readers. If you find yourself drawn irresistibly to a familiar activity, however, you can still delight your readers by presenting it in a way they had never before considered.

A profile writer has one further concern: to be sensitive to readers' knowledge of a subject. Since readers must imagine the person, place, or activity being profiled and understand the new information offered about it, writers must take extreme care in assessing what their readers are likely to have seen and to know. The decisions of a writer addressing readers who have never seen a rodeo will be very different from those of a writer addressing readers who have often sat near the chutes in rodeo arenas watching saddle bronc riding. Given Ehrlich's care in presenting specific action and vivid details, she appears to be thinking of readers who have never (or not recently) seen a rodeo.

Profile writers must also consider whether readers know all the terms they want to use. Since profiles involve information, they inevitably require definitions and illustrations. For example, Noonan carefully defines many terms: *craniectomy, craniotomy, supracerebellar infratentorial approach, Leksell rongeurs, dura, cerebellum,* and *brainstem glioma.* (In doing so, he relies on several of the sentence-definition strategies illustrated in Chapter 16: Defining.) However, he does not bother to define other technical terms like *angiogram* and *meningioma.* Since profile writers are not writing technical manuals (or medical textbooks), they can choose which terms must be defined in order for readers to follow what is going on. Some concepts or activities will require extended illustrations, as when Noonan describes in detail what is involved in "opening the brain" or scrubbing up before entering the operating room.

BASIC FEATURES OF PROFILES

Profiles have intriguing, well-focused subjects, centered on a controlling theme, presented vividly, and proceeding at an informative, entertaining pace.

An intriguing,
well-focused subject

The subject of a profile is typically a specific person, place, or activity. In this chapter, John McPhee shows us J. Anthony Lukas, pinball player extraordinaire; Brian Cable describes a particular place, the Goodbody Mortuary; David Noonan and Gretel Ehrlich both present activities, brain surgery and saddle bronc riding. Although they focus on a person, place, or activity, these profiles contain all three elements: they examine certain people performing a special activity at a particular place.

Writers make even the most mundane subjects interesting by presenting them in a new light. They may simply take a close look at a subject usually taken for granted, as Cable does when he examines a mortuary. Or they might surprise us by revealing something we never expected to see, as McPhee does when he portrays his pinball enthusiasts as moral outlaws. Whatever they examine, profile writers bring attention to the uniqueness of the subject, showing what is special, definitive, or simply remarkable about it.

A controlling theme

Profiles thus center on a theme that nearly always reveals surprise or contrast in the subject or in the writer's response to it. Noonan, for instance, points to a discrepancy between the impersonality of neurosurgery and the extraordinary intimacy of such an operation. McPhee contrasts the seediness of pinball with the respectability of his two pinball players. Cable's thematic focus is his personal realization about how Americans seem to capitalize on death almost as a way of coping with it. Ehrlich wants us to value rodeo as an expression of Western life and values. This focus or controlling theme makes profiles something more than reporterlike writeups of observations and more than descriptive exercises. Profiles interpret their subjects, and they reveal the writer's attitude and point of view. The theme provides a point to a profile, a reason for the writer to be writing to particular readers. Along with awareness of purpose and readers, a controlling theme guides all the writer's decisions about how to organize the material and present it vividly and memorably.

A vivid presentation

Profiles particularize their subjects—one night at the rodeo, an actual operation, a real pinball-playing Pulitzer Prize–winning author, the Goodbody Mortuary—rather than generalize about them. Profile writers are more interested in presenting individual cases than in making generalizations. Consequently, profiles present people, places, and activities vividly and in detail.

Successful profile writers master the writing strategies of describing, regularly using sensory imagery and figurative language. For example, the profiles in this chapter evoke the senses of sight (a "dusty-pink building" that "looked a bit like a church—tall, with gothic arches and stained glass—and somewhat like an apartment complex—low, with many windows stamped out of red brick"); touch ("a thin, tough, leathery membrane"); smell ("a faint odor of burning bone"); and hearing ("his voice, rich and dense, pours out like cigarette smoke filtered through a New England prep school"). Similes ("his voice . . . pours out like cigarette smoke") and metaphors ("Tenth Avenue in the low Forties—a pocket of the city known as Coin Row") also abound.

Profile writers often describe people in graphic detail ("an aristocratic, olive-skinned Andalusian sort of man, with deep eyes in dark wells"). They reveal personal habits and characteristic poses ("As he listened, he bit his lips and squeezed his adam's apple somewhat nervously"). They also use dialogue to suggest speakers' characters and their relationship:

"I love my Bally."
"The Bally is the Corvair of pinball machines. I don't even care for the art on the back-glass. Williams and Gottlieb are the best. Bally is nowhere."

Narrating may be even more important to profile writing than describing since narration is used by many writers to organize their essays. Some profiles read like stories. They create tension and suspense and build to a dramatic climax. McPhee, for instance, sets up his essay so that it will end in a dramatic showdown between the two best pinball players in New York City, Lukas and Buckley. Noonan's dramatization has two climaxes, first when the brain is exposed and second when the tumor is discovered. The climax of Cable's narrative of his visit to a mortuary occurs at the end when he touches a corpse. Each of these writers relies on pacing to develop and sustain tension and drama in their narratives.

An informative, entertaining pace

Successful profile writers know that if they are to keep their readers' attention, they must entertain as well as inform. It is for this reason that they tell their stories dramatically and describe people and places vividly. They also carefully pace the flow of information. This kind of pacing is as important as narrative pacing.

Profiles present a great deal of factual detail about their subject, but this information is woven into the essay—conveyed in dialogue, interspersed throughout the narrative, given in the description. Noonan, for instance, tells us about the brain's parts (dura, cerebellum, brainstem), about surgical procedures (preparation of the patient and the surgeons, the difference between craniectomy and craniotomy), as well as about the attitudes of surgeons toward brain surgery. All of this information is given to us in bits and pieces rather than in one large chunk.

Parceling out information in this way increases the chances of comprehension because it allows readers to master one part of the information before going on to the next. Perhaps even more importantly, pacing the information injects a degree of surprise and thus makes readers anticipate what will come next. Profiles that vary the pacing of information may, in fact, actually keep readers reading.

GUIDE TO WRITING

Write an essay about an intriguing person, place, or activity in your community. With the advice of your instructor, you have several options in completing this assignment: a brief profile of an event, place, or activity observed once or twice; a brief profile of an individual based on one or two interviews; or a longer, more fully developed profile of a person, place, or activity based on several observational visits and interviews. Observe your subject closely and then present what you have learned in a way that both informs and entertains readers.

Preparing to write a profile involves several activities: choosing a subject, exploring your preconceptions of it, planning your project, posing some preliminary questions, and finding a theme or focus for your profile.

Choosing a subject When you choose a subject, you consider various possibilities, select a promising subject, and check that particular subject's accessibility.

Listing possibilities. You may already have chosen a subject for your profile. If so, turn now to Checking on Accessibility. But it might be advisable to take a few minutes now to consider some other possible subjects. The more possibilities you consider, the more confident you can be about your choice.

Before you list possible subjects, consider realistically the time you have available to complete this writing project. Think about the scope of the observing and interviewing you will be able to accomplish. Whether you have a week to plan and write up one observational visit or interview or a month to develop a full profile will determine what kinds of subjects will be appropriate for you. Consult with your instructor if you need help defining the scope of your writing project.

Following are several ideas you might use as a starting point for your list of subjects. Try to extend your list to ten or twelve possibilities. Consider every subject you can think of, even the unlikeliest. Begin your list with subjects you are already familiar with but would like to know more about. Then add unfamiliar subjects—people or places or activities you find fascinating or bizarre or perhaps even forbidding. Take risks. People like to read about the unusual.

People

- [ ] Anyone with an unusual job or hobby—a private detective, chimney-sweep, beekeeper, classic-car owner, dog trainer
- [ ] A homecoming queen candidate or weight-lifting contestant
- [ ] A TV celebrity, newspaper editor, radio disc jockey
- [ ] A popular local personality—parent of the year, a labor organizer, political activist, consumer advocate
- [ ] Campus president, ombudsman, fundraiser, distinguished teacher or researcher

Places

- [ ] A weight-reduction clinic, tanning salon, body-building gym, health spa
- [ ] Small claims court, Juvenile Hall, consumer fraud office, Internal Revenue Service office
- [ ] A used-car lot, old movie house, used-book store or specialized bookshop, antique shop, auction hall
- [ ] A hospital emergency room, hospice, birthing center, psychiatric unit, physical therapy center
- [ ] A place to eat—campus dining commons; a local diner; the oldest, biggest, quickest, or most expensive restaurant in town; a vegetarian restaurant
- [ ] Campus radio station, computer center, agricultural research facility, student center, faculty club, museum, newspaper office, health center
- [ ] Book, newspaper, or magazine publisher; florist shop, nursery, or greenhouse; pawnshop; boatyard; automobile restorer or wrecking yard; professional sports team office
- [ ] Recycling center; fire station; airport control tower; theater, opera, or symphony office; refugee center; orphanage; convent or monastery

Activities

- [ ] A citizens' volunteer program—voter registration, public TV auction, meals-on-wheels project
- [ ] An unusual sports event—a marathon, frisbee tournament, chess match, bicycle race
- [ ] Folk dancing, roller skating, rock climbing, poetry reading

Making a choice. Look over your list and select a subject that you find personally fascinating, something you want to know more about. It should also be a subject that you think you can make interesting to readers.

If you choose a subject with which you are familiar, it is a good idea to study it in an unfamiliar setting. Let us say you are a rock climber and decide to profile rock climbing. Do not rely on your own knowledge and authority. Seek out other rock-climbing enthusiasts and even some critics of the sport to get a more objective view of the subject. Then you would enjoy the advantage of knowing the questions to ask but be less likely to predict the answers. When research is predictable for the writer, it will probably lead to dull and uninspired writing.

Stop now to focus your thoughts. In a sentence or two, identify the subject you have chosen and explain why you think it is a good choice for you and for your readers.

Checking on accessibility. Once you have chosen a subject, you need to make sure you will be able to visit or observe it. Begin by finding out who might be able to give you information. If necessary, make some preliminary phone calls and explain that you need information for a school research project. You will be surprised how helpful and informative people can be when they have the time. If you are unable to contact knowledgeable people or get access to the place you need to observe, you may not be able to write on this subject. Therefore, try to make initial contact now.

Exploring your preconceptions Before you begin observing or interviewing, you should explore your initial thoughts and feelings about your subject. Write for about ten minutes, using the following questions as a guide:

- [ ] What do I already know about this subject?
  How would I define or describe it?
  What are its chief qualities or parts?
  Do I associate anyone or anything with it?
  What is its purpose or function?
  How does it compare to other, similar subjects?
- [ ] What is my attitude toward this subject?
  Why do I consider this subject intriguing?
  Do I like it? Respect it? Understand it?
  What about it interests me?
- [ ] What do I expect to discover as I observe the subject?
  What would surprise me about it?
  Do I anticipate any troubling discoveries?
  Might I find anything amusing in it?
  Are there likely to be any notable incongruities—for example, between what the people are trying to do and what they are actually doing?
- [ ] How do my preconceptions about this subject compare with other people's?
  What makes my point of view unique?
  What attitudes and values relating to this subject do I share with other people?

Planning your project Whatever the scope of your project—single observation, interview with follow-up, repeated observations and interviews for a full profile—you will want to get the most out of your time with your subject. Chapter 20: Field Research offers complete guidance in observing and interviewing. It will give you an idea of how much time will be required to plan, carry out, and write up an observation or interview.

Take time now to write out a tentative research schedule. Figure out first the amount of time you have to complete your essay, then decide what visits you will need to make, whom you will need to interview, and (in the case of a full profile) what library work you might want to do. Estimate the time necessary for each.

You might put your plan on a chart like the following one:

Date	Time Needed	Purpose	Preparation
10/23	1 hour	observation	bring map and directions, pad of paper
10/25	1/2 hour	library	bring reference, notebook, change for copy machine
10/26	45 minutes	interview	read brochure and write questions
10/30	2 hours	observe and interview	prepare questions, confirm appointment, bring pad

This plan will probably need to be modified once you actually begin work, but it is a good idea to keep some sort of schedule in writing.

If you are developing a full profile, your first goal is to get your bearings. Some writers begin by observing the place or activity, while others start with an interview. Many read up on the subject before doing anything else, though it may be best to read about the subject as soon as you can to get a sense of its main elements and concerns. You may also want to read about other people, places, or activities that are similar to the one you have chosen to investigate. Save your notes for use later when you draft your essay.

Posing some
preliminary questions Try writing some questions for which you would like to find answers. These questions will provide orientation and focus for your visits. As you continue your project, you will find answers to many of these questions. Also, add questions to this list as they occur to your, and delete any that come to seem irrelevant.

Each subject invites its own special questions, and every writer has his or her own particular concerns. Here is an example of questions one student posed for a profile of a campus rape-crisis center:

☐ Is rape a special problem on college campuses? On this particular campus? Why?

☐ How much support does the center receive from the college administration? How much from students?

☐ How well qualified are the people working in the center? What do they actually do? Do they counsel women who have been raped? Advise women on avoiding rape? Teach women how to defend themselves?

☐ Do the police do anything to prevent rape on campus?

☐ Are most of the rapes on campus committed by known sex offenders? Or are they date rapes, committed by "friends"?

Finding a tentative theme When you have completed your visits (one or several), you must decide on a tentative theme for your profile. Do the following activities to help you review your project. Complete them both at one sitting, one right after the other.

Write a narrative of your visits and research. Write nonstop for about fifteen minutes, telling the story of your project—what you did first, what happened next, where you went, who you met. Do not consult your notes, but try to include everything you recall. Also, do not worry if details are omitted or events are out of order.

Write an analysis of your project. Do not bother to reread your narrative, but immediately begin writing an analysis. Do not retell the story of what you did. Instead, try to answer as many of the following questions as you can:

☐ What was the most important thing I learned? Why does it seem so important?

☐ If I could find out the answer to one more question, what would be the question? Why is this question so crucial?

☐ Were there any incongruities, surprises, or contradictions? If so, what do they tell me about the subject?

☐ What is most memorable about the people I observed and talked to?

☐ What visual or other sensory impression is most memorable about the place I observed? What do I associate with this sensory impression?

☐ What is most striking about the activity I witnessed?

☐ What about this subject says something larger about our lives and times?

☐ What generalization or judgment do these personal reactions lead me to?

Stop and take a few moments to reflect on what you have discovered in doing these activities. Then, in a sentence or two, state what now seems to you to be a promising theme or focus for your profile. What do you want readers to see as they read your profile?

PLANNING AND DRAFTING

As preparation for drafting, you need to review your invention or research notes to see what you have, organize your profile, and set goals for yourself.

Seeing what you have   You may now have a great deal of material from a variety of sources—notes from observational visits, interviews, or reading; some idea of your preconceptions; a list of questions, perhaps with some answers; and both a narrative and an analysis of your project. You should also have a tentative theme or focus for your profile.

Read it all over now to sort through your material. Some writers find it helpful to put promising ideas or key information on index cards so they can try out various combinations and arrangements. Others try arranging their materials graphically, by clustering them around the central theme. However you prefer to sort and arrange your material, your aim now is to digest all the information you have gathered; to pick out the promising facts, details, anecdotes, and quotes; and to see how well your tentative theme focuses all the material you plan to include in the essay.

As you sort through your material, look at it in some of the following ways. They may help you find an even better theme or clarify the theme you already have.

- ☐ Contrast your preconceptions with your findings.
- ☐ Juxtapose your preliminary questions against the answers you have been able to find.
- ☐ Compare what different people say about the subject.
- ☐ Look for discrepancies between people's attitudes and values and their behavior.
- ☐ Compare your personal reactions to the reactions of the people directly involved.
- ☐ Contrast the place's appearance with the activity that occurs there.
- ☐ Juxtapose bits of information, looking for contrasts, incongruities, or dissonances.
- ☐ Look at the subject from the perspective of someone totally unfamiliar with it—a visitor from another country or even from another planet.
- ☐ Examine the subject as an anthropologist or archaeologist might, looking for artifacts that would explain what role the people, place, or activity had in the society at large.

Setting goals   The following questions will help to establish particular goals for your first draft. Consider each one briefly now, and return to them as necessary as you draft.

Your readers

☐ Are my readers likely to be at all familiar with my subject? If not, what details do I need to provide to help them visualize it?

☐ If my readers are familiar with my subject, how can I present it to them in a new and engaging way? What information do I have that is likely to be new or entertaining to them?

☐ Is there anything I can say about this subject that will lead readers to reflect on their own lives and values?

The beginning

The opening plays an especially important role in profiles. Because readers are unlikely to have any particular reason to read a profile, the writer must work hard to arouse their curiosity and interest. The best beginnings are surprising and specific, the worst are abstract. Here are some strategies you might consider:

☐ Should I open with a striking image or vivid scene, as Noonan does?

☐ Should I begin with a statement of the central theme, as McPhee does?

☐ Should I start with an intriguing epigraph, as Cable does?

☐ Do I have an amazing fact that would catch readers' attention?

☐ Is there an anecdote that captures the essence of the subject?

☐ Should I open with a question, perhaps a rhetorical one then answered in the essay?

☐ Do I have any dialogue that would serve as a good beginning?

The general organization

If I organize my material chronologically:

☐ How can I make the narrative dramatic and intense?

☐ What information should I integrate into the narrative?

☐ What information will I need to suspend the narrative for? If I must suspend the narrative, how can I minimize the disruption and resume the dramatic pace?

☐ What information should I quote and what should I present in summary form?

☐ How can I set the scene vividly?

If I organize my material analogically:

☐ How can I group my material in a way that best presents the subject, informs readers, and yet holds their interest?

☐ How can I sequence the groupings to bring out contrasts, juxtapositions, or incongruities in my material?

☐ Can readers make connections between groupings, or should I provide transitions?

☐ At what point should I describe the place, people, or activity? How can I make any descriptions true and vivid?

The ending

☐ Should I try to frame the essay by repeating an image or phrase from the beginning or by completing an action?

☐ Would it be good to end by restating the theme?

☐ Should I end with a telling image, anecdote, or bit of dialogue?

Outlining the profile   Profile writers basically use two methods of organizing their material: they either arrange it chronologically in a narrative or analogically by grouping related materials.

If you plan to arrange your material chronologically by using narrative, you should construct a timeline of the key events. Star the event that you consider the high point or climax.

If you plan to arrange your material by grouping related information, you might use the clustering or outlining strategies described in Chapter 11: Invention and Revision to get a graphic view of the interconnections. Both these strategies enable you to divide and group the information you have. After classifying your material, you might list the items in the order in which you plan to present them.

The following outlines illustrate the differences between chronological and analogical organization. The first is a *chronological outline* of Ehrlich's profile on saddle bronc riding:

   horsemanship and partnerships: what ranching is all about
   sit behind the chutes
   cowboys prepare to ride
   *one complete ride
   other riders named
   walk across the street to hotel
   observe scene in coffee shop
   the point of rodeo

If Ehrlich had wanted to emphasize the scene in the arena, the variety of activities, and the actors and equipment—rather than the drama of individual events—she might have made observations that could be grouped as follows in an *analogical outline*:

   one complete ride (an opening for dramatic effect, but narrated more briefly than in the actual profile) panorama of rodeo arena

cowboys (dress, manner, names, hometowns)

chute boss, stock contractors, announcer, clown

saddle bronc riding (animals, equipment, rules)

calf roping (animals, equipment, rules)

steer wrestling (animals, equipment, rules)

bull riding (animals, equipment, rules)

social scene at hotel

point of rodeo

The organization you choose will reflect the possibilities in your material and in your theme, purpose, and readers. Your decision must, at this point, be tentative. As you begin drafting, you will almost certainly discover new ways of organizing your material. Once you have a first draft, you and others may see ways to reorganize the material to achieve better your purpose with your particular readers.

Drafting a profile   Before actually beginning to write, you might look at the general advice on drafting in Chapter 1. By now, of course, you are not starting from scratch. If you have followed this guide, you will already have done a great deal of invention and planning. Some of this material may even fit right into your draft with little alteration.

Be careful not to get stuck trying to write the perfect beginning. Start anywhere. Worry about perfecting your beginning at the revision stage.

Once you are actually writing, try not to be interrupted. Should you find you need to make additional visits for further observations and interviews, do it only after you have completed a first draft.

READING A DRAFT WITH A CRITICAL EYE

At this point you are ready to have someone else read your draft. The following guidelines will help you to analyze someone else's profile draft closely in order to see its possibilities and problems. (Before you begin, you might want to review the general advice on reading another's draft critically in Chapter 1.)

First general   Read quickly through the draft first to get an overall impression. Note down
impression   your immediate reaction. What do you consider most interesting in the essay? State the theme, and indicate whether or not it is well focused. Is the profile adequately informative? Can you see any holes or gaps? Did it hold your interest? You should not try to write a detailed critique now, but rather articulate the general impression the profile gives.

Pointings One good way to maintain a critical focus as you read the essay is to highlight noteworthy features of the writing with *pointings*. A simple system of lines and brackets, these pointings are quick and easy to do, and they can provide a lot of helpful information for revision. Use pointings in the following way:

☐ Draw a straight line under any words or images that impress you as especially effective: strong verbs, specific details, memorable phrases, striking images.

☐ Draw a wavy line under any words or images that seem flat, stale, or vague. Also put the wavy line under any words or phrases that you consider unnecessary or repetitious.

☐ Look for pairs or groups of sentences that you think should be combined. Put brackets [ ] around these sentences.

☐ Look for sentences that are garbled, overloaded, or awkward. Put parentheses ( ) around these sentences. Put parentheses around any sentence that seems even slightly questionable; don't worry now about whether or not you're certain about your judgment. The writer needs to know that you, as one reader, had even the slightest hesitation about understanding a sentence.

Analysis Now read the draft more closely to analyze its strengths and failings. As you read, consider the following points.

1. Examine the pace of information. Point to any places where you felt bogged down or overwhelmed with information. These may be parts where there was too much new information or where the information was not clearly presented.

2. If narrative is used as an organizing strategy, see how well the narrative itself is paced. Point to any places where the narrative seemed to drag as well as where it seemed most dramatic and intense. Tell the writer what you think is the climax or high point of the narrative.

3. Consider what use the writer has made of specific narrative action—people moving, gesturing, talking. Suggest ways to strengthen any sections of specific action. Point out any places in the general narrative where specific action might be appropriate.

4. If the profile is organized analogically by topical grouping of related material, tell the writer whether any grouping presents too little or too much material and whether groupings might be sequenced differently or connected more explicitly.

5. Look specifically at the description of objects, scenes, or people. Point out places where the description is vivid and specific. Also point to places where it is vague or blurred.

6. Evaluate any anecdotes. Indicate which seem to have little impact or relevance. Suggest places where anecdotes might strengthen the profile.

7. Skim the essay for definitions. Indicate whether any definitions in the essay seem unnecessary. Also point out any terms that need defining.

8. Reread the beginning, and decide whether it is effective. Tell the writer whether it captured your attention. See whether there is any quotation, fact, or anecdote elsewhere in the draft that might make a better opening.

9. Look again at the ending. Let the writer know if it leaves you waiting for more, if it seems too abrupt, or if it oversimplifies the material. Suggest another ending, possibly by moving a passage or quotation from elsewhere in the essay.

REVISING AND EDITING

You now are ready to revise your profile. Review any critical reading notes from your instructor or other students. You may find that you have only a little work to do, or you may have to make substantial changes to move you closer to realizing your goals for your particular readers. This section provides guidance in planning your revision.

Revising a profile   The guidance here can be used in tandem with the revision plan found in Chapter 11. You may now want to turn to Chapter 11 and follow that general plan for revising until you reach the section Read Again To Identify Problems. At that point, you should substitute the following specific guidelines for revising a profile.

Revising to clarify the theme

☐ Reconsider the focus. If your readers had difficulty describing the theme or suggested focusing on something different, you should either clarify or revise your theme. Clarifying your theme might involve making it more explicit or eliminating material that seems to contradict the point you are trying to make.

☐ Eliminate any dialogue, description, anecdote, or factual detail that does not contribute to the general theme.

Revising for vivid presentation

☐ Consider whether your draft offers readers enough descriptive details so that they can imagine the person, place, or activity. Where might you add details to increase the vividness of your subject?

☐ Reflect on whether you have made good use of all the possibilities for sensory detailing—sight, sound, smell, texture. Would broadening the range of detailing help your readers imagine your subject more fully?

Revising for pacing and readability

☐ Reconsider the pacing of information. If readers felt bogged down at any point, either reorganize the information or eliminate some of it.

☐ Reconsider the pacing of the narrative. Dramatize promising moments through specific narrative action. Summarize activity to speed the story along.

☐ If readers were confused or felt juxtapositions were too abrupt, add appropriate transitions or revise sentences for smoother reading.

☐ If any anecdotes have little impact, consider eliminating them or try speeding them up and sharpening their focus.

☐ Define any words that need explanation and eliminate any unnecessary definitions.

☐ If the opening fails to engage readers' attention, look back at the suggestions for beginning in Setting Goals.

Editing and proofreading

As you revise a draft for the final time, you must edit it closely. Though you probably corrected obvious errors in the drafting and revising stages, usage and mechanics were not your first priority. Now, however, you must find and correct any errors of mechanics, usage, and punctuation.

After you have revised the draft and produced the final copy, you must proofread carefully before handing in your essay.

LEARNING FROM YOUR OWN WRITING PROCESS

If you are asked to write about your experience writing this essay, begin by reviewing your invention and planning materials. Note how you came to select your subject and how you then defined your theme. Point out any special problems you encountered when gathering information for this profile.

Then reread your draft. What major problems did you encounter in this first draft and how did you solve them? Look over any critical reviews of your draft, and then reread your revision. What worked well in the first draft, and what needed reworking? How exactly did you go about reworking your draft? Where did you begin? What changes did you make, and how do you feel about them now? What other changes would you still like to make?

A WRITER AT WORK

THE INTERVIEW NOTES AND REPORT

When interviewing people for a profile, writers usually take notes. After the interview they may summarize their notes in a short report. In this section we will look at the interview notes and report Brian Cable prepared for his profile of a mortuary, printed earlier in this chapter.

For his essay Cable first visited the mortuary and then conducted two interviews—with the funeral director and the mortician. Before each interview he divided some paper into two columns and then used the left-hand column for descriptive details and personal impressions, the right-hand column for questions he posed and information he found. Here we will see Cable's notes and report for his interview with the funeral director, Mr. Deaver.

Cable wrote out a few questions in advance of the interview and then took brief notes during the interview. He kept his attention fixed on Deaver, however, trying to keep the interview comfortable and conversational. He did not concern himself too much with note-taking during the actual interview because he planned to spend a half-hour directly afterward to complete his notes. During the interview, he noted down just enough to jog his memory, and to catch anything especially quotable. The typescript of Cable's interview notes follows.

The interview

DESCRIPTIVE DETAILS &
PERSONAL IMPRESSIONS   QUESTIONS

    1. How do families of deceased view the
       mortuary business?
    2. How is the concept of death approached?
    3. How did you get into this business?

    INFORMATION

weird looking   "Call me Howard"
tall   How things work: Notification pick up body
long fingers   at home or hospital, prepare for viewing, re-
big ears   store distorted features—accident or illness,
low, sloping forehead embalm, casket—family selects, chapel
Like stereotype—skin services (3 in bldg.), visitation room—pay
colorless   respects, family & friends.

    Can't answer questions about death—
    "Not bereavement specialists. Don't handle
    emotional problems. Only a trained therapist
    can do that."
    "We provide services for dead, not counseling
    for the living." (great quote)
    Concept of death has changed in last 40 yrs
    (how long he's been in the business)
    Funeral cost $500–600, now $2000

plays with lips blinks plays with adam's apple desk empty—phone, no paper or pen	Phone call (interruption) "I think we'll be able to get him in on Friday. No, no, the family wants him cremated." *Ask about Neptune Society—cremation Cremation "Cheap, quick, easy means of disposal."
angry disdainful of the Neptune Soc.	Recent phenomenon. Neptune Society—erroneous claim to be only one. "We've offered them since the beginning. It's only now it's come into vogue." Trend now back towards burial. Cremation still popular in sophisticated areas 60% in Marin and Florida
	Ask about paperwork—does it upstairs, lives there with wife Nancy
musty, old stained glass sunlight filtered	Tour around (happy to show me around) Chapel—Large service just done, Italian.
man in black suit roses wooden benches	"Not a religious institution—A business." casket—"beautiful craftsmanship"—admires, expensive
contrast brightness fluorescent lights plexiglass stands	Display room—caskets about 30 of them Loves to talk about caskets "models in every price range" glossy (like cars in a showroom) cardboard box, steel, copper, bronze $400 up to $1800. Top of line: bronze, electronically welded, no corrosion—$5000

Cable's notes include many descriptive details of Deaver as well as of various rooms in the mortuary. Though most entries are short and sketchy, much of the language will find its way into the essay. In describing Deaver, for example, Cable notes the fact that he fits the stereotype. Cable will make much of this in his essay.

He puts quotation marks around Deaver's actual words. Some of the quotes are complete, whereas others are only fragmentary. We will see how he fills these quotes in when he writes up the interview. Cable caught many of Deaver's words and even several of his sentences. In only a few instances does he take down more than he can use. Even though profile writers want good quotes, they should not quote things they can better put in their own words. Direct quotation has a special, enlarged function in a profile—both to provide information and to capture the mood or character of the person speaking. Quoting is as much a means of characterization as of presenting information.

As you can see, Deaver was not able to answer any of Cable's questions. The gap between the questions and Deaver's responses led Cable to recognize some of his own misperceptions about mortuaries—namely, that they serve the living by helping them adjust to the death of their loved ones. This misperception becomes an important theme of his essay.

After filling in his notes following the interview, Cable took some time to reflect on what he had learned. Here are some of his thoughts:

> I was surprised how much Deaver looked like the undertakers in scary movies. Even though he couldn't answer any of my questions, he was friendly enough. It's obviously a business for him (he loves to talk about caskets and to point out all their features, like a car dealer kicking a tire). Best quote: "We offer services to the dead, not counseling to the living." I have to arrange an interview with Tim, the mortician.

Writing up an account of the interview a short time afterward helped Cable to fill in more details and to reflect further on what he had learned. His report shows him already beginning to organize the information he had gained from his interview with Deaver.

A report on the interview

I. His physical appearance.

Tall, skinny with beady blue eyes embedded in his bony face. I was shocked to see him. He looked like the undertakers in scary movies. His skin was white and colorless, from lack of sunshine. He has a long nose and a low sloping forehead. He was wearing a clean white shirt. A most unusual man—have you ever seen those Ames Home Loan commercials? But he was friendly, and happy to talk to me. "Would I answer some questions? Sure."

II. What people want from a mortuary.

A. Well first of all, he couldn't answer any of the questions I had expected. As to how families cope with the loss of a loved one, he didn't know. "You'd have to talk to a psychologist about that," he said. He did tell me how the concept of death has changed over the last ten or so years.

B. He has been in the business for forty years. (forty years?!!?) One look at him and you'd be convinced he'd been there at least that long. He told me that in the old times everyone was buried. Embalmed, put in a casket, and paid final homage before being shipped underground forever and ever. Nowadays, many people choose to be cremated instead. Hence comes the success of the Neptune Society and those like it. They specialize in cremation. You can have your ashes dumped anywhere. "Not that we don't offer cremation services. We've offered them since the beginning," he added with a look of disdain. It's just that they've become so popular recently because they offer a "quick, easy, and efficient means of disposal." Cheap too—I think it is a reflection of a "no nonsense" society. The Neptune Society has become so successful because they claim to be the only ones to offer cremations as an alternative to expensive burial. "We've offered it all along. It's just only now come into vogue."

Sophisticated areas (I felt "progressive" would be more accurate) like Marin County have a cremation rate of over 60 percent. The phone rang. "Excuse me," he said. As he talked on the phone, I noticed how he played with his lips, pursing and squeezing them. He was blinking all the time too. Yet he wasn't a schitzo or anything like that. I meant to ask him how he got into this business, but I forgot. I did find out his name and title. Mr. Deaver, general manager of Goodbody Mortuaries (no kidding, that's the real name). He lived on the premises upstairs with his wife. I doubt if he ever left the place.

III. It's a business!

Some people have the idea that mortuaries offer counseling and peace of mind—a place where everyone is sympathetic and ready to offer advice. "In some mortuaries, this is true. But by and large this is a business. We offer services to the dead, not counseling to the living." I too had expected to feel an awestruck respect for the dead upon entering the building. I had also expected green lawns, ponds with ducks, fountains, flowers, peacefulness—you know, a "Forest Lawn" type deal. But it was only a tall, Catholic-looking building. "Mortuaries do not sell plots for burial," he was saying. "Cemeteries do that, after we embalm the body and select a casket. We're not a religious institution." He seemed hung up on caskets—though maybe he was just trying to impress upon me the differences between caskets. "Oh, they're very important. A good casket is a sign of respect. Sometimes if the family doesn't have enough money, we rent them a nice one. People pay for what they get just like any other business." I wonder when you have to return the casket you rent?

I wanted to take a look around. He was happy to give me a tour. We visited several chapels and visiting rooms—places where the deceased "lie in state" to be "visited" by family and friends. I saw an old lady in a "fairly decent casket," as Mr. Deaver called it. Again I was impressed by the simple businesslike nature of it all. Oh yes, the rooms were elaborately decorated, with lots of shrines and stained glass, but these things were for the customers' benefit. "Sometimes we have up to eight or nine corpses here at one time, sometimes none. We have to have enough rooms to accommodate." Simple enough, yet I never realized how much (trouble?) people were after they died. So much money, time, and effort go into their funerals.

As I prepared to leave, he gave me his card. He'd be happy to see me again, or maybe I could talk to someone else. I said I would arrange to call for an appointment with the mortician. I shook his hand. His fingers were long, and his skin was warm.

Writing up the interview thus helped Cable probe his subject more deeply. It also helped him to develop a witty voice for his essay. Although Cable's report is quite informal, some writers choose to make their reports as formal as published interviews.

Reporting Information

For distribution to the media, a staff member of the U.S. Bureau of the Census writes a report on population changes between 1980 and 1985, using data from one of the Bureau's *Current Population Reports*. The report centers on a table that indicates for each state its 1985 population, 1980 population, percent change from 1980 to 1985, and net migration. The staff member emphasizes in the report that every state in the Midwest lost more people than it gained, while ten of thirteen Mountain and Pacific states gained more people than they lost.

A new edition of *Jane's Fighting Ships*, the British publication that is the standard reference on the world's navies, includes an article about a new Swedish antisubmarine cruiser. The article contains technical information, along with drawings and photographs. In focusing on the innovative features of this new ship, the writer compares it to several antisubmarine ships in other national navies.

Two authors noted for their research on cats write an article for a popular magazine on the history of the cat. The article explains the religious and economic importance cats held in ancient Egypt, China, Greece, and Rome and then shows how they spread throughout Europe during the period of the Roman Empire.

A college professor is writing a textbook for an introductory course in linguistics. In the chapter on syntactic development, he plans to trace children's gradual control of sentences from the earliest two-word sentences through all basic sentence patterns. After reviewing research and other reports on syntactic development, he divides the information into stages of development and describes what children do within each stage. He includes brief transcripts of children's spoken monologues and conversations to illustrate each stage of development. He also discusses the contributions of key researchers and cites their major publications. Because he is writing for beginning students of linguistics, he carefully defines all special linguistic terms.

A student reporter for a college newspaper writes a feature article on a continuing campus controversy over the status of a gay and lesbian student group. The Student Association executive committee has voted to recognize the group as an official student organization, adding it to the list of association-sponsored organizations. Students are divided over the decision. The reporter interviews students on both sides of the controversy and in her article clarifies the issue and contrasts the views of both sides. She avoids taking a side herself and concentrates instead on reporting the controversy.

Asked to write an essay for his freshman English class on an activity at which he is an expert, a student chooses Scrabble, a game he has played since childhood. He reads several articles on the invention and development of the game and on experts' strategies for playing it. In his essay he narrates the history of the game, concentrating on its invention in the 1930s, production during the late 1940s and early 1950s, and its widespread popularity by the 1950s. Assuming his readers have played the game, he describes its basic strategies only briefly and then reports various strategies experts have devised to achieve high scores. He also includes many unusual words that produce high scores.

□ For an American history term paper a student decides to write about Susan B. Anthony. Her specific focus is on Anthony's contributions to the women's suffrage movement. The student lists these contributions and discusses the importance of each one as well as reporting several historians' assessments of them.

All writing reports information. Autobiographies, poems, even postcards all include some kind of information. But each of the situations listed to the left call for a special type of informative writing—one in which the writer's main purpose is to increase readers' understanding of a subject. For example, the authors of the article on cats assume that even readers who have cats are likely to know little if anything about the history of the cat as revealed in written documents, painting, and sculpture. By reporting information new to readers, they may increase their readers' understanding of and appreciation for cats.

Comprising much of the writing done in the world every day, informative writing predominates in newspapers, magazines, textbooks, how-to articles, technical manuals, and research reports. Most of the reading you will do in college and on the job is of this type.

Reports of information relay knowledge held by some people to those who do not have it, and either want or need it. Personal experiences may be included, but only as illustration, not as autobiographical disclosure. Similarly, reports on controversies strive to present a balanced view and avoid taking a position. The writing situation for an informational report, then, differs from that of an autobiography (Chapter 2) or a position paper (Chapter 6), and is like that of the profile (Chapter 4). The difference between profiling and reporting information is that the profile writer relies mainly on his or her own recent firsthand observations, whereas a report writer relies mainly on secondhand information learned from others.

A report writer nearly always writes for readers who know less than the writer about the subject, as the selections in this chapter illustrate. In college, however, you will be asked regularly to explain what you have learned to an instructor who knows more than you do about the subject, a problematic writing situation your writing instructor can advise you about. You will also find advice about this special writing situation in Chapter 23: Essay Examinations. Your writing instructor will help you identify appropriate readers for the essay you write in this chapter.

The following readings illustrate a wide range of topics and strategies. All are based on secondhand information, but only one actually cites its sources. Some adopt a personal tone and go to some lengths to engage readers' interests in the subject, while others write more impersonally. Each reading is followed by questions, which will direct you to central issues and possibilities in this kind of writing. These readings will also give you many ideas for essays you yourself might write.

READINGS

The first reading is a chapter from *A Country Year: Living the Questions* by Sue Hubbell, a writer and commercial beekeeper and honey producer who lives in the Ozark Mountains of southern Missouri. In this selection, Hubbell writes about chiggers, a tiny orange mite that thrives in southern Missouri's hot, humid summers. As you read, notice Hubbell's strategies for engaging and holding readers' interest while informing them about chiggers. How is her essay different from an entry in a reference book on mites?

CHIGGERS
SUE HUBBELL

Last winter was extraordinarily mild, and as a result the chiggers are abun- 1
dant this summer. Ozark humor is an understated sort of thing, and folks here are asking one another if they happened to attend one of the funerals held for the five chiggers that died during the cold weather.

Once the timber has been cut from these hills, the thin soil will barely support 2 cattle or hog farming and crops won't grow here, so many of the clearings and old pastures go to scrubby second growth and blackberries. That kind of cover and the hot steamy summers make it a prime place for chiggers.

Yesterday a friend of mine from the city was here and went out to pick 3 blackberries for a cobbler. By evening, he was covered with red, ferociously itching chigger bites. They will itch for weeks, although I did not have the heart to tell him so. I was sympathetic because for the first few years I lived here I, too, spent my summers scratching continuously, often in socially unacceptable places. Like many people, after a couple of years I gained a tolerance to them, and so I believe I have now earned the right to take a longer view.

Bad as chiggers are, they have had a worse press than they deserve because 4 their name so closely resembles that of another pesty being, the chigoe, which is found only in the deep South. Chigoes are insects, tropical fleas that burrow under the skin to lay their eggs; since both chigoes and chiggers are tiny and their names sound so similar, people often confuse them and think that chiggers burrow too. They do not, and they are not insects.

Chiggers are mites and, like their spiderish kin, have unsegmented bodies 5 and eight legs when they grow up. They belong to the class Arachnida, not Insecta. There are more than seven hundred species of chiggers throughout the world, and of these fewer than fifty feed on humans. In the Orient one variety spreads scrub typhus, but on this continent the worst that they can do is make us itchy. One of our most common species is *Trombicula alfreddugesi*, a mouthful because it is named for Alfred Dugès, who studied them around the turn of the century. Dugès was a celebrated mite man, but my own favorite chigger expert is James M. Brennan, a government entomologist who once took more than 4,000 chiggers from a single woodchuck in the Bitterroot valley of Montana. Counting out 4,000 tiny chiggers would be an heroic task, and so I was pleased when I read that scientist Brennan had a whole genus named for him.

From a human standpoint, one of the most significant facts about chiggers 6 is that they are so small we cannot see them and seldom realize they have been feeding on us until we begin to itch like my friend the blackberry picker.

Adult chiggers, it is true, are quite visible to the naked eye, attaining a 7 whopping one tenth of an inch. Even I, with my middle-aged eyes, sometimes see them. They are bright orangy red, the color of butterfly weed (or chigger plant, as it is called in the Ozarks). When looked at through a hand lens, the mites can be seen to be covered with feathery hairs, and are rather handsome. However, as they feed on plant and animal debris and an occasional tiny insect egg, our paths seldom cross. But they do lay the minute eggs from which larval chiggers hatch, and it is the larvae that we human beings mind so much.

The eggs, only a hundred microns big, are laid in the soil. Instead of hatching 8 directly, they break open into a second egg, called a deutovum. This second egg hatches the orange larva, a larva so small that it would take a hundred and twenty-five of them, lined up snout to rear, to come up to the inch mark. These larvae must find a meal before they can metamorphose to their next nymphal stage. They crawl up blades of grass, brambles or bushes to find a suitable vertebrate host on which to feed. Their preference would be a lizard, turtle, bird or even a woodchuck; from a chigger's standpoint, a human is a poor host, but should the mite end up on one, it starts to climb to find a protected spot on which to feed. For this reason chiggers most often chose places where clothing fits tightly, and our itches are usually clustered around the ankles, crotch, waist and armpits. Some Ozarkers swear that the best way to avoid getting "chigger bit" is to conduct one's outdoor activities stark naked. Presumably the chiggers would then wander up one side of the body and down the other, discouraged by finding no suitable spot on which to feed. I have never nerved myself to plunge into a blackberry thicket naked, so I cannot report if this is true.

Once a larval chigger has found a good location, he settles down for a feed. 9 Technically speaking, chiggers do not bite at all; their mouth parts are too delicate. Instead, they inject a digestive enzyme into the skin which dissolves a bit of flesh; the chigger then sucks it up. Chiggers are not interested in blood, but feed on liquefied skin and lymph. If left undisturbed, the chigger stays in the same place, using the enzyme to make a small well or tube called a stylostome. If the larva can stay on his host long enough to have a full feed—about three days—he drops off when engorged and crawls to a protected place on the ground, where he rests and prepares to undergo transformation. Inside, his body parts melt down and reconstitute themselves into a legless, pupa-like protonymph, which in turn changes into an active deutonymph, a predator like the adult he eventually will become. The change from nymph to adult is also in two stages. Once again the chigger settles quietly, while within tissue dissolves and reforms into a legless, pupa-like tritonymph or pre-adult, which does not move, but from which emerges the adult, the bright-red, velvety, sexually mature chigger.

All of which is most elegant and complex, but easily the most curious thing 10 about chiggers from a human standpoint is our own reaction to them. When a chigger commences to feed on us, our bodies overreact by setting off a full battalion of allergy alarm bells, making us itch and scratch. It is actually an overreaction, because it serves no purpose either for us or for the chigger. Those of us who have happily developed a tolerance to chiggers serve as calm, non-scratching chigger hosts. And the chigger is not served by provoking that allergy either. The allergic reaction caused by the venom of the honeybee sting preserves the bee colony and its food stores, but when a chigger provokes an allergic reaction, we scratch it off before it has fed its fill and usually kill it in the process.

Mulling over this curiosity, G. W. Krantz, an eminent acarologist says, '' . . . 11 the intense itching reaction experienced by man . . . reflects a lack of host adaptation.'' In other words, it is all a Terrible Mistake.

This is one of those biological puzzles that I find cheering—untidy, unre- 12 solved, a reminder that the results are not yet all in, that we do not have the final forms, nor all the answers. We are still in process, chiggers, humans and the rest. There are probably better answers somewhere on down the pike.

Questions for analysis   1. Did you find Hubbell's essay easy or hard to read? Point to specific sections, and try to explain why they seemed easy or hard to you. As a writer, what can you conclude about making unfamiliar information easy or hard for readers?

2. What readers do you think Hubbell had in mind? What assumptions does she seem to have made about these readers' knowledge and interests?

3. Readers are always influenced by the tone of an essay. Tone reveals the writer's attitude toward the subject and readers. How would you describe the tone of Hubbell's essay? Point to specific word choices as an illustration. Given Hubbell's readers, what seems to you appropriate or inappropriate about this tone?

4. Hubbell knows something personally about chiggers, but she also knows facts that she could only have acquired by reading. How many different sources and what kinds of sources might she have consulted? How can you tell?

5. In paragraphs 8 and 9, Hubbell presents a chigger's development in a process narrative, a strategy for reporting information that sets out the temporal stages. How does Hubbell organize this narrative? What purpose does it serve in the essay?

6. Do you have a special interest in some insect or arachnid, wild or domestic animal, kind of plant or tree, or particular natural phenomenon like waves, thunder, hurricanes, or bird migration? Think about what subject you would like to learn more about and report on. How would you engage and hold readers' interest?

Commentary   This reading shows three features basic to all essays reporting information: a general subject, a specific subject, and a thesis. Hubbell's general subject is chiggers. Her specific subject is chiggers' developmental cycle and humans' inadvertent (and uncooperative) role in that cycle. Her thesis seems to be that humans' reaction to the chigger poses a biological puzzle suggesting that evolution is not yet complete. These distinctions—general subject, specific subject, thesis—show how a writer focuses on a limited subject within a larger subject and then makes an assertion, a thesis, about that specific subject. In essays presenting information, the thesis engages, holds, and focuses a reader's attention. It is the main point and thus determines how the writer selects and organizes information.

The thesis is generally stated concisely in one or two sentences, but it may be presented indirectly as part of a larger discussion. Whether stated or implied, a thesis usually mentions or forecasts other key points of the essay as well as giving some indication of the overall plan. Hubbell hints at her thesis in the opening anecdote about her itching friend, but she does not state it explicitly until the final paragraph. Writers reporting information usually state the thesis early in an essay so that it can focus readers' attention. Hubbell, however, chooses to lead readers toward her thesis along a route of personal experience, human interest, and specific information about chiggers. Readers are not necessarily disadvantaged by having to wait for her thesis—the larger significance of humans' relation to chiggers—until the final paragraph.

The thesis makes clear the writer's purpose in presenting the information. As you plan and draft your own essay, you will need to discover and clarify your purpose in presenting the information to your particular readers. This purpose—made explicit in your thesis—will enable you to decide what information to include and how to organize it effectively.

Besides centering her essay around a focusing thesis, Hubbell attempts to create and maintain readers' interest in chiggers. She begins by telling a chigger joke, then mentions an itchy blackberry-picking friend and an enormously patient entomologist. She tries to avoid a dry account of facts about chiggers by injecting humor and by connecting chiggers to humans, not just humans in general, but to two particular humans: her friend and the entomologist. In nearly every paragraph, even those paragraphs dense with facts, Hubbell mentions humans: "it is the larvae that we human beings mind so much" (paragraph 7); "our itches are usually clustered around the ankles, crotch, waist and armpits" (paragraph 8); "we scratch it off before it has fed its fill and usually kill it in the process" (paragraph 10).

Report writers must not only engage readers' interest, but also devise a strategy for introducing and pacing information. They must be careful not to introduce too much information too soon nor to pack in the information so densely that readers lose interest. Hubbell begins humorously, lightly considering how chiggers affect humans and briefly contrasting the chigger with the chigoe. Not until paragraph 5 does she get to any real technical information. Immediately, however, she shifts back to a story about the patient entomologist. The next paragraph (6) gives us only one fact about chiggers (their small size) and ends by mentioning the blackberry picker. You can see that she introduces information very gradually and then keeps returning to her human-interest angle. Only in paragraphs 7, 8, and 9 does she present sustained information about chiggers, and even here she inserts humor and a startling visual image at the end of paragraph 8 in order not to go beyond the limits of her readers' tolerance for new information.

The next selection was written by Isaac Asimov, a distinguished science fiction writer *(The Foundation Trilogy)*, who is also noted for his books and articles explaining scientific concepts. About explaining things clearly, he has said, "In addition to knowing your subject and knowing your reader, you have to have a certain amount of self-assurance. . . . I don't in the least mind being simple, using simple language and trying to describe things in colorful metaphors."

This essay from the *Los Angeles Times* presents a subject—cholesterol— that Asimov can probably assume is already familiar to his newspaper readers. As you read, ask yourself how Asimov interests readers in learning more about this familiar subject. What colorful metaphor does he use in this essay?

ISAAC ASIMOV
CHOLESTEROL

Cholesterol is a dirty word these days, and every report that comes out seems 1 to make it worse. A government study of more than 350,000 American men between 35 and 37 years old was reported last month and 80% of them had cholesterol levels of more than 180 milligrams per 100 milliliters of blood. Anything over the 180 mark indicates an increased probability of an early death from heart disease. The higher the measurement the higher the probability.

And yet this grinning death mask is not the only face that cholesterol bears. 2 Cholesterol happens to be absolutely essential to animal life. Every animal from the amoeba to the whale (including human beings, of course) possesses cholesterol. The human body is about one-third of 1% cholesterol.

The portion of the animal body that is richest in cholesterol is the nervous 3 system. There we encounter masses of nerve cells which, in bulk, have a grayish appearance and are therefore referred to as "gray matter."

Each nerve cell has fibers extending from it, including a particularly long one 4 called the "axon" along which electrical impulses travel from nerve cell to nerve cell, coordinating the body and making it possible for us to receive sense-impressions, to respond appropriately and, above all (for human beings), to think.

The axon is surrounded by a fatty sheath, which presumably acts as an 5 insulating device that enables the electrical impulse to travel faster and more efficiently. Without its insulating powers, it is possible that nerve cells would "short-circuit" and that the nervous system would not function.

The fatty sheath has a whitish appearance so that those portions of the 6 nervous system that are made up of masses of axons are called the "white matter."

As it happens, two out of every five molecules in the fatty sheath are cho- 7
lesterol. Why that should be, we don't know, but the cholesterol cannot be
dispensed with. Without it, we would have no nervous system, and without a
nervous system, we could neither think nor live.

So important is cholesterol that the body has the full power to manufacture 8
it from simpler materials. Cholesterol does not need to be present in the diet at
all.

The trouble is, though, that if, for any reason, the body has more cholesterol 9
than it needs, there is a tendency to get rid of it by storing it on the inner surface
of the blood vessels—especially the coronary vessels that feed the heart. This is
"atherosclerosis," and it occurs in men more often than in women. The cholesterol deposits narrow the blood vessels, stiffen and roughen them, make internal
clotting easier and, in general, tend to produce heart attacks, strokes and death.

Why is that? Why should such a vital substance, without which we could 10
not live, present such a horrible other face? Why haven't we evolved in such a
way as not to experience such dangerous cholesterol deposits?

One possible answer is that until the coming of modern medicine, human 11
beings did not have a long life span, on the average. Most people, even in
comparatively good times, were dead of violence or infectious disease before
they were 40, and by that time atherosclerosis had not had time to become
truly dangerous.

It is only since the average human life span has reached 75, in many parts 12
of the world, that atherosclerosis and other "degenerative diseases" have become of overwhelming importance.

What to do? There is the matter of diet, for one thing. Apparently, flooding 13
the body with high-cholesterol items of diet (eggs, bacon, butter and other fatty
foods of animal origin) encourages a too-high level of cholesterol in the blood
and consequently atherosclerosis.

As it happens, plants do not contain cholesterol. They have related com- 14
pounds, but not cholesterol. Therefore, to cut down on fatty animal food in the
diet (the cholesterol is in the fat) and to increase plant food lowers the chance
of atherosclerosis.

In fact, since most primates (apes and monkeys) are much more vegetarian 15
in their diet than human beings, can it be that we have not yet had time to fully
adapt to the kind of carnivorous diet we have grown accustomed to? This is
particularly so in prosperous Western countries. People of the Third World countries eat far less meat than Westerners do. They may have troubles of their own,
but atherosclerosis, at least, is a minor problem.

We may also develop drugs that interfere with the body's ability to deposit 16
cholesterol in the blood vessels. A new drug called lovastatin had been recently
reported to show promising effectiveness in this direction. There is hope.

Questions for analysis   1. Asimov's general subject is cholesterol. What are his specific subject
and thesis? How does he present his thesis? (See the analysis of these features
following the Hubbell essay.) Given his audience and informative purpose,
how appropriate does this thesis seem?

2. Like Hubbell, Asimov does not cite any of the sources of the considerable amount of information in his report. Why do you think he does not? What advantages or disadvantages for a writer in Asimov's situation can you see in not citing sources?

3. Do you find Asimov's essay easier or harder to read than Hubbell's? Specifically, why is it easier or harder? Comparing these two essays, what can you conclude about ease and difficulty in writing that reports information?

4. In addition to providing information, Asimov asks several questions. Why do you think he asks questions when his primary purpose is to inform? What do you think each question adds to the essay?

5. In paragraphs 3, 4, and 5, explaining the role of cholesterol in the nervous system, Asimov uses several *which* clauses (called adjective or relative clauses). Such clauses can play an important role in essays reporting information, enabling the writer to define terms or combine information in sentences. Underline the *which* clauses in Asimov's essay and decide how he uses each one.

6. Writers of informative essays must read substantial amounts of material and understand it well so that they can summarize it accurately and confidently. Summary is essential to reporting information. To practice writing summary, briefly summarize Asimov's essay. (Chapter 11: Invention and Revision outlines a plan for summarizing.)

7. Consider medical problems, scientific principles or discoveries, or technological breakthroughs that interest you. Choose one you might write about. How would you learn more about it? How would you present it to readers unfamiliar with the details of it? How would you engage and hold your readers' interest?

Commentary   Asimov's essay on cholesterol illustrates essential strategies for reporting information: transitions, cohesive ties, and defining. Like a line of people holding hands, Asimov's paragraphs are linked by explicit transitions—important cues that readers require to stay on track. The first sentence in paragraph 2, for example, connects this paragraph to the preceding one through the word "death"; and the opening phrase "and yet" signals the contrast between the first and second paragraphs, a contrast that remains central to the essay. These transitions seem logical and even obvious. They provide the links between the major sections, contributing significantly to coherence and enabling us to follow easily and understand more readily. When you write your own essay reporting information, you will want to pay close attention to establishing strong links between sections and paragraphs.

Just as readers require explicit transitions at paragraph breaks, they also require transitions from sentence to sentence. We talk about these sentence transitions in terms of cohesion, the connections that tie one sentence to the previous one throughout an essay. In reports, readers typically expect all the connections to be explicit. Writers have many resources for creating cohesion, resources outlined in Chapter 12: Cueing the Reader. Some of these cohesion devices are evident in Asimov's brief paragraph 7. In the first sentence, "fatty sheath" repeats the same words in the previous paragraph. In the second sentence, "cholesterol" repeats the same word in the first paragraph. (You can see the relationships easily if you circle these words and then draw a line from one circle to the next.) In addition to repeating key words, pronouns forge coherence. In the second sentence, for example, "that" refers to the entire first sentence, while in the third sentence, "it" refers to "cholesterol" in the second sentence.

Finally, Asimov's essay illustrates some of the strategies for defining that are so important in essays reporting information. In fact, you might view Asimov's essay as an extended definition of cholesterol. Paragraphs 4–6 define "axon" by describing this nerve cell fiber's appearance, function, and purpose. Notice Asimov's use of sentences with *which* and *that* clauses and *-ing* phrases. Though he does not define cholesterol chemically—perhaps assuming his readers would not understand such a definition and do not need it anyway—he does describe its origins, as well as its positive and negative role in human life. When you write your own report, you will probably have to define certain terms for your readers. A quick phrase or sentence definition (like a dictionary definition) may suffice; or, like Asimov, your essay might be an extended definition of an important concept or principle. (Chapter 16: Defining illustrates many strategies of defining.)

The next selection was written by Anastasia Toufexis for *Time* magazine. After several years as a writer and editor for medical journals, she joined *Time* as its medical editor. This essay reports on the controversy surrounding a proposal to trace the sexual contacts of AIDS victims. Newspapers and magazines often feature reports that try to present both sides of an issue, without taking a position on it. As you read, ask yourself whether Toufexis successfully remains objective.

TRACING A KILLER
ANASTASIA TOUFEXIS

"Good afternoon. This is a disease specialist at the department of public 1 health. Can you talk privately? The reason I'm calling is because one of your previous sexual partners has a sexually transmitted disease. Would you mind coming in to undergo a few tests to see if you've been exposed?"

"What type of tests? What kind of sexually transmitted disease?"   2

"One of your previous sexual partners has AIDS."   3

It is a chilling phone call, still rarely made but likely to become more common 4 as the disease spreads and more and more public-health authorities begin tracing the sexual intimates of AIDS victims. Calls of this kind, known in public-health jargon as contact notification, have long been accepted as part of the effort to curb the spread of sexually communicable diseases like syphilis and gonorrhea.

But when used to battle AIDS, the practice has aroused a storm of criticism and has raised some thorny ethical issues.

Untangling the skein of someone's sexual contacts can be a time-consuming 5 and onerous process. San Francisco's public-health department, for example, has been tracing the partners of heterosexual AIDS victims since April 1985. (Tracing would serve little purpose among San Francisco's estimated 90,000 bisexuals and homosexuals; 50% to 70% are thought to be infected with the virus.) Of 114 heterosexuals with AIDS, the department was able to interview 50, who identified 93 other people with whom they had been intimate. Of the 93, only 42 were located in the Bay Area, and of these, 27 agreed to be interviewed, counseled and tested. Seven proved positive for the AIDS virus.

Though such numbers may seem small, proponents claim that contact trac- 6 ing will help contain the spread of the disease, primarily among heterosexuals and in communities where it is not already prevalent. Those with AIDS, they say, have a moral duty to warn those they have put at risk. Critics of mandatory tracing charge that it may feed panic and hysteria. They stress that, unlike syphilis or gonorrhea, AIDS is so far incurable. Indeed, says Dr. Kevin Cahill, a member of New York City's board of health, some people who were told that they had been exposed to the virus have attempted suicide—even though they showed no symptoms of the disease.

Opponents of tracing also fear that breaches in the confidentiality of contact 7 lists could lead to greater discrimination in housing, jobs and insurance. Some places—San Francisco and Minnesota, for example—protect privacy by destroying the lists, but Colorado's health department is preserving its files on all contacted partners. "You can't do this stuff anonymously," explains Beth Dillon, manager of Colorado's AIDS-education program. "If I could have contacted, traced and counseled the 150 gay men in Denver in 1981 who tested positive, we wouldn't have 20,000 infected in 1986." Yet critics counter that such actions may send AIDS victims underground, thus undercutting the effectiveness of programs that still rely on voluntary cooperation. Says Nan Hunter, an American Civil Liberties Union attorney: "You can't torture people for names."

Instead, Hunter and other foes of tracing insist that mass educational pro- 8 grams are the answer. But even with the extensive publicity about AIDS and safe sex, many heterosexuals who risk exposure are apparently indifferent to the danger and feel no need to change their ways. Contact notification accompanied by counseling, say its proponents, might bring home the message to such people and spur them to take the AIDS test. Then those who test positive might feel a responsibility to their sexual partners and adopt safer practices. Those with negative results, having been given a scare, might be encouraged to moderate their activities. Either way, the spread of AIDS would be slowed. Says Michael Osterholm, a Minneapolis epidemiologist: "Only those people who have been given a personal sense of vulnerability seem to be willing to make changes in their sexual habits."

Questions for analysis   1. The organization of this essay may seem obvious, even inevitable. But unlike narrative writing, which has its own inherent logic, informational reports ordinarily can be organized in many different ways. To understand and evaluate Toufexis's plan, make a scratch outline of her essay. Then, consider how else she might have arranged the jumble of facts and opinions she has gathered.

2. What is Toufexis's purpose? How can you tell? Where does she present her thesis?

3. How does Toufexis seek to engage readers' interest at the beginning of her essay? What advantages or disadvantages do you see in this particular strategy? Compare Toufexis's beginning with Hubbell's and Asimov's. From these three beginnings, what can you conclude about writers' strategies for beginning reports of information?

4. What does Toufexis seem to assume about her readers? What does she assume they know about AIDS? About tracing sexual contacts of AIDS victims? Do you think she assumes that most of her readers favor tracing or that they oppose it? What makes you think so?

5. Review the quotations from authorities in Toufexis's essay. Who are these authorities? Do they seem well chosen to represent both sides of the controversy? What contribution does each quotation make to the report?

6. Think of campus, community, or national controversies that concern you. If you could review the arguments on both sides of one such controversy and report them objectively to readers, which controversy would you choose? How would you go about discovering differing views of the controversy?

Commentary   Toufexis's writing situation demands that she withhold her own opinion in the interests of balanced, objective reporting. To be able to consider a controversy in this way is more than a writing skill—it is an important intellectual achievement, requiring the ability to remain cool even when your feelings are strong. In the next chapter (6: Taking a Position), you will have the opportunity to argue for your own position on a controversial issue and will undoubtedly discover that your best chance of getting readers to take your views seriously is by demonstrating that you understand their position and can describe it objectively and fairly.

While Hubbell and Asimov rely on published sources of information, Toufexis relies on interviews, as reporters often must to meet publication deadlines. She uses interviews not to profile an individual, as you might have done in Chapter 4, but solely as sources of information. Though she almost certainly has read reports about AIDS, she relies on interviews for nearly all the arguments she includes from both sides of the controversy.

Toufexis's essay also illustrates how useful a comparison/contrast strategy can be to a writer reporting information. Beginning in paragraph 6, each paragraph contrasts the views of those supporting and those opposing tracing. For example, in paragraph 6, Toufexis explains that while proponents believe tracing will contain the spread of AIDS, opponents are persuaded tracing will cause panic and hysteria. On the issue of confidentiality, she contrasts the argument that the risk is worth the gain with the counter-argument that fear of discrimination may send AIDS victims underground. This alternation of views is an especially appropriate and effective strategy for presenting opposing views on a controversial issue. (See Chapter 18: Comparing and Contrasting for further information.)

Like Toufexis, the author of the next selection, David Green, reports on a current controversy; but, unlike her, he relies solely on published sources of information. For his freshman composition class, Green reports on the controversy over a new sound recording and playback system—digital audio tape, or DAT. Japanese electronics manufacturers want to market this technology in America, but American recording companies and musical artists want to prevent such sales until DAT machines contain an anticopying device. Behind this controversy lies an older one over home recording or copying that dates back to 1971, when copyright law was broadened to cover sound recordings. As you read, notice what use Green makes of the sources he cites.

THE DIGITAL AUDIO TAPE CONTROVERSY

DAVID GREEN

By now most of us have heard music played on a compact disc (CD). A few of us even own CD machines, now that they are priced in the $200 to $600 range. Anyone who has listened to music on a CD has been impressed by the quality of sound reproduction. Just as we are adjusting to this welcome electronic breakthrough, however, another looms on the horizon—digital audio tape (DAT). It is smaller and lighter than a CD; in fact, it is only two-thirds the size of a conventional audiocassette, and yet it offers two full hours of playing time. Its compactness will lead to even smaller portable recording machines. Best of all, it offers studio-recording sound quality, "the best, most authentic sound to ever emerge from a speaker system" (McDougal 1).

The DAT cassette "pushes the familiar audiocassette to new limits" (Schiffres 54). DAT achieves its crystal clear tone by storing every millisecond of music as a digitalized number on a magnetic tape. Then, when DAT is in the playback mode on a DAT machine, a microprocessor in the tape player converts the digital numbers to music. Compared to conventional audio tape, which records the music as it is heard, the precise digitized audio tape is free of distortion and bothersome background hiss.

This new sound technology, invented by Japanese electronics firms who are eager to market it around the world, may be a long time arriving on American retailers' shelves, however. It has produced a controversy that now involves the U.S. Congress. "DAT could eliminate our industry," says Jason S. Berman, president of the Recording Industry Association of America (Buell 112). Wary that the introduction of DAT in the fall of 1987 will encourage unauthorized copying and thus severely cut their profits, record companies are pushing for Congress to pass legislation that would require Japanese manufacturers to insert an anticopying device into their DAT machines. Record companies are also worried about the possibility of abruptly falling CD sales as consumers await DAT and then switch over to it. For the time being, CDs will have an advantage because of the lack of prerecorded DAT software. Digital audio tape machines could also sell for anywhere from $1500 to $2000 when they first hit the market (Buell 112).

But that advantage does not buoy the confidence of American record com- 4 panies. At costs of about $8 for a DAT and roughly $15 for a CD, record executives fear that the consumer will take either of these options: purchase a blank DAT and record a borrowed CD onto it, or record their music from a borrowed DAT onto another blank one (Buell 112). In either case, the record industry could be losing money to copiers. For an industry that says it already loses one and a half billion dollars annually to people who copy music from their friends, the record industry is fearful of that number growing astronomically (Buell 112).

Record company executives, not taking any chances about how the con- 5 sumer will react to DAT, have taken up the issue on Capitol Hill. The industry has presented Congress with two plans. The first one would make it mandatory for all DAT machines to be built with an anticopying device. This plan has been introduced as legislation by Henry Waxman (D-California), whose Hollywood district includes much of the entertainment industry. Waxman's bill requires that all DAT machines contain a special microchip that "would pick up a signal in compact discs, analog tapes, and records that would tell the DAT to stop recording" (Morehouse 1235). The second plan proposed by industry opponents of DAT would settle for an import tariff on DAT players. Some industry insiders have been speaking of a tariff as high as 35 percent. The first proposal seems to have President Reagan's approval. The President's State of the Union report included this statement: "We will seek a 'technological' solution to the potential problem of unauthorized copying of copyrighted material on digital audio tape recorders" (Buell 112). Like Waxman, the Reagan administration has introduced legislation that would require anticopying devices. While Waxman's bill requires the device for three years so that Congress can study the effects of DAT, the administration's bill requires it permanently (Morehouse 1235).

American record company executives are taking action, but Japanese elec- 6 tronics firms are not sitting still. Economic pressure from abroad, resulting from the extremely strong yen, has Japanese electronics executives distressed over profits. To them, DAT is the product that could become the high volume and profit item that they feel they need to boost their economic spirits. Worldwide sales of DAT are predicted to be only 230,000 units in 1987 and no more than 550,000 units in 1988 (Buell 112). The Japanese attribute these low figures to the high price of DAT players and the limited availability of DAT equipment. Electronics executives in Japan, however, are confident that as the price of DAT players drops and prerecorded digital audio tapes become more available, DAT sales will account for a considerable number of all audio sales. Thus, American record executives feel their fear is justifiable.

American lobbyists for Japanese electronics manufacturers have been ener- 7 getically making the case in Congress for unrestricted importation of DAT machines without anticopying devices. The Electronics Industry Association argues that anticopying devices "would distort or otherwise damage the quality of the digital audio tape system" (McDougal 4). They say that since DAT is the recorded music system of the future, it should not be opposed. Just as conventional audiocassette tapes replaced vinyl LP albums and increased recording companies' profits, so will DAT replace CDs and increase profits (McDougal 4).

American record company executives have met with Japanese electronics 8
firms and urged them to adopt the anticopying device. The Japanese are defiantly against the plan because they believe people would be dissuaded from purchasing the DAT machines if they lacked recording capabilities. Said one Japanese electronics luminary, "It would be like trying to sell a car that can only go 55 miles an hour" (Buell 112). The Japanese have put forth a compromise that would allow themselves to sell DAT players with copy-guard protection. This technological defense against copying means that the players will have no input jack to connect a DAT machine up to a CD player. But consumers would still be able to pass the music through speakers and then record onto a blank DAT. The Japanese argue that the result would be a recording of lesser quality than DAT or CD. But record executives in the United States are not budging from their demand for a total prevention of recording ability.

The DAT debate will not go away. DAT players and software are expected 9
to arrive in American stores in the fall of 1987. There are now no laws that would prevent their importation. Both sides have launched an advertising campaign and have stepped up their lobbying efforts. Congress has asked the National Bureau of Standards to decide whether one already developed anticopying device will affect the quality of DAT music. It wants to know the result before debating pending legislation. Congressman Waxman has said, "It's important . . . to get the legislation in place before the DATs are dumped on our shore" (Morehouse 1236).

At the only congressional hearing on the issue so far, on May 14, 1987, the 10
debate focused on home copying. Country singer Emmylou Harris testified, "I can't think of any other business in America today where people would think they're entitled to a second item for free just because they paid for the first one. Maybe people think they're flattering us by copying our music. But the simple truth is they're choking off our livelihood" (Morehouse 1235). Opponents, however, argue that home taping actually helps musicians and the record industry. Charles Ferris, a lawyer for the Home Recording Rights Coalition says, "Home taping has the documented effect of encouraging purchases of prerecorded music, either of entire albums that have only been partially taped, or of other albums by the artist or composer whose work was taped" (Morehouse 1236).

For recorded-music enthusiasts, this debate will be interesting to follow. Its 11
outcome will determine the kind of home music we will all have available in the next few years. CD music isn't bad at all, but DAT music clearly has advantages. Since anticopying devices are not presently required in any other audio or video machines and since the Supreme Court has even ruled that home copying is legal (Morehouse 1236), opponents of DAT may have a difficult time obtaining any special restrictions on its copying capabilities.

WORKS CITED

Buell, Barbara. "Record Executives Are on Pins and Needles." *Business Week* 16 February 1987: 112.

Schiffres, Manuel. "The New Sound of Music." *U.S. News & World Report* 26 January 1987: 54–55.

McDougal, Dennis. "DAT Recorder Debate Erupts." *Los Angeles Times* 22 June 1987: 1, 4.

Morehouse, Macon. "Digital Tape Recorders Spark Lobbying War." *CQ Weekly Report* 13 June 1987: 1235–1237.

Questions for analysis

1. How successfully does Green present opposing views? Is his presentation fair? Where is he most successful? Least successful?

2. Why do you think Green begins by defining DAT? What defining strategies does he use? (Chapter 16: Defining discusses several strategies.)

3. Both Toufexis and Green present opposing views in a controversy. Compare their plans, tones, and general strategies. From your comparison, what can you conclude about reporting controversies?

4. Examine Green's sources in his "Works Cited" list. Given his purpose and readers, how might you evaluate the appropriateness of these sources?

5. Examine the frequency, pattern, and types of citations in Green's essay. What do you notice about his citation strategy?

6. Consider current controversies in the news or in subjects you are studying. Which controversy might you write about? What kinds of research would you need to do in order to report on the controversy authoritatively? How would you define or describe the subject of the controversy and establish its importance to your readers?

Commentary

One of the most important decisions a writer reporting information must make is whether to cite sources. As with all writers' decisions, this one depends on your purpose and readers—on the writing situation in which you find yourself. In college, the general expectation is that students will use and cite sources. The chapter on the research paper provides general guidelines for deciding when to quote, summarize, or paraphrase as well as information on compiling reference lists and citing sources in your essay. If you cannot decide whether to quote, summarize, or paraphrase a source, you might bring a copy to class and consult your instructor. You can also find a detailed discussion of how David Green made his decisions in the Writer at Work section later in this chapter.

PURPOSE AND AUDIENCE

The central purpose of essays reporting information is easier to understand if contrasted with the purposes of two other kinds of informative or explanatory writing: news and directions. For example, newspaper weather reports or sports reports provide news about familiar and well-understood subjects. Personal computer manuals, game rules, or cake recipes offer directions for repeating a process exactly as the writer has designed and tested it.

The essays in this chapter, however, all report information for the purpose of enhancing readers' understanding. They assume readers want to learn something new about the subject: chiggers, cholesterol, tracing sexual partners of AIDS patients, controversy over digital audio tape recorders. While a daily weather report is news, weather is a subject about which any reader could be better informed. An essay reporting what is known about conditions that generate hurricanes in the Caribbean would be informative, but a newspaper report on damage caused by a particular hurricane would simply be news. While a report on last night's baseball game is news, there is information about sports—the history of baseball, for example—that would add to a reader's fundamental understanding of baseball. Anyone with a serious interest in food as a subject knows that cakes, like baseball, have a history. They have a chemistry, too. Articles about the origins of chocolate cake or its chemistry would be informative. A recipe for chocolate chiffon cake is merely directions. In this chapter you will not write news or directions; instead, you will write an essay informing and educating your readers.

Knowing these contrasts in purposes of different types of explanatory writing—information, news, directions—will sharpen your understanding of the special purpose in informative essays like the one you will write in this chapter. Still another contrast will be helpful, a contrast between the purpose of informative writing and the purposes of other types of writing in this text. In autobiographical writing (Chapters 2 and 3), the writer's purpose is to share significant personal experiences in so engaging a way that readers reflect on their own lives. In persuasive writing (Chapters 6–10), the writer's purpose is to convince readers to take seriously a claim or assertion the writer has made about a controversy, problem, trend, or work of literature. The writer intends readers to take action or to think deeply about their own opinions. In profiles (Chapter 4), where the purpose is closest to that in reports of information, the writer's purpose is to inform readers in an entertaining way, enabling them to imagine (just as in autobiography or prose fiction) the person, place, or activity and to understand something about it.

Like the profile you may have written in Chapter 4, the essay reporting information purposefully informs readers. Though it may seek to engage readers' interests, it gives prominence to the facts about its subject. It aims at readers' intellects rather than their imaginations. It is determined to instruct rather than entertain.

To set out to increase readers' understanding of a subject is an audacious undertaking. To succeed, you must know your subject so well that you can explain it simply, without jargon or obfuscation. You must be authoritative without showing off or talking down.

You must also know your readers. Primarily, you must understand what they already know about the subject in order to decide which facts will be truly new to them. You will want to define unfamiliar words and pace the information carefully so that your readers are neither bored nor over-whelmed.

BASIC FEATURES OF ESSAYS REPORTING INFORMATION

From your analysis of the readings, you know that essays reporting information display certain basic features. This section summarizes those features.

A subject and a thesis

At the basis of every report are a subject and a thesis. The subject may be selected by the writer, or it may be assigned by someone else. Once the general subject is determined, the writer must narrow the topic somewhat by deciding on a specific subject. Finally, within this specific subject, the writer must develop a thesis, which is the main point of the report.

The thesis is the assertion the writer wishes to make about the specific subject. As such, it controls the entire essay, determining what information is included and how it is organized.

An appeal to readers' interests

In reporting information, good writers try to make a direct appeal to their readers' interests. They try to capture their readers' interest with an engaging beginning. For example, Sue Hubbell begins with an Ozark joke about the five chiggers who died during the winter. Throughout her essay, she tries to connect to readers' natural human interest in chiggers. Anastasia Toufexis opens with a dramatic telephone call from a health official to a previous sexual partner of an AIDS victim. Isaac Asimov begins with engaging tough talk about a health menace: "Cholesterol is a dirty word these days, and every report that comes out seems to make it worse." The danger, the threat, the possibility of worrisome new information draws us in.

A logical plan

Reports must follow a clear path to keep readers on track. For organizing reports and cueing readers, writers rely on many strategies. They divide the information in such a way that supports the thesis and then alert readers to these divisions with forecasting statements and transitions. They try to frame the essay for readers by relating the ending to the beginning. We have seen these features repeatedly in the readings in this chapter. Toufexis, for example, after presenting the context for her report on the AIDS contact tracing controversy, organizes her essay around three of the main issues about which there is sharp disagreement. She forecasts the disagreements when she writes, " . . . the practice [of tracing] has aroused a storm of criticism and has raised some thorny ethical issues." She frames her essay by concluding with a quote from a doctor who argues that only those who feel personally vulnerable will change their sexual habits, reminding us of the person called by the health worker at the opening of the essay. In the three paragraphs presenting the disagreements, the transition sentences continually remind readers of Toufexis's plan and even her purpose: the first mentions "proponents," the next "opponents," and the last "foes."

Good writers never forget that readers need many signals. Because a writer knows the information so well and is aware of how it is organized, it is difficult to see it the way someone reading the essay for the first time would. That is precisely what must be done, however, to be sure that the essay includes all the signals the reader will need to stay on track in a first reading.

Clear definitions Essays reporting information depend on clear definitions. In order to relate information clearly, a writer must be sensitive to the readers' knowledge; any terms that are likely to be misunderstood must be explicitly defined. Asimov, for example, provides an extended definition of *axon*. In defining the term *atherosclerosis*, Asimov first describes the conditions that produce it before introducing this medical term. Using the same strategy, Hubbell first identifies a *deutovum*, "a second egg," before mentioning the term. She does the same with *stylostome*, "a small well or tube." Green carefully defines *digital audio tape*. Sometimes writers reporting information include definitions and explanations as sidelights to the main discussion. At other times, writers center the entire essay on straightforward definitions of key terms and concepts. (Many more examples of definitions are discussed in Chapter 16: Defining.)

Appropriate writing Writers have available many strategies for presenting information. The strate-
strategies gies they use are determined by the point they want to make and the kind of information they have to work with. Following are some of the writing strategies that are particularly useful in reports.

Classification. Organization is possible in informative writing only through classification. To classify is to discover what goes with what in order to create groupings or patterns from the information on a subject. Classification is more than a way of organizing an essay, however. It is basically a way of understanding the world.

In this chapter, for example, Toufexis classifies her material around specific disagreements in the controversy over whether to trace sexual partners of AIDS victims. Hubbell classifies some of her material by biological stages in chiggers' development.

Writers of informative essays are sometimes able to classify their information successfully before they start drafting. Often, however, they begin with a tentative classification—a plan, even an outline—and then change it as they draft or as they reflect on a completed draft. The classification that finally determines the plan, sequence, and focus of the essay reflects the nature of information, the writer's purpose, and the writer's estimation of readers' knowledge about the subject. (Chapter 17: Classifying provides further information on this important thinking process and writer's strategy.)

Narration. Writers may sometimes illustrate a subject with anecdotes, which can convey information directly as well as indirectly by setting up contrasts. Storytelling is important even in the most practical academic and professional writing—reporting information. For example, Hubbell dramatizes the inconvenience caused by chiggers with the anecdote of her blackberry-picking friend. She also narrates the process of chiggers' egg and larval development. Toufexis presents a possible anecdote—a scenario really—in the conversation between the health worker and the sexual partner of an AIDS victim. If you were to write about a historical figure, you might rely on anecdotes to characterize this figure vividly. Reporting on both sides of a campus controversy, you might narrate anecdotes involving people on both sides. (Narrative strategies are analyzed and illustrated in more detail in Chapter 13: Narrating.)

Illustration. Illustration is the life's blood of informative writing. Concrete, elaborated illustrations establish the writer's authority and enable readers to understand and remember a subject. Illustrations may take the form of developed examples, lists of facts, statistics, even anecdotes and scenarios. For example, Toufexis illustrates the results of AIDS contact tracing in San Francisco by providing statistics on contacts, interviews, and positive tests for AIDS. Asimov lists foods that do and do not contain high amounts of cholesterol. Green illustrates congressional debate on the digital audio tape controversy by quoting testimony of country singer Emmylou Harris. (These and other forms of illustration are discussed in Chapter 15: Illustrating.)

Comparison and contrast. This strategy is especially useful in presenting information because it helps readers to understand something new by showing how it is similar to or different from things they already know. Every essayist in this chapter makes use of contrast. Toufexis organizes her essay around contrasting views on tracing the sexual partners of AIDS victims. Asimov contrasts cholesterol as deadly and as essential to life, and Hubbell contrasts chiggers and chigoes. In order to describe digital audio tape technology, Green contrasts it with compact disc technology. He focuses on differing views of the impact of digital audio tape. (See Chapter

18: Comparing and Contrasting for a more detailed discussion of this writing strategy.)

GUIDE TO WRITING

THE WRITING TASK

Write an essay that reports information for the purpose of increasing readers' understanding of a subject. Choose a subject that you can write about with confidence and some authority; if necessary, do research to get more information.

INVENTION AND RESEARCH

The following activities are designed to help you write a focused, developed, interesting report. They will help you to find a subject and a thesis, evaluate your choice of subject, analyze your readers, figure out what you know about the topic and what you need to learn. Together, these invention and research activities will enable you to write a draft that will be truly informative for your particular readers.

Finding a subject   You may already have a topic in mind. Your work, recreation, travels, and reading may suggest topics. Even if you already have a subject in mind, you might want to complete these activities in order to be certain yours is the best possible choice.

Listing subjects. The possibilities may seem limitless. Remember, however, that some subjects—war, politics, and religion, for example—are so general that they would be extraordinarily difficult to discuss in a short essay. Other subjects may be inappropriate because you would not have sufficient time to find out enough about them.

Consider each of the categories that follows, listing as many subjects as you can under each one. The longer your list, the more likely you are to find just the right subject for your essay. And, should your first choice not work out, you will have a ready list of alternatives.

Include topics you already know something about as well as some you know only slightly and would like to research further. If any of the following examples of subjects interest you, add them to your list.

- ☐ An important academic breakthrough: Newton's law of gravity, Darwin's theory of evolution, Leeuwenhoek's microscope, DNA, Einstein's theory of relativity, Freud's theory of the unconscious, Marx's analysis of class conflict

- ☐ A significant academic principle or theory: *cohort size* in economics, the *uncertainty principle* in physics, *invention* in composition, *irony* in literature, *existentialism* in philosophy, *osmosis* in biology, *I.Q.* in psychology, *phonology* in linguistics, *ionic bonds* in chemistry, *socialization* in sociology

- ☐ An animal, insect, spider, bird, flower, shrub, or tree you know something about and would like to know still more about

- ☐ A significant but complicated graphic—chart, table, drawing, figure, photograph—(you would present the graphic and help your readers understand it)

- ☐ Any ordinary event you might like to know more about: sunsets, cloud formations, potholes, jet lag, sneezing, yawning

- ☐ A current danger to public health, the environment, or the social order: acid rain, high-fat diets, inflation, malnutrition, oil spills, car accidents, rape, child abuse (Your essay would report what is presently known about the danger, not take a position or propose a solution.)

- ☐ A common object you would like to know something about: baseballs, pianos, fingernail clippers, microwave ovens, microprocessors, automatic bank tellers

- ☐ An activity at which you are an expert: playing the flute, speed skating, raising pigs, growing cactuses, photographing tornadoes, managing a restaurant, playing poker (Your essay would describe the activity so that readers could understand and appreciate it, not present rules or directions for readers to follow.)

- ☐ The historical context for some current issue: handgun control, capital punishment, abortion, government subsidies for private schools, social security, federal price supports for agricultural products, congressional filibusters (Remember that your purpose would not be to argue your opinion or propose a solution.)

- ☐ A landmark or historic site: the Mississippi River, Mount Rushmore, Lincoln Memorial, the Watts Towers, the Brooklyn Bridge, the Alamo, Gettysburg, Alcatraz

- ☐ An influential nonfiction book, article, commission report, or newspaper series that you could summarize

- ☐ An important current controversy, issue, or problem, one that you could present objectively

- ☐ A topic you are currently studying (or reporting on) for another course

Choosing a subject. Now look over your list and select one subject to explore. Pick a subject that interests you and that might interest others. Write a few sentences about the subject: say what it is, describe how you first learned about it, explain why you remain interested in it.

Probing your subject To find out whether this is a good subject for an essay, invest a few minutes to explore it in writing, using the next three activities as guides.

Finding out what you already know. Take about ten minutes to jot down everything you know about this subject. Write quickly, putting down your thoughts just as they occur. You may fill in any details later. Feel free to write in sentences, or phrases, or lists. Make drawings or charts. The goal is to get everything you know about this subject down on paper.

Writing generalizations. Review what you have written, and reflect further on your subject. Now write a few very general statements about it: define it, describe it, sum up its importance, note anything unusual about it. Making such statements may help you to narrow the subject and find a thesis.

Asking questions. List any questions you have about your subject. Next, try to imagine what questions readers might have. Which of these questions would your essay attempt to answer? These questions may help you focus the subject and ultimately may suggest a thesis.

Asserting a tentative thesis Review your general statements and questions thoughtfully to find the thesis, or main point, you wish to write about. The thesis must interest you and should be manageable in a brief essay. It ought to be an assertion that you will be able to illustrate. Write down this thesis, and then state in writing why you consider it a good choice.

Attempting to state your thesis now will help you focus further invention and research. You may have to tinker with your thesis to get it right, perhaps even drafting several different versions. As you continue invention and research, you may want to revise or change your thesis. You may even find it necessary to revise or change your thesis as you plan and draft your essay.

Testing your choice Now stop to examine your topic to see whether it is worth reporting on and whether you will be able to do so. The following questions can help you to test your choice.

- ☐ Do I have a strong personal interest in this subject?
- ☐ Are my readers likely to be interested in this subject?
- ☐ Do I know enough about it already, or can I find out what I need to know about it within the time available?

☐ Can I discuss this specific subject well in a short essay?

☐ Does my tentative thesis provide a clear, forceful focus for the essay?

You may want to reconsider these questions later, as you invent and plan and draft. If at any point you feel unable to answer the questions affirmatively, you should consider finding a different specific subject and thesis, or even a whole new general subject.

Analyzing your readers Decide who your readers will be, and think carefully about the interests, knowledge, and expectations they will bring to your essay. Your readers are a very important consideration, one that will help determine what information you include and that will influence the way you pace the information. Even if you are writing only for your instructor, you must be aware of his or her knowledge of your subject.

Write for at least ten minutes describing your readers. Consider the following questions as you write:

☐ Who are my readers? Are they all similar, or are they a diverse group?

☐ How much are they likely to know about this subject? What assumptions might they have about the subject?

☐ Why might they want to read about this subject?

☐ How can I engage and hold their interest?

☐ Are there any aspects of my subject that may surprise my readers?

Finding out more about your subject Depending on your subject and readers, you may be able to rely on information you already have at your command. Your instructor may prefer that you do that. On the other hand, your instructor may expect you to research your subject and cite your sources, or your subject may require that you do so. To find additional information, you will probably need to do some research at the library or perhaps even to seek help or advice from an expert on the topic.

Finding information at the library. The best place to start your research is your college library. Figure out the subject headings that you should consult for information on your topic, and then look in the card catalog, in encyclopedias (both general and specialized), in bibliographies, and in periodical indexes. If your library has open stacks, you can probably find a lot of information just by finding the right area and browsing. Chapter 21: Library Research provides detailed guidance for finding information at a library.

One thing you should look for in your research is authoritative opinions and information. Once you have identified the experts on your topic, look for articles, books, and interviews by and with them. Find out their opinions, and see if anything they have said helps you understand your subject better.

You can quote them directly, or you can summarize or paraphrase their words. (See Chapter 22: The Research Paper for discussion of quoting, summarizing, and paraphrasing.) If you photocopy any pages from which you plan to take material, your instructor can help you decide whether to quote, summarize, or paraphrase and how to integrate quotations smoothly into your draft.

Consulting an expert. Is there someone very knowledgeable about your subject who might be helpful? If you are writing about a subject from another college course, for example, the teaching assistant or professor might be someone to consult. Not only could such a person answer questions, but also he or she might direct you to important or influential articles or books. At the very least, he or she could advise you on who the preeminent people in the field are. See Chapter 20: Field Research for specific advice on interviewing.

Refocusing your thesis statement   You have already written a tentative thesis statement. Now you should look at it closely to see that it does indeed say something significant about your information.

Look at what you wrote about your readers. Now think about any additional information you have found about your subject. Does your original thesis still ring true, or does it seem weak? If you are not satisfied, try to determine what is wrong—is it too general? too bland? too reckless? too hard to illustrate? If need be, compose a whole new thesis. Remember that it is the thesis that provides the focus of the report; it must be as good as you can make it.

Defining key terms   Make a list of the key terms your readers need to understand. These terms might refer to general concepts, steps in a process, parts of an object, or aspects of a place. Then decide which terms may be unfamiliar to your readers.

Write definitions of those terms. Consider what kinds of definitions are necessary—a simple synonym, a single sentence, an example, or an extended definition. (Strategies for writing definitions are presented in Chapter 16: Defining.)

PLANNING AND DRAFTING

Here are some activities that should help you to get the most out of your invention writing, to decide on some specific goals for your essay, and to write a first draft.

Seeing what you have   Reread everything you have written so far. This is a critically important time for reflection and evaluation. Before beginning the actual draft, you must decide whether your subject is worthwhile and whether you have sufficient information for a successful essay.

It may help as you read to annotate your invention writings. Look for details that will support your thesis and appeal to your readers. Underline or circle key words, phrases, or sentences; make marginal notes. Your goal here is to identify the important elements in what you have written so far.

Be realistic. If at this point your notes do not look promising, you may want to select a different general subject or specific subject to write about. If your notes seem thin but promising, you should probably do further research to find more information before continuing.

Setting goals   Successful writers are always looking beyond the next sentence to larger goals. Indeed, the next sentence is easier to write if you keep larger goals in mind. The following questions can help you set these goals. Consider each one now and then return to them as necessary while you write.

Your readers

☐ How much are my readers likely to know about this subject? How can I build on their knowledge?

☐ What new information can I present to them?

☐ How much information will be enough and how much will be too much?

☐ How can I organize my essay so that my readers will be able to follow it easily?

☐ What tone would be most appropriate? Would an informal tone like Hubbell's suit my purpose, or would a formal tone like Asimov's be more appropriate?

The beginning

☐ How shall I begin? Should I open with a surprising fact, as Asimov does? Should I begin with an anecdote, as Hubbell does? a quotation? a question? What kind of opening would be most likely to capture my readers' attention?

☐ Should I assert my thesis immediately, as Asimov does? Or should I first set the context?

☐ How can I best forecast the plan my report will follow? Should I offer a detailed forecast? Or is a brief description sufficient?

The ending

☐ How shall I end?

☐ Should I relate the ending to the beginning, as Asimov and Green do, so as to frame the essay?

Special writing strategies

☐ How much do I need to define my terms? Can I rely on brief sentence definitions or will I need to write extended definitions?

☐ Should I include any tables, charts, or graphs?

☐ Do I need to include any particular examples?

☐ Would comparison or contrast help readers to understand the information?

☐ Should I include any anecdotes?

☐ Do I need to explain any processes? Or describe any historical events?

Outlining the report   Now you should give some thought to organization. Many writers find it helpful to outline their material before actually beginning to write. Whatever organizing you do before you begin drafting, consider it only tentative. Never be a slave to an outline. As you draft, you will usually see some ways to improve on your original plan. Be ready to revise your outline, to shift parts around, to drop or add parts. Chapter 11: Invention and Revision includes a thorough discussion of outlining.

Consider the following questions as you plan:

☐ How should I divide the information? (See Chapter 17: Classifying.)

☐ What order will best serve my thesis?

☐ Where should the thesis go?

☐ What kinds of transitions will I need between the main parts of my essay? (See Chapter 12: Cueing the Reader for a discussion of transitions.)

Drafting the report   Before you begin drafting your report, take time to review the general advice about drafting in Chapter 1. As you write, keep your mind on your thesis statement. Remember that this assertion is the reason for your report; everything you include must in some way support the thesis. Remember also the needs and expectations of your readers; organize and define and explain with them in mind. Your goal is to increase their understanding of your subject.

READING A DRAFT WITH A CRITICAL EYE

Now is the time to try to find someone else to read your draft. The following guidelines will help you analyze the particular features of essays that report information. (Before you begin, you might want to review the general advice on reading another's draft critically in Chapter 1.)

First general impression Read the essay straight through to get a quick general impression. Write down your reactions in a few sentences. Is the report readable? Is it informative? Did it hold your interest? Did anything surprise you? What do you like best about it? Does anything seem weak? This reading should not be for detailed analysis, but rather to express your first reaction.

Pointings One good way to maintain a critical focus as you read the report is to highlight noteworthy features of the writing with *pointings*. A simple system of lines and brackets, these pointings are quick and easy to do, and they can provide a lot of helpful information for revision. Use pointings in the following way:

☐ Draw a straight line under any words or images that seem especially effective: strong verbs, specific details, memorable phrases, striking images.

☐ Draw a wavy line under any words or images that seem flat, stale, or vague.

☐ Also put the wavy line under any words or phrases that you consider unnecessary or repetitious.

☐ Look for pairs or groups of sentences that you think should be combined into one sentence. Put brackets [ ] around these sentences.

☐ Look for sentences that are garbled, overloaded, or awkward. Put parentheses ( ) around these sentences. Put them around any sentence that seems even slightly questionable; don't worry now about whether or not you are sure of your impression. The writer needs to know that you, as one reader, had even the slightest hesitation about understanding a sentence.

Analysis Now make a more thorough analysis of the draft. As you read, consider the following things.

1. Describe the subject in your own words. Is it too big? Too small? Can you think of ways to refocus the subject that might make the essay more successful?

2. Identify the thesis. What is the main point? Is it stated directly or implied? If it is implied, state in your own words what you understand the thesis to be. If you recognize no thesis (stated or implied), suggest one.

3. Look at the way the report is organized. Is the information logically divided? Can you suggest another way to organize it? Consider also the order—can you suggest a better way of sequencing the information?

4. Describe the tone of the report. Is it appropriate for the intended readers? Does the tone remain the same throughout the report?

5. Evaluate the beginning. Does it pull you into the essay and make you want to continue? Does it adequately forecast the direction of the essay? You may be able to suggest alternative beginnings to the writer.

6. Find the obvious transitions in the draft. Are they helpful? If not, can you improve any of them? Can you see any places where additional transitions would be helpful?

7. Consider the use of facts and examples. Is the draft too factual? Too general? Point out any places where more facts or examples are needed. Look also at any anecdotes—are they interesting? Do they contribute to the overall report, or do they stray from the point?

8. Think about the draft's content. Does it seem complete? Does it tell you all that you want to know right now about this subject? Specify any additional information you think should be included. Is there any information you consider superfluous? What questions do you have about the subject that have not been answered?

9. Examine the definitions. Are they clear? Is everything defined that needs to be?

10. Evaluate the ending. Is it effective? Does it frame the report? Should it? Can you suggest any alternative endings?

11. Now imagine someone with limited time reading this essay. This reader wants—and needs—to proceed at an even, quick pace, with as little effort as possible. Where might this draft slow a reader down?

REVISING AND EDITING

You are now ready to revise your essay. Review any critical reading notes from your instructor or other students. You may find that you have only a little work to do, or you may have to make substantial changes to realize your goals for your particular readers. This section provides guidance in planning your revision.

Revising an informative essay   The guidance offered here works in tandem with the comprehensive plan for revising in Chapter 11. You may wish to turn now to Chapter 11 and follow the plan for revising until you reach the general guidelines for revising (Read Again To Identify Problems). At that point, you should substitute the following specific guidelines for revising a report.

Revising to sharpen the focus   ☐ Reconsider your thesis. Make sure that it focuses on the right point and that it is neither overstated nor understated.

☐ Remove any information that is not directly relevant to your thesis. Unrelated details, no matter how fascinating, merely detract from the main point.

Revising to clarify
the organization

☐ Look once more at the way you divided your information. Be sure the divisions are parallel and do not overlap.

☐ Reconsider the sequence of information. Be sure that the most important information receives the proper emphasis—should it be placed first or last? Is there any information that must be presented first?

Revising to enrich
the content

☐ Reconsider the total content to be sure nothing seems vague or unexplained. If necessary, do additional reading or other research.

☐ Evaluate the information your report gives. Consider whether it is too familiar; if so, try to replace some unsurprising facts with new or unexpected information.

Revising for
readability

☐ Consider other beginnings to be sure that you forecast your plan and engage your readers' interest as well as possible.

☐ Look over all the cues you provide readers to be sure they are sufficient and helpful.

☐ Reconsider your conclusion; does it frame the report? If not, should it?

☐ Scrutinize each sentence. Does it repeat the previous sentence? Does it say exactly what you want it to say? Does it have clear connections to the sentences around it? Should it be broken into two sentences or combined with another sentence?

Editing and
proofreading

Once you revise a draft for the last time, you must edit it closely. As you were drafting, you surely corrected obvious errors of usage and style, but correctness probably was not your first priority. Now, though, you must look at your draft critically and objectively in order to find and correct any errors of mechanics, usage, punctuation, or style.

After you have edited the draft and produced your final copy, proofread your report to be certain that it contains no mistakes.

LEARNING FROM YOUR OWN WRITING PROCESS

Your instructor may ask you to think or write about the process you followed in producing this essay. If so, begin by skimming your invention writing and then reread your draft and revision. Look at specific changes you made between draft and revision, and explain why you made them. Think about any problems you encountered choosing a subject and gathering information. Decide what pleases you the most about your final draft and what you would try to improve if you had more time. What did you learn about writing to report information?

A WRITER AT WORK

David Green, whose essay "The Digital Audio Tape Controversy" appears earlier in this chapter, first became aware of the controversy he was to write about while reading an issue of *Business Week*. The DAT controversy caught his attention because he prides himself on knowing about the latest technology for playing recorded music. Since he already owned a compact disc (CD) machine and a portable audiocassette machine, he knew that he would almost certainly buy a digital audio tape (DAT) machine as soon as he could afford one.

Four months later, when assigned an essay reporting information and encouraged to consider current controversies for a topic, Green listed the DAT controversy among his possible topics. Before committing himself to this topic, he went to the library to see whether he could find the *Business Week* article he remembered, as well as other sources. He found three articles listed in the *Readers' Guide to Periodical Literature*, all from weekly news magazines:

Barbara Buell, "Record Executives Are on Pins and Needles," *Business Week* (This was the article Green remembered reading.)

Manuel Schiffres, "The New Sound of Music," *U.S. News & World Report*

"DAT Spat," *Time* (no author indicated)

Though these sources were similar and limited, they provided more information than he could use in his first draft. Buell and the unidentified *Time* writer outlined the essential facts of the controversy. Schiffres outlined the basic information about DAT, contrasting it with CD and conventional audiocassette technology. Green might have found further articles about DAT technology; since the technology itself was not to be the focus of his report, however, he sensed that Schiffres provided all the information he would need to define DAT adequately for his readers.

Just before he began revising his draft, Green came across a useful feature article in the *Los Angeles Times*, "DAT Recorder Debate Erupts," by Dennis McDougal. Longer than any of the magazine articles, it contained information to strengthen his presentation of the American electronics industry and Japanese side of the controversy. This article also briefly reviewed activity in Congress and confirmed Green's instructor's suggestion that he examine the Congressional debate by looking at *CQ Weekly Report*, a weekly review of Congressional hearings and legislation. In his revision, Green relied on an article in the *CQ Weekly Report*, by Macon Morehouse, for new information about hearings and legislation. Morehouse, along with McDougal, provided several of the direct quotations Green included in his revision.

After dropping the *Time* magazine article, Green cited four sources in his revision: the two magazine articles by Buell and Schiffres, McDougal's newspaper feature article, and Morehouse's Congressional report. These four sources provided about 6,000 words of information on the DAT controversy, which Green had to integrate into his own 1,200-word essay.

After completing the invention activities in the Guide to Writing, Green had a clear sense of purpose (to report the DAT controversy objectively) and a good understanding of his readers (students in his composition class). He also had a workable thesis. Consequently, he could plan the draft and select information with some confidence. Responses from other students and the instructor confirmed that his first draft was basically sound but needed further, more substantive sources on the controversy. These became available in McDougal and Morehouse.

Guided by a good understanding of his writing situation, Green selected, paraphrased, and quoted directly from his sources. Instead of summarizing all or nearly all the information in the four sources, he selected a limited amount of information to paraphrase. (Summary reduces and rewords information, while paraphrase retains and rewords information. You can find out more about summary and paraphrase in Chapter 11: Invention and Revision.)

Green's quoting and paraphrasing strategy can be seen by comparing paragraphs from the Schiffres article with Green's opening paragraphs. Following are three paragraphs from the original article:

> Technologically, DAT is less revolutionary than the CD. It pushes the familiar audiocassette to new limits, but doesn't leapfrog it. In use for six years to make professional recordings, DAT stores music on magnetic tape as discrete units of computer data in contrast to analog tape, which captures sound in a form analogous—hence the name—to the waves transmitted through the air. And in the DAT playback mode, a microprocessor converts the digits back to analog waves so they can be heard.
>
> The main advantages: Sound can be reproduced without the distortions and the low-grade background hiss that now plague even the best analog tape cassettes. And the range of signals captured on DAT is equivalent to CD in richness. Other pluses include 2 hours of playing time for music and a tinier cassette. Once DAT catches on, it will inevitably lead to more miniaturized playback gear for joggers and other on-the-go types.
>
> CDs however, have the edge over DAT in other important areas. For one thing, it's possible to go to a selection almost instantaneously on CD, while it takes about 36 seconds to scan a 2-hour DAT cassette. Aside from the convenience, compact discs are extremely durable, while digital tapes, like other magnetic-type transports, can jam or break, ruining the entire recording.

Now look at Green's paragraphs incorporating this source:

By now most of us have heard music played on a compact disc (CD). A few of us even own CD machines, now that they are priced in the $200 to $600 range. Anyone who has listened to music on CD has been impressed by the quality of sound reproduction. Just as we are adjusting to this welcome electronic breakthrough, however, another looms on the horizon—digital audio tape (DAT). It is smaller and lighter than CD; in fact, it is only two-thirds the size of a conventional audiocassette, and yet if offers two full hours of playing time. Its compactness will lead to even smaller portable recording machines. Best of all, it offers studio-recording sound quality, "the best, most authentic sound to ever emerge from a speaker system" (McDougal 1).

The DAT cassette "pushes the familiar audiocassette to new limits" (Schiffres 54). DAT achieves its crystal clear tone by storing every millisecond of music as a digitalized number on a magnetic tape. Then, when DAT is in the playback mode on a DAT machine, a microprocessor in the tape player converts the digital numbers to music. Compared to conventional audio tape, which records the music as it is heard, the precise digitized audio tape is free of distortion and bothersome background hiss.

Notice first of all that Green ignores the information in Schiffres's third paragraph. Green's essay focuses on the controversy over DAT's recording capabilities. Though he must define DAT carefully at the beginning, he needs to provide only enough information so that readers can follow his report on the controversy over it. Green wisely adopts Schiffres's strategy of defining DAT by contrasting it with CD and conventional audiocassettes, but he does not need to elaborate the contrast to the extent that Schiffres does.

From Schiffres's three paragraphs Green quotes only one phrase, at the beginning of his second paragraph. This direct quotation seems to be part of Green's strategy of establishing the importance of his subject. He wants readers to see the significance and novelty of DAT so that they will take seriously the controversy about it. As part of this strategy, Green also quotes McDougal, who claims DAT is superior to all other forms of sound recording. Only one other place in Green's essay (paragraph 10) offers back-to-back quotations like this. Quite clearly, Green quotes very sparingly and only for a particular purpose. To confirm this, you can examine the few other direct quotations in his complete essay. (Information on using sources and integrating direct quotations smoothly into your own texts appears in Chapter 22: The Research Paper.)

In addition to the direct quotations from Schiffres and McDougal, elsewhere in his complete essay Green selects three direct quotations each from Buell and Morehouse. These six quotations are quotes of quotes; that is,

Green selects significant quotations secondhand from writers who had selected them from firsthand, or primary, sources—Buell from interviews, Morehouse from the *Congressional Record*, a daily transcript of hearings and legislation in Congress. In some writing situations, this secondhand selection of quotations could be questionable. With more time, Green could have read the same transcripts as Morehouse (college libraries shelve both the *CQ Weekly Report* and the daily *Congressional Record*) and then selected his own quotations, perhaps deciding in the end that Morehouse's choices really were the most appropriate. Checking Buell's primary sources would have meant interviewing the same people, which was not possible since he did not know how to get in touch with them. In your own research, you should resist quoting sources others have quoted. If possible, check the original source yourself. You may find a better quote, or you may discover that the quote comes from a context inappropriate for your report. If you do quote other's quotes, you can indicate that with "quoted from" as part of your in-text citation.

If you compare Schiffres's and Green's first two paragraphs, you will see that, except for the fact about DAT's equivalence to CD in quality, Green uses every fact in Schiffres's paragraphs. Instead of reducing this information by summarizing, he paraphrases it by reorganizing and rewording it, not simply to avoid quoting it, but to suit his own purposes. For his definition of DAT he is more interested than Schiffres in the contrast between DAT and conventional audiocassettes, because he assumed that more of his readers buy audiocassettes than CDs. Green might have cited Schiffres as the source of this information, but he justifiably did not because the information is noncontroversial and familiar by now even to newspaper and magazine readers.

Taking a Position

For a sociology class, a student writes a term paper on surrogate mothering. She first learned about the subject from the television news, but feels that she needs more information in order to write a paper on it. In the library, she finds several newspaper and magazine articles that help her better understand the pros and cons of the issue. In her paper, she presents the strongest arguments on each side, but concludes that, from a sociological perspective, surrogate mothering is bad because it exploits poor women by creating a class of professional breeders.

A college journalism student writes an editorial for the campus newspaper condemning the practice of hazing fraternity pledges. He acknowledges that most hazing is harmless, but argues that hazing can get out of hand and even be lethal. He refers specifically to two incidents reported in the national news in which students died as a result of hazing. In one case, the student died of alcohol poisoning after drinking too much liquor; in the other, the student had a heart attack after running the track many times. To show that the potential for similar tragedy exists on his own campus, the writer recounts hazing anecdotes told to him by several students. He concludes with a plea to the fraternities on campus to curtail their hazing practices before someone gets seriously hurt or killed.

A parents group upset by the school board's plan to provide information on AIDS to students in the district decides to write a letter arguing against the plan. Although all the parents oppose AIDS education, they find that they have different reasons for their opinions. Everyone agrees to the principle that parents and not teachers are responsible for children's sexual education, however, so a volunteer drafts a letter based on this principle. After some discussion and revision, they all sign the letter and mail it to the school board the next day.

For a political science class, a student is assigned to write an essay either supporting or attacking the right of public employees to strike. Having no strong opinion on the issue herself, she discusses it with her mother, a nurse in a county hospital, and her uncle, a firefighter. Her mother feels that public employees like hospital workers and teachers should have the right to strike, but that police officers and firefighters should not because public safety would be endangered. Her uncle disagrees, arguing that allowing hospital workers to strike would jeopardize public safety as much as allowing firefighters to strike. He insists that the central issue is not public safety, but individual rights. In her essay, the student supports the right of public employees to strike but argues that a system of arbitration should be used where a strike might jeopardize public safety.

6

☐ A committee made up of business and community leaders investigates the issue of regulating urban growth. They prepare a report for the City Manager in which they explain the controversy, summarize the pro and con arguments, and argue their own opinion that growth should be unregulated. The reasons they give for their conclusion are that supply and demand will regulate development without governmental interference, that landowners should be permitted to sell their property to the highest bidder, and that developers are guided by the needs of the market and thus serve the people.

As these examples suggest, we often must examine a complex issue and construct a reasoned argument for any position we wish to present. Taking a position after thoughtful deliberation enables us to air our differences constructively and learn to understand one another. It leads us to find or to create common ground on which we can meet.

Writing a position paper can be intellectually challenging and also very satisfying. In examining an issue, you will uncover your own basic values, assumptions, and beliefs as well as those of others. Constructing an argument tests and develops your reasoning powers. You must distinguish between opinion and fact, draw conclusions from particular examples, and evaluate evidence. Reading and writing position papers can also heighten your sensitivity to language. You will learn to choose your words carefully—both to convince your readers and to clarify your own thinking.

The position paper differs from the other writing presented so far in this book. You do not write primarily to inform your readers, as in profiles (Chapter 4) or reports (Chapter 5). Nor is your aim basically to express yourself, as in autobiography (Chapters 2 and 3). In a position paper, you seek not only to inform readers about the issue and to express your view, but also to convince readers to take your position seriously, whether or not they change their views to conform with yours.

This chapter is the first in a series of chapters (6–10) on argumentative writing. The types of writing presented in these chapters—position paper, proposal, evaluation, cause, and interpretation—all have the same general purpose: to convince readers that your inquiry is fair and thoughtful, and that your conclusion makes sense. The strongest arguments, as you will see when you read the following selections, appeal to readers in several ways. They appeal to logic by making a sound, well-reasoned, and well-supported argument. They appeal to emotion by making the reader care about the outcome. And they appeal to trust by establishing the writer's credibility.

Reading and analyzing these selections will help you to understand the special demands of this type of writing. You may also find ideas about how to write effective position papers of your own.

READINGS

The first position paper involves a campus controversy. In March 1986, the staff of *The Harvard Crimson* decided not to run the following advertisement:

> *Playboy*'s photographer is now on campus. *Playboy* photographer David Chan is now interviewing students for *Playboy*'s "Women of the Ivy League" pictorial. To qualify, you must be a female student 18 years of age or older, registered full- or part-time at any Ivy League college. Call now for more information and to schedule an interview.

The decision not to run the ad led to considerable debate. *The Crimson* published several articles on the controversy, including the following by editorial staff member Kristin Goss.

Before reading her essay, think for a moment about the controversy. What do you suppose is at issue? What reasons might *The Crimson* have had for deciding not to publish the *Playboy* announcement?

**TAKING A STAND
AGAINST SEXISM**

KRISTIN A. GOSS

The Crimson's decision not to run *Playboy*'s advertisement recruiting Harvard women for its October "Women of the Ivy League" issue was both the very most and the very least the newspaper could do to fight the institutionalized exploitation of women. 1

Those who claim the staff endeavored to "censor" *Playboy*, or to protect Harvard women from themselves, miss the point of the majority's intentions, just as they did seven years ago when *The Crimson* rejected the same ad. 2

The question is clearly not one of hiding information or of paternalism, but of refusing to support, either tacitly or overtly, a publication whose *raison d'être* is the objectification of women and the exploitation of womankind. It is a question of integrity. 3

Playboy editors must not expect us—a group of undergraduates who are ourselves either morally repulsed by the pornography racket or in the very least respectful of such feelings of collective degradation in our peers—to aid and abet their objectionable cause. 4

They should also not expect us to keep silent, as they attempt to make sex objects out of our classmates by offering five times as much money to those who take their clothes off as to those who remain clothed. This is not sexuality; it is sexism. 5

Those who say *The Crimson* singlehandedly stifled *Playboy*'s message have no argument. *Playboy* could have spent the same amount of money that running 6 an ad in *The Crimson* would cost to make somewhere in the neighborhood of 10,000 photocopied posters, which would have effectively reached every under-graduate, professor and administrator on this campus, and then some. It could have run an advertisement on WHRB. It did run one in the *Independent* and in the *Boston Herald*.

The Crimson's rejection of the ad clearly did not compromise *Playboy*'s right 7 to freedom of expression. The newspaper has not as an institution prevented *Playboy* photographer David Chan from coming to campus.

Nor has it implied that Harvard women cannot decide for themselves 8 whether to pose before him; they can and will make a proper, reasoned decision in either case.

Nor has *The Crimson* censored *Playboy*; the newspaper is in fact on record 9 as supporting pornography's First Amendment right to exist.

The newspaper staff has used its editorial discretion to state that its toleration 10 of pornography—by default, because the alternative would be worse—does not preclude protest. It has expressed the view held by many of its editors that while *Playboy* and other forms of institutionalized sexism may be "socially acceptable," they should not be so.

Social acceptability is a function of which group controls society and to what 11 extent minority voices can influence the spectrum of opinion. Just as racist ads of 50 years ago were socially acceptable to a white-dominated society, so are sexist ads today threatening to females who, despite the women's liberation movement, still have a long way to go to gain equality.

Any woman who has walked down the street and been verbally harassed; 12 and any woman who has feared rape while walking alone in her own neigh-borhood at night—I might add there is not one female who has not—knows that fighting the image of woman-as-object, woman-as-silenced-victim, woman-as-sex-organ remains among her most urgent tasks.

Sexism is most dangerous when it's subtle, when it is so deeply embedded 13 in a culture that it becomes socially acceptable, as *Playboy* has. And so, you speak out, you yell, you rant and you rave when you recognize this subtle destruction. There is no other way to jar society out of its passive acceptance of the objectification of women, even though in this society it happens to be legal.

In not running the ad, *The Crimson* has taken that initiative. Seven years 14 from now, when *Playboy* again decides to try its luck with a whole new batch of Ivy League women, we can only hope all Ivy League newspapers will decide not to extend their helping hands. It is both the most and the least they can do.

Questions for analysis   1. Goss states one of her basic assumptions in the opening paragraph when she refers to "the institutionalized exploitation of women." How do you react to this premise? In your view, does society exploit women? If so, in what way is this exploitation institutionalized in your own school or workplace, for example?

2. Study the opening and closing paragraphs to see how Goss frames the essay (echoes something from the beginning at the end). What purpose

does framing appear to serve in this particular essay? How effective or in-effective does this strategy seem?

3. Because the essay was published in *The Crimson*, we know that Goss was writing specifically for her fellow Harvard students. What assumptions do you think she makes about her audience? Specifically, what values does she assume they share with her?

4. How would you describe the overall tone of this essay? (Tone reveals the writer's attitude toward the audience and the subject, and usually affects readers' willingness to accept the writer's argument.) Point to particular word choices that illustrate this tone. How does it affect your acceptance of Goss's argument?

5. Refuting opposing views plays an important part in most position papers. How does Goss respond to the view that *The Crimson* is guilty of censoring *Playboy*? What is her strongest argument in refuting this view? Her weakest?

6. Goss's argument depends on certain terms like *censorship, pornography,* and *sexism*. How does she define these terms? How would you define them?

7. If *Playboy* photographers came to your campus and invited female students to pose, would you oppose or favor publishing the advertisement in the campus newspaper? What issues are currently being debated on your campus, at work, or in your community? What controversy might you write about? What basic assumptions affect your thinking on this issue?

Commentary   Because they are addressing readers with whom they may disagree, writers of position papers must carefully consider their readers' knowledge, values, and assumptions in order to find areas of common ground. The argumentative strategy they employ will reflect their purpose as well as their expectations about their audience.

Goss's ultimate purpose seems to be to inspire readers to take up the fight against sexism. She apparently assumes that her readers oppose sexism and that if she can enlighten them, they will eventually reject *Playboy*'s subtle form of sexism. To succeed, however, she must first defend *The Crimson* against charges of censoring *Playboy* because, she seems to assume, her audience dislikes censorship even more than sexism.

We can see this strategy at work in the way Goss presents her thesis. Her thesis statement, that the decision "was both the very most and the very least the newspaper could do to fight the institutionalized exploitation of women" makes clear her position. The decision not to run the *Playboy* announcement, she asserts, is "the very most" *The Crimson* can do because newspapers are limited in what they can do. They can express opinion through editorials (as Goss tries to do with her essay). They can also refuse to sell advertising space. At the same time, Goss admits, the decision was "the very least" that the newspaper could do because its action does very little to alleviate sexism.

It is a symbolic action and can therefore be successful only to the extent that it raises people's consciousness and inspires them to take action themselves.

By placing her thesis in the opening paragraph, Goss follows the conventions of editorial writing, conventions that also lead to her reliance on short, one- or two-sentence paragraphs. But her decision on where to place the thesis also reflects her special purpose and audience. Because she is writing to Harvard students who already know something about *The Crimson*'s controversial decision, she must state her position emphatically at the outset. It would not do for her to begin, for example, with an extended description of the issue. Her readers already know the issue. Identifying the issue is necessary, but it can be done (as Goss shows) in the thesis statement. (For further discussion of thesis statements in argumentative writing, see Chapter 19: Arguing.)

Goss's writing strategy also determines how she deals with counterarguments, arguments made by those with opposing views. She refers to two counterarguments: that *The Crimson*'s decision is an act of censorship, and that it is paternalistic toward Harvard women. Both charges are important, but Goss apparently decided to focus on the former, possibly because it appeals to the same liberal attitudes she hopes to arouse with her sexism argument. She offers several reasons to refute the censorship counterargument. (See Chapter 19: Arguing for further discussion of counterarguments.)

Finally, as we look at the way Goss justifies *The Crimson*'s action, we see further evidence of her strategy. To defend the decision, she must establish that *Playboy* is sexist and that, moreover, its brand of sexism is particularly pernicious because it has become so ingrained that people cannot even see it is objectionable. This strategy leads her to define and classify *Playboy*'s brand of sexism. It also leads her to compare *Playboy*'s sexist ads to the racist ads that were acceptable fifty years ago but are now seen as repugnant. This analogy is calculated to have a powerful effect on readers who consider themselves enlightened and would thus not even want to be compared to racists. (Strategies of defining are discussed in Chapter 16, classifying in Chapter 17, and comparing in Chapter 18.)

In planning and writing your own position paper, you will also want to develop an argumentative strategy that reflects thoughtful consideration of your purpose and audience. How you decide to present your thesis, acknowledge counterarguments, and support your position will all depend on this strategy.

While Goss writes about a local issue, the next author, Rachel Richardson Smith, takes up an issue—abortion—that has been debated nationally for some time. In fact, few issues excite more impassioned argument than abortion. Writing in the "My Turn" section of *Newsweek,* Smith, a theology student and mother, exhibits a keen awareness of the issue's complexity.

Before reading her essay, recall what you already know about this issue. What does each side claim? What are their chief arguments? Which arguments do you find most convincing?

ABORTION, RIGHT AND WRONG

RACHEL RICHARDSON SMITH

I cannot bring myself to say I am in favor of abortion. I don't want anyone 1 to have one. I want people to use contraceptives and for those contraceptives to be foolproof. I want people to be responsible for their actions, mature in their decisions. I want children to be loved, wanted, well cared for.

I cannot bring myself to say I am against choice. I want women who are 2 young, poor, single or all three to be able to direct the course of their lives. I want women who have had all the children they want or can afford or their bodies can withstand to be able to decide their future. I want women who are in bad marriages or destructive relationships to avoid being trapped by pregnancy.

So in these days when thousands rally in opposition to legalized abortion, 3 when facilities providing abortions are bombed, when the president speaks glowingly of the growing momentum behind the anti-abortion movement, I find myself increasingly alienated from the pro-life groups.

At the same time, I am overwhelmed with mail from pro-choice groups. 4 They, too, are mobilizing their forces, growing articulate in support of their cause, and they want my support. I am not sure I can give it.

I find myself in the awkward position of being both anti-abortion and pro- 5 choice. Neither group seems to be completely right—or wrong. It is not that I think abortion is wrong for me but acceptable for someone else. The question is far more complex than that.

Part of my problem is that what I think and how I feel about this issue are 6 two entirely different matters. I know that unwanted children are often neglected, even abandoned. I know that many of those seeking abortions are children themselves. I know that making abortion illegal will not stop all women from having them.

I also know from experience the crisis an unplanned pregnancy can cause. 7 Yet I have felt the joy of giving birth, the delight that comes from feeling a baby's skin against my own. I know how hard it is to parent a child and how deeply satisfying it can be. My children sometimes provoke me and cause me endless frustration, but I can still look at them with tenderness and wonder at the miracle of it all. The lessons of my own experience produce conflicting emotions. Theory collides with reality.

It concerns me that both groups present themselves in absolutes. They are 8 committed and they want me to commit. They do not recognize the gray area where I seem to be languishing. Each group has the right answer—the only answer.

Yet I am uncomfortable in either camp. I have nothing in common with the 9 pro-lifers. I am horrified by their scare tactics, their pictures of well-formed fetuses tossed in a metal pan, their cruel slogans. I cannot condone their flagrant misuse of Scripture and unforgiving spirit. There is a meanness about their position that causes them to pass judgment on the lives of women in a way I could never do.

The pro-life groups, with their fundamentalist religious attitudes, have a fear 10 and an abhorrence of sex, especially premarital sex. In their view abortion only compounds the sexual sin. What I find incomprehensible is that even as they are opposed to abortion they are also opposed to alternative solutions. They are squeamish about sex education in the schools. They don't want teens to have contraceptives without parental consent. They offer little aid or sympathy to unwed mothers. They are the vigilant guardians of a narrow morality.

I wonder how abortion got to be the greatest of all sins? What about poverty, 11 ignorance, hunger, weaponry?

The only thing the anti-abortion groups seem to have right is that abortion 12 is indeed the taking of human life. I simply cannot escape this one glaring fact. Call it what you will—fertilized egg, embryo, fetus. What we have here is human life. If it were just a mass of tissue there would be no debate. So I agree that abortion ends a life. But the anti-abortionists are wrong to call it murder.

The sad truth is that homicide is not always against the law. Our society 13 does not categorically recognize the sanctity of human life. There are a number of legal and apparently socially acceptable ways to take human life. "Justifiable" homicide includes the death penalty, war, killing in self-defense. It seems to me that as a society we need to come to grips with our own ambiguity concerning the value of human life. If we are to value and protect unborn life so stringently, why do we not also value and protect life already born?

Why can't we see abortion for the human tragedy it is? No woman plans 14 for her life to turn out that way. Even the most effective contraceptives are no guarantee against pregnancy. Loneliness, ignorance, immaturity can lead to decisions (or lack of decisions) that may result in untimely pregnancy. People make mistakes.

What many people seem to misunderstand is that no woman wants to have 15 an abortion. Circumstances demand it; women do it. No woman reacts to abortion with joy. Relief, yes. But also ambivalence, grief, despair, guilt.

The pro-choice groups do not seem to acknowledge that abortion is not a 16 perfect answer. What goes unsaid is that when a woman has an abortion she loses more than an unwanted pregnancy. Often she loses her self-respect. No woman can forget a pregnancy no matter how it ends.

Why can we not view abortion as one of those anguished decisions in which 17 human beings struggle to do the best they can in trying circumstances? Why is abortion viewed so coldly and factually on the one hand and so judgmentally on the other? Why is it not akin to the same painful experience families must sometimes make to allow a loved one to die?

I wonder how we can begin to change the context in which we think about 18 abortion. How can we begin to think about it redemptively? What is it in the trauma of loss of life—be it loved or unloved, born or unborn—from which we can learn? There is much I have yet to resolve. Even as I refuse to pass judgments on other women's lives, I weep for the children who might have been. I suspect I am not alone.

1. Contrast this essay with Goss's. While Goss is quite definite in her view of the issue, Smith seems ambivalent, genuinely torn. Are you surprised to find a position paper that emphasizes the writer's indecision? What does this imply about why people write position papers?

2. Smith appears to weigh impartially the pros and cons, rejecting some arguments and accepting others. Upon close examination, how impartial do you think she really is? Does she treat each side equally? To help you analyze the essay, make a chart outlining the pro-life and pro-choice arguments Smith cites and her judgments of them.

3. Smith claims that both camps—pro-life as well as pro-choice—"present themselves in absolutes." Why does she apparently assume that thinking in absolutes is wrong? What do you think?

4. Consider how this selection begins, noticing the repetition of sentence structure in the first two paragraphs. What exactly is repeated and what effect does this repetition have? From this way of beginning, what can you infer about Smith's argumentative strategy? How effective would you say it is?

5. In paragraphs 12 and 13, Smith addresses the question of whether or not abortion constitutes murder. For many, this is the heart of the issue. How does she handle this crucial question? Given her argumentative strategy, how convincing is this part of her argument?

6. Think of an issue about which you feel ambivalent. What exactly are your contradictory feelings on this issue? If you were to write a position paper on this issue, how would you construct your argument? What points would you have to consider further and learn more about?

This essay illustrates two special strategies writers depend on, particularly when writing about highly emotional issues: establishing credibility by building a bond of trust with readers and defining the key terms of the argument.

Writers who want to affect their readers' thinking on an issue must make a special effort to win their confidence. Smith tries to gain her readers' trust by establishing a bond of shared feelings and values between herself and her audience. To build this bond, Smith admits that she feels torn by "conflicting emotions" about abortion. Her ambivalence, she tells us, derives from the disparity between theory and reality. By theory, Smith means an ideal world where abortion would be unnecessary, contraceptives would be foolproof, and people would always be responsible. People would have all the children they wanted and could afford. However, Smith knows, and assumes all reasonable people know, that reality inevitably falls short of theory. So, she concludes, if abortion is evil (and Smith seems to agree that it is), it may be a necessary evil.

Not only does Smith try to give readers the impression that she, like them, is honestly struggling to make a reasonable decision, but she also presents herself as an independent thinker by criticizing both camps. She describes herself as "horrified" and "alienated" by their tactics. Ticking off the arguments proposed by each side, she agrees with some and disagrees with others. By seeing merit as well as weakness in both sides, she demonstrates that she is fair-minded. In this way, Smith attempts to establish a bond with readers who also want to think of themselves as caring and reasonable, independent and fair-minded.

In addition to noticing how Smith establishes her credibility, you might also consider how she uses definition to support her position. While definition is an essential strategy used in every kind of writing, position papers nearly always depend on this strategy. Smith relies on defining as her primary argumentative strategy. By defining abortion as "the taking of human life," she appears to concede an important point to the pro-life advocates. In effect, she agrees with them that a fetus, though unborn, should still be regarded as a human life. This idea is crucial to the pro-life argument because it enables them to argue that abortion is murder. But Smith will not go this far. While she concedes that "abortion ends a life," she disagrees that it is murder. She draws a distinction—some would say too fine a distinction— between taking a human life and murder. Definition always involves classification, and Smith classifies homicide (the taking of a human life) into two categories: justifiable homicide (in which she includes the death penalty, war, killing in self-defense, and abortion) and unjustifiable homicide (which she also calls murder).

Readers may or may not be convinced, but nearly everyone can admire the ingenuity of her argument. Basing an argument on definition is not a sure bet; as this example illustrates, it is just as risky as any other kind of reasoning. When you write your own position paper, you will have to decide what your key terms are and how best to define them.

Writing in the popular magazine *Science '81*, biology professor Albert Rosenfeld addresses the issue of animal experimentation. The debate over vivisection is as old as science itself. Before reading the essay, think about your own view of this issue. Should scientists be allowed to experiment on live animals? What sorts of restrictions—if any—should be placed on such research? Then, as you read, consider how well Rosenfeld answers your own and others' concerns.

**ANIMAL RIGHTS VER-
SUS HUMAN HEALTH**
ALBERT ROSENFELD

Stray dogs and cats by the hundreds of thousands roam the streets of our 1
cities. Usually they wind up in animal shelters, where hard-pressed staffs must find ways to dispose of them. One legitimate disposal route has been the research laboratory. But in southern California—with its impressive collection of research centers—antivivisectionists and animal rights groups recently have been leaning hard on animal shelters, effectively cutting off much of the supply.

About 30 years ago Los Angeles voters soundly defeated a proposal to pro- 2
hibit the release of animals for laboratory use. But today, with new proposals

being submitted to city councils and county boards, the results could well be different. And the new proposals are much more sweeping. They would, for instance, create review boards for all animal experimentation, requiring researchers to justify in advance any experiment they were planning and to submit a detailed research protocol before even applying for a grant. Alarmed, a group of southern California investigators have organized a committee for animal research in medicine.

"Most scientists don't realize the danger," says Caltech neurobiologist John 3 M. Allman, who uses monkeys to study the organization of the brain. "Such movements in the past—in this country, at least—have largely been the efforts of small, fragmented, and relatively ineffective groups. But this new movement is carefully orchestrated, well organized, and well financed. Moreover, this is not just a local issue. It is going on intensively at the national and even at the international level. We'd be foolish to underestimate these people. They have clout. And if they attain their goals, it will effectively kill a lot of important research."

To doubly ensure the protection of human experimental subjects, a number 4 of restrictions and regulations that admittedly are burdensome have been adopted over recent years. They take a great deal of time and energy. They generate a considerable amount of extra paper work. They often slow research (indeed, make some projects impossible) and render it much more difficult and costly at a time when budgets are shrinking and inflation is making further inroads. While these procedures are accepted as the price of seeing that human subjects volunteer freely and with fully informed consent, are we willing to pay a similar price on behalf of animal subjects who can in no way either give or withhold consent?

It is easy to look at the history of animal experimentation and compile a 5 catalog of horrors. Or, for that matter, to look around today and find research projects that might be hard to justify. But the day is long past when a researcher can take any animal and do anything he pleases to it with a total disregard for its welfare and comfort. "People don't realize," says Allman, "that we are already extensively reviewed. In my work I must follow the ethical codes laid down by the National Institutes of Health and the American Physiological Society, among others. And we might have a surprise visit at any time from the U.S. Department of Agriculture's inspectors. It's the USDA field veterinarians who do the enforcing. Believe me, these inspections are anything but routine, and these fellows have a great deal of power. Because their reports can adversely affect federal funding, their recommendations are, in reality, orders.

"More than that, we are all required to keep detailed reports on all our 6 animal experiments. And if pain or surgery is involved, we must tell them what anesthetics we used and in what dosages, what postoperative pain relievers and care were given, and so on. These reports are filed annually with the USDA, and they keep tabs on what goes on all over the country."

For all these precautions, however, it is fair to say that millions of animals— 7 probably more rats and mice than any other species—are subjected to experiments that cause them pain, discomfort, and distress, sometimes lots of it over long periods of time. If you want to study the course of a disease with a view to figuring out its causes and possible therapies, there is no way that the animal to whom you give the disease is going to be happy about it. All new forms of medication or surgery are tried out on animals first. Every new substance that is released into the environment, or put on the market, is tested on animals.

In fact, some of the tests most objected to by animal advocates are those 8 required by the government. For instance, there is a figure called the LD-50 (short for "lethal dose for 50 percent") that manufacturers are required to determine for any new substance. In each such case, a great many animals are given a lot of the stuff to find out how much it takes to kill half of them—and the survivors aren't exactly in the pink.

The animal rights advocates, except for the more extreme and uncompro- 9 mising types, are not kooks or crackpots. They tend to be intelligent, compassionate individuals raising valid ethical questions, and they probably serve well as consciousness raisers. It is certainly their prerogative—or anyone's—to ask of a specific project: Is this research really necessary? (What's "really necessary" is of course not always obvious.)

But it's important that they not impose their solutions on society. It would 10 be tragic indeed—when medical science is on the verge of learning so much more that is essential to our health and welfare—if already regulation-burdened and budget-crunched researchers were further hampered.

In 1975, Australian philosopher Peter Singer wrote his influential book called 11 *Animal Liberation*, in which he accuses us all of "speciesism"—as reprehensible, to him, as racism or sexism. He freely describes the "pain and suffering" inflicted in the "tyranny of human over nonhuman animals" and sharply challenges our biblical license to exercise "dominion over the fish of the sea, and over the fowl of the air, and over every living thing that moveth upon the Earth."

Well, certainly we are guilty of speciesism. We do act as if we had dominion 12 over other living creatures. But domination also entails some custodial responsibility. And the questions continue to be raised: Do we have the right to abuse animals? To eat them? To hunt them for sport? To keep them imprisoned in zoos—or, for that matter, in our households? Especially to do experiments on these creatures who can't fight back? To send them into orbit, spin them on centrifuges, run them through mazes, give them cancer, perform experimental surgery?

Hardly any advance in either human or veterinary medicine—cure, vaccine, 13 operation, drug, therapy—has come about without experiments on animals. And it may be impossible to get the data we need to determine the hazards of, say, radiation exposure or environmental polutants without animal testing. I certainly sympathize with the demand that we look for ways to get the information we want without using animals. Most investigators are delighted when they can get their data by means of tissue cultures or computer simulations. But as we look for alternative ways to get information, do we meanwhile just do without?

I wonder about those purists who seek to halt all animal experimentation 14 on moral grounds: Do they also refuse, for themselves and others, to accept any remedy—or information—that was gained through animal experimentation? And do they ask themselves if they have the right to make such moral decisions on behalf of all the patients in cancer wards and intensive care units and on behalf of all the victims of the maladies that afflict our species? And what of the future generations that will be so afflicted—but who might not have been—had the animal rightists not intervened?

Questions for analysis   1. In this essay, Rosenfeld focuses on the expediency or advisability of animal experimentation. Those who oppose using live animals for laboratory experiments, however, usually argue that it is a moral, not a practical issue. How do you respond to these two different approaches to the issue? Are they equally legitimate, or do you favor one over the other? Why?

2. Look closely at the opening paragraphs of this selection. How does Rosenfeld present the issue? How does he establish its importance? What does he want readers to believe is at stake? As one reader, how do you react to this part of his argument?

3. At what point do you first become aware of Rosenfeld's position on the issue of animal experimentation? Where does he state his thesis most explicitly?

4. Rosenfeld cites an authority, John Allman, whom he apparently interviewed. How does he establish Allman's credentials? How convincing is Allman's expert testimony? What can you conclude from this essay about using authorities to support an argument?

5. Look closely at how Rosenfeld tries to refute Peter Singer's counterargument. From Rosenfeld's summary, what do you think Singer means by "speciesism"? How effective is his refutation?

6. In the last few paragraphs, Rosenfeld rests his argument on a series of rhetorical questions, questions that he does not expect readers to answer but poses for effect. How effective does this strategy of arguing seem to you? What are its possible advantages and disadvantages?

7. Did you ever have to kill a frog or dissect an earthworm in a science course? If so, how did you feel about experimenting on animals? What other issue pertaining to science concerns you? If you were to take a position on this issue, what counterarguments would you anticipate and how would you respond to them?

Commentary   Writers of position papers attempt to establish their credibility by the way that they present their argument, in particular by the tone they adopt. Rosenfeld tries to present the issue neutrally, giving the impression that he is objective. This appearance of objectivity is basic to his argumentative strategy: to make readers think he is uninvolved and, therefore, more likely to be right.

The opening paragraphs are designed to make the essay seem more a report informing readers about the controversy (like the reports by Toufexis and Green in Chapter 5) than a position paper on it. He explains the role performed by research laboratories to solve the problem of strays, tells us of proposals—new and old—to regulate animal experimentation, and announces the formation of a committee of scientists who oppose restricting experimentation. Even when he explicitly raises the issue, he does so in a question (at the end of paragraph 4) that implies but does not assert his own position.

Rosenfeld maintains this tone even as he argues forcefully for his view. He does this by acknowledging counterarguments and accommodating them in his argument. He begins paragraph 5, for example, by acknowledging that problems existed in the past and may even continue in the present. He argues that the situation is much improved, however, quoting Allman to prove that researchers are already adequately regulated.

In paragraph 7, Rosenfeld acknowledges another counterargument when he agrees that animals suffer pain from experiments. He responds to this criticism in two ways: by asserting that pain relievers are regularly prescribed, and by admitting that the suffering of some animals is unfortunate but unavoidable. Although he seems to be conceding a point here, notice how he tries to play it down by adding that "more rats and mice" suffer than any other species. Rosenfeld knows that most readers feel more sympathy toward dogs, cats, and monkeys than they do to rats and mice. This preference for animals that are higher on the evolutionary ladder could be used by critical readers as evidence of speciesism, the attitude of superiority mentioned in the essay.

Although Rosenfeld skillfully maintains his neutral tone, close attention to his language suggests that he is actually a strong advocate. Even the opening sentences reveal his partisanship, speaking of *stray* dogs and cats not as objects of sympathy but as a public nuisance. He is concerned not about finding good homes for these animals but about disposing of them. The research laboratory, he says, is a "legitimate" means of disposal.

As a writer of position papers, you should also try to establish your credibility with readers, but keep in mind that a writer's credibility is fragile. If readers suspect that you are being false or condescending—as they might with Rosenfeld—they could lose confidence in you and distrust your argument, no matter how well reasoned it is.

The final selection was written by Sydney Young for her freshman English class. It concerns the controversy surrounding Gary Hart's withdrawal in May 1987 from the race for the Democratic nomination for president. As you read Young's essay, pay special attention to her tone. How would you describe it? Do you react favorably or unfavorably to it? Why?

JOURNALISTIC ETHICS
SYDNEY YOUNG

On May 8, 1987, Gary Hart was forced to once again relinquish his goal of 1 becoming President of the United States. Four years earlier, he had been defeated by another candidate. This time, he was defeated by scandal. While some critics claim that Hart really defeated himself, it seems to me that the media was primarily responsible for Hart's withdrawing from the race before a single vote was cast. By probing into his personal life, journalists from the *Miami Herald* began a process that ultimately cost Hart the presidency. In this particular case, the media overstepped the boundaries of fairness. Its actions raise important questions about journalistic ethics. Journalists should report only the facts relevant to the campaign—not sensationalize the candidate's life.

What led to Hart's premature withdrawal from the presidential race can only 2 be described as a bizarre sequence of events. Frustrated because the media seemed interested in reporting on his personal life instead of his ideas, Hart issued a challenge to the press: "Follow me around. I don't care. If anybody wants to put a tail on me, go ahead. They'd be very bored" (Morganthau 22). One newspaper, the *Miami Herald*, took up Hart's challenge after receiving a tip that while his wife was out of town, Hart was with another woman, a Miami actress named Donna Rice. *Herald* reporters staked out Hart's Washington townhouse and broke the story that Rice spent the night and the following day with Hart in his home. From the beginning, Hart has denied any impropriety. But the story would not go away, even though the *Herald* admitted that Hart's back door was unwatched for several hours.

Whether or not a public figure has a right to privacy has long been a con- 3 troversial issue. Where should the fine line be drawn in terms of how much personal information the public needs to know about a political candidate? It comes down to a question of relevance. What about the candidate's personal life is relevant to his ability to be an effective president? To consider this question, we have to separate the issues. One issue is adultery: Is a candidate's faithfulness to his wife relevant? Another is lying: If he committed adultery and then lied about it, is that any more relevant? The final issue is the media's role in all this: Is it right for the media to hound candidates and to report stories that may not be true?

Adultery is not something that should be tolerated or condoned, but neither 4 should it be a significant issue in a political campaign. Hart claims that whether he committed adultery is a personal matter and not a political one. Any unfaithfulness is, as the candidate phrased it, "between me and Lee [his wife] and me and God" (Shapiro 17). Lee Hart herself bluntly stated her agreement, "If it doesn't bother me, I don't think it ought to bother anyone else" (Shapiro 17).

Those who disagree say that it has as much bearing on the campaign as any 5 other issue. Supporters of the *Herald*'s surveillance of Hart's townhouse feel that his actions rendered his character questionable. "What counts with a candidate for President is his character," claims George Reedy, press secretary to former President Lyndon Johnson, "and nothing shows it like his relationship with women" ("Private" 33). If this is true, then one wonders why adultery has never been a campaign issue before. We now know that Harding, Franklin Roosevelt, Eisenhower, and Kennedy all had mistresses. But the press did not stake out their homes. What makes Hart an exception? The times may have changed, but an opinion poll by *Time* magazine shows that only 7% of the people asked today would be bothered if Hart had had sex with Rice ("After" 26).

In determining the relevancy of a candidate's personal life, the press needs 6 to carefully scrutinize the point in question. For instance, in the sex scandal involving Jim Bakker, the press had every right to investigate and let the full story be known because evangelism is Bakker's vocation. The question of Bakker's faithfulness is pertinent because he preaches a religion that forbids adultery. In Hart's case, unfaithfulness is not pertinent because he is a politician, not a preacher. Sex has no relevance to politics. In the words of former vice-presidential candidate Geraldine Ferraro:

> The issue is not whether the press has the right to investigate. It's *what* they are investigating. The public is entitled to know if he is a person who has good judgment, the right to know if he is smart, the right to know if he understands what's going on. If the *Miami Herald* had reported that Gary Hart had invited to his house a *contra* leader, then I'd be very angry, because he has taken a strong stand against the *contras*. I don't find the Donna Rice story relevant to the campaign. ("Private" 33)

Still others object to Hart's actions because they believe he lied in an effort 7 to save his campaign. According to Brandeis University philosophy professor Sissela Bok, what's an issue is "not whether he's a perfect husband" but "whether or not the man is telling the truth" ("Private" 33). Most Americans share Bok's opinion. According to the *Time* poll, 69% said that it would bother them more if Hart had not told the truth than if he had committed adultery ("After" 26). There can be no doubt that a candidate's truthfulness is relevant, but we should not judge Hart before we know whether he's lying. Both Hart and Rice insist that "their friendship was platonic" (Morganthau 24). Hart's wife appears to accept his word. Moreover, the *Herald* admits that its stakeout was sloppy and that Rice could have left Hart's house, as they both claim.

Because we will probably never know the truth, we should be very careful 8 not to judge Hart on the basis of unsubstantiated reports. The thing about rumors is that they persist, regardless of whether they are true or not. Hart withdrew from the campaign because he realized that he could never put the rumors to rest. For this reason, journalists have a special responsibility to report only what they know to be true. Political reporting is a big business, and every reporter knows that scandals, especially sex scandals, sell papers. Reporter Jon Margolis acknowledges that "personal scandals, with or without sex, always have been bigger stories" (C-1). Even though the public seems to have an insatiable curiosity about the rich and famous, reporting scandal sometimes backfires. "Two out of three" people polled by *Newsweek* magazine, for example, "think Hart was treated unfairly in an effort to attract large audiences" ("Down" 25). Unfortunately, the people never had a chance to voice their opinion by voting.

Today, the press puts political candidates and their families on public display 9 in a way they never were before. Hart claims that the media's close scrutiny invades the candidate's privacy and threatens to destroy the election process by reducing the press "to hunters and presidential candidates to being hunted" (Morganthau 22). Perhaps after seeing the humiliation Hart has suffered, whether he's at fault or not, the media will be more discriminating next time. The American public, not the media, should elect its officials. Let us hope that the stone will not be cast again before the vote.

WORKS CITED

"After the Fall." *Time* 18 May 1987: 26.

"Down on the Press." *Newsweek* 18 May 1987: 25.

Margolis, Jon. "The Media and the Candidates." *San Diego Union* 17 May 1987: C–1.

Morganthau, Tom. "The Sudden Fall of Gary Hart." *Newsweek* 18 May 1987: 22–28.

"Private Life, Public Office." *Time* 18 May 1987: 33.

Shapiro, Walter. "Fall from Grace." *Time* 18 May 1987: 16–20.

Questions for analysis

1. Young argues that the issue should not be Hart's alleged unfaithfulness or how that reflects on his character but how the media handled the scandal. How do you react to this argument? Do you think that Young has missed the main point or has she put her finger on it? Can you imagine any other way of defining this particular issue?

2. Find the thesis statement. Chapter 19 explains that the claim of an argument should be clear, unambiguous, and appropriately qualified. According to these criteria, how do you rate this essay's claim?

3. Why do you think Young bothers to tell what happened? Look closely at her word choice and selection of detail in paragraph 2. What does her narrative accomplish?

4. In paragraph 6, Young contrasts the Hart scandal with another sex scandal involving a television evangelist named Jim Bakker. What does this contrast add to her argument? How could she develop the contrast further?

5. How balanced is Young's argument? Does she anticipate counter-arguments and represent them fairly? To answer this question, skim the essay and note in the margin which of her sources support her position and which express opposing views.

6. Young is writing about a controversy that received enormous attention from the news media at the time. What issues are currently receiving attention? Which of these could you imagine writing about? What do you think is the heart of this issue?

Commentary Young's essay illustrates one further strategy you will want to consider when you write your own position paper: dividing the issue. Because arguments over controversial issues tend to be very complicated, writers need to help readers follow their reasoning. One way of doing this is by separating the issue into its various components.

Young attempts in paragraph 3 to separate the issue. She begins by identifying the central question: "Where should the fine line be drawn in terms of how much personal information the public needs to know about a political candidate?" She then divides this question into two separate questions: What personal information is relevant? And what role should the media play in gathering and communicating this information? She further divides the question of relevance to cover two different questions—whether a candidate has been faithful in marriage, and whether he or she has been truthful to the electorate.

After separating the issue into these questions, Young takes up each in turn. She treats the question of the relevance of Hart's alleged adultery in paragraphs 4–6, his alleged lying in paragraph 7, and the media's role in paragraphs 8–9. Thus her paragraph separating the issue also forecasts the plan of her essay.

PURPOSE AND AUDIENCE

Because position papers intentionally challenge other views on the issue, the writer must seek to understand these views and try to discover common ground for potential agreement. While position papers chiefly address readers who hold opposing opinions, they may also address other groups of readers. These may include readers who are undecided and even those who basically agree with the writer. Whoever your readers may be, your aim is always essentially the same: to examine the issue thoughtfully and to develop a carefully reasoned, well-supported argument for your position.

When writing primarily to readers with whom you disagree, your purpose should probably be to convince them to take your position seriously and to reflect on their own viewpoint and even to reconsider it. Changing readers' minds can be very difficult, particularly when their views are based on deeply held assumptions, values, and beliefs. To influence these readers, you must not only make a logical case but also ease their concerns and show that you respect and share their values. Most writers feel satisfied if they can simply win their readers' respect for their views.

Of course, your chances of persuading your readers are better if they have not yet made up their minds. You may be able to offer these readers a new way of seeing the issue that leads them to accept your view of the issue.

Your success may depend on how you describe the issue, how well you construct your argument, how you come across to readers—or a combination of all these factors.

Your audience may also include readers who already accept your position but are curious to see how you construct your argument. These readers will be particularly interested in your reasoning and supporting evidence. Reading an especially compelling argument or discovering new evidence can also strengthen their understanding and commitment.

We ultimately write position papers for ourselves as well as for others. Constructing an argument requires us to probe our underlying assumptions, values, and beliefs. It forces us to examine our reasoning, and expose flaws in our logic as well as gaps in our evidence. It encourages us to put our thoughts into simple, direct language. Writers often gain as much satisfaction from shaping a thoughtful argument as they do from convincing others to respect their views.

BASIC FEATURES OF POSITION PAPERS

Position papers generally share the following basic features: a well-defined issue, a clear position, a convincing argument, and a reasonable tone.

A well-defined issue   Position papers concern controversial issues, matters of deliberation on which reasonable people disagree. The issue may arise from a particular occasion (as in the Goss and Young essays) or be part of an ongoing debate (as in the Smith and Rosenfeld selections). In either case, the writer must clearly explain the issue.

Kristin Goss, because she is writing about a campus controversy, can safely assume that her immediate readers, Harvard students, will be familiar with the issue. Nevertheless, she reminds them that it centers on *The Crimson*'s decision not to print a *Playboy* ad recruiting Harvard coeds. Similarly, although Sydney Young can probably assume that her readers already know about Gary Hart's withdrawal from the presidential race and the controversy surrounding it, she devotes an entire paragraph to describing what happened.

Disagreements over issues often hinge on different ways of defining the issue. In the debate on animal experimentation, for example, Albert Rosenfeld sees the issue as a question of expediency, a judgment about the best means of achieving a desired end, while opponents like Peter Singer regard the issue as a question of simple morality, a judgment about what is right and wrong. Goss defines the issue as sexism, whereas her opponents think it involves censorship. Young argues that the issue is not Hart's moral character but journalistic ethics.

A clear position In addition to defining the issue, your essay should also clearly state your position. Writers of position papers may qualify their views to accommodate strong counterarguments, but they should avoid equivocating or hedging.

Writers very often declare their position in a thesis statement early in the essay. The advantage of announcing the thesis in the beginning is that it lets the audience know right away where the writer stands. Goss, for instance, opens her essay with a sentence that both defines the issue and announces her position: "*The Crimson*'s decision not to run *Playboy*'s advertisement recruiting Harvard women . . . was both the very most and the very least the newspaper could do to fight the institutionalized exploitation of women." Similarly, Young concludes her opening paragraph with the assertion that "journalists should report only the facts relevant to the campaign—not sensationalize the candidate's life."

The thesis may also appear at a later point in the essay. Postponing the announcement of the thesis is particularly appropriate when the writer wants to weigh the pros and cons before taking a position. We see this strategy in Rosenfeld's essay on animal experimentation. He states his thesis most explicitly in paragraph 10: "It would be tragic indeed—when medical science is on the verge of learning so much more that is essential to our health and welfare—if already regulation-burdened and budget-crunched researchers were further hampered."

Sometimes, the thesis is modified in the course of the argument. Rachel Richardson Smith announces her position on abortion in paragraph 5: "I find myself in the awkward position of being both anti-abortion and pro-choice. Neither group seems to be completely right—or wrong." This statement, which is echoed in the title, may be taken to express the essay's thesis. Certainly it expresses Smith's indecision. Toward the end of the argument, however, her word choice seems to suggest that she has made up her mind in favor of pro-choice. By acknowledging that abortion is "not a perfect answer," Smith implies that it may be the only answer for some people.

In writing your own essay, your purpose and audience will determine where you place your thesis statement. The main object, though, is to be clear and unambiguous. Your readers deserve to know exactly where you stand on the issue. You may want to consider the possibilities thoroughly, but you should avoid being vague or wishy-washy. (See Chapter 19: Arguing for further discussion of making claims and Chapter 12: Cueing the Reader for more information on the thesis statement.)

A convincing argument Writers of position papers cannot merely assert their views. To convince their readers, they must support their claims with sound reasoning and solid evidence, and also anticipate possible counterarguments.

Sound reasoning and solid evidence. To be sure that readers will be able to follow your argument, the main points supporting your claim should not only be stated clearly but also explained and fully developed. Goss, for example, explains that protesting *Playboy*'s brand of sexism is particularly important because it is so subtle. She develops this point by describing *Playboy* as an example of "socially acceptable" sexism. Then, arguing by analogy, she compares *Playboy*'s sexism to the kind of racism that was once socially accepted but is now widely condemned. Readers may or may not be convinced by this argument, but by explaining and developing it fully, Goss makes sure that they will be able to understand her reasoning.

To support their claims, writers cite various kinds of evidence, including facts, examples, authorities, and statistics. Facts have great persuasive power once their veracity is accepted. Writers, however, may question the status of facts that have not been verified. Young, for example, questions whether or not Hart actually committed adultery. She argues that until proven, we should not accept the allegation as fact.

Examples are used to bolster an argument and to illustrate the writer's point. Rosenfeld gives examples to support his assertion that today research is regulated whereas in previous years it was not. He lists several institutions that now impose "ethical codes" on researchers.

Testimony from authorities enhances the credibility of an argument. Rosenfeld quotes an authority, John M. Allman, whom he identifies as a Caltech neurobiologist. Writers usually give the credentials of their authorities in order to establish them as believable experts. We infer that Rosenfeld got his quotations from Allman during an interview. Young takes her expert testimony from published sources.

Statistics are another common kind of evidence. Young, for instance, cites statistics, the results of opinion polls conducted by *Newsweek* and *Time* magazines. Her purpose in citing these statistics is to demonstrate that other people share her view of the issue. (Chapter 19: Arguing discusses further how writers use these and other kinds of evidence to support their claims.)

In constructing your own argument, consider carefully the reasons and evidence you offer readers. Writers of position papers usually find that they need to do some research to discover facts, examples, authorities, and statistics they can cite. (See Chapter 20: Field Research for advice on interviewing and Chapter 21: Library Research for guidance on finding published sources.)

Anticipating counterarguments. It is often not enough to present your own reasons and evidence. You may also need to acknowledge arguments offered by those with opposing points of view. To show that you are flexible, you may want to accommodate any counterarguments that seem reasonable to you. Accommodating a counterargument basically involves admitting that it has validity and qualifying your own view to account for it. Other counterarguments may strike you as wrong; these you may wish to refute. Refuting a counterargument means trying to show how it is wrong.

Rosenfeld offers a good example of a writer accommodating reasonable counterarguments. Acknowledging that animal experimentation has been cruel to animals (paragraph 5), he agrees that animal research should be carefully regulated to prevent abuses, and goes on to cite examples of regulations now in force. Goss's essay, on the other hand, demonstrates how writers refute counterarguments. To identify the counterargument and represent it fairly, Goss uses the opposition's own language: they "claim the staff endeavored to 'censor' *Playboy*." To refute this counterargument, Goss argues that *The Crimson*'s action does not fit the definition of censorship.

Some writers appear to accommodate counterarguments but actually refute them. In debating the issue of abortion, for example, Smith accepts as fact the argument that a fetus is a human life (paragraph 12). Since this point is the crux of the anti-abortion argument, it would seem that by accommodating it Smith is conceding the whole argument. However, she turns around and refutes the anti-abortion argument by arguing that homicide is sometimes justifiable. These examples from Goss and Smith also indicate how important definition is in constructing a convincing argument.

You should consider addressing counterarguments in your own position paper. Anticipating counterarguments shows readers that you are not narrow-minded but that you take opposing views seriously. (Anticipating counterarguments is illustrated extensively in Chapter 19: Arguing.)

A reasonable tone   Because writers of position papers want readers to take them seriously, they adopt a tone that will be likely to gain readers' confidence and respect. They attempt to demonstrate their sincerity both by the way they reason and the language they use. In other words, through their tone writers seek to create a favorable impression.

Goss, for example, adopts an impassioned tone when writing about sexism. When she calls attention to the plight of women, her tone carries the conviction of personal experience. When she defends political protest as the only means of fighting sexism, she seems genuinely frustrated and angry. Even readers who oppose her view on the issue are likely to respect her feelings. Some readers, however, may react negatively to her use of such feminist buzzwords as *exploitation, sexism,* and *sex object.* (A buzzword is a term or phrase associated with a particular ideology.) Buzzwords are a shortcut; they signal a writer's affiliation and establish common ground with sympathetic readers. But an argument cannot be based on buzzwords alone. They may resonate for those who already agree, but are unlikely to convince anyone else.

The first two paragraphs of Smith's essay on abortion strike a heartfelt, confessional tone. She gives the impression of someone who sees both sides of a complicated issue, but when she characterizes the sides as camps vying for her support, her tone changes. She criticizes both sides—the pro-choice advocates for treating abortion "coldly and factually," and the pro-lifers for their "meanness" and "unforgiving spirit." Some readers may respond negatively to Smith's name-calling. Because she seems so sincere, however, many readers are apt to forgive this harshness.

GUIDE TO WRITING

THE WRITING TASK

Write a position paper on a controversial issue. Examine the issue critically, take a position on it, and develop a reasoned argument in support of your position.

INVENTION AND RESEARCH

Following are some activities to help you choose and explore an issue, consider your purpose and audience, formulate your thesis, test your choice, develop your reasoning, and anticipate counterarguments.

Choosing an issue to write about Writing a position paper offers an opportunity to think deeply about an important issue. Following are some activities that can help you choose a promising issue and that may suggest ways to begin thinking about it.

Listing issues. Begin by making a list of the issues you might be interested in writing about. Put them in the form of questions, like the following examples. Make the list as long as you can. Include issues on which you already have ideas, but do not limit yourself to these. Add new and unfamiliar issues, ones you do not know much about but would like to explore further.

Your choice may be influenced by whether you have time for research or whether your instructor requires it. You would have to research issues like creationism and abortion before you could adequately define the issue, explore it fully, anticipate counterarguments, and decide what argumentative strategy to adopt for your own position. Issues like these have been debated for years and written about repeatedly. Such issues make excellent topics for extended research projects. Other issues like rock music and searches of student lockers may be approached more confidently from personal experience or from limited research in recent publications. Even with this kind of topic surprises may occur, however. For example, the issue of locker searches has a substantial legal history. Nevertheless, you might argue it convincingly without research if you have firsthand knowledge and can discuss it with others. Still other topics may be more suitable if your time is limited or your instructor wants you to exercise your position-taking strategies without doing research, topics like separate college organizations for black and Hispanic students, sex before marriage, special academic assistance for athletes, and the timing of marriage. You could define and explore fully issues like these with your classmates or other friends; and, with care, you could identify a wide range of counterarguments.

To help you start your own list of possible topics, here are some examples:

- [ ] Should capital punishment be abolished?
- [ ] Should drug testing in sports and industry be required?
- [ ] Should the lyrics of rock music be censored?
- [ ] Should high school officials be permitted to search students' lockers?
- [ ] Should school boards be able to keep certain books out of school libraries and prevent teachers from assigning them?
- [ ] Should the primary purpose of a college education be job preparation?
- [ ] Should creationism be taught as a science along with evolution?
- [ ] Should parents strictly limit the amount of television their children watch?
- [ ] Should parents avoid divorce at all costs for the sake of their children?
- [ ] Should marriage wait until you have established a career and saved enough money to buy a house?
- [ ] In light of the current epidemic of sexually transmitted diseases, should couples engage in sex before marriage?
- [ ] Should schools attempt to teach spiritual and moral values?
- [ ] Should police officers be permitted to pose as undercover high school students in order to identify sellers and users of drugs?
- [ ] Should history and literature be taught in high schools so that all graduates have a common American cultural experience?
- [ ] Should extended training in music performance or art making (drawing, painting, sculpting) be required of all high school students?
- [ ] Should college admission be based solely on academic achievement?
- [ ] Should college students work part time?
- [ ] Should affirmative action programs continue in America's colleges?
- [ ] Since fraternity hazing practices have caused injuries and even deaths, should fraternities be banned from college campuses?
- [ ] Should college athletes receive tutoring and other special academic assistance with their academic work, assistance not readily available to other students?
- [ ] Should black or Hispanic students have their own separate organizations on college campuses?
- [ ] Should self-expression and self-development take priority over family and social responsibilities?

Choosing an intriguing issue. Select an issue from your list that seems especially interesting, one that you would like to know more about. It should be an issue about which people disagree.

Defining the issue. To begin thinking about the issue, write for about five minutes trying to define it. Do not take sides or present an argument; just state what you presently think the issue is. Explain what kind of issue it is and what other issues it may be related to. Define the issue as well as you can for now, even if you plan eventually to research it.

Exploring the issue   To understand the issue and the rhetorical situation better, you will need to examine the pros and cons and to identify possible readers for your essay.

Determining the pros and cons. Begin by dividing a page vertically into two columns. Write the word *Pro* at the top of the left-hand column, and *Con* at the top of the right-hand column. Then, in the appropriate column, list the arguments on each side of the issue. Try to be as thorough as you can now, even if you find later that you need to do research.

Identifying possible readers. Having explored different views of the issue, you should be able to identify, by name or in some other way, people who take these particular positions. Go back to your Pro/Con chart, and at the bottom of each column describe the people who take that side. Then, decide to whom you would like to address your position paper. You may change your mind as you learn more about the issue and your readers, but it will help to have possible readers in mind as you explore further.

Researching the issue   You may have found that you do not know very much about the issue or the opposing views on it. If this is the case, then you probably need to do some research before continuing. You can gather information by talking to others or by reading what others have written. Refer to Chapter 20: Field Research if you are thinking of interviewing an expert or surveying opinion. Chapter 21: Library Research offers guidelines on doing library research.

If you do not have enough time for research but do not feel confident that you know enough to write a thoughtful essay, perhaps you should consider another subject, one about which you are better informed. Return to your list of possible issues and start over again.

Considering your purpose and audience   Given what you now know about the issue and the various views people hold, you are ready to consider your purpose and audience, and to state your thesis tentatively.

Analyzing your purpose and audience. Write a couple of paragraphs analyzing your purpose and readers. Try to determine from this analysis what your best argumentative strategy might be. Consider the following questions as you write.

☐ Given these particular readers, what argumentative strategy should I adopt?
☐ How do they define the issue?
☐ What basic values or assumptions about the issue do we share?
☐ What kinds of evidence are they likely to find convincing?

You should consider several different ways of appealing to your readers. By considering various strategies now, you prepare yourself to make thoughtful decisions later.

Stating your thesis. Write a sentence or two stating your thesis. Choose your words carefully. Try to make your claim clear and arguable, and be sure to qualify it appropriately.

You will have ample opportunity to revise your thesis as you learn more about the issue and develop your argument. Stating it now, even tentatively, will help you to focus the rest of your invention and planning.

Testing your choice This is a good time to evaluate whether or not you should proceed with this particular issue. To make this decision, ask yourself the following questions:

☐ Does this topic really interest me?
☐ Do I know enough about it now or can I learn what I need to know in the time I have remaining to plan and write my essay?
☐ Is the topic small and manageable enough for my time and space limits?
☐ Do I have a good sense of how others view this issue and what readers I might address in my essay?
☐ Have I begun to understand the issue and to formulate my own view of it?

As you explore the issue further and develop your argument, you will want to reconsider these questions. If at any point you decide that you cannot answer them affirmatively, you may want to choose a different issue to write about.

Developing your reasoning To construct a convincing argument, you should list reasons for your position, choose the strongest ones, and develop them fully.

Listing reasons. Write down every plausible reason you could give to convince readers that your position on this issue should be taken seriously.

To get started, it might help to think of your reasons as *because* clauses attached to your thesis statement.

Choosing the strongest reasons. Review your list with your readers in mind. Put an asterisk next to the reasons that you think would carry most weight with these particular readers. If none of your reasons seems very strong, you might need to reconsider your position, do some more research, or even pick another topic.

Developing your best reasons. Take each of the strongest reasons in turn and write for five minutes on each one, explaining it to your readers and providing evidence to support it. You may discover at this stage that you need some specific information. Do not stop now to locate it, but make a note about what you need and continue writing. If you decide not to include some of these reasons, you may not need the information after all. Later, before drafting or even when revising your draft, you will be able to follow up and locate any information you still need.

Anticipating counterarguments

This section will help you to anticipate counterarguments (reasons for the opposing view) and to decide which ones you will accommodate and which ones you will refute.

Listing counterarguments. Begin by listing all the counterarguments you can think of. You will have discovered some in the process of exploring and researching the issue. If you cannot think of any counterarguments at all, write out an imaginary conversation with someone with whom you disagree on the issue.

Accommodating counterarguments. Review your list of counterarguments, and decide which of them you think you should accommodate. Write a few sentences for each one indicating how you will have to modify or qualify your thesis. Also, briefly explain why you are conceding this point.

Refuting counterarguments. Review the list to find counterarguments that you can refute. For each one, write for five minutes developing your refutation. Be careful not to criticize unfairly those who present the counterarguments. Try to explain to them why you do not find the arguments convincing. They may be irrelevant, only partially true, or not true at all. If you need to check facts or find some other information, do it later. It will be most efficient at this point simply to list the points you need to check and to save the research until you take a break.

Restating your thesis

Now that you have developed your argument, you may want to reformulate your thesis. Consider whether you should change your language to qualify or limit your claim.

PLANNING AND DRAFTING

Before you begin drafting your essay, take some time to review your notes and see what you have discovered, to set goals for your essay, and to prepare an outline.

Seeing what you have If you have completed all the invention activities, you will have accumulated several pages of notes. Much of this writing will be rambling and fragmentary. Review your notes carefully to see what you might use in your draft. Mark passages that seem especially promising. Indicate any that show conviction, have vivid writing, contain pointed examples, demonstrate strong reasoning. Note places where you reach out to readers, share their concerns and values, acknowledge their feelings, and modify your own views to accommodate theirs.

If your invention notes are skimpy, you may not have given enough thought to the issue or know enough at this time to write a convincing essay about it. You have several alternatives. You can do more invention and research, possibly using the general invention activities in Chapter 11: Invention and Revision. You can go on to write a draft, hoping that you will get more ideas as you write. Or you can begin again with a new topic without losing much more time.

Setting goals Experienced writers set overall goals for themselves before drafting their essays. They decide what they will try to achieve and how they will go about it. To help you set realistic goals, consider the following questions now. You may also find it helpful to return to some of these questions as you outline and draft your essay.

Your purpose and audience

☐ What can I realistically hope to accomplish by addressing these particular readers? Are they deeply committed to their opinions? Should I try, as Goss does, to make readers see that their view is mistaken? Should I appeal, as Smith does, to their ambivalence?

☐ Can I address readers' special concerns, acknowledge the legitimacy of their feelings, or define the issue in terms that appeal to common values and beliefs? Shall I appeal, as Rosenfeld does, to their desire for practical results or to their sense of morality? Can I demonstrate, as Goss and Young do, that I am aware of the need to protect the freedom of the press?

☐ Can I draw on any common experiences that relate to this issue? Could I share my own experience, as Smith and Goss do?

The beginning

☐ How shall I open the essay to engage readers' attention immediately? Should I begin by identifying the controversy and stating my thesis, as Goss does? Should I use a rhetorical question, a surprising example, a personal anecdote, or startling statistics to draw readers into the argument?

☐ How much do I need to explain about the controversy and define the terms before proceeding with my argument? Should I summarize the facts, as Young does? Should I summarize both sides, as Goss does?

Your argument

If I have more than one reason, how should I order the reasons? From strongest to weakest? From the most to the least predictable? From simplest to hardest? Can I sequence them logically, so that one leads inevitably to the next?

Which counterarguments should I mention, if any? Shall I acknowledge and rebut them all, as Goss does? Shall I focus, as Rosenfeld does, on one that I can easily dismiss? Can I concede anything, as Rosenfeld does? What would I gain from conceding? What would I lose?

Avoiding logical fallacies

Can I avoid making *sweeping generalizations* (offering broad statements without providing specific details to support them)?

Will I be able to avoid *oversimplifying* the issue (concentrating on only one or a few aspects of an issue and ignoring its complexity)?

Will I be able to avoid committing an *either/or fallacy* (unjustly limiting the issue to only two alternatives)?

Can I avoid an *ad hominem* argument (making a personal attack against my opponents rather than addressing the issue)?

How can I avoid building a *straw man* (representing the opposition's argument unfairly so that I can knock it down easily)?

The ending

How can I conclude my argument effectively? Should I repeat my thesis, as Goss does? Shall I look to the future, possibly to redefine the issue, as Smith does?

Can I end on a note of agreement by reminding readers of the common concerns and values we share? Shall I look forward, as Smith does, to a new way of understanding the issue that transcends our differences?

Outlining the
position paper

Some position papers include everything—an extended definition of the is-sue, an elaborate argument with multiple reasons and evidence, and several counterarguments, some of which are accommodated while others are re-futed. Your essay may not be so complicated, but you will still have to decide how to arrange the different parts. In the previous section, you considered strategies for beginning and ending your essay, and determined how you might order your reasons. Now you should consider the organization of your position paper more carefully and prepare a tentative outline.

If you assume your readers are aware of the issue and might favor the opposing side, then, like Goss, you may first want to refute counterargu-ments before offering your own reasons. Your position paper might follow this plan:

identifies issue and states thesis

introduces counterarguments

refutes counterarguments

argues for her own reason

restates thesis

Or you could, like Smith, weigh the pros and cons before arriving at your own position on the issue. The outline of your essay might then look like this:

introduces both sides without advocating either

considers the strengths and weaknesses of the argument offered by one side

considers the strengths and weaknesses of the argument offered by the other side

states thesis advocating a new way to view the issue

These are by no means the only ways to arrange your essay. Indeed, every writer will see different possibilities in the material. Making an outline before drafting your essay, though, will help you to get started. An outline presents a route, neither the only one nor necessarily the best, but one that will get you going in the right direction.

Drafting the
position paper

With an outline and goals as your guide, you should be able to draft your essay fairly quickly. Before you begin, you might want to review the general advice on drafting in Chapter 1. As you draft, remember the importance of audience in a position paper. Keep your audience in mind by writing to a particular (real or imaginary) reader. Think of your writing as a transcript of what you would say to this person. Also keep in mind your purpose in writing to this particular reader. Remember that establishing common ground depends on acknowledging readers' intelligence, experience, values, and concerns.

Use your outline to guide your drafting, taking each point separately. As you pick up momentum, you may leave the outline behind. If you get stuck, refer to it again. But do not worry if you diverge from your original plan. Writing sometimes has a logic of its own that carries the writer along.

READING A DRAFT WITH A CRITICAL EYE

At this point you are ready to have someone else read your draft. The following guidelines will help you to analyze the particular features of a position paper. (You might want to review the general advice on reading another's draft critically in Chapter 1 before you begin.) As you read, keep this general question in mind: given the audience to whom this essay is addressed, how could the argument be made more convincing?

First general impression   Read the essay through quickly to get a sense of its argument. Then, write a few sentences describing your initial reaction. Does the issue interest you? What is your personal view of it? What did you find most convincing in the essay? Least convincing?

Pointings   It is important to maintain a critical focus as you read the essay now; one way to do this is by highlighting notable features of the writing with *pointings*. A simple system of marking a draft with underlining and brackets, these points are quick and easy to do and provide helpful information for revising the draft. Use pointings in the following way:

☐ Draw a straight line under any words or images that impress you as especially effective: strong verbs, precise descriptive details, memorable phrases, striking images.

☐ Draw a wavy line under any words or images that seem flat, stale, or vague. Also put a wavy line under any words or phrases that seem unnecessary or repetitious.

☐ Look for pairs or groups of sentences that you think should be combined. Put brackets [ ] around these sentences.

☐ Look for sentences that are garbled, overloaded, or awkward. Put parentheses ( ) around these sentences. Parenthesize any sentence that seems even slightly questionable; don't spend time worrying about whether it actually is incorrect. The writer needs to know that you, as one reader, had even the slightest difficulty understanding a sentence.

Analysis   1. The essay should center on a well-defined controversial issue. Check to see how the writer presents the issue. Is it clearly arguable? How well defined is it? Let the writer know what kind of issue you think it is.

2. The writer's position on this issue should be stated clearly and appropriately qualified. Indicate at what point in the essay you think the thesis is most explicitly stated. Tell the writer if you think it is clear and appropriately qualified.

3. Study the reasons given to support this thesis. Indicate which reasons you find most convincing and which least convincing. Point to any reasons that need more development or support. Comment on the order in which the reasons are given. If you have any objections to the argument, explain them.

4. Focus on the evidence supporting these reasons. Note whether any of the evidence seems unbelievable or irrelevant. Also indicate where you think more evidence is needed.

5. Look for any reference to the opposition or to their counterarguments (the arguments they offer to support their opinion). Is the opposition represented fairly? If the writer accommodates any counterarguments, is the thesis modified accordingly? Should it be?

6. Focus on the passages in which counterarguments are refuted. Tell the writer what is most and least convincing in the refutation. If you have any suggestions on how to strengthen the argument, offer them.

7. If the writer defines any terms in the essay, indicate whether or not you accept the definitions. Point to any terms that you think need to be defined.

8. Look again at the beginning and the ending of the essay. Explain why you think they are or are not effective. If you have a problem with the beginning or the ending, suggest an alternative.

9. Skim the essay, paying special attention to the tone the writer adopts. Offer some adjectives to describe the tone (or tones). Indicate how you, as one reader, respond to the essay's tone.

10. If you suspect that there are any logical fallacies in the essay, point them out. (A list of logical fallacies appears in Chapter 19: Arguing.)

REVISING AND EDITING

All writers, from student to professional, find it necessary to revise their writing. Because position papers concern controversial issues and usually address unsympathetic readers, you must pay particular attention to revising your draft. This section provides guidance in planning your revision.

Revising a position paper If you have received comments on your draft from another student or from your instructor, you will have some idea of what needs attention. You might also turn to Chapter 11, where you will find a general plan for revising. When you reach the section Read Again To Identify Problems, you can substitute the following specific suggestions on revising a position paper for the general suggestions in that chapter.

Revising to strengthen your argument

☐ Given your purpose, can you accommodate your readers any better? Could your tone be more conciliatory? If you refute counterarguments, can you find any common ground with readers by acknowledging the legitimacy of their concerns? Have you put your argument in terms that are familiar and acceptable to your readers? Can you emphasize the areas of agreement? Can you make concessions without undermining your position?

☐ Can you convince your readers to look at the issue in the same way you do? What personal experiences could you include to show readers how important the issue is to you? What examples and anecdotes could you include to put the issue in human terms? In defining the issue, could you use terms that are already used by your readers? By showing where you agree as well as disagree, could you avoid polarizing opinion? Can you rely on an authority your readers respect?

☐ Can you make your argument seem more understandable and reasonable? Restate your position, qualifying your language so that it does not seem so extreme. Explain each reason more fully, developing your point by using the writer's strategies of narration, description, definition, classification, illustration, and comparison/contrast. Offer a range of evidence and show exactly how the evidence supports your point.

Revising for readability

☐ Outline your draft to determine whether your argument follows logically.

☐ Add forecasting to alert readers to your plan and transitions so that they can see where each point ends and the next begins.

☐ Reconsider the opening. Would a vivid example or startling fact help to introduce the issue? Should you explain the controversy or describe the opposition? Should you put your thesis statement up front to clarify your position for readers?

☐ Look for writing that is abstract or unclear. Use familiar words instead of unusual ones. Rewrite convoluted sentences by beginning with the subject and putting the action in the verb.

☐ Reconsider the ending. If the essay seems to fade away, can you add a brief summary of your argument or a memorable image to make it more emphatic? Should you frame the essay by repeating something from the beginning? Can you extend the scope of the argument at the end by looking to the future or to broader implications of the issue?

Editing and proofreading As you revise your draft for the final time, edit it carefully and correct any errors of mechanics, usage, punctuation, or style. If you habitually misspell certain words or make certain types of punctuation or grammatical errors, read specifically for these mistakes. After you have produced the final copy, be sure to proofread it carefully before handing it in.

LEARNING FROM YOUR OWN WRITING PROCESS

Spend a few moments reflecting on the process you followed in writing this essay. Review your invention writing, drafts, critical reading notes, and final revision. What problems did you encounter in constructing your essay? Could you have avoided any of them by gathering more information, by understanding your purpose and readers better, by having more time to plan your draft, or by some other means?

What have you learned about writing an argumentative essay from this experience? Is it very different from the other kinds of writing you have done in this course? What would you do differently next time?

A WRITER AT WORK

DEFINING THE ISSUE

Young had no difficulty choosing an issue for her position paper; from the start, she wanted to write about the Gary Hart scandal. She had watched it unfold on the television news and had read reports and editorials in the newspaper and newsmagazines. She never seriously considered any other topic, although she did list several other possibilities, including divestment of stock in American companies doing business in South Africa, television commercials for condoms to fight the spread of AIDS, and overcrowding of dormitories.

The first step was easy for her, but the next one—defining the issue—turned out to be hard because she felt so strongly about the issue that she could not resist stating her position. She knew she was supposed to be objective and to simply say what the issue is about, but she found herself also expressing outrage. Here is what she wrote:

Gary Hart was made to withdraw from the campaign by rumors spread by the media. This situation points up a serious problem with our democracy. In a nation where freedom of the press is an inalienable right, I find that this right is often abused. This abuse is seen every time there is a major political campaign. By probing into Gary Hart's personal life, journalists from the <u>Miami Herald</u>, in effect, began a process which destroyed a presidential candidate. Hart had no choice but to forfeit his campaign. The media ultimately caused the loss of his and his family's dignity.

She found the next step—constructing a pro/con chart—particularly helpful because it made her stop and think about other points of view. It also helped her realize how important the question of relevance was going to be in her argument. She began by opposing the right of privacy to the right of a free press. Then she went back and forth between the pro and con sides, trying to balance each point and writing phrases instead of whole sentences—a shorthand that would later jog her memory.

PRO	CON
--Press invaded Hart's privacy	--As public figures, candidates give up their right to privacy
--Media set itself up as judge and jury	--Media has right and duty to report
--Adultery is irrelevant to campaign, between husband and wife	--Adultery shows weak character
--Lying is understandable, human nature	--Lying is even worse
--Media should report on important issues	--Adultery is a relevant issue

Later in developing her argument and anticipating counterarguments, Young was able to build upon this initial exploration of the issue. Her list of reasons repeats many of the points she originally entered on the pro side, and her list of counterarguments repeats those on the con side. She tried to develop two reasons from her list: that even candidates have a right to privacy and that whether Hart committed adultery is irrelevant to the campaign. This is how she developed the latter reason:

It is not relevant to the campaign whether Hart committed adultery. Hart said the question of unfaithfulness is between "me and Lee and me and God." There is no reason why others should be involved. "Adultery is not a crime. It's a sin." His wife, Lee, agrees. She said, "If it doesn't bother me, I don't think it ought to bother anyone else." Why should this non-issue become so important? Why doesn't the press cover Hart's stand on nuclear arms or foreign policy and other political issues? Adultery doesn't have anything to do with it? It's a way to divert attention away from the real issues. Why would the press want to do that, except for money? The <u>Miami Herald</u> rushed the story into print in order to be first and sell more papers. What do most people feel? Do they care? <u>Time</u> or <u>Newsweek</u> had an opinion poll—check.

Of the counterarguments she listed, Young decided to accommodate the criticism of Hart for lying but to try to refute the argument that adultery is relevant because it shows weak character. In her invention writing and first draft, Young accepts the fact that Hart lied. However, she tries to explain away his lying as a perfectly natural reaction. After going over the draft with her instructor, Young changed her mind and decided to refute rather than to accept this criticism since the charge that he lied has not and probably will never be proved.

Young's invention work records her attempt to refute the counterargument about character and shows Young struggling to understand why some people consider it so important. She begins by trying to define character.

Some people argue that committing adultery is relevant because it shows that the candidate has a weak character. Character is defined as strength of mind and purpose. And a man's actions are a portrait of his character. If Hart was unfaithful to his wife, does that show he wouldn't be a good leader? So many leaders had affairs—like Eisenhower, Roosevelt, and Kennedy. They were some of our best presidents. Maybe they were also unhappily married. People stay married just for show like Ted Kennedy until he got divorced and gave up hope of ever becoming president.

Maybe I'm wrong, but I don't think that people nowadays think of character in the same way they used to. Morals used to be stricter. Now people are more accepting. They see adultery as something personal, between husband and wife. It's their business and if the wife doesn't mind, then no one else should.

As you can see from this overview of her invention process, Young's argument did not fall neatly into place all at once. She wrote the draft fairly quickly, relying on the ideas and even using some of the language from her invention writing. But she still was not satisfied. In fact, the essay did not come up to her expectations until after she had revised it in response to critical readings she received from a classmate and her instructor. You can find a description of Young's revising process in Chapter 11: Invention and Revision.

Proposing Solutions

☐ The business manager of a large hospital writes a proposal to the board of directors requesting the purchase of a new word-processing and billing system that she recently saw demonstrated at a convention. She argues that the new system would both improve efficiency and save money. In support of her proposal she reminds the board of the limitations of the present system and points out the advantages of the new one.

☐ Researchers at an oceanographic institute write a proposal to the National Science Foundation for funding to study the effects of ocean temperatures on weather patterns. To convince the foundation that their research should have priority over other proposed projects, they argue that the world economy is being adversely affected by erratic weather conditions. They discuss in detail the case of the El Niño phenomenon of 1983, with its extreme temperatures and severe storms, as evidence of the catastrophic effects changes in ocean temperature can have.

☐ For a political science class, a student analyzes the problem of the four-year presidency. Citing examples from recent history, she argues that American presidents spend the first year of each term getting organized and the fourth year either running for re-election or as a lame duck. Consequently, they are fully productive for only half of their four-year terms. She proposes a six-year nonrenewable presidential term, claiming that it would remedy the problem by giving presidents 4 or 5 years to put their programs into effect. She acknowledges that this change could make presidents less responsive to the public will, but insists that the system of legislative checks and balances would make that problem unlikely.

☐ A newspaper columnist writes about the problem of controlling the spread of AIDS. Since symptoms take years to appear, she notes, people with AIDS unwittingly pass it on to their sexual partners. She discusses three solutions that have been proposed by others: having only one sexual partner, engaging in safe sexual practices, or notifying and testing the sexual partners of those found to have the disease. She argues that the first solution would solve the problem, but may not be feasible, and that the second solution would not work because safe sexual practices are not absolutely reliable. In support of the third solution—tracing of sexual partners—she argues that tracing has worked in controlling other communicable diseases and that it should be even more effective with AIDS because it would help overcome a major obstacle in controlling the epidemic—namely, the false assumption that heterosexuals cannot contract AIDS.

☐ Several students in the predentistry program at a large state university realize how uncertain they are about requirements, procedures, and strategies for applying to dental school. One of them writes a proposal to the head of the program suggesting the need for a handbook for predentistry students. To dramatize that a problem exists and is considered serious by students, he points out their students' declining rates of admission to dental schools and includes an informal survey of students presently in the program. He also mentions several other programs that offer this kind of pamphlet for their students. Realizing that few faculty members would take time for such a project, he proposes that students would do the actual writing as well as handle the printing and distribution; two faculty members would serve simply as advisers. He asks that the publication costs be borne by the predentistry program, however, pointing out that students would donate their time.

☐ A college student who works part-time at a pizzeria near campus notices certain problems created by high turnover of employees. Newcomers often misplace things, forget procedures for cleaning up, and interrupt other employees to ask for help operating the espresso machine. Since the company offers cash awards for innovative ideas for improving procedures or service, the student writes a letter to the owners suggesting ways to reduce these problems. Knowing that high turnover is inevitable in such a job, she concentrates on procedures for orienting and training new employees.

Proposals serve an important role in a democracy, informing citizens about problems affecting their well-being and that of the society and also suggesting actions that could be taken to remedy these problems. As these examples demonstrate, people write proposals every day in business, government, education, and the professions. Proposals are a basic ingredient of the world's work. The writing students do in their academic studies often involves problem analysis and solution as well.

This chapter follows the one on taking a position because writing position papers is a more general kind of argumentation than proposing solutions to problems. When you write a position paper, your concerns are broader. How well the problem is solved may be only one thing to consider, if it is considered at all. Writing a proposal, however, requires you to offer a specific solution, perhaps even outlining how the solution can be implemented.

Problem solving is a way of thinking basic to most disciplines and professions: for example, scientists use the scientific method, a systematic form of problem solving; engineers regularly employ problem-solving techniques; attorneys find legal precedents to solve their clients' problems; physicists pose questions about universal laws. Problem solving depends on a questioning attitude, what is called critical thinking. In addition, problem solving demands imagination and creativity. To solve a problem, you need to see it anew, to look at it from new angles and in new contexts. The writing guide in this chapter will help you to develop your problem-solving ability by presenting activities you can use to invent a solution to your problem.

Since a proposal tries to convince readers that its way of defining and solving the problem makes sense, proposal writing also helps writers become more sensitive to readers' needs and expectations. As you plan and draft your proposal, for instance, you will want to determine whether your readers are aware of the problem and whether they recognize its seriousness. In addition, you will want to consider whether any other solutions have been proposed and what your readers think of them. Knowing your readers is crucial to developing a persuasive argumentative strategy.

The reading selections that follow illustrate many of the strategies proposal writers use to analyze a problem and persuade readers to accept their solution. You will find that all the writers in this chapter address fairly well-defined audiences. Knowing what your readers know, what their assumptions and biases are, what kinds of arguments will be appealing to them is a central part of proposal writing, indeed of all good argumentative writing. You will be asked to direct your own proposal essay in this chapter to specific readers who want to think seriously about the problem or find a solution to it in their own lives. As you read the following selections, you may see strategies you find effective and wish to use in your own writing.

READINGS

The first selection proposes a solution to the problem of teenage pregnancy. It was written by Adam Paul Weisman for the *New Republic*, a national news magazine. As you read, ask yourself how Weisman's admission that his solution is not original—that it, in fact, has already been tried—affects your reaction to it.

BIRTH CONTROL IN THE SCHOOLS: CLINICAL EXAMINATION

ADAM PAUL WEISMAN

Should contraceptives be distributed to teenagers in public schools? A research panel of the National Academy of Sciences spent two years studying adolescent pregnancy in America, and decided they should. Its 1986 report, *Risking the Future*, prompted a new wave of angry debate about how to reduce the high rate of teenage pregnancy in the United States. 1

No one disputes the severity of the problem. Teen pregnancy ruins young lives and perpetuates a tragic cycle of poverty. According to the Alan Guttmacher Institute, the rate of pregnancy among American women aged 15 to 19 was almost ten percent in 1981. That far outstrips the next closest industrialized nation, England, where the rate is less than five percent. Guttmacher estimates that more than 80 percent of teenage pregnancies in the United States are unintended and unwanted. Every year about four in 100 women aged 15 to 19 have an abortion. But those looking for ways to reduce these statistics have divided into two distinct camps: one favoring contraception, the other, sexual abstinence. 2

The contraception advocates point out that a majority of teenagers have already rejected abstinence. In 1986, 57 percent of 17-year-olds say they have had sex. This camp believes that schools, as a central location in young peoples' lives, are a good place to make contraceptives available. Three recent studies (by the National Academy of Sciences, the Guttmacher Institute, and the Children's Defense Fund) have taken this view, while also calling for programs geared toward postponing adolescent sexual involvement and including parents in school sex education classes. 3

The abstinence advocates believe the answer lies in inculcating values based 4
on a clear understanding that sex is simply wrong for teenagers. They say that
moral lessons are best taught by parents in the home, but that schools should
continue the job by teaching a chaste morality. Secretary of Education William
Bennett has been the most outspoken proponent of this view. Exposing students
to "mechanical" means of pregnancy prevention, he says, encourages "children
who do not have sexual intimacy on their minds to . . . be mindful of it."

Bennett concedes that "birth control clinics in schools may prevent some 5
births." And indeed, whatever the drawbacks, the contraception advocates have
one strong advantage in this debate: their approach works. The only rigorous
study of a pregnancy prevention program for urban teenagers was conducted
in Baltimore from 1982 to 1983 by researchers from Johns Hopkins Medical
School. The Hopkins-run birth-control clinic, located across the street from one
school and nearby another, reduced the pregnancy rate in the schools it served
by 30 percent while pregnancy rates in control schools soared 58 percent.

"Why did this program work?" asks Dr. Laurie Zabin, the program's director, 6
in her report on the experiment. "Access to high-quality, free services was probably crucial to its success. Professional counseling, education, and open communications were, no doubt, also important. All these factors appear to have
created an atmosphere that allowed teenagers to translate their attitude into
constructive preventive behavior." And what of those students who were vir-
gins? According to Zabin, that group of girls (not very large) delayed initiation
of sexual activity an average of seven months longer than those in the control
groups, strong evidence that awareness of contraception is not directly linked
to promiscuity.

But the existing school-based clinics that distribute or arrange for birth con- 7
trol are not just rooms plastered with Planned Parenthood posters where contraceptives are handed out. They are full-service health clinics that came into
existence to provide young people with comprehensive health care. Public health
officials, including many who have doubts about distributing contraceptives in
schools, agree that in many places, particularly the inner city, health care for
adolescents is inadequate. The school-based clinic, like the school lunch program, seeks to make all students healthy enough to get the most out of
education.

This is not to say that school-based clinics don't do a lot in the way of 8
contraception. According to Douglas Kirby, director of research for the Center
for Population Options, a group that advocates and monitors school-based clinics, 15 percent to 20 percent of visits to clinics are for family planning. The
majority are for general health care. Twenty-eight percent of the clinics actually
dispense contraceptives or other prescription drugs. About half of the clinics
write prescriptions that are filled off-campus; the rest diagnose and counsel
teens before making referrals to outside health agencies.

These clinics also seem to help reduce unintended pregnancies. In St. Paul 9
33 percent of girls made use of the clinic's contraceptive services, and birth rates
dropped by 50 percent. Thanks to the clinic's counseling, four out of five of the
girls who did have children stayed in school, and only 1.4 percent of them had

another pregnancy before graduation. Nationally, about 17 percent of teenage mothers become pregnant again within a year.

Bennett argues that distributing birth control is "not what school is for," 10 and that doing so represents "an abdication of moral authority." Many educators have similar concerns. They fear that communities and government are trying to dump another social problem—like drug counseling and AIDS education—on the schools when they could better be handled in the home. Diane Ravitch, an adjunct professor of history and education at Teachers College in New York, says, "Schools are increasingly being pushed to be social service centers, and they don't do that well."

Yet clearly schools do more than teach students the three R's. Schools are 11 where many teenagers learn to drive, weld, and cook. And numerous surveys reveal that over 80 percent of parents think it is a proper place for their children to learn about sex. Dr. Stephen Joseph, health commissioner for New York City, explains that if it weren't for the involvement of schools, the United States never could have achieved 100 percent immunization rates, a worthy goal that "wasn't perceived as the role of the school either at that time."

If the pressing health crisis were non-sexual in nature—tuberculosis, for ex- 12 ample—it's hard to believe that educators such as Bennett wouldn't be the first to volunteer schools as a locus for a solution. And of course, if the problem of teen pregnancy is one that the schools shouldn't be expected to deal with, that would exclude any program of anti-sex indoctrination as well as the distribution of contraceptives. Putting such indoctrination into the curriculum is, arguably, more intrusive on the schools' basic function than the existence of a birth control or general health clinic. Bennett's speeches rule out the very real possibility that schools could prosecute a moral agenda and *also* support a clinic.

Despite the success of Zabin's off-campus model, there is a good reason 13 school-based clinics receive such wide support in the health services community: teenagers are notoriously lazy. As Cheryl Hayes, director of the NAS study explains, "If teenagers have to wait in the rain for a bus to take them to a clinic, there is a good chance they will never make it to the clinic." If the goal is providing health care and family planning services to teenagers, it is unlikely that anything will work as well as locating those services where most teenagers are: at school.

Of course the real question that excites people isn't whether teenagers 14 should get birth control at school, but whether they should get it at all. There is no hard evidence linking exposure to contraception with promiscuity, and it is unlikely any teenager who watches prime-time television is less than "mindful" (as Bennett puts it) of sexual intimacy. Although Bennett has dismissed the recommendations of *Risking the Future* as "stupid," the opponents of making contraception available to teenagers have yet to offer an effective alternative. As for the "parental authority" that birth control availability is said to undermine, a 1986 Planned Parenthood survey of 1,000 teenagers revealed that 31 percent of parents discuss neither sex nor birth control with their children. The failure of parental authority is manifest in the almost 900,000 unintended teenage pregnancies in 1983. *Risking the Future* only makes that failure painfully clear.

Questions for analysis

1. As a student yourself, how do you react to Weisman's proposal that school-based health clinics be permitted to distribute birth-control information and contraceptives? Do you think it is appropriate for schools to play such a role?

2. How does Weisman set the stage for his argument in the title and opening paragraph? How effectively does his proposal begin? What criteria do you think are appropriate for judging the effectiveness of a proposal's beginning?

3. In the opening paragraph, Weisman appears to be a neutral reporter rather than an advocate for a particular solution. How does this paragraph convey an objective reporter's tone? Is this tone maintained consistently throughout the essay? Point to passages where the same tone is evident or where a different tone emerges. How does the neutral reporter's tone serve Weisman's overall argumentative strategy?

4. In paragraph 5, Weisman cites the example of the Johns Hopkins University birth-control clinic. How does he use this example to support his argument? How effective is the example?

5. What are the advantages of Weisman's proposed solution? How does he present these advantages so that they will appeal to supporters of the abstinence solution? What common values and concerns does he call upon?

6. In paragraph 12, Weisman uses the writer's strategy of comparing and contrasting. Why do you think he compares teenage pregnancy to tuberculosis? How well does this comparison support his point? (The strategy of comparing and contrasting is discussed in Chapter 18.)

7. Teenagers are the problem in this proposal, but they can also play a positive role in solving certain social problems. For example, high school students can teach illiterate adults to read, help rebuild tenements, or refurbish playgrounds and parks. Think of a problem that students in high school or college might be able to help solve. If you were to write a proposal suggesting a solution to this problem, how would you explain the problem? How would you go about convincing other students that they should participate?

Like writers of position papers, proposal writers must develop an argumentative strategy designed for their particular readers. After carefully considering what their readers know and think about the problem, writers try to anticipate how they will react to the proposed solution. Understanding their readers enables proposal writers to develop an argument that appeals to readers' basic values and needs.

Weisman's purpose in this proposal is obviously to convince his readers that distributing contraceptives through school clinics would help solve the problem of teenage pregnancy. He knows, however, that some readers oppose the idea on moral grounds because they believe that giving birth control information to teenagers condones and may even encourage sexual activity. He also knows that some readers object to using the schools for anything involving sex education. Because he anticipates both of these objections, Weisman can develop an argumentative strategy that acknowledges his readers' concerns.

This strategy is evident in the way Weisman presents the problem as well as in the way he argues for his solution. Like all good proposal writers, Weisman does not assume that his readers will accept as fact his definition of the problem. He must first establish that there is a problem and define precisely what the problem is. He begins by asserting that "no one disputes the severity of the problem." By making this assertion, Weisman tries to establish common ground with his readers, in effect, inviting them to agree with him. At the same time, he checks potential disagreement by citing statistics to support his assertion. Since few readers are likely to have an alternative set of statistics at hand, they are likely to accept the ones he offers. Moreover, the very fact that he offers supporting evidence for his statement may well reassure some readers that he is reasonable and fair. (See Chapter 19: Arguing for further discussion of supporting evidence.)

After establishing the problem, Weisman introduces the two solutions that have been proposed: encouraging teenagers to abstain from sexual activity, and providing birth control information to them. To demonstrate his fairness, Weisman presents the abstinence solution objectively, even sympathetically. He accepts the legitimacy of this proposed solution and objects only on the grounds that it does not work.

The fact that Weisman's proposed solution does appear to work is the cornerstone of his argument. He uses Secretary Bennett's own words to convince advocates of abstinence that the contraception solution, in contrast to their own, actually works. The Johns Hopkins study gives additional credence to his argument. Furthermore, by noting that birth-control counseling "delayed initiation of sexual activity" for some of the teenagers, he makes a forceful appeal to those in favor of abstinence.

Not only does Weisman support his solution with reasons and evidence, but he also anticipates and refutes a major objection to his argument. This counterargument deals with the use of schools to solve social and moral problems. He refutes it in two ways. First, he reasons that the problem of teenage pregnancy is a health crisis and that there is ample precedent for dealing with such problems through the schools. This argument appeals to humanitarian concerns, but is unlikely to convince those who consider it a moral issue, not a health problem. To these readers, he offers a second argument: if birth-control information is excluded from the schools, then "any program of anti-sex indoctrination" must also be excluded. In other words, the argument against school-based birth-control clinics could also be made against teaching sexual abstinence. Both are forms of sex education.

(Chapter 19: Arguing provides further information on anticipating counter-arguments.)

Weisman's argumentative strategy in this proposal is to show that he understands and respects the values of those who advocate alternative solutions, and that he shares their desire to remedy the problem. He appeals to them on practical grounds, arguing that his solution will get the job done. As you plan your own proposal, you will want to think carefully about your own argumentative strategy, deciding not only what you want to say but also how you should say it in order to convince your particular readers.

Weisman's proposal illustrates a writer's readiness to acknowledge readers who prefer an alternative solution. David Owen, the author of the following proposal, tries to convince his readers that a solution that they have come to accept has itself become the problem. The subject of his proposal is the Scholastic Aptitude Test (SAT), a standardized test originally developed to remove social and economic bias from college admissions procedures.

As you read this selection, taken from Owen's book *None of the Above: Behind the Myth of the Scholastic Aptitude* (1985), look closely at Owen's argumentative strategy. To whom does he address his argument? How does he attempt to establish common ground with these readers?

TESTING AND SOCIETY: WHAT CAN BE DONE?
DAVID OWEN

In the winter of 1979, I spent a semester posing as a senior at a large public high school in Stratford, Connecticut. In English class, we spent six weeks reading a fifty-five-page book and devoted most of the rest of our time to memorizing lists of vocabulary words and solving SAT-like multiple-choice word problems: antonyms, analogies, sentence completions. We almost never had to write anything and, aside from our weekly ten-page assignments, we didn't have to read. In large measure our time was spent doing multiple-choice busywork. One of the reasons for this, I think, is that over the years ETS has made busywork seem like real work. With its PSATs, SATs, GREs, GMATs, LSATs, and dozens of other tests, the company has given the multiple-choice question a credibility it does not deserve.

This is not to suggest that teachers would immediately start assigning papers again if ETS disappeared. But as school budgets have declined, ETS has given teachers an easy rationalization for abandoning time-consuming assignments. If multiple-choice tests are good enough for the experts down in "Princeton," they must be good enough for English 12. As long as the tests provide, or seem to provide, the standard by which society's rewards are allocated, schools will inevitably remake themselves in the image of the tests. When this transformation also lightens the loads of overworked teachers, it takes place all the more quickly.

The impact of the SAT is not felt equally by all our schools. Students still read books at Exeter and Andover, even if they also take coaching courses. But in schools where money is scarce and incentives are few, tests like the SAT provide a plausible excuse for cutting back. If the SAT can see through the differences in schools, as the official mythology states, does it matter if a city's poorest school district stops offering algebra, chemistry, and French? By emphasizing "ability" over content, the SAT sends a tragic signal to teachers and administrators.

In a broader social sense, ETS perpetuates the very inequalities it sometimes 4 claims to eliminate and sometimes claims merely to measure. For all its sermonizing about equal opportunity, ETS is the powerful servant of the privileged. The company's executives wax lyrical about ghetto children rescued from poverty by their 600s. But the real beneficiaries of "aptitude" testing are the offspring of the advantaged, who ascend from privilege to privilege on the strength of their scores and come to view those numbers as a moral justification for the comforts that are the trappings of their class. Tests like the SAT convert the tainted advantages of birth and wealth into the neutral currency of merit, enabling the fortunate to believe they have earned what they have merely been given.

The exam-based system jumbles up the pieces of society, but it puts them 5 back together largely as they were before, justifying each new version of the old order on the basis of merit. As ETS extends its reach through American society, the impact of the meritocratic fallacy becomes more pervasive and more insidious. Do we really want to grant a company like ETS such a vast responsibility for ordering our lives?

The SAT isn't perfect, many people would concede; but what would you 6 put in its place? This question is thought by the test's defenders to be unanswerable; critics of ETS, confronted by it, throw up their hands and vanish in puffs of gray smoke. But there are excellent alternatives to the SAT and other standardized tests. There are even some excellent alternatives to ETS.

What would I put in place of the SAT? I don't think we *need* to put anything. 7 If the SAT simply disappeared tomorrow, admissions officers would squawk for a year or so, the foundations of ETS's Henry Chauncey Conference Center would tremble, and life would go on as before. The SAT plays virtually no useful role in college admissions right now. Getting rid of it would not, by itself, make admissions very different.

As long as we're being so radical as to chuck the SAT, though, we might as 8 well take the opportunity to improve college admissions procedures in general. I think there are a number of fairly modest changes that would not only simplify the lives of many admissions officers but also raise the quality of our high schools and colleges. I don't see these proposals as *alternatives* to the SAT; I see them as improvements on an irrational system in which the SAT is, at best, superfluous.

The one inescapable fact about any method of selection is that people who 9 want to be selected are going to try to improve their chances of being selected. If Columbia University suddenly decided to base admissions on the results of the New York State lottery, people who wanted to go to Columbia would buy more lottery tickets than people who didn't. If the SAT is believed to be important in determining who goes to which college, then students who want to go to college are quite understandably going to try to improve their SAT scores. They may not buy desks with built-in alarm clocks, but they may very well enroll in coaching schools. No amount of sermonizing (or outright lying) by ETS or the College Board is going to change that. As long as admissions officers continue to speak idolatrously about SAT scores, multiple-choice busywork and test-taking strategies are going to be facts of life in classrooms, and coaching schools are going to continue to make their owners rich.

Since students are going to expend all this effort anyway, why not adopt a 10 selection method that would encourage them to expend it in some more obviously useful manner? ETS and the College Board pay lip service to this principle, since they maintain that one of the chief virtues of the SAT is that scores can't be improved except through genuine, high-quality education. But no one except them believes this.

One plausible alternative to this sort of testing would simply be an increased 11 emphasis on academic requirements for admission, to *encourage* readiness rather than merely attempt to measure it indirectly. Colleges are in an excellent position to improve the quality of their own applicant pools by encouraging high schools to be better at preparing their students for higher education.

All selective colleges have at least some requirements. Students are supposed 12 to take so many years of science, so many years of math, perhaps a year of a foreign language. But most colleges' requirements aren't much more detailed than that. What if colleges were very specific about what they expected their applicants to have accomplished in high school? What if a group of colleges announced tomorrow that they would no longer admit students who hadn't had four years of high school English (and that courses in film comedy don't count as English courses), that certain books have to be read, that a certain number of papers have to be written, and so on? One of the many crimes of the SAT is that it has led both colleges and high schools to behave as though differences in course content—Shakespeare versus Groucho—were less important than differences in, say, size of vocabulary. An emphasis on genuine accomplishment would be a useful corrective to the superficiality promoted by the SAT.

Most selective colleges strongly favor students who take uniformly solid 13 courses rather than gimmicky electives. Some schools, like Stanford, even recalculate student grade point averages to reflect the presumed seriousness of courses taken. But few colleges, in the materials they send to potential applicants, are explicit about what sort of courses they like and what sort of courses they don't or about how they compare different transcripts. Frivolous high school courses would lose much of their appeal if students knew they were reducing their prospects for college by taking them. Nervous parents would stop demanding SAT preparation in the schools and start demanding term papers.

A model for reform is the Advanced Placement (AP) program, in which 14 participating high schools offer accelerated courses based on specifications promulgated by ETS and the College Board. The AP program as it is currently set up is a joke, but the form is appealing. The nice thing about the concept is that it emphasizes serious learning and promotes the notion that taking challenging courses is a good thing. Couldn't high schools and colleges come up with a similar program that would encourage real education and at the same time give admissions officers something resembling a common ground on which to judge candidates from different schools? An organization like the College Board could serve as a neutral forum at which high schools and colleges could meet to iron out what these courses ought to cover, how they might be taught, and what sort of materials they should use. The new program could simply be built on the bones of the old one. As with the AP, it would be possible to give teachers substantial leeway while at the same time making certain that general standards were upheld.

With colleges providing steady, systematic guidance to high schools, I don't 15 think there would be any need for a national admissions testing program (indeed, I don't think there's a need for one even *without* such steady, systematic guidance). If colleges can't bear the thought of giving up test scores, however, then we need tests that are very different from the ones we have now. Once again, I think the AP program, for all its many faults, provides a general outline for what such testing might be.

Like AP tests, any new admissions tests should be directly tied to curriculum 16 so that learning and "coaching" would be indistinguishable. But unlike AP tests, any new tests should not contain multiple-choice questions, and they should not be so trivial or transparent that they encourage short-cut preparation. They should be incorporated directly into the curricula they measure and be treated as a part of the educational process rather than as a "barometer" of the quality of schools. Like AP exams, they should be conducted by the schools and not by ETS or the College Board. At the very least, admissions testing, if it is done at all, should not take place in a single hour on a single Saturday morning.

Such testing would be enormously expensive (unless colleges were willing 17 to dispense with centralized grading and let teachers mark the tests themselves and incorporate scores into class grades, perhaps in accordance with some common formula). But we shouldn't fool ourselves into thinking that a test like the SAT is good simply because it can be administered and scored with ease. The features of the SAT that make it quick and easy are the same ones that make its content so superficial and unfair and its effect on schools so pernicious.

An admissions system centered on explicit requirements and guidelines 18 would not necessarily be any fairer to the underprivileged than a system based on SAT scores. As Leon Botstein, the president of Bard College, pointed out at the College Board's annual meeting in 1982, colleges can effectively exclude minorities simply by requiring their applicants to take courses that aren't taught (because they're too expensive or because qualified teachers can't be found) in inner-city schools. Given this fact, it seems to me that colleges have an additional responsibility to help less fortunate schools fulfill commonly accepted requirements for admission. It is in the interest of colleges to make this possible. The only way to produce qualified minority students is to ensure that they have a chance to learn what they must know to succeed.

To meet this goal, colleges need literally to invest in disadvantaged schools 19 and school systems. Harvard recently spent five years raising a third of a billion dollars for its already oceanic endowment. A number of other prestigious colleges have raised similar sums, and still others are planning monumental fund drives of their own. Why not spend some of this money on helping high schools prepare qualified candidates (or on helping elementary schools prepare qualified high school students)? A useful role for an organization like the College Board would be as an intermediary between colleges and high schools, channeling expertise, subsidized teaching materials, and other aid to needy schools. The Board and ETS loudly extol the idea of equal opportunity, but they have never done anything to bring it about. The SAT, as I have argued, actually undermines such efforts by creating the illusion that differences in school quality don't matter. Since all colleges would be better off if high school students were better prepared, colleges could look at such contributions as expressions of pure self-interest. Many colleges now have expensive and time-consuming remedial programs. But colleges wouldn't have to offer high-school-level courses if high schools did.

Reforming schools and admissions systems along these or similar lines would 20 not be terribly difficult, but it would require a conscientious effort by the colleges and high schools. Is such an effort likely to be made? I don't think so. The simple fact is that the selection of applicants at the vast majority of colleges isn't terribly important to the colleges: schools that have few applicants worry more about filling dormitories than about making fine distinctions between candidates; prestigious colleges with vast surpluses of qualified applicants (that are thus forced to turn away students who would succeed if admitted) know that the consequences of "incorrect" decisions are very slight.

If colleges put a little effort into helping high schools produce better can- 21 didates, the colleges would benefit too, and professors wouldn't complain so much about the shortcomings of the students they're forced to teach. Professors have tended to moan about inadequate high schools without realizing that they are in an excellent position to do something about improving them. After all, colleges created the multimillion-dollar coaching industry and transformed high school curricula simply by requiring their applicants to take the SAT; what would happen if they explicitly required their applicants to read books, write papers, and take challenging courses?

The first step in creating both a humane admissions system and healthy 22 secondary schools is as simple as shifting emphasis from the rewarding of "aptitude" to the fostering of preparation. Before we can do this, we have to abandon the notion, cultivated by ETS, that each of us harbors a finite consignment of merit to be bartered for educational and economic opportunity. We will never eliminate inequalities and injustices from our schools or our society by maintaining an "objective" testing system that perpetuates both.

Questions for analysis   1. As someone who may have recently taken the SAT or a comparable aptitude test to get into college, how do you react to Owen's proposal? Do you regard aptitude testing a problem? What do you think should be the basis for college admission?

2. Where is the problem stated most explicitly in this proposal? What do you think are the advantages—and possible disadvantages—of putting this statement at this point in the essay?

3. This proposal opens with a personal anecdote. What does it contribute to the essay? What impression of the author do you get from this beginning?

4. In paragraph 3, Owen refers to the "official mythology" of the SAT; in paragraph 4, he describes the ETS as "sermonizing" about equal opportunity. What tone do these particular word choices suggest? Find other instances of this same tone in the proposal. How do you react to the tone? Does it make you more or less receptive to Owen's argument?

5. Owen actually offers two solutions to the problem he has identified. What are they? Why do you think he includes both? How are they related to one another and to the problem they are meant to solve?

6. Look closely at the passages in which Owen argues that the multiple-choice SAT should be replaced with an AP-like test. What objection to his argument does he anticipate? How effectively does he refute this counter-argument?

7. This proposal addresses a problem in the present system of college admissions. Think of other problems relating to high school or college that disturb you. Identify one particular problem that you think needs to be solved. How would you solve this problem? Who would you address your proposal to and what argumentative strategy would you use for these particular readers?

Commentary Owen, as suggested earlier, faces a difficult writing situation in this proposal. Understanding how he appeals to different readers will help you to appreciate how well he handles the rhetorical situation and may suggest strategies that you can use in your own proposal.

Owen addresses six general groups of readers, each with its own values and concerns: high-school students, their teachers and parents, college administrators, professors, and the general public. He first acknowledges the plight of high-school students, the most obvious victims of the SAT. In the opening paragraph, Owen explicitly identifies himself with high-school students and shows that he understands their situation. His description of a typical English class shows how boring and pointless high-school courses can be under the tyranny of the verbal section of the SAT. His proposed change to AP-like tests would clearly benefit high-school students by giving them the opportunity to study something more valuable.

Since he identifies with high-school students, you might expect Owen to lack sympathy for their teachers. He is critical of high-school teachers; in paragraph 2, for example, he says that ETS's emphasis on multiple-choice tests "has given teachers an easy rationalization for abandoning time-consuming assignments." At the same time, however, he does acknowledge that teachers are overworked. Later, in paragraph 14, he appeals to teachers' professionalism by suggesting that they be given "substantial leeway" as graders of the AP-like tests he proposes to substitute for the SAT.

Owen's appeal to parents is both direct and indirect. At the end of paragraph 13, he directly addresses parents' concerns about their children's test scores, advising them to "stop demanding SAT preparation in the schools and start demanding term papers." He acknowledges parents' concerns about college admissions, but suggests that they should be more concerned about their children's education than about their test scores. Owen indirectly addresses parents when he admits in paragraph 17 that his proposed AP-like tests would probably increase the cost of taking the test. He acknowledges that quality testing may have to carry a higher price tag; however, he also implies that quality testing will lead to improved teaching in the high schools.

High-school students, their teachers, and parents are all interested parties, and Owen acknowledges the legitimacy of their interests. But the most important readers of his proposal are the college administrators and professors who could actually implement the change he recommends. Owen argues that colleges would benefit from his proposal. The change in testing would make the college admissions process easier and lead to a bigger pool of well-educated applicants. Moreover, if colleges invested in disadvantaged high schools, minority students also would be better prepared for college. Colleges, Owen claims in paragraph 19, would save money because they would not have to provide "expensive and time-consuming remedial programs." In paragraph 21, he speaks directly to college professors who "moan about inadequate high schools without realizing that they are in an excellent position to do something about improving them."

One theme recurs throughout this essay, the theme of equal opportunity. Owen uses this theme to appeal to all of his readers. He asks us—student, teacher, parent, administrator, and professor—to transcend our differences and act as citizens to promote our common values. The proposed reform of the college admissions process, together with increased aid to disadvantaged schools, would, he argues, bring us closer to realizing our dream of equal educational opportunity.

Proposal writers often address a variety of readers, as Owen does in this selection. Because Owen recognizes that many people would be affected by a change in the college admissions system, he tries to address them all. He singles out each interest group, shows that he understands and sympathizes with its concerns, and argues that the changes he proposes would benefit everyone individually as well as collectively. As you plan and write your own proposal, you may want to consider the different interests of your readers in addition to their shared values and concerns.

The next selection was written by Carol Bly, a writer who lives in rural Minnesota. Her essay, which originally appeared in *Minnesota Monthly*, proposes the institution of a special high school class for farming communities. The problem she is trying to solve with this solution is serious but somewhat abstract. In the title, she calls it "greed," but later describes it as a lack of moral consciousness. As you read her proposal, look closely at the way Bly tries to define this problem and to convince readers that her solution will help alleviate it.

TO UNTEACH GREED
CAROL BLY

For the moment, at least, we are stuck with advising high schoolers that they must expect to take jobs they don't look forward to, because the interesting ones are too rare. In my hometown, for example, six or seven of each high school class express an interest in forestry, parks, and similar outdoor work, but the vocational school that trains for those jobs, Brainerd, has only thirteen openings a year. Girls want to be dental assistants, but St. Cloud, which has the appropriate program, gets three hundred applications for its forty places. Minnesota city dwellers may find it odd but it is nonetheless true that to get into farming—and I use the term here to mean just to get a job as a hand—you have to "know somebody." The good jobs, which by their nature are satisfying to sense and sensibility, are cruelly hard to land.

Therefore, a realistic high school counselor teaches kids to get ready for disappointment. He or she may seem a villain in steering young people to the 600,000 clerk-typist openings when they want forestry, or in not making a whole lot out of the Phillips (Andover, Massachusetts) Academy's imaginative Short Term institutes—six weeks' programs for high school kids from around the country, designed to give them the idea of knowledge-for-the-joy-of-it before they get washed into the Vo-Tech stream of cost/benefit thinking. It seems tough to advise kids that someone must work in the deafening assembly lines; why not advise them someone must staff the top offices everywhere, and raise their expectations to that?

The counselors are being realistic, and their advice isn't cruel. What *is* cruel is that we do not teach a decent philosophical way to look at life; so that those in our countryside who work with hands or head are misled, and waste years finding their inner life. People are taught to be drones.

Only once in a public information meeting in my part of the country have I heard the farm populace approached as if they were people with anything but money making in their heads. In countless Countryside Council meetings, countless Democratic party meetings, countless senior citizens' group meetings (which I went to when working on a minibus task force) and nearly always in Lutheran Church meetings—where the ministers are constantly saying, "We think too much of money," as if money consciousness were a uniform, requisite sin—in all these public meetings the audience was regarded as people wanting profit or high income only. The schools assume that even the children will be interested only in profit and high income. Once I saw a sixth-grade movie against shoplifting in which the two motives provided for not shoplifting were

1. you might be caught, and if you have a police record it will be hard to get a job;
2. shoplifting indirectly raises prices so you eventually will have to pay more for things;

both reasons being self-interest. Nowhere did the movie say,

1. it is mean to shoplift;
2. you do not want to be an unkind person.

The single occasion on which I heard an adult group out here addressed as 5 if they had any moral nature or philosophical nature at all was April 2, 1977, at a 208 Water Quality meeting arranged by the 6-W Regional Development Commission. The speaker, Judge Miles Lord, said, "You farmers can act on motivations beyond greed . . . you can think of natural resources in terms of sharing what we all have, not just in terms of exploitation."

It was rather a surprising address. One farmer, a panelist, was querulous 6 because a Minnesota law made it illegal for us to dye our potatoes with that poisonous red dye but Missouri farmers could still dye theirs, so it was hard for a Minnesota potato producer and shipper to compete with the Missouri people (housewives still being ignorant enough of the chemical danger to buy potatoes because of the handsome color). The speaker's reply to this was "There speaks the voice of greed!" The audience was a little surprised. It was refreshing to hear the word aloud—*greed*—and to be expected to do better.

How refreshing it is to get to think about the moral aspect of things! How 7 immensely boring our countryside life in Minnesota is, despite its beauty, for the simple reason we never get to consider the morals of things—together, publicly.

I have a practical suggestion to make to raise the moral consciousness out 8 here. I suggest we keep or make English required of our juniors and seniors but with the following two strict conditions:

1. That *no techniques* of literature be taught or discussed ever. All approaches to stories being read must be to what they show of life—inner life, feelings, public life, morals.
2. And that we teach courses with a rural-literature emphasis.

Technique is the enemy of philosophy and goodness. The "technique or 9 form creates content" attitude of the 1940s New Criticism makes for cold treatment of stories, deliberate mental superiority over literature—as if literature were something to be seen through. You see it in the frosty way English departments of universities and colleges, still stuck with that interest in technique, handle their freshman curricula. Tolstoy has a terrific passage in *Anna Karenina* against technique. Some art "appreciators" are in a painter's studio, looking at a picture he has just passionately finished in which Christ is one of the figures.

"Yes—there's a wonderful mastery!" said Vronsky. . . . "There you have technique." . . . The sentence about technique had sent a pang through Mihailov's [the painter's] heart, and looking angrily at Vronsky he suddenly scowled. He had often heard this word technique, and was utterly unable to understand . . . a mechanical facility for painting or drawing, entirely apart from its subject.

Here is a tentative format for an Ag Lit course:

Akenfield, especially the chapters about Muck Hill Farm and the Young Farmers' League, and the one about the old Scot who couldn't adjust to the new gardening ways

"How Much Land Does a Man Need?" from Tolstoy's *Russian Stories and Legends*

Growing Up in Minnesota, especially Robert Bly's strange chapter about the sheriff railroading a farmhand to jail in Madison, Minnesota

All Things Bright and Beautiful and *All Creatures Great and Small*

"To a Mouse" by Burns

"Home Burial" and "The Hill Wife" by Frost

Furrow's End, edited by D. B. Greenberg, especially the story of the young sheepherder and his girl from squatter background—one of the most terrific young-love stories with a farming scene

Winesburg, Ohio

My Antonia

String Too Short to Be Saved, Donald Hall's autobiography, with a terrific chapter on a hired hand whose sole passion in life was Mounds bars

These stories and poems should be read by people who are going to live in 10
Minnesota small towns and on farms if they're lucky; and if the stories and verse are studied in the spirit in which they were written, instead of in the spirit of methodology, the young people may come to like English, and enjoy seeing what people think about life.

We especially need to do this if we can't have the jobs we want. If the 11
competitive profit-making part of our lives is going to fall short, and it will for most, then the reflective, intuitive part of life had better be more rewarding than it is. A very nice by-product of an Ag Lit course would be something for men and women to talk about besides Starsky and Hutch. We need a thousand more things to ruminate about together out here. We need conversations that take in the moral aspect of things as well as their moneymaking aspect. It will bring to the countryside a sorely needed gentleness.

Questions for analysis   1. In the first three paragraphs, Bly establishes the context for her proposal by discussing the job prospects for high-school graduates in rural Minnesota. How effective is this opening? How do you react to the news that "the good jobs, which by their nature are satisfying to sense and sensibility, are cruelly hard to land"? What do you think she means by defining good jobs as "satisfying to sense and sensibility"?

2. If Bly is addressing students and townspeople in this proposal, why does she describe students as being "taught to be drones" (paragraph 3) or

the townspeople as seeming to care only about "profit or high income" (paragraph 4)? What risk is she taking? Why?

3. Bly uses examples throughout her essay. Make a list of the examples and the purpose for which she uses each example. What generalizations can you make about Bly's use of examples? How do they serve her overall argumentative strategy?

4. In one of her examples, Bly refers to Judge Miles Lord. How does she use the Judge as an authority to lend credibility to her argument?

5. In paragraph 8, Bly announces that her proposed solution is "practical." Why do you think she makes a point of it being practical? Just how practical is her suggestion? What might be the advantages of making a practical proposal to help solve a problem of the kind Bly identifies?

6. Writers sometimes conclude an essay with a rhetorical device known as *framing,* returning to something mentioned in the beginning of the essay. How does Bly frame her essay? Why do you think framing is an especially effective way to end this proposal?

7. Can you think of a practical proposal to solve an important cultural or moral problem? Name a particular problem. What might you propose to solve this problem? How could your proposal be put into practice? How exactly would it help to solve the problem?

Commentary   Some readers of this proposal may question the relationship between Bly's solution and the problem she identifies. For a proposal to succeed, it must not only establish the problem clearly but also present a convincing argument that the proposed solution will actually help to alleviate the problem. When we understand that the problem Bly identifies is not the lack of interesting jobs or even the desire for profit, but rather the lack of any moral values apart from self-interest, then her solution begins to make sense. Bly is talking here about the need for a moral education, which she believes can be supplied, at least in part, through the study of literature.

Her argument assumes that literature holds up a mirror to human nature. The stories, plays, and poems we read tell us about ourselves and about human nature in general. As we consider a character's motives, for example, we reflect upon our own motives and the motives of those around us. In addition, literature frees us from our narrow self-interest, enabling us to transcend our own limiting experience.

But, as Bly argues, everything depends on how literature is read. That is why she insists on two conditions: that the course not teach techniques and that it emphasize rural literature. Bly opposes the teaching of technique because she believes it makes people look for the wrong thing. The New Criticism to which she refers sought to explain *how* a poem means as opposed to *what* it means; it emphasized the form and craft over ideas and feelings. Bly does not want the students to maintain this kind of critical distance, but to become involved in the works they read and to reflect on what their reading reveals about human experience. Her condition that the books relate to students' immediate experience makes it even easier for them to respond personally to their reading.

Bly presents her solution as a "practical suggestion." Her proposal for an Ag Lit course is feasible and specific. It can be easily implemented. She even recommends a reading list. The difficulty in this proposal is whether her suggested solution will in fact solve the problem. Whether such a course could actually raise moral consciousness is up to readers to decide because the argument depends on a causal connection that can be asserted but never really proven. As you prepare to write your own proposal, think carefully about how you might support your claim that the proposed solution actually will help alleviate the problem.

In our final selection, a college student proposes changes in the operation of a research project. She addresses her proposal to the research group leader—that is, to the very person who can best implement her suggestions. Unfortunately, this group leader is also the person most directly responsible for the problem this proposal sets out to correct.

Wendy Jo Niwa, the writer, is therefore faced with an awkward rhetorical situation: how to convince her reader of the seriousness of the problem without making him feel he is being criticized. As you read, notice how Niwa handles this delicate writing problem.

A PROPOSAL TO STRENGTHEN THE LANGUAGE ACQUISITION PROJECT

WENDY JO NIWA

Our present research project involving content analysis of mother-and-child 1 conversations has exciting possibilities. The data we have gathered thus far promise conclusions about some perplexing questions about language acquisition. However, we do not yet have an efficient system of analyzing the data and our progress is therefore quite slow. Many mistakes and inconsistencies occur because we lack specific criteria for counting mean length of utterances or for verifying or coding the transcripts. Too often, we decide how to do something only *after* the task has been completed. Consequently, we have to take time to recheck the transcripts once again, thus spending twice the time necessary on the task. Not only does this kind of disorganization jeopardize the validity and reliability of the study, but also it lowers the morale of everyone working on it. Students become frustrated, you have more to worry about, and everything takes more time than it should. Whereas we students suffer simply because our work on the project is less than satisfying, you have a lot to lose, as the disorganization could affect the quality of your dissertation. This is most unfortunate, for we have so much to learn from working with you—just as you have something to gain from any help we can give to your project.

One of the main causes of these problems is a lack of communication among 2 group members. Information and decisions concerning the transcripts are not always passed along, which results in disruptive and confusing inconsistency. Because we do not keep a record of important decisions, they are often forgotten. Confusion results. Without specific guidelines, we often find ourselves merely guessing, and individual biases are introduced into your work.

Some blame must be placed on the independent study program itself. Unfortunately, the Psychology Department has offered little guidance to any of us. Your focus is understandably on your project, and students' needs must come second. If we could get the Psychology Department to assume some oversight responsibility, students' educational needs could be better balanced with the project's needs. Perhaps they would show more interest in the program if they realized that our dissatisfaction may deter other students from participating in future research projects. 3

If these problems continue to be ignored, the result could be lower quality work. Misleading conclusions may be drawn from the study, or significant findings may fail to surface due to the inconsistency among student assistants. Should the findings become too inconsistent, they may not serve to support a conclusion. The research would then have failed. 4

Since you are the researcher and are the one most likely to be hurt by these problems, I am directing this proposal to you. I see several ways of improving the quality and effectiveness of our research program, ways that I feel sure would be beneficial to us all. I propose that we meet at least once a week for around an hour. At the meetings we could discuss any problems or questions we may have involving the transcripts and doublecheck procedures followed. Such meetings should promote much greater consistency and enable us to monitor progress and to plan for the next stage in the research. If there were no problems or business involving the project to discuss, we could use the time as a workshop to discuss relevant topics in the field. In this way, we would learn from your experience and expertise in developmental psychology. 5

To find a time when we could all attend such a meeting, we would each submit our class schedules and preferred meeting times. A meeting time convenient for everyone could then be chosen. In addition, a sign-up sheet could be posted in the lab for workshop presentations. Each student would be responsible for one workshop a month when he or she would summarize background reading on a chosen topic and prepare a short presentation on the topic. These topics would either concern our specific research project or developmental psychology in general. 6

We would keep a record of all plans and decisions made at the meetings. Responsibility for keeping this record would rotate. This record would be typed and made available to everyone in the lab. Surely such a record would be useful to you when you later must describe research procedures in your final paper. 7

There are several reasons why you should find my proposal valuable. First, these weekly meetings would only help eliminate any major inconsistencies and prevent other problems from occurring which might require us to go back and review the transcripts. Thus, time would be saved and the study would progress at a much faster pace. Second, the workshops should help to increase student enthusiasm for the project and therefore improve everyone's work. Third, keep- 8 ing a record of all decisions made would ensure that we all follow the same criteria rather than our own individual criteria, thus improving the reliability of your research. Also, putting the plans in print would help since all of us have a tendency to forget things when they are not written down. Best of all, this solution would be easy to implement.

You may be concerned that the meetings would interfere with our work on 9 the transcripts. I feel sure that the meetings would take less time than is used presently in going back over finished transcripts several times. Not only would our work be much more efficient if we discussed problems and issues together, but also we could get through many more transcripts if we were clearer on what we were doing. We could, however, meet outside of the ten hours we are required to work on the project.

You might think that we should have the meetings but not the workshops, 10 or that we should meet only to deal with the research and that if there are no problems, there should be no meetings. If all we do is work on transcripts, however, the independent study program will not be as valuable a learning experience as it might be. One of the purposes of the program is to give under-graduates a chance to learn from others who have more education, experience, and expertise. It is of course true that we could meet individually with you without having to organize a group. That would obviously require more time on your part, however, and would not solve the inconsistency problem in your project. Also, individual meetings may not be as productive as group meetings, since individuals tend to be stimulated by the exchange of ideas.

My proposal to have a group meeting once a week is the best way to solve 11 all of our problems at once. Besides being the most efficient and fair way, it would be easy to implement: All we need is an hour each week. The most important reason to accept this proposal, however, is that the final results of your study would be obtained sooner and the quality of your research would improve. The meetings would enhance group cohesiveness, which would facil-itate communication among members. Morale would be lifted and interest heightened as a result of the attention from you that we received in the work-shops.

Questions for analysis   1. Why do you think Niwa spends one third of the proposal (paragraphs 1–4) defining the problem? How exactly does she avoid blaming her reader and forge an alliance of common interests? Cite specific passages as examples.

2. Why do you suppose Niwa mentions the independent study program (paragraph 3)?

3. Niwa does not mention consulting with any other student assistants about either the problem or her proposed solution. How could this lapse affect the chances of her proposal being accepted? Suppose she had discussed her proposal with her colleagues: how could she have best made this known in the essay?

4. What objections or counterarguments does she anticipate? How does she handle them?

5. What alternative solutions does she discuss? What reasons does she give for rejecting them? Does she present any evidence in support of these reasons?

6. How does Niwa present herself in this essay? Point to specific places in the essay where you get a sense of her as a person. How would you describe her tone? Is it consistent throughout or does it change?

7. How does Niwa conclude her proposal? How does she avoid repeating herself?

8. Have you ever had occasion to write a proposal to solve a problem at school—in one of your classes, in your department, in your high school or college, in a lab, library, or other facility? Think of a particular problem you might propose a solution for. How would you go about trying to convince others of the importance of the problem? Would you address your proposal to the person able to resolve it (as Niwa does) or to those affected by the problem (as Bly does in the preceding selection)?

Commentary   Niwa does what all proposal writers must do: she builds a bridge of shared concerns between herself and her reader. This is essential if she has any hope of solving the problem. If she were to blame or even criticize the research group leader, he would be unlikely to respond positively to her proposal.

One obvious way Niwa forges an alliance between herself and the reader is by using the pronoun *we*. Instead of establishing an adversary *us* (the student assistants) against *you* (the group leader) relationship, she shows from the first sentence that she considers herself a partner with her reader, working together on an important research project.

She also shows her respect for her reader by indicating that she values the project. It is, after all, his dissertation project. Niwa makes it clear in the first paragraph that the problem she is writing about threatens the success of a project both she and her reader care a great deal about. Furthermore, she makes it seem that she regards him highly when she says that weekly workshops would be valuable because students could "learn from your experience and expertise" (paragraph 5).

PURPOSE AND AUDIENCE

More than any other kind of writing, proposals depend on the writer's anticipation of readers' needs and concerns—because most proposals are calls to action. They attempt not only to convince readers but also to inspire them, to persuade them to support or to put into effect the proposed solution. How you decide to construct your argumentative strategy will naturally depend on your understanding of the rhetorical situation in which you are writing. What your particular readers know about the problem and what they are capable of doing to solve it determines how you address them.

Readers of proposals are often unaware of the existence of the problem. In this case, your task is clear: present them with facts that will convince them of the problem's existence. These facts may include statistics as well as testimony from witnesses or experts. Example can be a particularly effective way of bringing home the reality of the problem to readers. You can also speculate about the causes of the problem and describe its ill effects.

Sometimes readers recognize the existence of a problem, but fail to take it seriously. When this is so, you may need to connect the problem directly to readers' own concerns. For instance, you might show how much they have in common with those directly affected by the problem. Or you might demonstrate how the problem affects them indirectly. However you connect to readers, you must do more than alert them to the problem; you must also make them care about it. You want to touch readers emotionally as well as intellectually.

There will be occasions when readers are aware of the problem but unaware of efforts to solve it. They may assume that someone else is taking care of the problem and that they need not become personally involved. Faced with this situation, you might want to show readers that those they thought were taking care of the problem have failed. Another assumption readers might make is that a solution they supported in the past has already solved the problem. You might point out that the original solution has proved unworkable or that new solutions have become available due to changed circumstances or improved technology. Your aim is to rekindle these readers' interest in the problem.

Many proposals are addressed to those who can take immediate action to remedy the problem. These are perhaps the most satisfying proposals to write. Your chances of writing such a proposal are good if you choose a problem faced by a group to which you belong. You not only understand the problem fully but can make practical suggestions that other members of the group will support. (You might informally survey others before you submit your proposal in order to test your definition of the problem and your proposed solution.) When you address readers who are in a position to take action, you obviously want to assure them that it is wise to do so. You must demonstrate that the solution is feasible, that it can be easily implemented without undue cost or effort, and that it will work.

BASIC FEATURES OF PROPOSALS

Effective proposals typically include the following features: a well-defined problem, a clear proposed solution, a convincing argument, and a reasonable tone.

A well-defined problem

Proposals are written to offer a solution to a problem. Before presenting the solution, a proposal writer must be sure that readers know what the problem is. Carol Bly spends the first eight paragraphs of her essay defining the problem, Wendy Jo Niwa the first four. All the writers in this chapter state the problem explicitly. Adam Paul Weisman identifies it as teenage pregnancy. David Owen explains that the solution—the SAT—has itself become the problem. Niwa describes a complex of problems: progress on the research is slow, tedious, and repetitive; mistakes and inconsistencies occur; student assistants are not learning what they hoped to.

Stating the problem is not enough, however: the writer must establish the fact that the problem indeed exists and that it is serious enough to need solving. Sometimes a writer may assume that the reader will recognize the problem. Niwa describes in detail problems on the research project, but does not give examples or statistical evidence because she knows her reader will not deny the problem's existence. She does argue for the problem's seriousness, though, pointing out potentially negative consequences her reader would be sure to take seriously.

Sometimes a writer is addressing readers who may not already be aware of the problem under consideration. Bly, for example, reminds readers how poor job prospects are for high school graduates and, therefore, how important it is for them to examine their basic values and needs.

In addition to stating the problem and establishing its existence and seriousness, a proposal writer must analyze the problem. It is necessary to examine the problem's causes and its consequences, its history and past efforts to deal with it. This information not only helps readers understand the problem, but it may also provide grounds for the proposed solution. When Owen explains that teachers design their curricula to prepare students for the test, he is setting the foundation for his proposal that AP-like essay exams be substituted for the multiple-choice SAT questions. In the same way, Niwa points out inconsistencies and delays that result from the lack of communication among researchers, laying the groundwork for her proposal to institute regular meetings.

A clear proposed solution

Once the problem is established, the writer presents and argues for a particular solution. As the writer's view of how the problem should be solved, this solution constitutes the thesis of the proposal. Weisman states his thesis thus: "Whatever the drawbacks, the contraception advocates have one strong advantage in this debate: their approach works." Owen places his thesis at the end: "The first step in creating both a humane admissions system and healthy secondary schools is as simple as shifting emphasis from the rewarding of 'aptitude' to the fostering of preparation."

A convincing argument

As an argument, the main purpose of a proposal is to convince readers that the writer's solution is the best way of solving the problem. Proposal writers argue for their solutions by demonstrating:

that the proposed solution will solve the problem

that it is a feasible way of solving the problem

that it is better than other ways of solving the problem

Arguing that the proposed solution will solve the problem. A writer must give reasons and evidence to show that the proposed solution will indeed solve the problem. Bly seems to assume that readers will immediately recognize how her proposed solution would solve the problem, asserting her solution with no discussion of how or why. Niwa, on the other hand, goes on to argue that her proposal would solve the problem by removing the cause (lack of communication). Owen points out that AP-like essay exams would cause teachers to alter the curriculum and that investing in disadvantaged high schools would make educational equality truly possible.

Arguing that the proposed solution is feasible. In arguing that the proposal is feasible, the writer must demonstrate how it can be implemented. The easier the proposed solution seems to implement, the more likely it is to win readers' support. Therefore, writers generally devote as much space as necessary to setting out the steps required to put the proposal into practice, an especially important strategy when the solution might seem difficult, time-consuming, or expensive to enact.

All the writers in this chapter offer specific suggestions for implementing their proposals. Niwa takes three paragraphs to discuss how her plan would be put into effect. Weisman points to an actual instance in which the proposal has been effectively implemented. By comparing his proposed essay test to the current AP program, Owen helps readers see how easy his proposal would be to implement. Bly offers a sample syllabus teachers could adopt for the course she proposes.

An important part of arguing that a proposal is feasible involves anticipating counterarguments. Counterarguments consist of any objections or reservations readers may have about the proposed solution. Weisman anticipates the counterargument that schools should not be used as "social service centers." He attempts to refute it by arguing that if birth-control information is banned from the schools, then teaching sexual abstinence must also be banned. Niwa allows that her reader might be concerned that meetings would actually take time away from research but argues against this counterargument by asserting that efficiency would be greatly increased, thus making time at meetings well spent. (Chapter 19: Arguing illustrates other ways writers anticipate counterarguments.)

Considering and rejecting alternative solutions. Finally, the writer has to convince readers that his or her solution is preferable to other solutions. This is done by examining alternative ways of solving the problem. Weisman considers the proposal that teenagers abstain from sexual activity. Niwa brings up one alternative after stating her own. Bly does not examine any alternatives, probably because no other practical solutions to this problem have been proposed.

The best way to reject an alternative solution is simply to demonstrate that it does not work, as Weisman tries to do. Another reason that might be offered is that the alternative solves only part of the problem. This is Niwa's strategy in rejecting the idea of individual instead of group meetings.

A reasonable tone   Regardless of the proposal or the argument made on its behalf, proposal writers must adopt a reasonable tone. The objective is to advance an argument without "having" an argument. That is, writers must never take an adversarial or quarrelsome stance with their readers. The aim is to bridge any gap that may exist between writer and readers, not widen it.

Writers build such a bridge of shared concerns by showing respect for readers and treating their concerns seriously. They discuss counterarguments as an attempt to lay to rest any doubts readers may have. They consider alternative solutions as a way of showing they have explored every possibility in order to find the best possible solution.

Most important, they do not criticize those raising counterarguments or offering other solutions. Never do they question anyone's intelligence or good will. Attacking people personally is called *argumentum ad hominem* (Latin for "argument against the man") and is considered a fallacy in arguing. (See Chapter 19: Arguing for information on fallacies.)

GUIDE TO WRITING

THE WRITING TASK

Write an essay proposing a solution to a particular problem. It should be one you are familiar with or can research. Choose a problem faced by a group to which you belong, and address your proposal either to one or more members of the group or to an outsider who might help solve the problem.

INVENTION AND RESEARCH

As you prepare to write a proposal, you will need to choose a problem you can write about, find a tentative solution to it, test your choice of problem and solution, identify your prospective readers, develop reasons for adopting your proposal rather than an alternative, and research any necessary information.

Choosing a problem to write about

One problem may come to mind immediately, and you may already have a solution for it. If not, you may want to think about various problems in various groups before settling on a topic.

If you have already made a choice, briefly describe the problem, explaining why it is a problem for you and others in your group. If you are not yet sure what problem you want to solve, the following listing activity should prove helpful.

Listing problems. Divide a piece of paper into two columns. In the left-hand column list three or four communities, groups, or organizations to which you belong, and in the right-hand column list two or three problems or conflicts existing within each group. Here is an example:

college	poor advising
	insufficient library hours
	noisy dorms
	too many required courses
soccer team	poor attendance at games
	disorganized coaches
	player disagreements
job	high employee turnover
	unsafe working conditions
	inefficient procedures
religious group	not enough youth activities
	insufficient support from church

Choosing an important problem. Choose a problem from your chart that you consider especially important. It should be one that seems solvable and that would concern others in the group. You should of course select a problem you can explore in detail—and one you are willing to discuss in writing.

Analyzing the problem. Think about the problem you have chosen. Start to analyze the problem by writing out answers to the following questions.

☐ Does the problem really exist? How serious is it? Will other members of the group agree that it is indeed serious?

☐ What caused the problem? Is it a new problem or an old one? Can I identify any immediate causes as well as any deeper causes?

☐ What bad effects might the problem cause? How is it hurting group members? Is it endangering any long-range goals of the group?

☐ Is it an ethical or moral problem—whether or not it has any bad consequences?

☐ Are there any other similar problems?

☐ Does the problem affect everyone in the group equally?

Finding a tentative solution Look at your analysis of the problem and think about your personal experience with it. Your analysis of the problem will probably lead you to possible solutions. If no solution is apparent, try the following creative problem-solving procedures.

Solving the problem. Creative problem solving generally involves looking at the problem in new ways. These activities should get you started. Write for around five minutes pursuing each possibility.

Solve one small aspect of the problem.

Find out how a comparable problem has been solved.

Develop a solution that eliminates one or more of the problem's causes.

Think of another way to categorize the problem.

Envision the problem in another medium or context.

Consider how another person you respect (someone you know personally or a historical or fictional figure) might solve the problem.

If you cannot think of an original solution, investigate ones that others have proposed. At some point, you will need to consider alternative solutions anyway and how they compare to your own. Remember that your solution does not have to be original, but it should be one you feel strongly about.

Solving problems takes time. Often the most imaginative solutions come only after we have struggled and given up. Be sure to give yourself enough time to let your ideas percolate.

Choosing the most promising solution. In a sentence or two state what you would consider the best possible way of solving the problem.

Listing specific steps. Write down each of the steps necessary to implement your solution.

Testing your choice Now you should examine the problem and solution you have selected to see whether they will result in a strong proposal. For guidance, ask yourself the following questions:

☐ Is this a significant problem? Do other people in the group really care about it, or can they be persuaded to care?

☐ Is my solution feasible? Will it really solve the problem? Can it be implemented?

As you plan and draft your proposal, you will probably want to consider these questions again and again. If at any point you decide that you cannot answer them affirmatively and confidently, you may want to choose a different problem to write about or find another solution.

Identifying your readers   You must decide whom you wish to address—everyone in the group, a committee, an individual, someone outside the group. Write down a few sentences describing your readers and stating your reason for directing your proposal to them.

Profiling your readers. Take ten minutes to write about your readers. Use these questions to stimulate your writing:

☐ How informed are they likely to be about the problem? Have they shown any awareness of it?

☐ Why would this problem be important to them? Why would they care about solving it?

☐ Have they offered or supported any proposals to solve the problem? If so, what do their proposals have in common with my proposal?

☐ Do they ally themselves with any particular group or philosophy that might cause them to favor or reject my proposal? Do we all share any values or attitudes that I could use as a bridge to bring us together to solve the problem?

☐ How have they responded to other problems? Can I infer anything from their reactions in the past that would suggest how they may respond to my proposal?

Talking with a reader. Imagine one reader, someone who would question your assessment of the problem or your tentative solution. If you have someone particular in mind, name that person. Try to imagine how he or she would react to your proposal. Write out a dialogue between the two of you, setting it up as Wendy Jo Niwa does (see the Writer at Work section at the end of this chapter). Imagine that there is some disagreement about your proposal—that is, assume you are forced to respond to questions or objections.

Take a minute to focus your thoughts. In two or three sentences, restate the problem and your proposed solution.

Defending your solution   Proposals have to be feasible—that is, they must be both reasonable and practical. Imagine that one of your readers opposes your proposed solution and confronts you with each of the following statements. Write several sentences refuting each one.

☐ It won't really solve the problem.

☐ We can't afford it.

☐ It will take too long.

☐ People won't do it.

☐ I don't even see how to get started on your solution.

☐ It's already been tried, with unsatisfactory results.

☐ You're making this proposal because it will benefit you personally.

Answering these questions now should help you to prepare responses to possible objections to your proposal. You may find that you need a better idea of how others are likely to feel about your proposal. You may want to talk to a few people involved. The more you know about your readers and their concerns, the better you will be able to anticipate any counterarguments they may offer or alternative solutions they might prefer.

Listing and developing reasons for adopting your proposal

To make a convincing case for your proposed solution you will need to offer your readers good reasons for adopting your proposal.

Listing reasons. Write down every plausible reason you could give that would persuade readers to accept your proposal. These reasons should be your answer to your readers' key question: "Why is this the best solution?" It might help to have a look at your writing from the preceding section. You should of course try to think of other reasons.

Choosing the strongest reasons. Keeping your readers in mind, look over your list and put an asterisk next to the best reasons. If you do not consider two or three of your reasons strong, you may anticipate difficulty developing a strong proposal and should reconsider your topic.

Developing your strongest reasons. Now look at these strongest reasons. Make a list of these reasons, explaining briefly why you think each one will be effective with your particular readers. Then take around five minutes to write about each reason, developing your argument on its behalf.

Comparing your solution to alternative solutions

Even if your readers are likely to consider your proposal reasonable, they will probably want to compare your proposed solution with other possible solutions. List several alternative solutions that might be offered by other members of the group, and consider the advantages and disadvantages of each one next to your solution. You might find it helpful to put together a chart like this:

Possible Solutions	Advantages	Disadvantages
[My solution]		
[Alternative Solution 1]		
[Alternative Solution 2]		
etc.		

Researching your proposal

Thus far you have relied upon your own knowledge, experience, and instincts for solving the problem. You may now feel that you need to know more. We have already suggested that you talk to potential readers in order to anticipate their counterarguments or alternative proposals. You might also want to discuss your solution with someone in the group; their questions and objections can tell you a great deal.

You may also need to do some further research: to learn more about the causes of the problem, perhaps, or to find more technical information about implementing the solution. Now is a good time—before beginning to draft—to get any additional information you need. (See Chapter 21 for guidelines on library research.)

PLANNING AND DRAFTING

To help you plan your essay and begin drafting, review what you have discovered about your topic, prepare an outline, and set some specific goals for yourself.

Seeing what you have

Reread your invention writings now, asking yourself whether you have a good topic—an interesting problem with a feasible solution. If at this point you are doubtful about the significance of the problem or unsure about the potential success of your proposed solution, you might want to look for a new topic. If your invention sequence is still weak, you cannot really expect to be able to produce a rich, persuasive draft.

If your invention material seems thin but promising, you may be able to strengthen it with additional writing. Consider the following questions in trying to fill out your writing:

☐ Could I make a stronger case for the seriousness of the problem?

☐ Could I find more reasons for readers to support my solution?

☐ Are there any other ways of refuting attractive alternative solutions or troubling counterarguments?

Setting goals

Before you actually begin your draft, you should think seriously about the overall goals of your proposal. Not only will the draft be easier to write once you have established clear goals, but it will almost surely be stronger and more convincing.

Following are goal-setting questions to consider now. You may find it useful to return to them while you are drafting, for they are designed to help you to focus on what exactly you want to accomplish with this proposal.

Your readers

☐ What do my readers already know about this problem?

☐ Are they likely to welcome my solution or resist it?

☐ Can I anticipate any specific reservations or objections they may have?

☐ How can I gain readers' enthusiastic support? How can I get them to help me implement the solution?

☐ What kind of tone would be most appropriate? How can I present myself so that I seem both reasonable and authoritative?

The beginning

☐ How can I begin so as to immediately engage my readers' interest? Shall I open with a personal anecdote or a dramatic one? Shall I begin by stating something surprising, as Bly does? Or should I open my proposal as Niwa does, by commenting on something positive before announcing the problem?

☐ What information should I give first?

Defining the problem

☐ Is this a problem people know about, or is it relatively unknown?

☐ How much do I need to say about its causes or history?

☐ How can I establish the seriousness of the problem?

☐ Is it an urgent problem? How can I emphasize this?

☐ How much space should I devote to defining the problem?

Proposing a solution

☐ How should I state my thesis? When should I announce it explicitly?

☐ How can I make the solution seem easy to implement? Can I present the first step so that it looks easy to take?

☐ How can I present my solution so that it looks like the best way to proceed?

Rejecting alternative solutions

☐ How many alternative solutions should I mention? Which ones should I discuss?

☐ Should I indicate where these alternatives come from? Should I name those who proposed them?

☐ How can I reject these other solutions without seeming to criticize their proponents?

☐ What reasons should I give for rejecting the alternative solutions? Can I offer any evidence in support of my reasons?

Refuting counterarguments

☐ Should I mention every possible counterargument to my proposed solution? How might I choose among them?

☐ Has anyone already proposed these counterarguments? If so, should I name the person in my proposal?

☐ How can I refute the counterarguments without criticizing anyone?

☐ What specific reasons can I give for refuting each counterargument? How can I support these reasons?

Avoiding logical fallacies

☐ Will I be committing an *either/or* fallacy by presenting my solution as the only possible solution: either mine or nothing? Can I ignore any of the likely alternative solutions?

☐ Can I present other proposed solutions in such a way that they are easily rejected without being accused of building a *straw man*? (A straw man is easy to push over.)

☐ How can I show my readers that I have *accepted the burden of proof*? Can I make a comprehensive argument for my proposed solution? Will readers feel that it is one they should accept?

☐ If I discuss the causes of the problem, can I avoid the fallacy of *oversimplified cause*? Have I identified significant causes, or are some of them minor contributing causes? Have I accounted for all of the major causes?

☐ How can I argue reasonably against other possible solutions? Can I criticize other proposals without attacking the people involved and thus committing the *ad hominem* (Latin for "to the man") fallacy?

The ending

☐ How should the proposal end? Shall I end with a practical plan, as Bly does? Or should I simply end by summarizing my solution and restating its advantages?

☐ Is there something special about the problem itself I should remind readers of at the end?

☐ Should I end with an inspiring call to action or a scenario suggesting the dreaded consequences of a failure to solve the problem?

☐ Would a shift to humor or satire be an effective way to end?

Outlining the proposal

The basic outline for a proposal is quite simple:

> the problem
>
> the solution
>
> the reasons for accepting the solution

This simple plan is nearly always complicated by other factors, however. In outlining your material you must take into consideration many other details: whether readers already recognize the problem, how much agreement exists on the need to solve the problem, how many alternative solutions are available, how much attention must be given to the other solutions, and how many counterarguments should be expected.

A possible outline for a proposal where readers may be unlikely to fully understand the problem and where other solutions have been proposed might look like this:

> presentation of the problem
>
> demonstration that the problem exists and is serious
>> causes of the problem
>
> consequences of failing to solve the problem
>
> description of the proposed solution
>
> list of steps for implementing the solution
>
> discussion of reasons to support the solution
>> acknowledgment of counterarguments
>> accommodation or refutation of counterarguments
>
> consideration of alternative solutions and statement of their disadvantages
>
> restatement of the proposed solution and its advantages

Your outline will of course reflect your own writing situation. As you develop an outline, think about what your readers know and feel. Concentrate on your own purpose and writing goals. Once you have a working outline, you should not hesitate to change it as necessary while writing. For instance, you might find it more effective to hold back on presenting your own solution until you have dismissed other possible solutions. Or you might find a better way to order the reasons for adopting your proposal as you draft. The purpose of an outline is to identify the basic features of your proposal, as the preceding example shows. Most of the information you will need to develop each feature can be found in your invention writing and research notes.

How much space you devote to each feature is determined by the topic, not the outline. Do not assume that each entry on your outline must be given one paragraph—in the preceding example, each of the reasons for supporting the solution may require a paragraph, but you might also discuss the reasons, counterarguments, and refutations all in one paragraph. The length of a proposal depends upon the topic. The important thing is that the proposal be coherently organized, and an outline helps you to do so.

Drafting the proposal   Before you consider the advice here about drafting a proposal, you might want to review the general advice on drafting in Chapter 1. Then review your outline. Let it help you write your proposal, but don't hesitate to change it if you find that drafting takes you in an unexpected direction. If you are really stuck, return to one of the invention activities to get yourself going again. You could explore the problem more fully, examine your readers once again, think about the advantages and disadvantages of your solution or reconsider alternate solutions, strengthen your defense against counter-arguments, or try to come up with still more reasons for adopting your solution.

As you draft, keep in mind the two main goals of proposal writing: (1) to establish that a problem exists that is serious enough to require a solution; and (2) to demonstrate that your proposed solution is feasible and is the best possible alternative.

READING A DRAFT WITH A CRITICAL EYE

At this point you are ready to have someone else read your draft with a critical eye. You may have the opportunity to read a classmate's draft in the same way.

A close reading of a proposal has three steps: reading quickly for a general impression, pointing to strengths and weaknesses in the writing, and analyzing the effectiveness of the proposal. (Before you begin, you might want to review the general advice on reading another's draft critically in Chapter 1.)

First general impression   Read the essay straight through to get a general impression. Put yourself in the position of a member of the group to whom the proposal is addressed. Try to assume the concerns of the group, and consider the proposal as if its suggestions were to affect you personally.

After this first reading, tell the writer how you understand the problem, whether it seems serious to you, and whether you would support the proposed solution.

Pointings   As you read, highlight noteworthy features with *pointings,* a simple system of lines and brackets that is especially useful for revising a draft. Use this system as follows:

☐ Draw a straight line under any words or images that seem especially effective: strong verbs, specific details, memorable phrases, striking images.

☐ Draw a wavy line under any words or images that sound flat, stale, or vague. Also put the wavy line under any words or phrases that you consider unnecessary or repetitious.

☐ Look for pairs or groups of sentences that you think should be combined. Put brackets [ ] around these sentences.

☐ Look for sentences that are garbled, overloaded, or awkward. Put parentheses ( ) around these sentences. Parenthesize any sentence that seems even slightly questionable; don't worry now about whether or not it is actually incorrect. The writer needs to know that you, as one reader, had even the slightest hesitation about reading a sentence, even on first reading.

Analysis The following questions will help you analyze the parts of the proposal and evaluate their effectiveness.

1. Evaluate the definition of the problem. Has the writer given enough information about its causes and consequences? Tell the writer if there is anything more you wish to know about the problem.

2. Restate in your own words the proposed solution. Is it clear? Look at the reasons in support of this solution—are they sufficient? Which are the most convincing reasons offered? Which are the least convincing ones? Why?

3. Look closely at the steps for implementing the proposal. Do they tell you everything you need to know? If not, ask specific questions to let the writer see what additional information a reader needs to know. Does the solution seem practical? If not, why not?

4. Consider the treatment of objections or counterarguments to the proposed solution. Point out any other counterarguments the writer may have missed. Cite the reasons and evidence refuting counterarguments that you found the most convincing. Indicate also which was the least convincing, and why.

5. Does the writer discuss any alternative solutions? If not, should any be mentioned? If any are mentioned, does the writer argue against them effectively? What are the most convincing reasons given against these other solutions? Which are least convincing, and why?

6. Consider the balance. Are the key features treated adequately and fairly? Or is there too much of one thing and too little of another? Perhaps there is too much attention given to alternative solutions, too little to counterarguments. Point out any elements that need more or less emphasis, and explain why.

7. Evaluate the beginning. Is it at all engaging? Did it capture your attention? Does it forecast the main ideas and alert the reader to the plan of the proposal? Should it? See if you can suggest other ways to begin.

8. Evaluate the ending. Does it frame the proposal? If not, how might it do so? Can you suggest a stronger conclusion?

9. Describe the tone of the proposal. Does it seem appropriate for its readers? Is it consistent from beginning to end? Point out any inconsistencies.

10. What final comments or suggestions can you offer to the writer? What is the strongest part of this proposal? What most needs additional work?

REVISING AND EDITING

You are now ready to revise your draft. Before considering the following specific suggestions for revising a proposal, you might want to refer to the plan for revising described in Chapter 11. Follow this revising plan until you reach the section Read Again To Identify Problems. At this point, you can substitute these specific suggestions for the general ones in Chapter 11.

Revising a proposal   Consider any advice you may have from other readers as you reread your draft and make plans for revision. If you can, you might have someone else read the draft to help you solve any particularly difficult problems. For example, if you are having trouble refuting one alternative solution, you might see if someone else can help.

Look now at the following tips on revising proposals.

Revising to strengthen the argument

☐ Reconsider your definition of the problem. Is it complete, or would it be stronger with more information? Should you add anything about its causes or potential dangers? Have you articulated its seriousness?

☐ Scrutinize your solution as closely as possible. Have you shown it to be both feasible and superior to all other possible solutions?

☐ Reread your argument with your readers in mind. Have you fully considered their experience and expectations, fears and biases? Think of all the factions within the group—does your argument appeal to them all? Should it?

☐ Look carefully at each part of your argument. Could you strengthen your proposal by rearranging these parts?

Revising for readability

☐ Are there any places where you tell readers more than they need to know? Less than they need to know?

☐ Reconsider your beginning. Would another beginning engage readers more quickly?

☐ Reconsider your ending. Does the proposal end gracefully and emphatically? Is the ending likely to appeal to your readers? Does it emphasize what you want it to?

☐ Look carefully at each sentence. Does it say what you want it to say? Does it repeat something said in the previous sentence? Does it state the obvious?

☐ Improve the flow of your writing by strengthening connections between sentences and paragraphs. See whether any sentences should be combined or separated into two sentences.

Editing and proofreading   As you revise a draft for the final time, you need to edit it closely. Though you probably corrected obvious errors in the drafting stage, usage and style were not your first priority. Now, however, you must find and correct any errors of mechanics, usage, punctuation, or style.

After you have edited the draft and produced the final copy, be sure to proofread carefully before turning in your essay.

LEARNING FROM YOUR OWN WRITING PROCESS

Take time now to look over all the work you have done on your proposal. Start with your invention materials—what was easiest? what was hardest? Did the readings influence your invention and drafting in any way? What difficulties did you encounter while you were drafting? How did you solve them?

Consider your final draft. What changes did you make from draft to revision? Did other readers' comments affect the final version? Look at specific changes you made, and explain why you made them.

What do you consider best about your proposal? What would you like to improve if you had still more time?

A WRITER AT WORK

ANALYZING THE READERS OF A PROPOSAL

One of the most important tasks facing all proposal writers is to analyze their prospective readers. Before beginning to write, they need to know who their readers will be, what they can be expected to know about the problem, and how they are likely to respond to the proposed solution. This section will examine how Wendy Jo Niwa went about analyzing her readers before drafting her proposal to improve a research project. (Niwa's final draft appears earlier in this chapter.)

Niwa began by deciding who she wanted her readers to be. Initially she had considered addressing her proposal to the other students on the project, but she decided they already agreed with her and could not do anything about the problem anyway. She also considered sending it to the Psychology Department, but she thought that would merely cause trouble for the group leader. Finally she realized that the most obvious choice was the group leader himself, since he was the only one who would have reason or power to implement her proposal.

Once she had identified who her reader would be, Niwa was able to plan her proposal with the sure knowledge that he was aware of the problem. She was not sure, however, why he did nothing to try to solve it himself. In one of her invention activities, Niwa wrote, "I guess he's just too busy handling problems as they come up and taking care of other parts of the project. He's probably too involved to see what needs to be done. Or maybe he's lazy. I don't think he realizes how bored and frustrated we all are."

Niwa spent a good deal of time on one invention activity, Talking with a Reader. Constructing an imaginary dialogue with the group leader helped her to know what material to include in her proposal. She worked out a plan to implement the proposal, anticipated her reader's counterarguments and figured out how to refute them, and found a way to bridge her own and her reader's concerns.

Because this invention activity was so productive for Niwa, it is printed here in its entirety.

NIWA: I think we should all meet together in a group at least once a week on a set day at a set time. We need to discuss difficulties we may be having with the transcripts, share knowledge, check progress.

READER: How are we going to find a time which will accommodate everyone?

NIWA: All we have to do is write down our schedules and preferred times to meet. We can choose a day and time from these lists.

READER: But this will cut into the time usually used for work—this project needs to get done!

NIWA: If everyone agrees, we can meet outside of the 10 hours per week required of us on the project. However, I bet that a one-hour meeting as a group will take less time than we now spend discussing difficulties among ourselves. Our work would be much more efficient if we discussed and cleared up problems all at once. We could get through a lot more transcripts if we were clearer on what we were doing.

READER: If there are no problems with transcripts, won't the time be wasted?

NIWA: No. We students are anxious to gain as much as possible from your experience. We could use the time to discuss topics of interest, research which is relevant to yours.

READER: What if no one has anything to discuss?

NIWA: We can make a schedule of tentative topics to discuss, and can take turns preparing brief presentations to guide discussion.

READER: What if the others are not willing to go along with your idea?

NIWA: If you make it a part of the requirement they will. Besides, many have already stated that they would be more than willing to put in extra effort and time.

READER: Why should I put in the extra time?

NIWA: I think you have an obligation to the students. Also it would be in your best interests. Correlations may be found which wouldn't have been had we not been consistent. Also your dissertation may be pushed along at a quicker pace.

READER: What type of organization are you talking about?

NIWA: Decide on whether each of us will be responsible for a different task or all working on the same task. A goal would make the work seem less tedious, morale would be lifted, and we'd all feel less frustration. By not staying on one task too long we'll all avoid getting burned out.

READER: What's wrong with the way it is now?

NIWA: Many students are frustrated, dissatisfied. The criteria is not well established. By trial and error, we end up spending twice as much time on a single task because we're always having to go back and redo it. We should establish the criteria clearly before we start work, not after.

Niwa concludes this section by restating the problem and her solution to it. Analyzing her reader helped her to clarify her goals in writing the proposal. She realized it was important not only to reduce boredom and frustration, but also to learn something from the group leader and from other students. Most of all, her imaginary conversation with the group leader made her appreciate how hard she would have to work to convince him.

Making Evaluations

In an article about the upcoming Rose Bowl game, a reporter for the *Los Angeles Times* evaluates the two competing Pacific Ten and Big Ten teams. She predicts victory for the Pacific Ten team, contending that it has a better-balanced offense as well as more depth and experience at each position. As support for her prediction, the reporter names several specific players and mentions some key plays from earlier games. To refute the likely counterargument that the Pacific Ten team won fewer games, she argues that it played a much tougher schedule than the Big Ten team.

The president of a large computer corporation writes a letter recommending one of his employees for an upper-level management position at another company. He praises her judgments, energy, and interpersonal skills, mentioning several incidents as support for his claims. He describes in detail her contributions to several specific projects.

A *Skiing* reporter writes an article evaluating two popular slalom skis. He assumes his audience to be made up of experienced downhill skiers who may not have actually done any slalom racing. Using one technical criterion, design, he argues that one make of ski is superior to the other. He cites specific differences in waist width, sidecut radius, camber, and shovel stiffness as support for his judgment.

In a column syndicated to college newspapers, a writer reviews two newly revised paperback thesauri. Both are selling well in college bookstores. The reporter compares the two on the criteria of size, price, and usefulness. The criterion of usefulness leads to further comparisons of format and specific sample entries. She concludes by recommending one thesaurus over the other.

For her senior thesis, a political science major evaluates a state senator whom she dislikes and distrusts. After researching the senator's legislative activities and voting record, she decides that the best criteria for evaluating a senator are three: responsibility in carrying out his legislative duties, voting record in support of public programs, and willingness to educate the voters on important issues. These criteria provide adequate support for her negative judgment: the senator is often absent for important votes, he votes consistently against antipoverty bills, and he makes little effort to provide his constituents with news about important issues. She documents each of these reasons—and all the others in her paper—with specific evidence gathered in her research. At several points in the paper she contrasts the senator's activities and voting record with the records of other state senators.

8

□ A mid-term exam for a literature course includes two poems by John Updike that the students are unlikely to have seen before. They are to decide which is the better poem and write an essay explaining why. Evaluating the poems according to criteria he learned in the class, one student argues that one is better because its rhythms are less predictable and more conversationlike and also because its imagery is more visual and hence more memorable. He provides several examples from the poems in support of each reason.

We all make judgments many times each day. We make evaluations spontaneously, in response to events, people, things. In everyday conversation we often state our evaluations without thorough justification or development. Rarely do we think out a reasoned, detailed argument based on appropriate criteria, although we constantly give reasons for our evaluations in a casual way. By contrast, we expect judgments stated in writing to be authoritative and persuasive. We expect a planned, coherent, reasoned argument. We assume the writer knows enough to use appropriate standards of evaluation, and we expect the argument based on these standards to be supported with reasons, evidence, and examples.

Evaluations are basic to thinking, learning, and writing. They underlie all types of argument, forming with cause-and-effect analysis the basic building blocks of argument. As a college student, you may be asked to write evaluations of books, art works, research reports, scientific discoveries, current events, or major contributions and contributors to your field of study. If your college has a system of student course evaluations (most do), you will regularly evaluate your instructors. On the job, you will be evaluated and will eventually evaluate others for promotions, awards, or new jobs. You will also be asked to evaluate various plans and proposals, and your success at these important writing tasks will in large part determine how quickly and how high you are promoted. In a more general and fundamental way, studying and writing evaluations contributes to your intellectual development. You learn to define the criteria that provide the standards for judging any subject you write about. You also learn to develop a reasoned argument, selecting evidence that will support your evaluation.

Your purpose in writing evaluations is to convince readers that you have made an informed judgment. You may want to convince them that a particular movie is worth seeing, the campus student health service poorly organized, a research report in your major field seriously flawed, a competitor's product brilliantly innovative, an applicant for a management position not the person to hire. In these and innumerable other writing situations in college and on the job, you must establish your authority and credibility in order to win the trust of your readers. You do that essentially by basing your judgment on appropriate criteria, demonstrating that your judgment is informed or educated, not simply personal or prejudicial. In addition to appropriate criteria, you must also provide convincing reasons supported by evidence. This evidence comes from a thorough analysis of your subject, an analysis that ensures a detailed and comprehensive understanding.

This chapter is designed to help you write an authoritative, convincing essay of evaluation. It is the third chapter of the five chapters in this book that are devoted to persuasive writing. Each of these chapters places you in a well-defined writing situation, requiring you to develop a special argumentative strategy; yet each situation shares characteristics common to all forms of argument: making claims and supporting them for particular readers in order to build a convincing argument. (All these common characteristics are illustrated fully in Chapter 19: Arguing.) The readings that follow will give you an idea of the specific strategies used by writers of evaluations.

READINGS

One of the most common forms of written evaluations is reviews—of movies, books, restaurants, vacation resorts, plays, concerts. Reviewers help us to decide where to go out for dinner, what movies to see, which novels to read.

The first essay is a review of a classic American movie, *The Treasure of the Sierra Madre*. Published in 1948, soon after the movie appeared, the review was written by James Agee. Agee was for many years a celebrated film critic for *The Nation;* in 1944 W. H. Auden called his reviews "the most remarkable regular event in American journalism today." He is best known for his novel *A Death in the Family,* for which he was posthumously awarded the Pulitzer Prize in 1958.

As you read Agee's review, pay close attention to the way he argues for his judgment that *The Treasure of the Sierra Madre* is an outstanding movie.

THE TREASURE OF THE SIERRA MADRE

JAMES AGEE

Several of the best people in Hollywood grew, noticeably, during their years 1 away at war; the man who grew most impressively, I thought, as an artist, as a man, in intelligence, in intransigence, and in an ability to put through fine work against difficult odds, was John Huston, whose *San Pietro* and *Let There Be Light* were full of evidence of this many-sided growth. I therefore looked forward with the greatest eagerness to the work he would do after the war.

His first movie since the war has been a long time coming, but it was certainly 2 worth waiting for. *The Treasure of the Sierra Madre* is Huston's adaptation of B. Traven's novel of the same title. It is not quite a completely satisfying picture, but on the strength of it I have no doubt at all that Huston, next only to Chaplin, is the most talented man working in American pictures, and that this is one of the movie talents in the world which is most excitingly capable of still further growth. *The Treasure* is one of very few movies made since 1927 which I am sure will stand up in the memory and esteem of qualified people alongside the best of the silent movies. And yet I doubt that many people will fully realize, right away, what a sensational achievement, or plexus of achievement, it is. You will seldom see a good artist insist less on his artistry; Huston merely tells his story so straight and so well that one tends to become absorbed purely in that; and the story itself—a beauty—is not a kind which most educated people value nearly enough, today.

This story and Huston's whole handling of it are about as near to folk art as 3 a highly conscious artist can get; both also approach the global appeal, to the most and least sophisticated members of an audience, which the best poetic drama and nearly all the best movies have in common. Nominally an adventure story, this is really an exploration of character as revealed in vivid action; and character and action yield revelations of their own, political, metaphysical, moral, above all, poetic. The story unfolds so pleasurably on the screen that I will tell as little as possible of it here. Three American bums of the early 1920s (Walter Huston, Humphrey Bogart, Tim Holt) run into lottery luck in Tampico and strike into the godforsaken mountains of Mexico in search of gold. The rest of the story merely demonstrates the development of their characters in relation to hardship and hard work, to the deeply primitive world these modern primitives are set against, to the gold they find, and to each other. It is basically a tragic story and at times a sickeningly harsh one; most of it is told as cheerfully brutal sardonic comedy.

This may be enough to suggest how rich the story is in themes, semi-symbols, 4 possible implications, and potentialities as a movie. Huston's most wonderful single achievement is that he focuses all these elements as simply as rays in a burning-glass: all you see, unless you look sharp, is a story told so truly and masterfully that I suspect the picture's best audience is the kind of men the picture is about, who will see it only by chance.

But this single achievement breaks down into many. I doubt we shall ever 5 see a film more masculine in style; or a truer movie understanding of character and of men; or as good a job on bumming, a bum's life, a city as a bum sees it; or a more beautiful job on a city; or a finer portrait of Mexico and Mexicans (compare it with all the previous fancy-filter stuff for a definitive distinction between poetry and poeticism); or a crueler communication of absolute deso-lateness in nature and its effect on men (except perhaps in *Greed*); or a much more vivid communication of hardship, labor, and exhaustion (though I wish these had been brutally and meticulously presented rather than skillfully sketched); or more intelligent handling of amateurs and semi-professionals (no-tably the amazing character who plays Gold-Hat, the bandit leader); or a finer selective eye for location or a richer understanding of how to use it; or scenes of violence or building toward violence more deeply authentic and communi-cative (above all in Huston's terrific use of listlessness); or smarter casting than that of Tim Holt as the youngest bum and that of Bruce Bennett as an intrusive Texan; or better acting than Walter Huston's beautiful performance; or subtler and more skillful collusions and variations of tempo (two hours have certainly never been better used in a movie); or a finer balance, in Ted McCord's perfect camera work, in every camera set-up, in every bit of editing, of unaffectedness, and sensitiveness. (As one fine example of that blend I recommend watching for the shot of Gold-Hat reflected in muddy water, which is so subtly photographed that in this noncolor film the hat seems to shed golden light.) There is not a shot-for-shot's sake in the picture, or one too prepared-looking, or dwelt on too long. The camera is always where it ought to be, never imposes on or exploits or over-dramatizes its subject, never for an instant shoves beauty or special meaning at you. This is one of the most visually alive and beautiful movies I have ever seen; there is a wonderful flow of fresh air, light, vigor, and liberty through every shot, and a fine athlete's litheness and absolute control and flexibility in every succession and series of shots. Huston shows that he is already capable of literally anything in movies except the profoundest kind of movie inventiveness, the most extreme kind of poetic concentration, artiness, soft or apathetic or sloppy or tasteless or excessive work, and rhetoric whether good or bad. His style is practically invisible as well as practically universal in its possible good uses; it is the most virile movie style I know of; and is the purest style in contemporary movies, here or abroad.

I want to say a little more about Walter Huston; a few thousand words 6 would suit me better. Rightly or wrongly, one thing that adds to my confidence that the son, so accomplished already, will get better and better, is the fact that the father has done that, year after year. I can think of nothing more moving or happier than every instance in which an old man keeps right on learning, and working, and improving, as naturally and eagerly as a child learns the fundamentals of walking, talking, and everything else in sight until his parents and teachers destroy his appetite for learning. Huston has for a long time been one of the best actors in the world and he is easily the most likable; on both counts this performance crowns a lifetime. It is an all but incredible submergence in a role, and transformation; this man who has credibly played Lincoln looks small and stocky here, and is as gaily vivacious as a water bug. The character is beautifully conceived and written, but I think it is chiefly Walter Huston who gives it its almost Shakespearean wonderfulness, charm, and wisdom. In spite of the enormous amount of other talent at large in the picture, Huston carries the whole show as deftly and easily as he handles his comedy lines.

There are a few weaknesses in the picture, most of which concern me so 7 little I won't even bother to mention them. Traven's Teutonic or Melvillean excitability as a poet and metaphysician sometimes, I think, misleads him—and John Huston; magnificently as Walter Huston does it, and deeply as he anchors it in flesh and blood, the Vast Gale of Purifying Laughter with which he ends the picture strikes me as unreal, stuck-onto-the-character, close to arty; yet I feel tender toward this kind of cliché, if I'm right that it is one. One thing I do furiously resent is the intrusion of background-music. There is relatively little of it and some of it is better than average, but there shouldn't be any, and I only hope and assume that Huston fought the use of it. The only weakness which strikes me as fundamental, however, is deep in the story itself: it is the whole character of the man played by Bogart. This is, after all, about gold and its effects on those who seek it, and so it is also a fable about all human life in this world and about much of the essence of good and evil. Many of the possibilities implicit in this fable are finely worked out. But some of the most searching implications are missed. For the Bogart character is so fantastically undisciplined and troublesome that it is impossible to demonstrate or even to hint at the real depth of the problem, with him on hand. It is too easy to feel that if only a reasonably restrained and unsuspicious man were in his place, everything would be all right; we wouldn't even have wars. But virtually every human being carries sufficient of that character within him to cause a great deal of trouble, and the demonstration of that fact, and its effects, could have made a much greater tragicomedy—much more difficult, I must admit, to dramatize. Bogart does a wonderful job with this character as written (and on its own merits it is quite a character), miles ahead of the very good work he has done before. The only trouble is that one cannot quite forget that this is Bogart putting on an unbelievably good act. In all but a few movies one would thank God for that large favor. In this one it stands out, harmfully to some extent, for everything else about the picture is selfless.

It seems worth mentioning that the only thing which holds this movie short 8 of unarguable greatness is the failure of the story to develop some of the most important potentialities of the theme. In other words, "Hollywood," for once, is accountable only for some minor flaws. This is what it was possible to do in Hollywood, if you were talented enough, had standing enough, and were a good enough fighter, during the very hopeful period before the November Freeze. God knows what can be done now. But if anybody can hope to do anything, I count on Huston, who made *San Pietro* and *Let There Be Light* as an army officer and *The Treasure of the Sierra Madre* as a Hollywood writer-director.

Questions for analysis

1. Agee describes John Huston as a "highly conscious artist" and praises *The Treasure of the Sierra Madre* for being an exploration of character and not simply an adventure movie. How do you react to the idea that movies are works of art with political, moral, and even poetic qualities? Is this possible? How is it true or not true of any movies you have seen recently?

2. Agee gives many reasons why he likes the movie. Some reasons he merely mentions, but others he develops with specific illustrations from the movie. What are those reasons? (Skim the review, listing each reason briefly in a phrase.) Which are mentioned, and which are developed? Why do you suppose Agee chooses to develop the ones he does?

3. Film critics nearly always draw comparisons between movies. What comparisons does Agee make? Would further comparisons strengthen the review? If so, what kinds of comparisons would you like to have seen?

4. Agee wrote this review after the movie was released. Because readers of such reviews must be assumed to be unfamiliar with the movie, the writer must describe it before evaluating it, yet without telling any more than he has to. What does Agee choose to summarize from the movie? Where does he place this summary? How much space does he devote to it?

5. In paragraph 7, Agee points out some of the movie's weaknesses. Why do you think he mentions its weaknesses? How does paragraph 7 affect your response to the review?

6. How does Agee begin and end his review? How effective do you find this beginning and ending?

7. What recent movie would you like to review in writing? How would you evaluate this movie? On what criteria important to judging films would you base your review? What reasons and evidence would you offer in support of your judgment?

Commentary   Agee's review has all the features we expect of an evaluation: a firm judgment based on appropriate criteria, reasons and evidence in support of the judgment, some description of the subject, and comparisons to similar things.

The thesis in an evaluation essay is simply the statement asserting the writer's judgment. Usually it is repeated in several ways throughout the essay. In paragraph 2, Agee states his thesis in an unmistakable way: he says the movie is "a sensational achievement" and predicts it will become a classic.

Evaluation essays have one special requirement: the writer must first decide on criteria, or standards, as a basis for judgment. The specific reasons and evidence supporting the writer's judgment derive from these criteria. Agee, for example, judges *The Treasure of the Sierra Madre* on the criteria of story line, theme, unity, cinematography, acting, and direction. The following table shows these criteria along with the specific reasons Agee gives to support his judgment:

Criteria: Reasons
story line: a masterfully told story
theme: a story rich in implications
unity: well-focused elements
cinematography: excellent camera work; skillful film editing
acting: excellent acting
direction: effective use of locations; director's style "invisible," "universal," and "virile"

Because Agee uses widely recognized criteria for evaluating movies, he does not define or justify his criteria because he knows they are shared by all moviegoers. In other situations, however, a writer might need to explain and justify criteria. For example, in an essay evaluating a teacher, a writer might first need to establish criteria for evaluating teachers. Whereas most people agree readily on appropriate criteria for evaluating movies, there exists no clear consensus about what makes a good teacher.

Notice that for some of Agee's criteria there is a one-to-one match with his reasons for judging the film so positively. For example, the movie criterion of "story line" underlies his reason "a masterfully told story." Some of his criteria, however, underlie more than one reason. For example, the criterion "cinematography" underlies the two reasons "excellent camera work" and "skillful film editing." When two or more reasons derive from a single criterion, then the concept of criteria becomes essential in analyzing evaluations. The concept enables readers to classify (or group) the reasons supporting the judgment and to analyze the *basis* of the writer's reasoning. When you plan your own essay of evaluation, you will want to list the criteria appropriate to judging your subject. Like Agee, you may not need to educate readers about your standards for judging your subject or convince them of the appropriateness of your criteria. You will still find that listing your criteria and thinking critically about appropriate standards for judging your subject will give you much greater confidence in developing your argument.

Often it is necessary to choose among many criteria; usually, writers will do so with their readers in mind. If Agee had reviewed the film for filmmakers, for example, rather than general moviegoers, he might have been concerned solely with cinematography, concentrating the whole review on camera work, editing and cutting, sound track, and quality of film stock.

It might be said that education is largely a matter of learning the criteria appropriate for judging any subject. For example, in psychology you learn how to evaluate educational practices or proposals for self-improvement. In biology you acquire standards for evaluating the usefulness and safety of diets, exercise regimens, and proposals for a cleaner environment and better health care. In a writing course like the one in which you are using this text, you learn how to evaluate many kinds of writing—autobiography, profiles, reports, and arguments. Learning cultivates judgment, making it sounder, more discriminating, less reckless, not merely "judgmental." When the writing situation requires it, such learning enables you to go beyond the reaction "I just happen to like it" or "Oh, I don't know—I just think it's a good idea."

Finally, Agee's review illustrates a very important component in all evaluative writing: a clear argumentative strategy. An argumentative strategy arises from a writer's purpose, subject, and readers—from the writer's understanding of all aspects of the writing situation. Early in the process of writing, this strategy may be only dimly defined; but as invention, planning, and drafting proceed, it must become gradually better understood and finally brought into focus on the final revision. Only if the writer achieves this focus—reflecting mastery of the writing situation—is there a chance the essay can succeed.

Agee's purpose is to persuade his readers to take the film seriously and, even more than that, to consider it a remarkable film. The confident, authoritative tone of his review suggests that Agee expects all of his readers to accept his judgment and see the film as soon as possible. (It is interesting to note that film history confirms Agee's judgment of Huston and *Treasure*.)

Given this writing situation, what is his argumentative strategy? He opens by praising the director, who he assumes already has a reputation among his readers, and then assertively states his judgment of the movie. Next, he briefly describes the movie so that readers who have not seen it will know the setting, main characters, and premise of the story. These sections take up the first third of the review. The remainder is devoted to "achievements" and weaknesses. The reasons and evidence supporting the judgment unfold as a wide-ranging list of "achievements" of style, casting, acting, camera work, and directing. Agee admires so many aspects of the movie that he seems to want to amass them in order to make an overwhelming case. Then, as if to respond to readers' growing doubts that any film could be perfect, Agee discusses several weaknesses he sees in the film. He concludes by asserting that even though the film is not perfect, it is about as good a film as readers can expect from a Hollywood studio in 1948.

People are always evaluating movies, but how often does anyone set out to review an entire region of the country? North Dakota poet Jane Greer does just that in the following selection. Her evaluation first appeared in *Chronicles: A Magazine of American Culture*. Before reading, think for a moment about people's loyalties to their own hometowns and regions and their prejudices against other places. As you read, notice how Greer handles the difficult task of defining an entire region.

THE MIDWEST: CLOSE TO HEAVEN

JANE GREER

This is not an invitation. Frankly, if you don't live here already, most of us would rather you stay where you are, although we can't blame you for *wanting* to come. Oh, some of our businessmen and bankers and ministers and mayors and tourism promoters might, in the prejudicial atmosphere of their workplaces, look down and mutter something about growth being good for everyone, but really, when we're home reading the paper or mowing the lawn, we like things here the way they are.

Still, just where—and what—*is* "here"? Do we draw the line at Nebraska or halfway through Wyoming? At Iowa or deep into Missouri? (My aunts and cousins still live in the little Iowa-Mississippi River town where I was born, a bicycle ride from Missouri, and have a suspicious-sounding twang in their voices. The first- and second-generation German-Americans in North Country, where I live now, tell me I still have a vestige of that same twang; they laugh nervously when they say it.) Does the Midwest go as far east as Ohio? Do cows really give better milk on Central Time?

See the problem? The harder we tread water trying to define that warm 3
spot, the more uncertain we become.

And yet, "here" *is* someplace special. Its boundary degenerates only under 4
a strictly objective eye, one that takes in nothing but stone-hard facts—which
have a way of becoming less unequivocally, vitally "true" in the company of
human beings. Subjectivity is sometimes the only way to get at the truth. We
fall in love because we cannot help it, not because we have weighed the good
and bad traits of our beloved. It's not blind love; it's a *knowing choice to be
faithful,* of the same species as patriotism. . . . My love for the Midwest, where
I was born and have lived always and where I hope I will die (a very long time
from now), grows stronger each year even though I get no closer to an objective
definition or justification of that love. A Southerner, who lives in perhaps the
best-defined U.S. region, would have the same problem—but just try denying
there is a "South."

One answer, however, the simplest of all, keeps returning to me: The Mid- 5
west is singular and love-deserving because it is as close to Heaven as we can
come on this earth.

Yes, I hear you falling out of your hammocks in Hawaii, pausing amid the 6
endless thunder of Big Sur to wonder what drugs *I've* been taking. The world
is full of fine places, and I'd love to visit them all someday. But capital-H Heaven
will not, I think, be a holiday. Something tells me we'll all have work to do there;
important, hard work; labors of real love for perhaps the first time. With the
labors of love will come understanding, and with understanding, acceptance
and the freedom it allows—and suddenly Paradise sounds an awful lot like Peoria
or Council Bluffs, only warmer. Around here, life is one long practice for the
real thing.

Even though God's Workshop on Earth is managed by bungling human 7
beings, the Midwest offers a nearly perfect blend of work and joy, freedom and
responsibility. There's lots of work to go around, and a relatively low unemployment rate. (Data can be massaged and facts used differently by different
groups. I know people who figure everyone has a constitutional *right* to a job;
to such people, even 1 percent "unemployment," regardless of how we arrive
at that figure, is a criminal violation.)

Farmers come to mind first, of course, when we're talking about really *hard* 8
work. Not much is harder than farming, even if you're fortunate enough to have
an air-conditioned tractor cab. All the farmers I've ever known have had dirty
fingernails and two-tone arms and grit in their eyes and up their noses, at least
until their nightly scrub-down. The smart, good ones manage to save a little
every year for their old age and to pass on to their children. The others go bust.
Even if you aren't a farmer, though, your days in the Midwest are most likely
made up of good, hard work, if you want it—at construction sites, in offices,
factories, hospitals, television stations, stores, or in your own studio. If you're
extraordinarily lucky, you'll have a job you love; if you're just everyday, Mid-
western-type lucky, you'll have a job.

Joy in the Midwest comes from many sources: human relationships, the 9
pursuit of hobbies and sports, work well done, and—were you wondering when

I'd get around to this?—the land we live on. Each state in the Midwest is larger than many countries; the Midwest is huge, its landscape as varied as America herself. Badlands moonscapes like ours in western North and South Dakota appear nowhere else in the world. The Midwest has prairie so flat and perfectly lush with wheat or corn or sunflowers it makes you dizzy to look around. Wooded hills tower over deep-cut, narrow rivers in Minnesota and Illinois; the flat pewter of the Missouri and Mississippi Rivers rests between small, much-older knobs of hills. It gets so hot here in the summer, sometimes, that our livestock suffocates and our cities have to ration electricity, and our winter cold spells regularly exceed 40 below.

Winter here, especially in the northern states, is an opportunity for personal 10 valor—an opportunity some Midwesterners prefer to pass up. My brother recently moved to Mesa, Arizona (he'd lived all his life in Iowa, South Dakota, and Minnesota), selling everything he had and arriving there without a job; I found out only then, and was surprised that I'd never noticed before, that he's always *hated* winter. He now works two jobs and makes less than he did at one in Minneapolis, and when I ask him what he likes so much about his new home, I get temperature and humidity statistics from him. A friend likes it here because he enjoys pitting himself against the elements every day: venturing out when he needn't, skiing, skating, snowmobiling. (He also jogs and lifts weights; in spite of all his exertions, I respect him.)

For me, winter is my once-yearly chance to dig in and see what I'm made 11 of, an amusement of which I have little time in other seasons. The long cold (and my resultant long colds) gives me an excuse to read a lot, walk a little, bundled in my thoughts and other paraphernalia, sit by the fire in the dark and listen to the wind howl. (Often the wind on our hill is so fierce we can't *start* a fire.) I feel—well, yes, I'll admit it—like a pioneer: self-reliant, ready for anything, tough as a scrub oak rooted in rock. I have the urge to see old friends more often. My tastes grow simpler, my desires calmer.

But let's say, just for the sake of argument (one more Midwestern winter 12 pastime), that another long drought ground us into a dustbowl, and another Depression savaged our jobs, and we were all out of work. And let's say, further—although the possibility is beyond my imagining—that we lost all our means of joymaking. It wouldn't matter as much as it would in some places, because what ultimately makes the Midwest special is that here, to an extent unparalleled anywhere else, we're *free.*

Now, that doesn't mean you may, with impunity, take a meathook to my 13 windshield if I perturb you, or that I am excused from paying my bills and acting responsibly. What it *does* mean—to a sometime bohemian who sometimes enjoys other bohemians—is that here in the Midwest we can all act a little crazy when we need to: without being arrested, usually without even being noticed, and still—this is the best part—without being *surrounded* by crazies. (Although, because we *are* such a large, diverse place, we do have our little ghettos of lunacy, especially in our bigger cities.) Think of it: We're neither California, where one's invitation to community seems to rest solely on one's aberration and pique at all things normal, nor Managua (we have no Managuas in this country), where what is not standard is quietly crushed.

Here is a cornucopia of disinterested goodwill towards oddities, an amused 14 politeness at the tender psyches of the genius and the *artiste* and the sometimes unbalanced (often indistinguishable); here we have both the security of being part of a sane, humdrum community and the stimulation of observing, or perhaps acting, the occasional eccentric. There's room here for the dance instructor grocery shopping in his lavender leotard; the militant feminist, and the shy bride who just wants to have babies and keep her house spotless; the teenager clad in leather and chains; the oil rig or coal mine or harvest itinerant from Texas or Mexico; the flamboyant Marxist professor and his colleague who spends his spare time translating Old High German lays; the buttoned-down shopowner and the layered-look artist and the turtlenecked writer; Born-agains and Jews and Muslims, Christian Scientists and Quakers and Moonies, Junior Leaguers and right-to-lifers and the Posse Comitatus.

Here I can run my business or my family or my love life the way I want, and 15 no one will think it proper to interfere unless it's obvious that I'm hurting someone else. Here privacy is considered a part of community, and license is answerable only to its own excesses. Outsiders might think we're "isolated" here, because fads and national paranoias are slow to reach us; the truth is that Midwesterners are too busy and involved with real life to spend much time fearing the corruption of civilization. And besides, it just won't *happen* here: decency, charity, dogged skepticism, and a heartfelt *laissez-faire* are our defense, as solidly a part of us as our suspicion of gratuitous change and our dependence on the livestock market.

It's no accident that, in addition to being the clearest hint of Heaven to come 16 our way, the Midwest is also, barring certain details, a compelling synecdoche for the nation whose heartland it is. With that in mind, perhaps this *should* be an invitation: What I believe about the nation should hold for the region, too. So: If you think you can handle the *sanity* here, and are content to help us do what we do best, come on in. There's plenty of room.

Questions for analysis   1. In her last paragraph, Greer asserts that the Midwest is a synecdoche for America. (A synecdoche is a part representing the whole.) Are the values she ascribes to the Midwest also the values of your region or community? Explain how they are alike and different.

2. Identify Greer's intended readers, her purpose, and argumentative strategy in this essay. Given her readers and purpose, how well do you think her argument succeeds?

3. Look closely at the first sentence in paragraph 7. What does it accomplish? How is it related to what precedes and follows it in the essay?

4. Greer asserts that the Midwest "is as close to Heaven as we can come on this earth," and that it "offers a nearly perfect blend of work and joy, freedom and responsibility." How does she define the key terms in her

claim—Heaven, joy, work, freedom, responsibility? What does she mean by these terms? How are they "singular" (or unique) to the Midwest?

5. What kinds of supporting reasons and evidence do you find in paragraphs 10 and 11? Why do you think Greer might have included this evidence, given her purpose and readers?

6. Skim the essay looking for places where Greer pointedly anticipates readers' disagreements, questions, doubts, or objections. Is she accommodating or challenging at these places? How do you evaluate her strategy? (See Chapter 19: Arguing for a discussion of anticipating counterarguments.)

7. How would you go about writing an evaluation of your neighborhood, city, state, or region of the country? What criteria are appropriate for such an evaluation? What reasons would you give to support your judgment? What evidence would you amass to develop your argument? For whom would you want to write such an evaluation?

Commentary Unlike Agee, who offers a very brief description of a well-defined object (a movie), Greer appears not to know the boundaries of her subject (a region of the country). In her first four paragraphs, she attempts not so much a description of the Midwest as a definition of it. Her efforts to define her subject remind us of the care with which writers of position papers and proposals would define their terms. By paragraph 4, however, Greer gives up any attempt at an "objective" definition and asserts that "Subjectivity is sometimes the only way to get at the truth." Since Greer's purpose is not to advertise the region as real estate for sale, but rather to evaluate it in terms of what it feels like to live there, most readers will understand, even if they do not accept, her judgment.

In addition to defining the subject, writers must seriously consider the criteria or standards that are the basis of any informed evaluation. Greer's wide-ranging reasons for her judgment all seem to derive from a single criterion: a living place's balance of "work and joy, freedom and responsibility." It is a criterion of harmony, of balancing or reconciling essential opposites in human existence. She seems to be saying that the most important standard for judging a place to live should be the way it fulfills basic human personal and social needs. By emphasizing the balance of opposites Greer gives this "quality of life" criterion a special twist. From this single criterion, stated in paragraph 7, Greer derives many of her reasons. Like Greer, you will need to discover criteria on which to base your argument. Like her also, you may think of criteria that might surprise readers initially but come to seem quite appropriate.

The next selection evaluates a person, Albert Einstein, easily the best-known scientist of the twentieth century. The author is the British philosopher and mathematician Bertrand Russell. The essay appeared in a British magazine,

The New Leader, just after Einstein's death. Russell writes about Einstein not for other scientists but for an educated public. How do you think he might evaluate a well-known public figure like Einstein? What might he assume his readers already know about Einstein's accomplishments?

THE GREATNESS OF ALBERT EINSTEIN
BERTRAND RUSSELL

Einstein was indisputably one of the greatest men of our time. He had in a high degree the simplicity characteristic of the best men of science—a simplicity which comes of a single-minded desire to know and understand things that are completely impersonal. He had also the faculty of not taking familiar things for granted. Newton wondered why apples fall; Einstein expressed "surprised thankfulness" that four equal rods can make a square, since, in most of the universes that he could imagine, there would be no such things as squares.

He showed greatness also in his moral qualities. In private, he was kindly and unassuming; toward colleagues he was (so far as I could see) completely free from jealousy, which is more than can be said of Newton or Leibniz. In his later years, relativity was more or less eclipsed, in scientific interest, by quantum theory, but I never discovered any sign that this vexed him. He was profoundly interested in world affairs. At the end of the First World War, when I first came in contact with him, he was a pacifist, but Hitler led him (as he led me) to abandon this point of view. Having previously thought of himself as a citizen of the world, he found that the Nazis compelled him to think of himself as a Jew, and to take up the cause of the Jews throughout the world. After the end of the Second World War, he joined the group of American scientists who were attempting to find a way of avoiding the disasters to mankind that are threatened as a result of the atomic bomb.

After Congressional committees in America began their inquisitorial investigations into supposed subversive activities, Einstein wrote a well publicized letter urging that all men in academic posts should refuse to testify before these committees or before the almost equally tyrannical boards set up by some universities. His argument for this advice was that, under the Fifth Amendment, no man is obliged to answer a question if the answer will incriminate him, but that the purpose of this Amendment had been defeated by the inquisitors, since they held that refusal to answer may be taken as evidence of guilt. If Einstein's policy had been followed even in cases where it was absurd to presume guilt, academic freedom would have greatly profited. But, in the general *sauve qui peut,* none of the "innocent" listened to him. In these various public activities, he has been completely self-effacing and only anxious to find ways of saving the human race from the misfortunes brought about by its own follies. But while the world applauded him as a man of science, in practical affairs, his wisdom was so simple and so profound as to seem to the sophisticated like mere foolishness.

Although Einstein has done much important work outside the theory of relativity, it is by this theory that he is most famous—and rightly, for it is of fundamental significance both for science and for philosophy. Many people (including myself) have attempted popular accounts of this theory, and I will not add to their number on this occasion. But I will try to say a few words as to how the theory affects our view of the universe. The theory, as everyone knows, appeared in two stages: the special theory in 1905, and the general theory in 1915. The special theory was important both in science and philosophy—first, because it accounted for the result of the Michelson-Morley experiment, which had puzzled the world for thirty years; secondly, because it explained the increase of mass with velocity, which had been observed in electrons; thirdly, because it led to the interchangeability of mass and energy, which has become an essential principle in physics. These are only some of the ways in which it was scientifically important.

Philosophically, the special theory demanded a revolution in deeply rooted ways of thought, since it compelled a change in our conception of the spatio-temporal structure of the world. Structure is what is most significant in our knowledge of the physical world, and for ages structure had been conceived as depending upon two different manifolds, one of space, the other of time. Einstein showed that, for reasons partly experimental and partly logical, the two must be replaced by one which he called "space-time." If two events happen in different places, you cannot say, as was formerly supposed, that they are separated by so many miles and minutes, because different observers, all equally careful, will make different estimates of the miles and minutes, all equally legitimate. The only thing that is the same for all observers is what is called "interval," which is a sort of combination of space-distance and time-distance as previously estimated.

The general theory has a wider sweep than the special theory, and is scientifically more important. It is primarily a theory of gravitation. No advance whatever had been made in explaining gravitation during the 230 years since Newton, although the action at a distance that it seems to demand had always been repugnant. Einstein made gravitation part of geometry; he said that it was due to the character of space-time. There is a law called the "Principle of Least Action," according to which a body, in going from one place to another, chooses always the easiest route, which may not be a straight line: It may pay you to avoid mountain-tops and deep valleys. According to Einstein (to use crude language, misleading if taken literally), space-time is full of mountains and valleys, and that is why planets do not move in straight lines. The sun is at the top of a hill, and a lazy planet prefers going round the hill to climbing up to the summit. There were some very delicate experimental tests by which it could be decided whether Einstein or Newton fitted the facts more accurately. The observations came out on Einstein's side, and almost everybody except the Nazis accepted his theory.

I suppose that, in the estimation of the general public, Einstein is still reckoned as a revolutionary innovator. Among physicists, however, he has become the leader of the Old Guard. This is due to his refusal to accept some of the innovations of quantum theory. . . . Quantum theory is more revolutionary than the theory of relativity, and I do not think that its power of revolutionizing our conceptions of the physical world is yet completed. Its imaginative effects are very curious. Although it has given us new powers of manipulating matter, including the sinister powers displayed in the atom and hydrogen bombs, it has shown us that we are ignorant of many things which we thought we knew. Nobody before quantum theory doubted that at any given moment a particle is at some definite place and moving with some definite velocity. This is no longer the case. The more accurately you determine the place of a particle, the less accurate will be its velocity; the more accurately you determine the velocity, the less accurate will be its position. And the particle itself has become something quite vague, not a nice little billiard ball as it used to be. When you think you have caught it, it produces a convincing alibi as a wave and not a particle. In fact, you know only certain equations of which the interpretation is obscure.

This point of view was distasteful to Einstein, who struggled to remain nearer 8 to classical physics. In spite of this, he was the first to open the imaginative vistas which have revolutionized science during the present century. I will end as I began: He was a great man, perhaps the greatest of our time.

Questions for analysis   1. Russell evaluates Einstein's moral qualities as well as his accomplishments. How appropriate do you think this criterion is in judging scientists?

2. What does Russell seem to assume his readers already know about Einstein? Point to specific places in the essay where he anticipates readers' knowledge of Einstein or science in general. Is he right in your case?

3. Given his readers, how would you describe Russell's purpose and argumentative strategy? What advantages and disadvantages do you see in this strategy?

4. What reasons does Russell give to support his claim for Einstein's greatness? What criteria underlie these particular reasons? To help you answer this question, you could make a table listing Russell's criteria and reasons. (For an example of such a table, see the Commentary following the Agee review.)

5. What role do paragraphs 4–6 play in this evaluation?

6. How important is comparison and contrast to this essay? Compare Russell's use of this strategy to that of Agee and Greer. What can you conclude about the usefulness of comparing and contrasting in evaluative writing?

7. If you were to evaluate a person, who would you choose? How would you establish your credibility with readers? What criteria would you use to evaluate this person? Do you think you would need to convince your readers that these criteria are appropriate?

Commentary   A great temptation when writing an evaluation of an individual is either to praise the person without qualification, making him or her into a cardboard saint, or to damn the person as an ogre, allowing for no redeeming virtues. Even people justly famous for great accomplishments or moral qualities are not perfect. Einstein, for example, refused to accept and champion some aspects of quantum theory. Russell explains what is revolutionary about quantum theory and seems to regret Einstein's opposition to it, yet he does not believe this failing prevents Einstein from being considered a great man.

To increase your credibility with your readers, you will want to avoid unqualified praise or damnation of your subject when you write your own evaluation essay. If you write to praise a teacher, politician, or discoverer, do not hesitate to mention a weakness or fault. If you value a movie, like Agee, you may want to mention one or two ways in which it falls short of greatness. Humor and irony perhaps enable Greer's unqualified enthusiasm for the Midwest to succeed, but if you write to praise your region or community, you will almost certainly want to mention its blemishes. This is not to say that you should waffle by seeking to balance the advantages and disadvantages and not offering your ultimate judgment. Evaluations must assert a firm judgment, but your argument will be more convincing if you can acknowledge readers' expectations that nothing is altogether perfect or terrible.

The final essay was written by a college freshman, Steven Weisman. In it, he evaluates his college newspaper. Before you read Weisman's essay, think about your own college newspaper. Do you read it regularly? What do you like best about it? Do you have any complaints about it? As you read, notice Weisman's argumentative strategy—how and where he states his thesis, the reasons supporting his thesis, his sequencing of reasons, use of evidence, and anticipations of readers' counterarguments.

**UNDEFENDED
BY OUR GUARDIAN**
STEVEN WEISMAN

The responsibility to inform a college campus of the many goings-on is 1 indeed a large one. This task becomes even more important with a school as large as the University of California, San Diego. The only way students can find out why the Dean of Third College was fired, how the Triton basketball team is doing, or where a lecture on metaphysics is taking place is through the school paper. *The UCSD Guardian* is this university's biweekly newspaper. It supplies campus news, sports, and other important information for students and faculty. However, the manner in which it performs this essential function is pitifully ineffective from visual, stylistic, and journalistic standpoints.

Visually, the *Guardian* suffers from a variety of plagues. Photographs are 2 rare. The *Guardian*'s pages two and three, reserved for either news or opinions, are almost always without a visual aid to liven up the monotony of print. Even when visuals are used, they seldom enhance the story. In a recent paper, two of three photos presented sports events and the other was of Governor Deukmejian. The front page of the January 12 issue is dominated by a photo of Deukmejian holding a pie and wearing a chef's apron. Glancing at it, the reader gets no clue as to the contents of the article. Only after reading the article about the university's budget for the year, does the photograph have any relevance.

A good photograph should always tell a story, and it will usually tell it better than a graphic or drawing. In the *Guardian,* however, graphics are used more frequently than photos and are usually so large that they clearly take up space for lack of interesting copy.

The *Guardian*'s layout is equally frustrating. While each page is labeled 3 "news," "sports," and so on, these categories do not accurately represent the kinds of articles printed on the page. Six pages in the January 12 issue are at least two-thirds full of ads. The remaining space is filled primarily with articles started on an earlier page. Rather than concentrating the advertisements on an entire page or two, the *Guardian* editors throw away these six pages. Flipping through any given issue, readers can find only three or four pages that will catch their attention, make them stop, and read. Poor layout inhibits readers from seeing or reading what is in three-fourths of the paper.

To make matters worse, the text itself is lifeless, even for newspaper writing. 4 This is due in part to the *Guardian*'s abundance of uninteresting and inappropriate article topics. The front page of the January 12 issue featured a story on increased state funding of schools, opinions on diplomacy or politics in the Middle East, and a feature on a hiking trip. Earlier this year, the *Guardian* covered the remedial writing program at UCSD, religion on campus, and fake I.D.'s, and addressed the futility of partying in a fictional piece. Having been editor-in-chief of a high school paper this past year and having used the last three article topics in our paper, I know that the *Guardian* is scraping the bottom of the idea barrel. Major publications such as the *L.A. Times* face the same problem, but unlike smaller papers, they are able to hide these "fillers" in the back. Granted, the *Guardian* has less to work with because of its much smaller scope; however, it also has less space to fill. The sixteen-page *Guardian* has an average of about five pages of advertisements per issue, plus calendars of upcoming events, a classifieds page, and two or three pages of sports. This leaves just five or six pages, including the front page, to be filled. Major universities such as UCLA and Stanford print daily publications. The *Guardian* comes out only twice a week. This should allow the staff plenty of time to brainstorm for creative ideas and develop intriguing articles.

Vague headlines give the reader few clues as to what an article is about. 5 What is "UC Gets a Bigger Slice of the Pie" about? The county fair? Is "MacCrone Faces Continued Legal Battles" about his divorce proceedings? No kickers or subheadings or enlarged type were used to explain, clarify, or emphasize the importance of the topics. These tactics are rarely employed by the *Guardian.* The problem with headlines may seem small, yet few readers take the time to delve into an article with a vague or ambiguous headline—a headline that doesn't tell them up-front how the following piece relates to them. Most of the *Guardian*'s news items involve all UCSD students. Sadly, many may never find out this information partly because the headlines are ineffective and partly because writers fail to reveal the subject matter to readers until the fourth or fifth paragraph, if at all. In a school or college newspaper, informing students of the effects an event will have on them is often, or should be, a greater priority than the actual events themselves.

Not only does the *Guardian* suffer from poor article topics—it suffers from 6 bad writing. The January 12 feature on a hiking trip, written by feature editor Suzanne Lifson, is an endless narrative dotted with such attempts at humor as, "I prepared myself by screaming at the top of my lungs," "It made all the tripping easier to take," and "Just what Perrier salesmen would love to exploit." This may amuse the author, but it is neither informative nor entertaining reading. With articles like Lifson's, a typical issue of the *Guardian* is as dull to read as it is to look at.

Guardian editors seem unwilling to trim and edit articles. The interest span 7 of a newspaper reader averages about five paragraphs. Even features or fiction longer than a thousand words are more than most people will bother to read. In the *Guardian,* features usually consume an entire page (sometimes more), while news articles run several paragraphs too many. Not including news "shorts" or sports articles, there are only five articles in the January 12 issue. That is pitifully few.

Though I consider the *Guardian* an embarrassment for a university like UCSD, 8 I will concede that it is not the worst paper I have ever encountered. The *Guardian* is indisputedly a neat looking paper. Headlines, columns, and boxes are all straight and evenly aligned. Likewise, the manipulation of white-space (blank areas surrounding headlines or articles) is professional. To the *Guardian*'s credit, most issues concerning the school are indeed covered in either the news or the sports sections. Also to their credit, most of the writers on the staff can spell and avoid grammar mistakes. Yet, considering all its problems, the *Guardian* is clearly in need of some quality control. No paper is without occasional uninteresting topics, weak writing, or fillers. Unfortunately, these lapses are the norm for the paper, as the January 12 issue illustrates. It is obvious that few on the *Guardian* staff are living up to the responsibility of creating a quality publication—one that informs, entertains, and enlightens its readers.

Questions for analysis   1. Since college students can receive local, state, and national news from daily newspapers and television, what, in your opinion, should be the function of a college newspaper? What kind of college newspaper would you like to read? How does your own college newspaper meet or fail to meet your expectations?

2. What do you find most and least convincing in Weisman's argument? Though his judgment is negative, does his evaluation seem fair to you? How would you expect the editors of the *Guardian* to respond?

3. In order to evaluate the sequencing of reasons supporting the judgment, make a scratch outline of Weisman's essay. (Scratch outlining is illustrated in Chapter 11: Invention and Revision.) What advantages or disadvantages do you see in the sequence?

4. Summarize Weisman's argumentative strategy. How appropriate do you think his tone is, given this strategy? What do you find most and least effective in his strategy?

5. What kinds of evidence does Weisman include? (Chapter 19: Arguing reviews the basic kinds of argumentative evidence.) How responsibly does he handle this evidence?

6. Why do you think Weisman does not define and defend the criteria on which he relies to evaluate the *Guardian*?

7. Think about the specialized newspapers and magazines you read regularly, those for readerships like college students, neighborhoods or communities, religious groups, hobbyists, or age groups. Which one might you evaluate? Consider how you would describe it for readers who have never seen it. On what basis would you evaluate it? To what other publications might you compare it?

Commentary   One of the virtues of Weisman's essay is that it is nearly impossible to go off track while reading it. Connections between sentences are seamless. Equally important, transitions at paragraph boundaries are unmistakable. Though he does not forecast all his reasons in the first paragraph, Weisman does promise to provide several reasons for his judgment. Then, at the beginning of each paragraph, he clearly identifies each new reason—ineffective visuals, clumsy layout, lifeless topics, vague headlines, bad writing, untrimmed articles. (You will find a comprehensive discussion of strategies for achieving coherence in Chapter 12: Cueing the Reader.)

The essay would be more convincing, however, if he had contrasted the *Guardian* with the two other student newspapers he mentions. Evaluation invites comparison and contrast. Without the contrast, we cannot tell whether the *Guardian* is as good as it could be, given the realistic constraints on publishing a college newspaper, or whether it is as comparatively bad as Weisman claims. Weisman might also be faulted for basing his evaluation on only one issue of the *Guardian*, because he does not demonstrate that the January 12 issue is representative. For examples to be persuasive, they must be typical. Otherwise, readers can simply dismiss them as anomalous. He could easily have supported his evidence about advertising space and layout by examining other issues, perhaps all the January issues or all the issues from September to December.

PURPOSE AND AUDIENCE

Your purpose in writing an essay of evaluation is to influence your readers' judgment of some subject. You assert your own judgment and then justify it by constructing a convincing argument of reasons and evidence. If readers are unfamiliar with your subject, you will need to describe it for them. To have any chance of influencing readers, you must appear knowledgeable, authoritative, and believable. Your essay must have a tone that invites trust.

You may want to acknowledge your readers' experience of your subject, perhaps revealing that you understand how they might judge it differently. You might even let readers know that you have anticipated their objections to specific reasons you advance or to a comparison you might make.

In some evaluative writing situations, you may want to influence readers to make a decision. For example, you might argue the advantages of one product over another in hopes of influencing readers to buy the one you prefer. Or you might review a movie or restaurant with the purpose of enticing readers to see it or visit it (or avoid it).

In a different evaluative writing situation, your purpose might be only to invite readers' admiration or appreciation of your subject. For example, you might evaluate a particular North American explorer as the very best of the early group of explorers. Or you might praise one of your college instructors as the best lecturer you have ever heard.

BASIC FEATURES OF EVALUATIONS

Presentation of the subject

Most evaluations include some description of the subject. For example, James Agee briefly summarizes *The Treasure of the Sierra Madre,* and Jane Greer offers subjective boundaries for the Midwest and later describes some of its geographic features. Such descriptions are generally selective and written to a well-focused purpose—to support the writer's judgment.

An authoritative judgment

Evaluation essays are focused on a judgment—an assertion about the value of something. This judgment is the thesis, or main point, of the essay. Such judgments assert that something is good or bad or that it is better or worse than something else. Usually this judgment is restated in various ways in the essay and repeated at the end. For example, in reviewing *The Treasure of the Sierra Madre,* Agee states his positive judgment of the movie in several ways:

> . . . I have no doubt at all that Huston [the director] . . . is the most talented man working in American pictures. . . .
>
> . . . [*Treasure*] will stand up in the memory and esteem of qualified people alongside the best of the silent movies.
>
> . . . a sensational achievement . . .
>
> . . . the story itself—a beauty . . .

Never are we in doubt about Agee's judgment.

In essays of evaluation we expect to hear an authoritative tone. Such a tone assures us that the writer has knowledge and self-confidence about the subject. Agee seems to understand quite fully the movie he is reviewing (we might guess that he saw it more than once), and he clearly knows a lot about movies in general. Likewise, Greer's essay leaves no doubt that she understands the Midwest and can write authoritatively about its virtues. In the same way, Bertrand Russell demonstrates that he knows about Einstein's life and work—and about other scientists as well.

A convincing *argument*

To be convincing, the evaluation must be based on relevant criteria appropriate for the intended readers of the essay. For example, Agee's criteria— story line, theme, unity, cinematography, acting, direction—are relevant to movies (but not to scientists) and appropriate for the average moviegoer who reads reviews in such magazines as *Rolling Stone, Time* or the *New Yorker.*

The argument of the evaluation is developed with reasons and evidence. Writers explain why they like or dislike something by giving us reasons, sometimes only one or two, other times many. These reasons are developed and supported with evidence from the subject being evaluated. Most of the discussion in an evaluation essay is taken up with this evidence.

For reasons and evidence to be persuasive, a writer must organize them into a convincing argument. The reasons must be arranged in some logical order with the most important reason either first or last. The most significant criterion is generally given the most weight (or space) in the essay. Also, the writer must be willing to acknowledge any weaknesses in something being praised (as Agee does in paragraph 7) or strengths in something being criticized (as Weisman does in his final paragraph). Usually writers of evaluations restate their thesis at the end to provide an emphatic conclusion and a frame for the essay.

Comparison

Comparison and contrast is not a requirement in written evaluations, but it is nearly always used. Our minds turn naturally to comparisons when we are making judgments because judgments are relative: if we are evaluating a movie, we judge it relative to other movies; if we are evaluating a scientist, we judge him relative to other scientists. The criteria for our evaluations derive from characteristics of all movies or all scientists.

Most of the evaluations in this chapter are positive. For such evaluations, writers draw comparisons to similar things of less value. The purpose of the comparison, of course, is to increase the value of that which they are praising. Agee compares Huston to Chaplin, and he contrasts the actors in *The Treasure of the Sierra Madre* on the basis of the strength and believability of their acting. Greer contrasts the Midwest with Hawaii, California, Arizona, and Managua (Nicaragua); Russell contrasts Einstein with Newton.

Since comparisons and contrasts are so useful in evaluations, you will want to test the possibilities of this strategy in your own evaluation. All the writers in this chapter use comparisons in a limited way. You could use them much more prominently, of course, organizing your entire essay around the particular subject you want to praise (or criticize) and an inferior (or superior) one you have chosen for contrast.

Strategies for presenting comparisons or contrasts in writing are analyzed and illustrated further in Chapter 18: Comparing and Contrasting.

GUIDE TO WRITING

THE WRITING TASK

Write an essay evaluating something you know about or can research. Carefully define your readers—are they familiar with the topic or is it perhaps new to them? Your evaluation cannot be merely subjective; it must be based on appropriate criteria and be supported by reasons and evidence.

INVENTION AND RESEARCH

Identifying a subject for evaluation

These writing activities will enable you to choose a subject, analyze it closely, and decide how you will argue to support your judgment. You may already have a good idea of what you would like to evaluate. Still, you may want to consider some other topics. This activity is designed to help you come up with some possibilities.

Listing possibilities. For each of the following categories list two or three things you might possibly evaluate.

- ☐ A poem, story, or novel
- ☐ A movie, play, or television series
- ☐ A musical recording or performance
- ☐ A noteworthy person—a professor, a political figure, an artist, an athlete
- ☐ A consumer product—a camera, a car, a computer
- ☐ A theory—supply-side economics, the big-bang theory, evolution
- ☐ An essay or other work of nonfiction
- ☐ A magazine (several issues), a writer's work (several publications)
- ☐ An engineering accomplishment, medical breakthrough, environmental policy, agricultural practice, energy source, educational practice
- ☐ A restaurant, fast-food place, coffeehouse, bar
- ☐ One aspect of your high school or college—science instruction, the counseling program, the student health service, the library

Choosing a tentative topic. Once you have a list of possibilities, review the list looking for a tentative topic. Choose something you have settled feelings about: you either like it or dislike it. Most important, select a subject you can evaluate with authority—you must know the proper criteria and have enough knowledge to give detailed examples. You might want to consider a topic you are now studying (a literary work, a scientific theory).

If you wish to evaluate a work of art—whether a story or a movie or a concert—you will be able to write a much stronger evaluation if you read it or see it now, even before you start writing about it.

You should write about a product only if you are very knowledgeable about it. A slight acquaintance with a product will never do: to write a convincing evaluation, you must have a great deal of experience using the product and be something of an expert about other models and types.

Examining your knowledge of the subject

Describe it. Describe your subject briefly in just a few sentences. What is it? How did you first encounter it?

Judge it. In a sentence or two state your judgment.

Explore it in writing. Write nonstop for about ten minutes, exploring your feelings and knowledge about the topic. The following questions can guide your writing here:

☐ How certain am I of my judgment? Do I have any doubts? Why do I feel the way I do?

☐ Do I like (or dislike) everything about my subject, or only certain parts of it?

☐ Are there any similar things I should consider (other products or movies, for example)?

☐ Is there anything I will need to do right away in order to evaluate this subject authoritatively? Will I need to do any research? Can I get the information I need?

Testing your choice

Now you should pause and test your choice. Before you invest any more time in this choice, consider the following questions:

☐ Do I know enough about this topic to describe it fully and to present detailed evidence to support an evaluation?

☐ Do I know (or can I find out) the appropriate criteria for evaluating such things?

☐ Do I have experience with other things of its type as a basis for comparison?

☐ Do I personally care enough about the topic and my judgment of it— positive or negative—to want to convince readers of the validity of my judgment?

You will want to keep these questions in mind and perhaps reconsider them as you invent and plan and later as you draft your essay. If you ever have trouble answering them affirmatively and confidently, you may want to choose another subject to evaluate.

Identifying criteria   Criteria are standards for judging something. They apply to a class of things, not to individuals in the class. If you own a jeep or a sports car, your particular reasons for liking or disliking that vehicle derive from criteria appropriate for evaluating jeeps or sports cars, not eighteen-wheel trucks. If you evaluate a fast-food restaurant, your criteria must be appropriate for such restaurants, not for gourmet restaurants. For evaluations to seem informed, thoughtful, convincing, they must be based on appropriate criteria.

Make a list of all the criteria you can think of for judging the topic you have chosen. You may want to brainstorm with other students about appropriate criteria. Consult with your instructor, or talk to a campus expert on the subject. The question you must answer is this: What are the criteria or standards for judging the class of things to which my particular subject belongs?

Your criteria should be impersonal (not based just on your personal tastes) and appropriate for the thing being evaluated. They should include nothing trivial, but instead should point to the most basic and important features.

Here are some possible lists of criteria for different subjects. A movie review might be based (as Agee's is) on criteria of story line, theme, unity, cinematography, acting, and direction. To evaluate a camera, you might begin with construction, optics, functions, and price. Evaluations of autobiographical essays rely on such criteria as style, coherence, opening, story, scene, characterization of people, evaluation of experience, significance to the writer, personal response of the reader, and framing.

Analyzing your readers   You will be trying to convince particular readers to consider your evaluation seriously, perhaps even to take some action as a result, like seeing a certain movie, or buying a particular sailboat. Consequently, you must analyze these readers very carefully. You should do so now, so that you can next select reasons that might appeal to these readers.

Write for at least ten minutes exploring your readers' knowledge of the topic. These questions may stimulate your exploration:

☐ Do my readers have any knowledge of or experience with the topic? If not, how thoroughly will I have to describe it?

☐ Have they experienced anything similar?

☐ Are they familiar with the criteria for evaluating such things? Must readers have any special knowledge to understand my evaluation?

☐ Are my readers likely to disagree with my judgment? Why? Might they find my judgment controversial or surprising?

Generating reasons and evidence

Consider now the reasons for your judgment: why do you like or dislike the essay or senator or city or whatever you are evaluating? Then see what factual evidence you can offer to support those reasons. A good way to do this is to make a table containing criteria, reasons, and evidence. (See a sample table in the Writer at Work section at the end of this chapter.)

Listing criteria and reasons. Divide a piece of paper into three columns. In the left-hand column list all the criteria you identified as necessary and appropriate for evaluating your subject, skipping about five lines between each item. Then, in the middle column, list all the reasons, criterion-by-criterion, for your judgment. Select the reasons with your readers' sensibilities in mind. You may find more reasons for some criteria than for others; also, you may think of reasons that seem to fit with none of your criteria.

Finding evidence. When you have listed as many reasons as you can, move on to the right-hand column, and add any evidence you can think of to illustrate each reason—personal anecdotes, illustrations (quotations, paraphrases, summaries, descriptive details, etc.), statistics, or testimony (someone else's statement).

You will probably find that the amount of evidence you can find to support each reason will vary. Some reasons will have only one piece of evidence, while others may have several supporting facts.

Charting your criteria, reasons, and evidence in table form can be useful in identifying which reasons need additional evidence. It shows you at a glance how well each of your arguments is supported.

Reconsidering your criteria. Look at all the criteria you have identified so far. Can you see any ways to narrow or broaden certain criteria, or to combine two or more? Can you think of any additional criteria? Revise or extend your table of reasons, criteria, and evidence.

Elaborating on the most convincing reasons

By now you have had a chance to explore fully all the elements necessary to writing an evaluation essay: the subject itself, your judgment of it, the criteria of judgment on which your argument will be based, the reasons and evidence to support your judgment, and your readers. Next you should perform a critical analysis of each reason, the relations among all your reasons, their relation to your judgment, and their appropriateness for your readers. This step will allow you to analyze the materials that may go into your draft and discover consistencies and strengths in your argument.

Selecting the best reasons. For your particular readers, which of your reasons would be most convincing? Reconsider your table and select three to five of your strongest reasons. Put an asterisk by these.

Analyzing the reasons. Analyze each of your best reasons. Guided by the questions that follow, write a few sentences of analysis for each one of your best reasons.

- ☐ How exactly does this reason directly support my judgment?
- ☐ Does the reason derive from an appropriate criterion?
- ☐ What is so important about this reason?
- ☐ Why did I choose this reason?
- ☐ Why will my readers find this reason convincing?
- ☐ What further evidence do I need to strengthen this reason?

Considering the set of reasons. Now analyze the reasons you selected as the best ones as an interrelated set. Guided by the following questions, write for at least five minutes on all of your best reasons:

- ☐ As a set, do my reasons slight an important criterion?
- ☐ Are any of the reasons similar? If so, might they be combined?
- ☐ Which reasons are the strongest? Why?
- ☐ Which ones are the weakest? Why?
- ☐ Should any reasons be dropped altogether?
- ☐ What would be the best sequence for presenting these reasons to my readers?
- ☐ Why would it be better than some other order?

Developing the reasons. To test how well you can integrate the evidence for a reason into a forceful argument, take your three most important reasons in turn and write quickly for at least five minutes on each one. These test writings may suggest that you need still further evidence to support a reason or that you have to figure out connections between bits of evidence.

PLANNING AND DRAFTING

Before you begin drafting, you will want to reflect on what you have discovered in your invention writings. You will also want to set goals to guide your drafting. This section helps you think about important goals of accommodating your readers, beginning and ending effectively, organizing for maximum effect, and avoiding logical fallacies.

Seeing what you have   You have by now done considerable thinking and writing about issues basic to all evaluative writing. You have chosen a subject and identified your readers, and you have charted the criteria, reasons, and evidence necessary to an evaluation. Reread it all thoughtfully to see what you have. Look for connections, patterns, surprises. Highlight anything promising by underscoring or making notes in the margin. Tinker with your criteria, reasons, and evidence to see that they all fit together. Try to decide what you need to research further.

If you are still not satisfied that you have enough material to develop a persuasive essay, you might want to select a different topic. Consider the questions under Testing Your Choice one last time.

Setting goals Before starting to draft, think about the important rhetorical goals for your essay. The following questions can help you to focus on particular decisions you will have to make as you plan and draft your essay.

Your purpose and audience

☐ What do I hope to achieve with this essay? What do I want my readers to think, believe, or do as a result of reading my essay?
☐ What do my readers already know about my subject?
☐ How much experience and knowledge do they have with the general subject?
☐ If readers are unfamiliar with my subject, how can I describe it to them?
☐ What is the most appropriate tone for these readers? Which tone will enhance my authority, win my readers' trust, and make my argument more convincing? Should I write a text that seems witty? serious? casual? impersonal?

The beginning

☐ How should I begin? How can I capture my readers' attention? Should I open by stating my judgment? Should I quote some authority on the topic? Should I begin with an anecdote?
☐ What information should I give first? Should I provide some background, or simply state my judgment?

The criteria, reasons, and evidence

☐ Will people recognize and accept the criteria on which I am basing my evaluation? Do I need to define or justify my criteria?
☐ Will readers question any of my reasons?
☐ Do I have evidence to support each of my reasons?
☐ Should I acknowledge any objections readers may have to my evaluation?
☐ Should I acknowledge any weaknesses or strengths my subject may have?

Avoiding logical fallacies

☐ Will I be able to base my argument on impersonal criteria and avoid considering my own *personal tastes* (praising a movie because the main character reminds me of my favorite uncle, for example)?

☐ Am I considering any *irrelevant criteria* (condemning a movie because I do not like the shirt worn by one of the characters, for example)?

☐ Am I considering any *unimportant criteria* (praising a movie because its outdoor scenes are filled with beautiful cumulus clouds, for example)?

☐ Am I guilty of *hasty generalization* (criticizing a movie because I disliked an earlier movie by the same director, for example, or praising a movie because I have always admired its leading actress)?

☐ Can I avoid making *weak comparisons*? (Should I acknowledge weaknesses in subjects I praise or strengths of those I criticize?)

☐ How can I show that I have *accepted the burden of proof*? Can I make a convincing argument for my evaluation, so that no one thinks I am exaggerating or overstating the case?

☐ Will I be committing an *either/or fallacy* if I claim that my subject is either all good or all bad?

☐ Can I compare my subject to something inferior without being accused of making a *straw man* argument? (A straw man is easily knocked down.)

The ending

☐ How can I leave my readers with an unmistakable (even memorable) impression of my judgment?

☐ Shall I end by summarizing the reasons for my judgment?

☐ Should I restate my judgment, as Russell does?

☐ Should my ending frame the essay by referring to the opening, as Greer's ending does?

Outlining the evaluation Evaluations may be organized in various ways. The important thing is to include all essential parts: a presentation of the subject, a judgment of some kind, and reasons and evidence to support the judgment.

If your readers are already familiar with the topic, your outline might look like this:

presentation of the subject

discussion of criteria to be considered (if you suspect your readers may not know appropriate criteria or may question or challenge yours)

judgment

reason 1
   evidence

reason 2
   evidence

reason 3
   evidence, with a comparison

(etc.)

consideration of an opposing judgment (if you suspect your readers might judge your subject differently)

conclusion

If your readers are unfamiliar with the topic, however, you will need to begin with some description of your subject, including perhaps some background discussion and definition of terms. These are, of course, the most basic elements; there are many other possible organizations.

You will want to arrange your reasons in some logical order: from most obvious to least obvious, most general to most technical, least convincing to most convincing, least important to most important.

Remember that an outline should serve only as a guide. It can help you to organize your invention materials and provide a sense of direction as you start drafting.

Drafting the evaluation Before you begin to draft, you might want to review the general advice about drafting in Chapter 1. Reread all your notes. If you are evaluating a published work (a poem, story, novel, etc.) reread it. If you are writing about a movie, go to see it again. Your subject must be completely fresh in your mind.

If you have trouble drafting, consider each element in your evaluation. Perhaps you should think of better reasons or add more evidence to support the reasons you give. You may need to take another look at your criteria. If you really get stuck, turn back to the invention activities to see if you can fill out your material.

READING A DRAFT WITH A CRITICAL EYE

Once you have completed your draft, you may want to have someone else read it. You may be able to read someone else's draft in the same way. Try to adopt a critical viewpoint, looking to see what works and what needs improvement. Try to put yourself in the position of the intended readers. Following are some guidelines to help you analyze the particular features of evaluative essays. (Before you begin, you might want to review the general advice on reading another's draft critically in Chapter 1.)

First general impression Read the essay straight through to get a quick, general impression. Write down a few sentences stating your immediate reaction. If you are reading someone else's evaluation, let the writer know whether you agree or disagree, whether the essay convinced you or left you with questions.

Pointings It is important to maintain a critical focus as you read the essay now; one way to do this is by highlighting notable features of the writing with *pointings*. A simple system of marking a draft with underlining and brackets, these pointings are quick and easy to do and provide helpful information for revising the draft. Use pointings in the following way:

☐ Draw a straight line under any words or images that impress you as especially effective: strong verbs, precise descriptive details, memorable phrases, striking images.

☐ Draw a wavy line under any words or images that seem flat, stale, or vague. Also put a wavy line under any words or phrases that seem unnecessary or repetitious.

☐ Look for pairs or groups of sentences that you think should be combined. Put brackets [ ] around these sentences.

☐ Look for sentences that are garbled, overloaded, or awkward. Put parentheses ( ) around these sentences. Parenthesize any sentence that seems even slightly questionable; don't spend time worrying about whether it actually is incorrect. The writer needs to know that someone had even the slightest difficulty understanding a sentence.

Analysis   Consider the following points as you analyze an evaluation essay.

1. The writer's judgment should be clearly stated. Look to see that there is a firm judgment, rather than just a balance of good and bad points. Is the judgment stated early enough in the essay? Identify the thesis statement.

2. If the criteria are not stated explicitly, what are they? Do any criteria need to be explained or justified? Mention important criteria that seem to have been overlooked.

3. List the reasons the writer gives for the judgment. Tell the writer whether these reasons seem relevant and convincing. Suggest other appropriate reasons.

4. Look closely at the way each reason is developed. What evidence does the writer provide? Not all reasons must be fully developed—some may only be listed—but all of them must be supported with evidence. Look then at the evidence—is it believable and authoritative?

5. Describe the order in which the reasons are given. Does one reason seem to lead logically to the next? Suggest a different order that might strengthen the argument.

6. Look at any comparisons in the draft. What is the basis for the comparison? Is it clear? Is it appropriate? Is it convincing? Think of other comparisons that would help to support the evaluation.

7. How does the writer describe the subject? Tell the writer whether you want to know more or less about the subject.

8. Describe the tone of the essay. Is it consistent from start to finish? Does it seem appropriate for the intended readers?

9. Does the writer use any terms that may be unfamiliar to the intended readers? Are they defined adequately?

10. Consider the balance of the draft. Are the key features treated adequately? Is there too much description? Too little? Too many reasons? Not enough? Look to see if any such elements could use more or less emphasis, and advise the writer about specific changes.

11. Consider the effectiveness of the beginning. Does it engage your interest? If so, how? If not, how do you react? Suggest alternative ways to open the essay.

12. Evaluate the ending. Is it graceful and satisfying? Can you suggest a different conclusion?

REVISING AND EDITING

With a period of invention and drafting behind you, you are now ready to revise your essay. Review any critical reading notes from your instructor or other students. Try to view your draft impersonally in order to see what you actually said, rather than what you intended to say. This section provides guidance in planning your revision.

Revising an evaluation

The following advice on revising an evaluation essay can be used together with the comprehensive plan for revising in Chapter 11. If you want more assistance, turn to Chapter 11 and follow the general revising plan until you reach the section Read Again To Identify Problems. At that point substitute for those general guidelines the following specific guidelines for revising an evaluation essay.

Revising to strengthen the argument

☐ Reconsider the criteria on which your evaluation is based. Are they clear, or do they need explaining? Are they all important, or are any trivial? Should you add any new criteria?

☐ Scrutinize your reasons. If you cannot improve a weak reason, drop it altogether.

☐ Examine all your evidence. Have you provided enough evidence to support your reasons? Have you given too much evidence anywhere? Should you add any new facts or details?

☐ Consider the order of your reasons. Would some other order be more persuasive?

☐ Think about the presentation of your subject. Do you need to reduce or expand your description?

☐ Reread your evaluation with your readers in mind. Have you fully considered their experiences, prejudices, and expectations? How might they challenge your evaluation? Respond to counterarguments.

☐ Listen again to the tone in your paper. Should you modulate it to make it more authoritative, credible, trustworthy, consistent? Is it appropriate for your readers?

Revising for readability

☐ Consider your introduction. Is it engaging? Will it attract a reader's attention? Is it helpful? Does it forecast your plan? Should it?

☐ Look at all the cues and transitions you provide. Are they sufficient?

☐ Reconsider your conclusion. Is it sufficiently emphatic? Does it frame the essay? Do you want it to do so? Does it end your essay with a proper focus?

☐ Examine each sentence. Does it say what you want it to say? Does it state the obvious?

☐ Read to see how your writing flows. Do the sentences fit together gracefully? Should any sentences be broken up or be combined with another sentence?

Editing and proofreading As you revise a draft for the final time, edit it carefully. When you were drafting your essay, your main focus was on figuring out what you wished to say; usage and style were not your first priority. Now, however, you must take the time to find and correct any errors of mechanics, usage, punctuation, or style.

After editing the draft and typing or writing out your final copy, proofread closely before submitting your essay to your instructor.

LEARNING FROM YOUR OWN WRITING PROCESS

Reflect now on the process you followed in writing this essay. Look over all your work—invention writing, draft, and revision. Think about the various problems you encountered choosing a subject or defining criteria or articulating reasons or finding evidence.

Study any changes you made between draft and revision and think about why you made them.

What are the strong points in your essay? What would you still like to improve?

A WRITER AT WORK

ANALYZING REASONS FOR AN EVALUATION

In planning an evaluation essay, a writer must decide what reasons will be most convincing to readers. These reasons must be based on appropriate criteria, and at least some of them must be supported by factual evidence. In this section we will see how Steven Weisman analyzed the reasons he gives in his essay "Undefended by Our Guardian," printed earlier in this chapter.

Following this chapter's Guide to Writing, Weisman charted his criteria, reasons, and evidence in the form of a table as he was planning his essay evaluating the university newspaper, *The Guardian*. Long before drafting, he analyzed this table in writing in order to see that his criteria were appropriate, his reasons sound, and his evidence sufficient. Here is his table.

CRITERIA	REASONS	EVIDENCE
visuals	poorly chosen photographs	January 12 issue: 3 photos, front pager of the governor holding pie
	graphics too large	
layout	ads crowd out articles	6 pages at least 2/3's filled with ads
interest	uninteresting topics	front page: school funding, Middle East politics, hiking trip. Earlier: remedial writing, religion on campus, fake ID's, partying. Only about 5 pages to fill twice weekly. UCLA and Stanford are daily.
	vague headlines	"UC gets a bigger slice of the pie," "MacCrone faces continued legal battles." No kickers, subheadings, or enlarged type
	untrimmed articles	articles too long—only 5 articles on January 12
style	bad writing	Lifson article

After completing the table, Weisman considered which reasons he should actually include in his essay. He decided that they were all good reasons backed by solid evidence and that they would be convincing to the readers he was addressing. After next analyzing each reason in writing, he considered all of the reasons together as a set. Together, these analyses helped him to test the appropriateness of each reason for his readers and the strength of the evidence supporting it, as well as the total effect of all the reasons.

Following is his written analysis.

Analyzing the reasons. Poorly chosen photographs should seem an important reason to students who read the Guardian. It will be easy to convince them that a photo should complement an article and its purpose should be clear, not just decorative. The Deukmejian photo is so silly and inappropriate that it should be evidence enough. Could look at other <u>Guardian</u> issues if I had time. Graphics are related to photos. Readers can easily see that the graphics are too large, really just in order to fill up space. I wonder, though, if all readers have thought about how editors choose photos and graphics. My experience as a newspaper editor is probably unusual. My criteria are not technical or specialized, but I may have to help readers see that they are relevant.

Layout is related to visuals. It gets to the heart of the design or plan of a newspaper, the way the parts are arranged on the page, especially ads in relation to graphics and articles. <u>Guardian</u> is so obviously clumsy about placing ads. Readers will see that this reason is important because ads can be such a distraction.

Uninteresting topics, vague headlines, and untrimmed articles are really the flaw no one can forgive. Even if the <u>Guardian</u> didn't look very pretty, it could still be interesting. I may have to convince readers that too-long articles are a bad idea. I'll have plenty of evidence to support these reasons from the January 12 issue.

Bad writing can't be overlooked. I think one article can show what I mean here.

Considering the set of reasons. I know from my own experience that the set covers all the important criteria in evaluating a newspaper: visuals, layout, interest, and style. There are more technical criteria in the newspaper business, but they wouldn't be appropriate for my readers. Each reason seems to identify a unique feature of a newspaper—no need to combine any of them. Probably the reasons having to do with interest are the most important, and maybe those should come last in my essay. Now that I think of it, maybe I should combine untrimmed articles with bad writing because both result from poor editing. An article that is too long loses readers, but the correction for it is the responsibility of staffers who are supposed to fix bad writing.

In both his draft and revision, Weisman makes good use of his table of criteria, reasons, and evidence and these analyses. The essay essentially follows the sequence of reasons in the table. As he discovers in his analysis, the problem of untrimmed articles and bad writing can be usefully combined.

Speculating About Causes

☐ The national sales manager for a toy company is at a loss to explain the disappointing Christmas sales of the company's perennial best seller. With limited time for research, the sales manager consults the business manager and then begins a telephone survey of company sales representatives and regional sales managers. Meanwhile, the business manager, an astute Texan, reads *The Wall Street Journal* and trade newsletters to see if there is any industry-wide reason to explain the decline. Their final report for the company president includes a graph showing the toy's sales history. The report attributes the decline to the immense popularity and increasing market share of two other toys made by a competing manufacturer. They flatly refuse to entertain the possibility that something is wrong with their toy, citing past sales as evidence of its acceptance in a cutthroat market.

☐ For a popular magazine, two anthropologists write an article in which they offer an explanation for the universal phenomenon of the "afternoon lull," the period of reduced energy after the midday meal. Referring to research studies, they reject the possibility that the lull is caused either by the biochemical effects of eating or by a change in body temperature. They also reject the possibility that the lull is due to laziness or a desire for diversion. They argue instead that the lull is caused by a human rhythm established during early human evolution in the tropics, where heat peaks in the early afternoon.

☐ In an essay for her college composition class, a black college student speculates about the causes of the decline in enrollment of black students, as a percentage of all college students. In order to demonstrate that the trend exists, she reports that from 1980 to 1985, during a time when the number of black high school graduates was rising, the proportion of black college undergraduates declined by 20 percent and of

9

graduates by 12 percent. She offers evidence for three possible causes: continuing prejudice against black students on college campuses, disproportionate financial limitations of black families, and black teenagers' doubts that they can succeed in college. Reporting anecdotes and cases from her own experience, she argues that this last reason may be more influential than people suspect because it is both cause and effect of the trend: black students who drop out return home with stories about finding no place for themselves in college, thus discouraging younger siblings and friends from going to college.

We all quite naturally attempt to explain causes. Because we assume everything has a cause, we predictably ask "Why?" when we notice something new or unusual or when we are puzzled by some familiar feature of daily life.

Many things can be fully and satisfactorily explained. When children ask "Why is the sky blue in the day and black at night?" parents can provide definite answers. But there are other questions we can answer only tentatively: Why do Pacific Ten teams nearly always defeat Big Ten teams in the Rose Bowl? Why did the United States become involved in Vietnam? Why do minority groups in American society continue to suffer discrimination? Phenomena and trends such as these often have only plausible, not definitive explanations because we cannot design a scientific experiment to identify the actual cause conclusively. The decline in SAT scores, for example, has been attributed to the rise in television viewing among children. Though this cause is plausible, we cannot know for certain that it is actually responsible for the drop in scores. Much of what we want to know about ourselves, other people, and the social order can never be known definitively and unarguably, but can only be speculated about on the basis of the best available evidence and experience. Writing that speculates about the causes of puzzling phenomena or trends clearly has an important role to play in academic and professional life, as well as in personal affairs.

In this chapter you will write an essay arguing for the causes of a phenomenon or a trend. A phenomenon is a notable fact of life—racial discrimination, lack of financial aid for college students, fear of failure, popularity of Japanese cars. A trend is a prevailing increase or decrease—in female ministers, political action groups, single-parent households, whatever. You first need to describe the phenomenon or trend and then to propose some causes and argue for one or more as the best available explanation. You do not have to prove that your explanation is right, but you must convince readers that it is plausible.

This chapter is the fourth in this book's persuasive writing sequence, which is designed to introduce you to the most common and important writing situations requiring argument. In this chapter you will explore ways to construct a convincing causal argument speculating about why things are the way they are or why things change. You will find this form of argumentative writing especially challenging and satisfying. Writing about the causes of a phenomenon or trend will help you to develop your powers of creativity as you speculate about possible causes, your powers of judgment as you weigh these possibilities and choose the most plausible ones, and your powers of reasoning as you devise an argumentative strategy to present your conclusions to your readers. All the thinking, planning, and writing strategies involved in this kind of writing will prepare you for many reading and writing situations that you will encounter in other college classes and later on in your career.

The readings that follow show several strategies writers use to establish the plausibility of their causes.

READINGS

The first selection is by Stephen King, America's best-known writer of horror fiction. Writing for *Playboy* magazine, King speculates about the popular appeal of horror movies. Before you begin reading, think about your own attitude toward horror films. Would you say you enjoy or even "crave" them? Are you repulsed by them? Indifferent?

As you read, notice how assertively King presents his assumptions about people, such as the one in the opening sentence. How does he try to get you to accept these assumptions? Is he successful?

**WHY WE CRAVE
HORROR MOVIES**
STEPHEN KING

I think that we're all mentally ill; those of us outside the asylums only hide 1
it a little better—and maybe not all that much better, after all. We've all known people who talk to themselves, people who sometimes squinch their faces into horrible grimaces when they believe no one is watching, people who have some hysterical fear—of snakes, the dark, the tight place, the long drop . . . and, of course, those final worms and grubs that are waiting so patiently underground.

When we pay our four or five bucks and seat ourselves at tenth-row center 2
in a theater showing a horror movie, we are daring the nightmare.

Why? Some of the reasons are simple and obvious. To show that we can, 3
that we are not afraid, that we can ride this roller coaster. Which is not to say that a really good horror movie may not surprise a scream out of us at some point, the way we may scream when the roller coaster twists through a complete 360 or plows through a lake at the bottom of the drop. And horror movies, like roller coasters, have always been the special province of the young; by the time one turns 40 or 50, one's appetite for double twists or 360-degree loops may be considerably depleted.

We also go to re-establish our feelings of essential normality; the horror 4
movie is innately conservative, even reactionary. Freda Jackson as the horrible
melting woman in *Die, Monster, Die!* confirms for us that no matter how far
we may be removed from the beauty of a Robert Redford or a Diana Ross, we
are still light-years from true ugliness.

And we go to have fun. 5

Ah, but this is where the ground starts to slope away, isn't it? Because this 6
is a very peculiar sort of fun, indeed. The fun comes from seeing others men-
aced—sometimes killed. One critic has suggested that if pro football has become
the voyeur's version of combat, then the horror film has become the modern
version of the public lynching.

It is true that the mythic, "fairy-tale" horror film intends to take away the 7
shades of gray. . . . It urges us to put away our more civilized and adult penchant
for analysis and to become children again, seeing things in pure blacks and
whites. It may be that horror movies provide psychic relief on this level because
this invitation to lapse into simplicity, irrationality and even outright madness is
extended so rarely. We are told we may allow our emotions a free rein . . . or
no rein at all.

If we are all insane, then sanity becomes a matter of degree. If your insanity 8
leads you to carve up women like Jack the Ripper or the Cleveland Torso Mur-
derer, we clap you away in the funny farm (but neither of those two amateur-
night surgeons was ever caught, heh-heh-heh); if, on the other hand, your
insanity leads you only to talk to yourself when you're under stress or to pick
your nose on your morning bus, then you are left alone to go about your business
. . . though it is doubtful that you will ever be invited to the best parties.

The potential lyncher is in almost all of us (excluding saints, past and present; 9
but then, most saints have been crazy in their own ways), and every now and
then, he has to be let loose to scream and roll around in the grass. Our emotions
and our fears form their own body, and we recognize that it demands its own
exercise to maintain proper muscle tone. Certain of these emotional muscles are
accepted—even exalted—in civilized society; they are, of course, the emotions
that tend to maintain the status quo of civilization itself. Love, friendship, loyalty,
kindness—these are all the emotions that we applaud, emotions that have been
immortalized in the couplets of Hallmark cards and in the verses (I don't dare
call it poetry) of Leonard Nimoy.

When we exhibit these emotions, society showers us with positive reinforce- 10
ment; we learn this even before we get out of diapers. When, as children, we
hug our rotten little puke of a sister and give her a kiss, all the aunts and uncles
smile and twit and cry, "Isn't he the sweetest little thing?" Such coveted treats
as chocolate-covered graham crackers often follow. But if we deliberately slam
the rotten little puke of a sister's fingers in the door, sanctions follow—angry
remonstrance from parents, aunts and uncles; instead of a chocolate-covered
graham cracker, a spanking.

But anticivilization emotions don't go away, and they demand periodic ex- 11
ercise. We have such "sick" jokes as, "What's the difference between a truckload of bowling balls and a truckload of dead babies?" (You can't unload a

truckload of bowling balls with a pitchfork . . . a joke, by the way, that I heard originally from a ten-year-old). Such a joke may surprise a laugh or a grin out of us even as we recoil, a possibility that confirms the thesis: If we share a brotherhood of man, then we also share an insanity of man. None of which is intended as a defense of either the sick joke or insanity but merely as an explanation of why the best horror films, like the best fairy tales, manage to be reactionary, anarchistic, and revolutionary all at the same time.

The mythic horror movie, like the sick joke, has a dirty job to do. It delib- 12
erately appeals to all that is worst in us. It is morbidity unchained, our most base instincts let free, our nastiest fantasies realized . . . and it all happens, fittingly enough, in the dark. For those reasons, good liberals often shy away from horror films. For myself, I like to see the most aggressive of them—*Dawn of the Dead*, for instance—as lifting a trap door in the civilized forebrain and throwing a basket of raw meat to the hungry alligators swimming around in that subterranean river beneath.

Why bother? Because it keeps them from getting out, man. It keeps them 13
down there and me up here. It was Lennon and McCartney who said that all you need is love, and I would agree with that.

As long as you keep the gators fed. 14

Questions for analysis

1. In this essay, King appears to be suggesting that horror films perform a social function by allowing us to exercise or possibly exorcise our "anti-civilization emotions." How do you react to this idea? What does it imply about the general role of literature, film, and art in society?

2. Do you find King's causal argument convincing? Which parts do you find most and least convincing? How convincing do you think his argument would be for readers of *Playboy*? Why?

3. A successful argument often depends on a careful definition of a key term. Which term does King define? What significance does the definition have for King's argument? How convincing do you find his definition? (You will find strategies for defining illustrated in Chapter 16: Defining.)

4. Why do you think King begins as he does? Given the causal argument that follows and his particular readers, what advantage do you see in this beginning?

5. Causal arguments must be carefully sequenced and logically developed. To discover King's plan, make a scratch outline of the selection. (Scratch outlines are discussed in Chapter 11: Invention and Revision.) Then, to follow one of his main cues for keeping readers on track, analyze the transitions at the beginning of each paragraph. Begin by underlining the word or phrase that makes the exact connection with the previous paragraph. (For information on transitions, see Chapter 12: Cueing the Reader.)

6. How effective do you find the analogy King uses in paragraph 3? To analyze its effectiveness, consider carefully the ways in which horror movies and roller coaster rides are similar and dissimilar. Can you think of another

analogy that would work? (Analogy in argument is illustrated in Chapter 18: Comparing and Contrasting.)

7. What phenomenon of popular culture interests you enough to speculate about its causes? (You may or may not be an enthusiastic participant in the phenomenon.) Have you ever wondered why adult romance novels are so popular? Police shows and soap operas on television? Survivalist war games? Singles bars? Computer hacking? How would you present the phenomenon to your readers and develop an argument for its causes?

Commentary   To understand King's argument, it may help to distinguish between the obvious and hidden causes. King begins with a cause that seems obvious but is still worth mentioning: we go to horror films because we want to prove that we can sit through them—that we can "dare the nightmare"—just as we ride roller coasters to show ourselves and others that we have the courage to do it (paragraph 3). This cause seems plausible, though not at all surprising. We can assume that King mentions it right away because he assumes readers will be thinking of it. It enables him both to connect to a very common experience of his readers and to set an obvious cause aside in order to move on to the not-so-obvious causes, which are the heart of his argument.

King next entertains a very different cause: we go to horror movies "to re-establish our feeling of essential normality." This cause is much less predictable than the first. It may even be somewhat puzzling, and King might have argued it further. He asserts that horror movies are conservative and gives one illustration about the attractiveness of their actors and actresses. However plausible this cause, it does move us from obvious causes toward the one hidden (unexpected, unlikely, risky) cause that King is to argue at length—we "crave" horror movies (not just attend them casually) in order to manage our uncivilized emotions of fear, violence, and aggression. We may not accept King's psychology or find this hidden cause convincingly argued, but we are almost certainly interested in the argument itself, perhaps intrigued, maybe even shocked by either the idea or the examples. Whatever our reaction, King has not bored us with causes so obvious that we could have predicted all of them before reading the selection. In your own causal analysis essay, your first goal will be to speculate creatively about your subject so that you can come up with at least one not-so-obvious cause. Like King, you may want to place this cause last, after discussing other more obvious causes, and to argue for it at length and with ingenuity.

Experienced writers address their arguments to particular readers, letting them know in the essay that they are taking into account their values and beliefs as well as anticipating their counterarguments. We see this strategy in the way King attempts to get us to accept his striking assertions about our basic nature: "we're all mentally ill" (paragraph 1), "the potential lyncher is in almost all of us" (paragraph 9), and "anticivilization emotions . . .

demand periodic exercise" (paragraph 11). Knowing these are debatable assertions, King defines his terms and qualifies them in a way that will enable most readers to consider his argument seriously, instead of rejecting it irritably. For example, he defines the disguised insanity in all of us in terms of all too familiar private habits and personal fears. Later he reminds us that sick jokes, which nearly all readers have told or laughed at from time to time, reveal our "anticivilization emotions." At the end of paragraph 11, King attempts to bridge the gap between himself and his readers by addressing them for solidarity as "we." He says, to paraphrase: "Look, I know you may be resisting my argument; but if I acknowledge that we all do share a brotherhood of man, then I think you should be able to acknowledge that we share an insanity of man, as I have been arguing. I'm not trying to encourage sick jokes or excuse aggression and violence but only to explain why we crave horror movies." This kind of direct acknowledgment of readers' points of view increases a writer's credibility and results in a more convincing argument. When you draft and revise your essay of causal analysis, you will want to give considerable thought to acknowledging readers—anticipating their objections to your argument as well as the causes they themselves might suggest. (Chapter 19: Arguing further illustrates this strategy of anticipating readers' counterarguments.)

To write an effective essay, you will have to develop an argumentative strategy, which includes anticipating your readers' views and sequencing the causes you consider. This strategy must be worked out in the context of your purpose and readers. It may be instructive to consider King's causal argument strategy in this selection. He begins assertively, even challengingly, trying to engage his readers' interests and ally himself with them immediately ("those of us outside the asylums"). He proposes "simple and obvious" reasons and then moves directly to his not-so-obvious reason, defining the "peculiar sort of fun" that draws us to horror movies. Much of his argument for this reason involves reminding readers of their dark side and its consequences and convincing them that horror movies and sick jokes (and presumably horror novels) help us exercise our dark fantasies harmlessly. In the end, his argument is psychological. His tone is tough but engaging. We know what his thesis is and where he is going with the argument. Whether or not we are convinced, we can admire his thoughtfulness and craftsmanship.

Like King, the author of the following selection, communications professor Joshua Meyerowitz speculates about the causes of a phenomenon: why some children seem so adult. As you read this *Newsweek* article, notice how carefully Meyerowitz describes the phenomenon he is speculating about; he devotes nearly half his essay to this description. As is often the case with causal analysis, Meyerowitz must first convince readers that the phenomenon or trend actually exists. Have you, too, noticed this phenomenon?

WHY CHILDREN DON'T SEEM CHILDLIKE ANYMORE
JOSHUA MEYEROWITZ

About six years ago I was eating lunch in a diner in New York City when a women and a young boy sat down in the next booth. I couldn't help overhearing parts of their conversation. At one point the woman asked: "So, how have you been?" And the boy—who could not have been more than seven or eight years old—replied, "Frankly, I've been feeling a little depressed lately." 1

This incident stuck in my mind because it confirmed my growing belief that children are changing. As far as I can remember, my friends and I didn't find out we were "depressed" until we were in high school. 2

The evidence of a change in children has increased steadily in recent years. Children don't seem childlike anymore. Children speak more like adults, dress more like adults and behave more like adults than they used to. The reverse is also true: adults have begun to speak, dress and act more like overgrown children. 3

It is not unusual to see children wearing three-piece suits or designer dresses, or adults in Mickey Mouse T shirts, jeans and sneakers. Adults now wear what were once considered play clothes to many work locations, including the White House. 4

Education, career choice and developmental stages were once discussed primarily in relation to children and adolescents. Now an increasing number of adults are enrolling in adult-education programs, changing careers in midlife and becoming concerned with their "life stages." Meanwhile, alcoholism, suicide, drug addiction and abortion have become children's issues. Children also commit adult crimes such as armed robbery and murder. 5

The merging of childhood and adulthood is reflected in the shifting image of children in entertainment. The Shirley Temple character of the past was a cute and outspoken child. Current child stars, such as Brooke Shields and Gary Coleman, seem to be adults imprisoned in children's bodies. 6

Whether this is good or bad is difficult to say, but it certainly is different. Childhood as it once was no longer exists. Why? 7

Human development is based not only on innate biological states, but also on patterns of access to social knowledge. Movement from one social role to another usually involves learning the secrets of the new status. Children have always been taught adult secrets, but slowly and in stages: traditionally, we tell sixth graders things we keep hidden from fifth graders. 8

In the last 30 years, however, a secret-revelation machine has been installed in 98 percent of American homes. It is called television. 9

Communication through print allows for a great deal of control over the social information to which children have access. Reading and writing involve a complex code of symbols that must be memorized and practiced. Children must read simple books before they can read adult books. 10

On TV, however, there is no complex code to exclude young viewers. There is no sharp distinction between the information available to the fifth grader, the high-school student and the adult. Even two-year-old children, unable to read or write their own names, find television accessible and absorbing. They watch over 27 hours a week. 11

While adults often demand more children's programming, children them- 12
selves prefer adult programs. In fact, everyone, regardless of age, tends to watch
similar programs. In 1980, for example, "Dallas," "The Dukes of Hazzard," "Love
Boat" and "The Muppets" were among the most popular programs in *all* age
groups in the country, including ages 2 to 11.

The world of children's books can be insulated to present kids with an 13
idealized view of adulthood. But television news and entertainment presents
children with images of adults who lie, drink, cheat and murder.

Reading skill no longer determines the sequence in which social information 14
is revealed to children. Through books, adults could communicate among themselves without being overheard by children. Advice books for parents, for example, can refer them to books that would be inappropriate for children. Similar
attempts on television are relatively useless because they are as open to children
as they are to adults. Advisory warnings on television often have a boomerang
effect by *increasing* children's interest in what follows.

Even early conservative programs such as "Father Knows Best" and "Leave 15
It to Beaver" reveal important social secrets to children. They portray adults
behaving one way in front of children and another way when alone. "Father
Knows Best," for example, reveals to the child viewer the ways in which a father
hides his doubts and manipulates his behavior to make it appear to his children
that he knows best.

Such programs teach children that adults play roles for their benefit and that 16
the behavior adults exhibit to children is not necessarily their real or only behavior. Television not only exposes adult secrets, it also exposes the secret of
secrecy. As a result, children become more suspicious of adults and adults may
feel it no longer makes sense to try to keep some things hidden from children.
Television undermines behavioral distinctions because it encompasses both children and adults in a single informational sphere or environment.

Many formal reciprocal roles rely on lack of intimate knowledge of the other. 17
If the mystery and mystification disappear, so do the formal behaviors. Stylized
courtship behaviors, for example, must quickly fade in the day-to-day intimacy
of marriage. Similarly, television's involvement of children in adult affairs undermines many traditional adult-child roles.

Given this analysis, it is not surprising that the first widespread rejection of 18
both traditional child and traditional adult behavior occurred in the late 1960s
among the first generation of Americans to have grown up with television. In
the shared environment of television, children and adults know a great deal
about each other's behavior and social knowledge—too much, in fact, for
them to play out the traditional complementary roles of innocence versus
omnipotence.

Questions for analysis   1. In the concluding sentence, Meyerowitz describes the traditional relationship of children and adults in terms of innocence and omnipotence.
What do you think he means by these terms? As a child, how was your
experience with your parents or other adults like or unlike this kind of
relationship?

2. How does Meyerowitz attempt to convince readers (in paragraphs 1–7) that "children don't seem childlike anymore"? What kinds of evidence does he cite? What does he mean by the term *childlike?* What behavior and attitudes does he associate with being childlike? How convincing is this part of his essay?

3. Meyerowitz proposes one cause to explain why children seem so adult—television. Beginning in paragraph 9, he argues for this cause trying to make it seem plausible to his readers. Does this cause seem predictable or obvious to you? What do you find most and least convincing in his argument?

4. List the points of contrast between books and television. Why do you think Meyerowitz develops this contrast? How does it support his argument?

5. Write several sentences outlining Meyerowitz's causal argument strategy—how he presents the subject, argues causes, and anticipates readers' assumptions given his writing situation (purpose and readers).

6. Meyerowitz and King wrote their pieces for readers of two well-known, popular national magazines. What features of the two pieces make them appropriate for a magazine?

7. What phenomena of human behavior have puzzled you lately? Have you wondered why people are lazy, jealous, determined, fickle, creative; why some people are able to solve problems, program computers, act, or get along with strangers superbly; why others are short-sighted, idealistic, reckless, childlike, old before their time, or unable to keep the gators fed, as King would say? Which of these phenomena might you write about? How would you describe the phenomena for your readers? What not-so-obvious causes could you come up with to explain it?

Commentary   Like King, Meyerowitz argues for not-so-obvious or "hidden" causes as the best explanation for the phenomenon he analyzes. In addition to the hidden cause, Meyerowitz's essay illustrates several other kinds of causes. Television can be thought of as the *immediate* or *precipitating* cause of children's new knowledge and attitudes because the change he describes occurred just as TV became widespread. You could say television started it all, and know approximately when it happened. Furthermore, you could argue that television is a *sufficient* cause of the change, that television alone could have caused it. Television may even be seen as a *necessary* cause if you were to argue that the change could not have occurred without it. Finally, you could classify television as a *perpetuating* cause, arguing that it perpetuates or continues the phenomenon, sustaining it now and into the future. In other words, childhood will never be the way it once was as long as children and adults continue to watch the same television programs.

This brief analysis of different kinds of causes introduces important concepts in causal analysis. Your own essay will be much more thoughtful and convincing if you have first analyzed the causes you are considering to determine whether you could argue that they are immediate, sufficient, necessary, or perpetuating causes of the phenomenon or trend.

If a cause is immediate or perpetuating, you will want to ask yourself what other causes might lay behind it because these might be more important and influential. You should also be careful to avoid the most common pitfall of causal reasoning: thinking that just because one thing follows another in time, the second was caused by the first. This fallacy is often called by its Latin name *post hoc, ergo propter hoc,* meaning "after this, therefore because of this."

The most convincing causal arguments demonstrate that the proposed cause is necessary. Being sufficient to cause the effect is not enough since something else could have actually caused it. If the cause can be shown to be necessary, however, there can be no doubt that the phenomenon or trend could not have happened without it. Nevertheless, take into consideration as you plan your argument that essays based on necessary causes may not be very interesting because these are often also the most obvious causes.

The next selection is from a book by Victor Fuchs, *How We Live: An Economic Perspective on Americans from Birth to Death* (1983). A professor of economics at Stanford, Fuchs has for many years been a research associate at the National Bureau of Economic Research. Here he speculates about the causes of a trend. (King and Meyerowitz speculate about the causes of phenomena.) As you begin reading, notice the care with which Fuchs documents the trend.

The tone of Fuchs's essay is more serious than King's. Fuchs does not let his personality show. His essay is not only impersonal, it is dryly factual; it seems to move slowly, but such slowness is actually a tribute to the rigor of Fuchs's careful reasoning and attention to detail.

As you read, pay attention to both the causes Fuchs rejects and the ones he proposes to explain the increase in suicides among young people.

SUICIDE AMONG YOUNG PEOPLE

VICTOR FUCHS

Although the vigor and vitality of most young people are the envy of their elders, a significant range of serious health problems are present at ages 15–24, including venereal disease, alcoholism, and drug abuse. Moreover, a large number of adolescents and youth are making themselves vulnerable to future health problems through cigarette smoking, poor diet, and inadequate exercise (Institute of Medicine 1978). One of the most disturbing trends is rising mortality among youth at a time when death rates at all other ages are declining rapidly. Male death rates at ages 15–19 and 20–24 were 12 percent *higher* in 1977 than in 1960, while mortality at other ages *declined* an average of 12 percent. A large differential in mortality trends by age is also evident for women. The

deaths of young people take a tremendous emotional toll and are also particularly costly because these men and women are at the threshold of productive
lives during which they and society could realize a return on the investment that
has been made in them.

The principal reason for the divergent trends in mortality by age is the in- 2
crease in self-destructive behavior by young men and women (see the tabulation
below). Among young men, suicide and motor vehicle accidents now account
for half of all deaths, and among women for well over 40 percent. More youth
die from suicide alone than from cancer, cardiovascular disease, diabetes, pneu-
monia, and influenza combined. The rising death rate from homicide also contributes to the rising death rate among the young. Homicide rates have approximately doubled at most ages, but because it is a relatively more important cause
of death among the young, this doubling has had more of an impact on their
overall rate. The high homicide rate among nonwhite men is particularly shocking, averaging about 50 per year per hundred thousand at ages 15–19 and over
100 per hundred thousand at ages 20–24. These rates imply that almost one
out of every 100 black youths who turn 15 becomes a homicide victim before
the age of 25! Apart from violent deaths, the trends in mortality of young men
and women have been as favorable as at older ages.

	Percent change in age-sex-specific death rates, 1960 to 1977	
	Ages 15–24	Ages 25 and over
Suicide	145	6
Motor vehicle accidents	25	−15
Homicide	113	83
All other causes	−22	−21

Why did suicide rates among young people increase so rapidly in the 1960s 3
and 1970s? It is much easier to rule out answers to this question than to find
ones that will withstand critical examination. For instance, it is highly unlikely
that the trend is a result of differences in the reporting of suicides, although
reporting practices do vary considerably over time and in different areas.
Changes in reporting, however, would affect the suicide rate at all ages, and
there was no comparable increase at other stages of life. The emotional trauma
of the Vietnam War was felt more keenly by young people and this may have
contributed to the increase in suicides, but there are two problems with this
explanation. First, after the war ended the suicide rate among young people
kept on rising, rather than falling back to prewar levels (see Figure 9.1). Second,
suicide rates at ages 15–24 in Canada and Sweden have been rising as rapidly
and are as high as in the United States. Neither country was much affected by
the Vietnam War.

Suicides have been blamed on deteriorating economic conditions, but Figure 4
9.1 shows that the rate has been rising in good times as well as bad; the long-

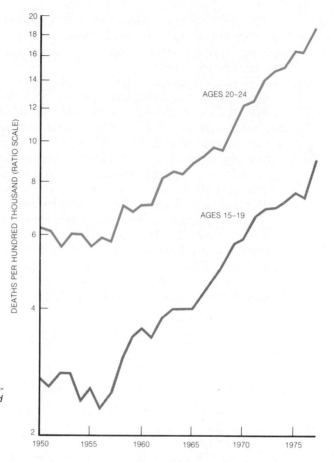

term trend is much stronger than any response to business cycle fluctuations. Furthermore, the suicide level is slightly higher among white than nonwhite youth and the rate of increase has been as rapid for whites as for nonwhites, despite the large race differentials in youth employment. One of the more mischievous arguments currently in vogue is that the problems of children and youth are the result of high unemployment and that their solution lies in better macroeconomic policies. Of course low unemployment is better than high, and price stability is preferable to inflation, but anyone who believes that the increases in suicides among youth, births to unwed mothers, juvenile crime, and one-parent homes are primarily the result of macroeconomic conditions is ignoring readily available evidence. All these problems were increasing particularly rapidly during the second half of the 1960s, when the unemployment rate averaged 3.8 percent and economic growth was extremely rapid.

Some mental health experts attribute the increases in suicides among the 5 young to the rapid changes in the American family. A study at Bellevue Hospital in New York City of 102 teenagers who attempted suicide showed that only one-third of them lived with both parents (*Newsweek,* August 28, 1978, p. 74). Parents may be failing to provide enough structure and security for children either because they are not present or because they are preoccupied with their own lives and careers, or simply because they are too permissive. In a review of psychosocial literature on adolescence, Elder (1975) concludes: "Adolescents who fail to receive guidance, affection, and concern from parents—whether by parental inattention or absence—are likely to rely heavily on peers for emotional gratification, advice, and companionship, *to anticipate a relatively unrewarding future,* and to engage in antisocial activities" (italics added). On the other hand, some experts contend that too many demands and the setting of unrealistic standards by parents also predispose young people toward suicide.

Some evidence of a relation between family background and suicide appears 6 in a long-term longitudinal study of fifty thousand male students of Harvard University and the University of Pennsylvania that compared the characteristics of 381 men who eventually committed suicide with a set of living control subjects randomly chosen from the same school and year as the suicides (Paffenbarger, King, and Wing 1969). One of the strongest results was a positive relation between suicide and loss of father. At the time of the original interview (average age 18) the future suicides were more likely than the controls to have a deceased father (12.4 percent versus 8.1 percent) or to have parents who had separated (12.6 percent versus 8.9 percent). The difference in paternal loss through death or separation was statistically significant at a high level of confidence. The future suicides also differed from the control by having a larger percentage of fathers who were college-educated (69.1 percent versus 56.6 percent) and who were professionals (48.8 percent versus 38.4 percent). Loss of mother did not differ between the suicides and the controls.

It must be emphasized that the rapid increase in suicide rates among youth 7 is unique to that age group—there is nothing comparable at other ages. By contrast, the doubling of death rates from homicide at young ages reflects a general increase in violent crime that has affected all age groups, although not in exactly equal degree.

For some problems, such as the sharp increase in suicides, no simple or even 8 moderately complex public policy solution is in the offing. Young people may be succumbing to what Abraham Maslow (1959) forecast as the ultimate disease of our time—"valuelessness." The rise in suicides and other self-destructive behavior such as motor vehicle accidents and drug abuse may be the result of weakening family structures and the absence of fathers, as suggested by the study of Harvard University and University of Pennsylvania students. We can't be sure of the cause, but if it's along the lines suggested above, the challenge to public policy is staggering.

REFERENCES

Elder, Glen H., Jr. 1975. Adolescence in the life cycle: An introduction. In *Adolescence in the life cycle: Psychological change and social context,* ed. Sigmund E. Dragastin and Glen H. Elder, Jr. New York: Halsted-Wiley.

Institute of Medicine. 1978. *Adolescent behavior and health.* Washington, D.C.: National Academy of Sciences.

Maslow, Abraham H. 1959. *New knowledge in human values.* New York: Harper and Brothers.

Paffenbarger, Ralph S. Jr.; Stanley H. King; and Alvin L. Wing. 1969. Characteristics in youth that predispose to suicide and accidental death in later life. *American Journal of Public Health* 59 (June): 900–908.

Questions for analysis

1. In this essay, Fuchs discusses the self-destructive behavior of young people. What kinds of self-destructive behavior are you aware of among young people you know? Why do you think they behave this way?

2. How does Fuchs demonstrate that there is a trend of increased suicide among young people? What role do the table and figure play? Has he convinced you that the trend actually exists?

3. What causes does Fuchs propose to explain the increasing number of suicides among young people? Analyze Fuchs's proposed causes in terms of the categories introduced earlier in this chapter: obvious, hidden, precipitating, perpetuating, necessary, and sufficient. (You may want to review the discussion of these categories in the commentary following the King and Meyerowitz essays.)

4. What kind of evidence does Fuchs offer for his proposed causes? How convincing do you find his argument?

5. In "ruling out answers" to his question at the beginning of paragraph 3, Fuchs rejects alternatives to his own proposed causes. List the alternative causes he rejects in paragraphs 3 and 4. In paragraph 7, Fuchs reiterates his objections to an alternative cause he had discussed earlier. Why do you think he does this? Why do you think he devotes so much space to considering alternatives that he then rejects?

6. How does Fuchs conclude his essay? Does he frame it by repeating some element of the beginning in the ending? How successful do you find his ending? Can you suggest a more effective conclusion?

7. Imagine that you had the opportunity to write about some recent trend in "how we live" (to borrow the title of the book from which this essay was taken). What important trends have caught your attention? Choose one. How would you demonstrate that the trend exists? What causes would you suggest?

Commentary

Fuchs's essay is easy to read because it follows a simple plan:

> beginning
> > context for suicide trend
> > demonstration of suicide trend
>
> consideration and rejection of alternative causes
> argument for proposed causes

> parental failure
> loss of father
> reiteration of why the most likely alternative cause should be rejected
> ending

Essays explaining trends nearly always begin by demonstrating the trend and then move on to the causes. The challenge in planning such an essay is in ordering the causes to make the most convincing argument. Another decision that must be made is where to take up alternative causes.

Writing about trends involving people and groups usually demands the kind of careful arguments Fuchs presents. It is the sort of argumentative writing we rely on for help making personal and social-policy decisions when there is no unarguable scientific evidence to tell us what to do. Such analysis helps us to consider plausible arguments, decide which is the best one, and then decide what to do.

Fuchs's essay provides causal analysis typical of the social sciences. You will encounter such analysis often in the texts you will be required to read as a college student as well as in the social or political analysis found on the editorial pages of newspapers and magazines. You may very well be asked to write a causal analysis yourself, either as an essay exam or as a term paper.

The documenting style in Fuchs's essay is the style favored in the social sciences, that of the American Psychological Association. The following student essay also uses the APA style. You might want to contrast this social science documentation with the style favored in the humanities, that of the Modern Language Association. The Green selection in Chapter 5 uses the MLA style. Chapter 22: The Research Paper provides detailed information on using each style.

The final essay, written by college freshman Kim Dartnell, looks at the plight of homeless American women. Like Fuchs's essay, it illustrates how a writer can use library research to analyze a trend. In her essay Dartnell documents the trend and defines its special characteristics.

Before reading the essay, recall what you know about the homeless in America and homeless women in particular. What reasons can you think of for men and women being without homes?

WHERE WILL THEY SLEEP TONIGHT?

KIM DARTNELL

On January 21, 1982, in New York City, Rebecca Smith died of hypothermia, [1] after living for five months in a cardboard box. Rebecca was one of a family of thirteen children from a rural town in Virginia. After graduating from high school and giving birth to a daughter, she spent ten years in mental institutions, where she underwent involuntary shock treatment for schizophrenia. It was when she was released to her sister's custody that Rebecca began wandering the streets of New York, living from day to day. Many New York City social workers tried unsuccessfully to persuade her to go into a city shelter. Rebecca died only a few hours before she was scheduled to be placed into protective custody. Rebecca Smith's story is all too typical. Rebecca herself, however, was anything but a typical homeless woman; not only did she graduate from high school, but she was the valedictorian of her class (Hombs and Snyder, 1982, p. 56).

Rebecca Smith is one of an increasing number of homeless women in America. Vagrant men have always been a noticeable problem in American cities, and their numbers have increased in the 1980s. Vagrancy among women is a relatively new problem of any size, however. In 1979, New York City had one public shelter for homeless women. By 1983 it had four. Los Angeles has just recently increased the number of beds available to its skid-row homeless women (Stoner, 1983, p. 571). Even smaller communities have noticed an increase in homeless women. It is impossible to know the number of homeless women or the extent of their increase in the 1980s, but everyone who has studied the problem agrees that it is serious and that it is getting worse (Hombs and Snyder, 1982, p. 10; Stoner, 1984, p. 3).

Who are these women? Over half of all homeless women are under the age of forty. Forty-four percent are black, forty percent white. The statistics for homeless men are about the same (Stoner, 1983, p. 570). There are several ways homeless women cope with their dangerous lifestyle. To avoid notice, especially by the police, some women will have one set of nice clothes that they wash often. They will shower in shelters or YWCA's and try to keep their hairstyle close to the latest fashions. An extreme is the small number of women who actually sleep on park benches, sitting up, to avoid wrinkling their clothes. On the other end of the spectrum is the more noticeable "bag lady," who will purposely maintain an offensive appearance and body odor to protect herself from rape or robbery. These women are almost always unemployed and poorly educated. "Homeless women do not choose their circumstances. They are victims of forces over which they have lost control" (Stoner, 1983, pp. 568, 569).

The question is, why has there been such an increase in the number of vagrant American women? There are several causes of this trend. For one thing, more and more women are leaving their families because of abuse. It is unclear whether this increase is due to an actual increase of abuse in American families, or whether it results from the fact that it is easier and more socially acceptable for a woman to be on her own today. Once on her own, however, the woman all too often finds it difficult to support herself. A more substantial reason is the fact that social programs for battered women have been severely cut back, leaving victims of rape, incest, and other physical abuse nowhere else to go. To take one example, the Christian Housing Facility, a private organization in Orange County, California, that provides food, shelter, and counseling to abused families, sheltered 1,536 people in 1981, a 300-percent increase from the year before (Stoner, 1983, p. 573).

Evictions and illegal lockouts force some women onto the streets. Social welfare cutbacks, unemployment, and desertion all result in a loss of income. Once a woman cannot pay her rent, she is likely to be evicted, often without notice.

Another problem is a lack of inexpensive housing. Of today's homeless 6 women, over fifty percent lived in single rooms before they became vagrants. Many of the buildings containing single-room dwellings or cheap apartments have been torn down to make way for land renovation. Hotels are being offered new tax incentives that make it economically unfeasible to maintain inexpensive single rooms. This is obviously a serious problem, one that sends many women out onto the streets every year.

Alcoholism has been cited as a major reason for the increase in the number 7 of homeless women. I don't feel this is a major contributing factor, however. First, there hasn't been a significant general increase in alcoholism to parallel the rise in homeless women; second, alcoholism occurs at all levels of financial status, from the executive to the homeless. Rather, I would like to suggest that alcoholism is a result of homelessness, not the cause.

Probably the biggest single factor in the rising numbers of homeless women 8 is the deinstitutionalization of the mentally ill. One study estimated that ninety percent of all vagrant women may be mentally ill (Stoner, 1983, p. 567), as was the case with Rebecca Smith. The last few years have seen an avalanche in the number of mental patients released. Between 1955 and 1980 the numbers of patients in mental institutions dropped by 75 percent, from about 560,000 to about 140,000. There are several reasons for this. New psychotonic drugs can now "cure" patients with mild disturbances. Expanded legal rights for patients lead to early release from asylums. Government-funded services such as Medicare allow some patients to be released into nursing or boarding homes. The problem is that many of these women have really not known any life outside the hospital and suddenly find themselves thrust out into an unreceptive world, simply because they present no threat to society, or are "unresponsive to treatment." Very few of them are ever referred to community mental health centers. Instead, many of them go straight out on the streets. They may live with family or in some other inexpensive housing, but sooner or later they are likely to end up in the streets. And once homeless, all funding stops, as someone without an address can't receive any benefits from the government.

Although deinstitutionalization seems to have been the biggest factor in the 9 increase in vagrant women, there is some evidence that the main cause is economic. In 1981, 3,500,000 Americans were living below the poverty line. Unemployment hit 10.1 percent in 1982, the highest it has been since 1940. Yet, that same year saw $2.35 billion cut from food-stamp programs. Reductions in Aid to Families with Dependent Children (AFDC) hit women particularly hard because four out of five AFDC families are headed by women, two thirds of whom have not graduated from high school. (All data are from Hombs and Snyder, 1982). Coupled with inflation, recession, unemployment, and loss of other welfare benefits, these cuts have effectively forced many women into homelessness, and can be expected to continue to do so at a greater rate in the years to come.

The United States may be one of the world's most prosperous nations, but 10 for Rebecca Smith and others like her, the American Dream is far from being fulfilled.

REFERENCES

Hombs, M. E., and Snyder, M. (1982). *Homelessness in America*. Washington, D.C.: Community for Creative Non-Violence.

Stoner, M. R. (1983). The plight of homeless women. *Social Service Review, 57*, 565–581.

Stoner, M. R. (1984). An analysis of public and private sector provisions for homeless people. *The Urban and Social Change Review, 17*.

Questions for analysis

1. Have you ever encountered a homeless person? How do you react to the fact that many people, including women, are homeless? Why do you think our society allows people to remain in this condition?

2. How convincing do you find Dartnell's explanation for the increasing numbers of homeless women? If you find it convincing, how would you explain its effectiveness? If it is not convincing, how could it be improved?

3. What is Dartnell's purpose in this essay? What does she seem to assume about her readers? Briefly describe her argumentative strategy.

4. In paragraph 7, Dartnell rejects an alternative cause that is frequently used to explain why women are homeless. How does she construct her refutation? How convincing do you find it? Why do you think Dartnell makes a point of refuting this particular argument?

5. Write out a brief scratch outline of this essay. How does Dartnell order her proposed causes? Given her argumentative strategy, what advantages or disadvantages do you see in this order?

6. How does Dartnell begin and end her essay? How effective is this way of beginning and ending a causal argument?

7. Think of another troubling social trend you might write about. How would you demonstrate its existence, and what causes would you propose to explain it?

Commentary

Dartnell's essay illustrates how important a small amount of research can be for an essay explaining the causes of a social trend. She uses only three sources, all located on one visit to the library, which provide adequate documentation both for the trend and her proposed causes. Her sources include two essays she found in social science journals and a book on the general topic of homelessness in America. Dartnell depends on these sources for her evidence—statistics and the particular case of Rebecca Smith. She also uses the authority of her sources to bolster her argument. She quotes from Stoner at the end of paragraph 3, for example, to persuade readers that they should not blame homeless women for their plight but rather should see them as victims. (See Chapter 19: Arguing for further discussion of these and other kinds of evidence.)

PURPOSE AND AUDIENCE

When you write an essay speculating about the causes of a phenomenon or trend, your chief purpose is to convince readers that your proposed causes are plausible. Whatever your subject, writing situation, or available evidence, you must construct a coherent, logical, authoritative argument, one that readers will take seriously. Sometimes, like King and Meyerowitz, you may want readers to look at a phenomenon or trend in a new way. You can challenge them to think more deeply by taking them beyond obvious or popular explanations. At other times, you may, like Fuchs and Dartnell, hope to influence policy decisions. You can assume that if policy makers hear sound arguments for possible causes of social problems, they may be influenced to take thoughtful action.

Causal arguments are tricky. Effects have a way of being mistaken for causes. Causes proposed as sufficient to explain a trend may not even be necessary to explain it. A proposed cause may turn out to have originated only after a trend started. Since careful, skeptical readers are quick to spot these reasoning errors, you must take the greatest care in constructing your argument. If readers are to take your causal speculations seriously, you must first win their respect, and you can do this by reasoning thoughtfully and supporting your argument with solid evidence.

BASIC FEATURES OF ESSAYS SPECULATING ABOUT CAUSES

Essays that explain the causes of a phenomenon or trend typically include three basic features: a presentation of the phenomenon or trend, a convincing causal argument, and a reasonable, authoritative tone.

A presentation of the phenomenon or trend

In an essay about the causes of a phenomenon, a writer must first describe the phenomenon. In the original essay from which his selection was excerpted, Stephen King elaborately describes horror movies. Because we have all seen horror movies, we do not need such a detailed description in order to understand his argument. The writer of an argument like King's, however, could very well begin by presenting one horror movie, perhaps the most terrifying the author has seen. Because Joshua Meyerowitz cannot be certain that we all recognize the phenomenon he wants to analyze—that children do not seem childlike these days—he devotes nearly half his essay to describing and illustrating the phenomenon.

Likewise, in an essay about a trend, a writer's first task is to demonstrate that the trend exists. Notice how Victor Fuchs very carefully documents the increase in youth suicides, presenting figures to show the sharp increase in suicides since 1960 as well as other statistics. In the same way, Kim Dartnell uses an example (a case of an actual homeless woman) and well-documented statistics to demonstrate that the number of homeless women is increasing. Because the situation she discusses is likely to be unfamiliar to some readers, she also describes some typical homeless women.

It is also necessary to provide some details—background, current status, likely direction. When did the trend start? Is it completed or continuing? Where did it take place? What did it look like? Are you sure this is a trend and not a mere fad? Is it *really* increasing or decreasing? Is this increase or decrease decelerating or accelerating? Where does your evidence come from? Is it authoritative? A thorough presentation of the trend will answer all these questions.

A convincing causal argument   At the heart of an essay that analyzes the causes of a phenomenon or trend is the causal argument itself—the presentation of the causes in an effective order, evidence in support of each cause, anticipation of counterarguments and alternative causes. If we could explain a phenomenon or trend scientifically by offering incontrovertible evidence for its causes, there would be no need for causal arguments. However, most phenomena or trends—especially troubling social or political ones—cannot be explained definitively. Instead, they must be argued—as logically and plausibly as possible. Some of these arguments play a critical role in our lives—for example, in affecting the way money is spent for research or for social and educational programs. Ultimately, they help to determine judges' decisions and legislators' votes.

Since an explanation of a phenomenon or trend must be argued, rather than simply announced, writers need to be very sensitive to their readers. They must present their causes in a logical order that readers will be able to follow. Thus Dartnell, writing for a somewhat uninformed readership, begins with immediate and personal causes (abuse) and concludes with background and perpetuating causes (economics). To be convincing, writers do not emphasize causes their readers would consider obvious or predictable.

Writers must marshal evidence for each cause they propose. They may use statistics, factual cases and examples, and anecdotes. Fuchs gives statistics (paragraphs 5 and 6) to support his argument about the most likely cause of the increase in suicide among today's youth. Similarly, Dartnell offers statistical evidence of the economic forces behind female homelessness. The best example of a case is found in Dartnell's essay, which opens with a short narrative about a particular homeless woman. Meyerowitz opens with an anecdote, a concrete, one-time incident that begins his presentation of the phenomenon about which he speculates. (All these kinds of argumentative evidence are discussed and illustrated further in Chapter 19: Arguing.)

Most important, writers must anticipate readers' possible objections to the proposed causes, as well as showing they have considered (and accepted or rejected) any other possible causes. Fuchs emphatically rejects several proposed causes before proposing his own explanation of the increase in youth suicides. Dartnell refutes the counterargument that many homeless women are alcoholics. Not only does she show evidence that alcoholism is not a cause of increased homelessness among women, but she goes on to suggest that it is actually an effect.

A reasonable, authoritative tone

Essays analyzing trends should be written in a tone readers can trust. It need not be a terribly serious one; it can even be personal or playful. But it must be reasonable and authoritative. Readers will not take any other tone seriously. This chapter's readings have tones that range from informal (King) to seriously academic (Fuchs). What they all have in common is authority and trustworthiness, a tone that emerges in the ways readers are addressed and the ways evidence is presented.

GUIDE TO WRITING

THE WRITING TASK

Write an essay that presents a well-thought out argument explaining why a phenomenon or a trend has occurred. The phenomenon or trend may be one you have observed firsthand, one you learned about in the news, or one you are learning about now in a course. Your essay should do two things: demonstrate the existence of the phenomenon or trend, and offer possible causes for it. Your purpose is to convince your particular readers that your proposed causes are plausible.

INVENTION AND RESEARCH

The following activities will help you find a subject, explore what you know about the subject, and do any necessary research.

Finding a subject

You will want to seek a subject among either current phenomena or completed or continuing trends. A phenomenon is a fact of life, not a one-time event. It is something you or others have noticed about the human condition or the social order. A trend is a noticeable change extending over many months or years. It can be identified by some sort of increase or decrease—a rise in the birthrate, a decline in test scores.

Some subjects can be approached as either phenomena or trends. For example, you could, like Fuchs, speculate about the increasing trend in teenage suicide; or you could speculate about the causes of teenage suicide as a phenomenon, ignoring whether it is increasing or decreasing. If you were to treat teenage suicide as a trend, however, you would have to explain why more or fewer teenagers are committing suicide, not simply why teenagers as a group commit suicide.

If you are undecided whether to choose a phenomenon or a trend as your subject, list possible examples of both.

Listing phenomena. List all historical or current phenomena you might possibly want to write about. Following are some categories that might give you ideas for your list.

☐ The workplace—job dissatisfaction, white-collar crime, cocaine use on the job, discrimination against women in hiring and promotion, cooperative spirit, too many bosses, boredom and repetition, reliance on part-time help, low productivity, lack of caring and commitment

☐ College—bad cafeteria food, noisy libraries, shortage of parking, a winning football team, an outstanding musical group or program, an award-winning research team, inaccessibility or aloofness of instructors, crowded classrooms, cheating on exams

☐ Personal life—fear of success, fickle relationships, competitiveness, hostility, idealism, creativity, dread of the future, popularity, jealousy, laziness, workaholic syndrome, procrastination, "superman" or "supermom" syndrome, "distant" father syndrome

☐ Community—failure or success of urban renewal, weak or strong community spirit, lack of leadership, continuing success of a major or influential city council member

☐ Politics and government—low quality of political candidates, low voter turnout for elections, weak Attorney Generals

☐ Environment—failure to reduce pollution, continued deforestation

☐ Emotional stages in life—the terrible two's, teenage alienation or rebellion, midlife crises, late divorces, abrupt career changes

☐ Popularity of current musical styles, dance styles, or art forms

☐ Continuing influence or popularity of a book, movie, actor or actress, novelist or screenwriter, athlete, politician, religious leader

Listing trends. List all the trends you can think of. Make your list as long as possible, considering trends you have studied and can research as well as those you know firsthand. Try to think of trends you would like to understand better.

Remember that a trend is an established, demonstrable change, as opposed to a fad, which is only a short-term, superficial change. For example, a new diet might become a fad if many overweight people try it out for a few months. But this would not make it a trend. It might, however, be considered part of a trend—a general increase in health-consciousness, for example. Be sure that the possibilities you list are trends, not fads.

Consider the following possibilities as you think about trends:

☐ Shifting patterns in education—increasing interest in science or computers, increasing interest in teaching as a career, increase in home schooling, increase in time required to complete college

☐ Changes in patterns of leisure or entertainment—increasing consumption of fast food, declining interest in a particular style of music, increase in competitive cycling

☐ Shifts in religious practices—decreasing support for television evangelists, increasing incidence of women ministers or rabbis, increasing interest in Asian religions, increased membership in fundamentalist churches, increasing numbers of ministers and priests entering political races

☐ New patterns of political behavior—increase in conservatism or liberalism, a growing desire for isolationism from world affairs, developing power of minorities and women

☐ Societal changes—increases in the number of women working, unmarried teenagers having babies, single-parent households

☐ Changes in politics or world affairs—the growing opposition to nuclear arms, increase in special action groups, increasing terrorist activity

☐ Changes in economic conditions—the long-term rise or fall of interest rates, increase in low-paying service jobs, increasing cost of medical care

☐ Changing patterns in attitude or philosophy—the diminishing concern about world hunger, the growing concern for personal success

☐ Completed artistic movements or historical trends—Impressionism, pop art, the struggle for female suffrage, industrialization

Choosing a subject. Now look over the possibilities you have listed and pick one subject to write about. You may or may not already have some ideas about why this phenomenon or trend occurred. As you analyze it in some detail, you will have the opportunity to weigh possible causes and to decide which ones are the most important.

Of the two types of subjects, a trend may be the more challenging because you must nearly always do research in order to demonstrate that the trend actually exists and has been increasing or decreasing over a number of years. Usually one or two references will be adequate. Since a trend begins at a specific point (it may have ended or reversed or be continuing as you write), you must take care that your proposed causes actually precede the onset of the trend. You may also need to differentiate between causes that launched the trend and those that perpetuate it. Though trend analysis is challenging, it may be a challenge you are ready to take on.

Stop now to focus your thoughts. In one or two sentences, describe the subject you have decided to analyze.

Exploring what you know about your topic

Do some thinking now about the subject you have chosen to analyze. Consider it, probe it, discover what you know about it, figure out why you are interested in it, compare it to other subjects, decide where you might find more information about it. Write for around ten minutes, noting down everything you seem to know about the phenomenon or trend itself.

Considering causes

Think now about what caused your subject, listing all the causes you can think of and then analyzing each one.

Listing causes. Write down all the things you can think of that might have caused this phenomenon or trend. There are several kinds of causes you should try to find, specifically:

- [ ] immediate, precipitating causes: those present just before the phenomenon or trend began
- [ ] remote, background causes: those from the more distant past
- [ ] perpetuating causes: those that may have helped the trend grow or keep going once it started
- [ ] obvious causes
- [ ] hidden causes

It might be helpful to list these causes in table form. Fold a piece of lined paper vertically to make two columns, the left-hand column narrower than the right-hand one. List the causes in the left-hand column, leaving five or six lines between each cause. (See the Writer at Work section at the end of this chapter for an example of such a table.)

Analyzing causes. In the right-hand column, next to each cause, explain why you think that potential cause is real and important. Consider each of the following questions as you analyze the causes.

- [ ] Is it a necessary cause? Without it, could the phenomenon or trend have occurred?
- [ ] Is it a sufficient cause? Could it alone have caused this phenomenon or trend?
- [ ] Would this cause affect everybody the same way?
- [ ] Would this cause always lead to phenomena or trends like this?
- [ ] Is there any statistical evidence showing that this *cause* increases or decreases as the *trend* increases or decreases?
- [ ] Are there any particular incidents that demonstrate the cause's importance?
- [ ] Have any authorities suggested it is an important cause?
- [ ] Is it actually a result of the phenomenon or trend or a side effect of it rather than a cause?
- [ ] Is it a remote cause or an immediate cause?

☐ Is it a perpetuating cause?

☐ Is it an apparent cause or a hidden cause?

Testing your choice Look at your analysis of all the possible causes. Have you identified enough solid causes to support a strong explanation? If not, you could do some research to find other possible causes. If none of your causes seems likely, and you really have no idea why the phenomenon or trend occurred, you could return to your original list and choose a new subject to write about.

Researching the topic Thus far you have relied solely on your own knowledge of your topic. Now you should decide whether you need to find further evidence. You might look for statements from authoritative sources or for definitive statistics. Doing research can be helpful in several ways: (1) to confirm your own hunches, (2) to suggest other causes, (3) to provide evidence in support of your proposed causes, and (4) to identify evidence against possible counter-arguments.

Some phenomena or trends can be explained fully and convincingly with your own knowledge and instincts. For new, emerging trends or for recent phenomena, you will be on your own to decide on the most plausible causes, for there may be no published explanations.

Library research may be required for other topics—completed historical trends, for instance. You might also find information or opinions on current phenomena or trends. In doing research you should look for additional proof that the phenomenon or trend really exists or existed, proposed causes, and more evidence—to support your causes or to reject other ones. As you do research and further analysis, continue adding to your table of causes and analyses.

Considering your readers Because you are trying to make a convincing case for some particular causes, you should know as much as possible about your prospective readers. Only after you have analyzed your readers can you confidently decide which causes will go into your essay. Take about ten minutes to answer the following questions:

☐ Whom do I expect to read this essay?

☐ Are they likely to be aware of the phenomenon or trend?

☐ If they are aware of the phenomenon or trend, what are they likely to know or think about it?

☐ What assumptions might my readers share about the causes of such a phenomenon or trend?

Making your explanation as convincing as possible Once you have figured out your expectations of your readers, review the table of causes and analyses in order to select the causes that will be most appealing to these readers. List the causes in the order you think most effective.

Choose the two or three most important causes and write about each one for around five minutes, summing up all the evidence you have found. Develop your argument with your readers in mind; remember that you must convince them that your causes are reasonable ones.

Anticipating and refuting counterarguments

You should expect readers to evaluate your essay critically, considering your reasons and evidence carefully before accepting your explanation. It would be wise, therefore, to account for any possible objections they could raise. Consider the two most likely objections or counterarguments and figure out a way to refute them. Write out a few sentences to prepare your refutation.

Rejecting alternative explanations

As they read your essay, your readers may think of other causes. Try to think of two or three alternative causes now and write a few sentences about each one explaining why you are rejecting it.

PLANNING AND DRAFTING

You will now want to review what you have learned about your topic and start to plan your first draft.

Seeing what you have

Pause now to reflect on your notes. Reread everything carefully in order to decide whether you can really prove that the phenomenon or trend exists (or existed) and whether you can name causes to offer a convincing explanation of why it came about.

Setting goals

Before you begin your draft, you should consider some specific goals for your essay. Not only will the draft be easier to write once you have established clear rhetorical goals, but it is likely to be stronger and more convincing.

Following are goal-setting questions to consider now. You may find it useful to return to them while you are drafting. They are designed to help you to focus on specific elements of an essay about a phenomenon or trend.

Your readers

☐ What are they likely to know about the topic?

☐ How much do I need to say about the phenomenon or trend in order to establish the fact that it exists?

☐ How can I make my readers interested in understanding why this phenomenon or trend occurred?

☐ How can I refute their potential counterarguments or reject their preferred explanations without unduly irritating them?

☐ How can I present myself to my readers so they will consider me reasonable, fair, and authoritative?

The beginning

☐ How can I make readers take this subject seriously and really want to think about what caused it? Should I personalize it? Should I begin with an anecdote, as Meyerowitz does? Should I cite statistics, as Fuchs does?

Special strategies for causal analysis

☐ How can I demonstrate conclusively that this phenomenon or trend really exists? If I am analyzing a trend, how can I demonstrate that it is increasing or decreasing, and that it is truly a trend and not just a fad?

☐ How can I anticipate and refute readers' counterarguments to my proposed causes?

☐ How should I deal with alternative causes—by refuting them, or by accepting them as part of my argument?

Avoiding logical fallacies

☐ How can I avoid the fallacy of *oversimplified cause*? Have I assumed that a mere contributing cause is a sufficient one? Have I really identified a sufficient cause? Have I mentioned only one or two causes when I should be accounting for several?

☐ How can I avoid the *post hoc, ergo propter hoc* fallacy? (Latin for "after this, therefore because of this") Have I mistakenly assumed that something that occurred prior to the beginning of the phenomenon or trend was therefore a cause?

☐ How can I be sure not to *confuse causes with effects*? Sometimes effects can be sustaining causes of a trend, but if that is so, I should acknowledge it as such. Are any of my causes also results? Are any of my causes actually results and not causes at all?

☐ How can I show readers that I have *accepted the burden of proof*? I must offer proof for all my assertions and not *shift the burden of proof* to my readers by assuming they will automatically understand certain assertions.

☐ How can I refute counterarguments without committing the *ad hominem* (Latin for "to the man") fallacy? Can I argue against them without ridiculing their proponents?

☐ How can I consider and reject alternative causes without committing the *straw man* fallacy? (A straw man is easy to push over.)

☐ Can I argue for one cause only without being accused of the *either/or fallacy*? Might readers find my argument more convincing if I acknowledge alternative causes?

The ending

☐ How should I end my essay? Should I frame it by referring back to the beginning? Do I need to summarize my causes? Should I conclude with a conjecture about larger implications, as Fuchs does?

Outlining the essay A causal analysis may contain as many as four basic features: (1) a description of the subject, (2) a presentation of proposed causes and reasons for them, (3) a refutation of counterarguments, and (4) the consideration and rejection of alternative causes.

If you wish to propose a single cause, you could begin with a statement about the subject, describing it and indicating its importance. Then state the cause and elaborate on the reasons it has contributed to the subject. In your conclusion you could then refer to—and explain—the absence of other explanations.

presentation of the subject

proposed cause

reasons for cause

conclusion

If you need to account for alternative causes, you could discuss them first and give your reasons for rejecting them before offering your own proposed cause. Many writers save their own cause for last, hoping to leave their readers with a clear picture of it.

presentation of the subject

alternative causes and reasons for rejecting them

proposed cause with reasons

conclusion

Another option is to put your own cause first followed by alternatives. This is a good way to show the relative advantage of your cause over each of the others. You might then end with a restatement of your cause.

presentation of the subject

proposed cause with reasons

alternative causes compared to your cause

concluding restatement of proposed cause

If you are offering several causes, you will have to present them in some logical order—by relative importance, perhaps. This approach could very well mention each proposed cause's shortcomings. The explanations themselves may be somewhat incomplete, becoming convincing only when viewed in combination. An outline of this plan might look like this:

presentation of the subject

explanation of each possible cause, mentioning reasons as well as short-comings

conclusion

There are of course many other possible ways to organize a causal analysis, but these outlines should help you to start planning your own essay.

Drafting the essay   In addition to the general advice on drafting given in Chapter 1, consider the following tips on writing an essay of causal analysis:

☐ Remember that in writing about causes of phenomena or trends you are dealing with probabilities rather than certainties; therefore, you should not try to claim you have the final, conclusive answer but only that your explanation is plausible. Qualify your statements and acknowledge the worth of opposing views.

☐ Try to appeal to your readers' interests and concerns. Causal analysis is potentially rather dry. Make an effort to enliven your writing and involve your readers.

☐ Remember that your outline is just a plan. Writers often make major discoveries and reorganize as they draft. Be flexible. If you find your writing taking an interesting, unexpected turn, follow it to see where it leads. You will have an opportunity to look at it critically later.

☐ If you run into a problem or find you need more information as you draft, pause for a few minutes and see whether any of the invention activities will help. If, for instance, you are having difficulty making the subject seem important, you could analyze your readers further, find a way to personalize the subject with a quotation or an anecdote, or look for some attention-getting statistical evidence.

☐ If you are having difficulty refuting counterarguments, try composing a dialogue between yourself and an imaginary reader.

☐ If you find you need more information, you might want to interview an expert, survey a group, or do further library research.

READING A DRAFT WITH A CRITICAL EYE

At this point you are ready to have someone else read your draft. (Before you begin, you might want to review the general advice on reading another's draft critically in Chapter 1.) As you read, keep in mind the following key question: given the prospective readers, how could the argument for the proposed causes be strengthened?

First general impression   Read the essay straight through to get a general impression. Write just a few sentences stating your first reaction. Did the essay hold your interest? What surprised you most? What did you like best? Did you find the explanation convincing?

Pointings   As you read, highlight noteworthy features with *pointings,* a simple system of lines and brackets that is especially useful for revising a draft. Use this system as follows:

- ☐ Draw a straight line under any words or images that seem especially effective: strong verbs, specific details, memorable phrases, striking images.
- ☐ Draw a wavy line under any words or images that sound flat, stale, or vague. Also put the wavy line under any words or phrases that you consider unnecessary or repetitious.
- ☐ Look for pairs or groups of sentences that you think should be combined. Put brackets [ ] around these sentences.
- ☐ Look for sentences that are garbled, overloaded, or awkward. Put parentheses ( ) around these sentences. Parenthesize any sentence that seems even slightly questionable; don't worry now about whether or not it is actually incorrect. The writer needs to know that you, as one reader, had even the slightest hesitation about reading a sentence, even on first reading.

Analysis   Following are some suggestions for analyzing the parts of the essay.

1. Look at the presentation of the subject. If the subject is a *phenomenon,* has the writer adequately defined or described it? If the subject is a *trend,* are you absolutely sure that it is a trend rather than a fad or a single event? Are you convinced that the trend exists (or existed)? Can you see a progression over time? What kind of evidence is offered to show this progression? Suggest specific ways to strengthen the presentation of the phenomenon or trend.

2. Focus on the proposed cause or causes. Are there too many? Too few? Can you recognize any sufficient cause? A necessary one? Are any of the suggested causes actually results? Can you think of any causes the writer has ignored? Is the total discussion of the causes convincing? Point out ways to improve the argument.

3. Look for counterarguments. How does the writer anticipate and refute possible counterarguments? Which refutations do you find most convincing? Least convincing? Why? Alert the writer to any other counterarguments.

4. Evaluate the treatment of alternative causes. Are they clearly presented? Is the argument against them convincing? Why or why not? Indicate any alternative causes that still seem plausible to you.

5. Consider the organization of the essay. Given the argumentative strategy, are the causes presented in an effective order? Try suggesting a better order.

6. Reread the beginning. Is it engaging? Does it make you want to read the essay? Try to suggest other ways to open the essay. Look for sections that could be moved to the beginning.

7. Describe the ending. Does the essay conclude decisively? Try to suggest an alternative ending.

8. What final thoughts do you have about this draft? Does anything still need work? What is the strongest part of the draft? What is the single most encouraging comment you could make?

REVISING AND EDITING

You are now ready to revise your draft. Review any critical reading notes from classmates or advice from your instructor. You may decide that you need only add or delete a small amount of material, or you may feel that substantial changes are necessary. The following revising plan will enable you to realize the potential of your draft.

Revising a causal analysis

The specific advice here on revising a causal analysis essay can be used in conjunction with the comprehensive plan for revising in Chapter 11. For further advice, follow the general plan in Chapter 11 until you reach the section Read Again To Identify Problems. The following specific guidelines for revising a causal analysis essay can be used in place of the more general ones in that section.

Revising to strengthen the argument

☐ Should you qualify your argument?

☐ Have you presented the causes with more certainty than is actually the case?

☐ Have you oversimplified your case?

☐ Have you shown (or at least argued) that each of the causes actually *did* contribute to the phenomenon or trend?

☐ Have you placed too much importance on any one cause?

☐ Have you given too full an explanation, tracing causes too far back in time, arguing for the causes of causes, so that your argument loses some impact?

Revising for clarity and readability

☐ If the phenomenon or trend did not impress readers as important, think of ways to strengthen your presentation of it.

☐ Reconsider the opening. Would another beginning be more engaging? Does it supply adequate forecasting?

☐ Look at the ending. Does it frame the essay? Should it? Is it sufficiently emphatic?

☐ Look carefully at each sentence. Does it say what you intend it to say? Does it repeat information given earlier? Does it explain the obvious?

☐ If readers had trouble following your argument, add or clarify transitions so as to make the parts of the essay cohere better.

Editing and proofreading   As you revise a draft for the final time, you need to edit it closely for any errors of mechanics, usage, punctuation, or style. These were not a priority in earlier stages, but they should be now. Proofread as carefully as possible before turning in your final essay.

LEARNING FROM YOUR OWN WRITING PROCESS

If your instructor asks you to analyze your own composing process, begin by rereading your draft and revision. Focus on the way you analyzed causes, mentioning uncertainties you may still have about your analysis. Point to some specific changes you made in your revision, and explain why you made them. Indicate what you like best about your revision, as well as what still seems to need work.

A WRITER AT WORK

ANALYZING CAUSES

For a writer planning an essay explaining the causes of a trend, the most important part of invention and research is analyzing the causes. Because the causes are the heart of the argument, it takes rigorous analysis of each cause during the invention stage to compose a convincing argument.

Here we will look at the table of causes and analyses that Kim Dartnell developed for her essay on homeless women. (The revised version of her essay appears earlier in this chapter.)

Dartnell began this invention activity intending to write about the trend of homelessness in general, without considering men and women separately. Only after she had started to do some research did she realize that not only was there an increasing number of homeless women but that there had been several recent reports on the subject.

She began her analysis before going to the library, entering the first four causes on her table and completing a partial analysis. After she decided to focus on women, she added the other causes and completed the analysis. Examine her table of causes and analyses now. As you study her analysis, remember the questions she was asking herself about each cause.

TABLE OF CAUSES AND ANALYSES

Causes	Analyses
1. unemployment	Necessary cause for this trend. Could be sufficient, would affect everybody the same way, causes loss of income. Precipitating cause that has grown in importance recently. Also an immediate cause of homelessness.
2. inflation	Relates to unemployment—as such, may be necessary but not sufficient by itself, especially affects unemployed and poor. Perpetuating, immediate, hidden cause.
3. alcoholism	Not necessary, not sufficient. Common conception is all homeless are drunks. Refute this cause since alcohol use hasn't risen in proportion to homelessness. Alcoholism is found at all levels of society, and so can't say that it causes homelessness. May be a result of unemployment or homelessness. No one really knows what causes alcoholism—or what it causes.
4. cutbacks in welfare	Necessary cause, could be sufficient. Affects women especially, causes loss of income, homelessness. Immediate cause—with no

	money, people forced to beg or move in with others.
5. abuse	There's always been abuse. Neither necessary nor sufficient. Affects women and children more. Research shows it's risen in proportion to homelessness (Stoner).
6. deinstitutionalization	Many women being released from mental institutions. Necessary, may be sufficient. Precipitating cause for the mentally ill. May be coupled with economic problems. Rebecca Smith is a good example. Evidence shows this is increasing as homelessness increases. Couldn't be a result. Perpetuates the trend. (Use Stoner, Hombs and Snyder data.)
7. evictions	Necessary and sufficient cause, due to economic reasons. Precipitating cause. Affects females more, but also affects men. As evictions increase, more homeless. Perpetuating cause.
8. lack of housing	Necessary and sufficient, but related to economic reasons. Cheap housing is harder to find due to redevelopment and gentrification. Renovation affects those already without housing more. Could mention Rebecca Smith. Perpetuating cause.

Once she had analyzed all these possible causes, Dartnell could decide how to use them to make the most convincing explanation. She had to decide which causes to emphasize, which ones to combine, which ones to omit entirely, and how to order them to produce the most effective argument. Also, she had to consider whether or not any of her causes should be refuted. Last, she had to try to find any potential objections to her arguments, which she would then have to answer. As it happened, she decided to use all of these causes in her argument except for alcoholism, which she would mention and refute.

She begins her essay with a discussion of abuse, thinking it was the one cause of homelessness that most affects women. She then discusses evictions and housing, treating each of these causes in a separate paragraph. Next she mentions—and refutes—alcoholism as a cause. Only then does she develop the cause for which she had the most evidence—deinstitutionalization. Finally, she combines several causes—unemployment, inflation, welfare cutbacks—into one paragraph on economic causes.

Certainly these causes might be presented in a different order—deinstitutionalization might be effectively placed either first or last, for example—but Dartnell's plan serves her topic well. By covering her topic so comprehensively and discussing it in a clear, logically organized manner, she presents a convincing argument.

Interpreting Literature

☐ For a history of science class, a student writes about the myth of the mad scientist in literature, focusing on two classic works: *Frankenstein* and *Dr. Jekyll and Mr. Hyde*. From her reading, she concludes that as a fictional figure, the mad scientist is socially isolated, obsessed with the desire for knowledge and power, and reckless of his own and others' safety. To demonstrate the accuracy of her analysis, the student quotes descriptions of the scientists in the two works and discusses their behavior.

☐ A journalist writing about the American newspaper publisher William Randolph Hearst (1863–1951) decides to model his article on the classic film about a Hearstlike character, *Citizen Kane*. He organizes his piece around a series of imagined interviews with people who knew and worked for Hearst. Throughout the article, he draws parallels between Hearst and his film counterpart to support the point that Hearst is finally as unknowable as Kane.

☐ In an introductory literature class, a student analyzes the structure and meaning of Edgar Allan Poe's poem "The Raven." As the thesis of her essay, she claims the poem's message of inescapable despair is conveyed by its repetition of words and sounds as well as by its monotonous rhythm. To underscore her conclusion, the student points to specific examples in the poem of repetition, alliteration, and rhythmic uniformity.

☐ A freshman in a composition course explores the relationship between setting and action in William Faulkner's story "Dry September." He argues that the setting can be viewed metaphorically, as a projection of the characters' emotions. To support his point, he draws parallels between descriptions of the setting and descriptions of the characters.

10

□ After seeing Henrik Ibsen's *A Doll's House*, a student decides to write about the play's feminist themes in her diary. She is disturbed by the decision of the play's protagonist, Nora, to leave her home and children. The student asks: if Nora felt she had never grown up or accepted responsibility, why was she leaving her children? To answer this question, she attempts to examine Nora's character in light of the expectations Nora's husband and society in general have of women.

Interpreting what we read is an intuitive as well as an intellectual process. We engage a story or poem with our feelings and values, our imaginations and minds. Not only do we examine its parts to see how they influence our understanding, but we also immerse ourselves in the language.

As we read works of literature and try to understand their meanings, we often see reflections of our own experience. We may recognize characters in a story and sympathize with them because we share their problems and motives, even if their situations differ radically from our own. From seeing our own lives mirrored in the stories of others, we can begin to appreciate how much we have in common. Thus, studying literature reinforces the bonds that hold people together.

Sharing our interpretations with others also forges shared understanding and connection. When we read and write about literature, we join an ongoing conversation, becoming members of what the literary critic Stanley Fish calls the "interpretive community." As members of this community, we exchange our views and share our insights. This process of inquiry and exchange enables us to clarify and deepen our understanding.

Writing an essay interpreting a work of literature means that we must probe our initial responses to the work, examining the work closely to find the basis for our thinking. This analysis of the work and of our reactions to it helps us to discover and create new meaning. But we do not write for ourselves alone, we also write for others. We present our interpretations as arguments. We make a claim about the story or play just as we would about an issue or problem. As with all argumentative writing, we must provide reasons and evidence to convince readers that our interpretation is plausible. Since literary works can be interpreted in different ways, we do not seek to prove that we have discovered the one correct or final meaning. Instead, we try to convince our readers—instructors, classmates, or other students of literature—that we have analyzed the work carefully and thoughtfully and have found a reasonable way of understanding it.

Although the preceding examples refer to many kinds of literature—short stories, novels, poems, films, and plays—this chapter focuses on essays interpreting stories. It opens with a short story by the renowned Irish writer James Joyce. The story is followed by a set of approaches for interpreting it. These approaches are followed by two interpretations of Joyce's story. By analyzing these essays with your instructor and other students, you will learn about the features and strategies characteristic of writing interpretations of literary texts.

James Joyce (1882–1941) was a native of Dublin, Ireland. "Araby," the short story that follows, appears in a collection of stories entitled *Dubliners*. Joyce completed the collection in 1907, but it was not published until 1914. Along with his other stories and novels, it is considered a major work of modern literature in English.

In every detail, "Araby" reflects Dublin around the turn of the century. As a boy, Joyce lived on the North Richmond street of the opening sentence of the story. He also attended the Christian Brothers' School for a short while. In 1894, the year that the Joyce family moved to North Richmond Street, the *Grand Oriental Fete, Araby in Dublin* attracted many visitors, the young Joyce almost certainly among them. Araby was a bazaar with various stalls selling cheap merchandise with an exotic Middle Eastern flavor. A special train, like the one mentioned in the story, carried visitors to the bazaar.

At the turn of the century, Ireland was a predominantly Catholic country, and the story is filled with religious references. The girl in the story ("Mangan's sister") cannot go to Araby because she must attend a special week of communal living and prayer arranged by her convent school. (The girl is not a nun.) The narrator's family lives in a house formerly occupied by a priest, whose possessions the narrator mentions. The story ends in an epiphany, a sudden insight. In Christianity, the Feast of Epiphany celebrates the revelation of Christ's divinity to the Magi, the three wise men who traveled to the scene of Christ's birth.

In the second paragraph, the narrator mentions three of the priest's books: *The Abbot* by Sir Walter Scott (1771–1832), a story about a poor boy in the court of Mary, Queen of Scots, who becomes important because he knows a valuable state secret; the *Devout Communicant*, a book of religious meditations; and *The Memoirs of Vidocq*, a sexually suggestive story about a criminal who becomes a detective.

Joyce chose the Dublin details with great care to create a story with significance far beyond its particular setting. It is this significance you will be inquiring into as you analyze the story and read what others have written about it.

ARABY

JAMES JOYCE

North Richmond Street, being blind, was a quiet street except at the hour 1
when the Christian Brothers' School set the boys free. An uninhabited house of
two storeys stood at the blind end, detached from its neighbours in a square
ground. The other houses of the street, conscious of decent lives within them,
gazed at one another with brown imperturbable faces.

The former tenant of our house, a priest, had died in the back drawing- 2
room. Air, musty from having been long enclosed, hung in all the rooms, and
the waste room behind the kitchen was littered with old useless papers. Among
these I found a few paper-covered books, the pages of which were curled and
damp: *The Abbot,* by Walter Scott, *The Devout Communicant* and *The Memoirs
of Vidocq.* I liked the last best because its leaves were yellow. The wild garden
behind the house contained a central apple-tree and a few straggling bushes
under one of which I found the late tenant's rusty bicycle-pump. He had been
a very charitable priest; in his will he had left all his money to institutions and
the furniture of his house to his sister.

When the short days of winter came dusk fell before we had well eaten our 3
dinners. When we met in the street the houses had grown sombre. The space
of sky above us was the colour of ever-changing violet and towards it the lamps
of the street lifted their feeble lanterns. The cold air stung us and we played till
our bodies glowed. Our shouts echoed in the silent street. The career of our
play brought us through the dark muddy lanes behind the houses where we
ran the gauntlet of the rough tribes from the cottages, to the back doors of the
dark dripping gardens where odours arose from the ashpits, to the dark odorous
stables where a coachman smoothed and combed the horse or shook music
from the buckled harness. When we returned to the street light from the kitchen
windows had filled the areas. If my uncle was seen turning the corner we hid
in the shadow until we had seen him safely housed. Or if Mangan's sister came
out on the doorstep to call her brother in to his tea we watched her from our
shadow peer up and down the street. We waited to see whether she would
remain or go in and, if she remained, we left our shadow and walked up to
Mangan's steps resignedly. She was waiting for us, her figure defined by the
light from the half-opened door. Her brother always teased her before he obeyed
and I stood by the railings looking at her. Her dress swung as she moved her
body and the soft rope of her hair tossed from side to side.

Every morning I lay on the floor in the front parlour watching her door. The 4
blind was pulled down to within an inch of the sash so that I could not be seen.
When she came out on the doorstep my heart leaped. I ran to the hall, seized
my books and followed her. I kept her brown figure always in my eye and, when
we came near the point at which our ways diverged, I quickened my pace and
passed her. This happened morning after morning. I had never spoken to her,
except for a few casual words, and yet her name was like a summons to all my
foolish blood.

Her image accompanied me even in places the most hostile to romance. On 5

Saturday evenings when my aunt went marketing I had to go to carry some of the parcels. We walked through the flaring streets, jostled by drunken men and bargaining women, amid the curses of labourers, the shrill litanies of shop-boys who stood on guard by the barrels of pigs' cheeks, the nasal chanting of street-singers, who sang a *come-all-you* about O'Donovan Rossa, or a ballad about the troubles in our native land. These noises converged in a single sensation of life for me: I imagined that I bore my chalice safely through a throng of foes. Her name sprang to my lips at moments in strange prayers and praises which I myself did not understand. My eyes were often full of tears (I could not tell why) and at times a flood from my heart seemed to pour itself out into my bosom. I thought little of the future. I did not know whether I would ever speak to her or not or, if I spoke to her, how I could tell her of my confused adoration. But my body was like a harp and her words and gestures were like fingers running upon the wires.

One evening I went into the back drawing-room in which the priest had 6 died. It was a dark rainy evening and there was no sound in the house. Through one of the broken panes I heard the rain impinge upon the earth, the fine incessant needles of water playing in the sodden beds. Some distant lamp or lighted window gleamed below me. I was thankful that I could see so little. All my senses seemed to desire to veil themselves and, feeling that I was about to slip from them, I pressed the palms of my hands together until they trembled, murmuring: "O love! O love!" many times.

At last she spoke to me. When she addressed the first words to me I was 7 so confused that I did not know what to answer. She asked me was I going to *Araby.* I forgot whether I answered yes or no. It would be a splendid bazaar, she said she would love to go.

"And why can't you?" I asked. 8

While she spoke she turned a silver bracelet round and round her wrist. She 9 could not go, she said, because there would be a retreat that week in her convent. Her brother and two other boys were fighting for their caps and I was alone at the railings. She held one of the spikes, bowing her head towards me. The light from the lamp opposite our door caught the white curve of her neck, lit up her hair that rested there and, falling, lit up the hand upon the railing. It fell over one side of her dress and caught the white border of a petticoat, just visible as she stood at ease.

"It's well for you," she said. 10

"If I go," I said, "I will bring you something." 11

What innumerable follies laid waste my waking and sleeping thoughts after 12 that evening! I wished to annihilate the tedious intervening days. I chafed against the work of school. At night in my bedroom and by day in the classroom her image came between me and the page I strove to read. The syllables of the word *Araby* were called to me through the silence in which my soul luxuriated and cast an Eastern enchantment over me. I asked for leave to go to the bazaar on Saturday night. My aunt was surprised and hoped it was not some Freemason affair. I answered few questions in class. I watched my master's face pass from amiability to sternness; he hoped I was not beginning to idle. I could not call my wandering thoughts together. I had hardly any patience with the serious work of life which, now that it stood between me and my desire, seemed to me child's play, ugly monotonous child's play.

On Saturday morning I reminded my uncle that I wished to go to the bazaar 13 in the evening. He was fussing at the hallstand, looking for the hatbrush, and answered me curtly:

"Yes, boy, I know." 14

As he was in the hall I could not go into the front parlour and lie at the 15 window. I left the house in bad humour and walked slowly towards the school. The air was pitilessly raw and already my heart misgave me.

When I came home to dinner my uncle had not yet been home. Still it was 16 early. I sat staring at the clock for some time and, when its ticking began to irritate me, I left the room. I mounted the staircase and gained the upper part of the house. The high cold empty gloomy rooms liberated me and I went from room to room singing. From the front window I saw my companions playing below in the street. Their cries reached me weakened and indistinct and, leaning my forehead against the cool glass, I looked over at the dark house where she lived. I may have stood there for an hour, seeing nothing but the brown-clad figure cast by my imagination, touched discreetly by the lamplight at the curved neck, at the hand upon the railings and at the border below the dress.

When I came downstairs again I found Mrs. Mercer sitting at the fire. She 17 was an old garrulous woman, a pawnbroker's widow, who collected used stamps for some pious purpose. I had to endure the gossip of the tea-table. The meal was prolonged beyond an hour and still my uncle did not come. Mrs. Mercer stood up to go: she was sorry she couldn't wait any longer, but it was after eight o'clock and she did not like to be out late, as the night air was bad for her. When she had gone I began to walk up and down the room, clenching my fists. My aunt said:

"I'm afraid you may put off your bazaar for this night of Our Lord." 18

At nine o'clock I heard my uncle's latchkey in the halldoor. I heard him talking 19 to himself and heard the hallstand rocking when it had received the weight of his overcoat. I could interpret these signs. When he was midway through his dinner I asked him to give me the money to go to the bazaar. He had forgotten.

"The people are in bed and after their first sleep now," he said. 20

I did not smile. My aunt said to him energetically: 21

"Can't you give him the money and let him go? You've kept him late enough 22 as it is."

My uncle said he was very sorry he had forgotten. He said he believed in 23 the old saying: "All work and no play makes Jack a dull boy." He asked me where I was going and, when I had told him a second time he asked me did I know *The Arab's Farewell to his Steed*. When I left the kitchen he was about to recite the opening lines of the piece to my aunt.

I held a florin tightly in my hand as I strode down Buckingham Street towards 24
the station. The sight of the streets thronged with buyers and glaring with gas
recalled to me the purpose of my journey. I took my seat in a third-class carriage
of a deserted train. After an intolerable delay the train moved out of the station
slowly. It crept onward among ruinous houses and over the twinkling river. At
Westland Row Station a crowd of people pressed to the carriage doors; but the
porters moved them back, saying that it was a special train for the bazaar. I
remained alone in the bare carriage. In a few minutes the train drew up beside
an improvised wooden platform. I passed out on to the road and saw by the
lighted dial of a clock that it was ten minutes to ten. In front of me was a large
building which displayed the magical name.

I could not find any sixpenny entrance and, fearing that the bazaar would 25
be closed, I passed in quickly through a turnstile, handing a shilling to a weary-
looking man. I found myself in a big hall girdled at half its height by a gallery.
Nearly all the stalls were closed and the greater part of the hall was in darkness.
I recognised a silence like that which pervades a church after a service. I walked
into the centre of the bazaar timidly. A few people were gathered about the
stalls which were still open. Before a curtain, over which the words *Café Chan-
tant* were written in coloured lamps, two men were counting money on a salver.
I listened to the fall of the coins.

Remembering with difficulty why I had come I went over to one of the stalls 26
and examined porcelain vases and flowered tea-sets. At the door of the stall a
young lady was talking and laughing with two young gentlemen. I remarked
their English accents and listened vaguely to their conversation.

"O, I never said such a thing!"   27

"O, but you did!"

"O, but I didn't!"

"Didn't she say that?"

"Yes. I heard her."

"O, there's a . . . fib!"

Observing me the young lady came over and asked me did I wish to buy 28
anything. The tone of her voice was not encouraging; she seemed to have
spoken to me out of a sense of duty. I looked humbly at the great jars that
stood like eastern guards at either side of the dark entrance to the stall and
murmured:

"No, thank you."   29

The young lady changed the position of one of the vases and went back to 30
the two young men. They began to talk of the same subject. Once or twice the
young lady glanced at me over her shoulder.

I lingered before her stall, though I knew my stay was useless, to make my 31
interest in her wares seem the more real. Then I turned away slowly and walked
down the middle of the bazaar. I allowed the two pennies to fall against the
sixpence in my pocket. I heard a voice call from one end of the gallery that the
light was out. The upper part of the hall was now completely dark.

Gazing up into the darkness I saw myself as a creature driven and derided 32
by vanity; and my eyes burned with anguish and anger.

APPROACHES TO INTERPRETING "ARABY"

Every reader of "Araby" finds it puzzling. Events seem strange and exaggerated. We wonder about the importance to the narrator of the Araby bazaar and of his relationship to Mangan's sister. Most of all, we wonder what to make of the narrator's final insight. For over 70 years, readers have been interpreting this story. To work out your own interpretation, you will need to find a way into the story. The following approaches present some of the ways experienced readers have successfully discovered meanings in puzzling stories. Each approach invites you to reread the story, looking at it from a new perspective, annotating what you notice, and then making an inventory of your annotations in order to discover patterns, relations, and insights. These approaches will help you interpret "Araby" and can be used also with other stories, as indicated in the Guide to Writing later in this chapter.

Surprising or puzzling statements

Readers often approach a story by starting from one statement in the story that surprises or puzzles them. Here are three statements that readers of "Araby" have found surprising and that eventually led them to understand the story better:

"Her image accompanied me even in places the most hostile to romance."

"I bore my chalice safely through a throng of foes."

"Gazing up into the darkness I saw myself as a creature driven and derided by vanity; and my eyes burned with anguish and anger."

You may find another surprising or puzzling statement to investigate. Begin by looking closely at the context of the statement: what is happening at that point in the story, what do the key words mean, and what attitudes and values are associated with them? Then, reread the entire story annotating words, images, events, and ideas that help you understand the importance of the statement. Inventory your annotations in order to probe the significance of the surprising statement.

Patterns of words and images

Another way to understand stories is through specific patterns of words and images. Such a pattern may lead a patient reader to a larger understanding of the story. Here are three of the many patterns of words and images you may discover in "Araby": religion, water, blindness and vision. Reread the story, annotating evidence of such a pattern of words and images. Inventory your annotations with the purpose of discovering what this particular pattern discloses about the meaning of the story.

Character and character change

Another useful approach is to analyze one or more characters closely in terms of their attributes and development in the course of the story. Reread the story, annotating information about each character you have chosen (physical characteristics, attitudes, values), key events in which the character is directly or indirectly involved, and important relationships or interactions with other characters. Your goal is to understand the characters you are studying as fully as possible, piecing together all the clues Joyce offers and making inferences from this evidence. It is important to notice not only what characters tell us about themselves and say about one another, but also to make your own judgments about their behavior and ways of thinking.

Point of view   Point of view refers to how the story is told, who tells it, and how much you can count on what the narrator tells us. Examining a story's point of view can be a productive first step in deciding what the story might mean. "Araby" is written in the first person, with the narrator telling his own story. Reread the story, annotating it with the following questions in mind. Your purpose is to probe the implications of the story being told by this narrator (rather than by some other possible narrator).

Who exactly is the narrator in "Araby"?

How does the narrator reveal his values and beliefs?

Are the events being narrated as they happen, soon after, or years later? How can you tell?

How well does the narrator seem to understand his experience? What are his perceptive insights? His blind spots?

In light of the revelation the narrator has at the end, can you find evidence of hindsight or of irony in the way he tells the story?

Can you trust the narrator? Why or why not?

Ironies or contradictions   Frequently, readers begin their analysis by noticing ironies or contradictions in the story. Something is ironic when it appears to say one thing but actually says something else. Here are three ironies readers have found in "Araby":

1. Mrs. Mercer appears to be religious and to serve the Church, but everything about her suggests money rather than spirit: her name, Mercer, means dealer in merchandise; her husband is a pawnbroker; even her church work involves acquisitiveness, collecting cancelled stamps, presumably to sell. She embodies the contradiction between the spiritual and the material that is evident throughout the story.

2. The boy appears to worship Mangan's sister as a religious object, yet he describes her in sensual, not spiritual, images. These images point to a contradiction in the way the boy feels and the way he allows himself to think, a contradiction between illusion and reality.

3. The boy likes the dead priest's book, *The Memoirs of Vidocq*, not because of its content but because of its appearance. Ironically, the book is about the criminal and sexual adventures of a notorious impostor. This irony points up the idea of disguise and suggests that below the surface respectability lurks something criminal or antisocial.

Some other irony or contradiction might strike you as you read. Reread the story with one of these ironies or contradictions in mind. Annotate any evidence you find of it elsewhere in the story—in events; in what the main character thinks, says, or does; in how characters relate to one another and to their environment.

Literary motifs   Araby is remarkable in that many of the most familiar literary motifs are reflected in it. Select one of the following motifs, or any other you happen to notice, and then reread the story carefully, annotating it as a story of that type.

- ☐ a journey or quest for something of value, like self-knowledge
- ☐ a conflict or disparity between appearance and reality—or what seems to be and what is
- ☐ individual in relation to society
- ☐ coming of age or initiation into new experience
- ☐ conflict between spiritual and material values
- ☐ relations between generations, genders, groups—children and parents, men and women, blacks and whites, employees and owners
- ☐ the double, in which two or more characters represent alternative realities, perhaps one good and one evil or one desired and one denied (consider the shop girl and Mangan's sister or the narrator and the bazaar girl's "gentlemen" as doubles)

Setting   The physical setting of particular scenes can often be a productive starting point for interpreting a story. In "Araby" the narrator mentions many details of setting, which create an unmistakable mood. Annotating and inventorying these details may lead you to a full understanding of the influence of setting on the characters' lives and the narrator's motives, feelings, and final insight.

You might choose one of these scenes—the Saturday evening streets, the drawing room of the narrator's house, the train the narrator rides to the bazaar, the bazaar—to examine closely. Look for connections between this scene and any other parts of the story, noticing especially how this scene and its events compare or contrast with other scenes and their events. Annotate what you notice. Your purpose is to understand the significance of the scene in the story and to let the scene lead you to a fuller understanding of the story.

Structure   Exploring structure or plot can lead to unexpected insights about the story. "Araby" is a straightforward narrative encompassing a few weeks in the narrator's life, moving through winter days of growing adoration for Mangan's sister to the time of the Araby bazaar. You could outline the story's narrative to identify conventional features of narrative structure such as foreshadowing, points of suspense, climax, and ending or denouement.

You could also look for structural relationships beyond the conventional narrative pattern. For example, you could see the story as organized into stages and annotate in order to discover what is revealed by the events in each stage and how they relate to one another. Or you might look for structural patterns—repeated or contrasting events such as the narrator's conversation with Mangan's sister and the Araby shop girl's conversation with the two men.

Historical, social, and economic context

Every story reflects a historical, social, and economic context specific to its time and place. You can deepen your understanding of the story by learning about these conditions from outside sources and by looking at the story's events and details for references to them.

"Araby," for example, subtly refers to the long-term political, religious, and economic tensions between the Irish and the British, who ruled Ireland until 1921. It also reflects a religious and patriarchal tradition of viewing women as either angel or whore. Read the story with one of these contexts in mind, annotating and inventorying what you find. Your aim is to discover how the story's particular context informs its meaning.

READINGS

The first essay on "Araby" comes from *Understanding Fiction*, a classic introduction to literary interpretation by Cleanth Brooks and Robert Penn Warren. As Brooks and Warren demonstrate, interpretations consist of two essential elements: general ideas about the story and particular details from the story. The key to constructing an interpretation is establishing clear and compelling relationships between the general ideas and the particular details. As you read this essay, notice Brooks and Warren's general ideas about the story. Also ask yourself how they tie these ideas together. What conclusion do these ideas lead to? How convincing do you find this interpretation of the story?

THE CHALICE BEARER
CLEANTH BROOKS AND
ROBERT PENN WARREN

On what may be called the simplest level "Araby" is a story of a boy's disappointment. The description of the street in which he lives, the information about the dead priest and the priest's abandoned belongings, the relations with the aunt and uncle—all of these items, which occupy so much space, seem to come very naturally into the story. That is, they may be justified individually in the story on realistic grounds. But when one considers the fact that such material constitutes the bulk of the story, one is led to observe that, if such items *merely* serve as "setting" and atmosphere . . . , the story is obviously overloaded with nonfunctional material. Obviously, for any reader except the most casual, these items do have a function. If we find in what way these apparently irrelevant items in "Araby" are related to each other and to the disappointment of the boy, we shall have defined the theme of the story.

What, then, is the relation of the boy's disappointment to such matters as 2 the belongings of the dead priest, the fact that he stands apart talking to the girl while his friends are quarreling over the cap, the gossip over the tea table, the uncle's lateness, and so on? One thing that is immediately suggested by the mention of these things is the boy's growing sense of isolation, the lack of sympathy between him and his friends, teachers, and family. He says, "I imagined that I bore my chalice safely through a throng of foes." For instance, when the uncle is standing in the hall, the boy could not go into the front parlor and lie at the window; or at school his ordinary occupations began to seem "ugly monotonous child's play." But this sense of isolation has, also, moments which are almost triumphant, as for example is implied when the porters at the station wave the crowds back, "saying that it was a special train for the bazaar" and was not for them. The boy is left alone in the bare carriage, but he is going to "Araby," which name involves, as it were, the notion of romantic and exotic fulfillment. The metaphor of the chalice implies the same kind of precious secret triumph. It is not only the ordinary surrounding world, however, from which he is cruelly or triumphantly isolated. He is also isolated from the girl herself. He talks to her only once, and then is so confused that he does not know how to answer her. But the present which he hopes to bring her from Araby would somehow serve as a means of communicating his feelings to her, a symbol for their relationship in the midst of the inimical world.

In the last scene at the bazaar, there is a systematic, though subtle, prepa- 3 ration for the final realization on the part of the boy. There is the "improvised wooden platform" in contrast with the "magical name" displayed above the building. Inside, most of the stalls are closed. The young lady and young men who talk together are important in the preparation. They pay the boy no mind, except in so far as the young lady is compelled by her position as clerk to ask him what he wants. But her tone is not "encouraging." She, too, belongs to the inimical world. But she, also, belongs to a world into which he is trying to penetrate: she and her admirers are on terms of easy intimacy—an intimacy in contrast to his relation to Mangan's sister. It is an exotic, rich world into which he cannot penetrate; he can only look "humbly at the great jars that stood like eastern guards at either side of the dark entrance to the stall. . . ." But, ironically, the young lady and her admirers, far from realizing that they are on holy, guarded ground, indulge in a trivial, easy banter, which seems to defile and cheapen the secret world from which the boy is barred. How do we know this? It is not stated, but the contrast between the conversation of the young lady and her admirers, and the tone of the sentence quoted just above indicates such an interpretation.

This scene, then, helps to point up and particularize the general sense of 4 isolation suggested by the earlier descriptive materials, and thereby to prepare for the last sentence of the story, in which, under the sudden darkness of the cheap and barnlike bazaar, the boy sees himself as "a creature driven and derided by vanity," while his eyes burn with anguish and anger.

We have seen how the apparently casual incidents and items of description 5 do function in the story to build up the boy's sense of intolerable isolation. But this is only part of the function of this material. The careful reader will have noticed how many references, direct or indirect, there are to religion and the ritual of the church. The atmosphere of the story is saturated with such references. We have the dead priest, the Christian Brothers' School, the aunt's hope that the bazaar is not "some Freemason affair," her reference, when the uncle has been delayed, to "this night of Our Lord." These references are all obvious enough. At one level, these references merely indicate the type of community in which the impressionable boy is growing up. But there are other, less obvious, references, which relate more intimately to the boy's experience. Even the cries of the shop boys for him are "shrill litanies." He imagines that he bears a "chalice safely through a throng of foes." When he is alone the name of Mangan's sister springs to his lips "in strange prayers and praises." For this reason, when he speaks of his "confused adoration," we see that the love of the girl takes on, for him, something of the nature of a mystic, religious experience. The use of the very word *confused* hints of the fact that romantic love and religious love are mixed up in his mind.

It has been said that the boy is isolated from a world which seems ignorant 6 of, and even hostile to, the experience of his love. In a sense he knows that his aunt and uncle are good and kind, but they do not understand him. He had once found satisfaction in the society of his companions and in his school work, but he has become impatient with both. But there is also a sense in which he accepts his isolation and is even proud of it. The world not only does not understand his secret but would cheapen and contaminate it. The metaphor of the chalice borne through a throng of foes, supported as it is by the body of the story, suggests a sort of consecration like that of the religious devotee. The implications of the references to religion, then, help define the boy's attitude and indicate why, for him, so much is staked upon the journey to the bazaar. It is interesting to note, therefore, that the first overt indication of his disillusionment and disappointment is expressed in a metaphor involving a church: "Nearly all the stalls were closed and the greater part of the hall was in darkness. I recognized a silence like that which pervades a church after a service. . . . Two men were counting money on a salver. I listened to the fall of the coins." So, it would seem, here we have the idea that the contamination of the world has invaded the very temple of love. (The question may arise as to whether this is not reading too much into the passage. Perhaps it is. But whatever interpretation is to be made of the particular incident, it is by just such suggestion and implication that closely wrought stories, such as this one, are controlled by the author and embody their fundamental meaning.)

Is this a sentimental story? It is an adolescent love affair, about "calf love," 7 a subject which usually is not to be taken seriously and is often the cause of amusement. The boy of the story is obviously investing casual incidents with a meaning which they do not deserve; and himself admits, in the end, that he has fallen into self-deception. How does the author avoid the charge that he has taken the matter over-seriously?

The answer to this question would involve a consideration of the point of 8 view from which the story is told. It is told by the hero himself, but after a long lapse of time, after he has reached maturity. This fact, it is true, is not stated in the story, but the style itself is not that of an adolescent boy. It is a formal and complicated style, rich, as has already been observed, in subtle implications. In other words, the man is looking back upon the boy, detachedly and judicially. For instance, the boy, in the throes of the experience, would never have said of himself: "I had never spoken to her, except for a few casual words, and yet her name was like a summons to all my foolish blood." The man knows, as it were, that the behavior of the boy was, in a sense, foolish. The emotions of the boy are confused, but the person telling the story, the boy grown up, is not confused. He has unraveled the confusion long after, knows that it existed and why it existed.

If the man has unraveled the confusions of the boy, why is the event still 9 significant to him? Is he merely dwelling on the pathos of adolescent experience? It seems, rather, that he sees in the event, as he looks back on it, a kind of parable of a problem which has run through later experience. The discrepancy between the real and the ideal scarcely exists for the child, but it is a constant problem, in all sorts of terms, for the adult. This story is about a boy's first confrontation of that problem—that is, about his growing up. The man may have made adjustments to this problem, and may have worked out certain provisional solutions, but looking back, he still recognizes it as a problem, and an important one. The sense of isolation and disillusion which, in the boy's experience, may seem to spring from a trivial situation, becomes not less, but more aggravated and fundamental in the adult's experience. So, the story is not merely an account of a stage in the process of growing up—it does not merely represent a clinical interest in the psychology of growing up—but is a symbolic rendering of a central conflict in mature experience.

Questions for analysis

1. Brooks and Warren say that the sense of isolation and disillusion that the boy experiences is not peculiar to childhood but is a fundamental fact of human experience. How familiar are you with these feelings? What is there about "Araby" that seems like or unlike what you know and feel?

2. Brooks and Warren suggest that the struggle to solve the problem of isolation and disillusion never ends, that we can devise only provisional solutions. In your view, what role does literature play in helping us understand such problems and discover possible solutions? What solutions, if any, do you find in "Araby"?

3. In paragraph 2, Brooks and Warren introduce the idea that the boy feels isolated. To develop this idea, they use the writing strategy of division and classification. How do they categorize his feeling of isolation? How do these distinctions contribute to your understanding of this idea? (For further discussion of this strategy, see Chapter 17: Classifying.)

4. Brooks and Warren argue that the boy's sense of isolation is particularized in the details used to set the scene at the bazaar. They use the writing strategy of comparison and contrast to reveal a pattern in the scene's details. What pattern do they find? How does this pattern illustrate their idea about the boy's feelings of isolation? (You can learn more about comparing and contrasting as writing strategies in Chapter 18: Comparing and Contrasting.)

5. In paragraphs 5 and 6, Brooks and Warren turn their attention to another pattern of details—language referring to religion and church ritual. What ideas do they connect to these details? How do they relate these ideas about the story's religious imagery to their idea about the boy's sense of isolation? How important do you think it is, in general, to relate different ideas in an essay of interpretation?

6. In the last two paragraphs, Brooks and Warren discuss the point of view from which "Araby" is told in order to argue that it is not just a "sentimental story" about a boy's growing up. Why do you think they challenge this interpretation? What does the word *sentimental* mean? In what ways does the story seem sentimental to you? How does it avoid sentimentality?

Commentary   Brooks and Warren seem to have relied on four approaches: character and character change, setting, patterns of words and images, and point of view. These approaches allow them to draw a conclusion about the meaning of "Araby" that serves as the thesis of their essay. The thesis, stated explicitly in the last sentence, claims that the story is "a symbolic rendering of a central conflict in mature experience," the conflict between reality and illusion.

Though Brooks and Warren present their thesis at the end of the essay, other writers about literature, as you will see, put their thesis near the beginning. Whether it appears in the first paragraph or in the last, the thesis represents the writer's conclusion. The thesis is not your initial idea about the story but the result of a process of inquiry that leads to the discovery of new meanings, even in familiar works of literature. As Brooks and Warren show us, it is not possible to know in advance what discoveries you will make or what connections you will find from using different approaches.

Brooks and Warren begin their analysis with two approaches: character and setting. Looking at the boy leads them to the idea that the story is about the boy's state of mind—specifically, his disappointment. Another approach—the setting—reveals many interesting details but, as Brooks and Warren explain, these seem to be unrelated to each other and to the idea of the boy's disappointment. For them, the key to interpreting "Araby," to defining the story's theme, is forging connections between these apparently unrelated ideas and details.

By considering the boy's disappointment in the context of the other characters and the setting, Brooks and Warren come up with the idea that the boy experiences a "growing sense of isolation." This sense of isolation, they note, has a positive as well as a negative side. His estrangement from others is painful; he feels "cruelly" isolated. But he also feels "triumphant" in being separate from and somehow raised above his ordinary surroundings. This contrast between the ordinary and extraordinary, or actual and ideal, provides the basis for Brooks and Warren's thesis about reality and illusion.

To this analysis of character and setting, Brooks and Warren add two more approaches: patterns of words and images, and point of view. In the story's religious references they find a pattern that suggests a distinction between romantic love and religious love. The boy, they argue, confuses these two kinds of love. By making his love for Mangan's sister a religious experience, the boy attempts to protect it, like the chalice, from everything that would, according to Brooks and Warren, "cheapen and contaminate it"—namely, from the real, material world.

By thinking about the story's point of view, Brooks and Warren are able to put their various discoveries into perspective. They observe that the story is told by the boy after he has grown up. This hindsight allows the narrator to understand the significance of the boy's experience: "The emotions of the boy are confused, but the person telling the story, the boy grown up, is not confused. He has unraveled the confusion long after, knows that it existed and why it existed." This insight enables Brooks and Warren to recognize that "Araby" is not simply about a particular boy's childhood experience, but presents a universal theme, the continuing conflict between the real and the ideal.

From this essay on "Araby," you can see how different approaches to interpreting a story might be productive. Brooks and Warren make use of several approaches. The writer of the next essay uses only one. As you plan and write an essay interpreting a story, you will need to decide which approach or approaches to use in developing your own interpretation.

The following essay was written by David Ratinov for his freshman composition class. Like most readers of "Araby," Ratinov wanted to understand what the narrator's final statement meant and what motivated it. Rereading and annotating the story, he gradually focused on the narrator's relationships with the other characters. As you read, notice how he uses evidence from these relationships to argue that self-delusion and hypocrisy are the central ideas of the story.

FROM INNOCENCE TO ANGUISHED INSIGHT: "ARABY" AS AN INITIATION STORY
DAVID RATINOV

"Araby" tells the story of an adolescent boy's initiation into adulthood. The story is narrated by a mature man reflecting upon his adolescence and the events that forced him to cross over the threshold from childhood innocence to a more mature understanding of the realities of the human condition. The minor characters play a pivotal role in this initiation process. The boy's infatuation with the girl ultimately ends in disillusionment, and Joyce uses the specific example of the boy's disillusionment with love to act as a metaphor for disillusionment with life itself. From the beginning the boy deludes himself about his relationship with Mangan's sister. Through this self-delusion, he increasingly resembles the adult characters, and later, at Araby, he realizes the parallel between his own self-delusion and the hypocrisy and vanity of the adult world.

From the beginning, the boy's infatuation with Mangan's sister draws him 2 away from childhood toward adulthood. He breaks his ties with his childhood friends and luxuriates in his isolation. He can think of nothing but his love for her: "From the front window I saw my companions playing below in the street. Their cries reached me weakened and indistinct and, leaning my forehead against the cool glass, I looked over at the dark house where she lived." The friends' cries are weak and indistinct because they are distant, emotionally as well as spatially. He imagines he carries his love for her as if it were a sacred object, a chalice: "Her image accompanied me even in places the most hostile to romance. . . . I imagined that I bore my chalice safely through a throng of foes." Even in the active, distracting marketplace, he is able to retain this image of his pure love. But his love is not pure.

Although he worships her as a religious object, his lust for her is undeniable. 3 He idolizes her as if she were the Virgin Mary: "her figure defined by the half-opened door. . . . The light from the lamp opposite our door caught the white curve of her neck, lit up her hair that rested there, and falling, lit up the hand upon the railing." Yet even this image is sensual with the halo of light accentuating "the white curve of her neck." The language makes obvious that his attraction is physical rather than spiritual: "Her dress swung as she moved her body and the soft rope of her hair tossed from side to side." His desire for her is strong and undeniable: "her name was like a summons to all my foolish blood"; "my body was like a harp and her words and gestures were like fingers running upon the wires." But in order to justify his love, to make it socially acceptable, he deludes himself into thinking that his love *is* pure. He is being hypocritical, although at this point he does not know it.

Hypocrisy is characteristic of the adults in this story. The characters of the 4 priest and Mrs. Mercer epitomize adult hypocrisy. The priest is by far the most obvious offender. What is a man of the cloth doing with books like *The Abbott* (a romantic novel) and *The Memoirs of Vidocq* (a sexually suggestive tale)? These books imply that he led a double life. Moreover, the fact that he had money to give away when he died suggests that he was far from saintly. Similarly, at first glance, Mrs. Mercer appears to be religious, but upon closer inquiry it seems that she too is materialistic. Her church work—collecting used stamps for some "pious purpose" (presumably to sell for the church)—associates her with money and profit. Even her name, Mercer, identifies her as a dealer in merchandise. In addition, her husband is a pawnbroker, a profession that the church frowns upon. Despite being linked to money, she pretends to be pious and respectable. Therefore, like the priest, Mrs. Mercer is hypocritical.

The uncle may not be hypocritical, but as the boy's only living male relative 5 he is a failure as a role model and the epitomy of vanity. He is a self-centered old man who cannot handle responsibility. When the boy reminds him on Saturday morning about the bazaar, the uncle brushes him off, devoting all his attention to his own appearance. After being out all afternoon the uncle returns home at 9:00, talking to himself. He rocks the hallstand when hanging up his overcoat. These details suggest that he is drunk. "I could interpret these signs" indicates that this behavior is typical of his uncle. The uncle is the only character in the story the boy relies upon, but the uncle fails him. Only after the aunt persuades him does the uncle give the boy the money he promised. From the priest, Mrs. Mercer, and his uncle, the boy learns some fundamental truths about the world, but it is only after his visit to Araby that he is able to recognize what he has learned.

Araby to the adolescent represents excitement, a chance to prove the purity 6 of his love and, more abstractly, his hope; however, Araby fulfills none of these expectations. Instead, the boy finds himself in utter disillusionment and despair. Araby is anything but exciting. The trip there is dreary, and uneventful, lonely and intolerably slow—not the magical journey he had expected. When he arrives, Araby itself is nearly completely dark and in the process of closing. With his excitement stunted, he can barely remember why he came (to prove the purity of his love by buying a gift for Mangan's sister). The trip is a failure. He does nothing to prove himself or his faithfulness, and as a result his illusion that his love for her is pure begins to break down.

The young lady selling porcelain and her gentlemen friends act as catalysts, 7 causing the boy to recognize the truth of his love for Mangan's sister. Their conversation is flirtatious—a silly lover's game that the boy recognizes as resembling his own conversation with Mangan's sister. He concludes that his love for her is no different than the two gentlemen's "love" for this "lady." Neither love is pure. He too had only been playing a game, flirting with a girl and pretending it was something else and that he was someone else.

His disillusionment with love is then extended to life in general. Seeing the 8 last rays of hope fading from the top floors of Araby, the boy cries: "I saw myself as a creature driven and derided by vanity; and my eyes burned with anguish and anger." At last he makes the connection—by deluding himself, he has been hypocritical and vain like the adults in his life. Before these realizations he believed that he was driven by something of value (such as purity of love) but now he realizes that his quest has been in vain because honesty, truth, and purity are only childish illusions and he can never return to the innocence of childhood.

Questions for analysis   1. Ratinov suggests "Araby" is about adolescence. How perceptive do you think the story is? Could you generalize, for example, from the boy's experience to your own? What role do you think literature should play in helping us understand our own experience and human experience in general?

2. In paragraphs 2 and 3, Ratinov quotes repeatedly from the story in order to supply the textual evidence essential to his argument. Examine each

quotation to see how it contributes to his argument and how he integrates it into his own text. Then compare Ratinov's use of quotation to Brooks and Warren's. What conclusions can you make about how literary critics use quotations from the texts they are interpreting? (For a discussion of ways to integrate quotations into your writing, see Chapter 22: The Research Paper.)

3. Ratinov analyzes three minor characters in "Araby"—the priest, Mrs. Mercer, and the uncle. Look back at the story to see which details Ratinov left out. Do these details support his interpretation or do they suggest some other meaning? How could Ratinov have used these details from the story as further evidence for his thesis? Should a writer use every detail from the story? What about details that contradict the writer's thesis? Should the writer ignore them?

4. In paragraph 7, Ratinov focuses on what happens at the bazaar, particularly the conversation the boy overhears between the shop girl and the two men. Look back at this conversation in paragraph 27 of "Araby." How convincing is Ratinov's interpretation of this conversation? What does it lead you to understand about the significance of the conversation for the boy?

5. In the last paragraph, Ratinov ties together his two main ideas: that the boy's love for Mangan's sister is an illusion, and that the boy's adult role models are either hypocritical or vain. How effectively does he connect these ideas? How could the connection be made even clearer?

Commentary   Like Brooks and Warren, David Ratinov presents an interpretation of "Araby." His audience, purpose, and argumentative strategy, however, differ markedly from theirs. Brooks and Warren wrote their piece for a book introducing literary interpretation to college students. They, therefore, sought to demonstrate how students might go about analyzing a story like "Araby." Ratinov, on the other hand, wrote his essay for his English teacher and classmates. His aim was to show that his interpretation of the story is plausible, carefully reasoned, and well-supported.

Their respective argumentative strategies reflect the special constraints of writing for a particular audience and purpose. Brooks and Warren arrange their argument inductively, ending with their thesis. This arrangement allows them to show how an interpretation develops from discoveries made by taking various approaches to the work. Ratinov arranges his argument deductively, beginning with the thesis. Organizing the essay deductively allows him to lay out his argument so that readers can judge his reasoning and evidence.

Ratinov sets forth his thesis in the opening sentence and elaborates it extensively in the first paragraph. This paragraph introduces the key terms and main ideas in his argument. The key terms in Ratinov's thesis are *innocence, disillusionment, self-delusion,* and *hypocrisy.* The clarity and coherence of an argument depends largely on its key terms. Terms that are vague or ambiguous lead to confusing writing. Writers, therefore, carefully define and explain their meaning in the context of the story they are analyzing. (See Chapter 19: Arguing for further discussion of criteria for making claims.)

The last two sentences of Ratinov's introductory paragraph forecast the main points of the essay and the order in which they are presented: that the boy deludes himself about his infatuation with Mangan's sister (paragraphs 2 and 3); that the adult characters are hypocritical (paragraphs 4 and 5); and finally that the boy's self-delusion parallels the adults' hypocrisy (paragraphs 6–8). In addition, each succeeding paragraph begins with a topic sentence that announces the point developed in that paragraph. This careful, systematic presentation of the thesis, forecast, and topic sentences ensures that the argument will be easy for readers to follow. (Chapter 12: Cueing the Reader discusses these writing strategies in detail.)

PURPOSE AND AUDIENCE

When you write an essay interpreting a literary work, your purpose is to present an idea about what the work means. This idea is your interpretation. Since your readers may favor other interpretations, your task is to convince them that yours is reasonable or plausible and that it reflects thoughtful analysis. Even if it were possible for all serious readers to agree about a general theme for a work, such readers might focus on quite diverse aspects of the work, just as the writers in this chapter do. A story, such as this one, can be interpreted in many different ways. A community of readers—your composition class or all English majors on your campus or all literary scholars who have written about "Araby"—accepts this diversity and enjoys it.

There is, then, no single or best interpretation. There are only interesting or plausible ideas, intriguing ideas presented convincingly. Consequently, in writing an essay interpreting a story you are not trying to win a contest or prove that only your idea should be taken seriously. Instead, you are trying to share your idea and to develop a reasonable and well-supported argument for it. Your readers will not immediately assume that they disagree with what you are about to say. Quite the contrary, as members of your community of readers, they will be anticipating a new intriguing idea about the story, one that may lead them to a new understanding and appreciation for it.

Your readers do not expect you to come up with a startling insight into the story, though they will be pleased if you do. What readers do expect is a logical argument supported by an interesting "reading" of the story. If you have been discussing the same story (like "Araby") or a group of stories by the same author (like Joyce's *Dubliners,* in which "Araby" appears), they may even find your thesis predictable or similar to their own. But a predictable thesis can be argued in an interesting way, showing readers new ways to look at the story. Your readers will be disappointed only if you propose an unclear or unfocused thesis with unworkable terms, propose a thesis that can be challenged by evidence in the text, argue illogically, neglect to include numerous examples and quotations from the text, or fail to provide the necessary cues to keep readers on track. Readers will be especially disappointed if they think you are summarizing the story rather than developing a particular idea about it.

BASIC FEATURES OF LITERARY INTERPRETATION

Writing about literature generally has only two key ingredients: an interpretation of the work and a convincing argument based on textual evidence for that interpretation.

The writer's interpretation

At the center of a literary interpretation lies the writer's analysis of how the work achieves its particular effects and meaning. This is the point the writer is trying to communicate to readers; it provides the main focus for the essay. Without such a central point, the essay would be just an accumulation of ideas about the work rather than a coherent, reasoned analysis of the work.

In literary interpretation, this main idea is usually given directly in a thesis statement. Something of a focal point, the thesis brings the parts of the essay into perspective, helping readers to understand how the ideas and details relate to one another as well as how they combine to illuminate the work.

For example, David Ratinov states his thesis in his opening paragraph: " 'Araby' tells the story of an adolescent boy's initiation into adulthood. . . . Through this self-delusion, he increasingly resembles the adult characters, and later, at Araby, he realizes the parallel between his own self-delusion and the hypocrisy and vanity of the adult world." The key terms in Ratinov's interpretation—*initiation, self-delusion,* and *hypocrisy* are clear, appropriate, and workable. Brooks and Warren begin with a general statement about the story ("On what may be called the simplest level 'Araby' is a story of a boy's disappointment.") that they explore in the essay. Their thesis, however, is not explicitly stated until the final sentence: "So, the story is not merely an account of a stage in the process of growing up . . . but is a symbolic rendering of a central conflict in mature experience."

Although literary critics may want their analysis to account for subtleties in the work, they do not want their readers to have difficulty understanding their interpretation. No matter how complex their interpretation, they strive to make their writing direct and clear. Therefore, writers usually alert readers to the points they will be making, giving readers a context in which to understand their analysis of the work. Ratinov, for example, forecasts in the last two sentences of the opening paragraph the main points he develops in the essay: "From the beginning, the boy deludes himself about his relationship with Mangan's sister. Through this self-delusion, he increasingly resembles the adult characters, and later, at Araby, he realizes the parallel between his own self-delusion and the hypocrisy and vanity of the 'adult world.' "

A convincing argument   In addition to stating their interpretation, writers must try to present a convincing argument for it. They may sometimes assume that readers are familiar with the work, but never can they expect readers to see it as they do or automatically to understand—let alone accept—their interpretation.

Writers argue for their interpretation not so much to convince readers to adopt it but rather to convince them that it makes sense. They must demonstrate to readers how they "read" the work, pointing out specific details and explaining what they think these details mean.

The primary source of evidence for literary interpretation, then, is the work itself. Writers quote the work, describe it, summarize it, and paraphrase it. They do more than just refer to a specific passage in the work, however: they explain the meaning of the passage in the light of their thesis. Since the language of literature is so suggestive, writers have to demonstrate to readers how they arrived at their understanding of the work by pointing to specific details in the work and explaining what these details mean to them. Cleanth Brooks and Robert Penn Warren, for example, paraphrase, summarize, and quote from the story throughout their essay. This textual evidence alternates with their serious and energetic explanation of its significance to their thesis. In paragraph 2 alone, in which they explore the idea of the boy's sense of isolation, they quote from the story three times and also summarize several events.

It is also possible to find ideas and evidence in support of an interpretation from outside sources—other critics, biographical information about the author, historical facts. Not only can such evidence provide insight into the work, but it may also increase the writer's authority and lend the argument credibility. Occasionally, writers may refer to other critics to build their own case not on, but in opposition to, alternative interpretations. Disagreements over interpretations are productive and healthy, leading to clearer insights and deeper understanding of the work.

GUIDE TO WRITING

THE WRITING TASK

Write an essay interpreting a work of short fiction to reveal how the work achieves its meaning. Your aim is not primarily to convince readers to adopt your view, but to convince them that your view is a reasonable one based on a thoughtful and imaginative reading of the work.

INVENTION AND RESEARCH

At this point you should choose a short story, analyze it carefully, develop a thesis, and find evidence in the story for that thesis.

Choosing a story   Your instructor may have asked you to write about a particular story. If this is the case, turn now to the next section, Approaching the Story.

   If you must choose a story on your own, you should consider—and read—several stories before deciding on one to write about. Choose a story that impresses you, one that excites your interest and imagination. You should not expect to understand the story completely on the first reading; just be sure to select a story that you want to study closely.

Approaching the story   To discover meaning in a story you need a strategy of inquiry, an approach to the story that will lead to ideas about it. This section provides such a strategy. Although it requires attentive rereading and various kinds of writing, it will richly reward your investment of time and attention.

   A strategy for approaching the story. This strategy involves selecting one of several approaches, rereading the story with the approach in mind, noting what you see, and then organizing and writing about your notes. Your goal is to write an essay interpreting the story you have read. These steps provide a starting point:

   1. *Read.* Read the story for pleasure, diversion, and insight—for the same reasons you always read stories and novels or watch movies.

   2. *Approach.* Look over the list of approaches that follows to find one that interests you. Any approach will enable you to begin serious analysis of a story to discover what it might mean. Since you will want to try at least two or three approaches, this first choice is not crucial. Review the approach you choose carefully so that you fully understand its possibilities. To ensure that your annotating and inventorying (Steps 3 and 4) are focused and productive, you should refer continually to the suggestions listed in the approach.

   3. *Annotate.* Reread the story with your pencil in hand, annotating anything you notice that is at all relevant to the approach you are taking. To annotate, mark on the text itself and write in the margins. (You will find illustrations and discussions of annotating in the Writer at Work section at the end of this chapter and in Chapter 11: Invention and Revision.) Look up any unfamiliar words in a college dictionary. Your annotating and subsequent inventorying may be severely limited if you do not take the time to do this. You will be shut off from exact details about characters, rich connotations in words or images, and suggestive historical allusions. (An espe-

cially valuable library source for word histories and connotations is the un-abridged *Oxford English Dictionary*.)

Since annotating is most productive if it is "layered up" over several readings, you will want to reread the story more than once, adding new annotations each time. Annotate freely. Annotating leads to unexpected connections and patterns that you cannot predict while you are annotating, so you should not limit yourself in this early stage of inquiry.

4. *Inventory.* Look over your annotations and inventory them. Inventorying involves classifying, connecting, or patterning your annotations. You *organize* your annotations. You can draw lines on the text to connect related annotations, number related text or marginal annotations, or list related items on a sheet of paper and then name the groupings. (You will find examples in the Writer at Work Section at the end of this chapter and in Chapter 11: Invention and Revision.)

5. *Write.* Analyze your inventory and write at least a page about the connections and patterns you have discovered. This writing will record what you have learned and may also lead you to still further discoveries. Answer this question as you write: What does this inventory reveal about the story?

6. *Assert.* Reflect on what you have learned through this approach. In a sentence or two, assert one or more ideas you now have about the story. Think of these ideas as generalizations about the story or as insights or conclusions. Assert them confidently. Writing one may suggest others. Write as many as you can. These assertions may lead you to a thesis for your essay. Remember that you may want to repeat these steps with more than one of the following approaches to interpreting stories.

A catalog of approaches. Used with the steps outlined earlier, these approaches enable you to analyze a story productively.

1. *Surprising or puzzling statements.* Select a surprising or puzzling statement that especially interests you, and begin by looking closely at the context in which it appears. Then reread, annotating to explore the significance of the statement throughout the story.

2. *Patterns of words and images.* To find patterns of related words or images, reread the story, watching for unusual words; words that suggest a particular feeling or mood; words identifying visual details (shape, color, texture), sounds, smells; words that form patterns of repetition, contradiction, or tension; images (simile, metaphor) and patterns of images. When you have identified a pattern, annotate the text carefully in order to discover what the pattern discloses about the story.

3. *Character and character change.* Examine the personality and state of mind of one or more characters. Annotate the story, noticing the character's name; way of talking; actions; reported thoughts; values, beliefs, motives, and goals; relations with other characters; differences from and similarities

to other characters; contradictions among the character's thoughts, words, and actions. Also notice any changes or development of the character from beginning to end of the story.

4. *Point of view.* Analyze how the story is told, who tells it, and how much this narrator knows. Consider how you learn about the narrator (whether through description, action, dialogue, statements that reveal attitudes and opinions, or other characters' statements); whether the narrator is a character or just a disembodied voice; whether the narrator knows everything, including characters' thoughts and feelings, or has only limited knowledge; whether the narrator focuses on one character, restricting information to what the character knows, sees, thinks, feels; whether the narrator can be trusted; how the work would be changed with a different narrator. Your goal is to decide just who the narrator is and how the story is shaped by this narrator.

5. *Ironies or contradictions.* Identify ironies or contradictions in events; in what characters think, say, or do; and in ways characters relate to one another and to their environment. Annotate the story with one or more ironies or contradictions in mind.

6. *Literary motifs.* Analyze the story as an example of a conventional literary motif, such as the conflict between the individual and society, coming of age or initiation, a journey or quest, the disparity between appearance and reality, and the double, in which two or more characters represent alternative realities.

7. *Setting.* Consider the physical setting of the story: place and time of the events; whether the setting or scene changes; relationship between different scenes; the way the writer presents the setting (features and objects singled out for attention or naming; particular colors, shapes, sizes, textures, sounds, smells); the mood the setting creates; whether the setting causes, reflects, or contradicts the characters' actions, values, or moods; how a different setting might alter the story's meaning.

8. *Structure.* Analyze the story in terms of its arrangement: the opening, foreshadowing, points of suspense or tension, the climax, the ending. Look for repetition, framing, unresolved conflicts, as well as stages in the story's development (repeated or opposite events).

9. *Historical, social, and economic context.* Analyze the story for specific historical, political, economic, social, or religious references. Stories are written in a particular time and place. If you know anything about the conditions at the time a story was written or the cultural and historical background of it, you can gain a valuable perspective on the story. You can also ask questions like the following: Who has the money, power, privilege, or status? Do the political, economic, and social conditions trivialize or enoble human activities and relationships? Are people trapped in limiting sexual or economic roles? Do institutions support or thwart human needs and dreams?

Finding a thesis   Your aim now is to find a thesis you will be able to develop and support with specific evidence from the story. You may already have a tentative thesis in mind, but it is still advisable to consider several other possibilities.

Listing generalizations. Begin by reviewing all the assertions or generalizations that you wrote as you completed each approach to the story. Start a new list now of the most promising ones. Select just two or three that express ideas about the story that especially interest you and that you might like to write about. Then add to this list any other ideas that have occurred to you since you completed working on the approaches to the story.

Choosing a possible thesis. From your list of promising generalizations, choose one to refine into a thesis for your essay. At this point, you cannot know for certain that your first choice will work out. Choose for now on the basis of the appeal to you of the idea. Consider carefully whether there is evidence in the story that could contradict your idea. Your idea does not have to accommodate all the evidence in the story, but it should not be easily challenged by a skeptical reader.

If you find that you do not have a generalization that meets these criteria, discuss your list with other students and your instructor. You may discover a way to modify a generalization to suit your purposes.

Writing and revising a tentative thesis statement. You now want to turn your favored generalization into a thesis statement. A useful thesis should offer an interesting idea about the story, be concise and well focused, preclude easy challenge, and include the key terms in which you will discuss the story. These key terms label the basic concepts in your interpretation of the story and will provide coherence and focus to your argument.

Try out your thesis statement on your instructor and classmates. You do not want to know whether they agree with it (if they have read the story you are interpreting) but whether they find it clear and workable.

Consider your thesis statement tentative at this stage. Once you begin collecting and organizing evidence to support your thesis, you may decide the evidence supports it only partially or even contradicts it. Be prepared to revise the thesis to fit your new understanding of the story.

Considering your   Before you proceed, you must consider your readers. In a composition class,
readers   your instructor is, of course, a reader. He or she may have invited you to identify other readers or have asked you to consider your classmates the primary readers.

Two things are essential to know about your readers: whether they are familiar with the story and whether they are likely to favor other interpretations.

If they are unfamiliar with the story, you will need to describe it for them briefly before proposing your interpretation to them. If you are interpreting the same story as your classmates, they will know the story well, and they will almost certainly propose interpretations different from yours. Knowing their interpretations (and even perhaps their reasons, evidence, or argumentative strategy) can influence your argumentative strategy, especially your choice of evidence.

Take a few moments to make some brief notes about your readers. State who they are, what they know about the story, and what interpretations they may favor. Try to predict how they will receive your interpretation. What questions might they raise?

Gathering textual evidence
Having settled on a tentative thesis and identified your readers, you now need to marshal evidence from the story to support your thesis. As you draft and revise your essay, you will be returning to the story for evidence. For now, however, you can begin to identify, organize, and evaluate evidence to support your thesis. You will find this evidence in the story and in your annotations, inventories, and exploratory writings about the inventories.

Identifying evidence. With your thesis in mind, search for evidence that will support it. Note everything you can find that seems relevant to your thesis—dialogue, events, descriptive details, key words, images. Annotate this evidence. You may also find evidence that contradicts your thesis. Do not ignore this evidence. Let it lead you to clarify and revise your thesis.

Organizing evidence. Your inventories and exploratory writings may provide partial organizations of evidence. You may now, however, see different ways to organize it. Or you may have identified new evidence that you overlooked in your earlier annotations and inventories.

Your goal is only to begin grouping evidence around probable ideas, rather than to organize it precisely, since you cannot predict the exact sequence of your argument at this point. One way to do this is to list the probable ideas, give each a number or letter code, and then review the evidence you have identified, coding each piece of evidence for the idea it seems to support. Another way is to make an ideas and evidence table. Divide a piece of paper into two columns. In the left column, list your ideas, skipping several lines after each one. Then, in the right column beside each idea, write down the evidence you have to support it.

Evaluating evidence. Determine whether you have sufficient evidence to support your thesis and develop a convincing argument for your particular readers. Also test the fit between your ideas and the available evidence. If you have trouble supporting your thesis and fitting evidence to it logically, you will need to revise your thesis or try out a different one.

Researching other critics' interpretations

Others may have published their interpretations of the story you have chosen in articles and books that you can find in the library. Of course, you need not read theirs for assurance that yours is appropriate, nor can their interpretations substitute for your own. After you have examined the story closely and have devised a thesis, however, your instructor may encourage you to search out other interpretations to help you clarify and develop your ideas. Reading what others have written is like entering a conversation about the story. You may agree or disagree, find your own ideas supported or challenged, discover new insights, or learn nothing at all. If you do research, be sure to cite any ideas from other critics that you use in your essay. You might acknowledge interpretations supporting your own or refute those that contradict yours. You could even mention different, but complementary, interpretations. Whether you quote, paraphrase, or summarize others' ideas, keep the focus on your own interpretive argument. Do not write a report surveying what others think about the story; write an essay arguing for your own interpretation.

If you read published interpretations, keep careful notes of your research, noting direct quotations you may use later. Keep a record of your sources, including page numbers.

PLANNING AND DRAFTING

As you prepare to draft your essay, you will need to review your notes, set goals for drafting, and make an outline.

Seeing what you have

Review your notes. If you wish, reread the story. As you review what you have discovered about the story, ask yourself these questions:

- ☐ Can I express my thesis more clearly?
- ☐ What are my reasons for holding this thesis?
- ☐ Can my evidence be interpreted in some other way?
- ☐ Have I overlooked any important evidence?
- ☐ Have I glossed over or ignored any contradictions or problems?

Decide now whether or not you need to do further research. Postpone starting to draft if you find problems that still need to be worked out.

Setting goals

Before you start to draft, consider the special demands of literary interpretation and of the story you are interpreting. Let the following questions guide you in setting goals.

Your readers

- ☐ Are my readers likely to know this story? If not, how much of the plot should I relate? If so, how can I lead them to see the story as I do?

☐ What interpretations will my readers favor? How does my interpretation complement or differ from theirs?

☐ What tone should I adopt to assure my readers that I consider them valued members of my interpretive community?

☐ How can I organize the essay so that my readers will find it easy to follow? What cues can I provide about my organization and sequence? How can I integrate textual evidence smoothly into my essay?

☐ What questions, objections, or challenges might my readers raise about my interpretation?

The beginning

☐ Must I begin by describing the work for readers who have not read it?

☐ Should I pose an interpretive problem about the work and ask a question about it, as Brooks and Warren do?

☐ Should I state my thesis and forecast my plan, as Ratinov does?

☐ Should I establish the significance of the story and the importance of probing its meanings?

The argument

☐ How can I ensure that my thesis focuses my argument throughout? What role will my key terms play throughout my argument?

☐ How can my argument be considered authoritative and at the same time thoughtful and reasonable?

☐ How should I sequence the main parts of my argument so that it seems both logical and cumulative?

☐ How much textual evidence must I include in order for my argument to seem informed and convincing?

☐ Should I acknowledge readers' possible objections to my argument or alternative interpretations?

Avoiding logical fallacies of literary interpretation

☐ Will I be committing an *either/or fallacy* by presenting my interpretation as the only possible interpretation?

☐ How can I show that I have accepted *the burden of proof*? Will my readers believe that I have taken responsibility for presenting a convincing argument for my interpretation?

☐ Can I avoid making a *straw man* of others' interpretations, oversimplifying or misrepresenting them to make my interpretation seem stronger? (Straw men are easier to push over than real men.)

☐ Can I avoid *hasty generalization* by offering adequate evidence for all the general statements I make about the work?

The ending

☐ Should I repeat my key terms, as all the writers in this chapter do?

☐ Should I restate my thesis, as Ratinov does?

☐ Should I end with a provocative question?

Outlining the essay　　At this point you should try to develop a plan for your draft. You may compose a formal outline, a simple list of key points, or a clustering diagram. (Each of these kinds of outlines is discussed in Chapter 11: Invention and Revision.) Whichever method you choose, remember that an outline is only a tentative plan. It need not be binding; if you have other thoughts along the way, try them out.

Drafting the essay　　If some time has gone by since you last read the story, reread it quickly before you begin to draft. Then review the general advice on drafting in Chapter 1.

As you draft, keep in mind the two goals of all literary analysis: presenting your interpretation and supporting that interpretation with textual evidence. Try to be as direct as you can. Explain your ideas fully. Make the relations between the thesis, the points you use to develop it, and the supporting evidence explicit for readers. Remember they will have different ways of reading and understanding the passages you quote or refer to. Show them how you are using specific evidence from the work to make your own point about the work.

READING A DRAFT WITH A CRITICAL EYE

At this point you are ready to have someone else read your draft critically to help you see how it can be strengthened. The following guidelines will help you analyze the particular features of an essay interpreting literature. (Before you begin, you might want to review the general advice on reading another's draft critically in Chapter 1.)

First general impression　　Read the essay straight through to get a quick, general impression. Write just a few sentences giving your first reaction. If you are familiar with the story, briefly tell the writer how you would interpret it. Did you find the essay logical and convincing? What did you learn about the story from reading the essay? Identify one problem and one strength you noticed in this first reading.

Pointings　　One good way to maintain a critical focus as you read the essay is to highlight noteworthy features of the writing with *pointings*. A simple system of lines and brackets, these pointings are quick and easy to do, and they can provide a lot of helpful information for revision. Use pointings in the following way:

☐ Draw a straight line under words or images that impress you as especially effective: strong verbs, specific details, memorable phrases, striking images.

☐ Draw a wavy line under any words or images that seem flat, stale, or vague. Also put the wavy line under any words or phrases that you consider unnecessary or repetitious.

☐ Look for pairs or groups of sentences that you think should be combined. Put brackets [ ] around these sentences.

☐ Look for sentences that are garbled, overloaded, or awkward. Put parentheses ( ) around these sentences. Put them around any sentence that seems even slightly questionable; don't worry now about whether or not you're certain about your judgment. The writer needs to know that you, as one reader, had even the slightest hestitation about understanding a sentence.

Analysis

1. To be convincing, literary interpretation must be grounded in specific textual evidence. Point to any places where evidence must still be provided.

2. Textual evidence should be clearly related to a specific point. Alert the writer to any evidence that is not tied to an idea.

3. Ideas must not only be supported with textual evidence, but they must also be fully explained. Point to any ideas that need more clarification or development.

4. Help the writer focus and clarify the thesis statement by explaining what each of the key terms in the thesis means to you. Identify terms that are especially valuable as well as those that are questionable.

5. Point out any ideas that seem unrelated to the thesis, disconnected from the other ideas, or contradictory.

6. Literary interpretation occasionally needs to relate details of the plot. Let the writer know, however, if too much space is devoted to plot summary and not enough to analysis.

7. How and where does the writer acknowledge readers' possible objections and preferred interpretations? Tell the writer if this feature should be played down or strengthened.

8. If other critics are cited, decide whether they strengthen or weaken the essay's argument. Explain your views.

9. Effective interpretations have direction and momentum. Point out places in the essay where the momentum slowed. Advise the writer if a different sequence for the main ideas would provide a more logical progression to the argument.

10. Evaluate the beginning. How does it prepare the reader for the essay? Suggest other ways to open.

11. Evaluate the ending. Is it too abrupt or mechanical? Does it oversimplify the argument or distort the thesis? Try to suggest an alternate ending.

12. What final comments or suggestions can you offer? Do you have any unanswered questions?

REVISING AND EDITING

You are now ready to revise your draft. Review any advice you have from classmates or your instructor. Before you begin, you may want to read the story again, especially if several days have passed since you worked with it. You will need the story at hand as you plan your revision.

Revising a literary interpretation

The specific advice here on revising a literary interpretation can be used with the plan for revising in Chapter 11. For further advice, follow the general plan in Chapter 11 until you reach the section Read Again To Identify Possible Revisions. The following specific guidelines for revising a literary interpretation can be used in place of the more general ones in that section.

Revising to strengthen the argument

☐ Reconsider your interpretation of the story. Can your thesis be refined? Should you add more evidence or explain more specifically how your evidence supports your thesis?

☐ Can you strengthen the logical connections among your ideas?

☐ Reread your argument with your readers in mind. Have you fully considered the likelihood that they might interpret the story in some other way and that therefore you need to show them not only how you see it but why you see it as you do?

☐ Consider each of the main ideas. Are they now in the best possible order, or should they be presented in some other order?

Revising for readability

☐ Reconsider the beginning. Could you better prepare readers to follow your argument? Does the essay need a forecasting statement?

☐ Do you need to provide more explicit transitions between sentences and paragraphs?

☐ Do you sometimes give more details than you need to? Or too few?

☐ Reconsider the ending. How can you improve it? Can you see any other point in the essay that would be a stronger place to end?

Editing and proofreading   As you revise a draft for the last time, you need to edit it closely. Though you no doubt corrected obvious errors of usage and style in the drafting stage, editing was not your first priority. Now, however, you must find and correct any errors of mechanics, usage, punctuation, or style. After you have edited the draft and produced the final copy, you must proofread it carefully for any careless mistakes.

LEARNING FROM YOUR OWN WRITING PROCESS

If your instructor asks you to write about what you learned from writing this essay, consider the following questions:

- ☐ How did my thesis evolve as I planned and drafted the essay?
- ☐ How did I go about analyzing the work?
- ☐ What problems, if any, did I have finding evidence to support the thesis?
- ☐ Why did I decide to organize the essay as I did?
- ☐ What specific revisions, if any, did I make in the draft and what were my reasons for making these changes?

A WRITER AT WORK

ANNOTATING AND INVENTORYING A LITERARY WORK

Annotating and taking inventory of annotations are basic tools for understanding and interpreting short stories. Together with various traditional approaches to analyzing stories, they provide an instructive strategy of critical reading, inquiry, and interpretation. Here you can see a portion of the results of one student's annotation and inventory of "Araby." The student is David Ratinov, whose revised essay appears earlier in this chapter.

Ratinov chose Character and Character Change and Literary Motifs as his approaches to analyzing "Araby." Following the instructions in the Guide to Writing, Ratinov reread the story and annotated it from these two perspectives, took inventory to discover connections and ideas among his annotations, wrote briefly about his discoveries, and then wrote several generalizations asserting his ideas about the story. One of these generalizations led to the thesis you see in the revised essay.

Here are Ratinov's annotations on paragraphs 13 through 23, which resulted from two careful analytical readings of the story. Notice the diversity of his annotations. On the text itself, he underlines key words, circles words to be defined, and connects related words and ideas. In the margin, he defines words, makes comments, poses questions, and expresses tentative insights, personal reactions, and judgments.

[Marginal annotations:]

2nd mention of uncle
fussing—vain? irritable?
rude
always unkind to the boy?
uncle's effect on the boy

uncle will be late
sudden change in mood:
big contrast

liberated from untrust-
worthy uncle?
isolated from friends

romantic, even sensual

merchandise
talkative
hypocritically or self-con-
sciously religious
boy doesn't seem to like or
trust any of the adults

uncle and Mercer both try
to give a false impression
aunt seems pious too

boy knows uncle is drunk
boy's fears are justified
excuses

aunt to the rescue

hypocritical
what a bore!
boy determined to go to
bazaar to buy girl a gift

[Main text:]

On Saturday morning I reminded my uncle that I wished to go to the bazaar in the evening. He was fussing at the hallstand, looking for the hatbrush, and answered me curtly:

"Yes, boy, I know."

As he was in the hall I could not go into the front parlour and lie at the window. I left the house in bad humour and walked slowly towards the school. The air was pitilessly raw and already my heart misgave me.

When I came home to dinner my uncle had not yet been home. Still it was early. I sat staring at the clock for some time and, when its ticking began to irritate me, I left the room. I mounted the staircase and gained the upper part of the house. The high cold empty gloomy rooms liberated me and I went from room to room singing. From the front window I saw my companions playing below in the street. Their cries reached me weakened and indistinct and, leaning my forehead against the cool glass, I looked over at the dark house where she lived. I may have stood there for an hour, seeing nothing but the brown-clad figure cast by my imagination, touched discreetly by the lamplight at the curved neck, at the hand upon the railings and at the border below the dress.

When I came downstairs again I found Mrs. Mercer sitting at the fire. She was an old garrulous woman, a pawnbroker's widow, who collected used stamps for some pious purpose. I had to endure the gossip of the tea-table. The meal was prolonged beyond an hour and still my uncle did not come. Mrs. Mercer stood up to go: she was sorry she couldn't wait any longer, but it was after eight o'clock and she did not like to be out late, as the night air was bad for her. When she had gone I began to walk up and down the room, clenching my fists. My aunt said:

"I'm afraid you may put off your bazaar for this night of Our Lord."

At nine o'clock I heard my uncle's latchkey in the halldoor. I heard him talking to himself and heard the hallstand rocking when it had received the weight of his overcoat. I could interpret these signs. When he was midway through his dinner I asked him to give me the money to go to the bazaar. He had forgotten.

"The people are in bed and after their first sleep now," he said.

I did not smile. My aunt said to him energetically:

"Can't you give him the money and let him go? You've kept him late enough as it is."

My uncle said he was very sorry he had forgotten. He said he believed in the old saying: "All work and no play makes Jack a dull boy." He asked me where I was going and, when I had told him a second time he asked me did I know *The Arab's Farewell to his Steed.* When I left the kitchen he was about to recite the opening lines of the piece to my aunt.

Annotating the story for the boy's character, Ravinov finds himself paying a lot of attention to the boy's relations with other characters. Taking inventory of these annotations for the entire story, Ratinov notices how negatively the narrator portrays the priest, Mrs. Mercer, and the uncle. He decides that what these characters have in common is hypocrisy. This notion would become a key term in his thesis and a major idea in his essay. In his essay, of course, he would have to prove with textual evidence that all these minor characters are hypocrites. In addition, he would have to be sure that no textual evidence challenged this idea.

Here Ratinov tries to organize his textual and marginal annotations in paragraphs 13 through 23 under the idea of hypocrisy:

adult hypocrisy
Mrs. Mercer
    name means "merchandise"
    pious—a religious hypocrite
    widow of pawnbroker—makes money by lending money to poor
       people for their possessions
    collected stamps—to sell for a church charity?
    gossip—talk about others behind their backs
Uncle
    a banker or manager
    brushes hat—obsessive about appearance
    fussy, vain, irritable, curt
    boy distrusts him, hides from him, seems to have no real relation-
       ship with him*
    lives in a big house only partly furnished and heated
    drinks, often drunk—Irish habit or stress of social pretense?
    "all work and no play"—uncle is the player—plays at social status,
       vain about appearance; also "plays" in bar (pub?) every night
       (most nights?)
    lets boy down—can't be trusted, irresponsible, insensitive to
       the boy's feelings, forgets, doesn't keep agreements or prom-
       ises*

*irresponsibility, not hypocrisy

You can see that Ratinov labels this portion of his inventory with the connection he makes among the adult characters. He then lists relevant annotations under the characters' names. (Ratinov also inventoried information about the priest, but it is not included here because the priest is not mentioned in paragraphs 13 through 23.) Many inventories of text annotations share these characteristics of labeling and listing. The labels indicate connections, patterns, or ideas about the story. The lists bring together annotations relevant to the labels. Although Ratinov's inventory collects annotations that appear close together on the story's text, some inventories collect widely scattered annotations.

When analyzing his inventory in writing, Ratinov produces these sentences about the section on hypocrisy:

Mrs. Mercer may be a good neighbor to the boy's aunt, but the boy dislikes her. Joyce plants many clues that she is a hypocrite. She

thinks of herself as a good religious Christian, but she is pious (an
exaggerated Christian, not a believable one), collects stamps to sell for
charity instead of doing good works firsthand (my guess), and she is
a gossip. Her husband got his money in an unchristian way. Does the
boy know all this or only the narrator much later? I'm sure the boy
senses it. He says he has to endure Mrs. Mercer and her gossip with
his aunt. Now that I look over the evidence for the uncle's hypocrisy,
it seems that his unguardianlike actions toward the boy, his irresponsibility toward him, is just as big a flaw as his hypocrisy. He seems to
be trying to hide something by drinking and being obsessive about his
appearance—a failure to advance at work? He tries to impress people
with a bigger house than he can afford. Says he believes in things
that don't apply to his own actions. I think I can show that he's a
hypocrite like Mrs. Mercer. Because the boy distrusts him, he must
sense this hypocrisy.

Writing about this portion of his inventory enables Ratinov to try out
his ideas about hypocrisy. He confirms that the term itself is workable for
discussing the story and that the evidence in the text supports the idea of
hypocrisy. He also makes the important discovery that some annotations
listed under the uncle reveal his irresponsibility and goes back to the inventory to asterisk these items. This discovery leads in his essay to a more
complex presentation of the uncle as a flawed adult inadvertently teaching
lessons the boy will discover at the Araby bazaar.

After completing his written analysis of his annotations involving the
boy's relations with other characters, Ratinov writes several generalizations
(or ideas or insights) about what he discovered.

All the adult characters are hypocrites.
If this is just a story about romance, then all the adult characters
wouldn't have to be so weak and flawed.
Mangan's sister is different from the adults, but through her he has
to face up to what the adult world is all about.
The adults are initiating the boy into adulthood, but he doesn't see it
until the end of the story.
Growing up means being able to see the world for what it actually is,
not what you want it to be.

From these generalizations about initiation, epiphany, romance, and hypocrisy, Ratinov devised the thesis for his essay.

PART TWO

Writing Strategies

Invention and Revision

The first part of this chapter presents a catalogue of invention and inquiry strategies writers use to explore their subjects and to find out what they have to say about them—before, during, and after the drafting stage of the writing process. In the second part we present a general plan for revision, to be followed once an initial draft is complete. You may use the invention strategies and revision plan in conjunction with the writing guides in Part I or on their own, as you plan, draft, and revise in other writing situations.

INVENTION AND INQUIRY

Writers are like scientists: they ask questions, inquiring about how things work, what they are, where they occur, and how more information can be learned about them. Writers are also like artists: they use what they know and have learned to create something new and imaginative, inventing meaning and form.

The invention and inquiry strategies described here are not mysterious or magical. They are tricks of the trade available to everyone and should appeal to your common sense and experience in solving problems. Developed by writers, psychologists, and linguists, they represent the ways writers, engineers, scientists, composers—in fact, all of us—creatively solve problems.

Once these general strategies become familiar, they will help you tackle any writing situation you encounter in college or on the job. The best way to learn these strategies is to use them as you write an actual essay. Part I, Chapters 2–10, shows you when these general strategies can be most helpful and how to make the most efficient use of them. The guides to invention and research in these chapters offer easy-to-use adaptations of these general strategies, adaptations designed to satisfy the special requirements of the essay you are writing.

The general strategies for invention and inquiry in this chapter are grouped into three categories:

Mapping: a brief visual representation of your thinking or planning

Writing: the composition of phrases or sentences to discover information and ideas and to find relationships among ideas

Reading: a systematic use of reading to understand and to explore information for its possibilities in your own writing

In each category individual strategies are arranged alphabetically.

The invention and inquiry strategies give you a powerful advantage in thinking and planning for writing. They enable you to explore and research a topic fully before you begin drafting, and they also help you solve problems as you are drafting and before you revise.

MAPPING

Mapping involves making a visual record of invention and inquiry. Writers use mapping strategies to help them think about a topic. In making maps, they usually use key words and phrases—their private shorthand or code—to record material they want to remember, questions they need to answer, and even new sources of information they want to check. The maps they create show the ideas, details, and facts they are examining. They also show possible ways materials can be connected and focused. Maps might be informal graphic displays with words and phrases circled and connected by lines to show relationships, or they might be formal sentence outlines. Mapping can be especially useful because it gives you an immediate visual representation of your thinking and planning. Mapping strategies include clustering, listing, and outlining.

Clustering   Clustering is an invention activity which reveals possible relations among facts and ideas. Unlike listing (the next mapping strategy), clustering requires a brief period of initial planning. You must first come up with a tentative division of the topic into subparts or main ideas. Clustering works as follows:

1. In a word or phrase, write your topic in the center of a piece of paper. Circle it.

2. Also in a word or phrase, write down the main parts or central ideas of your topic. Circle these, and connect them to the topic in the center.

3. The next step is to generate facts, details, examples, or ideas related in any way to these main parts. Cluster these around the main parts.

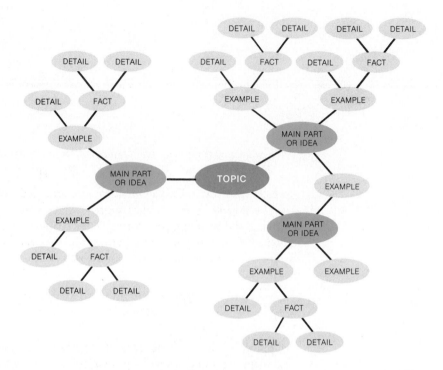

Clustering can be useful for any kind of writing. Writers use it in the early stages of planning an essay in order to find subtopics in a topic or to organize information. They may try and discard several clusters before finding one that is promising. Writers also use clustering to plan brief sections of an essay as they are drafting.

Listing   Listing is a familiar activity. We make shopping lists and lists of errands to do or people to call. A list of things to accomplish can reassure us when we are behind in our work or facing deadlines.

Listing can also be a great help in planning an essay. It enables you to recall what you already know about a topic and suggests what more you may need to find out. It is an easy way to get started doing something productive, instead of just worrying about what you will write. A list has an interesting way of riding along on its own momentum. The first item in the list leads easily to the next.

Listing has always been a basic activity for writers. It can be especially useful for those who have little time for planning—for example, reporters facing deadlines or college students taking essay exams. Listing lets you put your ideas in order quickly. It can also help as a first step in discovering possible writing topics.

Listing is a solitary form of brainstorming, a popular technique of problem solving in groups. If you were working with a group to generate ideas for a collaborative writing project, then you would be engaged in true brainstorming.

Here is how listing works best as an invention activity:

1. Give your list a title.

2. Write as fast as you can, relying on short phrases.

3. Include anything that seems at all useful. Do not try to be judgmental at this point.

4. After you have finished, or even as you write, reflect on the list and organize it in the following way. This is a very important step, for it may lead you to further discoveries about your topic.

> put an asterisk by the most promising items
>
> number key items in order of importance
>
> put items in related groups
>
> cross out items that do not seem promising
>
> add new items

Outlining Outlining is both a way of planning and a means of inventing. An outline may, of course, provide the plan for an essay. Yet, as soon as you start making an outline, you will begin to see new possibilities in your subject. You may discover new ways of dividing or grouping information. You can estimate whether you have adequate information to develop each major point. You will know whether there is an appropriate plan for presenting the information necessary for your thesis. If not, you may need to revise your thesis.

There are three main forms of outlining: scratch, topic, and sentence. (Keep in mind that clustering is also a way of outlining.)

A scratch outline is an informal outline, really only a rough list of the main points (and sometimes subpoints as well) of an essay. You have no doubt made scratch outlines many times—both to clarify difficult reading and to plan essays or essay exams. As an example, here is a scratch outline for Victor Fuchs's essay in Chapter 9: Speculating About Causes.

SUICIDE AMONG YOUNG PEOPLE

death rate rising for 15–24 year olds

mainly more murders and suicides

why more suicides?—not a result of new ways of reporting suicides or of Vietnam War or of bad economy

causes probably in family—divorce, no discipline, loss of father

increase in suicide really is unique to this age group

no simple solution possible

We can imagine Fuchs making such a scratch outline before he began drafting his essay. (A different scratch outline emphasizing strategies of causal analysis rather than content follows Fuchs's essay.)

Scratch outlines can help you organize information while you are still gathering it. Before you begin a first draft, organize your invention and research notes in a scratch outline. As you draft, you may need to change this scratch outline. Once you have had advice on your draft and a chance to consider revising it, you may need a new scratch outline for a differently organized revision. The writing guide for each chapter in Part I offers possibilities for outlining the kind of writing you are working on in that chapter.

Items in a scratch outline do not necessarily coincide with paragraphs, although they may. Sometimes two or more items may be developed in the same paragraph. At other times one item may represent two or more paragraphs. Whether outline items represent paragraphs or not, they rarely indicate the extent to which that item is developed in the essay.

Topic and sentence outlines are more formal than scratch outlines. They follow a conventional format of numbered and lettered headings and subheadings. Some instructors require topic or sentence outlines with essays or research papers. Following is a *topic* outline of Fuchs's essay:

SUICIDE AMONG YOUNG PEOPLE

I. Increasing death rate in the 15–24 age group
II. Increase explained by self-destructive behavior
    A. Homicide
    B. Suicide
III. Unacceptable causes of the increase
    A. Change in reporting of suicides
    B. Attitudes toward Vietnam War
    C. Unemployment and weak economy
IV. Probable causes of the increase
    A. Divorce or lack of discipline
    B. Loss of father
V. Increase in suicides unique to 15–24 age group
VI. Challenge of this problem for public policy

Notice that a period follows the Roman numerals and capital letters. The items in the outline are words or brief phrases, not sentences. Items are not followed by a period, but the first word in each case is capitalized. It is customary in a topic outline for items at the same level of indentation to be grammatically parallel. Under Item IV, for instance, the A and B items both begin with nouns:

A. *Divorce* or lack of discipline
B. *Loss* of father

The items would not be grammatically parallel if B began with an infinitive phrase (*to* plus a verb), like this:

A. *Divorce* or lack of discipline
B. *To lose* a father

Following is a *sentence* outline of Fuchs's essay. The items are complete sentences, with the first word capitalized and the last word followed by a period.

SUICIDE AMONG YOUNG PEOPLE

I.   The death rate is rising only for Americans in the age group 15–24.
II. This increase is a result of self-destructive behavior.
     A. The homicide rate is rising in the 15–24 age group, especially among blacks.
     B. The suicide rate is also increasing.
III. Many explanations have been offered for the increasing suicide rate.
     A. The trend is not the result of a change in ways of reporting suicides.
     B. The trend cannot be explained by attitudes toward the Vietnam War.
     C. The trend cannot be explained by unemployment or a bad economy.
IV. The causes of the trend can most probably be located in family situations.
     A. Children in families where little guidance is provided or where parents are divorced are more likely to commit suicide.
     B. Children who have lost a father are more likely to commit suicide.
V.   The increase in suicide rates is unique to the 15–24 age group.
VI. Whatever the cause of the increasing suicide rate among young people, since there is no apparent solution, it creates a serious challenge to public policy.

Sentence outlines can be considerably more detailed than this one, to the point of containing most of the information in the essay; but for an essay the length of Fuchs's they are usually about as detailed as this one. Should you want to make a more detailed outline, you would probably need more levels of information than the preceding two outlines contain. You would follow this convention for identifying levels:

I.   (Main topic)
     A. (Subtopic of I)
     B.
        1. (Subtopic of I.B)
        2.
           a. (Subtopic of I.B.2)
           b.
              (1) (Subtopic of I.B.2.b.)
              (2)
                 (a) (Subtopic of I.B.2.b.(2))
                 (b)
                 (c)

Any division of a topic at one level must result in at least two items in the level beneath it.

Not surprisingly, writers rely heavily on writing to find out what they know about a topic. Writing itself is a powerful tool for thinking. By writing, you can recall details of scenes or people, remember facts and ideas, find connections in new information you have collected.

Unlike most mapping strategies, writing strategies of invention invite you to produce complete sentences. The sentence provides considerable generative power. Because sentences are complete statements, they take you further than listing or clustering. They enable you to explore ideas and define relationships, to bring ideas together or show how they differ, to identify causes and effects. Sentences can follow one another naturally and develop a chain of thought.

This section presents several invention and inquiry strategies which invite you to formulate complete sentences and thus produce brief exploratory pieces of writing. Some are guided, systematic strategies, while others are more flexible. Even though they call for complete sentences that are related to one another, they do not require planning or polishing. They may be associational or logical, playful or serious.

The writing strategies for invention and revision include cubing, dialogues, diaries, dramatizing, drafting and dictating, journals, looping, and questioning.

Cubing   Cubing is useful for quickly exploring a writing topic. It lets you probe the topic from six different perspectives. (It is known as cubing because a cube has six sides.) Following are the six perspectives in cubing:

Describing: What does your subject look like? What size is it? Color? Shape? Texture? Name its parts.

Comparing: What is your subject similar to? Different from?

Associating: What does it make you think of? What connections does it have to anything else in your experience? Be creative here. Include any connection you can think of.

Analyzing: How is it made? Where did it come from? Where is it going? How are its parts related?

Applying: What can you do with it? What uses does it have?

Arguing: What arguments can you make for it? Against it?

Here are some rules that may help you use cubing productively:

1. Select a topic, subject, or part of a subject. This can be a person, scene, event, object, problem, idea, or issue. Hold it in focus.

2. Limit yourself to three to five minutes for each perspective. The whole activity will then take no more than a half hour.

3. Keep going until you have written about your subject from *all six* perspectives. Remember that the special advantage of cubing is the quick *multiple* perspectives it provides.

4. As you write from each perspective, begin with what you know about your subject. However, do not limit yourself to your present knowledge. Indicate what else you need to know about your subject, and suggest where you might find that information.

5. Reread what you have written. Look for bright spots, surprises. Recall the part that was easiest for you to write. Recall the part where you felt a special momentum and pleasure in the writing. Look for an angle or an unexpected insight. These special parts may suggest a focus or a topic within a larger subject, or they may provide specific details to include in a draft.

Dialogues   A dialogue is a conversation between two or more people. You can use dialogue to search for topics, find a focus, explore ideas, or consider opposing viewpoints. As an invention activity, writing a dialogue requires you to make up all parts of the conversation. Imagine two particular people talking, or hold a conversation yourself with some imagined person, or simply talk out loud to yourself. Follow these steps:

1. Write a conversation between two speakers. Label the speakers "1" and "2," or make up names for them.

2. If you get stuck, you might have one of the speakers ask the other a question.

3. Write brief responses in order to keep the conversation moving fast. Do not spend much time planning or rehearsing responses. Write what first occurs to you—just as in a real conversation, where people take quick turns to prevent any awkward silences.

You can find examples of dialogues in the Writer at Work sections at the end of Chapter 2: Remembering Events and Chapter 7: Proposing Solutions. In the dialogue in Chapter 2 a college writer is re-creating a conversation with someone in an event she plans to write about.

Dialogues can be especially useful with personal experience essays about events, people, and places. For these kinds of writing, dialogues help you remember relationships and rehearse conversations you might want to include in a draft. Dialogues can also help you recall conversations with significant people in an activity or a place you are profiling or anticipate counterarguments to any of your points in an opinion essay, a proposal, an evaluation, or a causal explanation.

Dramatizing   Dramatizing is an invention activity based on the idea that people behave very much like actors in a play. It was developed by the philosopher Kenneth Burke as a way of thinking about how people interact in real life and as a way of analyzing literature and the arts.

Thinking about human behavior in dramatic terms can be very productive for writers. Drama has action, actors, setting, motives, and methods. Since stars and acting go together, you can use a five-pointed star to remember these five points of dramatizing:

METHOD

MOTIVES   ACTION

SETTING   ACTORS

Each point provides a different perspective on human behavior. We can think of each point independently and in various combinations. Let us begin by looking at each point in order to see how it helps us analyze people and their interactions.

Action. An action is anything that happens, has happened, will happen, or could happen. Action includes events that are physical (running a marathon or eating a meal), mental (discovering a solution to a problem or thinking about a book you have read), and emotional (falling in love or feeling depressed). This category also refers to the results of activity (a term paper or a sweater).

Actor. The actor is involved in the action. He or she may be responsible for it or simply be affected by it. The actor does not have to be a person. It can be a force, something that causes an action. For example, if the action is a rise in the price of gasoline, the actor could be increased demand or short supply. Dramatizing may also include a number of co-actors working together or at odds with one another.

Setting. This is the situation, the background of the action. We usually think of setting as the place and time of an event, but it can be the historical background of an event or the childhood of a person.

Motive. The motive is the purpose or reason for an action. It refers to the intention actors may have or the end an action serves.

Method. Method is the way an action occurs, the techniques an actor uses. It refers to whatever makes things happen.

Each of these points suggests a simple invention question:

Action = What?
Actor = Who?
Setting = When and where?
Motive = Why?
Method = How?

This list looks like the familiar newspaper reporter's invention activity for remembering to include all the essential details in a report of an event. But dramatizing goes further, in that it enables us to answer a much fuller set of invention questions generated by considering relations or interactions between the five elements of a dramatic situation. We can think about actors' motives, the effect of the setting on the actors, the relations between actors, and so on.

We have adapted Burke's invention activity for use in exploring human motivations and relationships in particular events or situations, fictional or real. Hence, you could use this activity to learn more about yourself in an event you were going to narrate, about other people you wanted to write about, or about significant people in a place you were going to write about. You could use it, as well, to explore characters in stories or movies you were analyzing or evaluating. It is also especially useful in analyzing readers who might resist your solution to a problem.

To use this activity, imagine the person you want to write about (yourself, another person, a fictional character) in a particular situation or event or series of events. Holding this image in focus, write answers to any questions in the following list that apply. You may draw a blank on some questions. You may have little to say to some and a lot to say to others. Be exploratory and playful. Write quickly, following digressions; relying on words, lists, phrases, even drawings; and composing sentences when you wish to do so.

☐ What did the person do?
☐ How did the person come to be involved in this situation or event?
☐ Why does the person do what he or she does?
☐ What goals is the person trying to accomplish?
☐ How is the person trying to accomplish these goals?
☐ To what extent do other people in the event recognize what the person is trying to accomplish?
☐ What might prevent this person from carrying out these goals?
☐ What might the person do that he or she is not doing?
☐ What do the person's actions reveal about the person?
☐ What does the person's language reveal about the person?

☐ How does the event's setting influence the person's actions?
☐ How does the time of the event influence what the person does?
☐ Where did this person come from?
☐ How is this person different from what he or she used to be?
☐ What might this person become?
☐ How is this person like others in the event?
☐ How is this person different from others in the event?

Drafting and dictating

Sometimes writers know approximately what they want to say. Sometimes, too, writers have time for only one draft and possibly a quick revision. Even in these situations, listing or clustering can be useful. Still, there are occasions when the appropriate thing to do is to write a complete draft, attempting to come as close as possible to the finished version you imagine. For example, an experienced newspaper reporter may type a brief news report that requires little revision by the copy editor. After many years on the job, the head of a National Weather Bureau station can confidently draft the brief hourly weather forecast that is broadcast locally. Once the research data are organized and interpreted, a medical researcher who has published dozens of reports in specialized journals can quickly draft a new report that conforms closely to the format required by those journals. A college senior who has just won a national prize for a collection of her photographs can readily explain what was new in that work in a letter to the high school art teacher who introduced her to photography.

These experts would probably concede that with more time for invention their writing would be even stronger. Nevertheless, in some writing situations an immediate attempt at a complete draft is a good strategy, and in such situations the goal is to come as close as possible to your best prose on the first attempt. There are two ways in which even this strategy is an invention activity, however: (1) all composing is a discovery of what you want to say and how to say it, and (2) some revisions are nonetheless required in nearly all attempts at drafting.

There are no special rules for immediate drafting. You will want to bypass one of the other invention strategies in this chapter and immediately attempt a full draft only under these conditions:

☐ You consider yourself unusually knowledgeable about the topic.
☐ You feel certain you already know essentially what you want to say. You have a focus, a thesis, a rough plan, even a vision of where it will all come out.
☐ You have written about the topic many times.

Even if you are desperately short of time, you cannot produce good writing unless you can meet these conditions.

As you write an immediate draft, you may get stuck. The clock is ticking. Your instructor or your colleagues expect a draft early tomorrow. You feel a twinge of panic. Under such conditions, make a diversion to listing, clustering, even a brief looping exercise (discussed later in this chapter) to get yourself unstuck.

Dictating is common in the business world for letters, memos, and brief reports. The person dictating attempts to construct written discourse orally. With experience, many people become surprisingly adept at this activity. In addition, a few professional writers, including some novelists, dictate early versions of their books. Here, they use dictation less as a shortcut to finished text than as a tentative, exploratory invention activity. These dictations nearly always require extensive revisions and sometimes are discarded as mere warmups.

The major limitation to dictation is that taped material must then be typed or written out. Since thirty minutes of dictation produces many pages of typescript, transcription can be time consuming and costly. However, this cost may not be a barrier for long. Researchers are close to solving the technical problems of converting talk instantaneously into print on a word processor, thus allowing writers to see immediately what they have said.

Journals   Professional writers often use journals to keep notes, and so might you. It is quite easy to start a writer's journal. Buy a special notebook, and start writing. Here are some possibilities:

☐ Keep a list of new words you encounter. Always include the full sentence in which you found the word.

☐ Write about concepts you learn in courses you take. These entries will help you clarify new concepts and remember them. You could also write about the progress and direction of your learning in particular courses— the experience of being in the course, your feelings about what is happening and what you are learning. For this journal activity—and others concerned with writing to clarify and elaborate new learning—write experimentally and playfully. You may sometimes want to start writing immediately, without planning or rehearsing, just to see what the act of writing itself will lead you to. Try different styles and voices. Do not worry too much about spelling or punctuation.

☐ Respond to your reading, assigned and personal. Write about your personal associations as you read, your reflections, reactions, evaluations. Try to explain new concepts. Paraphrase difficult passages. Summarize important passages. Copy memorable sentences and short passages and comment on them. (This last activity—copying and commenting—has been practiced by students and writers for centuries, keeping what is called a *commonplace book*. In a commonplace book writers copied notable passages from books and then commented on them.)

☐ Write to prepare for particular class meetings. If you know the topic of the lecture or discussion, write about the main ideas you have learned from assigned readings. Write about the relation of these new ideas to other ideas in the course or to information you have picked up elsewhere. List questions you have about the topic. After class, write to summarize what you have learned. List questions you have about the ideas presented or discussed in class.

Writing in this way to prepare for classes, or to summarize them, is quite different from the writing that you will collect in your class note-book, where you will record a portion of the content of the lecture or discussion. Recording on the spot the information being passed along by others is an important part of being a student, but it does not involve reflecting, evaluating, interpreting, synthesizing, summarizing—the kinds of thinking and writing we recommend for your learner's journal. Writing to learn and remember is active, engaged writing. It requires judgment and critical thinking. By contrast, notetaking during a lecture, though it requires you to make choices, is relatively passive.

☐ Record observations and overheard conversations.

☐ Write for ten or fifteen minutes every day about whatever is on your mind in connection with recent observations and learning. Focus these medi-tative writings outwardly on your new experiences and your understand-ings, interpretations, and reflections on them. Write only what you would be willing to share with others. Writing about deeply personal matters and about your own emotional development is private and so would be better put in a diary.

☐ Write sketches of people—friends or strangers who catch your attention.

☐ Organize a day or a week. You could write about your goals and prior-ities. You could list specific things to accomplish.

☐ Keep a log over several days or weeks about a particular event unfolding in the news—a sensational trial, an environmental disaster, a political campaign, a campus controversy, the fortunes of a sports team.

If you begin a journal, you may think of still other ways to use it. There are many possibilities. All of the writing in your journal has value for learn-ing, observing experience closely, and organizing your life. It may also end up in other writing—essay tests, essays, reports, letters.

Some writers organize their logs into well-defined sections, one section for new words, one for continuing events, one for entries about a particular course, and so on.

Looping   Looping—the strategy of writing quickly but *returning* to your topic—is especially useful for the first stages of exploring a topic. From almost any starting point, no matter how general or unfocused, looping enables you to find a center of interest and eventually a thesis. The rules are simple:

1. Write down your area of interest. You may know only that you have to write about another person or a movie or a cultural trend that has caught your attention. Or, you may be searching for a topic in a broad historical period or one related to a major political event. Although you may wander from this topic as you write, you will want to keep coming back to it. Your purpose is to find a focus for writing, or even a thesis.

2. Write nonstop for ten minutes. Start with the first thing that comes to mind. Write rapidly, without looking back to reread or to correct anything. *Do not stop writing. Keep your pencil moving.* That is the key to looping. If you get stuck for a moment, rewrite the last sentence. Trust the act of writing to lead you to new insights. Follow diversions and digressions, but keep returning to your topic.

3. At the end of ten minutes, pause to reread what you have written. Decide what is most important—a single insight, a pattern of ideas, an emerging theme, a visual detail, anything at all that stands out. Some writers call this a "center of gravity" or a "hot spot." To complete the first loop, express this center in a single sentence.

4. Beginning with this sentence, write nonstop for ten minutes.

5. Summarize in one sentence again to complete the second loop.

6. Keep looping until one of your summary sentences produces a focus or thesis. You may need only two or three loops; you may need more.

Questioning   Asking questions about a problem or topic is a way to learn about it and decide what to do or say. However, when we first encounter a problem, our questions may be scattered. Also, we are not likely to think right away of all the important questions we ought to ask. The advantage of a basic list of questions for invention, like the ones for cubing and for dramatizing discussed earlier in this chapter, is that it reminds you of all of the ways of viewing a subject and hence of important questions to ask. It is a useful and systematic approach to exploring a problem.

The questions we are concerned with here come from classical rhetoric (what the Greek philosopher Aristotle called "topics") and a modern approach to invention called *tagmemics*. Tagmemics, based on the work of American linguist Kenneth Pike, provides questions about all the ways we make sense of the world, all the ways we sort and classify experience and come to understand it.

Here are the steps in using questions for invention: (1) Think about your subject. (By "subject," we mean any event, person, problem, project, idea, or issue—in other words, anything you might write about.) (2) Start with the first question, and move right through the list. Try to answer each question at least briefly with a word or phrase. Some questions may invite several sentences, or even a page or more of writing. You may draw a blank on a few questions. Skip them. Later, with more experience with questions for invention, you can start anywhere in the list. (3) Write your responses quickly, without much planning. Follow digressions or associations. Do not screen anything out. Be playful.

What is your subject?

- [ ] What is your subject's name?
- [ ] What other names has it had?
- [ ] What other names do people use for your subject now?
- [ ] Why do people call it something you do not call it?
- [ ] Imagine a photograph of your subject. What would it look like?
- [ ] What word, besides its name, best summarizes it?
- [ ] What would you put into a time capsule to stand for your subject?
- [ ] Where did it come from?
- [ ] What caused it?
- [ ] Why does it exist?
- [ ] What are its results?
- [ ] How would your subject look from different vantage points or perspectives?
- [ ] What particular experiences have you had with the subject? Do these experiences remind you of problems you have had with the subject? Do these experiences remind you of what you know about the subject?

What parts does your subject have and how are they related?

Think about your subject as having several parts or characteristics:

- [ ] Name the parts.
- [ ] Describe each part using the questions in the preceding subject list.
- [ ] How is each part related to the other parts?

How is your subject similar to and different from other subjects?

- [ ] What is your subject similar to? In what ways is it similar?
- [ ] What is your subject different from? In what ways is it different?
- [ ] Of all the things in the world, what seems to you most unlike your subject? In what ways are they unlike each other? Now, just for fun, note how they are alike.

How much can your subject change and still remain the same?

- [ ] How has your subject changed from what it once was?
- [ ] How is it changing now? From moment to moment, day to day, year to year?

☐ How much can it change and still remain the same?

☐ What are some different forms your subject takes?

☐ How does the subject change each time you see it or think about it?

☐ What does it become when it is no longer itself?

Where does your subject fit in the world?

☐ When and where did your subject originate?

☐ Has your subject always existed?

☐ Can you imagine a time in the future when your subject will not exist?

☐ When and where do you experience it?

☐ Is this subject part of something larger?

☐ Is the subject an important part of this larger thing?

☐ Does the subject cause this larger thing or result from it?

☐ Is the subject always separate from this larger thing of which it is a part, or does it sometimes blend into it?

☐ What do other people think of your subject?

READING

In many situations, writers must rely on information in books, films, maps, photographs, documents, archives, or museums. Their invention and inquiry in these situations involves gathering, analyzing, selecting, and organizing information from such sources.

Most of the writing you will do in college or on the job will be based at least in part on printed texts. This section presents several strategies for invention and inquiry that will enable you to write about ideas and information you acquire in your reading. The strategies include annotating, inventorying, outlining, paraphrasing, and summarizing. They will help you write about your reading in the following ways:

to gather and organize new information from your reading

to understand the new information

to connect information from different sources

to relate information to what you already know, believe, and feel

to condense and record information so that you can use it when writing exams, research papers, and arguments about issues and policies.

Annotating Annotations are the notes we make in margins of books we own. Annotations can be exclamations of outrage or of insight, questions, brief summaries, sequential labeling of arguments or main points, even doodles—anything at all that records succinctly what the reader is learning and feeling. Some readers do it consistently, even obsessively, filling margins with notes. Others rarely do it. Most also underline important sentences or passages, or they may highlight them with colored markers.

Annotations and underlining serve two purposes: (1) to record reactions, questions, and understandings, and (2) to organize the text for reviewing, studying, or writing about it. As a preliminary step to writing, annotations can be a very important invention activity: crucial details, examples, quotations, and main points that would be required in a summary, essay, or research report, are marked.

Annotating involves a number of specific activities:

☐ Writing words, phrases, or sentences: these writings can comment, question, evaluate, define, relate, challenge

☐ Underlining or highlighting words or phrases

☐ Circling or boxing words or phrases

☐ Connecting related items with lines

☐ Numbering a sequence of related items: arguments, examples, names

☐ Bracketing a part of the text, either within the text itself or with a line in the margin.

Annotating can be light or heavy, depending on the difficulty of the material and your plans for writing about it. For a literary text you plan to analyze and interpret, your annotations may be heavy and quite varied. You will make some annotations the first time you read it and more when you reread it. Here is the way one reader annotated one paragraph of James Joyce's "Araby." The complete story appears in Chapter 10: Interpreting Literature.

When the short days of winter came dusk fell before we had well eaten our dinners. When we met in the street the house had grown sombre. The space of sky above us was the colour of ever-changing violet and towards it the lamps of the street lifted their feeble lanterns. The cold air stung us and we played till our bodies glowed. Our shouts echoed in the silent street. The career of our play brought us through the dark muddy lanes behind the houses where we ran the gauntlet of the rough tribes from the cottages, to the back doors of the dark dripping gardens where odours arose from the ashpits, to the dark odorous stables where a coachman smoothed and combed the horse or shook music from the buckled harness. When we returned to the street light from the kitchen windows had filled the areas. If my uncle was seen turning the corner we hid in the shadow until we had seen him safely housed. Or if

Margin annotations (left):
light, faint

circular movement—from light, to dark, back to light

why hide from uncle?

Margin annotations (right):
time of year: winter

time of day: dusk

career = play, not job

repetition of "where" clauses

again—light to shadow to light

Mangan's sister came out on the doorstep to call her
brother in to his tea we watched her from our shadow peer
up and down the street. We waited to see whether she
would remain or go in and, if she remained, we left our
shadow and walked up Mangan's steps resignedly. She was
waiting for us, her figure defined by the light from the half-
opened door. Her brother always teased her before he
obeyed and I stood by the railings looking at her. Her dress
swung as she moved her body and the soft rope of her hair
tossed from side to side.

*enticing, almost sex-
ual image of friend's
sister (light)—older
than boys?*

At a glance you can see how many different annotating activities this
writer found useful: writing comments and questions, connecting related
items, circling unusual or unknown words, underlining certain words, and
bracketing part of the text in the margin. The written comments indicate
that the reader actively sought to understand the story. (You might want to
compare this annotation of "Araby" to the one that appears in the Writer at
Work section at the end of Chapter 10.)

Annotating an informational text is different from annotating a story or
a poem. You are not so much probing for meaning as you are organizing
and clarifying information. Consequently, in annotating an informational
text, you might want to concentrate on underlining main ideas, deciding
how the information is organized, and marking the most important facts.
Here is the way one student annotated a paragraph in an essay on Native
American writing systems.

The Native American groups which, despite all obstacles,
have developed traditions of literacy in their own languages
seem to share certain characteristics. All of them, of course,
have preserved some sort of social organization, at least at
the local community level. It would seem that such groups
have also found one or more functions for their own literacy. Thus the spread of Fox, Winnebago, Cherokee, and
Mahican literacy occurred at the same time that these several tribes were divided by migrations. In all four cases it
seems reasonable to suppose that the first individuals to
become literate were motivated by a desire to communicate
with relatives who had departed for the west or, as the case
may be, had lingered behind in the east. The Aleuts and
Yupiks were never forcibly "removed" or broken into separate reservation communities; but their dispersed settle-
ments and frequent hunting and fishing expeditions made
the ability to read and write letters a useful skill. Motivation
for literacy is not always based on the need to correspond
with absent friends and relatives, however. The Cherokee

*what kinds of
obstacles?*

*certain characteristics—
social organization, literacy
functions (letters, religious
services, records)*

*forcibly removed or broken
by whom?*

seven different tribes mentioned—strong evidence

syllabary, for example, has long been used in the context
of <u>religious services</u> and religious instruction where those
to whom messages are read are all present in the same
room with those who are reading. Likewise, the Cherokee
medical practitioners who <u>record</u> curing formulas in the syllabary do so primarily for their own reference, not for un-
specified readers at some remote place and time. <u>The factors that tend to perpetuate native literacy, then, need not</u>
<u>include a felt need to communicate with distant members</u>
<u>of a tightly knit society; but they do seem to include the</u>
<u>perception of literacy as a useful skill which enables the</u>
<u>literate to achieve some worthwhile objective.</u>

main point

Inventorying

Inventorying is a useful activity for understanding, analyzing, and interpreting reading. It is a natural follow-up to annotating. When you annotate you
try to identify significant information. Inventorying helps you find relationships and patterns in this information, which in turn helps you to decide
how you might interpret or evaluate it. Once you have a thesis, inventorying
enables you to review the reading for evidence to support your thesis.

An early inventory to find patterns in a text involves making several lists
of related items. Consider the following possibilities:

- [ ] Recurring images (similes, metaphors)
- [ ] Noticeable stylistic features
- [ ] Repeated descriptions
- [ ] Consistent ways of characterizing people or events and of defining terms
- [ ] Repeated words and phrases
- [ ] Repeated subjects or topics
- [ ] Repeated examples or illustrations
- [ ] Reliance on particular writing strategies.

What patterns you discover depend on the kind of reading you are analyzing. Here is an inventory a student made from the annotations of the
excerpt from James Joyce's "Araby."

<u>Movement between light and darkness</u>
space of sky
lanterns
bodies glowed
dark muddy lanes
dark dripping gardens
ashpits
dark odorous stables
light from kitchen windows
shadow ... shadow ... shadow
light from half-opened door

Mangan's sister enticing to narrator
figure defined by the light
dress swung as she moved her body
soft rope of her hair tossed from side to side
I stood by the railings looking at her

Childishness of narrator
played till our bodies glowed
our shouts echoed in the quiet streets
walked up to Mangan's steps resignedly

You may want to inventory your annotations of a literary work before you write about it as recommended in the writing guide to Chapter 10. (Also, you could compare this inventory to the one in that chapter's Writer at Work section.) You may also want to inventory the reading you do to find information for a report, evidence demonstrating that a trend exists, or background on an activity you are profiling. In inventorying a long work, you might want to include page numbers of items in your lists. For much of the writing you do as a college student, you will find inventorying (and annotating) not just helpful but essential.

Outlining   Outlining an essay or a chapter in a book can help you understand and remember the material. An outline displays the main features or main ideas in an essay. It presents only the framework and hence is quite general, even abstract. Some inventories move toward outlines when they involve comprehensive lists of the parts of a story or an essay.

An outline may be an informal list of phrases, a formal numbered and indented set of sentences, or a visual cluster. Each of these types of outlines is illustrated in the earlier discussion of mapping strategies.

Paraphrasing   In many of the writing activities in this book and in much of the writing you do in college, you will use information from printed sources. The three basic ways of integrating this information into your own writing are by means of quotation, paraphrase, and summary. One of the most important writing decisions you will have to make again and again is which one of these to use.

A quotation is an exact reproduction of the language in the source. (Strategies for integrating quoted material smoothly into your writing are demonstrated in Chapter 22: The Research Paper.)

A paraphrase is a presentation in your own words of *all* the information in a brief passage. Paraphrase alternates with quotations and with your own analysis or commentary. When you summarize, you present in your own words just the main ideas in a passage.

Here is how one student paraphrased the first five sentences of a paragraph from the article on Native American writing systems printed earlier in this chapter.

Original

The Native American groups which, despite all obstacles, have developed traditions of literacy in their own languages seem to share certain characteristics. All of them, of course, have preserved some sort of social organization, at least at the local community level. It would seem that such groups have also found one or more functions for their own literacy. Thus the spread of Fox, Winnebago, Cherokee, and Mahican literacy occurred at the same time that these several tribes were divided by migrations. In all four cases it seems reasonable to suppose that the first individuals to become literate were motivated by a desire to communicate with relatives who had departed for the west or, as the case may be, had lingered behind in the east.

Paraphrase

Native American groups had to overcome many obstacles in order to develop writing systems in their own languages. The groups that did develop writing are alike in several ways: they maintained their social structure, and they were able to put writing to good use. For example, writing became more common in the Fox, Winnebago, Cherokee, and Mahican tribes after they were separated through migration. Tribal members probably wanted to write to relatives they could no longer see regularly.

The first thing to note about the paraphrase is that it contains *all* the information in the original. It is not just a summary. It is a complete reproduction in the student's own words. Although it has the same number of sentences as the original, the information is grouped into sentences in somewhat different ways. In using this information in an essay, the writer might quote the original; but, unless it contains crucial evidence or memorable language, it probably should be paraphrased.

Without changing the information significantly, paraphrase aims to clarify and simplify the original. It may explain difficult material, or it may restate a complicated argument. Paraphrase is also useful as a strategy of inquiry. It is a way of understanding difficult material by restating it in your own words. It is very time-consuming, though, and should only be used with short passages.

Summarizing A summary is a selection of main ideas. All talking and writing involves some degree of summary. If we tell someone what our day was like, we summarize. When we write, we summarize our experience or knowledge.

As you write, you occasionally summarize your own writing, especially in longer essays or reports: you pause to remind the reader what you have said so far and forecast what is to come next. Some endings to essays are summaries. Summaries, an important writing strategy, are mentioned prominently in Chapter 5: Reporting Information.

As a writer, you also summarize information from other writers. In informative and argumentative essays, essay exams and research reports, you interweave your own analysis and commentary with quotations, paraphrases, and summaries from other writers. Just as you must indicate the source of quotations, you must also indicate the source of paraphrased or summarized material. (Chapter 22 illustrates ways to document your sources.)

Here is one student's summary of the paragraph from the essay on Native American writing systems that appeared earlier in this chapter. Read the complete paragraph, and then examine the student's summary.

Summary

Native Americans developed their own writing systems in order to write letters and keep records.

The preceding sentence is one possible summary of the main idea of the paragraph. It does not leave out any important part of the main idea, nor does it include any of the examples or illustrations. It is stated in the student's own language, not the language of the original, though, of course, certain key terms must be repeated.

To summarize a longer selection, you would read and reread it carefully, annotating as you go. You could then inventory or outline the selection in order to be certain you have identified all the main ideas. You would then be able to write a coherent summary.

A PLAN FOR REVISING

Even after productive invention or careful planning, a draft rarely satisfies its author's expectations. Unless a deadline precludes revising, you should always expect to revise your initial draft. Revising will move your draft closer to the essay you imagine. At the same time, it will help you re-envision the essay. Rereading your draft—perhaps with the critical comments of other readers—will show many opportunities for improvement. Not only might you notice a misspelled word or a garbled sentence but, most important, you may well see ways to clarify and extend your ideas by moving, deleting, rewriting, and adding material.

Successful revision depends on what you know about the type of essay you are attempting. By the time you begin revising an essay for one of the assignments in this book, you should have learned a great deal about the type of writing you have been asked to do. You will have studied several selections and considered the features and strategies basic to that type of essay. You will be able to use this knowledge as you plan your revision.

To be effective, you need to focus your attention carefully as you revise. Central to any revision are some very close readings of the draft; since attention and memory have certain natural limitations, and since written texts are so complex, you must be selective as you read, shifting your attention to focus on different aspects of the text on successive rereadings.

Here is a plan for revising that will help to focus your attention and to use what you know about the type of essay you are writing. The plan will help you to refine your writing purpose to suit the needs of your readers and to make your draft better realize that purpose. This plan has three basic steps: (1) reread, (2) re-envision, (3) rewrite.

You *reread* first to get a more objective view of your draft and to identify those problems you yourself recognize in it. At this stage, you will benefit immensely from another reader's perspective. A constructive, critical reading of the draft by one or more other readers will help you achieve this objectivity. Your aim, at this point, is to see what the draft actually says (as opposed to what you were trying to say) and to identify specific problems or shortcomings.

This series of rereadings leads to the second step, re-envisioning. To *re-envision* the essay, you need to reformulate your purpose by reconsidering what you were trying to accomplish in the light of the direction your writing has taken. Now is the time to bring your new intentions into line with the needs and expectations of your readers. Your aim, at this point, is to develop a plan of action based on your understanding of the draft's problems and your new vision of its possibilities.

Finally, you *rewrite*. This is the stage where you put your plan into action by reworking the draft. Your revisions may be minor or major, focus on one small part of the draft, or reconstruct the entire essay. To work efficiently, you should move systematically from "global" to "local" revisions—revising first for overall meaning; second for coherence, clarity, and grace; and last for correctness.

Look now at the initial draft of "Journalistic Ethics," an essay written by Sydney Young for her freshman English class. Young's assignment was to write a position paper on a controversial issue, following the Guide to Writing in Chapter 6. (The final revision of her essay appears in that chapter.)

On May 8, 1987, presidential candidate Gary Hart was forced to once again relinquish his goal of the presidency of the United States, though this time not by losing to his opponents. The campaign scandal which ensued after being questioned about adultery by a reporter left Hart no choice but to withdraw from the race. Exercising its right of freedom of the press, the media eliminated a candidate before a single vote was cast. By probing into Gary Hart's personal life, journalists from The Miami Herald in effect began a process which ultimately cost Hart not only the loss of the presidency, but also the loss of his and his entire family's dignity. In this particular case, the media over-stepped the boundaries of discretion and thereby raised questions of professional ethics in the field of journalism. As the source of information for the entire nation, journalists should adhere to reporting just the facts relevant to the issue—not try to sensationalize it.

Whether or not a public figure has a right to privacy has long been a bone of contention. Where should the fine line be drawn in terms of how much a public figure needs to divulge personal information? The response to this question is uncertain, but it is only common decency to allow an individual, public figure or not, some vestige of privacy. If no other job applicant in the United States is required to disclose all facets of his/her life, then neither should a political candidate. The question at hand is not whether Gary Hart did or did not commit adultery. Any unfaithfulness toward his wife on Hart's part is as the candidate phrased it, "between me and Lee [his wife] and me and God." Hart also stated that "adultery is not a crime. It's a sin." Why then has the media set itself up as judge and jury in a trial which no one is sinless enough to be entitled to preside over? Adultery is not something which should be tolerated or condoned, but neither should it be a significant issue in a political campaign.

Many would say that it has as much bearing on the campaign as any other issue. Supporters of The Miami Herald's surveillance of Hart's townhouse feel that his actions rendered his character questionable. If a man's character is defined as strength of mind and purpose then how does being with a woman other than his wife weaken his character— especially when positive proof of infidelity has not been provided? Lee Hart herself has bluntly stated, "If it doesn't bother me, I don't think it ought to bother anyone else."

Mrs. Hart's statement brings another point to mind. The American public does not elect its president in order to take comfort in the stability of his marriage or family life. If this were the basis by which presidents were elected, then many of our previous effective leaders would never have made it to the Oval Office.

Sex has no role in politics and only becomes relevant when the media forces it to be so. In the words of former vice presidential candidate Geraldine Ferraro, who experienced much the same heat from the press as Hart:

> The issue is not whether the press has the right to investigate. It's what they are investigating. The public is entitled to know if he is a person who has good judgment, the right to know if he is smart, the right to know if he understands what's going on. If the Miami Herald had reported that Gary Hart had invited to his house a contra leader, then I'd be very angry, because he has taken a strong stand against the contras. I don't find the Donna Rice story relevant to the campaign." ("Private" 33)

In determining the relevancy, the press needs to carefully scrutinize the point in question. For instance, in the sex scandal involving Jim Bakker the press had every right to investigate and let the full story be known because evangelism was Bakker's vocation. Whether Bakker was faithful or not was pertinent to the matter of contention because he preached a religion which forbids adultery. In Hart's situation, unfaithfulness is not pertinent because his political platform has no resemblance whatsoever to a sermon on the importance of fidelity.

Still others object to Hart's actions because he lied in an effort to save his campaign. In a Time magazine opinion poll, 7% of the respondents replied that that it would bother them more if Hart had sex with this woman while 69% replied that it would bother them more that he had not told the truth about it ("After" 26). Realistically, what choice did Hart have? The media cornered Hart with such guilt implicating circumstantial evidence that he had no choice but to find any method possible to salvage his campaign. Although his lies are unacceptable, Hart reacted using his human instincts. Can he be faulted for reacting in the only way he knew how, particularly since journalists probed so deeply into his personal life? A political candidate is a man, not a quasi-God who bears no imperfections.

Because the public has increasingly demanded more intimate details concerning political candidates, the press has strived to meet that demand. "Personal scandals, with or without sex, always have been bigger stories" (Margolis C-1).

Manipulations of the press have caused the political candidates of today to put not only themselves on display on the platform, but also to drag their families up with them. Perhaps after seeing the tremendous amount of humiliation suffered by Hart, whether he's at fault or not, the media will be more discriminant the next time an issue of this nature arises. The American public, not the media, should elect its officials. Hopefully, the stone will not be cast again before the vote.

After completing her initial draft, Young began the process of rereading, re-envisioning, and rewriting. Using Young's process as an example, the sections that follow illustrate a general plan for revising to be used in various writing situations.

Reread   To get an objective image of your initial draft, you should first read simply to see what the draft says. Then see if you can gain another reader's perspective. Finally, you should read with an eye for problems to solve.

Read first to see what the draft says. Read the complete draft straight through, trying to understand its central meaning. The meaning you find may or may not be the one you intended or remember drafting, but your concern should not be with such discrepancies at this stage. Just try to get a sense of what the draft actually says. A good way of doing so is making a scratch outline of the draft. You should then summarize your goals for the draft by writing out a statement of your purpose, audience, and strategy.

The scratch outline, as its name suggests, can be quite sketchy, but it should follow the development of the entire essay. Here is Young's outline. Note that she simply summarizes the main point of each paragraph.

1. The media is responsible for Hart's premature withdrawal.
2. Even public figures have the right to privacy; the central issue is not whether Hart committed adultery, but the role of the media.
3. Some think Hart's character is the issue, but what has character to do with it?
4. Marital fidelity has never been an issue before, why now?
5. Ferraro says the press should focus only on relevant issues.
6. Relevancy must be determined: a sex scandal is relevant for a minister but not for a political candidate.
7. Most people are more troubled about Hart's lying than his committing adultery, but his reaction is understandable.
8. The press pursues and emphasizes scandal to sell papers.
9. The public, not the media, should select candidates.

After outlining your draft, reconsider your purpose. It is best to do this in writing: state your purpose (including any thesis), your intended readers, and your basic writing strategy. Following are Young's notes.

Purpose: Stated in the thesis, in the opening paragraph: "...journalists should adhere to reporting just the facts relevant to the issue...."

Audience: The American public. They should be concerned about the election process and the press's interference in it.

Writing strategy: To provide evidence that the issue is not whether Hart committed adultery, but that reporting rumors that he did so is not relevant to the campaign. The key term is relevance.

Consider the draft from another reader's perspective. You should now try to see the draft as your readers see it. When you planned your essay, you thought about your readers. You tried to anticipate their needs and expectations and formulated your purpose with them in mind. As you wrote, you addressed the draft to these readers, hoping to make it understandable and convincing for them.

Audience may have figured prominently as you drafted, but until now your concept of audience has inevitably been abstract, based on guesses and assumptions about what your potential readers know, value, and feel. If you can get one or more people to read your draft and tell you what they see in it, you can make that abstract idea of audience concrete and revise with a sense of how your draft actually comes across to readers.

To sharpen your new, objective image of the draft, review any readers' comments thoroughly, referring to the draft on each point. See if you can figure out what led the reader to make a particular comment. Try not to react defensively. Rather, look at the comments as information that can help you see your draft as readers see it. Make notes on your draft if you wish, but do not make changes. At this stage, your goal is to look closely at what you have written and to recognize its potential problems.

Two people looked over Young's draft—a fellow student and her instructor. Let's look first at the written responses from Young's classmate, Jason Stakey, who read the draft during a workshop session in class and wrote out answers to the critical reading questions in the Chapter 6 writing guide.

First General Impression.   This is a great paper. I watched Ted Koppel and Barbara Walters last night and it is clear that this is, and always will be, a controversial issue. You take a definite stand at the beginning and support it throughout the paper. I found your insistence on relevancy convincing, but I'm not sure about the way you handled the character question. I think Hart's character is at issue. Some people talk about it in terms of bad judgment or self-destructiveness. Who wants a president with either of these qualities?

Analysis
1. The issue is well-defined, although I think your way of defining it as a question of journalistic ethics won't convince everyone. As I said before, it's also a character issue.
2. The thesis is made clear at the beginning, in the last sentence of the first paragraph.
3. I think your best reason supporting your thesis is the one about relevancy. In fact, it seems to be your only reason. Am I right?
4. In terms of evidence, I'm not sure about the comparison with Bakker since they're both moral leaders of a sort. The Ferraro quote about sex being irrelevant and the one about scandals being big stories are both good.
5. In paragraph 3 you acknowledge that some take the adultery thing seriously, but seem to dismiss it by simply quoting Hart and his wife. Isn't it still a question? I know we all know they did it, but it's not been proved. Maybe, you should bring this up.
6. Your response to the lying issue is weak. If Hart's instinct when cornered is to lie, then he'd do the same thing as president. Remind you of anyone?
7. Character is a key term in paragraph 3, but it's not developed very convincingly. Relevance is also a key term and is handled well.
8. The essay begins well but some readers might not know what happened. You might add that. The ending is good, but the stuff about humiliation of Hart and his family seems a little manipulative.

9. I'd describe your tone as apologetic or at least making excuses. It's morally upright, especially about journalistic ethics, but not so much about adultery. Serious, formal, maybe a little sad or angry. Were you a Hart supporter?

10. This question about logical fallacies is hard. Going down the list in Chapter 19, the only one that seems to apply is overreliance on authority because of all the quotes you use. Also, I suggested before that the ending is a little manipulative. I don't know which one this is, but sometimes you don't really argue, you just say it doesn't really matter, like with the lying issue.

Young's instructor commented on the draft during a brief conference, as noted in the following notes:

Opening too extreme ("media eliminated"). Didn't Hart dare reporters? Need facts. Pres. candidate not just a job applicant. Why isn't the main question whether he committed adultery? Too many rhetorical questions—weak refutation. No proof of adultery imp't. Character issue evaded not explored. Lying issue imp't. Bring in lack of fact. Excuses not convincing. Manipulation not proved. Ending strong.

Main points:
1. It doesn't explore issue, just defends claim. Sounds like a Hart supporter trying to find excuses. Need to entertain counterarguments more—character issue especially.

2. Words like sensationalize and manipulate to describe media need support, otherwise seem slanted. They're reporting rumors not facts. Character assassination.

3. Watch out for rhetorical questions. Not persuasive.

These critical comments helped Young to see that her draft still needed some basic work. She referred to the comments of her readers repeatedly as she took the next step in the rereading process.

Read again to identify problems. At this point your task is to reread the draft to identify problems. Divide a page in half vertically. At the top of the left-hand column write *Problems;* at the top of the right-hand column write *Possible Actions.* As you read, list in the left-hand column the problems you now think require attention. Later, you will consider specific actions to solve the problems.

Consider any notes you have from other readers. If you are using one of the writing guides in Chapters 2–10 refer to the suggestions under Revising in the appropriate guide. In addition, you should look for the following general kinds of problems:

☐ Changes in tone or inappropriate tone
☐ Slow or boring spots

☐ Flat or dull writing
☐ Vague or overly abstract passages
☐ Simplistic or obvious material
☐ Repetitious or irrelevant material
☐ Misplaced material
☐ Missing material, lapses, or gaps

These are some of the problems Young identified in her draft:

unconvincing treatment of the "character" issue
weak handling of the lying issue
tone: overly defensive, even pro-Hart
incorrect assumption that readers know all the details

Re-envision You should by now have an objective image of the draft, an understanding of how your audience sees it, and a list of particular problems to solve. Before trying to solve these problems, you may need to gather more information or review what you already know. You may also need to reconsider your purpose, audience, and overall writing strategy.

Review your materials and gather additional information. The problems you list will suggest what kind of information you still need. It may be that you already have what you need in your invention notes, but you might need to do further thinking or research. Look through your notes and determine what is required. If necessary, return to the pertinent invention activities in the writing guide or supplement these with activities from the Invention and Inquiry section at the beginning of this chapter. If you need more information, revisit the library or consult other outside sources.

Young recognized that she particularly needed to acknowledge additional counterarguments. Luckily, she had used only a small portion of the material she had researched. Upon rereading her research notes, she found all the additional material she would need.

Reconsider your original purpose. Look back at the statement you wrote after rereading your draft, and revise it to reflect any changes in your thinking. You may have changed your mind about your thesis, refocused your sense of your audience, or decided to modify your writing strategy. Revising your intention in light of what you have learned about your draft's strengths and weaknesses will guide you as you plan your revision.

Although Young's goals for her essay remained essentially the same, she did recognize the need to acknowledge counterarguments more completely. This change was reflected in her revision of the Audience portion of her goal statement. Compare her original description of Audience to this revision:

Audience: The American public. They share my concern about the media but are more troubled about Hart's character, particularly the possibility that he lied. I need to show that since we do not now and may never know whether or not he lied, it's crucial that we do not allow the press to make up our minds for us. This will help me emphasize their need to be concerned about the election process and the press's interference in it.

List possible solutions to any problems. Return now to your list of problems. In the right-hand column, note actions you might take to resolve these problems. The actions will probably consist of things to *cut, move, change, add, look up,* or *consider further*. You do not have to know at this time specifically how you will change the language or what you will add in the rewriting stage. You need only note the *kind* of solution needed. After tentatively deciding what actions you might take, your next step is to determine the sequence in which you will tackle the problems.

Among the actions Young listed were these:

To add some explanation of exactly what happened

To cut the definition of character

To remind readers that we don't know the facts: maybe he isn't lying

To tone down apologies and to quote others for support

Determine a sequence of actions. Review your list of problems and possible actions. Then number the actions in the order you think you should attempt them. You may decide to begin with an easy problem or to take on the hardest one first. Whether easy or hard, you should begin with global revisions, ones that affect the overall meaning and effectiveness of your essay.

Plan to move from global to local revisions—revising first for overall meaning, second for coherence, clarity, and grace, and finally for correctness. By fixing the draft's central problems before going on to the peripheral ones, you will discover that many of the peripheral problems have disappeared by the time you get to them.

Also plan to begin by producing new ideas and sentences, not on tinkering with imperfect—but still usable—sentences. Once you have added new material, and moved or deleted other sections, you can shift your focus to perfecting language and style.

Rewrite Carry out your revision plan by beginning with your first-numbered action. Be flexible with your plan, but avoid being diverted by minor problems before you have addressed the major ones. After you have made the major revisions, shift your focus to problems of coherence, clarity, grace, and correctness.

Make major revisions. A comparison of Young's draft to her revised essay as it appears in Chapter 6 shows the major revisions she made. She added material, moved passages around, cut some sentences, and changed others. Here is a partial list of her revisions:

> Added a new paragraph (paragraph 2 in the revision) to fill readers in on the background, as suggested by my classmate
>
> Added several quotes to reflect anticipation of counterarguments
>
> Moved the Ferraro quote, attaching it to the next paragraph (paragraph 6 in the revision)
>
> Cut paragraph 4, but used the idea in another place (paragraph 5 in the revision)

Make sentence-level revisions. Once you have made your major revisions, you can turn to sentence-level problems. Some of these will be noted in the Pointings section of a complete critical reading. Read slowly and carefully to locate others. Reading aloud can also help.

Young's revisions of the two sentences in the next to last paragraph of her draft demonstrate the difference such thoughtful improvements can make. Young originally expressed her ideas as follows:

> Because the public has increasingly demanded more intimate details concerning political candidates, the press has strived to meet that demand. "Personal scandals, with or without sex, always have been bigger stories" (Margolis C-1).

Note how she expresses the same ideas in the final version of her essay:

> Political reporting is a big business and every reporter knows that scandals, especially sex scandals, sell papers. Reporter Jon Margolis acknowledges that "personal scandals, with or without sex, always have been bigger stories" (C-1).

In her revision of these sentences, she both ties her ideas more directly to her thesis and provides a stronger introduction to the quotation.

Editing to correct any remaining errors. Although you may have already corrected some obvious errors, errors were not your first priority in the rewriting you did up to this point. Now, however, you must find and correct any errors of mechanics, usage, punctuation, and spelling, before preparing and submitting a final draft.

Note, for example, the way Young revised sentence four in her opening paragraph one when she recognized the possibility of confusion it created:

> By probing into Gary Hart's personal life, journalists from The Miami Herald in effect began a process which ultimately cost Hart, not only the loss of the presidency, but also the loss of his and his entire family's dignity.

Young not only cut out the reference to the Hart family's loss of dignity, which she recognized as being exaggerated; she also realized that the process did not cost Hart "the loss of" the presidency, as she originally wrote, but rather "cost Hart the presidency" itself. In order to use this idiomatic expression correctly and clearly, she deleted the words *the loss of*.

Making corrections such as this is the important, final stage of the entire revision process.

You might now turn back to Chapter 6, to look at its final essay: "Journalistic Ethics," by Sydney Young. Having read her first draft and seen examples of her revision work, you should now be able to appreciate the final result.

A SUMMARY OF THE REVISING PLAN

This brief outline of the general revision plan can be used for easy reference as you revise your drafts, to guide you through all the main steps of rereading, re-envisioning, and rewriting your essays.

Reread Read first to see what the draft says.

☐ Make a scratch outline of the draft.
☐ Write a statement of your purpose, audience, and overall writing strategy.

Consider the draft from another reader's perspective.

☐ Get one or more critical readings of your draft.
☐ Reread your draft in light of these critical readings, making notes on the draft but no changes.

Read again to identify problems.

☐ Divide a page into two columns, labelling one *Problems* and the other *Possible Actions*.
☐ List problems you find, following the general suggestions in this chapter and the specific suggestions in the Revising section of the writing guide to the chapter you are working on.

Re-envision Review your materials and gather additional information.

☐ Look over your list of problems.
☐ Search for solutions by returning to pertinent invention activities in the writing guide or trying additional activities in the Invention and Inquiry section at the beginning of this chapter.
☐ Do further library or field research.

Reconsider your original purpose.

- ☐ Reread your statement of purpose.
- ☐ Rewrite it to reflect any new understanding of your purpose, audience, and overall writing strategy.

List possible solutions to any problems.

- ☐ Examine your list of problems.
- ☐ In the right-hand column next to each problem, note an action you could take to solve that problem.

Determine a sequence of actions.

- ☐ Study your lists of problems and possible actions.
- ☐ Number the actions in the order you think you should attempt them.

Rewrite   Make major revisions.
Make sentence-level revisions.
Edit to correct any remaining errors.

Cueing the Reader

In order to guide readers through a piece of writing, writers provide four basic kinds of cues or signals: (1) thesis and forecasting statements to orient readers to ideas and organization; (2) paragraphing to group related ideas and details; (3) cohesive devices that connect ideas to one another and bring about coherence and clarity so that the writing makes sense; and (4) transitions to signal particular relationships or shifts in meaning. In this chapter, we will examine how each of these cueing strategies works to aid readers.

ORIENTING STATEMENTS

To help readers find their way, especially in difficult and lengthy works, writers provide two kinds of orienting information: thesis statements that declare the main point and forecasting statements that, in addition to stating the thesis, preview the way the thesis will be developed.

Thesis statements Although they may have a variety of forms and purposes, all essays are essentially assertive. That is, they assert or put forward the writer's point of view on a particular subject. We call this point of view the essay's *thesis,* or main idea.

To help readers understand what is being said about a subject, writers often provide a thesis statement early in the essay. The *thesis statement* is usually a single sentence that declares the essay's main idea. It operates as a cue by letting readers know which is the most important, general idea among the writer's many ideas and observations. Like the focal point of a picture, the thesis statement directs the reader's attention to the one idea that brings all the other ideas and details into perspective. Here are some thesis statements from essays in Part I:

> Two great partnerships are celebrated in this Oklahoma arena: the indispensable one between man and animal that any rancher or cowboy takes on, enduring the joys and punishments of the alliance; and the one between man and man, cowboy and cowboy.   Gretel Ehrlich, Chapter 4

> *The Crimson*'s decision not to run *Playboy*'s advertisement recruiting Harvard women for its October ''Women of the Ivy League'' issue was both the very

most and the very least the newspaper could do to fight the institutionalized exploitation of women.   Kristin A. Goss, Chapter 6

In the shared environment of television, children and adults know a great deal about each other's behavior and social knowledge—too much, in fact, to play out the traditional complementary roles of innocence versus omnipotence.   Joshua Meyerowitz, Chapter 9

EXERCISE 12.1
Read one of the essays by Ehrlich, Goss, or Meyerowitz; then briefly explain how its thesis statement brings the ideas and details of the essay into perspective.

Each of the three preceding thesis statements is expressed directly in a single sentence. But sometimes writers need several sentences to state their thesis, and sometimes they imply the thesis rather than state it directly. For example, Rachel Richardson Smith in "Abortion, Right and Wrong" (Chapter 6) states her thesis this way:

> I find myself in the awkward position of being both anti-abortion and pro-choice. Neither group seems to be completely right—or wrong. It is not that I think abortion is wrong for me but acceptable for someone else. The question is far more complex than that.   Rachel Richardson Smith, Chapter 6

Smith presents her thesis in terms of a dichotomy between two extremes, neither of which she finds acceptable. Rather than imposing a single viewpoint directly, Smith suggests the complexity of the matter of abortion and, in the course of her argument, encourages her readers to regard abortion less in ideologically single-minded terms than in terms of the variety of difficult human, ethical, and political questions involved.

Autobiographical writing often tends not to have explicit thesis statements; readers usually must infer the implied general point. For example, television journalist Linda Ellerbee, in describing her immediate response to winning a job on the *Weekend* news broadcast because her competition (reporter Jessica Savitch) dropped out (Chapter 2), comes close to suggesting a thesis when she connects her feelings to the profession as a whole:

It bears witness to the competitiveness or outright insanity of journalists that my first reaction to getting what I wanted was a terrible, fierce anger. Nobody left Gary Cooper standing in the middle of the street with his gun hanging out, waiting for the other guy to show up. I mean, I was *ready*. Where the devil was Jessica?   Linda Ellerbee, "The Lost Weekend"

EXERCISE 12.2

Read "A Hanging" by George Orwell or "Smooth and Easy" by Russell Baker, both in Chapter 2. What would you say is the thesis? If you cannot find an explicit statement of the thesis, express it in your own words. Then, briefly explain how the thesis brings the essay's ideas and details into focus for you.

Readers by necessity look for something that will tell them the point of an essay, a focus for the many diverse details and ideas they encounter as they read. The lack of an explicit thesis statement can make this task more difficult. Therefore, careful writers keep in mind the needs and expectations of readers as they make the important decision whether or not to state the thesis explicitly.

A further important decision is where to place the thesis statment in the text. Most readers expect to find some information early in the text that will give them a context for the essay. They expect essays to open with thesis statements, and they need such statements to orient them, particularly if they are reading about a new and difficult subject. A thesis statement placed at the beginning of an essay helps give readers a sense of control over the subject, enabling them to anticipate the content of the essay and more easily understand the relationship between its various ideas and details.

Occasionally, however, particularly in fairly short, informal essays and in some argumentative essays, writers will save a direct statement of the thesis until their conclusion. Such a thesis is designed to bring together the various strands of information or evidence introduced over the course of the essay and to suggest the essay's overall point; in many cases, a concluding thesis is also used to point the way toward future developments or goals. Examples in Part I of essays with concluding thesis statements are Sue Hubbell's examination of chiggers in Chapter 5 and Victor Fuchs's analysis of teenage suicide in Chapter 9.

Forecasting statements   Actually a special kind of thesis statement, a *forecasting statement* not only identifies the thesis but also gives an overview of the way that thesis will be developed. The opening paragraph of an essay by William Langer on the bubonic plague illustrates the role of the forecasting statement:

In the three years from 1348 through 1350 the pandemic of plague known as the Black Death, or, as the Germans called it, the Great Dying, killed at least a fourth of the population of Europe. It was undoubtedly the worst disaster that has ever befallen mankind. Today we can have no real conception of the terror under which people lived in the shadow of the plague. For more than two centuries plague has not been a serious threat to mankind in the large, although it is still a grisly presence in parts of the Far East and Africa. Scholars continue to study the Great Dying, however, as a historical example of human behavior under the stress of universal catastrophe. In these days when the threat of plague has been replaced by the threat of mass human extermination by even more rapid means, there has been a sharp renewal of interest in the history of the 14th-century calamity. <u>With new perspective, students are investigating its manifold effects: demographic, economic, psychological, moral and religious.</u>   William Langer, ''The Black Death''

This paragraph informs us that Langer's article is about the effects of the Black Death. His thesis, however, is not stated explicitly. It is implied by the forecasting statement that concludes the paragraph. With this sentence, Langer states that the study of the plague currently is focused on five particular categories. As a reader would expect, Langer then goes on to divide his essay into analyses of these five effects, taking them up in the order in which they appear in the forecasting statement.

EXERCISE 12.3
Look back at Jane Greer's essay "The Midwest: Close to Heaven" in Chapter 8. Find the forecasting statement in her essay, and then write a few sentences explaining how this forecasting sentence helps you anticipate the organization of the final part of the essay.

PARAGRAPHING

Paragraph cues   The indentation that signals the beginning of a new paragraph is a relatively modern printing convention. Old manuscripts show that paragraph divisions were not always marked. In order to make reading easier, scribes and printers began to use the symbol ¶ to mark paragraph breaks. Later indenting became common practice, but even that relatively modern custom has changed in some forms of writing today. Instead of indenting, most writers in business now set paragraphs apart from the rest of the text by leaving an extra line of space above and below each paragraph.

The lack of paragraph cues makes reading extremely difficult. To illustrate this fact, the paragraph indentions have been removed from the following introductory section of a chapter in Stephen Jay Gould's book *Ever Since Darwin*. Even with proper paragraphing, this selection might be difficult because it includes unfamiliar information and technical language. Without paragraphing, however, Gould's logic becomes hard to follow, and the mind and the eye long for a momentary rest. (Each of the thirty sentences in the selection is numbered at the beginning.)

(1) Since man created God in his own image, the doctrine of special creation has never failed to explain those adaptations that we understand intuitively. (2) How can we doubt that animals are exquisitely designed for their appointed roles when we watch a lioness hunt, a horse run, or a hippo wallow? (3) The theory of natural selection would never have replaced the doctrine of divine creation if evident, admirable design pervaded all organisms. (4) Charles Darwin understood this, and he focused on features that would be out of place in a world constructed by perfect wisdom. (5) Why, for example, should a sensible designer create only on Australia a suite of marsupials to fill the same roles that placental mammals occupy on all other continents? (6) Darwin even wrote an entire book on orchids to argue that the structures evolved to insure fertilization by insects are jerry-built of available parts used by ancestors for other purposes. (7) Orchids are Rube Goldberg machines; a perfect engineer would certainly have come up with something better. (8) This principle remains true today. (9) The best illustrations of adaptation by evolution are the ones that strike our intuition as peculiar or bizarre. (10) Science is not "organized common sense"; at its most exciting, it reformulates our view of the world by imposing powerful theories against the ancient, anthropocentric prejudices that we call intuition. (11) Consider, for example, the cecidomyian gall midges. (12) These tiny flies conduct their lives in a way that tends to evoke feelings of pain or disgust when we empathize with them by applying the inappropriate standards of our own social codes. (13) Cecidomyian gall midges can grow and develop along one of two pathways. (14) In some situations, they hatch from eggs, go through a normal sequence of larval and pupal molts, and emerge as ordinary, sexually reproducing flies. (15) But in other circumstances, females reproduce by parthenogenesis, bringing forth their young without any fertilization by males. (16) Parthenogenesis is common enough among animals, but the cecidomyians give it an interesting twist. (17) First of all, the parthenogenetic females stop at an early age of development. (18) They never become normal, adult flies, but reproduce while they are still larvae or pupae. (19) Secondly, these females do not lay eggs. (20) The offspring develop live within their mother's body—not supplied with nutrient and packaged away in a protected uterus but right inside the mother's tissues, eventually filling her entire body. (21) In order to grow, the offspring devour the mother from the inside. (22) A few days later, they emerge, leaving a chitinous shell as the only remains of their only parent. (23) And within two days, their own developing children are beginning, literally, to eat them up. (24) *Micromalthus debilis,* an unrelated beetle, has evolved an almost identical system with a macabre variation. (25) Some parthenogenetic females give birth to a single male offspring. (26) This larva attaches itself to his mother's cuticle for about four or five days, then inserts his head into her genital aperture and devours

her. (27) Greater love hath no woman. (28) Why has such a peculiar mode of reproduction evolved? (29) For it is unusual even among insects, and not only by the irrelevant standards of our own perceptions. (30) What is the adaptive significance of a mode of life that so strongly violates our intuitions about good design?   Stephen Jay Gould, *Ever Since Darwin*

A major difficulty in reading this selection is the need to hold the meaning of each sentence "in suspension" as you read ahead, because the meaning of an earlier sentence may be affected by the meaning of succeeding sentences. For instance, the second sentence in the Gould passage clarifies the meaning of the first sentence by giving specific examples; the third sentence restates the idea, while sentences 4 through 7 clarify and illustrate it. Without paragraphing, you are forced to remember each sentence separately and even to anticipate such close connections among sentences in order to make sense of the text.

EXERCISE 12.4

Here is the way the Gould selection divides into its six original paragraphs: sentences 1–7, 8–10, 11–12, 13–23, 24–27, 28–30. Put a paragraphing symbol ¶ in your own book immediately before the opening sentence of each paragraph. Later exercises will ask you to analyze some aspects of Gould's paragraphing.

Paragraphing helps readers by signaling when a sequence of related sentences begins and ends. The use of such paragraph signals tells you when you can stop holding meaning in suspension. The need for this kind of closure is a major consideration of writers. Gould, for example, begins a new paragraph with sentence 8 in order to draw a sharp distinction between the examples and the general principle. Similarly, he begins a new paragraph with sentence 24 to signal a shift from a description of the reproductive mode of the cecidomyian gall midge to that of *Micromalthus debilis*. In this way, paragraphing keeps readers from being overloaded with information and at the same time helps them follow the development of ideas.

Paragraphing also helps readers judge what is most important in what they are reading. Writers typically emphasize important information by placing it at the two points where readers are most attentive—at the beginning and ending of a paragraph. Many writers position information to orient readers at the beginning of a paragraph (as discussed under Topic-sentence Strategies later in this section), while they save the most important bit of information for last, as Gould does when he ends a paragraph with sentence 27.

Writers can give special emphasis to information by placing it in a paragraph of its own. Gould, for example, puts sentences 11 and 12 together in a separate paragraph. These two sentences could have been attached to either the preceding or following paragraphs. But Gould gives them a separate paragraph in order to emphasize the general point he is making. In addition, this paragraph serves as an important transition between the general discussion of how science explains things that go against intuition and the specific example of the bizarre adaptation of the cecidomyian gall midge.

Paragraph conventions Some writing situations call for fairly strict conventions for paragraphing. Readers may not be conscious of these conventions, but they would certainly notice if custom were not observed. For example, readers would be surprised if a newspaper did not have narrow columns and short paragraphs. This paragraphing convention is not accidental; it is designed to make newspaper reading easy and fast and to allow the reader to take in an entire paragraph at a glance. Business writing also tends to adhere to the convention of short paragraphs. Memo readers frequently do not want an excess of details or qualifications. Instead, they prefer a concise overview, a capsule that is easy to swallow.

College instructors, on the other hand, expect students to qualify their ideas and support them with specifics. They care less about how long it takes to read a paragraph than about how well developed the writing is. Therefore, paragraphs in college essays usually have several sentences. In fact, it is not unusual to find quite long paragraphs, as this example from an undergraduate history essay on the status of women in Victorian England illustrates:

> A genteel woman was absolutely dependent upon the two men in her life: first her father, and then her husband. From them came her economic and social status; they were the center of her thoughts and the objects of any ambitions she might have. The ideal woman did not live for herself; she barely had a self, because her entire existence was vicarious. Legally, a woman had almost no existence at all. Until her marriage, a daughter was completely in the power of her father; upon her marriage, she was legally absorbed by her husband. Any money she had became his, as did all of her property, including her clothes and even those things that had been given her as personal gifts before her marriage. Any earnings she might make by working belonged to her husband. A woman could not be sued for debt separately from her husband because legally they were the same person. She could not sign a lease or sue someone in court without having her husband be the complainant, even in cases of long separation. In cases of a husband's enmity, she had almost no legal protection from him. Under English law, divorces could be obtained, in practice, only by men. A man could divorce his wife on the grounds of adultery, but the reverse was not the case.

If any rule for paragraphing is truly universal, it is this: paragraphs should be focused, unified, and coherent. That is, the sentences in a paragraph should be meaningfully related to one another, and the relationships among the sentences should be clear. The following sentences—although they may look like a paragraph—do not constitute a meaningful paragraph because they lack focus, unity, and coherence.

> Maturity and attitude go together because both determine why you want to become a model. I went to the university for two years, not because I wanted to but because I was pushed into it. I used to think models were thought of as dumb blondes, but after being here at the university I realized that people still have respect for modeling and know all the hard work put in it.

Even though each of these sentences mentions either modeling or the university or both, the two topics are not connected. With each sentence, the focus shifts—from the general desire to become a model, to the writer's attending university, to the attitude of people toward models. There is no unity because there is no single idea controlling the sentences. The various elements of the writing do not "stick together" to form a coherent meaning, and the reader may well become disoriented. The topic-sentence strategies discussed in the following section are useful for ensuring this crucial sense of coherence.

EXERCISE 12.5

Look at the Gould passage earlier in this chapter. Analyze how Gould's paragraphing helps you follow his meaning. Would you have paragraphed this passage differently? Explain how and why.

Topic-sentence strategies   A *topic sentence* lets readers know the focus of a paragraph in simple and direct terms. It is a cueing strategy for the paragraph much as a thesis or forecasting statement is for the whole essay. Because paragraphing usually signals a shift in focus, readers expect some kind of reorientation in the opening sentence. They need to know whether the new paragraph is going to introduce another aspect of the topic or develop one already introduced. This need is especially strong when readers are under pressure to read quickly and efficiently.

Announcing the topic. Some topic sentences simply announce the topic. Here are a few examples taken from Barry Lopez's book *Arctic Dreams:*

> A polar bear walks in a way all its own.
>
> The surface of the great expanse of ice covering Bering Sea in April and May is infinitely varied.
>
> What is so consistently striking about the way Eskimos used parts of an animal is the breadth of their understanding about what would work.
>
> Distinctive landmarks that aid the traveler and control the vastness, as well as prominent marks on the land made inadvertently in the process of completing other tasks, are very much apparent in the Arctic.

The Mediterranean view of the Arctic, down to the time of the Elizabethan mariners, was shaped by two somewhat contradictory thoughts.

These topic sentences do more than merely identify the topic; they also indicate how the topic will be developed in subsequent sentences—by citing examples, describing physical features, presenting reasons and evidence, relating anecdotes, classifying, defining, comparing, or contrasting. Paragraphs may be developed in any one of these ways or by a combination of strategies. (See Chapters 13 through 19.)

Following is one of Lopez's paragraphs that shows how the topic in the first sentence is developed:

> <u>What is so consistently striking about the way Eskimos used parts of an animal is the breadth of their understanding about what would work.</u> Knowing that muskox horn is more flexible than caribou antler, they preferred it for making the side prongs of a fish spear. For a waterproof bag in which to carry sinews for clothing repair, they chose salmon skin. They selected the strong, translucent intestine of a bearded seal to make a window for a snowhouse—it would fold up for easy traveling and it would not frost over in cold weather. To make small snares for sea ducks, they needed a springy material that would not rot in salt water—baleen fibers. The down feather of a common eider, tethered at the end of a stick in the snow at an aglu, would reveal the exhalation of a quietly surfacing seal. Polar bear bone was used anywhere a stout, sharp point was required, because it is the hardest bone.   Barry Lopez, *Arctic Dreams*

EXERCISE 12.6

Read "Birth Control in the Schools: Clinical Examination," the argument written by Adam Paul Weisman in Chapter 7. Indicate which paragraphs begin with topic sentences and briefly explain how these topic sentences help you anticipate the paragraph's topic and suggest its method of development.

Forecasting subtopics. Other topic sentences do more than simply announce the topic and indicate how it will be developed. They actually give readers a detailed overview or forecast of subtopics that will be developed. The following paragraph shows how the subtopics mentioned in the opening sentence appear later in the paragraph. The subtopics are <u>underscored</u> in the first sentence and then connected by lines to the point in the paragraph where they subsequently appear.

Notice that the subtopics are taken up in the same order they are presented in the opening sentence: education first, followed by economic independence, power of office, and so on. This correlation between topic sentence and paragraph organization makes the paragraph easy to follow. Even so, such a structure is not necessarily mechanical in its execution. One subtopic may be developed in a sentence while another requires two or more sentences. The last two subtopics in Millett's piece—equality of status and recognition as human beings—are not directly brought up but are implied in the last sentence.

> Oppressed groups are denied education, economic independence, the power of office, representation, an image of dignity and self-respect, equality of status, and recognition as human beings. Throughout history women have been consistently denied all of these, and their denial today, while attenuated and partial, is nevertheless consistent. The education allowed them is deliberately designed to be inferior, and they are systematically programmed out of and excluded from the knowledge where power lies today—e.g., in science and technology. They are confined to conditions of economic dependence based on the sale of their sexuality in marriage, or a variety of prostitutions. Work on a basis of economic independence allows them only a subsistence level of life—often not even that. They do not hold office, are represented in no positions of power, and authority is forbidden them. The image of woman fostered by cultural media, high and low, then and now, is a marginal and demeaning existence, and one outside the human condition—which is defined as the prerogative of man, the male.   Kate Millett, *Sexual Politics*

Asking a question about the topic. Writers occasionally put their topic sentences in a question-answer format, posing a rhetorical question in one sentence which is then answered in the next sentence. Here is a paragraph illustrating this strategy.

> What about motion that is too slow to be seen by the human eye? That problem has been solved by the use of the time-lapse camera. In this one, the shutter is geared to take only one shot per second, or one per minute, or even one per hour—depending upon the kind of movement that is being photographed. When the time-lapse film is projected at the normal speed of twenty-four pictures per second, it is possible to see a bean sprout growing up out of the ground. Time-lapse films are useful in the study of many types of motion too slow to be observed by the unaided human eye. James C. Rettie, "But a Watch in the Night"

EXERCISE 12.7

Look at the selection by Rachel Richardson Smith in Chapter 6, or the one by David Owen in Chapter 7. Where does the writer use the rhetorical question as a topic-sentence strategy? Analyze how the rhetorical question is answered.

Question-answer topic sentences do not always appear at the beginning of a paragraph. On occasion, a question at the end of one paragraph may combine with the first sentence of the following paragraph. For an example, see paragraphs 1 and 2 in the selection by Linda Ellerbee in Chapter 2.

Making a transition. Not all topic sentences simply point forward to what will follow. Some also refer back to earlier sentences. Such sentences work both as topic sentences, stating the main point of the paragraph, and as transitions, linking that paragraph to the previous one. Here are a few topic sentences from *Aristotle for Everybody* by Mortimer J. Adler which use specific transitional terms (underscored) to tie the sentence to a previous statement:

Nevertheless there is something permanent in this special kind of change.

Like sensations, ideas are neither true nor false.

On the other hand, a piece of music—a song that is sung over and over again—does not exist just at one place and at one time.

So, too, are teachers.

There is one further difference between a song or a story and a painting or a statue.

Not only must these basic biological needs be satisfied beyond the level of the barest minimum required to sustain life but, in addition, many other human needs must be satisfied in order to approach the fulfillment of all our capacities and tendencies.

Sometimes the first sentence of a paragraph serves as a transition, while a subsequent sentence—in this case the last—states the topic. The under-scored sentences illustrate this strategy in the following example:

. . . What a convenience, what a relief it will be, they say, never to worry about how to dress for a job interview, a romantic tryst, or a funeral! Convenient perhaps, but not exactly a relief. Such a utopia would give most of us the same kind of chill we feel when a stadium full of Communist-bloc athletes in identical sports outfits, shouting slogans in unison, appears on TV. Most people do not want to be told what to wear any more than they want to be told what to say. In Belfast recently four hundred Irish Republican prisoners "refused to wear any clothes at all, draping themselves day and night in blankets," rather than put on prison uniforms. Even the offer of civilian-style dress did not satisfy them; they insisted on wearing their own clothes brought from home, or nothing. Fashion is free speech, and one of the privileges, if not always one of the pleasures, of a free world. Alison Lurie, *The Language of Clothes*

Occasionally, particularly in long essays, whole paragraphs serve as transitions, linking one sequence of paragraphs with those that follow. Even though we have taken the next transition paragraph out of its context, you can see that it summarizes what went before (evidence of contrast) and sets up what will follow (evidence of similarity):

Yet it was not all contrast, after all. Different as they were—in background, in personality, in underlying aspiration—these two great soldiers had much in common. Under everything else, they were marvelous fighters. Furthermore, their fighting qualities were really very much alike.   Bruce Catton, "Grant and Lee: A Study in Contrasts"

Positioning the topic sentence. Although topic sentences may occur anywhere in a paragraph, stating the topic in the first sentence has the advantage of giving readers a sense of how the paragraph is likely to be developed. The beginning of the paragraph is therefore the most commonly favored position for a topic sentence.

A topic sentence that does not open a paragraph is most likely to appear at the end. When placed in the concluding position, topic sentences usually summarize or generalize preceding information. In the following example, the topic is not stated explicitly until the last sentence.

> Every moment of the day the world bombards the human speaker with information and experiences. It clamors for his attention, claws his senses, intrudes into his thoughts. Only a very small portion of this total experience is language—yet the speaker must use this small portion to report on all the experiences that exist or ever existed in the totality of the world since time began. Try to think about the stars, a grasshopper, love or hate, pain, anything at all—and it must be done in terms of language. There is no other way; thinking is language spoken to oneself. <u>Until language has made sense of experience, that experience is meaningless.</u>   Peter Farb, *Word Play*

When a topic sentence is used in a narrative, it will often appear as the last sentence. This concluding topic sentence often evaluates or reflects on events, as illustrated in the following paragraph from Russell Baker's autobiography:

> I hadn't known she could play the piano. She wasn't playing very well, I guess, because she stopped occasionally and had to start over again. She concentrated intensely on the music, and the others in the room sat absolutely silently. My mother was facing me but didn't seem to see me. She seemed to be staring beyond me toward something that wasn't there. All the happy excitement died in me at that moment. <u>Looking at my mother, so isolated from us all, I saw her for the first time as a person utterly alone.</u>
> Russell Baker, *Growing Up*

EXERCISE 12.8
Look back at Russell Baker's "Smooth and Easy" in Chapter 2. Pick out the paragraphs that have their topic sentences at the end.

In rare cases, the topic sentence for one paragraph will appear at the end of the preceding paragraph, as in this example:

. . . And apart from being new, psychoanalysis was particularly threatening. French psychiatrists tended to look at the sufferings of their patients either as the result of organic lesions or moral degeneration. In either case, the boundary between the "healthy" doctor and the "sick" patient was clear. Freud's theory makes it hard to draw such lines by insisting that if the psychiatrist knew himself better, he would find more points in common with the patient than he might have thought. . . .   Sherry Turkle, *Psychoanalytic Politics*

In addition, it is possible for a single topic sentence to introduce two (or occasionally more) paragraphs. Subsequent paragraphs in such a series consequently have no separate topic sentence of their own. Following is an example of a two-paragraph sequence in which the topic sentence opens the first paragraph:

Almost without exception all human languages have built into them a polarity, a veer to the right. "Right" is associated with legality, correct behavior, high moral principles, firmness, and masculinity; "left," with weakness, cowardice, diffuseness of purpose, evil, and femininity. In English, for example, we have "rectitude," "rectify," "righteous," "right-hand man," "dexterity," "adroit" (from the French "*à droite*"), "rights," as in "the rights of man," and the phrase "in his right mind." Even "ambidextrous" means, ultimately, two right hands.

On the other side (literally), we have "sinister" (almost exactly the Latin word for "left"), "gauche" (precisely the French word for "left"), "gawky," "gawk," and "left-handed compliment." The Russian "*nalevo*" for "left" also means "surreptitious." The Italian "*mancino*" for "left" signifies "deceitful." There is no "Bill of Lefts."   Carl Sagan, *Dragons of Eden*

EXERCISE 12.9

Now that you have seen several topic-sentence strategies, look again at the Gould passage earlier in this chapter and identify the strategies he uses. Then evaluate how well his topic sentences work to orient you as a reader.

COHESIVE DEVICES

In addition to thesis and forecasting statements, paragraphing strategies, and topic sentences, writers also use certain cohesive devices to guide the reader. Cohesive devices help readers follow a writer's train of thought by connecting key words and phrases throughout a passage. Among such devices are pronoun reference, repetition of words, use of synonyms, repetition of sentence structure, and collocation.

Pronoun reference   One common cohesive device is pronoun reference. As noun substitutes, pronouns refer or point to nouns that either precede or follow them, and thus serve to connect phrases or sentences. The nouns that come before the pronouns are called antecedents. In the following paragraph, the pronouns (all *it*) form a chain of connection with their antecedent, *George Washington Bridge*.

> In New York from dawn to dusk to dawn, day after day, you can hear the steady rumble of tires against the concrete span of the George Washington Bridge. The bridge is never completely still. It trembles with traffic. It moves in the wind. Its great veins of steel swell when hot and contract when cold; its span often is ten feet closer to the Hudson River in summer than in winter. Gay Talese, "New York"

In the preceding example, there is only one pronoun-antecedent chain, and the antecedent comes first so all the pronouns refer back to it. When there are multiple pronoun-antecedent chains with references forward as well as back, writers have to make certain that readers will not mistake one pronoun's antecedent for another's (see Lack of Pronoun-Antecedent Agreement in the Handbook).

Word repetition To avoid confusion, a writer will often use a second cohesive device: the repetition of words and phrases. This device is used especially if a pronoun might confuse readers:

> The first step is to realize that in our society we have permitted the kinds of vulnerability that characterize the victims of violent crime and have ignored, where we could, the hostility and alienation that enter into the making of violent criminals. No rational person condones violent crime, and I have no patience with sentimental attitudes toward violent criminals. But it is time that we open our eyes to the conditions that foster violence and that ensure the existence of easily recognizable victims.   Margaret Mead, "A Life for a Life: What That Means Today"

The next example illustrates how a writer uses several overlapping chains of word repetition to avoid confusion and help the reader follow the development of ideas:

> Natural selection is the central concept of Darwinian theory—the fittest survive and spread their favored traits through populations. Natural selection is defined by Spencer's phrase "survival of the fittest," but what does this famous bit of jargon really mean? Who are the fittest? And how is "fitness" defined? We often read that fitness involves no more than "differential reproductive success"—the production of more surviving offspring than other competing members of the population. Whoa! cries Bethell, as many others have before him. This formulation defines fitness in terms of survival only. The crucial phrase of natural selection means no more than "the survival of those who survive"—a vacuous tautology. (A tautology is a phrase—like "my father is a man"—containing no information in the predicate ["a man"] not inherent in the subject ["my father"]. Tautologies are fine as definitions, but

not as testable scientific statements—there can be nothing to test in a statement true by definition.)   Stephen Jay Gould, *Ever Since Darwin*

Notice that Gould uses repetition to keep readers focused on the key concepts of "natural selection," "survival of the fittest," and "tautology." These key terms may vary in form—*fittest* becomes *fitness* and *survival* changes to *surviving* and *survive*—but they continue to serve as links in the chain of meaning.

Synonyms In addition to repeating the same word, writers also use synonyms, words with identical or very similar meanings, to connect important ideas. In the following example, the author develops a careful chain of synonyms and word repetitions:

> Over time, small bits of knowledge about a region accumulate among local residents in the form of stories. These are remembered in the community; even what is unusual does not become lost and therefore irrelevant. These narratives comprise for a native an intricate, long-term view of a particular landscape. . . . Outside the region this complex but easily shared "reality" is hard to get across without reducing it to generalities, to misleading or imprecise abstraction.   Barry Lopez, *Arctic Dreams*

Note the variety of synonym sequences: "region," "particular landscape"; "local residents," "community," "native"; "stories," "narratives"; "accumulate," "remembered," "does not become lost," "comprise"; "intricate long-term view," "complex . . . reality," "without reducing it to generalities." The result is a coherence of paragraph development that constantly reinforces the point the author is making.

Sentence-structure Writers occasionally repeat the same sentence structure in order to emphasize
repetition the connections among their ideas. Following is an example from Isaac Asimov:

> But the life forms are as much part of the structure of the Earth as any inanimate portion is. It is all an inseparable part of a whole. If any animal is isolated totally from other forms of life, then death by starvation will surely follow. If isolated from water, death by dehydration will follow even faster. If isolated from air, whether free or dissolved in water, death by asphyxiation will follow still faster. If isolated from the Sun, animals will survive for a time, but plants would die, and if all plants died, all animals would starve.   Isaac Asimov, "The Case Against Man"

From the third sentence to the last, Asimov repeats the "If this . . . then that" sentence structure to emphasize the various points he is making.

Collocation   Words collocate when they occur together in expected ways around a particular topic. For example, in a paragraph on a high school graduation, a reader might expect to encounter words such as *valedictorian, diploma, commencement, honors, cap and gown,* or *senior class.* Collocations occur quite naturally to a writer, and they usually form a recognizable network of meaning for readers.

In the paragraph that follows, five collocation chains are used:

1. housewife—cooking—neighbor—home
2. clocks—calculated cooking times—progression—precise
3. obstinacy—vagaries—problem
4. sun—clear days—cloudy ones—sundial—cast its light—angle—seasons—sun—weather
5. cooking—fire—matches—hot coals—smoldering—ashes—go out—bed-warming

The seventeenth-century housewife not only had to make do without thermometers, she also had to make do without clocks, which were scarce and dear throughout the sixteen hundreds. She calculated cooking times by the progression of the sun; her cooking must have been more precise on clear days than on cloudy ones. Marks were sometimes painted on the floor, providing her with a rough sundial, but she still had to make allowance for the obstinacy of the sun in refusing to cast its light at the same angle as the seasons changed; but she was used to allowing for the vagaries of sun and weather. She also had a problem starting her fire in the morning; there were no matches. If she had allowed the hot coals smoldering under the ashes to go out, she had to borrow some from a neighbor, carrying them home with care, perhaps in a bed-warming pan.   Waverly Root and Richard de Rouchement, *Eating in America*

EXERCISE 12.10

The preceding section illustrates the following cohesive devices: pronoun reference, word repetition, synonyms, sentence-structure repetition, and collocation. Look again at the Gould passage on adaptation earlier in the chapter, and identify the cohesive devices you find in it. How do these cohesive devices help you to read the essay and make sense of it?

TRANSITIONS

The final type of cueing discussed in this chapter is the transition. A *transition,* sometimes called a connective, serves as a bridge, connecting one paragraph, sentence, clause, or word with another. Not only does a transition signal a connection, it also identifies the kind of connection by indicating to readers how the item preceding the transition relates to that which follows it. Transitions help readers anticipate how the next paragraph or sentence will affect the meaning of what they have just read. Following is a discussion of three basic groups of transitions, based on the relationships they indicate: logical, temporal, and spatial.

Logical relationships   Transitions help readers follow the logic of an argument. How such transitions work is illustrated in this tightly—and passionately—reasoned paragraph by James Baldwin:

> The black man insists, by whatever means he finds at his disposal, that the white man cease to regard him as an exotic rarity <u>and</u> recognize him as a human being. This is a very charged and difficult moment, <u>for</u> there is a great deal of will power involved in the white man's naivete. Most people are not naturally malicious, <u>and</u> the white man prefers to keep the black man at a certain human remove <u>because</u> it is easier for him <u>thus</u> to preserve his simplicity <u>and</u> to avoid being called to account for crimes committed by his forefathers, <u>or</u> his neighbors. He is inescapably aware, <u>nevertheless,</u> that he is in a better position in the world <u>than</u> black men are, <u>nor</u> can he quite put to death the suspicion that he is hated by black men <u>therefore.</u> He does not wish to be hated, <u>neither</u> does he wish to change places, <u>and</u> at this point in his uneasiness he can scarcely avoid having recourse to those legends which white men have created about black men, the most unusual effect of which is that the white man finds himself enmeshed, so to speak, in his own language which describes hell, <u>as well as</u> the attributes which lead one to hell, <u>as being</u> black as night.   James Baldwin, "Stranger in the Village"

Following is a partial list of transitions showing logical relations:

To introduce another item in a series: first, second; in the second place; for one thing . . . for another; next; then; furthermore; moreover; in addition; finally; last; also; similarly; besides; and; as well as.

To introduce an illustration or other specification: in particular; specifically; for instance; for example; that is; namely.

To introduce a result or a cause: consequently; as a result, hence; accordingly; thus; so; therefore; then; because; since; for.

To introduce a restatement: that is; in other words; in simpler terms; to put it differently.

To introduce a conclusion or summary: in conclusion; finally; all in all; evidently; clearly; actually; to sum up; altogether; of course.

To introduce an opposing point: but; however; yet; nevertheless; on the contrary; on the other hand; in contrast; conversely; still; neither . . . nor.

To introduce a concession to an opposing view: certainly; naturally; of course; it is true; to be sure; granted.

To resume the original line of reasoning after a concession: nonetheless; all the same; even though; still; nevertheless.

Temporal relationships In addition to showing logical connections, transitions indicate sequence or progression in time (temporal relationships), as this example illustrates:

> That night, we drank tea and then vodka with lemon peel steeped in it. The four of us talked in Russian and English about mutual friends and American railroads and the Rolling Stones. Seryozha loves the Stones, and his face grew wistful as we spoke about their recent album, "Some Girls." He played a tape of "Let It Bleed" over and over, until we could translate some difficult phrases for him; after that, he came out with the phrases at intervals during the evening, in a pretty decent imitation of Jagger's Cockney snarl. He was an adroit and oddly formal host, inconspicuously filling our teacups and politely urging us to eat bread and cheese and chocolate. While he talked to us, he teased Anya, calling her "Piglet," and she shook back her bangs and glowered at him. It was clear that theirs was a fiery relationship. After a while, we talked about ourselves. Anya told us about painting and print-making and about how hard it was to buy supplies in Moscow. There had been something angry in her dark face since the beginning of the evening; I thought at first that it meant she didn't like Americans; but now I realized that it was a constant, barely suppressed rage at her own situation.
> Andrea Lee, *Russian Journal*

Following is a partial list of temporal transitions:

To indicate frequency: frequently; hourly; often; occasionally; now and then; day after day; again and again.

To indicate duration: during; briefly; for a long time; minute by minute; for many years.

To indicate a particular time: now; then; at that time; in those days; last Sunday; next Christmas; in 1995; at the beginning of August; at six o'clock; first thing in the morning; two months ago; when this first started.

To indicate the beginning: at first; in the beginning; since; before then; in the preceding weeks.

To indicate the middle: in the meantime; while this was going on; meanwhile; as it was happening; at that moment; at the same time; simultaneously; next; then.

To indicate the end and beyond: eventually; finally; at last; in the end; subsequently; later; afterwards.

Spatial relationships   Spatial transitions orient readers to the objects in a scene, as illustrated in this paragraph:

> On Georgia 155, I crossed Troublesome Creek, then went <u>through</u> groves of pecan trees aligned <u>one with the next</u> like fenceposts. The pastures grew a green almost blue, and syrupy water the color of a dusty sunset filled the ponds. <u>Around</u> the farmhouses, <u>from</u> wires strung high <u>above</u> the ground, swayed gourds hollowed out for purple martins.
>   The land rose <u>again on the other side</u> of the Chattahoochee River, and Highway 34 went to the ridgetops where long views <u>over</u> the hills opened <u>in all directions</u>. <u>Here</u> was the tail of the Appalachian backbone, its gradual descent <u>to</u> the Gulf. <u>Near</u> the Alabama stateline stood a couple of LAST CHANCE! bars. . . .   William Least Heat Moon, *Blue Highways*

Following is a partial list of transitions showing spatial relationships:

To indicate closeness: close to; near; next to; alongside; adjacent to; facing; here.

To indicate distance: in the distance; far; beyond; away; on the far side; there.

To indicate direction: up or down; forward(s) or backward(s); sideways; along; across; at an angle; to the right or left; in front of or behind; above or below; inside or outside.

EXERCISE 12.11

Return to the Gould passage on adaptation earlier in this chapter, and underline the logical, temporal, and spatial transitions he uses. How do they help you to relate different kinds of details and ideas?

Narrating

Narration is a basic writing strategy for presenting action. Writers use narration for a variety of purposes: they illustrate and support their ideas with anecdotes, entertain readers with suspenseful or revealing stories, predict what will happen with scenarios, and explain how something generally happens (or should happen) with process narrative. This chapter focuses on how writers make their narratives work—how they sequence narrative action, shape narrative structure, and present the narrative from various points of view. Finally, it looks at one special use of narrative: to present a process.

SEQUENCING NARRATIVE ACTION

One of the most important elements writers must consider in presenting action is sequencing. One way writers sequence action is by presenting it along a narrative time line. Simple chronological sequencing can be best illustrated with process narrative. Because these narratives present instructions for readers to follow, each action must be carefully identified and set out in a clear, straightforward order. How this simple sequencing works is illustrated in the following selection from a piece by Jim Villas on cutting up a whole chicken for frying:

> Placing whole chicken in center of cutting board (breast-side up, neck toward you), grab leg on left firmly, pull outward and down toward board, and begin slashing down through skin toward thigh joint, keeping knife close to thigh. Crack back thigh joint as far as possible, find joint with fingers, then cut straight through to remove (taking care not to pull skin from breast). Turn bird around and repeat procedure on other thigh.   Jim Villas, "Fried Chicken."

Such play-by-play narrating occurs occasionally in fiction as well. Here is an example from "Big Two-Hearted River: Part II," a story by Ernest Hemingway. This excerpt shows the actions Nick takes while fishing with grasshoppers as bait.

> Holding the rod in his right hand he let out line against the pull of the grasshopper in the current. He stripped off line from the reel with his left

hand and let it run free. He could see the hopper in the little waves of the current. It went out of sight.

There was a tug on the line. Nick pulled against the taut line. It was his first strike. Holding the now living rod across the current, he brought in the line with his left hand.   Ernest Hemingway, *In Our Time*

EXERCISE 13.1

Look at George Orwell's essay "A Hanging" in Chapter 2. Read it carefully and make a list of the major events in the story. Compare your list with those of others in your class. Did you all include the same events? Did you put the events in the same order? How do you account for any differences among these lists of major events?

EXERCISE 13.2

Think of something memorable you did that you could narrate in some detail. You might recall a race you ran in, a school play you performed in, an unusual activity you participated in, or an adventure in a strange place. Reflect on what you did, making a list of the events in the order in which they occurred. Then, write a narrative following the chronological sequence set out in your list. (You will be able to use this narrative in subsequent exercises.)

On occasion, writers complicate the narrative sequence by referring to something that occurred earlier, with a *flashback*, or that will occur later, with a *flashforward*. Film and modern fiction have made flashbacks familiar to us as methods of presenting past events dramatically or contrasting the past with the present. One way to introduce a flashback is in the form of a vivid memory which intrudes on the character's thoughts.

Flashbacks Here is an example of a flashback from a narrative by Annie Dillard. Dillard has been telling how she spent a day observing praying mantis egg cases hatch. In the following excerpt she interrupts the forward movement of her narrative to tell about an experience she had years before.

Night is rising in the valley; the creek has been extinguished for an hour. . . . The scene that was in the back of my brain all afternoon, obscurely, is beginning to rise from night's lagoons. It really has nothing to do with praying mantises. But this afternoon I threw tiny string lashings and hitches with frozen hands, gingerly, fearing to touch the egg cases for a minute because I remembered the Polyphemus moth. . . .

<u>Once, when I was ten or eleven years old</u> . . .   Annie Dillard, *Pilgrim at Tinker Creek*

Flashforwards   Not only do writers flash back to actions in the distant past, they also flash forward to actions occurring some time after the main action they are presenting. The following excerpt from an autobiographical narrative by John Edgar Wideman (reprinted in full in Chapter 2) offers an example of this kind of complex action:

Darryl knew damn well that wasn't the problem. Together we might have been able to say the right things. Put the white boy in his place. Recapture some breathing space. But Darryl had his own ghosts to battle. His longing for his blonde, blue-eyed Putney girl friend whose parents had rushed her off to Europe when they learned of her romance with a colored boy who was Putney school president. His ambivalence toward his blackness <u>that would explode one day and hurl him into the quixotic campaign of the Black Revolutionary Army to secede from the United States.</u> So Darryl cooled it that afternoon in his room and the choked feeling never left my throat. <u>I can feel it as I write.</u>   John Edgar Wideman, *Brothers and Keepers*

Narratives usually move in forward chronological sequence, from earliest action to most recent action, interrupted by occasional flashbacks or flashforwards. But, as the next passage shows, a narrative can also move in reverse chronology, from most recent action to actions increasingly earlier in time:

The crowd was excited to see Caudill and Guidugli spill their blood, yes, but if the truth be told, <u>they had been even happier several minutes earlier, when</u> Stanton Long, a machine operator, had staggered to the side of the ring and, in great pain, vomited the entire contents of his stomach onto the concrete floor below. And <u>they had laughed mightily when</u> Raymond Morris, a forty-five-year-old bartender, had convulsed on the mat after taking a beating from a man twenty-two years his junior. . . .

<u>Three weeks earlier,</u> the posters had gone up in the bars and factories around Dayton. HOW TOUGH ARE YOU? read the headline that stood next to a large drawing of a man's fist.   Bob Greene, "That's Entertainment"

Narrative time signals   Writers use three methods to signal shifts in narrative time: clock time, temporal transitions, and verb tense. You can see all three at work in the following passage from "Death of a Pig," an essay by E. B. White. The essay is about what happened when the pig White was raising to be butchered became ill and died. The pages that follow refer back to this passage often to illustrate the three methods of signaling time shifts. For now, just read the passage:

It was about four o'clock in the afternoon when I first noticed that there was something wrong with the pig. He failed to appear at the trough for his supper, and when a pig (or a child) refuses supper a chill wave of fear runs through any household, or ice-household. After examining my pig, who was stretched out in the sawdust inside the building, I went to the phone and cranked it four times. Mr. Dameron answered. "What's good for a sick pig?" I asked. (There is never any identification needed on a country phone; the person on the other end knows who is talking by the sound of the voice and by the character of the question.)

"I don't know, I never had a sick pig," said Mr. Dameron, "but I can find out quick enough. You hang up and I'll call Henry."

Mr. Dameron was back on the line again in five minutes. "Henry says roll him over on his back and give him two ounces of castor oil or sweet oil, and if that doesn't do the trick give him an injection of soapy water. He says he's almost sure the pig's plugged up, and even if he's wrong, it can't do any harm."

I thanked Mr. Dameron. I didn't go right down to the pig, though. I sank into a chair and sat still for a few minutes to think about my troubles, and then I got up and went to the bar, catching up on some odds and ends that needed tending to. Unconsciously I held off, for an hour, the deed by which I would officially recognize the collapse of the performance of raising a pig; I wanted no interruption in the regularity of feeding, the steadiness of growth, the even succession of days. I wanted no interruption, wanted no oil, no deviation. I just wanted to keep on raising a pig, full meal after full meal, spring into summer into fall. I didn't even know whether there were two ounces of castor oil on the place.

Shortly after five o'clock I remembered that we had been invited out to dinner that night and realized that if I were to dose a pig there was no time to lose. The dinner date seemed a familiar conflict: I move in a desultory society and often a week or two will roll by without my going to anybody's house to dinner or anyone's coming to mine, but when an occasion does arise, and I am summoned, something usually turns up (an hour or two in advance) to make all human intercourse seem vastly inappropriate. I have come to believe that there is in hostesses a special power of divination, and that they deliberately arrange dinners to coincide with pig failure or some other sort of failure. At any rate, it was after five o'clock and I knew I could put off no longer the evil hour.

When my son and I arrived at the pigyard, armed with a small bottle of castor oil and a length of clothesline, the pig had emerged from his house and was standing in the middle of his yard, listlessly. He gave us a slim greeting. I could see that he felt uncomfortable and uncertain. I had brought the clothesline thinking I'd have to tie him (the pig weighed more than a hundred pounds) but we never used it. My son reached down, grabbed both front legs, upset him quickly, and when he opened his mouth to scream I turned the oil into his throat—a pink, corrugated area I had never seen before. I had just time to read the label while the neck of the bottle was in his mouth. It said Puretest. The screams, slightly muffled by oil, were pitched in the hysterically high range of pig-sound, as though torture were being carried out, but they didn't last long; it was all over rather suddenly, and, his legs released, the pig righted himself.   E. B. White, "Death of a Pig"

Clock time. White uses clock time to orient readers and to give a sense of duration. He tells us that the action lasted a little over an hour, beginning at about four o'clock and ending a little after five. He indicates that he called Mr. Dameron as soon as he had assessed the situation and then had to wait five minutes for him to call back. More important, he makes clear that once he learned what to do, he spent most of the hour avoiding the task.

In the following brief example by George Simpson, clock time serves the writer's purpose by making readers aware of the speed with which actions were taken:

9:05 P.M. An ambulance backs into the receiving bay, its red and yellow lights flashing in and out of the lobby. A split second later, the glass doors burst open as a nurse and an attendant roll a mobile stretcher into the lobby. When the nurse screams, "Emergent!" the lobby explodes with activity as the way is cleared to the trauma room. Doctors appear from nowhere and transfer the bloodied body of a black man to the treatment table. Within seconds his clothes are stripped away.   George Simpson, "The War Room at Bellevue"

EXERCISE 13.3

Look at Linda Ellerbee's narrative in Chapter 2. Read the essay quickly, noting the use of clock time in paragraphs 11–13. What do you think is Ellerbee's purpose for using clock time in this selection? What effect does it have on you?

Temporal transitions. Another means of showing the passage of time is with temporal transitions, words and phrases that locate a point in time or relate one point to another. Some familiar ones include *then, when, at that time, before, after, while, next, later, first,* and *second;* see Chapter 12: Cueing the Reader for a more detailed discussion of these time markers. Look back at the first paragraph of the White passage from "Death of a Pig." White uses several temporal transitions in the paragraph: *when* (twice), *first,* and *after.*

Process narrative uses many temporal transitions, as you can see in this passage from an essay about wasps and spiders:

When the grave is finished, the wasp returns to the tarantula to complete her ghastly enterprise. First, she feels it all over once more with her antennae. Then her behavior becomes more aggressive. She bends her abdomen, protruding her sting, and searches for the soft membrane at the point where the spider's legs join its body—the only spot where she can penetrate the horny skeleton. From time to time, as the exasperated spider slowly shifts

ground, the wasp turns on her back and slides with the aid of her wings, trying to get under the tarantula for a shot at the vital spot. <u>During</u> all this maneuvering, which can last <u>for several</u> minutes, the tarantula makes no move to save itself. <u>Finally</u> the wasp corners it against some obstruction and grasps one of its legs in her powerful jaws. <u>Now at last</u> the harassed spider tries a desperate but vain defense. The two contestants roll over and over on the ground. It is a terrifying sight and the outcome is always the same.
Alexander Petrunkevitch, "The Spider and the Wasp"

EXERCISE 13.4

Look back at the narrative you wrote for Exercise 13.2. Did you use temporal transitions in your own writing? If you did, try to explain why. If you did not, would your writing be improved if you added temporal transitions? Which ones would you add, and where? Explain why you would add these particular transitions at these places.

Verb tense. Verb tense also plays an important role in presenting time in narrative. It indicates when the actions occur and whether they are complete or in progress. White, for example, sets most of his narrative in the simple past tense, complicating his narrative only when he reports actions occurring simultaneously: "When my son and I arrived at the pigyard, . . . the pig had emerged from his house and was standing in the middle of his yard. . . ." To convey the time relations among these actions, he uses three past tenses in one sentence:

simple past to indicate a completed action: "my son and I arrived"

past perfect to indicate the action occurred before another action: "the pig had emerged"

past progressive to indicate an ongoing action that had been in progress for some time: the pig "was standing"

Note that, in addition to these past tense forms, White also uses the present tense, to distinguish habitual, continually occurring, actions: "When a pig (or a child) refuses supper a chill wave of fear runs through any household." In fact, whole narratives may be written primarily in the present tense. This is generally the case for process narratives, as illustrated by the excerpt from "The Spider and the Wasp" in the preceding discussion. In addition, contemporary writers of profiles often use the present tense to give their writing a sense of "you-are-there" immediacy. The pieces by Gretel Ehrlich, David Noonan, and John McPhee in Chapter 4 are good examples of this use of the present tense.

Verb tense and temporal transitions can be used in various ways to distinguish actions that occurred repeatedly from those that occurred only once. In the following passage, for example, Willie Morris uses the tense marker *would* along with the time markers *many times* and *often* to indicate recurring actions. When he moves from action which occurred repeatedly to action which occurred only once, he shifts to the simple past tense, signaling this shift with the phrase *on one occasion*.

> <u>Many times</u>, walking home from work, <u>I would see</u> some unknowing soul venture across that intersection against the light and <u>then</u> freeze in horror when he saw the cars ripping out of the tunnel toward him. . . . Suddenly, the human reflex <u>would take</u> over, and the pedestrian <u>would jackknife</u> <u>first</u> one way, <u>then</u> another, arms flaying the empty air, and <u>often</u> the car <u>would</u> literally *skim* the man, brushing by him so close it <u>would touch</u> his coat or his tie. . . . <u>On one occasion</u>, feeling sorry for the person who had brushed against the speeding car, I <u>hurried</u> across the intersection after him to cheer him up a little. Catching up with him down by 32nd I <u>said</u>, "That was good legwork, sir. Excellent moves for a big man!" but the man <u>looked</u> at me with an empty expression in his eyes, and <u>then moved</u> away mechanically and trancelike, heading for the nearest bar.   Willie Morris, *North Toward Home*

EXERCISE 13.5

Look at Sue Hubbell's examination of chiggers in Chapter 5. Note the verb tenses Hubbell uses in the two narrative passages (paragraphs 3 and 8–9). How and why are they different? What reasons might an author have for using different tenses in the same essay?

SHAPING NARRATIVE STRUCTURE

In addition to clear sequencing of action, writers of effective narrative create a structure to give their stories interest and to focus the action. Among the devices for shaping narrative structure are conflict, tension, and narrative pace.

Conflict and tension   The basic device writers use to turn a sequence of actions into a story is *conflict*. Conflict adds the question "So what?" to "What happened next?" It provides motivation and purpose for the actions of characters. In this way, conflict gives narrative its dramatic structure.

The conflict in most narrative takes the form of a struggle between the writer (or the writer's subject) and an opposing force. This force may take many forms—another person or creature, nature, society's rules and values, internal characteristics such as conflicting values or desires.

In this excerpt from George Orwell's "A Hanging" (reprinted in full in Chapter 2), the conflict is between the narrator's sense of the sanctity of life and his duty to perform his role in the execution. As the dog tries to turn the death march into a game, the conflict between the forces that celebrate life and those that take it away is brought into the open.

> We set out for the gallows. Two warders marched on either side of the prisoner, with their rifles at the slope; two others marched close against him, gripping him by arm and shoulder, as though at once pushing and supporting him. The rest of us, magistrates and the like, followed behind. Suddenly, when we had gone ten yards, the procession stopped short without any order or warning. A dreadful thing had happened—a dog, come goodness knows whence, had appeared in the yard. It came bounding among us with a loud volley of barks, and leapt round us wagging its whole body, wild with glee at finding so many human beings together. It was a large woolly dog, half Airedale, half pariah. For a moment it pranced round us, and then, before anyone could stop it, it had made a dash for the prisoner and jumping up tried to lick his face. Everyone stood aghast, too taken aback even to grab the dog.   George Orwell, "A Hanging"

EXERCISE 13.6

What is the conflict in the narrative you wrote for Exercise 13.2? Write a few sentences, stating what you see as the central conflict of your narrative.

EXERCISE 13.7

Look at "Inside the Brain" by David Noonan in Chapter 4. What do you think is the central conflict in this essay? Write a few sentences describing this conflict.

Along with conflict in a narrative comes *tension,* and this tension is what makes readers want to read on to find out what will happen. Tension in narrative does not refer to hostility or anxiety, but to tautness. This sense of tension comes from its Latin root, *tendere,* meaning "to stretch." By setting up an unresolved conflict, a writer can stretch the narrative line, creating a sense of tautness or suspense. Readers thus are involved in the action because they care about the ultimate resolution of the conflict.

Conflict also imposes structure on narrative action in another way: by focusing the action toward some purpose. That is, instead of the simple "and then-and then-and then" structure which a time line gives, conflict provides a one-thing-leads-to-another structure. Each part of the action then plays an instrumental role in the narrative. In this way, it can help to support the theme of the narrative.

EXERCISE 13.8

Look at Russell Baker's essay in Chapter 2. Although this narrative has a fairly simple "and then" structure, it also has a lot of tension. Read the story quickly, paying special attention to your response to it. At what points do you feel excited? When do you have a sense of anticipation or suspense? How do these feelings affect your enjoyment of the story?

Narrative pace   Although writers may place actions in the context of clock time, they do not really try to reproduce time as it is measured by clocks. Clock time moves at a uniform rate. Five minutes always takes the same time no matter what is happening during that period. Imagine writing about an action that took five minutes and using the same number of words (or syllables) to present what happened in each minute. No minute would have more space than another; none would have more emphasis. If everything were emphasized equally, readers would be unable to distinguish the importance of actions. Such a narrative would be monotonous and unnatural.

Pace refers to the techniques writers use to vary the passage of narrative time. They pace narratives by emphasizing more important actions and deemphasizing less important ones. To emphasize a sequence of action, a writer heightens the drama, thus making the action last longer or seem more intense. Common techniques for doing this are concentration on specific narrative action, presentation of action through dialogue, and sentence rhythm.

Specific narrative action. The writer George Plimpton participated in the Detroit Lions football training camp in order to write a book about professional football. In this passage from his book, Plimpton tells what happened when he had his big chance in a practice scrimmage.

> Since in the two preceding plays the concentration of the play had been elsewhere, I had felt alone with the flanker. Now, the whole heave of the play was toward me, flooding the zone not only with confused motion but noise—the quick stomp of feet, the creak of football gear, the strained grunts of effort, the faint *ah-ah-ah,* of piston-stroke regularity, and the stiff calls of instruction, like exhalations. "Inside, inside! Take him inside!" someone shouted, tearing by me, his cleats thumping in the grass. A call—a parrot squawk—may have erupted from me. My feet splayed in hopeless confusion as Barr came directly toward me, feinting in one direction, and then stopping suddenly, drawing me toward him for the possibility of a buttonhook pass, and as I leaned almost off balance toward him, he turned and came on again, downfield, moving past me at high speed, leaving me poised on one leg, reaching for him, trying to grab at him despite the illegality, anything to keep him from getting by. But he was gone, and by the time I had turned to set out after him, he had ten yards on me, drawing away fast with his sprinter's run, his legs pinwheeling, the row of cleats flicking up a faint wake of dust behind.   George Plimpton, *Paper Lion*

Although the action lasted only a few moments, Plimpton gives a close-up of it. He focuses on what we are calling *specific narrative action*—specific

and concrete movements, gestures, and activities. Instead of writing "Someone ran by me shouting," he writes:

> "Inside, inside! Take him inside!" someone <u>shouted,</u> (verb) <u>tearing</u> by me,
> (participial phrase) <u>his cleats thumping</u> in the grass. (absolute phrase)

The underlined verbs and verb phrases identify a player's specific actions:
shouting, tearing by, thumping cleats. In the long fifth sentence Plimpton
gives us another series of specific narrative actions: "feet splayed," "came
directly toward me," "feinting in one direction," "stopping suddenly,"
"drawing me toward him," "leaned almost off balance," "turned and came
on again," and then "moving/leaving/reaching/trying" in quick succession.
The specific actions slow the narrative pace and heighten the tension. In
addition, because they are concrete, they enable us to imagine what is
happening.

EXERCISE 13.9
Look at the selection by Maya Angelou in Chapter 3. Note particularly
what happens in paragraph 18. How does Angelou's use of specific narrative
action here contribute to the overall effectiveness of the selection?

EXERCISE 13.10
Choose a paragraph or two from one of the selections in Chapter 4:
Writing Profiles. Underline each instance of specific narrative action in the
excerpt you choose. What is the effect of this technique on the pacing of the
narrative?

EXERCISE 13.11
Look back at the narrative you wrote for Exercise 13.2. How effectively
have you used specific narrative action to pace your narrative and make it
concrete? Choose a sentence or a series of sentences to revise, emphasizing
a particular part of your narrative by adding specific narrative action. Then,
compare the two versions, analyzing the different effects of pacing.

Dialogue. Another way of dramatizing narrative action is dialogue.
Writers use it to reveal conflict directly, without the narrator's intruding
commentary. Dialogues are not mere recordings of conversation, but pointed
representations of conversation. Through dialogue, readers gain insight into
the personality and motives of the characters.

Through dialogue, Richard Wright shows what happened when a white
man confronted a black delivery boy. Notice that the dialogue does not have
the free give-and-take of conversation. Instead, it is a series of questions
which get evasive answers: "he said" . . . "I lied" . . . "he asked me" . . .
"I lied." The dialogue is tense, revealing the extent of the boy's fear and
defensiveness.

I was hungry and he knew it; but he was a white man and I felt that if I told him I was hungry I would have been revealing something shameful.

"Boy, I can see hunger in your face and eyes," he said.

"I get enough to eat," I lied.

"Then why do you keep so thin?" he asked me.

"Well, I suppose I'm just that way, naturally," I lied.

"You're just scared, boy," he said.

"Oh, no, sir," I lied agan.

I could not look at him. I wanted to leave the counter, yet he was a white man and I had learned not to walk abruptly away from a white man when he was talking to me. I stood, my eyes looking away. He ran his hand into his pocket and pulled out a dollar bill.

"Here, take this dollar and buy yourself some food," he said.

"No, sir," I said.

"Don't be a fool," he said. "You're ashamed to take it. God, boy, don't let a thing like that stop you from taking a dollar and eating."

The more he talked the more it became impossible for me to take the dollar. I wanted it, but I could not look at it. I wanted to speak, but I could not move my tongue. I wanted him to leave me alone. He frightened me.

"Say something," he said.   Richard Wright, *Black Boy*

Wright does not try to communicate everything through dialogue. He intersperses information which supports the dialogue—description, reports of the boy's thoughts and feelings, as well as some movement—in order to help readers understand the unfolding drama.

Writers also use dialogue to reveal a person's character and show the dynamics of interpersonal relationships. Notice, for instance, the way Lillian Hellman uses dialogue to write about a long-time friend, Arthur W. A. Cowan:

. . . Cowan said, "What's the matter with you? You haven't said a word for an hour." I said nothing was the matter, not wishing to hear his lecture about what was. After an hour of nagging, by the repetition of "Spit it out," "Spit it out," I told him about a German who had fought in the International Brigade in the Spanish Civil War, been badly wounded, and was now very ill in Paris without any money and that I had sent some, but not enough.

Arthur screamed, "Since when do you have enough money to send anybody a can to piss in? Hereafter, I handle all your money and you send nobody anything. And a man who fought in Spain has to be an ass Commie and should take his punishment."

I said, "Oh shut up, Arthur."

And he did, but that night as he paid the dinner check, he wrote out another check and handed it to me. It was for a thousand dollars.

I said, "What's this for?"

"Anybody you want."

I handed it back.

He said, "Oh, for Christ sake take it and tell yourself it's for putting up with me."

"Then it's not enough money."

He laughed. "I like you sometimes. Give it to the stinking German and don't say where it comes from because no man wants money from a stranger."   Lillian Hellman, *Pentimento*

This dialogue is quite realistic. It shows the way people talk to one another, the rhythms of interactive speech and its silences. But the dialogue does something more: it gives readers real insight into the way Hellman and Cowan were with each other, their conflicts and their shared understanding. Such dialogue allows readers to listen in on private conversations.

The Hellman passage also exemplifies two methods of presenting dialogue: quoting and summarizing. In summarizing, writers choose their own words instead of quoting actual words used; this allows them to condense dialogue as well as to emphasize what they wish. When Hellman writes "I told him about a German . . . ," she is summarizing her actual spoken words.

EXERCISE 13.12

John McPhee uses dialogue in his profile of pinball player Anthony Lucas in Chapter 4. Read McPhee's piece, concentrating on the concluding scene between Lucas and Tom Buckley in paragraphs 12-23. How does the dialogue here reveal the characters of the two competitors and their relationship to one another? Describe the effect of this dialogue on your response to McPhee's article as a whole, analyzing how you think the dialogue creates its particular effect.

EXERCISE 13.13

Write several paragraphs of narrative, including some dialogue. Write about an incident that occurred between you and someone you consider a close friend or associate—a friend, a relative, an enemy, a boss. Try to compose a dialogue that conveys the closeness of your relationship.

Read over your dialogue, and reflect on the impression it gives. In a sentence or two, state what you think the dialogue reveals about your relationship with this person.

Sentence rhythm. Sequences of short sentences and phrases also contribute to narrative pace. You can see how this works in an example from Russell Baker's piece on flying in Chapter 2—particularly in the way Baker sets up the climax of the crucial flight test. Look back at paragraph 16 to see how the pace quickens until it reaches an apex in the dramatic series of quick phrases that make up the last sentence:

First, a shallow dive to gain velocity, then push the stick slowly, firmly, all the way over against the thigh, simultaneously putting in hard rudder, and there we are, hanging upside down over the earth and now—keep it rolling, don't let the nose drop—reverse the controls and feel it roll all the way through until—coming back to straight-and-level now—catch it, wings level with the horizon, and touch the throttle to maintain altitude precisely at 5,000 feet.   Russell Baker, *Growing Up*

EXERCISE 13.14

When you wrote about the Baker selection for Exercise 13.8, did you select paragraph 16 as an exciting or suspenseful part? Look back at the context of this paragraph, particularly the events leading up to it. What role do you think these events play in making this passage dramatic?

In addition to techniques that heighten the pace of narrative action, writers also have techniques to interrupt the flow of action or bring it to a halt for purposes of transition. Two such techniques are reporting feelings and thoughts, and summarizing action.

Reporting feelings and thoughts. Look at Piri Thomas's account of a fight he once had with a street gang. Notice how he changes the pace of the action when he reports his thoughts during the fight. Every time he mentions his thoughts (in italics), the action pauses:

Big-mouth came at me and we grabbed each other and pushed and pulled and shoved. *Poppa, I thought, I ain't gonna cop out. I'm a fighter, too.* I pulled away from Tony and blew my fist into his belly. He puffed and butted my nose with his head. I sniffed back. *Poppa, I didn't put my hands to my nose.* I hit Tony again in that same weak spot. He bent over in the middle and went down to his knees.   Piri Thomas, *Down These Mean Streets*

EXERCISE 13.15

Read the complete selection by John Edgar Wideman in Chapter 2. Mark those places where the narrative pauses while the author explores his thoughts and feelings about the confrontation that is taking place. Would you say that, in slowing down the pace of action, these pauses diminish the tension of the scene or add to it? Why?

Summarizing action. The next selection, about a soccer game in Central America, uses summary to alter the pace of the narrative. In this passage, the author tells us what happened when the ball repeatedly went into the stands. He tells about the first time (paragraphs 1–6) in great detail, using specific narrative action and dialogue to dramatize the event. In telling about the second time, he changes the pace by presenting fewer details and no dialogue, simply stating that the announcer made a threat. In effect, he summarizes what happened the second time, giving this action much less space (only one paragraph rather than the six before).

Some minutes later the ball was kicked into the Shades section. It was thrown back onto the field, and the game was resumed. Then it was kicked into the Suns section. The Suns fought for it. One man gained possession, but he was pounced upon and the ball shot up and ten Suns went tumbling after it. A Sun tried to run down the steps with it. He was caught and the ball wrestled from him. A fight began, and now there were scores of Suns punching their way to the ball. The Suns higher up in the section threw bottles and cans and wadded paper on the Suns who were fighting, and the shower of objects—meat pies, bananas, hankies—continued to fall. The Shades, the Balconies, the Anthill, watched this struggle.

And the players watched, too. The game had stopped. The Mexican players kicked the turf, the Salvadorean team shouted at the Suns.

Please return the ball. It was the announcer. He was hoarse. *If the ball is not returned, the game will not continue.*

This brought a greater shower of objects from the upper seats—cups, cushions, more bottles. The bottles broke with a splashing sound on the concrete seats. The Suns lower down began throwing things back at their persecutors, and it was impossible to say where the ball had gone.

The ball was not returned. The announcer repeated his threat.

The players sat down on the field and did limbering-up exercises until, ten minutes after the ball had disappeared from the field, a new ball was thrown in. The spectators cheered but, just as quickly, fell silent. Mexico had scored another goal.

Soon, a bad kick landed the ball into the Shades. This ball was fought for and not thrown back, and one could see the ball progressing through the section. The ball was seldom visible, but one could tell from the free-for-alls—now here, now there—where it was. The Balconies poured water on the Shades, but the ball was not surrendered. And now it was the Suns' turn to see the slightly better-off Salvadoreans in the Shades section behaving like swine. The announcer made his threat: the game would not resume until the ball was thrown back. The threat was ignored, and after a long time the ref walked onto the field with a new ball.   Paul Theroux, *Old Patagonian Express*

EXERCISE 13.16

Look at the profile of a rodeo competition by Gretel Ehrlich in Chapter 4, particularly her account of the saddle broncs ride (paragraphs 2–3). Analyze the way Ehrlich paces her narrative in these paragraphs through the use of specific narrative action and summary.

TAKING A POINT OF VIEW

In narrative writing, point of view refers to the narrator's relation to the action at hand. Basically, writers use two points of view: first person and third person.

First person is used to narrate action in which the writer participated. For instance, when Piri Thomas writes, "Big-mouth came at me and we grabbed each other and pushed and pulled and shoved," he is using a first-person point of view. Third person, on the other hand, is used to narrate action performed by people other than the narrator. When Paul Theroux writes, "The Suns fought for it. One man gained possession, but he was pounced upon and the ball shot up and ten Suns went tumbling after it," he is using a third-person point of view. Because they are telling about their own experiences, autobiographers typically write first-person narrative, using the first-person pronouns *I* and *we,* as Piri Thomas does. When writers tell another person's story, as in biography, they use the third-person pronouns *he, she,* and *they* instead of the first-person *I* or *we.*

Of course, first-person narrators often observe and report on the actions of others. In such cases they may shift, perhaps for long stretches, into what seems to be primarily a third-person point of view. This is especially true when the writer is neither participating in the action nor introducing personal thoughts or feelings. However, the presence of the narrative "I" at any point in a piece of writing suggests a first-person point of view throughout.

EXERCISE 13.17

In Chapter 4, compare the profiles written by John McPhee and by Brian Cable, noting particularly each writer's point of view, first-person or third-person. Take a paragraph from each profile and rewrite it, using another point of view. What is the effect of the change of point of view in each case?

EXERCISE 13.18

Think of a brief incident involving you and one other person. Write about the incident from your own, first-person, point of view. Then write about the incident from the third-person point of view, as though another person is telling it. What impact does a change in point of view have on your story?

PRESENTING A PROCESS

Process narrative typically explains how something is done or how to do it. For example, in *Oranges,* a book about the Florida citrus industry, John McPhee tells how the technical operation of bud grafting is done. He is not writing directions for readers to follow. If he were, his narrative would be much more detailed and precise. Instead, he tells us as much as he thinks nonspecialists need or want to know.

One of Adams' men was putting Hamlin buds on Rough Lemon stock the day I was there. He began by slicing a bud from a twig that had come from a registered budwood tree—of which there are forty-five thousand in groves around Florida, each certified under a state program to be free from serious virus disease and to be a true strain of whatever type of orange, grapefruit, or tangerine it happens to be. Each bud he removed was about an inch long and looked like a little submarine, the conning tower being the eye of the bud, out of which would come the shoot that would develop into the upper trunk and branches of the ultimate tree. A few inches above the ground, he cut a short vertical slit in the bark of a Rough Lemon liner; then he cut a transverse slit at the base of the vertical one, and, lifting the flaps of the wound, set the bud inside. The area was bandaged with plastic tape. In a couple of weeks, Adams said, the new shoot would be starting out of the bud and the tape would be taken off. To force the growth of the new shoot, a large area of the bark of the Rough Lemon would be shaved off above the bud union. Two months after that, the upper trunk, branches, and leaves of the young Rough Lemon tree would be cut off altogether, leaving only a three-inch stub coming out of the earth, thick as a cigar, with a small shoot and a leaf or two of the Hamlin flippantly protruding near the top.   John McPhee, *Oranges*

EXERCISE 13.19

Look at the selection by Brian Cable in Chapter 4. Read it carefully, noting the way the author tells about the funeral home's process of dealing with a "client." Why do you think Cable includes this process narrative in his essay? Write a few sentences explaining Cable's purpose.

In contrast to the McPhee example, here is a process narrative that provides both information and directions. This selection comes from an article written for the *American Journal of Physiology*. Notice all the precise detail, technical terminology, and careful, step-by-step narrating. Because objectivity is important to such writing, the writers use the passive voice.

Ten 20- to 25-kg male baboons *(Papio anubis)* were tranquilized with ketamine, 10 mg/kg, intubated, mechanically ventilated, and anesthetized with halothane, 1.5 vol%. Instrumentation was implanted through a thoracotomy in the fifth left intercostal space. A miniature pressure transducer (Konigsberg P22, Konigsberg Instruments, Pasadena, CA) was implanted in the left ventricle through a stab wound in the apex, and a pair of ultrasonic transducers was implanted on opposing endocardial surfaces of the left ventricle. Tygon catheters were implanted in the left atrium and aorta. The transducer wires and catheters were run subcutaneously and buried in the interscapular area. Steven F. Vatner and Michael Zimpfer, "Brainbridge Reflex in Conscious, Unrestrained, and Tranquilized Baboons"

EXERCISE 13.20

Read through the essays by Sue Hubbell and Isaac Asimov in Chapter 5, noting where each writer presents a process. What is the purpose of the process narrative in each instance?

Like the Vatner and Zimpfer passage, our final selection is also an example of scientific writing, but it is much less technical because it is written for nonspecialists. Written by a biologist for a college textbook, it explains the process by which viruses were discovered. Process narratives of this kind are fairly common in science writing. They tend to be quite entertaining and to satisfy their readers' curiosity about the process of scientific discovery.

The discovery of viruses. By the latter part of the nineteenth century the idea had become firmly established that many diseases are caused by microorganisms. Pioneer bacteriologists such as Louis Pasteur and Robert Koch had isolated the pathogens for a number of diseases that afflict human beings and their domestic animals. But for some diseases, notably smallpox, biologists, try as they might, could find no causal microorganism. As early as 1796 it had been known that smallpox could be induced in a healthy person by something in the pus from a smallpox victim, and Edward Jenner had demonstrated that a person vaccinated with material from cowpox lesions developed an immunity to smallpox. Yet no bacterial agent could be found.

A crucial experiment was performed in 1892 by a Russian biologist, Dmitri Iwanowsky, who was studying a disease of tobacco plants called tobacco mosaic. The leaves of plants with this disease become mottled and wrinkled. If juice is extracted from an infected plant and rubbed on the leaves of a healthy one, the latter soon develops tobacco mosaic disease. If, however, the juice is heated nearly to boiling before it is rubbed on the healthy leaves, no disease develops. Concluding that the disease must be caused by bacteria in the plant juice, Iwanowsky passed juice from an infected tobacco plant through a very fine porcelain filter in order to remove the bacteria; he then rubbed the filtered juice on the leaves of healthy plants. Contrary to his expectation, the plants developed mosaic disease. What could the explanation be?

Iwanowsky suggested two possibilities. Either bacteria in the infected plants secrete toxins, and it is these rather than the bacterial cells themselves that are present in infectious juice. Or the bacteria that cause this disease are much smaller than other known bacteria and can pass unharmed through a fine porcelain filter. When it was later demonstrated that the infecious material in filtered juice could reproduce in a new host, Iwanowsky abandoned his first explanation in favor of the second—that some type of extremely small bacterium was the causal agent of the disease. During the next several decades many other diseases of both plants and animals were found to be caused by infectious agents so small that they could pass through porcelain filters and could not be seen with even the best light microscopes. These microbial agents of disease came to be called filterable viruses, or simply viruses. They were still assumed to be very small bacteria.

There were, however, a few hints that viruses might be something quite different from bacteria. First, all attempts to culture them on media customarily used for bacteria failed. Second, the virus material, unlike bacteria, could be precipitated from an alcoholic suspension without losing its infectious power. But not until 1935 was it conclusively demonstrated that viruses and bacteria are two very different things. In that year W. M. Stanley of the Rockefeller Institute isolated and crystallized tobacco mosaic virus. If the crystals were injected into tobacco plants, they again became active, multiplied, and caused disease symptoms in the plants. That viruses could be crystallized showed that they were not cells but must be much simpler chemical entities.   William Keeton, *Biological Science*

EXERCISE 13.21

Write a simple process narrative, explaining how to do something—make a sandwich, build a doghouse, write a poem, perform a scientific experiment, fly a kite. Address your narrative to someone who knows nothing about performing the task you are telling about.

Describing

To describe, writers must notice what their senses tell them. Noticing is only half of describing, however; the other half is finding the language to record the fine discriminations their senses make. To do this, writers develop a vocabulary that is rich, subtle, and specific enough to allow them to describe what they observe with particularity and precision.

For scientific, engineering, and other technical purposes, writers try to describe things as objectively and impersonally as possible. For many purposes, however, writers want their descriptions not only to reflect accurately the objects they observe but to be suggestive as well. They want to suggest or evoke subjective, personal associations and feelings about what they are describing.

Here are two pieces of description, one more objective than the other. The first, part of an essay on Lake Mead, was written by a geology student:

> Lake Mead was formed when the Colorado River was impounded by Hoover Dam in the Black Canyon, approximately 420 miles upstream from the river's mouth in the Gulf of California. The present morphology of the Lake Mead area consists of a series of steep, narrow canyons separating wide sloping basins. The river cut through the softer material to form these deep, narrow valleys and thus left the wide sloping basins. The major reaches of the reservoir from the upper end to Hoover Dam are Pierce, Iceberg, and Gregg basins, Virgin Canyon, Virgin and Boulder basins, and the Overton arm extending northward from Virgin basin. When filled to its maximum operating level (1,229 feet above mean sea level), Lake Mead has a depth of up to 589 feet above the original stream bed, a shoreline of 550 miles, and a surface area of 225 square miles; it extends upstream 115 miles. The weight of the total impounded water has been estimated at 40×10^{19} tons, of which approximately 60% is located in the Virgin and Boulder basins. An additional 4×10^{6} acre-feet of interstitial water are located in the subsurface sedimentary formations surrounding the lake.

The writing in this passage is highly objective and technical. The writer describes the lake by giving its history (formation), describing its shape (morphology), naming its divisions (major reaches), and citing its vital statistics—depth, shoreline and upstream dimensions, surface area, weight, and water volume. This description is full of detail—factual, mostly quantifiable information. The writer does not refer to her sensory impressions of the lake: the sound of the dam, the appearance of the lake and the surrounding landscape, the smell or the feel of the breeze off the lake. Nor does she place herself in the scene by indicating her vantage point. In fact, nothing in her language suggests that she has ever observed the lake firsthand.

In the next selection, M. F. K. Fisher recalls a "fairy palace" of her childhood, a stylish Los Angeles ice cream parlor called the Pig 'n' Whistle. Fisher's description is very personal, revolving around her own sensory impressions and feelings as a child. Although she points out many items, she gives little quantifiable information, few vital statistics. She is more interested in re-creating the atmosphere and evoking the mood of the place than in citing facts about it.

> This scarlet den of sin and iniquity . . . had wide shiny windows out onto the street with the insigne of a capering little pig playing a golden whistle as he danced and smiled. He was adorable.
>
> Inside, his palace was a wonderland of quiet elegance. The paneled walls were a soft grey, after one passed the long marble counters where people drank through straws from tall silver goblets, and there was lots of gold on the carved edgings and the magical little lights that glowed down onto at least a hundred pictures that had been bought in a cultural frenzy after the Exposition was held in 1915 in San Francisco. They were misty and vague, mostly of young women gazing at butterflies or looking down at their Secret Diaries or perhaps a love letter. They were discreet girls, almost piled with filmy clothes, but there was a fine sunniness about them.
>
> Anne and I were permitted to walk silently over the thick carpeting to peer up at these artifacts . . . as we moved languourously back to Mother's booth and our melting scoops of ice cream in their long silver boats.
> M. F. K. Fisher, *As They Were*

Fisher's subjective description is as true as the geology student's objective description, although Fisher's is true to her personal experience and the student's is true to the verifiable facts. Descriptive writing ranges between these extremes of objectivity and subjectivity, as the descriptions you will read in this chapter illustrate. A writer decides how objective or subjective to make a description based on the purpose for writing and the readers' needs and expectations.

Regardless of whether a description is to be more or less objective, describing involves three basic strategies: naming, detailing, comparing.

To describe, writers point to and name objects or features of their subjects. In the following passage, for example, Annie Dillard identifies the face, chin, fur, underside, and eyes of a weasel she once encountered in the woods:

> He was ten inches long, thin as a curve, a muscled ribbon, brown as fruit-wood, soft-furred, alert. His <u>face</u> was fierce, small and pointed as a lizard's; he would have made a good <u>arrowhead</u>. There was just a dot of <u>chin</u>, maybe two brown hairs' worth, and then the pure white <u>fur</u> began that spread down his <u>underside</u>. He had two black <u>eyes</u> I didn't see, any more than you see a window.   Annie Dillard, *Teaching a Stone to Talk*

The underscored nouns name the parts of the weasel on which Dillard focuses her attention. The nouns she uses are concrete: they refer to actual, tangible parts of the animal. They are also fairly specific: they identify parts of one particular animal, the weasel she saw.

In looking for the right word to name something, writers can usually choose from a variety of words. Some words may be concrete (referring to tangible objects or actual instances), while others are abstract (referring to ideas or qualities). *Nose, tooth,* and *foot* are concrete words, whereas *love, faith,* and *justice* are abstract.

Some words may be specific (referring to a particular instance or individual), while others are general (referring to a class which includes many particular instances). *Specific* and *general* are relative terms. That is, the specificity of a word cannot be measured absolutely but only by contrasting it with other words that could be substituted for it. For example, *vegetable* is more specific than *food* but more general than *carrot.*

If you compare the following description to Dillard's, you will see how each writer has made particular word choices:

> The expression of this snake's <u>face</u> was hideous and fierce; the <u>pupils</u> consisted of a vertical slit in a mottled and coppery <u>iris</u>; the <u>jaws</u> were broad at the base, and the <u>nose</u> terminated in a triangular projection.   Charles Darwin, *The Voyage of the Beagle*

Like Dillard, Darwin uses the word *face,* though he specifies the expression on the snake's face. He could have used *eyes,* as Dillard does, but he uses the more specific *pupils* and *iris* instead. *Chin,* however, would not substitute for *jaws* because *jaws* refers to the bone structure of the lower face, while *chin* refers to something different—the prominence of the lower jaw. Darwin could have used the technical terms *maxilla* and *mandible,* the names of the upper and lower jaw bones. He chose not to use these words, even though they are more specific than *jaws,* possibly because they might be unfamiliar to readers or more specific than necessary. As a rule of thumb, writers prefer more specific nouns for naming, but they adjust the degree of specificity to the particular needs of their readers.

EXERCISE 14.1
This is an exercise in close observation and naming. Go to a place where you can sit for a while and observe the scene. It might be a landscape or a cityscape, indoors or outdoors, crowded or solitary. Write for five minutes, listing everything in the scene that you can name.

Then, for each noun on your list, try to think of two or three other nouns you could use in its place. Write these other names down.

Finally, write a paragraph describing the scene. Use the nouns you think go together best, assuming your readers are unfamiliar with the scene.

In addition to naming perceivable objects and features, writers name sensations (stink and plunk) and qualities (the sweetness of the lumber):

> When the sun fell across the great white pile of the new Telephone Company building, you could smell the stucco burning as you passed; then some liquid sweetness that came to me from deep in the rings of the freshly cut lumber stacked in the yards, and the fresh plaster and paint on the brand-new storefronts. Rawness, sunshiny rawness down the end streets of the city, as I thought of them then—the hot ash-laden stink of the refuse dumps in my nostrils and the only sound at noon the resonant metal plunk of a tin can I kicked ahead of me as I went my way.   Alfred Kazin, *A Walker in the City*

EXERCISE 14.2
Read "Father," the personal essay by student Jan Gray printed in Chapter 3, and notice how much naming she uses in her description. Then, write a few sentences explaining why you think Gray uses so much naming in this passage. What impression does all this naming make on you? How specific is her naming? How subjective or objective is it?

DETAILING

Although nouns can be quite specific, detailing is a way of adding more specificity to them, thus making description even more particular and precise. Naming answers the questions "What is it?" and "What are its parts or features?" Detailing answers questions like these:

☐ What size is it?

☐ How many are there?

☐ What is it made of?

☐ Where is it located?

☐ What is its condition?

☐ What is its use?

☐ Where does it come from?

☐ What is its effect?

☐ What is its value?

To add details to names, writers add modifiers—adjectives and adverbs, phrases and clauses. Modifiers make nouns more specific by supplying additional information about them.

Notice, in this passage about a weasel, how many modifying details Annie Dillard provides. She indicates size, shape, color, texture, value, and amount.

> He was <u>ten inches long</u>, <u>thin</u> as a curve, a <u>muscled</u> ribbon, <u>brown</u> as fruit-wood, <u>soft-furred</u>, <u>alert</u>. His face was <u>fierce</u>, <u>small</u> and <u>pointed</u> as a lizard's; he would have made a <u>good</u> arrowhead. There was just a <u>dot</u> of chin, maybe <u>two brown hairs'</u> worth, and then the <u>pure white</u> fur began that spread down his underside. He had <u>two black</u> eyes I didn't see, any more than you see a window.   Annie Dillard, *Teaching a Stone to Talk*

Like names, details can be more or less specific. For example, because "ten inches long" is a measurable quantity, it is more precise than the relative term *small*. Other detailing words like *good* and *pure* are also relative. Even *brown*, although it is more precise than the general word *color*, could be specified further, as Dillard does, by comparing it to the color of fruitwood.

EXERCISE 14.3

Choose a common household item like a clock, vacuum cleaner, television set, or toaster which you can examine closely. Study this object for at least ten minutes. Then describe it for someone who has never seen it, using as many specific naming and detailing words as you can.

Modifiers are also used to identify a person's character traits, as the following passage about Maya Angelou's mother illustrates:

> By no amount of agile exercising of a wishful imagination could my mother have been called <u>lenient</u>. <u>Generous</u> she was; <u>indulgent</u>, never. <u>Kind</u>, yes; <u>permissive</u>, never.   Maya Angelou, *Gather Together in My Name*

EXERCISE 14.4

Look at Richard Rodriguez's description of his parents in the excerpt from his autobiography printed in Chapter 3. What modifiers does he use to describe his parents' personalities? How does this detailing contribute to the overall impression the selection gives you of Rodriguez's parents?

COMPARING

Whereas naming and detailing call on the power of observation, comparing brings the imagination into play. Comparison makes language even more precise and description more evocative. Look again at Annie Dillard's description of a weasel to see how she uses comparison:

> He was ten inches long, thin as a curve, a muscled ribbon, brown as fruit-wood, soft-furred, alert. His face was fierce, small and pointed as a lizard's; he would have made a good arrowhead. There was just a dot of chin, maybe two brown hairs' worth, and then the pure white fur began that spread down his underside. He had two black eyes I didn't see, any more than you see a window.   Annie Dillard, *Teaching a Stone to Talk*

This passage illustrates two kinds of comparison: simile and metaphor. Both figures of speech compare things that are essentially dissimilar. A *simile* directly expresses a similarity by using the word *like* or *as* to announce the comparison. Dillard uses a simile when she writes that the weasel was "thin as a curve." A *metaphor*, on the other hand, is an implicit comparison by which one thing is described as though it were the other. Dillard uses a metaphor when she describes the weasel as "a muscled ribbon."

Here are more examples of comparison used to describe:

> Sometimes I rambled to pine groves, standing like temples, or like fleets at sea, full-rigged, with wavy boughs, and rippling with light. . . .   Henry David Thoreau, *Walden*

> Just below the path, raising their heads above the endless white crosses of a soldier's cemetery, were strange red flowers.   Alfred Kazin, *A Walker in the City*

Comparing enhances a description by showing readers the thing being described in a surprising new way that can be suggestive and revealing. Although this strategy is called comparing, it includes both comparing and contrasting because differences can be as illuminating as likenesses. Once two things are connected, put into context with one another through comparing, they play off each other in unexpected ways.

EXERCISE 14.5

Most writers use comparison only occasionally to achieve particular effects. Notice that John Edgar Wideman, in the excerpt from his autobiography printed in Chapter 2, uses simile (in paragraphs 3 and 11) and metaphor (in paragraph 17) to describe the nameless white student who antagonizes him. What exactly do these figures of speech add to Wideman's overall portrayal of the white student and to the effect of the selection as a whole?

Useful as comparison is, there are a few pitfalls to avoid with this strategy. Be sure that the connection between the two things being compared is clear and appropriate to your description. Avoid using clichéd expressions, comparisons which are so overused that they have become predictable and consequently do not reveal anything new. Following are some examples of comparisons that have been worn out and thus do not enrich a description:

The kiss was as sweet as honey.

I am as busy as a bee.

That picture stands out like a sore thumb.

EXERCISE 14.6

Take five minutes to list as many clichés as you can think of. Then, pair up with another student, and discuss your lists to decide whether the entries are all clichés. When you are done, figure out what turns a comparison into a cliché for you, and together write a sentence defining a cliché.

EXERCISE 14.7

In Chapter 3 Kate Simon describes her friend Martha's mother (paragraph 3). Look particularly at the description of Mrs. Albert's face in the first half of the paragraph and analyze this description in terms of naming, detailing, and comparing. What impression of Mrs. Albert does the language of this description give you? How does this brief description reinforce the overall impression you get of Mrs. Albert in this selection from Kate Simon's memoirs?

USING SENSORY DESCRIPTION

Writers use three basic strategies in describing—naming, detailing, and comparing—but they have many language resources, and some limitations, for reporting their sense impressions. These resources help convey sights, sounds, smells, touches, and tastes.

In describing, the sense of sight seems to have primacy over the other senses. *Describere,* the Latin root for describe, even means "to sketch or copy." In general people rely more on the sense of sight than on the other senses. Certainly our vocabulary for reporting what we see is larger and more varied than our vocabulary for reporting any other sense impression.

For the other senses, quite a few nouns and verbs designate sounds; a smaller number of nouns, but few verbs, describe smells; and very few nouns or verbs convey touch and taste. Furthermore, these nonvisual sensations do not invite as much naming as sights do because they are not readily divided into constituent features. For example, we have many names to describe the visible features of a car, but few to describe the sounds a car makes. Nevertheless, writers detail the qualities and attributes of nonvisual sensations—the loudness or tinniness or rumble of an engine, for instance.

The sense of sight
When people describe what they see, they identify the objects in their field of vision. As the following passages illustrate, these objects may include animate as well as inanimate things and their features. Details may range from words delineating appearance to those evaluating it.

The first selection, by Henry David Thoreau, depicts a nature scene with a lot of activity; the second passage, by Ernest Hemingway, describes F. Scott Fitzgerald's face.

> As I sit at my window this summer afternoon, hawks are circling about my clearing; the tantivy of wild pigeons, flying by twos and threes athwart my view, or perching restless on the white pine boughs behind my house, gives a voice to the air; a fish hawk dimples the glassy surface of the pond and brings up a fish; a mink steals out of the marsh before my door and seizes a frog by the shore; the sedge is bending under the weight of the reed-birds flitting hither and thither. . . .   Henry David Thoreau, *Walden*

> Scott was a man then who looked like a boy with a face between handsome and pretty. He had very fair wavy hair, a high forehead, excited and friendly eyes and a delicate long-lipped Irish mouth that, on a girl, would have been the mouth of a beauty. His chin was well built and he had good ears and a handsome, almost beautiful, unmarked nose.   Ernest Hemingway, *A Moveable Feast*

EXERCISE 14.8
Using Hemingway's description of Fitzgerald's face as a model, write a few sentences describing someone's face. Do not rely on memory for this exercise: describe someone who is before you as you write. You can even look in the mirror and describe your own face.

When you are done, read what you have written and assess the impression it gives of the person. If you feel it gives a weak or contradictory impression, revise your description. Then, in a sentence or two, explain what impression it gives and why you think it gives this impression rather than another.

The sense of hearing
In reporting auditory impressions, writers seldom name the objects from which the sounds come without also naming the sounds themselves: the murmur of a voice, the rustle of the wind, the squeak of a hinge, the sputter of an engine. *Onomatopoeia* is the term for names of sounds that echo the sounds themselves: *squeak, murmur, hiss, boom, tinkle, twang, jangle, rasp.* Sometimes writers make up words like *plink, chirr, sweesh-crack-boom,* and *cara-wong* to imitate sounds they wish to describe. Qualitative words like

powerful and *rich* as well as relative terms like *loud* and *low* often specify sounds further. Detailing of sounds sometimes involves the technique called *synesthesia*, applying words commonly used to describe one sense to another, such as describing sounds as *sharp* and *soft*.

To write about the sound of Yosemite Falls, John Muir uses all these naming and describing techniques. He also uses comparison when he refers metaphorically to the water's powerful "voice":

> This noble fall has far the richest, as well as the most powerful, voice of all the falls of the Valley, its tones varying from the sharp hiss and rustle of the wind in the glossy leaves of the live oaks and the soft, sifting, hushing tones of the pines, to the loudest rush and roar of storm winds and thunder among the crags of the summit peaks. The low bass, booming, reverberating tones, heard under favorable circumstances five or six miles away, are formed by the dashing and exploding of heavy masses mixed with air upon two projecting ledges on the face of the cliff, the one on which we are standing and another about 200 feet above it. The torrent of massive comets is continuous at time of high water, while the explosive, booming notes are wildly intermittent, because, unless influenced by the wind, most of the heavier masses shoot out from the face of the precipice, and pass the ledges upon which at other times they are exploded. John Muir, *The Story of My Boyhood and Youth*

The following passage describes the Doppler effect, the rise and fall of sound as something loud passes quickly by. The author uses a few distinct nouns to name and discriminate kinds of sound and also uses modifiers to detail gradations in sound. But his most interesting technique here is the way he suddenly shifts senses—from hearing to touch—when the car passes by.

> At first a faint sighing, like wind in the tops of distant trees. Then the birth of another sound within the sigh, a sharper sound, very faint but growing steadily, a kind of whine, first heard as a pinpoint in the higher registers, building rapidly to a full hum across the spectrum, growing louder and louder, and then (at the very instant a shock wave of air slammed softly across my shoulders) overtaking the sigh, reversing itself, and plunging down the scale of a steady hum. I watched the black car racing away ahead of me. Frank Conroy, *Stop-time*

EXERCISE 14.9

Find a noisy spot—a restaurant, a football game, a nursery school, a laundry room—where you can perch for a half hour or so. Listen attentively to the sounds of the place and make notes about what you hear. Then, write a paragraph describing the place through its sounds.

When you are done, read your description. In a sentence or two, sum up what impression it gives and why you think it gives this particular impression. If it does not give a strong impression, you may want to revise your paragraph before writing your analysis.

EXERCISE 14.10

George Orwell identifies various sounds in "A Hanging," printed in Chapter 2. Read the essay quickly, looking for each time he names a sound. Notice the contrast between the moments of noise and the moments of silence. How do the sounds contribute to the impact this story has on you?

The sense of smell   The English language has a meager stock of words to express the sense of smell. In addition to the word *smell*, only about ten commonly used nouns name this sensation: *odor, scent, vapor, aroma, fragrance, perfume, bouquet, stench, stink.* Although there are other, rarer words like *fetor* and *effuvium*, writers tend not to use them, probably for fear their readers will not know them. Few verbs describe receiving or sending odors—*smell, sniff, waft*—but a fair number of detailing adjectives are available: *redolent, pungent, aromatic, perfumed, stinking, musty, rancid, putrid, rank, foul, acrid, sweet,* and *cloying*.

In the next passage, Conroy uses comparing in addition to naming and detailing. Notice how he describes the effect the odor has on him:

> The perfume of the flowers rushed into my brain. A lush aroma, thick with sweetness, thick as blood, and spiced with the clear acid of tropical greenery. My heart pounded like a drowning swimmer's as the perfume took me over, pouring into my lungs like ambrosial soup.   Frank Conroy, *Stop-time*

In reporting smells, naming the objects from which they come can also be very suggestive:

> It is the smells of the school that I remember best; the sour smell of the oil they rubbed the desks with; the classroom smell of chalk dust and old pulled-down maps; the smell of fuller's earth scattered in wide arcs along the corridors, ahead of the pushbrooms that formed fat kittens out of the dirt tracked daily in by some 300 pairs of feet; the smell of a master's unlighted pipe; the smell that would periodically drift through the school late in the morning to tell us that we were going to have corned beef and cabbage for lunch; the steamy, chlorinated smell of the indoor pool; the smell of the gym, which was a mixture of wintergreen oil and sneakers.   Stephen Birmingham, "New England Prep School"

EXERCISE 14.11

Go someplace with noticeable, distinctive smells where you can stay for ten or fifteen minutes. You may choose an eating place (a cafeteria, a donut shop, a cafe), a place where something is being manufactured (a saw mill, a bakery, a pizza parlor), or some other place that has distinctive odors (a fishing dock, a garden, a locker room). Take notes while you are there on what you smell, and then write a paragraph describing the place through its smells.

The sense of touch   Writers describing the sense of touch tend not to name the sensation directly or even to report the act of feeling. Probably this omission occurs because only a few nouns and verbs name tactile sensations besides words like *touch, feeling, tickle, brush, scratch, sting, itch, tingle*. Nevertheless, a large stock of words describe temperature *(hot, warm, mild, tepid, cold, arctic)*, moisture content *(wet, dry, sticky, oily, greasy, moist, papery, crisp)*, texture *(gritty, silky, smooth, crinkled, coarse, soft, sharp, leathery)*, and weight *(heavy, light, ponderous, buoyant, feathery)*. Read the following passages with an eye for descriptions of touch.

> The midmorning sun was deceitfully mild and the wind had no weight on my skin. Arkansas summer mornings have a feathering effect on stone reality.   Maya Angelou, *Gather Together in My Name*

> It was an ordeal for me to walk the hills in the dead of summer for then they were parched and dry and offered no shade from the hot sun and no springs or creeks where thirst could be quenched.   William O. Douglas, *Go East, Young Man*

EXERCISE 14.12
Briefly describe the feel of a cold shower, a wool sweater, an autumn breeze, a raw steak, bare feet on hot sand, or any other tactile sensation you might think of. Then explain what impression your description makes and why you think it makes this particular impression.

EXERCISE 14.13
In his profile of a funeral home in Chapter 4, notice how student Brian Cable uses a description of the sense of touch in his conclusion (paragraph 28). What is the effect of this description on your overall response to Cable's profile?

The sense of taste   Other than *taste, savor,* and *flavor,* few words name the gustatory sensations directly. Certain words do distinguish among the four types of taste—*sweet (saccharine, sugary, cloying); sour (acidic, tart); bitter (acrid, biting); salty (briny, brackish),* while several other words describe specific tastes *(piquant, spicy, pungent, peppery, savory,* and *toothsome).*

In addition to these words, the names of objects tasted and other details may indicate the intensity and quality of a taste. Notice Hemingway's descriptive technique in the following selection.

> As I ate the oysters with their strong taste of the sea and their faint metallic taste that the cold wine washed away, leaving only the sea taste and the succulent texture, and as I drank their cold liquid from each shell and washed

it down with the crispy taste of the wine, I lost the empty feeling and began to be happy and to make plans.   Ernest Hemingway, *A Moveable Feast*

Possibly more than any other sense, taste is closely associated with other senses. In the next passage James Agee provides a rich context of sense impressions to describe a meal served in a poor, rural home:

> The biscuits are large and shapeless, not cut round, and are pale, not tanned, and are dusty with flour. They taste of flour and soda and damp salt and fill the mouth stickily. They are better with butter, and still better with butter and jam. The butter is pallid, soft, and unsalted, about the texture of cold-cream; it seems to taste delicately of wood and wet cloth, and it tastes "weak." The jam is loose, of little berries, full of light raspings of the tongue; it tastes a deep sweet purple tepidly watered, with a very faint sheen of a sourness as of iron. Field peas are olive-brown, the shape of lentils, about twice the size. Their taste is a cross between lentils and boiled beans; their broth is bright with seasoning of pork, and of this also they taste. The broth is soaked up in bread. The meat is a bacon, granular with salt, soaked in the grease of its frying: there is very little lean meat in it. What there is is nearly as tough as rind; the rest is pure salted stringy fat. The eggs taste of pork too. They are fried in it on both sides until none of the broken yolk runs, are heavily salted and peppered while they fry, so that they come to table nearly black, very heavy, rinded with crispness, nearly as dense as steaks. Of milk I hardly know how to say; it is skimmed, blue-lighted; to a city palate its warmth and odor are somehow dirty and at the same time vital, a little as if one were drinking blood. There is even in so clean a household as this an odor of pork, of sweat, so subtle it seems to get into the very metal of the cooking-pans beyond any removal of scrubbing . . . and it seems to be this odor, and a sort of wateriness and discouraged tepidity, which combine to make the food seem unclean, sticky, and sallow with some invisible sort of disease.   James Agee, *Let Us Now Praise Famous Men*

EXERCISE 14.14

Describe the taste of a particular food or meal as Agee does in the preceding passage. Then explain what impression your description makes and why you think it makes this particular impression.

CREATING A DOMINANT IMPRESSION

The most effective description creates a dominant impression, a mood or atmosphere that reinforces the writer's purpose. In particular, writers attempt to create a dominant impression when they describe a place in order to set a *scene* and its atmosphere. Naming, detailing, and comparing—all the choices about what to include and what to call things—come together to create this effect, as the following passage by Mary McCarthy illustrates. Notice that McCarthy directly states the idea she is trying to convey in the last sentence, the paragraph's topic sentence.

> Whenever we children came to stay at my grandmother's house, we were put to sleep in the sewing room, a bleak, shabby, utilitarian rectangle, more office than bedroom, more attic than office, that played to the hierarchy of chambers the role of a poor relation. It was a room seldom entered by the other members of the family, seldom swept by the maid, a room without pride; the old sewing machine, some cast-off chairs, a shadeless lamp, rolls of wrapping paper, piles of pins, and remnants of material united with the iron folding cots put out for our use and the bare floor boards to give an impression of intense and ruthless temporality. Thin, white spreads, of the kind used in hospitals and charity institutions, and naked blinds at the windows reminded us of our orphaned condition and of the ephemeral character of our visit; there was nothing here to encourage us to consider this our home.   Mary McCarthy, *Memories of a Catholic Girlhood*

Everything in the room made McCarthy and her brothers feel unwanted, discarded, orphaned. The room itself is described in terms applicable to the children. (Like them it "played to the hierarchy of chambers the role of a poor relation.") The objects she names, together with their distinguishing details—"cast-off chairs," "shadeless lamp," "iron folding cots," "bare floor boards," "naked blinds"—contribute to this overall impression, thus enabling McCarthy to convey her purpose to her readers.

Writers sometimes comment directly during their descriptions. McCarthy, for instance, states that the sewing room gave "an impression of intense and ruthless temporality," everything serving to remind the children that they were orphans and did not live there. Often, however, writers want description to speak for itself. They *show* rather than tell, letting the descriptive language evoke the impression by itself. Such is the case in the following description by George Orwell of a room for hire:

> Hanging from the ceiling there was a heavy glass chandelier on which the dust was so thick that it was like fur. And covering most of one wall there was a huge hideous piece of junk, something between a sideboard and a hall-stand, with lots of carving and little drawers and strips of looking-glass, and there was a once-gaudy carpet ringed by the slop-pails of years, and two gilt chairs with burst seats, and one of those old-fashioned armchairs which you slide off when you try to sit on them. The room had been turned into a bedroom by thrusting four squalid beds in among the wreckage. George Orwell, *The Road to Wigan Pier*

EXERCISE 14.15

Write a paragraph or two describing your bedroom or some other room where you have spent a lot of time. Describe the room in a way that conveys a strong mood or atmosphere. Then write a few sentences describing the dominant impression you want your description to make, explaining your purpose in describing the room this way and the techniques you used.

EXERCISE 14.16
Look at Orwell's account of a hanging in Chapter 2. Read the piece quickly, noting how Orwell describes the scene. What dominant impression does his description give? How does the scene reinforce the story?

ASSUMING A VANTAGE POINT

Writing effectively about a scene requires taking a vantage point—that is, selecting the point or position from which to describe the scene. By presenting objects and features from a particular vantage point, the writer creates a perspective by which readers can enter the scene.

A stationary vantage point

A writer of description who stays still assumes a fixed or stationary vantage point. In the following passage, the author takes a position in a subway station and describes what he sees without moving around the station:

Standing in a subway station, I began to appreciate the place—almost to enjoy it. First of all, I looked at the lighting: a row of meager electric bulbs, unscreened, yellow, and coated with filth, stretched toward the black mouth of the tunnel, as though it were a bolt hole in an abandoned coal mine. Then I lingered, with zest, on the walls and ceiling: lavatory tiles which had been white about fifty years ago, and were now encrusted with soot, coated with the remains of a dirty liquid which might be either atmospheric humidity mingled with smog or the result of a perfunctory attempt to clean them with cold water; and, above them, gloomy vaulting from which dingy paint was peeling off like scabs from an old wound, sick black paint leaving a leprous white subsurface. Beneath my feet, the floor was a nauseating dark brown with black stains upon it which might be stale oil or dry chewing gum or some worse defilement; it looked like the hallway of a condemned slum building. Then my eye traveled to the tracks, where two lines of glittering steel—the only positively clean objects in the whole place—ran out of darkness into darkness above an unspeakable mass of congealed oil, puddles of dubious liquid, and a mishmash of old cigarette packets, mutilated and filthy newspapers, and the debris that filtered down from the street above through a barred grating in the roof. As I looked up toward the sunlight, I could see more debris sifting slowly downward, and making an abominable pattern in the slanting beam of dirt-laden sunlight. I was going on to relish more features of this unique scene: such as the advertisement posters on the walls—here a text from the Bible, there a half-naked girl, here a woman wearing a hat consisting of a hen sitting on a nest full of eggs, and there a pair of girl's legs walking up the keys of a cash register—all scribbled over with unknown names and well-known obscenities in black crayon and red lipstick; but then my train came in at last. . . .   Gilbert Highet, "The Subway Station"

Although Highet stays still, he shifts his field of vision. He uses these shifts to order the description of what he sees, looking first at the lights, then at the walls and ceilings, at the floor, at the tracks, toward the sunlight, and finally at the posters on the wall. Although Highet seems to describe objects as they catch his attention, writers sometimes give details in a more orderly pattern—for example, from left to right, top to bottom, big to small.

A moving point of view   Instead of remaining fixed in one spot, a writer may move through a scene. Such is the case with the next author, who describes what he sees as he drives along a highway:

The highway, without warning, rolled off the plateau of green pastures and entered a wooded and rocky gorge; down, down, precipitously down to the Kentucky River. Along the north slope, man-high columns of ice clung to the limestone. The road dropped deeper until it crossed the river at Brooklyn Bridge. The gorge, hidden in the table and and wholly unexpected, was the Palisades. At the bottom lay only enough ground for the river and a narrow strip of willow-rimmed.

Houses on stilts and a few doublewides rose from the damp flats like toadstools. Next to one mobile home was a partly built steel boat longer than the trailer.   William Least Heat Moon, *Blue Highways*

Notice how the author uses spatial transitions like *down, along, from,* and *next* to orient his readers to his movements. An extended discussion of transitions and a list of transitions commonly used to indicate spatial relations are in Chapter 12: Cueing the Reader.

Combined vantage points   Writers sometimes use more than one stationary vantage point or combine stationary and moving vantage points. In these cases, the important thing is to orient the readers to any change in position.

In the next selection, Willie Morris begins with a moving vantage point and then uses several stationary points.

One walked up the three flights through several padlocked doors, often past the garbage which the landlords had neglected to remove for two or three days. Once inside our place, things were not bad at all. There was a big front room with an old floor, a little alcove for a study, and to the back a short corridor opening up into a tiny bedroom for my son and a larger bedroom in the back. The kitchen was in the back bedroom. I had not been able to find a view of an extensive body of water at popular prices, but from the back window, about forty-yards out, there *was* a vista of a big tank, part of some manufacturing installation in the building under it, and the tank constantly bubbled with some unidentified greenish substance. From this window one could see the tarred rooftops of the surrounding buildings, and off to the right a quiet stretch of God's earth, this being the parking lot next door.   Willie Morris, *North Toward Home*

EXERCISE 14.17

Look back at the paragraph you wrote for Exercise 14.1. What vantage point did you take in that description? Is your vantage point always clear? If you can improve it, revise the paragraph.

EXERCISE 14.18

In Chapter 8, Jane Greer writes in praise of the American Midwest. Note her encompassing description of the region in paragraph 9 of the selection. What vantage point or points does she use here? What is the effect of her use of vantage point in this description?

Illustrating

In order to explain or support any ideas or assertions, writers need to move beyond generalities and provide readers with specific, detailed information. One way of doing this is through *illustration,* which comes from the Latin *illustrare,* meaning "to illuminate or shed light on." Like pictorial illustrations, written illustrations bring focus and clarity to what may not be obvious or easy to imagine. They help writers go beyond the simple statement of an idea to communicating an understanding of the ideas to readers.

This chapter looks closely at two forms of illustration: examples and lists. Each can help make your writing more specific, more informative, and more memorable. Other forms of illustration, useful in persuasive writing, are discussed in Chapter 19: Arguing.

EXAMPLES

An example is the basic form of illustration. Essentially it consists of a general statement with a few sentences of more detailed explanation and elaboration. Sometimes the example is specifically signaled by the phrase *for example* or *for instance.*

Here are the opening paragraphs of a chapter on lenses from one of Annie Dillard's books:

> You get used to looking through lenses; it is an acquired skill. When you first look through binoculars, for instance, you can't see a thing. You look at the inside of the barrel; you blink and watch your eyelashes; you play with the focus knob till one eye is purblind.
>
> The microscope is even worse. You are supposed to keep both eyes open as you look through its single eyepiece. I spent my childhood in Pittsburgh trying to master this trick: seeing through one eye, with both eyes open. The microscope also teaches you to move your hands wrong, to shove the glass slide to the right if you are following a creature who is swimming off to the left—as if you were operating a tiller, or backing a trailer, or performing any other of those paradoxical maneuvers which require either sure instincts or a grasp of elementary physics, neither of which I possess.
> Annie Dillard, *Teaching a Stone to Talk*

15

The first sentence (a topic sentence) introduces the two examples that follow. Dillard develops the topic by inviting readers to remember what it was like to use binoculars and microscopes for the first time. She concentrates on the actions of viewers—blinking, playing with the knob, keeping both eyes open, moving the glass slide.

This second sample of illustration by example is from Mark Twain. There are two examples here, each demonstrating a different way that the Mississippi River keeps shifting its location. Twain's strategy is to use the consequences of each type of shift to develop the example.

The Mississippi is remarkable in still another way—its disposition to make prodigious jumps by cutting through narrow necks of land, and thus straightening and shortening itself. More than once it has shortened itself thirty miles at a single jump! These cutoffs have had curious effects: they have thrown several river towns out into the rural districts, and built up sand bars and forests in front of them. The town of Delta used to be three miles below Vicksburg: a recent cutoff has radically changed the position, and Delta is now *two miles above* Vicksburg.

Both of these river towns have been retired to the country by that cutoff. A cutoff plays havoc with boundary lines and jurisdictions: for instance, a man is living in the State of Mississippi today, a cutoff occurs tonight, and tomorrow the man finds himself and his land over on the other side of the river, within the boundaries and subject to the laws of the State of Louisiana! Such a thing, happening in the upper river in the old times, could have transferred a slave from Missouri to Illinois and made a free man of him.

The Mississippi does not alter its locality by cutoffs alone: it is always changing its habitat *bodily*—is always moving bodily *sidewise*. At Hard Times, La., the river is two miles west of the region it used to occupy. As a result, the original *site* of that settlement is not now in Louisiana at all, but on the other side of the river, in the State of Mississippi. *Nearly the whole of that one thousand three hundred miles of old Mississippi River which La Salle floated down in his canoes, two hundred years ago, is good solid dry ground now.* The river lies to the right of it, in places, and to the left of it in other places.

Although the Mississippi's mud builds land but slowly, down at the mouth, where the Gulf's billows interfere with its work, it builds fast enough in better protected regions higher up: for instance, Prophet's Island contained one thous⸺ J five hundred acres of land thirty years ago; since then the river has added seven hundred acres to it.

But enough of these examples of the mighty stream's eccentricities for the present—I will give a few more of them further along in the book.
Mark Twain, *Life on the Mississippi*

Like Dillard, Twain develops a single topic with two examples. A new paragraph clearly signals the beginning of the second example in both selections. Both Dillard and Twain rely on definition and division as the basis for illustration. (See Chapter 16: Defining and Chapter 17: Classifying, for techniques of definition and division.) Dillard divides her topic into binoculars and microscopes, but she does not define anything because she assumes readers know what binoculars and microscopes are. Twain divides his topic into cutoffs and sidewise shifts, and he also defines each of these river maneuvers for us. The examples in each case provide specific illustration of the writer's general statement.

Some examples are not quite so tidy as these pieces from Dillard and Twain. Here is a much less symmetrical example from John McPhee:

Among outdoor-equipment suppliers in the United States, Bean's is more or less the source pond—a business begun in 1912, when the Maine Hunting Shoe was developed by a noted woodsman, Leon Leonwood Bean. Boots with leather tops and rubber bottoms, they are of considerable utility in the quagmires of the north woods, and Bean's still sells them—eighty-eight thousand pairs a year. Bean's-boots simulacra are in the mail-order catalogues of nearly all the other outdoor suppliers in the country. Adding item after item over the years, Bean, who died in 1967, built a national reputation. In recent times, the company has further expanded, somewhat disturbingly, to become a kind of balsam-scented department store, but, for all its Japanese pot holders and Seventh Avenue jumpers, it still has truly serviceable woods equipment in sufficient variety to hold position in the field. If you travel in bush Alaska, you find Bean's catalogues in cabin after cabin there, and Bean's boots and garments on the people. Most transactions are by mail, but the home store, in Freeport, in Cumberland County, is open twenty-four hours a day seven days a week. I know people who have gone shopping at Bean's at four o'clock in the morning and have reported themselves to have been by no means the only customers there. The store is a rampant mutation of New England connective architecture—an awkward, naïve building, seeming to consist of many wooden boxes stacked atop one another and held together by steel exterior trusses. There is nothing naïve about the cash register. Sometimes it is necessary to go off to the woods for indefinite periods to recover from a visit to Bean's. John Kauffmann and I have stopped there at nine in the morning, fanned out for boots, mink oil, monoculars, folding scissors, Sven saws, fishing gear, wool shirts, met at noon by the windproof-match bin, gone out to lunch (lobsters—four—on the wharf at South Freeport), and returned to Bean's for a good part of the afternoon. Saltonstall, in his travels, makes regular visits to Bean's and, among trusted friends, is not too shy to admit it.   John McPhee, *Giving Good Weight*

This selection works by a strategy that could be called *additional comment*. The many examples are organized under a general topic sentence—L. L. Bean's outdoor equipment business is the best known in the country—but some examples are developed more fully than others. The examples shift rapidly across quite varied topics: history of the business, initial products, comparison to department stores, catalogues in Alaska, store operation, its architecture, a typical shopping trip there. And yet, despite all this rapid shifting, the selection is coherent because each new group of examples flows naturally from the one that precedes it.

The preceding selections illustrate very well how flexible this writing strategy is. Watch how writers vary the strategy of illustration by examples. Experiment with it yourself. Be guided by your readers' needs: readers respond with interest to a dense pattern of detailed examples, but they can become confused and lose interest if the examples are not grouped logically or do not seem pertinently related to the general idea.

EXERCISE 15.1

Write a one- or two-sentence general statement based on one of the following topics. Then illustrate the statement with one or two developed examples. Avoid the temptation to keep restating the general statement. Go immediately to your first example. Direct your illustration to an audience of other students in your class.

a change in your hometown
a popular trend (music, movies, TV)
the image of a particular group of people projected by advertising
an important quality of leadership
a useless modern invention

EXERCISE 15.2

Analyze the following paragraphs from selections in Part I. For each paragraph, describe how the writer develops the example. Also identify the purpose of the example within the selection as a whole. What does it contribute?

Chapter 2, "The Lost Weekend," Linda Ellerbee, paragraph 7
Chapter 4, "Inside the Brain," David Noonan, paragraphs 4 and 21
Chapter 5, "Tracing a Killer," Anastasia Toufexis, paragraphs 5 and 7
Chapter 8, "The Treasure of the Sierra Madre," James Agee, paragraph 5

Listing, a special form of illustration, is a writing strategy used in all types of writing. Poets, novelists, reporters, and scientists all use it to make their ideas concrete, informative, and memorable. Listing involves simply the quick accumulation of specific examples without taking time to develop any of them. It looks easy, but choosing the items for the list can be tricky. They need to suggest the range and variety of the scene or topic, and they need to create a single dominant impression.

One of John McPhee's recent pieces, "Giving Good Weight," reports what he learned about fresh fruit and vegetable markets in New York City. As part of his research he visited farms, and he also worked at the markets, weighing and selling vegetables. Very early in this long profile appears a list of people he observed at a Brooklyn farmers' market:

> The people, in their throngs, are the most varied we see—or that anyone is likely to see in one place west of Suez. This intersection is the hub if not the heart of Brooklyn, where numerous streets converge, and where Fourth Avenue comes plowing into the Flatbush-Atlantic plane. It is also a nexus of the race. "Weigh these, please." "Will you please weigh these?" Greeks. Italians. Russians. Finns. Haitians. Puerto Ricans. Nubians. Muslim women in veils of shocking pink. Sunnis in total black. Women in hiking shorts, with babies in their backpacks. Young Connecticut-looking pantssuit women. Their hair hangs long and as soft as cornsilk. There are country Jamaicans, in loose dresses, bandannas tight around their heads. "Fifty cents? Yes, dahling. Come on a sweetheart, mon." there are Jews by the minyan, Jews of all persuasions—white-bearded, black-bearded, split-bearded Jews. Down off Park Slope and Cobble Hill come the neobohemians, out of the money and into the arts. "Will you weigh this tomato, please?" And meantime let us discuss theatre, books, environmental impacts. Maybe half the crowd are men—men in cool Haspel cords and regimental ties, men in lipstick, men with blue eyelids. Corporate-echelon pinstripe men. Their silvered hair is perfect in coif; it appears to have been audited. Easygoing old neighborhood men with their shirts hanging open in the summer heat are walking galleries of abdominal and thoracic scars—Brooklyn Jewish Hospital's bastings and tackings. (They do good work there.)   John McPhee, *Giving Good Weight*

Notice how well this engaging list illustrates the opening general statement. The selection is a particularly strong example of the way general statements relate to specific illustrative details. This relationship can be stated as a working rule for writers: use many details and very few general statements. McPhee might have described the market as follows:

> The people are the most varied we see. They come from a great many different places in the city. In their accents and dress we get a sense of their

different origins. They talk about many things. Some dress informally, and some dress formally. They are all ages.

In other words, he might have given all general statements. Instead, he gives us a wide variety of authentic details. As you can see, listing is a powerful illustrator of generalities.

EXERCISE 15.3

Choose some busy activity you can observe conveniently. Make a general statement about the activity, and then illustrate it with a list of visual details you see at the scene of the activity. Select and present the list so that it conveys a dominant impression of the activity.

EXERCISE 15.4

Analyze the lists in the following selections from Part I. For each list, consider these questions: How long is the list? What kinds of items does it include? What dominant impression does it give? What is the purpose of the list within the whole selection?

Chapter 3, "Martha," Kate Simon, paragraph 1
Chapter 3, "My Parents," Richard Rodriguez, paragraphs 12 and 13
Chapter 4, "The Pinball Philosophy," John McPhee, paragraph 7
Chapter 8, "The Midwest: Close to Heaven," Jane Greer, paragraph 14

Defining

Defining is an essential strategy for all kinds of writing. Autobiographers, for example, must occasionally define objects, conditions, events, and activities for readers likely to be unfamiliar with particular terms. The following example (with definitions underlined) is from Chapter 3 on personal writing in Part I.

> My father's hands are grotesque. He suffers from psoriasis, <u>a chronic skin disease that covers his massive, thick hands with scaly, reddish patches that periodically flake off, sending tiny pieces of dead skin sailing to the ground.</u>
> Jan Gray, "Father"

Writers sharing information or explaining how to do something must very often define important terms for readers who are unfamiliar with the subject. This example comes from the selection by Isaac Asimov in Chapter 5.

> The trouble is, though, that <u>if, for any reason, the body has more cholesterol than it needs, there is a tendency to get rid of it by storing it on the inner surface of the blood vessels—especially the coronary vessels that feed the heart.</u> This is "atherosclerosis,". . .   Isaac Asimov, "Cholesterol"

To convince readers of a position or an evaluation or to move readers to take action on a proposal, a writer must often define concepts important to an argument. This example comes from Chapter 6.

> Social acceptability is <u>a function of which group controls society and to what extent minority voices can influence the spectrum of opinion.</u>   Kristin A. Goss, "Taking a Stand Against Sexism"

As these examples illustrate, there are many kinds of definitions and many forms that they take. This chapter illustrates the major kinds and forms of definitions, beginning with those that we find in dictionaries and other reference sources. After dictionary definitions come various forms of sentence definition. This type of definition, the most common form in writing, relies on various sentence patterns to provide concise definitions. Following this are illustrations of multi-sentence extended definitions, including definition by etymology, or word history, and by stipulation.

16

DICTIONARY DEFINITIONS

The most familiar source of definitions is the dictionary, where words are defined briefly with other words. In a short space, dictionaries tell us a lot about words: what they mean, how they are pronounced, how they look in context in a sample phrase or clause, where they originated, what forms they take as they function differently in sentences. Here is an example from *The American Heritage Dictionary:*

definition ——————————————————

part of speech ——————————————

syllabification ——————————————

pronunciation ——————————————

in-trep-id (ĭn-trĕp'ĭd) *adj.* Marked by reso-

illustrative use ——————————————

lute courage; fearless and bold: *an intrepid*

etymology ——————————————

mountaineer. [Fr. *intrépule* < Lat. *intrepidus*

: *in-,* not + *trepidus,* alarmed.] —in'tre-pid'i-

ty (-trə-pĭd'ĭ-tē), in-trep'id-ness *n.* —in-

other forms ——————————————

trep'id-ly *adv.*

Other dictionary entries may include still more information. For example, if a word has more than one meaning, all of its meanings will be presented. From the context in which you read or hear the word, you can nearly always tell which meaning applies.

A good dictionary is an essential part of your equipment as a college student. It should always be within reach when you are reading so that you can look up unfamiliar words in order to understand what you read and to expand your vocabulary. When you are writing, you can use a dictionary to check spellings and the correct forms of words as well as to make sure of the meanings of words you might not have used before.

You may want to ask your instructor for advice about which dictionary to buy in your college bookstore. A good current dictionary like *The American Heritage Dictionary* or *Webster's New Collegiate Dictionary* is most useful.

461

Though a hardback dictionary version will cost two or three times more than a paperback, it will be a sound and relatively inexpensive investment (about fifteen dollars). Hardback dictionaries usually have the advantages of more entries, fuller entries, larger type, and a thumb index.

To present a great deal of information in a small space, dictionaries have to rely on many abbreviations, codes, and symbols. These differ somewhat from one dictionary to the next, but you can learn the system of abbreviations in your dictionary by reading the front matter carefully. You will also find a range of interesting topics and lists in the front and end matter of some dictionaries: articles on usage and language history, reviews of punctuation rules, biographical entries, geographical entries, and lists of colleges and universities.

Any dictionary you are likely to buy for desk use would be an *abridged* dictionary, which does not include many technical or obsolete words. Much larger *unabridged* dictionaries contain every known current and obsolete word in the language. Two unabridged dictionaries are preeminent: *Oxford English Dictionary* and *Webster's Third New International Dictionary,* the latter the standard reference for American English. Libraries have these impressive dictionaries available for specialized use.

A special dictionary called a *thesaurus* can be useful for a writer, but only if it is used judiciously. It is a dictionary of synonyms, words with identical or very similar meanings. The motive for searching out synonyms should be to use just the right word, not to impress readers. Straining to impress readers with unusual words will more often than not lead to the embarrassing use of a word in the wrong context.

Here is an example from *Roget's II, The New Thesaurus.* It offers alternatives to *brave,* used as an adjective. Among the synonyms for *brave* is *intrepid,* noted in the dictionary definition on the preceding page.

brave *adjective*
Having or showing courage: *a brave effort to rescue the drowning child.* **Syns:** audacious, bold, courageous, dauntless, doughty, fearless, fortitudinous, gallant, game, gutsy (*Informal*), gutty, heroic, intrepid, mettlesome, plucky, stout, stouthearted, unafraid, undaunted, valiant, valorous.

Some thesauri also offer antonyms, words opposite in meaning to the word of interest. (An antonym of *brave,* for example, would be *cowardly.*)

The great limitation of a thesaurus is that it does not tell you which synonym is most appropriate for a particular writing situation. *Brave* and *intrepid* are not simply interchangeable. Which word you might use would depend on your readers, your purpose, your subject, and the exact meaning you hoped to convey with the sentence in which the word appears. In the preceding list, the only clue to appropriateness is the information that *gutsy* is informal. Checking each word in a good dictionary would be necessary to select the most appropriate word from a set such as the preceding one. Because of this troublesome limitation, a thesaurus is most useful in reminding you of a synonym whose shades of meaning you are already closely familiar with.

A solution to the limitations of a thesaurus is a dictionary of synonyms with words in a set like the preceding one but with each synonym defined, contrasted, and illustrated with quotations. An excellent source is *Webster's New Dictionary of Synonyms,* which provides enough information to let you make an appropriate choice among words with similar meanings. Your college bookstore will have this book for about the cost of a hardback dictionary. This volume's entry for *brave,* for example, notes eleven common synonyms for *brave* as an adjective, ranging from *courageous* to *audacious.* Each synonym is defined and then quoted in context from a respected source, as this portion of the entry shows:

brave *adj* **Brave, courageous, unafraid, fearless, intrepid, valiant, valorous, dauntless, undaunted, doughty, bold, audacious** are comparable when they mean having or showing no fear when faced with something dangerous, difficult, or unknown. **Brave** usually indicates lack of fear in alarming or difficult circumstances rather than a temperamental liking for danger ⟨the *brave* soldier goes to meet Death, and meets him without a shudder—*Trollope*⟩ ⟨he would send an explosion ship into the harbor . . . a *brave* crew would take her in at night, right up against the city, would light the fuses, and try to escape—*Forester*⟩ **Courageous** implies stouthearted resolution in contemplating or facing danger and may suggest a temperamental readiness to meet dangers or difficulties ⟨I am afraid . . . because I do not wish to die. But my spirit masters the trembling flesh and the qualms of the mind. I am more than brave, I am *courageous*—*London*⟩ ⟨a man is *courageous* when he does things which others might fail to do owing to fear—

Russell⟩ **Unafraid** simply indicates lack of fright or fear whether because of a courageous nature or because no cause for fear is present ⟨enjoy their homes *unafraid* of violent intrusion—*MacArthur*⟩ ⟨a young, daring, and creative people—a people *unafraid* of change—*MacLeish*⟩ **Fearless** may indicate lack of fear, or it may be more positive and suggest undismayed resolution ⟨joyous we too launch out on trackless seas, *fearless* for unknown shores—*Whitman*⟩ ⟨he gives always the impression of *fearless* sincerity . . . one always feels that he is ready to say bluntly what every one else is afraid to say—*T. S. Eliot*⟩ **Intrepid** suggests either daring in meeting danger or fortitude in enduring it ⟨with the *intrepid* woman who was his wife, and a few natives, he landed there, and set about building a house and clearing the scrub—*Maugham*⟩ ⟨the *intrepid* guardians of the place, hourly exposed to death, with famine worn, and suffering under many a perilous wound—*Wordsworth*⟩

This entry shows that *brave* and *intrepid* are very close in meaning, but that *intrepid* would be the better choice if you wanted to suggest "daring in meeting danger" rather than "lack of fear" in facing danger when it comes. You might call a person setting off on a solo sea voyage in a small craft an *intrepid sailor,* but a flight attendant who faced down a potential hijacker is better described as brave.

To summarize our advice about dictionaries: buy a respected hardback dictionary for looking up the meanings of new words you encounter and for checking spellings and correct usage. Buy an inexpensive paperback thesaurus for a quick look at sets of synonyms. Buy a respected hardback dictionary of synonyms in order to discriminate among synonyms and pick the most appropriate word. These resources will enable you to write essays with correct spellings and verb forms and using just the right words.

SENTENCE DEFINITIONS

Every field of study and every institution and activity has its own unique concepts and terms. Coming to a new area for the first time, a participant or a reader is often baffled by the many unfamiliar names for objects and activities. In college, a basic course in a field often seems like an entire course in definitions of new terms. In the same way, a sport like sailing requires newcomers to learn much specialized terminology. In such cases, writers of textbooks and sailing manuals rely on brief sentence definitions, involving a variety of sentence strategies.

Following are some sentence strategies from one widely used introductory college biology text, Sylvia Mader's *Inquiry into Life*. These examples illustrate some of the sentence strategies an author may use to name and define terms for readers. Coming from one book, these examples show how a particular writer relies again and again on each of these strategies. The names we have given the strategies come either from key words, characteristic punctuation, or grammatical function.

The most obvious sentence strategies simply announce a definition. (In each of the following examples the word being defined is in italics, while the definition is underlined.)

Strategy A: *means*

Homo habilis means handyman.

Strategy B: *which means that*

These patterns are *ritualized*, which means that the behavior which is stereotyped, exaggerated, and rigid is always performed in the same way so that its social significance is clear.

Strategy C: *is/are*

An environmental factor that increases the chances of a mutation is a *mutagen*.
Somatic mutations are mutations that affect the individual's body cells.

Strategy D: *called/termed*

At the time of ejaculation, sperm leaves the penis in a fluid called *seminal fluid.*

Strategy E: *refers to*

Morphogenesis refers to the shaping of the embryo and is first evident when certain cells are seen to move, or migrate, in relation to other cells.

Strategy F: *or*

In humans the *gestation period,* or length of pregnancy, is approximately nine months.

Strategy G: *insert with parentheses* (Either the definition or the word to be defined can be inserted.)

Viral infections can spread from the nasal cavities to the sinuses *(sinusitis),* to the middle ears *(otitis media),* to the larynx *(laryngitis),* and to the bronchi *(bronchitis).*

Thus an ecosystem contains both a *biotic* (living) and *abiotic* (nonliving) environment.

Strategy H: *insert with dashes*

The human blastula, termed the blastocyst, consists of a hollow ball with a mass of cells—*the inner cell mass*—at one end.

EXERCISE 16.1

This is the first of three exercises on sentence strategies for brief definitions. The exercises become steadily more difficult in that you will be writing structurally more complex sentences. Nevertheless, most of the sentences will be manageable, even easy. Doing all of them, including the easy ones, will give you a quick, comprehensive survey of most of the possibilities open to you when you need to define a term concisely in a sentence.

All three exercises include words you may not know, so you will have the challenge of inserting an unfamiliar dictionary definition into a particular sentence form, a form that you might actually use in your own writing. Though you will have to use the dictionary to complete nearly all of the sentences, these are not exercises in the use of the dictionary, nor is their purpose to increase your vocabulary. They are writing exercises of a special kind—practice with many of the sentence forms writers use to define unfamiliar terms.

Write out each of the following sentences, filling in the blanks with definitions in a current dictionary. As an alternative to this exercise, make up your own sentences in these same patterns, using new terms either from a course you are now taking or from a sport or hobby you know well. (Each particular strategy is identified by letter after each exercise item.)

1. A *clinometer* is _____ . (C)
2. *Ecumenism* refers to _____ . (E)
3. The report said the thieves resorted to a *subterfuge,* which means that they _____ . (B)
4. _____ is called an *ectomorph.* (D)
5. They danced the *habana*— _____ —and the *samba*— _____ . (H)
6. Instead of a *eulogy* (_____), he delivered a *harangue* (_____). (G)
7. That fall marked the return of the *tabard,* or _____ , to fashion news. (F)
8. To a fencer, a *riposte* means _____ . (A)

The sentence strategies listed so far all declare in a straightforward way that the writer is defining a term. Other strategies, signaled by certain sentence relationships, are less direct but still quite apparent. They can be identified by the word introducing the subordinate sentence part that contains the definition.

Strategy I: *which/that/where*

Fraternal twins, which originate when two different eggs are fertilized by two different sperm, do not have identical chromosomes.
The grasslands of all continents support populations of *grazers* that feed on grasses and *browsers* that feed on shrubs and trees.
The region of the inguinal *canal,* where the spermatic cord passes into the abdomen, remains a weak point in the abdominal wall.

Strategy J: *because*

Hemophilia is called the bleeders disease because the afflicted person's blood is unable to clot.

Strategy K: *when*

When a mutagen leads to an increase in the incidence of cancer it is called a *carcinogen.*

Strategy L: *if*

If the thyroid fails to develop properly, a condition called *cretinism* results.

These sentence parts—all of them subordinate clauses—play an important role in sentences by adding details, expressing time and cause, and indicating conditions or tentativeness. In all these examples from *Inquiry into Life*, however, the clauses have a specific defining role to play in the sections of the text where they appear. In this specialized way, they are part of a writer's repertoire for sentence definitions.

EXERCISE 16.2

To try out these kinds of clauses as defining strategies, write out the following sentences, using your dictionary for the definitions required in the blank spaces. As an alternative, you may create your own sentences in these pattens from specialized subject matter in a course you are now taking or from the special terms in a sport or hobby.

1. *Bureaucratese,* talk and writing which _____ , is the curse of the land. (I)

2. It was considered a *buyer's market* because _____ . (J)

3. Because _____ , the poem could be classified as a *Shakespearean sonnet.* (J)

4. When someone _____ , it is called *plagiarism.* (K)

5. When _____ , the diagnosis is *senile dementia.* (K)

6. If _____ , *edema* results. (L)

In addition to those already discussed, writers may choose several other defining strategies. One of the most common is the appositive phrase. Here one noun defines another noun in a brief inserted phrase called an appositive. Sometimes the appositive contains the definition; other times it contains the word to be defined. Because this is such an important defining strategy, here are illustrations of several variations.

Strategy M: *appositive*

Sperm are produced in the testes, but they mature in the *epididymus,* a tightly coiled tubule about twenty feet in length that lies just outside each testis.
Breathing consists of taking air in, *inspiration,* and forcing air out, *expiration.*

Certain specific phrases can also be used to point out words to be defined and thus indirectly introduce definitions.

Strategy N: *in the case of*

In the case of *hyperthyroidism* (too much thyroxin), <u>the thyroid gland is enlarged and overactive, causing a goiter to form and the eyes to curiously protrude.</u>

Strategy O: *according to*

According to the *Malthusian view,* <u>the depletion curve tells us that there are limits to growth and that we are rapidly approaching those limits.</u> . . .

Sometimes a writer can assume that readers will be familiar with the Latin, Greek, or other root of a word. In this case the writer may just point to these definitions.

Strategy P: *as the name implies*

As their name implies *monosaccharides* <u>are simple sugars with only one unit.</u>

Finally, in a comparative definition, two or more terms are defined in part by comparison or contrast with each other. For these multiple definitions, writers rely on a great variety of syntactic and stylistic strategies including the two illustrated below: (1) a series of phrases following either the main verb or a colon and (2) contrasting clauses beginning with words or phrases like *even though, in spite of,* or *whereas.* The various parts of the comparison are always grammatically parallel, that is, similar in form.

Strategy Q: *comparative*

The special senses include the *chemoreceptors* <u>for taste and smell,</u> the *light receptors* <u>for sight,</u> and the *mechanoreceptors* <u>for hearing and balance.</u>
Whereas a *miscarriage* <u>is the unexpected loss of an embryo or fetus,</u> an *abortion* <u>is the purposeful removal of an embryo or fetus from the womb.</u>

EXERCISE 16.3

With the aid of a dictionary, complete the following sentences. Alternatively, you may compose sentences in these patterns from information in courses you are taking or from the special terms in a sport or hobby.

1. According to the *Calvinists,* _____ . (O)
2. In the case of *caricature,* _____ . (N)
3. *Aerobics,* as the name implies, _____ . (P)
4. To remember large numbers of facts for an exam, some students rely on a *mnemonic,* _____ . (M)

5. Human hormones include *testosterone*, which _____ , and *estrogen*, which _____ . (Q)

6. In the human eye, the *rod cells* _____ whereas the *cone cells* _____ . (Q)

7. The three most common classifications of human body type are *endomorphic*, _____ ; *mesomorphic*, _____ ; and *ectomorphic*, _____ . (Q)

EXERCISE 16.4

Turn to the essay by David Noonan in Chapter 4, and analyze the sentence definitions in paragraphs 2, 6, 9, 13, and 18. (Some of these paragraphs contain more than one sentence definition.) Classify each definition as one of the preceding sentence types. What is the purpose of all these definitions in the selection as a whole?

EXTENDED DEFINITIONS

Rather than a brief sentence definition, a writer may need to go further and provide readers with a fuller definition extending over several sentences. Here, for example, is how Mark Twain defines a word he learned on a trip to New Orleans.

We picked up one excellent word—a word worth traveling to New Orleans to get; a nice limber, expressive, handy word—"lagniappe." They pronounce it lanny-*yap*. It is Spanish—so they said. We discovered it at the head of a column of odds and ends in the Picayune, the first day; heard twenty people use it the second; inquired what it meant the third; adopted it and got facility in swinging it the fourth. It has a restricted meaning, but I think the people spread it out a little when they choose. It is the equivalent of the thirteenth roll in a "baker's dozen." It is something thrown in, gratis, for good measure. The custom originated in the Spanish quarter of the city. When a child or a servant buys something in a shop—or even the mayor or the governor, for aught I know—he finishes the operation by saying—

"Give me something for lagniappe."

The shopman always responds; gives the child a bit of licorice root, gives the servant a cheap cigar or a spool of thread; gives the governor—I don't know what he gives the governor; support, likely.

When you are invited to drink—and this does occur now and then in New Orleans—and you say, "What, again?—no, I've had enough"; the other party says, "But just this one more time—this is for lagniappe." When the beau perceives that he is stacking his compliments a trifle too high, and sees by the young lady's countenance that the edifice would have been better with the top compliment left off, he puts his "I beg pardon—no harm intended," into the briefer form of "Oh, that's for lagniappe." If the waiter in the restaurant stumbles and spills a gill of coffee down the back of your neck, he says, "For lagniappe, sah," and gets you another cup without extra charge.   Mark Twain, *Life on the Mississippi*

This extended definition relies on a variety of strategies—word history, personal experience, many examples, and even dialogue.

A science text provides another example of the way certain important concepts require extended definition. This definition comes from the expanding field of ecology.

Demes   A deme is a small local population, such as all the deer mice or all the red oaks in a certain woodland or all the perch in a given pond. Although no two individuals in a deme are exactly alike, the members of a deme do usually resemble one another more closely than they resemble the members of other demes, for at least two reasons: (1) They are more closely related genetically, because pairings occur more frequently between members of the same deme than between members of different demes; and (2) they are exposed to more similar environmental influences and hence to more nearly the same selection pressures.

It must be emphasized that demes are not clear-cut permanent units of population. Although the deer mice in one woodlot are more likely to mate among themselves than with deer mice in the next woodlot down the road, there will almost certainly be occasional matings between mice from different woodlots. Similarly, although the female parts of a particular red oak tree are more likely to receive pollen from another red oak tree in the same woodlot, there is an appreciable chance that they will sometimes receive pollen from a tree in another nearby woodlot. And the woodlots themselves are not permanent ecological features. They have only a transient existence as separate and distinct ecological units; neighboring woodlots may fuse after a few years, or a single large woodlot may become divided into two or more separate smaller ones. Such changes in ecological features will produce corresponding changes in the demes of deer mice and red oak trees. Demes, then, are usually temporary units of population that intergrade with other similar units.   William T. Keeton, *Biological Science*

As a writer drafting an essay, your choice of appropriate definition strategies will be guided by your awareness of what you want to accomplish and by your knowledge of who your readers will be. You need not even be consciously aware of particular choices while you are writing a first draft. Later, though, when you are revising this first draft, you will have a special advantage if you can look critically at the way you have defined key terms. If your repertoire of defining strategies includes all the variations illustrated so far in this chapter, you will be able to revise with much more confidence and power. Sometimes you may need only a brief sentence definition. At other times, you may need an extended definition that includes brief anecdotes and examples as in the extended definitions by Twain and Keeton.

Though it happens fairly rarely, some published essays and reports are concerned primarily with the definition of a little understood or problematic concept or thing—for example, the essay about chiggers by Sue Hubbell or the one about cholesterol by Isaac Asimov in Chapter 5. Usually, however, definition is only a part of an essay. A long piece of writing, like a term paper or a textbook or a research report, may include many kinds of brief and extended definitions, all of them integrated with other writing strategies.

EXERCISE 16.5

Choose one term that names a complex concept or feature of central importance in an activity or subject you know well. Choose a word with a well-established definition, one agreed on by everyone knowledgeable about the topic.

Write an extended definition of several sentences for this important term. Write for readers your own age who will be encountering the term for the first time when they read your definition.

EXERCISE 16.6

Read "To Unteach Greed," Carol Bly's essay in Chapter 7, and analyze the extended definition of *technique* in paragraph 9. How does she define this term? What purpose does the definition have within the whole selection?

HISTORICAL DEFINITIONS

Writers will occasionally trace the history of a word—from its first use, to its adoption into other languages, to its shifting meanings over the centuries. Such a strategy can be a rich addition to an essay, bringing to the definition of an important concept a surprising depth and resonance. An historical definition usually begins with the roots of a word, but it extends well beyond that to trace the word's history over a long period of time. Such a history should always serve a writer's larger purpose, as the example here shows.

In this example, from a book discussing the recent rise of witchcraft and paganism in America, the writer uses an historical definition of the word *pagan* as background to her own definition and also as a way of instructing us in how we should feel about the new pagans.

> *Pagan* comes from the Latin *paganus*, which means a country dweller, and is itself derived from *pagus*, the Latin word for village or rural district. Similarly, *heathen* originally meant a person who lived on the heaths. Negative associations with these words are the end result of centuries of political struggles during which the major prophetic religions, notably Christianity,

won a victory over the older polytheistic religions. In the West, often the last people to be converted to Christianity lived on the outskirts of populated areas and kept to the old ways. These were the Pagans and heathens—the word Pagan was a term of insult, meaning "hick."

Pagan had become a derogatory term in Rome by the third century. Later, after the death of Julian, the last Pagan emperor, in 362 A.D. the word *Pagan* came to refer to intellectual Pagans like Julian. Gore Vidal, in his extraordinary novel *Julian*, wrote a fictional description of this event in which the Pagan orator Libanius, after attending the funeral of a Christian notable, writes in his journal: "There was a certain amount of good-humored comment about 'pagans' (a new word of contempt for us Hellenists) attending Christian services. . . . " Julian, by the way, has long been one of Neo-Paganism's heroes, and an early Neo-Pagan journal was called *The Julian Review*. Centuries later the word *Pagan* still suffers the consequences of political and religious struggles, and dictionaries still define it to mean a godless person or an unbeliever, instead of, simply, a member of a different kind of religion.

Pagan is also often associated with hedonism. This makes some sense, since many ancient Pagan religions incorporated sexuality into ecstatic religious practice. One scholar, writing on the use of mystical experience by young people in the 1960s, observed that a characteristic of many groups was "the idea of paganism—the body is a temple in which there is nothing unclean, a shrine to be adorned for the ritual of love." New attitudes toward sexuality play a part in some, but not all, Neo-Pagan groups, and the old Pagan religions had their share of ascetics, but generally, Neo-Pagans seem to have healthy attitudes toward sex.

I use *Pagan* to mean a member of a polytheistic nature religion, such as the ancient Greek, Roman, or Egyptian religions, or, in anthropological terms, a member of one of the indigenous folk and tribal-religions all over the world. People who have studied the classics or have been deeply involved with natural or aboriginal peoples are comparatively free of the negative and generally racist attitudes that surround the word *Pagan*.   Margot Adler, *Drawing Down the Moon*

EXERCISE 16.7

Any good dictionary tells the origins of words. Historical, or etymological, dictionaries, however, give much more information, enough to trace changes in use of a word over long periods of time. The preeminent historical dictionary of our language is the *Oxford English Dictionary*. Less imposing is *A Dictionary of American English*, and even less imposing is *A Dictionary of Americanisms*.

Look up the historical definition of any one of the following words in *A Dictionary of Americanisms*, and write several sentences on its roots and development. As an alternative, you may choose any word with a complex history from one of these dictionaries.

basketball	eye-opener
bazooka	filibuster
bedrock	gerrymander
blizzard	jazz
bogus	pep
bonanza	picayune
bushwhack	podunk
canyon	rubberneck
carpetbag	sashay
dugout	two bits

STIPULATIVE DEFINITIONS

The historical definition of pagans in the preceding section concludes with a stipulative definition: "I use *Pagan* to mean a member of a polytheistic nature religion. . . ." *To stipulate* means to seek or assert agreement on something. A stipulative definition is one in which the writer declares a certain meaning, generally not one found in the dictionary.

Stipulative definitions have a variety of important functions, several of which are illustrated here. In the next example, a prominent historian of science proposes a stipulative definition of the word *ecology*.

> Ernst Haeckel, the great popularizer of evolutionary theory in Germany, loved to coin words. The vast majority of his creations died with him a half-century ago, but among the survivors are "ontogeny," "phylogeny," and "ecology." The last is now facing an opposite fate—loss of meaning by extension and vastly inflated currency. Common usage now threatens to make "ecology" a label for anything good that happens far from cities or anything that does not have synthetic chemicals in it. In its more restricted and technical sense, ecology is the study of organic diversity. It focuses on the interactions of organisms and their environments in order to address what may be the most fundamental question in evolutionary biology: "Why are there so many kinds of living things?"   Stephen Jay Gould, *Ever Since Darwin*

Important concepts in technical fields like biology may gradually take on fuzzy or overly broad popular definitions. The specialists may then have to rescue a concept by redefining it, as Gould does here. He is asking his readers to agree with him that *ecology* means "the study of organic diversity." He stipulates a redefinition and asks us to use the word only as he defines it, at least for the duration of his book.

Another use of stipulative definition is to sort through alternative definitions of a problematic concept—*pure breed of cats* in the next example—in order to reject these alternative definitions and argue for another definition the writer favors.

What is a pure breed of cats, and what constitutes a pure-bred animal? These terms can have a number of meanings. One of the simplest is merely to regard as pure-bred a cat that has been properly registered with a responsible body (such as the Governing Council of the Cat Fancy [GCCF] in Britain, or the Cat Fanciers' Association [CFA] or one of the other similar associations in the United States). Such a cat will have a pedigree of similarly registered parents, grandparents and so on for a given number of generations—normally at least four. This ensures that the cat has "respectable" parentage and is likely to be a representative specimen of the breed—though it says nothing about its quality.

However, the process of registration and the writing of pedigrees is, in a sense (and without meaning to be derogatory), merely window dressing. They simply set a seal upon a more fundamental definition of pure breeds of cats. This relates to the characteristics of the individuals constituting a recognized breed and how these may differ from those of other cats: from alley cats and from other recognized breeds. In one sense, a breed is a group of animals that sufficient people are mutually agreed to recognize as such. This is not enough in itself, however; the group must have coherent distinguishing features that set them apart from all other cats, and hence distinctive underlying genetic characteristics.   Michael Wright and Sally Walters, *The Book of the Cat*

EXERCISE 16.8

In his proposal regarding birth control in schools in Chapter 7, Adam Paul Weisman offers a stipulative definition of the role schools play in the lives of students (paragraph 11). Read Weisman's essay, paying particular attention to this definition. What function does it serve in the essay as a whole?

EXERCISE 16.9

Write several sentences of a stipulative definition for one of the following alternatives.

1. Define in your own way TV game shows, soap operas, police dramas, or horror movies. Try for a stipulative definition of what these (or some other form of TV or movie entertainment) are generally like. In effect, you will be saying to your readers, other students in your class who are familiar with these forms of entertainment, "Let's agree for now to define X this way."

2. Do the same for some hard-to-define concept—like *loyalty, love, bravery, shyness, sportsmanship, male chauvinism,* or *worthwhile college courses.*

3. Think of a new development or phenomenon in contemporary romance, music, TV, leisure, fashion, or eating habits. Invent a name for it, and write a stipulative definition for it.

Classifying

In a variety of situations, writers are faced with the task of sorting various scattered observations and facts into an orderly presentation. A common strategy for doing so is *classifying*—combining items into a number of discrete groupings and then labeling each new combination. In many instances classifying is a matter of *dividing* a topic into its constituent parts in order to discuss the elements of each part separately.

Writers using classification and division are particularly concerned with organization, clearly defined principles of division, and coherence.

ORGANIZATION

The strategy of classification and division is primarily a means of organization, of creating a framework for the presentation of information, whether in a few paragraphs of an essay or an entire book. As discussed later, other strategies—definition, illustration, contrast—are necessary to develop the topic in detail.

Authors of technical discussions and textbooks often rely on classification and division as an organizing principle. In the following example from a book on the computer revolution, a three-part division of the topic is announced in the first sentence, and each part is labeled. Based on the order forecast by the opening sentence, each part is then defined and discussed in a separate paragraph and specific examples are classified according to category.

> There are essentially three categories of machine: simple machines, programmable machines and robots.
>
> Simple machines, to all intents and purposes, are nothing more than powerful mechanical muscles; they are either controlled by a human being, or have been designed and constructed to perform an endless series of repetitive acts. Hydraulic excavators, steam engines and motor cars all fall into this category.
>
> Programmable machines are more sophisticated. They are devices which can be programmed to do any of a number of different tasks or, in the more ambitious cases, a sequence of tasks. The program is set into the device by the human who controls it. They have only become widely used in recent years, though some of the very earliest versions were invented at around the

same time as the first simple machines. Jacquard's loom was a programmable machine—and it was also one of the first true machines.

The robot is different, and in an important way. It, too, is capable of performing a variety of tasks, or a sequence of tasks, but the choice of tasks at any particular moment is determined not only by a pre-set program, but also by some information *fed into it from the outside world which is relevant to the task it is performing.* The information it absorbs is fed into it through sensing devices attached to its own structure, and not by command signals from a human. A simple machine, or even a programmed one, is capable of performing quite a complex task, but it will go on doing it indefinitely in really blockheaded fashion until something intervenes to stop it; a robot, on the other hand, will take account of change in its environment and adjust its behavior accordingly.   Christopher Evans, *The Micro Millennium*

The division of a topic into parts can be used for a variety of purposes. See how Ernest Hemingway uses the strategy to open a chapter in *Death in the Afternoon,* his classic book on bullfighting in Spain. To help us understand how a bullfight develops, Hemingway describes it as divided into three acts, each of which is named for the major action (the trial of the lances, the banderillas, and the death). Hemingway subdivides the third act further, into three parts (or scenes, to continue his analogy between a bullfight and a play). Finally, he summarizes his discussion in terms of a three-act "tragedy."

There are three acts to the fighting of each bull and they are called in Spanish los tres tercios de la lidia, or the three thirds of the combat. <u>The first act, where the bull charges the picadors, is the suerte de varas, or the trial of the lances.</u> Suerte is an important word in Spanish. It means, according to the dictionary: Suerte, f., chance, hazard, lots, fortune, luck, good luck, haphazard; state, condition, fate, doom, destiny, kind, sort; species, manner, mode, way, skillful manœuvre; trick, feat, juggle, and piece of ground separated by landmark. So the translation of trial or manœuvre is quite arbitrary, as any translation must be from the Spanish.

The action of the picadors in the ring and the work of the matadors who are charged with protecting them with their capes when they are dismounted make up the first act of the bullfight. When the president signals for the end of this act and the bugle blows the picadors leave the ring and the second act begins. There are no horses in the ring after the first act except the dead horses which are covered with canvas. Act one is the act of the capes, the pics and the horses. In it the bull has the greatest opportunity to display his bravery or cowardice.

Act two is that of the banderillas. These are pairs of sticks about a yard long, seventy centimetres to be exact, with a harpoon-shaped steel point four centimetres long at one end. They are supposed to be placed, two at a time, in the humped muscle at the top of the bull's neck as he charges the man who holds them. They are designed to complete the work of slowing up the bull and regulating the carriage of his head which has been begun by the picadors: so that his attack will be slower, but surer and better directed. Four pair of banderillas are usually put in. If they are placed by the banderilleros or peones they must be placed, above all other considerations, quickly and in the proper position. If the matador himself places them he may indulge in a preparation which is usually accompanied by music. This is the most picturesque part of the bullfight and the part most spectators care for the most when first seeing fights. The mission of the banderilleros is not only to force the bull by hooking to tire his neck muscles and carry his head lower but also, by placing them at one side or another, to correct a tendency to hook to that side. The entire act of the banderillas should not take more than five minutes. If it is prolonged the bull becomes discomposed and the fight loses the tempo it must keep, and if the bull is an uncertain and dangerous one he has too many opportunities to see and charge men unarmed with any lure, and so develops a tendency to search for the man, the bundle, as the Spanish call him, behind the cloth when the matador comes out for the last act with the sword and muleta.

The president changes the act after three or at most four pairs of banderillas have been placed and the third and final division is the death. It is made up of three parts. First the brindis or salutation of the president and dedication or toasting of the death of the bull, either to him or to some other person by the matador, followed by the work of the matador with the muleta. This is a scarlet serge cloth which is folded over a stick which has a sharp spike at one end and a handle at the other. The spike goes through the cloth which is fastened to the other end of the handle with a thumb screw so that it hangs in folds along the length of the stick. Muleta means literally crutch, but in bullfighting it refers to the scarlet-serge-draped stick with which the matador is supposed to master the bull, prepare him for killing and finally hold in his left hand to lower the bull's head and keep it lowered while he kills the animal by a sword thrust high up between his shoulder blades.

These are the three acts in the tragedy of the bullfight, and it is the first one, the horse part, which indicates what the others will be and, in fact, makes the rest possible. It is in the first act that the bull comes out in full possession of all of his faculties, confident, fast, vicious and conquering. All his victories are in the first act. At the end of the first act he has apparently won. He has cleared the ring of mounted men and is alone. In the second act he is baffled completely by an unarmed man and very cruelly punished by the banderillas so that his confidence and his blind general rage goes and he concentrates his hatred on an individual object. In the third act he is faced by only one man who must, alone, dominate him by a piece of cloth placed over a stick, and kill him from in front, going in over the bull's right horn to kill him with a sword thrust between the arch of his shoulder blades. Ernest Hemingway, *Death in the Afternoon*

The way a topic is divided can be illustrated with a diagram showing the breakdown of its parts and subparts. Here is such a diagram of the organization of Hemingway's excerpt:

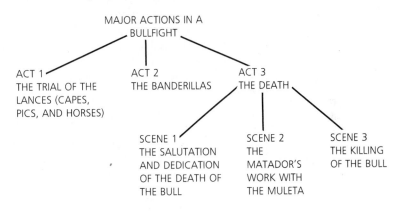

Using this division, the various actions of the bullfight can be classified according to the "act" in which they occur.

PRINCIPLES OF DIVISION

Each division and subdivision of a topic must meet the basic requirements of significance, consistency, exclusiveness, and completeness. These may be defined as follows:

Significance The principle of division must be appropriate to the writer's purpose.

Consistency The parts resulting from the division must all be based on the same principle of division.

Exclusiveness Parts resulting from the division should not overlap.

Completeness No important parts should be omitted in the division.

The Hemingway excerpt illustrates each of these requirements. The point, or *significance*, of Hemingway's division is to suggest the formalized, tragic drama of a bullfight and to highlight the contribution of the key action in each act to the noble defeat of the bull. This division is *consistent* in that the parts, or acts—the trial of the lances, the banderillas, and the death—are all formed on the same principle. Each one is a primary segment of the drama and revolves around a particular major action. The division is *exclusive* because there is no overlap: actions in one act do not usually occur again in other acts. It is *complete* because Hemingway's acts include all the actions responsible for the defeat of the bull. (Note that the subdivision of the third act into the major activities of the matador fulfills these same requirements.)

The principle of division one uses depends primarily on one's purpose. Most topics can be divided in a number of ways. For example, based on the purpose of the study, a team of sociologists might divide a survey's respondents according to age, education level, income, geographic location, or answer given to a particular question. Similarly, a landscape gardener choosing deciduous trees suitable for a midwestern park might be concerned, among other matters, with variations in leaf coloration or in shade-giving characteristics and thus divide the subject into groupings such as one of the following:

DECIDUOUS TREES OF THE MIDWEST

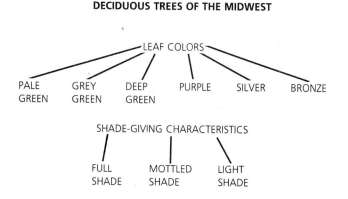

LEAF COLORS

PALE GREEN   GREY GREEN   DEEP GREEN   PURPLE   SILVER   BRONZE

SHADE-GIVING CHARACTERISTICS

FULL SHADE   MOTTLED SHADE   LIGHT SHADE

Writers likewise divide topics according to principles based on their purposes for writing. The division itself results from the writer's analysis of the topic and of all information gathered regarding the topic plus any ideas or insights he or she may have. Only full and thoughtful analysis of the topic and a carefully defined principle of division can assure that the division or system of classification will be consistent, exclusive, and complete.

EXERCISE 17.1

Diagram the division in the first example in this chapter, the selection from *The Micro Millennium* by Christopher Evans. Then decide whether the division is consistent, exclusive, and complete. What would you say is the significance or point of the division?

EXERCISE 17.2

Pick at least two of the following topics, and divide them according to two or three different principles of division. Diagram each division, and then state its significance, or point. Be sure that, for the point it makes, each division is consistent, exclusive, and complete.

teachers	crimes
dreams	poets
lies	popular music groups
restaurants	tools for writing
bars	ways of avoiding writing
cars	football offenses
movies	field hockey defenses
students	

STRATEGIES FOR COHERENCE

Writers must take care to present any division of information in a way that allows readers to follow it easily. Biologist Sylvia Mader's *Inquiry into Life*, featured in Chapter 16: Defining, illustrates a high level of such coherence. In the following example from a section of that book, Mader offers a straightforward three-part division to identify the parts of the human ear. In the larger context of the chapter in which it appears, its purpose is to name and classify the parts so that the reader will be able to follow a discussion of the function of the ear.

The ear has three divisions: outer, middle, and inner. The **outer ear** consists of the **pinna** (external flap) and **auditory canal**. The opening of the auditory canal is lined with fine hairs and sweat glands. In the upper wall are modified sweat glands that secrete earwax to help guard the ear against the entrance of foreign materials such as air pollutants.

The **middle ear** begins at the **tympanic membrane** (eardrum) and ends at a bony wall in which are found two small openings covered by membranes. These openings are called the **oval** and **round windows.** The posterior wall of the middle ear leads to many air spaces within the **mastoid process.**

Three small bones are found between the tympanic membrane and the oval window. Collectively called the **ossicles,** individually they are the **hammer** (malleus), **anvil** (incus), and **stirrup** (stapes) because their shapes resemble these objects. The hammer adheres to the tympanic membrane, while the stirrup touches the oval window.

The eustachian tube extends from the middle ear to the nasopharynx and permits equalization of air pressure. Chewing gum, yawning, and swallowing in elevators and airplanes helps move air through the eustachian tubes upon ascent and descent.

Whereas the outer ear and middle ear contain air, the inner ear is filled with fluid. The **inner ear,** anatomically speaking, has three areas: the first two, called the vestibule and semicircular canals, are concerned with balance; and the third, the cochlea, is concerned with hearing.

The **semicircular canals** are arranged so that there is one in each dimension of space. The base of each canal, called the **ampulla,** is slightly enlarged. Within the ampullae are little hair cells.

The **vestibule** is a chamber that lies between the semicircular canals and the cochlea. It contains two small sacs called the **utricle** and **saccule.** Within both of these are little hair cells surrounded by a gelatinous material containing calcium carbonate granules, or **otoliths.**

The **cochlea** resembles the shell of a snail because it spirals. Within the tubular cochlea are three canals: the vestibular canal, the **cochlear canal,** and the tympanic canal. Along the length of the basilar membrane, which forms the lower wall of the cochlear canal, are little hair cells, and just above them is another membrane, called the **tectorial membrane.** The hair cells plus the tectorial membrane are called the **organ of Corti.** When this organ sends nerve impulses to the cerebral cortex, it is interpreted as sound. Sylvia Mader, *Inquiry into Life*

The Ear

	Outer Ear	Middle Ear	Inner Ear Cochlea	Sacs plus semicircular canals
Function	Directs sound waves to tympanic membrane	Picks up and amplifies sound waves	Hearing	Maintains equilibrium
Anatomy	Pinna Auditory canal	Tympanic membrane Hammer (malleus) Anvil (incus) Stirrup (stapes)	Vestibular canal Tympanic canal Cochlear canal Contains organ of Corti Auditory nerve starts here	Saccule and utricle (contain otoliths and hair cells) Semicircular canals (contain hair cells in ampullae)
Media	Air	Air (eustachian tube)	Fluid	Fluid

Path of vibration: Sound waves—vibration of tympanic membrane—vibration of hammer, anvil, and stirrup—vibration of oval window—fluid pressure waves of fluids in canals of inner ear lead to stimulation of hair cells—bulging of round window.

Mader's plan for her division is a *spatial* one, moving from inside to outside. (Note, in contrast, that Hemingway's division of the bullfight into three acts follows a *temporal* plan.) In the initial statement of the division,

Mader forecasts the plan of the presentation and names the three divisions in the order in which she will take them up: outer, middle, and inner ear. Each division is then introduced in a new paragraph and always with the same syntax at the beginning of a sentence: "The outer ear . . . The middle ear . . . The inner ear . . ." Furthermore, Mader includes a chart to diagram the division and to classify all the main anatomical terms within each part. (She also provides several drawings of the ear, not included here.)

With each of these strategies, Mader helps readers to understand and to follow her explanation easily and without confusion. General strategies for coherence are discussed in more detail in Chapter 12: Cueing the Reader.

EXERCISE 17.3

Look again at the first selection in this chapter (from *The Micro Millennium* by Christopher Evans) to examine the strategies the writer uses to present a coherent division of information. Does the initial statement of the division name all the groups and forecast the order in which they will be discussed? What other writing strategies does the writer use to steer the reader through the presentation?

THE IMPORTANCE OF OTHER WRITING STRATEGIES

The last example in this chapter comes from a book that attempts to explain the new physics to nonphysicists.

There are two kinds of mass, which means that there are two ways of talking about it. The first is gravitational mass. The gravitational mass of an object, roughly speaking, is the weight of the object as measured on a balance scale. Something that weighs three times more than another object has three times more mass. Gravitational mass is the measure of how much force the gravity of the earth exerts on an object. Newton's laws describe the effects of this force, which vary with the distance of the mass from the earth. Although Newton's laws describe the effects of this force, they do not define it. This is the mystery of action-at-a-distance. . . .

The second type of mass is inertial mass. Inertial mass is the measure of the resistance of an object to acceleration (or deceleration, which is negative acceleration). For example, it takes three times more force to move three railroad cars from a standstill to twenty miles per hour (positive acceleration) than it takes to move one railroad car from a standstill to twenty miles per hour. . . . Similarly, once they are moving, it takes three times more force to stop three cars than it takes to stop the single car. This is because the inertial mass of the three railroad cars is three times more than the inertial mass of the single railroad car.

Inertial mass and gravitational mass are equal. This explains why a feather and a cannonball fall with equal velocity in a vacuum. The cannonball has hundreds of times more gravitational mass than the feather (it weighs more) but it also has hundreds of times more resistance to motion than the feather (its inertial mass). Its attraction to the earth is hundreds of times stronger than that of the feather, but then so is its inclination not to move. The result is that it accelerates downward at the same rate as the feather, although it seems that it should fall much faster.

The fact that inertial mass and gravitational mass are equal was known three hundred years ago, but physicists considered it a coincidence. No significance was attached to it until Einstein published his general theory of relativity.   Gary Zukav, *The Dancing Wu Li Masters: An Overview of the New Physics*

This example illustrates the relation of classification and division to other essential writing strategies. Zukav divides his topic into two kinds of mass: gravitational and inertial. Then he defines each one. In the first paragraph, to define gravitational mass, he relies in part on the illustration of an ordinary balance scale. In the second paragraph, to define inertial mass, he contrasts the action of three railroad cars with that of one railroad car. These two paragraphs show how naturally dividing and classifying lead to definition, illustration, and contrast.

The point of Zukav's division is the general physical principle he states at the beginning of the third paragraph. Once he has roughly and quickly identified the two kinds of mass, he considers how they are related—namely, that they are equal—which he then illustrates by contrasting a feather with a cannonball.

As this example and the others in this chapter indicate, classification and division are basically a strategy of organization rather than of development. Only when supplemented with other writing strategies can the topic under examination be explained fully.

EXERCISE 17.4

Analyze the following classifications, each from a selection in Part I of this book. First, within the context of the whole selection, decide the point or significance of the division and the principle used. Then decide whether the division is consistent, exclusive, and complete. To focus your analysis, you might want to make a diagram of the division.

Chapter 7, "Birth Control in the Schools: Clinical Examination," Adam Paul Weisman, paragraphs 2–5

Chapter 7, "Testing and Society: What Can Be Done?" David Owen, paragraph 3

Chapter 7, "A Proposal to Strengthen the Language Acquisition Project," Wendy Jo Niwa, paragraphs 5–7

Chapter 8, "The Greatness of Albert Einstein," Bertrand Russell, paragraphs 4–5

Chapter 9, "Suicide Among Young People," Victor Fuchs, paragraph 2 and table

EXERCISE 17.5

Choose one of the following writing activities. Each one asks for some division; be sure that your analysis observes the principles of a good division: significance, consistency, exclusiveness, and completeness. Include in your writing appropriate strategies of coherence, such as forecasting, paragraphing (optional in a brief piece), and repeated sentence patterns.

1. Write several sentences in which you identify the major periods in your life. Label and briefly define each period.

2. Describe a familiar activity (running, sleeping, eating Chinese food) in a new way by dividing it into stages. Label and define each stage.

3. Develop in writing one of the classification systems you created in Exercise 17.2.

Comparing and Contrasting

Writers use comparison to analyze and evaluate two or more things. You might compare two people you know well, three motorcycles you are considering buying for a cross-country tour, four Stephen King novels, three tomato plants being grown under different laboratory conditions, or two theories about the causes of inflation and unemployment. But as soon as comparison begins, contrast edges its way in, for rarely are two things totally alike. The contrasts, or differences, between the three motorcycles are likely to be more enlightening than the similarities, many of which may be so obvious as to need no analysis. *Comparison,* then, brings similar things together for examination, to see how they are alike. *Contrast* is a form of comparison that emphasizes their differences.

Comparison and contrast is more than a writing strategy, of course. It is a basic way of thinking and learning. We compare objects, events, and ideas as readily as we evaluate them. A basic principle of learning theory says that we acquire new concepts most readily if we can see how they are similar to or different from concepts we already know.

Professional writers say that comparison and contrast is a basic strategy they would not want to be without. For some writing situations (like the ones above) it has no substitute. Indeed, some writing is essentially extended comparison. But for all lengths and kinds of writing, comparison and contrast regularly alternates with other writing strategies in presenting information.

Chances are good that you will confront many test questions and essay assignments, asking you to compare and contrast some things—two poems, three presidents, four procedures for surveying public opinion. This is a popular format with instructors in all academic disciplines, because it requires critical, analytical thinking and writing. They see it as one of the best ways to challenge students intellectually.

TWO WAYS OF COMPARING AND CONTRASTING

There are two ways to organize comparison and contrast in writing: in chunks and in sequence. In *chunking,* each object of the comparison is presented separately; in *sequencing,* the items are compared point by point. For example, a chunked comparison of two motorcycles would first detail all pertinent features of the Pirsig 241X and then consider all features of the Kawazuki 500S, whereas a sequenced comparison would analyze the Pirsig and the Kawazuki feature by feature. In a chunked comparison discussion is organized around each separate item being compared. In a sequenced comparison it is organized around characteristics of the items being compared.

Look now at an example of chunked comparison, one that contrasts the effects westward migration had on American men in the nineteenth century with its effects on women:

> The westward move for many men was the physical expression of a break with the past and a setting out for a new life. The journey occurred when the rhythms of maturity were primed for a change. The determination to go West was either the initial separation from a man's parental family or the second major move, the move "upward" in the search for economic mobility and success. The adventure took on the color of some "dramatic rite of passage to mastery and adulthood" in the life cycle of frontier men.
>
> But the journey could have no natural place in the life cycle of the women. The journey was a violation of life's natural rhythms for women of childbearing years. There was simply no way that the rigorous exertions of the overland journey could be considered "normal" for a pregnant woman. And yet a woman's pregnancy mattered very little to emigrant families; certainly it was not sufficient cause to defer the trip.
>
> Even with the best of care, childbirth was a precarious business in the nineteenth century. It was even more risky on the open road, followed by immediate travel in a wagon with no springs and with very little access to water for drinking or for bathing. Any complications of delivery proved critical. And frailty in the newborn was life-threatening. The prospect of childbirth on the Trail must have meant months of heightened anxiety to women.
> Lillian Schlissel, *Women's Diaries of the Westward Journey*

The two parts of the comparison—men and women—are discussed separately, first one and then the other. The shift from the first discussion to the contrasting one is signaled by the word *but* and by a new paragraph. Each discussion begins with a general statement which is then developed by examples.

A biology text provides another example of a chunked comparison. This selection, from a chapter on evolution, contrasts Lamarckian and modern views of evolutionary change. (Have you ever wondered how giraffes got their long necks?) Here the shift to the second half of the discussion occurs at the beginning of the last paragraph. The writer signals the contrast with an unmistakable transitional expression: *on the other hand*.

> The theory of *evolution by natural selection* proposed by Darwin and Wallace had an influential rival during the nineteenth century in the concept of *evolution by the inheritance of acquired characteristics*—an old and widely held idea often identified with Jean Baptiste de Lamarck (1744–1829), who was one of its more prominent supporters in the early 1800s.
>
> The Lamarckian hypothesis was that somatic characteristics acquired by an individual during its lifetime could be transmitted to its offspring. Thus the characteristics of each generation would be determined, in part at least, by all that happened to the members of the preceding generations—by all the modifications that occurred in them, including those caused by experience, use and disuse of body parts, and accidents. Evolutionary change would be the gradual accumulation of such acquired modifications over many generations. The classic example (though by now rather hackneyed) is the evolution of the long necks of giraffes.
>
> According to the Lamarckian view, ancestral giraffes with short necks tended to stretch their necks as much as they could to reach the tree foliage that served as a major part of their food. This frequent neck stretching caused their offspring to have slightly longer necks. Since these also stretched their necks, the next generation had still longer necks. And so, as a result of neck stretching to reach higher and higher foliage, each generation had slightly longer necks than the preceding generation.
>
> The modern theory of natural selection, <u>on the other hand</u>, proposes that ancestral giraffes probably had short necks, but that the precise length of the neck varied from individual to individual because of their different genotypes. If the supply of food was somewhat limited, then individuals with longer necks had a better chance of surviving and leaving progeny than those with shorter necks. This means, not that all the individuals with shorter necks perished or that all with longer necks survived to reproduce, but simply that a slightly higher proportion of those with longer necks survived and left offspring. As a result, the proportion of individuals with genes for longer necks increased slightly with each succeeding generation.   William T. Keeton, *Biological Science*

Schematically, a chunked comparison looks simple enough. As the two preceding examples show, it is easy to block off such a discussion in a text and then provide a clean transition between the various parts. And yet it can in fact be more complicated for a writer to plan than a sequenced comparison. Sequenced comparison may be closer to the way people perceive and think about similarities or differences in things. For example, while your awareness that two navy blazers are different might come all at once, you would identify the specific differences—buttons, tailoring, fabric—one at a time. A sequenced comparison would point to the differences in just this way—one at a time—whereas a chunked comparison would present all the features of one blazer and then do the same for the second. Thus the chunked strategy requires that a writer organize all the points of comparison before starting to write. With sequencing, however, it is possible to take up each point of comparison as it comes to mind.

In the next example, from David Attenborough's natural history of the earth, sequencing is used to draw an elegant contrast between bird wings and airplane wings:

> Bird wings have a much more complex job to do than the wings of an aeroplane, for in addition to supporting the bird they must act as its engine, rowing it through the air. Even so the wing outline of a bird conforms to the same aerodynamic principles as those eventually discovered by man when designing his aeroplanes, and if you know how different kinds of aircraft perform, you can predict the flight capabilities of similarly shaped birds.
>
> Short stubby wings enable a tanager and other forest-living birds to swerve and dodge at speed through the undergrowth just as they helped the fighter planes of the Second World War to make tight turns and aerobatic manoeuvres in a dog-fight. More modern fighters achieve greater speeds by sweeping back their wings while in flight, just as peregrines do when they go into a 130 kph dive, stooping to a kill. Championship gliders have long thin wings so that, having gained height in a thermal up-current they can soar gently down for hours and an albatross, the largest of flying birds, with a similar wing shape and a span of 3 metres, can patrol the ocean for hours in the same way without a single wing beat. Vultures and hawks circle at very slow speeds supported by a thermal and they have the broad rectangular wings that very slow flying aircraft have. Man has not been able to adapt wings to provide hovering flight. He has only achieved that with the whirling horizontal blades of a helicopter or the downward-pointing engines of a vertical landing jet. Hummingbirds have paralleled even this. They tilt their bodies so that they are almost upright and then beat their wings as fast as 80 times a second producing a similar down-draught of air. So the hummingbird can hover and even fly backwards.   David Attenborough, *Life on Earth*

The important thing to note about this example is the limited, focused basis for the comparison: the shape of wings. Attenborough specifies this basis in the second sentence of the passage (underscored here). Though birds and planes both fly, there is almost nothing else they have in common. They are so obviously different that it would even seem silly to compare them in writing. But Attenborough finds a valid—and fascinating—basis for comparison and develops it in a way that is both informative and entertaining. A successful comparison always has these qualities: a valid basis for comparison, a limited focus, and information that will catch a reader's attention.

EXERCISE 18.1

Pick any one of the following subjects and write several sentences comparing and contrasting. Be careful to limit the basis for your comparison, and underline the sentence that states that basis.

two sports

two explanations or theories

two ways of achieving the same goal (travel by bus or subway, using flattery or persuasion to get what you want)

two things that seem to be unlikely subjects for comparison (a child and a puppy, soccer and ballet)

EXERCISE 18.2

Analyze the specified comparisons in the following selections from Part I. How is each comparison organized? (It may or may not be neatly chunked or sequenced.) Why do you think the writer organizes the comparison in that way? What is the role of the comparison in the whole piece? How effective do you consider the comparison?

Chapter 2, "The Lost Weekend," Linda Ellerbee, paragraph 9

Chapter 4, "Inside the Brain," David Noonan, paragraphs 21–23

Chapter 5, "Chiggers," Sue Hubbell, paragraph 4

Chapter 8, "The Treasure of the Sierra Madre," James Agee, paragraph 2

Chapter 8, "The Greatness of Albert Einstein," Bertrand Russell, paragraph 7

Chapter 9, "Why Children Don't Seem Childlike Anymore," Joshua Meyerowitz, paragraphs 3–6

Chapter 9, "Suicide Among Young People," Victor Fuchs, paragraph 2

EXERCISE 18.3

Some of the selections in Part I are organized around comparisons. Identify and evaluate the comparisons in each of the following pieces. (Remember that the comparison may be stated or implied.)

Chapter 2 "Smooth and Easy," Russell Baker

Chapter 3, "My Parents," Richard Rodriguez

Chapter 4 "The Pinball Philosophy," John McPhee

Chapter 5, "Tracing a Killer," Anastasia Toufexis

Chapter 5, "The Digital Audio Tape Controversy," David Green

Chapter 6, "Abortion, Right and Wrong," Rachel Richardson Smith

ANALOGY

One special form of comparison is the *analogy*, in which one part of the comparison is used simply to explain the other. See how John McPhee uses two different analogies—the twelve-month calendar and the distance along two widespread arms—to explain the duration of geologic time.

> In like manner, geologists will sometimes use the calendar year as a unit to represent the time scale, and in such terms the Precambrian runs from New Year's Day until well after Halloween. Dinosaurs appear in the middle of December and are gone the day after Christmas. The last ice sheet melts on December 31st at one minute before midnight, and the Roman Empire lasts five seconds. With your arms spread wide again to represent all time on earth, look at one hand with its line of life. The Cambrian begins in the wrist, and the Permian Extinction is at the outer end of the palm. All of the Cenozoic is in a fingerprint, and in a single stroke with a medium-grained nail file you could eradicate human history. Geologists live with the geologic scale. Individually, they may or may not be alarmed by the rate of exploitation of the things they discover, but, like the environmentalists, they use these repetitive analogies to place the human record in perspective—to see the Age of Reflection, the last few thousand years, as a small bright sparkle at the end of time.   John McPhee, *Basin and Range*

You may have seen other analogies to geologic time. Because it takes a great imaginative leap to comprehend this concept, writers consistently rely on analogy to explain it.

Scientists have always made good use of analogy—in both their thinking and their writing. Modern physics, in particular, is full of concepts that strain the comprehension and imagination of the nonscientist. One such concept is the uncertainty principle, a concept that is very difficult for anybody but a physicist to define. In the following excerpt, Gary Zukav does so with an analogy—likening the uncertainty principle to a movie projector that is always slightly out of focus.

> The uncertainty principle reveals that as we penetrate deeper and deeper into the subatomic realm, we reach a certain point at which one part or another of our picture of nature becomes blurred, and there is no way to reclarify that part without blurring another part of the picture! It is as though we are adjusting a moving picture that is slightly out of focus. As we make the final adjustments, we are astonished to discover that when the right side of the picture clears, the left side of the picture becomes completely unfocused and nothing in it is recognizable. When we try to focus the left side of the picture, the right side starts to blur and soon the situation is reversed. If we try to strike a balance between these two extremes, both sides of the

picture return to a recognizable condition, but in no way can we remove the original fuzziness from them.

The right side of the picture, in the original formulation of the uncertainty principle, corresponds to the position in space of a moving particle. The left side of the picture corresponds to its momentum. According to the uncertainty principle, we cannot measure accurately, at the same time, both the position *and* the momentum of a moving particle. The more precisely we determine one of these properties, the less we know about the other. If we precisely determine the position of the particle, then, strange as it sounds, there is *nothing* that we can know about its momentum. If we precisely determine the momentum of the particle, there is no way to determine its position.   Gary Zukav, *The Dancing Wu Li Masters: An Overview of the New Physics*

Notice what a strong visual image Zukav's analogy produces—it is very easy to imagine alternating sides of the movie screen going in and out of focus. Explanatory analogies almost always use very familiar objects for comparison, probably because they are trying to explain something very unfamiliar.

EXERCISE 18.4

As part of his discussion of Albert Einstein in Chapter 8, Bertrand Russell offers what he calls a "crude" analogy to explain a difficult concept of physical science, Einstein's space-time theory (paragraph 6). After reading the selection by Russell, discuss how you recognize this description as an analogy. Why do you suppose Russell warns that the analogy is "misleading if taken literally"?

Analogies can also be used for subjects other than abstract, scientific concepts. Indeed, writers often offer analogies to make nontechnical descriptions of explanations more vivid and entertaining. Here is a sports analogy from a sociological study of Hamilton, Ohio. It comes from a chapter describing a hearing held to examine a school board's decision to fire one teacher, Sam Shie. In it, the writer uses analogy to describe Shie's three lawyers, comparing them to an aggressive basketball team.

The cross-examination of Dr. Helms was conducted by Randy Rogers, the young associate of Holbrock's. Rogers was tall and strongly built, lacking by only a couple of inches the height of a professional basketball player who weakens the opposition by fouling often and drawing fouls in return. This was close to the function Rogers performed for the defense. With Hugh Holbrock, Robert Dunlevey, and Randy Rogers all ranged against Carl Morgenstern, it was sometimes hard to tell just who the underdog was at the hearings. Sam Shie, to be sure, was a lone teacher up against a community's educational establishment which was trying to purge him. But at the hearings themselves, almost all the spectators were on Shie's side; he was being supported by the Ohio Education Association, and he had three articulate, variously styled lawyers who disputed virtually everything Carl Morgenstern or one of his witnesses said. Each came at Morgenstern from a different angle with a new tactic, trying to wear him down the way a basketball team will use a full-court press, a fast break, the setting of a pick or screen, the switching of defensive assignments to bewilder an opponent. Hugh Holbrock made long, arcing, oratorical shots from outside the key, Robert Dunlevey dribbled spectacularly around any position Morgenstern took, and Randy Rogers would try to provoke Morgenstern into exchanges of anger and procedural wrangles. Rogers was surly to Morgenstern, who would respond by being loftily sardonic. A few times Morgenstern slipped and got mad at Rogers, who was polite to witnesses but steeled himself to a single pitch of fury when he was addressing Morgenstern. The rest of the time Rogers sat moodily at the defense table—in effect on the bench—while Holbrock and Dunlevey performed their own specialties.   Peter Davis, *Hometown*

Analogies are tricky. They may at first seem useful, but actually it is a rare analogy that is consistently useful at all the major points of comparison. Some analogies break down early; others are downright misleading. To be successful, a writer must carry out a conceptual analysis to be sure the analogy really holds.

Thus, most writers exercise caution with analogy, using it less often than illustration, definition, or classification. Nevertheless, you will run across analogies regularly; indeed, it would be hard to find a book without one. For certain very abstract information as well as some writing situations, analogy is the writing strategy of choice.

EXERCISE 18.5

Choose a principle or process that you know well. You might select a basic principle from the natural or social sciences; or you could consider a complex bodily movement, a physiological process, or a process of social change.

Write an analogy of several sentences that explains this principle or process to a reader who is unfamiliar with it. Look for something very familiar to compare it with that will help the reader understand the principle or process without a technical explanation. You may find yourself making some false starts, where your analogy holds up for only a few sentences. Writing out the analogy lets you discover whether it is plausible, consistent, and truly explanatory.

EXERCISE 18.6

In Chapter 2 Linda Ellerbee uses an analogy to express her attitude toward the contest for the anchorperson job on the *Weekend* news broadcast (paragraphs 10–17). What advantages or disadvantages do you see in this analogy? Why do you think Ellerbee chose it? Evaluate its effectiveness within the essay as a whole.

Arguing

The word *arguing*, in common parlance, connotes a dispute—raised voices, doors slammed, names called. As a writing strategy, however, arguing means something quite different. It means presenting a carefully reasoned, well-supported argument that takes into account other points of view. Arguing here, then, connotes both inquiry and advocacy, presenting a position in a thoughtful and convincing way.

This chapter presents the basic argumentative strategies available to a writer, focusing first on the structure of an argument—making claims, offering supporting reasons and evidence, and handling counterarguments—and then on common abuses or errors in arguing.

MAKING A CLAIM

Central to any writer's argument is a claim. The claim is whatever view or thesis or conclusion the writer puts forth about the subject. Argumentative essays present the claim in a thesis statement.

Here are some claims that appear as thesis statements in argumentative essays in Part I of this book:

> *The Crimson*'s decision not to run *Playboy*'s advertisement recruiting Harvard women for its October "Women of the Ivy League" issue was both the very most and the very least the newspaper could do to fight the institutionalized exploitation of women.   Kristin Goss, "Taking a Stand Against Sexism" (Chapter 6)

> I think there are a number of fairly modest changes that would not only simplify the lives of many admissions officers but also raise the quality of our high schools and colleges. I don't see these proposals as *alternatives* to the SAT; I see them as improvements on an irrational system in which the SAT is, at best, superfluous.   David Owen, "Testing and Society: What Can Be Done?" (Chapter 7)

> The Midwest is singular and love-deserving because it is as close to Heaven as we can come on this earth.   Jane Greer, "The Midwest: Close to Heaven" (Chapter 8)

> The mythic horror movie, like the sick joke, has a dirty job to do. It deliberately appeals to all that is worst in us. It is morbidity unchained, our

most base instincts let free, our nastiest fantasies realized . . . and it all happens fittingly enough, in the dark.   Stephen King, "Why We Crave Horror Movies" (Chapter 9)

"Araby" tells the story of an adolescent boy's initiation into adulthood. . . . From the beginning, the boy deludes himself about his relationship with Mangan's sister. Through this self-delusion, he increasingly resembles the adult characters, and later, at Araby, he realizes the parallel between his own self-delusion and the hypocrisy and vanity of the adult world.   David Ratinov, "From Innocence to Anguished Insight: 'Araby' As an Initiation Story" (Chapter 10)

Claims can be classified according to the kinds of questions they seek to answer. Each of the preceding thesis statements, for example, illustrates a different kind of claim:

Claim of judgment: What is your position on the issue? (Goss)

Claim of policy: What should be done to solve the problem? (Owen)

Claim of value: What is something worth? (Greer)

Claim of cause: Why is something the way it is? (King)

Claim of interpretation: What does something mean? (Ratinov)

Chapters 6–10 contain essays that argue for each of these kinds of claims, along with guidelines for constructing a reasoned argument to support such a claim.

Successful claims must be arguable, clear, and appropriately qualified. Following is a discussion of each of these characteristics of successful claims.

Arguable statements   To be arguable, a claim must have some probability of being true. It should not, however, be generally accepted as true. In addition, a claim must be arguable on objective grounds.

Facts are unarguable as claims because they are objectively verifiable. Facts are easy to verify—whether by checking an authoritative reference book, asking an authority, or observing it with your own eyes. For example, these statements assert facts:

Jem will be eighteen years old on May 6, 1988.

I am nearly five feet tall.

Eucalyptus trees were originally imported into California from Australia.

Each of these assertions can be easily verified. To find out Jem's age, you can do many things including asking him and looking up his school records. To determine a person's height, you can use a tape measure. To discover where California got its Eucalyptus trees, you can refer to a source in the library. There is no point in arguing over such statements (though you might question the authority of a particular source or the accuracy of someone's measurement). If a writer were to claim something as fact and attempt to support the claim with authorities or statistics, the essay would not be considered an argument but a report of information. Facts, as you will see in the next section, are used in arguments as evidence to support a claim and not as claims themselves.

Like facts, expressions of personal preference are not arguable claims. While facts are unarguable because they can be definitively proven true or false, claims of personal preferences are unarguable because they are purely subjective. The grounds for such claims are personal. A personal preference can be explained, but it cannot be used to convince others to accept as their own.

You can declare, for example, that you love rocky road ice cream or that eight o'clock classes are torture, but you cannot offer an argument to support such claims. All you can do is explain why you feel as you do. You might explain that the combination of chocolate, marshmallow, and nuts in rocky road feels good in your mouth. Similarly, even though many people undoubtedly share your dislike of eight o'clock classes, it would be pointless to try to convince anyone that you are right in your feelings. If, however, you were to restate the claim as "Eight o'clock classes are counterproductive," you could then construct an argument to support your claim that does not depend solely on your subjective feelings, memories, or preferences. Your argument could be based on reasons and evidence that are objective and that apply to others as well as to yourself. For example, you might argue that students' ability to learn is at an especially low ebb after breakfast and provide scientific as well as statistical evidence as support.

Clear and exact wording

The way a claim is worded is as important as whether or not it is arguable. The wording of a claim, especially its key terms, must be clear and exact. Two common kinds of imprecision are vagueness and ambiguity.

Consider the following claim: "Democracy is a way of life." The meaning of this claim is vague and uncertain. The problem stems both from the abstractness of the word *democracy* and the inexactness of the phrase *way of life*. Abstract ideas like democracy, freedom, and patriotism are by their very nature hard to grasp, and they become even less clear with overuse. Too often, such words take on connotations that may obscure their original meaning. *Way of life* suffers from fuzziness: What does it mean? Moreover, can a form of government be a way of life? It depends on what is meant by *way of life*. Does it refer to daily life, to a general philosophy or attitude toward life, or to something else?

A related problem is ambiguity. While a claim is considered vague if its meaning is unclear, it is ambiguous if it has more than one possible meaning. For example, the statement "my English instructor is mad" can be understood in two ways: The teacher is either angry or insane. Obviously, these are two very different claims. You wouldn't want readers to think you mean one when you actually mean the other.

In any argumentative writing, you should pay special attention to the way you phrase your claims and take care to avoid vague and ambiguous language.

Appropriate qualification

In addition to being arguable and clear, the forcefulness with which a writer asserts a claim should be appropriate to the writing situation. If you are confident that your case is so strong that readers will accept your argument without question, you will want to state your claim emphatically and unconditionally. If, however, you expect readers to challenge your assumptions or conclusions, then you will want to qualify your statement. Qualifying the extremity or forcefulness of a claim makes it more likely that readers will take it seriously. Expressions like *probably, very likely, apparently, it seems* all serve to qualify a claim.

It is also possible to qualify a statement in more subtle ways. Jane Greer, for example, asserts that the Midwest "is as close to Heaven as we can come on this earth." An unqualified—and unbelievable—claim would be "the Midwest *is* Heaven on earth." By phrasing her claim as she does, Greer anticipates objections her readers would be sure to voice. She pulls back only a little, but this strategic retreat enables her to accommodate her readers and at the same time put forward a claim that will surprise and possibly even amuse readers. Ways of anticipating reader reaction are discussed later in this chapter.

EXERCISE 19.1

Write a claim of judgment that asserts your position on one of the following controversial issues: capital punishment, abortion, mercy killing. These issues are complicated and have been debated for a long time. Constructing a persuasive argument would obviously require careful deliberation and probably some research as well. For the limited purpose of practicing writing claims, however, try simply to construct a claim that is arguable, clear, and appropriately qualified.

EXERCISE 19.2

Find the claim in any one of the selections in Chapter 6 and read the entire essay. Then decide whether the claim meets the three requirements of successful claims: that it be arguable, clear, and appropriately qualified.

SUPPORTING CLAIMS WITH REASONS AND EVIDENCE

Claims are supported with reasons and evidence. Whether you are taking a stand, proposing a solution, making an evaluation, speculating about causes, or interpreting a literary work, you need reasons and evidence to construct a convincing argument.

Reasons can be thought of as the main points supporting a claim. Often they are the answers to the question "Why do you make that claim?" For example, you might value a movie highly *because* of its challenging ideas, unusual camera work, and memorable acting. You might oppose mandatory drug testing for college athletes *because* it singles out one group for unusual treatment, cannot be conducted reliably with current technology, and in your view violates athletes' civil rights. These *because* phrases are the reasons you make your claim. You may have one or many reasons for a claim, depending on your subject and writing situation. These reasons need evidence in order for them to be convincing and in order for your whole argument to succeed with your readers.

The main kinds of evidence writers use to construct arguments include facts, statistics, authorities, anecdotes, scenarios, cases, and textual evidence. Following is a discussion of each one, along with criteria for judging the reliability of that particular kind of evidence and examples from published works. In each example, you will be able to see readily how the evidence supports a main point or reason in a larger argument.

Facts Facts may be used as supporting evidence in all types of arguments. A fact is generally defined as a statement accepted as true. Facts refer to a reality that can be measured or verified by objective means. The reliability of facts depends on their accuracy (they should not distort or misrepresent reality), completeness (they should not omit important details), and the trustworthiness of their sources (sources should be qualified and unbiased). Facts come from such sources as almanacs, encyclopedias, and research studies, as well as from our own observations and experience.

In this example, a scholar who studies Mexican migration to the United States uses facts to argue against three assumptions about illegal migrants, assumptions he asserts are false.

> The case for a more restrictive immigration policy is based on three principal assumptions: that illegal aliens compete effectively with, and replace, large numbers of American workers; that the benefits to American society resulting from the aliens' contribution of low-cost labor are exceeded by the "social costs" resulting from their presence here; and that most illegal aliens entering the United States eventually settle here permanently, thus imposing an increasingly heavy, long-term burden upon the society.

There is as yet no direct evidence to support any of these assumptions, at least with respect to illegal aliens from Mexico, who still constitute at least 60 to 65 percent of the total flow and more than 90 percent of the illegal aliens apprehended each year.

Where careful independent studies of the impact of illegal immigration on local labor markets have been made, they have found no evidence of large-scale displacement of legal resident workers by illegal aliens. Studies have also shown that Mexican illegals make amazingly little use of tax-supported social services while they are in the United States, and that the cost of the services they do use is far out-weighed by their contributions to Social Security and income tax revenues.

There is also abundant evidence indicating that the vast majority of illegal aliens from Mexico continue to maintain a pattern of "shuttle" migration, most of them returning to Mexico after six months or less of employment in the United States. In fact, studies have shown that only a small minority of Mexican illegals even aspire to settle permanently in the United States.

While illegal aliens from countries other than Mexico do seem to stay longer and make more use of social services, there is still no reliable evidence that they compete effectively with American workers for desirable jobs. The typical job held by the illegal alien, regardless of nationality, would not provide the average American family with more than a subsistence standard of living. In most states, it would provide less income than welfare payments.

Certainly in some geographic areas, type of enterprises, and job categories, illegal aliens may depress wage levels or "take jobs away" from American workers. But there is simply no hard evidence that these effects are as widespread or as serious as most policy-makers and the general public seem to believe.   Wayne A. Cornelius, "When the Door Is Closed on Illegal Aliens, Who Pays?"

Notice that Cornelius refers to facts as "hard evidence." They are considered hard or solid evidence because once accepted, a fact carries a great deal of weight in an argument. To encourage readers to accept his statements as fact, Cornelius says they come from "careful independent studies." Although he does not cite the sources of these studies here, they are included in the list of works cited at the end of the book in which this selection appears. Citing sources is especially important when your facts are not commonly accepted. Skeptical readers can review the research cited, as well as other relevant research, and draw their own conclusions.

Any facts you include in an argument should be current because what is accepted as "the facts" does change as new observations and studies are completed. In addition, you should use only those facts relevant to your argument, even if it means leaving out interesting peripheral information. Cornelius, for example, does not include facts about the kind of transportation Mexican illegals rely on because he wants to keep the focus on their brief periods of employment in the United States.

EXERCISE 19.3

Select one essay from Chapters 6–9 and evaluate its use of fact. Identify the statements presented as fact and comment on their reliability.

Statistics　In many kinds of arguments about economic, educational, or social issues, statistics may be essential. When you use statistics in your own arguments, you will want to ensure that they come from reliable sources. Your readers will expect you to explain the statistics clearly and present them fairly.

The following example, from Ken Auletta's book on America's underclass, presents statistics on violent crime, especially murder. In order to develop his argument that a permanent urban underclass is a growing threat to the social order, Auletta uses statistics in two ways: to show the increase in crime and to demonstrate that we have much more violent crime than other countries.

> For the average person, the most worrisome group are the violent criminals. Crime in America is now both more violent and more random. Crime statistics tell part of the story. In 1970, there were about 1,500 murders in the entire state of California. Nine years later, there were 1,975 murders in Los Angeles County alone. St. Louis, Missouri, which ranked as the murder capital of the nation, had 230 reported murders in 1978. In 1979, its murder rate jumped 24 percent. Eighty-four percent of the victims were black. Killings in Atlanta rose from 141 in 1978 to 231 in 1979; in Houston, from 462 to 632. Nationally, according to the FBI, violent crimes have risen in eleven of the past twelve years.
>
> In 1979 and 1980, violent crime jumped 11 percent. In 1980, New York City averaged five homicides a day (1,814)—more than triple the murder rate in all of Canada and ten times the declining murder rate in Tokyo, which has 40 percent more people. That same year New York had 3,711 rapes, 43,476 assaults, 210,703 burglaries and 249,421 cases of theft. There were an estimated 23,044 murders in the United States in 1980; in all of England and Wales in 1979, there were but 629.　Ken Auletta, *The Underclass*

Here, the author selected statistics to show the size of the problem and some of its results. The American numbers alone seem huge and worrisome. The contrast with the much smaller numbers in other countries makes the American numbers seem even bigger.

The next statistics come from a book by the prominent economist Lester Thurow, a book proposing a solution to the problem of America's economic decline. To convince readers that the problem is serious, Thurow argues early in the book that American productivity is falling behind that of some of our chief competitors. The statistics in the table are key evidence in his argument.

> The data in Table 2 show the level of manufacturing productivity for seven leading industrial countries in 1983. As the data show, the United States has already been surpassed by Germany and France. Since we know

that most of the small northern European countries (Switzerland, Sweden, Norway, Holland, Austria) have productivity rates similar to those of Germany and France, all of northern Europe with the exception of Ireland and the United Kingdom may now have moved slightly ahead of the United States in manufacturing productivity.

TABLE 2
MANUFACTURING PRODUCTIVITY 1983

Country	Output Per Hour of Work (1983 prices)	Rate of Growth 1977–82	1983
United States	$18.21	0.6%	4.2%
Germany	20.22	2.1	4.6
France	19.80	3.0	6.1
Italy	17.72	3.6	0.6
Japan	17.61	3.4	6.2
Canada	17.03	−0.3	6.9
United Kingdom	11.34	2.7	6.1

To some it will come as a surprise that Japanese productivity is still slightly behind that of the United States. This is due to the fact that the Japanese manufacturing economy is a peculiar mixture of the superefficient and the real dogs. In America we see only the exporting superefficient industries whose productivity is second to none. Japan's inefficient industries do not export and as a result are simply invisible to American eyes. While average Japanese productivity may be slightly inferior to that of America, it is well to remember that it is possible to drown in a river which is "on average" two feet deep. Where it counts—in exporting industries such as steel, autos, and consumer electronics—the Japanese are second to none.   Lester Thurow, *The Zero-Sum Solution*

Thurow comments on the table, explaining the information it contains and why it is important. He then immediately (and throughout the chapter in which the table appears) uses it to support his argument.

Chapter 21: Library Research describes strategies to help you locate statistics. Whenever possible, use sources in which statistics first appeared rather than summaries or digests of others' statistics. For example, you would want to get medical statistics from a reputable and authoritative professional periodical like the *New England Journal of Medicine* rather than from a popular news weekly. If you are uncertain about the most authoritative sources, ask a reference librarian or a professor who is a specialist on your topic.

EXERCISE 19.4
Analyze the use of statistics in one of the following selections in Part I of this book:
Chapter 7, "Birth Control in the Schools," Adam Paul Weisman

Chapter 9, "Suicide Among Young People," Victor Fuchs
Chapter 9, "Where Will They Sleep Tonight?" Kim Dartnell

Identify the sources of the statistics. Do they seem to be the original sources? How might you find out whether the sources are authoritative and reputable?

How does the writer integrate the statistics into the text of the selection? By direct quotation from the source? By paraphrase or summary? In tables or figures?

What part do the statistics play in the selection? Do you find the statistics convincing?

Authorities　To support their claims and reasons, writers do not hesitate to cite authorities. They establish their credentials and quote them. Quoting a respected authority on a topic generally adds weight to an argument.

From Loretta Schwartz-Nobel's book on starvation in America comes a typical example. The writer cites an authority, a researcher at a well-known oceanographic institute, to support her argument that we now have technical resources to eliminate hunger in America.

> Dr. John Ryther, a highly respected and well-known marine biologist at the Woods Hole (Massachusetts) Oceanographic Institution, points out that there are about one billion acres of coastal wetlands in the world. If only one-tenth of these wetlands were used to raise fish, the potential yield of fish using improved methods of production would be one hundred million tons a year. This is the equivalent of the yield from the entire world's commercial fisheries.
>
> Dr. Ryther has also devised a complex continuous culture system which produces oysters, seaweed, worms, flounder, and abalone. It ultimately becomes a biological sewage treatment plant returning clean water to the sea.
>
> If this kind of system were implemented on a large scale it could produce a million pounds of shellfish a year from each one-acre production facility. By using advanced culture techniques like those developed at Woods Hole, Dr. Ryther estimates that the yield could well be multiplied tenfold within the next three decades.　Loretta Schwartz-Nobel, *Starving in the Shadow of Plenty*

The writer could simply have mentioned a system for wetland culture, but instead she emphasizes that it comes from a respected expert—thereby adding to her own authority and to the credibility of her material. (After all, she is not an expert on all the technical aspects of her topic.) Instead of quoting the expert directly, she paraphrases the information from him.

EXERCISE 19.5

Analyze the way authorities are used in one of the following selections from Part I of this book. Decide whether you find the use of authorities convincing. How might you find out whether the authorities are respected? How does the writer establish each authority's credentials?

How does the writer integrate the authority's words or opinions into the text of the selection? By direct quotation? By paraphrase or summary in the writer's own language? What role does the authority have in the piece as a whole?

Chapter 6, "Animal Rights Versus Human Health," Albert Rosenfeld
Chapter 6, "Journalistic Ethics," Sydney Young
Chapter 7, "Birth Control in the Schools," Adam Paul Weisman
Chapter 9, "Suicide Among Young People," Victor Fuchs

Anecdotes   Anecdotes are brief stories that can very effectively provide evidence in an argument. Their specificity may be quite convincing if they seem to readers true to life. A physician opens an essay arguing that funerals are good for people with this anecdote:

> While attending a medical meeting about a year ago, I ran into a fellow I'd known in residency. "What are you doing here, Bill?" he asked. "Giving a talk on the responses to death," I replied. "It will cover the psychological value of funerals as well as—"
>
> "Funerals!" he exclaimed. "What a waste *they* are! I've made it plain to my wife that *I* don't want a funeral. Why spend all that money on such a macabre ordeal? And why have the kids standing around wondering what it's all about?"
>
> "Look, Jim," I said patiently, "I've seen case after case of depression caused by the inability of patients—young and old—to work through their feelings after a death. I've found that people are often better off if they have a funeral to focus their feelings on. That lets them do the emotional work necessary in response to the loss." My friend still looked doubtful. And, as we parted company, I wondered how many other physicians are also over-looking the psychological value of funerals.   William A. Lamers, Jr., "Funerals Are Good for People"

Notice that the anecdote characterizes one particular occurrence. Anecdotes are different from generalized narratives, which summarize recurring or typical events. They are also different from scenarios, which tell about something that might happen, and cases, which summarize observations made over a period of time. Anecdotes make a special contribution to argument through their concreteness. (Strategies for writing anecdotes are reviewed in Chapter 2: Remembering Events and Chapter 13: Narrating.)

In the next example, a historian repeats a secondhand anecdote to argue that we should take extrasensory perception more seriously than we do:

> At six o'clock one evening Swedenborg, while dining with friends in the town of Gothenburg, suddenly became excited and declared that a danger-

ous fire had broken out in his native city of Stockholm, some three hundred miles away. He asserted a little later that the fire had already burned the home of one of his neighbors and was threatening to consume his own. At eight o'clock of that same evening, he exclaimed with some relief that the fire had been checked three doors from his home. Two days later, Swedenborg's every statement was confirmed by actual reports of the fire, which had begun to blaze at the precise hour that he first received the impression.

Swedenborg's case is only one among hundreds of similar instances recorded in history and biography of the great, the near-great, and the obscure. At some time in their lives Mark Twain, Abraham Lincoln, Saint-Saëns, to name but a few, had, according to their biographers and in some cases their own accounts, strange sudden visions of events taking place at a distance, or events that took place, down to the last minute detail, months or years later in their own lives. In the case of Swedenborg the ability to see at a distance developed later into a powerful and sustained faculty; in most other cases, the heightened perceptivity seemed to arise only in a moment of crisis.   Gina Cerminora, *Many Mansions*

EXERCISE 19.6

Analyze the use of anecdote in one of the following selections from Part I of this book. How long is the anecdote in relation to the length of the whole essay? Does the writer comment on the significance of the anecdote or leave it to the reader to infer its importance? What role does the anecdote play in the selection as a whole? Do you find the anecdote convincing?

Chapter 7, "To Unteach Greed," Carol Bly

Chapter 9, "Why Children Don't Seem Childlike Anymore," Joshua Meyerowitz

Scenarios   While an anecdote tells about something that actually happened, a scenario is a narrative that describes something that might happen. Writers create scenarios to make their arguments more vivid and convincing. Scenarios raise and answer the question "What if?"

The first example comes from a book on illiteracy in America. To help readers understand illiterates' plight, the author creates a scenario from a dream:

Since I first immersed myself within this work I have often had the following dream: I find that I am in a railroad station or a large department store within a city that is utterly unknown to me and where I cannot understand the printed words. None of the signs or symbols is familiar. Everything looks strange: like mirror writing of some kind. Gradually I understand that I am in the Soviet Union. All the letters on the walls around me are Cyrillic. I look for my pocket dictionary but I find that it has been mislaid. Where have I left it? Then I recall that I forgot to bring it with me when I packed my bags in Boston. I struggle to remember the name of my hotel. I try to ask somebody for directions. One person stops and looks at me in a peculiar way. I lose the nerve to ask. At last I reach into my wallet for an ID card. The card is missing. Have I lost it? Then I remember that my card was confiscated for some reason, many years before. Around this point, I wake up in a panic.

This panic is not so different from the misery that millions of adult illiterates experience each day within the course of their routine existence in the U.S.A.   Jonathan Kozol, *Illiteracy in America*

The next example comes from an essay on the threat of nuclear war. Like analogies, scenarios use the familiar to define or illustrate the unknown. If you know Chicago, you will readily appreciate the devastation represented in this scenario of the effects of a nuclear bomb dropped on that city:

On the freeways radiating from the Loop, automobiles, trucks, and buses were simultaneously evaporated and blown away, their particles sucked up into the fireball to become components of the radioactive cloud.

Along the Stevenson Expressway, some seven or eight miles from Ground Zero, scores of oil storage tanks exploded—ruptured by the shock wave and then ignited from the grass and shrubbery burning around them.

At this range, too, aluminum siding on homes evaporated and some concrete surfaces exploded under thermal stress. The few buildings still standing were in danger of imminent collapse—and all were engulfed by flames. Highway spans caved in. Asphalt blistered and melted.

Clothing caught fire, and people were charred by intense light and heat. Their charcoal limbs would, in some instances, render their shapes recognizably human.

With greater distance from Ground Zero, the effects diminished. About ten miles from the Loop, in the area around the Brookfield Zoo, the fireball was merely brighter than a thousand suns. Glass did not melt, but shattered window fragments flew through the air at about 135 miles per hour. All trees were burning even before the shock wave uprooted most of them.

Railroad bridges collapsed, and railroad cars were blown from their tracks. Automobiles were smashed and twisted into grotesque shapes. One- and two-story wood frame homes, already burning, were demolished by the shock wave, which also knocked down cinderblock walls and brick apartment buildings.

Those who had taken shelter underground—or, more probably, just happened to be there—survived for fifteen minutes or a half hour longer than those who were exposed. They suffocated as oxygen was drawn away by the firestorm that soon raged overhead.

At O'Hare Airport, the world's busiest, aircraft engaged in landing or takeoff crashed and burned. Planes on the ground were buffeted into each other and adjacent hangars, their fuselages bent and partially crushed by the shock wave. Some thirty seconds before the shock wave struck, aluminum surfaces facing the fireball had melted and the aircraft interiors had been set aflame.   Erwin Kroll and Theodore Pastol, ''The Day the Bomb Went Off''

EXERCISE 19.7

Writers often use scenarios to discuss the possible effects of trends or phenomena. Choose one of the following trends or phenomena, and write a scenario illustrating the possible effects.

1. The effects of cable TV's popularity on commercial and public TV

2. The effects of the widespread popularity of aerobic dancing and exercise on Americans

3. The effects of increasing tuition costs on college students

4. The effects on American society if colleges were available only to the very wealthy

5. The effects on American culture if the United States ran out of gasoline

Cases   Like an anecdote, a case is an example that comes from a writer's firsthand knowledge. Cases summarize observations of people. They are meant to be typical or generalized. Case histories are an important part of the work of psychologists, doctors, and social workers. These cases may be quite lengthy, sometimes following the life of one individual over many months or years. In persuasive writing, however, cases are presented briefly as evidence for a claim or reason.

This example comes from a publication for school administrators. It was written by two sociologists studying the psychological problems of adolescents, particularly alienation. Notice how they use the John Kelly case both to define alienation and to argue that it is a serious problem.

Since the beginning of man's awareness of ''self'' and ''other,'' alienation has frayed the fabric of social institutions. In recent decades the term has become a euphemism for every kind of aberrant behavior from drug use to rejection of the political system. Adolescents are especially affected by this malaise. Let us consider the case of John Kelly, for example.

When John Kelly was 10, he was curious and energetic, the mascot of his family. His inquisitiveness led him to railroad yards, museums, and bus adventures downtown alone. In school, he was charming, cooperative, and interested. At 13, John suddenly changed. His agreeable nature vanished as he quarreled endlessly with his older brothers. He became moody and sullen, constantly snapping at his parents. He began to skip school and disrupt class when he did attend. When he was finally expelled, his parents enrolled him in another junior high school, hoping the change would solve some of John's problems. Instead, his difficulties intensified as he dropped his boyhood friends, stopped communicating with his parents, and withdrew into himself. Now, 16-year-old John bears little resemblance to the loving, active child his family once knew. He has been suspended from yet another school, hangs out with an older crowd, and comes home only to sleep. His parents feel hurt, bewildered, frustrated, and frightened.

As John Kelly's case makes clear, adolescent alienation is a teenager's inability to connect meaningfully with other people. At its root is aloneness, a feeling that no one else is quite like you, that you are not what other people want you to be.　James Mackey and Deborah Appleman, ''Broken Connections: The Alienated Adolescent in the 80s''

As examples and evidence in persuasive writing, cases are usually brief, rarely longer than this one. Writers nearly always know much more about their cases than they tell us. They select just the details from the case that will support the claim they are making.

To be effective, a case must ring true. Readers need specific details: dress, manner, personal history. Though the person in this case is an abstraction, meant to represent many people like him or her, we still recognize a real person.

EXERCISE 19.8
Evaluate the use of a case in "Where Will They Sleep Tonight?" by Kim Dartnell (Chapter 9). Decide whether the case is relevant to the argument and whether it rings true. What does the case contribute to the essay?

Textual evidence   When you argue claims of value (Chapter 8) and interpretation (Chapter 10), textual evidence may be very important. If you are criticizing a controversial book that your readers have not yet read, you may want to quote from it often so that readers can understand why you think the author's argument is not credible. If you are interpreting a novel for one of your classes, you may need to include numerous excerpts to show just how you arrived at your conclusion. In both these situations, you are integrating bits of the text you are evaluating or interpreting into your own text and building your argument on these bits.

In the following example, a literary critic uses textual evidence to support the claim that the main character in James Joyce's story "Araby" is involved in a "vivid waiting." (You can read "Araby" in Chapter 10). As you read, notice how the writer continually refers to events in the story and also regularly quotes phrases from the story.

''Araby,'' wrote Ezra Pound, ''is much better than a 'story,' it is a vivid waiting.'' It is true; the boy, suspended in his first dream of love, is also held up by circumstance, and the subjective rendering of this total experience is indeed vivid. . . .

Every morning the boy kept watch from his window until Mangan's sister appeared, and then with a leaping heart he ran to follow her in the street until their ways diverged, hers toward her convent school. Of an evening, when she came out on the doorstep to call her brother to tea, the boys at play would linger in the shadows to see whether she "would remain or go in"; then while she waited they would approach "resignedly," but while Mangan still teased his sister before obeying, the boy of this story "stood by the railings looking at her," seeing "her figure defined by the light from the half-opened door" and waiting upon a summons of another kind. He must wait too for his uncle's late return and for the money to fetch the girl a present from the bazaar Araby; then the special train, almost empty, waited intolerably and he arrived late. Still he drove toward his goal, paying a shilling to avoid further delay in looking for a sixpenny entrance. Once inside, he found the place half-darkened and the stalls mostly closed. Though there was nothing for him to buy, he lingered still, baffled, stultified, prolonging only pretense of interest. What awaits him as the lights are being put out is a facing "with anguish and anger" of his obsessive mood and its frustration, of himself as "a creature driven and derided by vanity"—like Stephen in *A Portrait* "angry with himself for being young and the prey of restless foolish impulses."   Warren Beck, *Joyce's Dubliners*

EXERCISE 19.9

Select one of the essays on "Araby" in Chapter 10 and analyze its use of evidence. Identify where "Araby" is quoted, paraphrased, summarized, or merely referred to. Indicate whether the evidence is simply cited or explained in some way.

ANTICIPATING READERS' COUNTERARGUMENTS

Claims, reasons, and evidence are essential to a successful argument. Thoughtful writers go further, however, by anticipating their readers' counterarguments. Counterarguments include any objections, alternatives, challenges, or questions. To anticipate counterarguments, try to imagine a reader's point of view on the subject, knowledge about the subject, and familiarity with the issues. Try also to imagine a reader's response to the argument as it unfolds step by step. What will readers be thinking and feeling? How will they react?

Anticipating readers' counterarguments, writers rely on three basic strategies: acknowledging, accommodating, and refuting counterarguments. They let readers know they are aware of their objections and questions (acknowledge), accept all or part of the objections into their argument (accommodate), or explicitly oppose (refute) the objections. Writers may use one or more of these strategies in the same essay. Research by communications specialists indicates that readers find arguments more convincing when writers have anticipated their readers in these ways.

At this point, you may have an objection: Isn't it manipulative to acknowledge and accommodate readers' counterarguments? In fact, cynical writers and speakers do try to manipulate their readers' responses. They may try to trick readers, sell something, ensure a donation, or win support for a policy based on lies and illegalities. However, unless readers are especially ignorant or emotionally vulnerable and willing to grant uncritically the writer's credibility, readers recognize and scorn manipulation. Anticipating counterarguments is convincing when it builds a bridge of shared concerns between writer and reader. The writer bases the anticipation (and the argument) on shared values, assumptions, goals, or criteria. This approach to acknowledging, accommodating, and refuting counterarguments wins readers' respect and attention—and sometimes even their agreement.

Acknowledgment of counterarguments

The primary purpose of argumentative writing is to influence readers. Therefore, careful writers seek to influence their readers with each choice of a word, each choice of a sentence. Sometimes writers may even address their readers openly, both to build a bridge of shared concerns and to acknowledge their questions or objections.

The first example comes from a book on hunger in America. The writer seeks to enlist readers' sympathies for neglected elderly people.

> This is South Philadelphia—a microcosm of America, a place where people have gone to work, raised children, and then retired. Their daughters are our secretaries, clerks, and teachers. Their sons are our policemen, longshoremen, bankers, doctors, and lawyers. Economically these retired people once represented America's middle class. Yet in this typical urban neighborhood with its tap dance school, businessmen's association, American Cancer Society chapter, and local fire station, a two-year survey conducted by the Albert Einstein Medical Center's Social Service Division concluded that "very few if any of the elderly were without need."
>
> These are men and women who have worked all their lives. These are our uncles, our aunts, our grandparents, our mothers, and our fathers. They live in a world of old newspaper clippings, pictures, and photographs of relatives who never visit.   Loretta Schwartz-Nobel, *Starving in the Shadow of Plenty*

Here the writer seems to anticipate that readers—as citizens, voters, and taxpayers in any part of the country—might question whether they have any personal responsibility for elderly people in South Philadelphia. Her strategy is to argue that South Philadelphia is a representative American community, not a peculiar place with unique problems. She implies that we are one big American family, with familylike responsibilities for aging relatives. Since she eventually argues for a national solution to what she believes to be a widespread problem, her success depends on convincing readers of their personal responsibility for needy elderly people anywhere in America.

The next example acknowledges readers' possible counterarguments even more directly. These are the opening paragraphs in an article arguing that some of America's homeless have chosen that way of life. The writer knows that readers may immediately doubt this surprising claim. It seems inconceivable that people would choose to sleep on sidewalks and eat out of garbage cans. Notice how the writer acknowledges three different counter-arguments.

> The homeless, it seems, can be roughly divided into two groups: those who have had marginality and homelessness forced upon them and want nothing more than to escape them, and a smaller number who have at least in part chosen marginality, and now accept, or, in a few cases, embrace it.
>
> I understand how dangerous it can be to introduce the idea of choice into a discussion of homelessness. It can all too easily be used for all the wrong reasons by all the wrong people to justify indifference or brutality toward the homeless, or to argue that they are getting only what they deserve.
>
> And I understand, too, how complicated the notion can become: Many of the veterans on the street, or battered women, or abused and runaway children, have chosen this life only as the lesser of evils, and because, in this society, there is often no place else to go.
>
> And finally, I understand how much that happens on the street can combine to create an apparent acceptance of homelessness that is nothing more than the absolute absence of hope.
>
> Nonetheless we must learn to accept that there may indeed be people on the street who have seen so much of our world, or have seen it so clearly, that to live in it becomes impossible.   Peter Marin, "Go Ask Alice"

You might think that acknowledging readers' objections in this way—addressing readers directly, listing their possible objections, and discussing each one—would weaken an argument. It might even seem reckless to suggest objections that not all readers would think of. On the contrary, however, readers respond positively to this strategy. The writer appears to have explained the issue thoroughly. He seems thoughtful and reasonable, more interested in inquiry than advocacy, more concerned with seeking the truth about the homeless than in ignoring or overriding readers' objections in order to win their adherence to a self-serving claim. By researching your subject and analyzing your readers, you will be able to use this strategy confidently in your own argumentative essays.

EXERCISE 19.10

Evaluate acknowledgment of readers in "Abortion, Right and Wrong" by Rachel Richardson Smith (Chapter 6). How does Smith adapt this strategy to her purposes? What is the approach to readers and the tone? What does the acknowledgment seem to contribute to the essay?

Accommodation of counterarguments

Careful argumentative writers often acknowledge their readers' objections, questions, and alternative causes or solutions. Occasionally, however, they may go even further. Instead of merely acknowledging their readers' objections, they accept them and incorporate them into their own arguments. You can imagine how disarming this strategy can be to readers.

This example comes from an essay arguing causes for people's interest in jogging. Before proposing his own cause (later in the essay), the writer acknowledges and then accommodates causes proposed by philosophers and theologists.

> Some scout-masterish philosophers argue that the appeal of jogging and other body-maintenance programs is the discipline they afford. We live in a world in which individuals have fewer and fewer obligations. The work week has shrunk. Weekend worship is less compulsory. Technology gives us more free time. Satisfactorily filling free time requires imagination and effort. Freedom is a wide and risky river; it can drown the person who does not know how to swim across it. The more obligations one takes on, the more time one occupies, the less threat freedom poses. Jogging can become an instant obligation. For a portion of his day, the jogger is not his own man; he is obedient to a regimen he has accepted.
>
> Theologists may take the argument one step further. It is our modern irreligion, our lack of confidence in any hereafter, that makes us anxious to stretch our mortal stay as long as possible. We run, as the saying goes, for our lives, hounded by the suspicion that these are the only lives we are likely to enjoy.
>
> All of these theorists seem to me more or less right. As the growth of cults and charismatic religions and the resurgence of enthusiasm for the military draft suggest, we do crave commitment. And who can doubt, watching so many middle-aged and older persons torturing themselves in the name of fitness, that we are unreconciled to death, more so perhaps than any generation in modern memory?   Carll Tucker, "Fear of Dearth"

Notice that this writer's accommodation is not grudging. He admits that the theorists (and any readers who favor them) are "more or less right," and he suggests reasons why they must be right. Considering alternative causes is very common in essays of causal analysis (see Chapter 9). Writers must include alternatives that their readers may be aware of and then either accommodate or refute these alternatives. To do anything less makes writers seem uninformed and weakens their credibility.

The second example, from an essay arguing for a solution to the nuclear arms race, begins with an assertive, unqualified claim that seems to challenge readers. Immediately, however, the writer acknowledges that certain readers will object to this claim. Notice how he accommodates their counterargument.

> To my mind, the nuclear bomb is the most useless weapon ever invented. It can be employed to no rational purpose. It is not even an effective defense against itself. It is only something with which, in a moment of petulance or panic, you commit such fearful acts of destruction as no sane person would ever wish to have upon his conscience.
>
> There are those who will agree, with a sigh, to much of what I have just said, but will point to the need for something called deterrence. This is, of course, a concept which attributes to others—to others who, like ourselves, were born of women, walk on two legs, and love their children, to human beings, in short—the most fiendish and inhuman of tendencies.
>
> But all right: accepting for the sake of argument the profound iniquity of these adversaries, no one could deny, I think, that the present Soviet and American arsenals, presenting over a million times the destructive power of the Hiroshima bomb, are simply fantastically redundant to the purpose in question. If the same relative proportions were to be preserved, something well less than 20 percent of those stocks would surely suffice for the most sanguine concepts of deterrence, whether as between the two nuclear superpowers or with relation to any of those other governments that have been so ill-advised as to enter upon the nuclear path. Whatever their suspicions of each other, there can be no excuse on the part of these two governments for holding, poised against each other and poised in a sense against the whole Northern Hemisphere, quantities of these weapons so vastly in excess of any rational and demonstrable requirements.   George Kennan, "A Proposal for International Disarmament"

The writer accepts the idea of deterrence and then uses it as the basis for arguing to reduce the size of the present American and Soviet arsenals. This strategy enables him to conclude this section of his argument with another assertive claim that has a good chance of winning readers' agreement.

EXERCISE 19.11

Exactly how does Albert Rosenfeld attempt to accommodate readers in his Chapter 6 essay, "Animal Rights Versus Human Health"? What seems successful or unsuccessful in Rosenfeld's strategy? What does accommodation contribute to the essay?

Refutation of counterarguments Readers' objections and questions cannot always be accommodated. Sometimes they must be refuted. When writers refute likely counterarguments, they assert that they are wrong and argue against them. Refutation does not have to be delivered arrogantly or dismissively, however. Writers can refute their readers' objections in a spirit of shared inquiry in solving problems, establishing probable causes, deciding the value of something, or understanding all the issues in a controversy. In argument, differences are inevitable. Argument remains centrally important in human discourse because informed, well-intentioned people disagree about issues and policies.

In this example, an economist refutes one explanation for the increasing numbers of women in the work force. First he describes a "frequently mentioned" counterargument. Then he concedes a point ("there is little doubt") before beginning his refutation.

> One frequently mentioned but inadequately evaluated explanation for the surge of women into paid employment is the spread of time-saving household innovations such as clothes washers and dryers, frozen foods, and dishwashers. There is little doubt that it is easier to combine paid employment with home responsibilities now than it was fifty years ago, but it is not clear whether these time-saving innovations were the *cause* of the rise in female labor force participation or whether they were largely a *response* to meet a demand created by working women. Confusion about this point is most evident in comments that suggest that the rapid growth of supermarkets and fast-food outlets is a cause of women going to work. Similar time-saving organizations were tried at least sixty years ago, but with less success because the value of time was much lower then. The absence of supermarkets and fast-food eating places in low-income countries today also shows that their rapid growth in the United States is primarily a *result* of the rising value of time and the growth of women in the work force, not the reverse. Victor Fuchs, "Why Married Mothers Work"

This selection illustrates very well that refutations must be argued. Writers cannot simply dismiss readers' counterarguments with a wave of the hand. Fuchs refutes a proposed cause of the trend by arguing that it is actually an effect or result of the trend. The last two sentences support his refutation.

The second example comes from a publication arguing for a revised English curriculum in the schools. In this section, the writers attempt to refute a predictable objection. Notice how they describe the objection and then assert their refutation.

> [An] argument against the teaching of literature, which enjoyed greater currency in the late 1960s and 1970s than it does now, goes something like this: Literature is an "elitist" discipline, a subterfuge for imposing ruling-class values on oppressed groups so that they will cooperate in their own exploitation. According to this argument, minority students will encounter a world view in literature classes that is either irrelevant to their own heritage or downright destructive of it. The rebuttal to this argument is straightforward: It is wrong. The treasure-house of literature is not oppressive; it is liberating—of the constraints of time, place, and personal experience into

which each of us as an individual is born. The real injustice would be to deny any child access to the wealth of insights that our best literature has to offer. To deny students the wisdom of our literary heritage may restrict their social mobility and limit the potential that schools have to create opportunities for students to develop their individual talents and to prepare for participation in our society.

Of course, in literature and the arts, local districts should adopt reading lists that recognize the natural desire of communities to maintain an ethnic identity. Quite rightly, black students are inspired by Alex Haley's *Roots* and Richard Wright's *Black Boy;* Hispanic students, by Rudolfo A. Anaya's *Bless Me, Ultima* and Peter Matthiessen's *Sal Si Puedes: Cesar Chavez and the New American Revolution;* Japanese-Americans, by Yoshiko Uchida's *Samurai of Gold Hill* and Monica Sone's *Nisei Daughter;* and so on. Like all great literature, these stories confer lasting benefits—intellectual, social, and spiritual—on those who read them. Furthermore, all students will profit from such literature to understand those whose experiences of America differ from theirs. The point is, far from being "elitist," the common culture belongs to all of us. And every child in the United States—rich or poor, male or female, black, Hispanic, Asian, or white—is entitled to experience it fully.

Our country was founded on the expectation that out of many traditions one nation could evolve that would be stronger and more durable than any single tradition. To argue that teaching a common core of literature in our pluralistic society is not feasible because there is no basis for consensus is to beg the question. It is, and always has been, precisely the task of the public schools to help form that consensus.

In a society that celebrates the prerogatives of the individual, the public schools are potentially one of the most meaningful forces for social cohesion. They are the modern equivalent of the village square—a forum for identifying the shared ethos of our diverse and cosmopolitan society; a place where all our children can come together and discover what it is that unites us as a people. Well-taught literature is an essential part of that consensus building. California State Education Department, *Handbook for Planning an Effective Literature Program*

This example and the previous one illustrate that effective refutation requires a restrained tone and careful argument. Although you may not accept the refutation, you can agree that it is thoughtfully argued. You do not feel attacked personally because the writers disagree with you.

The writers of the second article make an important concession in the second paragraph. They acknowledge the value of minority literature while still arguing for a common literature in school English programs. Here, accommodation blends with refutation.

EXERCISE 19.12

Analyze and evaluate the use of refutation in any one of the essays in Chapter 6. How does the writer manage the refutation? Does the objection seem to be clearly and accurately described? How is the refutation asserted and argued for? What seems most convincing and least convincing in the argument? What is the tone of the refutation?

EXERCISE 19.13
Briefly refute any of the refutations you analyzed in the preceding exercise. State the writers' refutation accurately, and argue your refutation of it convincingly. Try to use a restrained tone.

EXERCISE 19.14
Return to the claim you wrote in Exercise 19.1. Imagine how you might develop an essay arguing for this claim with reasons and evidence. Then identify one likely objection or question from your readers, and write a refutation of it. State the objection accurately, and argue your refutation in a way that will not alienate your readers.

LOGICAL FALLACIES

Fallacies are errors or flaws in reasoning. Although essentially unsound, fallacious arguments seem superficially plausible and often have great persuasive power. Fallacies are not necessarily deliberate efforts to deceive readers. They may be accidental, resulting from a failure to examine underlying assumptions critically, establish solid ground to support a claim, or choose words that are clear and unambiguous.

Here, listed in alphabetical order, are the most common logical fallacies:

☐ *Begging the question.* Arguing that a claim is true by repeating the claim in different words. Sometimes called circular reasoning.
☐ *Confusing chronology with causality.* Assuming that because one thing preceded another, the former caused the latter. Also called *post hoc, ergo propter hoc* (Latin for "after this, therefore because of this").
☐ *Either/or reasoning.* Assuming that there are only two sides to a question, and representing yours as the only correct one.
☐ *Equivocating.* Misleading or hedging with ambiguous word choices.
☐ *Failing to accept the burden of proof.* Asserting a claim without presenting a reasoned argument to support it.
☐ *False analogy.* Assuming that because one thing resembles another, conclusions drawn from one also apply to the other.
☐ *Overreliance on authority.* Assuming that something is true simply because an expert says so and ignoring evidence to the contrary.
☐ *Hasty generalization.* Offering only weak or limited evidence to support a conclusion.

☐ *Oversimplifying.* Giving easy answers to complicated questions, often by appealing to emotions rather than logic.

☐ *Personal attack.* Demeaning the proponents of a claim instead of their argument. Also called *ad hominen* (Latin for "against the man").

☐ *Red herring.* Attempting to misdirect the discussion by raising an essentially unrelated point.

☐ *Slanting.* Selecting or emphasizing the evidence that supports your claim and suppressing or playing down other evidence.

☐ *Slippery slope.* Pretending that one thing inevitably leads to another.

☐ *Sob story.* Manipulating readers' emotions in order to lead them to draw unjustified conclusions.

☐ *Straw man.* Directing the argument against a claim that nobody actually holds or that everyone agrees is very weak.

PART THREE

Research Strategies

Field Research

In universities, government agencies, and the business world, field research can be as important as library research or experimental research. In specialties such as sociology, political science, anthropology, polling, advertising, and news reporting, field research is the basic means of gathering information.

This chapter is a brief introduction to three of the major kinds of field research: observations, interviews, and questionnaires. The writing activities involved are central to several academic specialties. If you major in education, communication, or one of the social sciences, you probably will be asked to do writing based on observations, interviews, and questionnaire results. You will also read large amounts of information based on these ways of learning about people, groups, and institutions.

Observations and interviews are essential for the essay in Chapter 4: Writing Profiles. Interviewing could be helpful, as well, in documenting a trend or phenomenon and exploring its causes (Chapter 9: Speculating About Causes), in case you wanted to consult a campus or community expert on the trend or conduct a survey to establish the presence of a trend. In proposing a solution to a problem (Chapter 7: Proposing Solutions), you might want to interview someone who could help you outline the steps in a somewhat technical or complicated solution; or, if many people are affected, you might want to find out what they know with a questionnaire. In writing a report on an academic subject (Chapter 5: Reporting Information), you might want to interview a faculty member who is a specialist on that subject, or you might want to plan a questionnaire study as a basis for a report. Although you probably will not wish to interview the person you write about in Chapter 3: Remembering People, interviewing often plays a major role in family and group histories.

OBSERVATIONS

This section offers guidelines for planning an observational visit, taking notes on your observations, and later writing them up. Some kinds of writing are based on observations from single visits—travel writing, social workers' case reports, insurance investigators' accident reports—but most observational writing is based on several visits. An anthropologist or sociologist studying

20

an unfamiliar group or activity might observe it for months, filling several notebooks with notes. If you are profiling a place (Chapter 4: Writing Profiles), you almost certainly will want to make two or three (or more) observational visits, some of them perhaps combined with interviews.

Second and third visits to observe further and to take more notes are important because as you learn more about a place from observations, interviews, or reading, you will discover new ways to look at it. Gradually you will have more and more questions that can only be answered by follow-up visits.

Planning the observational visit

To ensure that your observational visits are worthwhile, you must plan them carefully.

Getting access. If the place you propose to visit is public, you probably will have easy access to it. If everything you need to see is within view of anyone passing by or using the place, you can make your observations without any special arrangements. Indeed, you may not even be noticed.

However, most observational visits that are part of special inquiries—reports for a sociology or education class, the profile in Chapter 4—require special access. Hence, you will need to arrange your visit, calling ahead or making a get-acquainted visit, in order to introduce yourself and state your purpose. Find out the times you may visit, and be certain you can gain access easily.

Announcing your intentions. State your intentions directly and fully. Say who you are, where you are from, and what you hope to do. You may be surprised at how receptive people can be to a student on assignment from a college course. Not every place you wish to visit will welcome you, and a variety of constraints on outside visitors exist in private businesses as well as public institutions. But generally, if people know your intentions, they may be able to tell you about aspects of a place or activity you would not have thought to observe.

Taking your tools. Take a notebook with a firm back so that you will have a steady writing surface, perhaps a small stenographer's notebook with a spiral binding across the top. Using this notebook, you can flip a page full of notes over and under and out of the way. Remember also to take a writing instrument.

Some observers dictate their observations into portable tape recorders. You might want to experiment with this method. We recommend, though, that for your first observations you record in writing. Your instructor or other students in your class may want to see your written notes.

Observing and taking notes

Following are some brief guidelines for observing and taking notes.

Observing. Some activities invite multiple vantage points, whereas others seem to limit the observer to a single perspective. Take advantage of every perspective available to you. Come in close, take a middle position, and stand back. Study the scene from a stationary position and also try to move around it. The more varied your perspectives, the more you are likely to observe.

Your purpose in observing is both to describe the activity and to analyze it. You will want to look closely at the activity itself, but you will also want to think about what makes this activity special, what seems to be the point of it.

Try to be an innocent observer: pretend you have never seen anything like this activity before. Look for typical features of the activity as well as unusual features. Look at it from the perspective of your readers. Ask what details of the activity would surprise and inform and interest them.

Taking notes. You undoubtedly will find your own style of notetaking, but here are a few pointers.

Write only on one side of the page. Later, when you organize your notes, you may want to cut up the pages and file notes under different headings.

Take notes in words, phrases, or sentences. Draw diagrams or sketches, if they help you see and understand the place.

Note any ideas or questions that occur to you.

Use quotation marks around any overheard conversation you take down.

Since you can later reorganize your notes in any way you wish, you do not need to take notes in any planned or systematic way. You might, however, want to cover these aspects of a place:

The setting. The easiest way to begin is to name objects you see. Just start by listing objects. Then record details of some of these objects—color, shape, size, texture, function, relation to similar or dissimilar objects. Although your notes probably will contain mainly visual details, you might also want to record sounds and smells. Be sure to include some notes about the shape, dimensions, and layout of the place as a whole. How big is it? How is it organized?

The people. Record the number of people, their activities, their movements and behavior. Describe their appearance or dress. Record parts of overheard conversations. Note whether you see more men than women, more members of one nationality or ethnic group than of another, more older than younger people. Most important, note anything surprising and unusual about people in the scene.

Your personal reactions. Include in your notes any feelings you have about what you observe. Also record, as they occur to you, any hunches or ideas or insights you have.

Reflecting on your observation

Immediately after your observational visit (within just a few minutes, if possible), find a quiet place to reflect on what you saw, review your notes, and add to your notes. Give yourself at least a half hour for quiet thought.

What you have in your notes and what you recall on reflection will suggest many more images and details from your observation. Add these to your notes.

Finally, review all of your notes, and write a few sentences about your main impressions of the place. What did you learn? How did this visit change your preconceptions about the place? What surprised you most? What is the dominant impression you get from your notes?

Writing up your notes

Your instructor may ask you to write up your notes as a report on the observational visit. If so, review your notes, looking for patterns and vivid details. You might find inventorying or clustering (Chapter 11: Invention and Revision) useful for discovering patterns and relationships in your notes.

Decide on the main impression you want readers to have of the place. Use this as the focus for your report.

Now draft a brief description of the place. Your purpose is to present a general impression of the place through a selection of the details in your notes. Assume your readers have never been to the place, and try to present a vivid impression of it. (See Chapter 14: Describing for a full discussion of strategies for descriptive writing.)

Follow-up visits

Rather than repeat yourself in follow-up visits, try to build on what you have already discovered. You should probably do some interviewing and reading before another observational visit so that you will have a greater understanding of the subject when you observe it again. It is also important to develop a plan for your follow-up: questions to be answered, hypotheses to be tested, types of information you would like to discover.

Like making observations, interviewing tends to involve four basic steps: (1) planning and setting up the interview, (2) notetaking, (3) reflecting on the interview, and (4) writing up your notes.

Planning and setting up the interview

The initial step in interviewing involves choosing an interview subject and then arranging and planning the interview.

Choosing an interview subject. First, decide whom to interview. If you are writing about some activity or enterprise in which several people are involved, choose subjects representing a variety of perspectives—a range of different roles, for example. If you are profiling a single person, most, if not all, of your interviews will be with that person.

You should be flexible because you may be unable to speak to the person you initially targeted and may wind up with someone else—the person's assistant, perhaps. Do not assume this interview subject will be of little use to you. With the right questions, you might even learn more from the assistant than you would from the person in charge.

Arranging an interview. You may be nervous about calling up a busy person and asking for some of his or her time. Indeed, you may get turned down. But if so, it is possible that you will be referred to someone who will see you, someone whose job it is to talk to the public.

Do not feel that just because you are a student you do not have the right to ask for people's time. You will be surprised how delighted people are to be asked about themselves, particularly if you reach them when they are not feeling harried. Most people love to talk—about anything! Usually, the problem is that no one will listen to them. And, since you are a student on assignment, some people may feel that they are doing a form of public service to talk with you.

A note about presenting yourself. When introducing yourself to arrange the interview, give a short and simple description of your project. If you talk too much, you could prejudice or limit the interviewee's response. At the same time, it is a good idea to exhibit some enthusiasm for your project. If you lack enthusiasm, the person may see little reason to talk to you.

Keep in mind that the person you are interviewing is donating time to you. Be certain that you call ahead to arrange a specific time for the interview. Be on time. Bring all the materials you need, and express your thanks when the interview is over.

Planning for the interview. The best interview is generally the planned interview. It will help if you have made an observational visit and done some background reading before the interview. In preparation for the interview, you should do two things in particular: consider your objectives and prepare some questions.

Think about your main objectives. Do you want an orientation to the place (the "big picture") from this interview? Do you want this interview to lead you to interviews with other key people? Do you want mainly facts or information? Do you need clarification of something you have heard in another interview or observed or read? Do you want to learn more about the person, or learn about the place through the person, or both? Should you trust or distrust this person?

The key to good interviewing is flexibility. You may be looking for facts, but your interview subject may not have any to offer. In that case, you should be able to shift gears and go after whatever your subject has to discuss.

Take care in composing the questions you prepare in advance; they can be the key to a successful interview. Any question that places unfair limits on respondents is a bad question. Two specific types to avoid are forced-choice questions and leading questions.

Forced-choice questions are unsatisfactory because they impose your terms on your respondents. Consider this example: "Do you think rape is an expression of sexual passion or of aggression?" A person may think that neither sexual passion nor aggression satisfactorily explain rape. A better way to phrase the question would be to ask, "People often fall into two camps on the issue of rape. Some think it is an expression of sexual passion, while others argue it is really not sexual but aggressive. Do you think it is either of these? If not, what is your opinion?" This form of questioning allows you to get a reaction to what others have said at the same time that it gives the person freedom to set the terms.

Leading questions are unsatisfactory because they assume too much. An example of this kind of question is this: "Do you think the increase in the occurrence of rape is due to the fact that women are perceived as competitors in a severely depressed economy?" This question assumes that there is an increase in the occurrence of rape, that women are perceived (apparently by rapists) as competitors, and that the economy is severely depressed. A better way of asking the question might be to make the assumptions more explicit by dividing the question into its parts: "Do you think there is an increase in the occurrence of rape? What could have caused it? I've heard some people argue that the economy has something to do with it. Do you think so? Do you think rapists perceive women as competitors for jobs? Could the current economic situation have made this competition more severe?"

Good questions come in many different forms. One way of considering them is to divide them into two types: open and closed.

Open questions give the respondent range and flexibility. They also generate anecdotes, personal revelations, and expressions of attitudes. Following are examples of open questions:

☐ I wonder if you would take a few minutes to tell me something about your early days in the business. I'd be interested to hear about how it got started, what your hopes and aspirations were, what problems you faced and how you dealt with them.

☐ Tell me about a time you were (name an emotion).

☐ What did you think of (name a person or event)?

☐ What did you do when (name an event) happened?

The best questions are those that allow the subject to talk freely but to the point. If the answer strays too far from the point, a follow-up question may be necessary to refocus the talk. Another tack you may want to try is to rephrase the subject's answer, to say something like "Let me see if I have this right," or "Am I correct in saying that you feel. . . ." Often, a person will take the opportunity to amplify the original response by adding just the anecdote or quotation you've been looking for.

Closed questions usually request specific information. For example:

☐ How do you do (name a process)?

☐ What does (name a word) mean?

☐ What does (a person, object, or place) look like?

☐ How was it made?

Taking your tools   As for an observational visit, you will need a notebook with a firm back so that you can write on it easily without the benefit of a table or desk. We recommend a full-size (8½ × 11) spiral or ring notebook.

In this notebook, divide several pages into two columns with a line drawn about one third of the width of the page from the left margin. Use the lefthand column to note details about the scene, the person, the mood of the interview, other impressions. Head this column DETAILS AND IMPRESSIONS. At the top of the righthand column, write several questions. You may not use them, but they will jog your memory. This column should be titled INFORMATION. In this column you will record what you learn from answers to your questions. (See Chapter 4 for an example.)

Taking notes during   Because you are not taking a verbatim transcript of the interview (if you
the interview   wanted a literal account, you would use a tape recorder or shorthand), your goals are to gather information and to record a few good quotations and anecdotes. In addition, because the people you interview may be unused to giving interviews and so will need to know you are listening, it is probably a good idea to do more listening than notetaking. You may not have much confidence in your memory, but, if you pay close attention, you are likely to recall a good deal of the conversation afterward. During the interview, you should take some notes: a few quotations; key words and phrases to jog your memory; observational jottings about the scene, the person, and the

mood of the interview. Remember that *how* something is said is as important as *what* is said. Pick up material that will give texture to your write-up of the interview—gesture, physical appearance, verbal inflection, facial expression, dress, hair, style, body language, anything that makes the person an individual.

Reflecting on the interview

As soon as you finish the interview, find a quiet place to reflect on it, and review your notes. This reflection is essential because so much happens in an interview that you cannot record at the time. You need to spend at least a half hour, maybe longer, adding to your notes and thinking about what you learned.

At the end of this time, write a few sentences about your main impressions from the interview. What did you learn? What surprised you most? How did the interview change your attitude or understanding about the person or place? How would you summarize your main impressions of the person? How did this interview influence your plans to interview others or to reinterview this person? What do you want to learn from these next interviews?

Writing up your notes

Your instructor may ask you to write up your notes as a report on the interview. If so, review your notes, looking for useful details and information. Decide what main impression you want to give of this person. Choose details that will contribute to this impression. Select quotations and paraphrases of information you learned from the person. Your task is to integrate this material into an essay presenting the person and what you learned about the subject.

To find a focus for your write-up, you might use looping. Clustering might give you suggestions for organizing the interview. Invention questions and dramatizing will help you consider the person from different perspectives. (All of these strategies are discussed in Chapter 11: Invention and Revision.)

QUESTIONNAIRES

Questionnaires let you survey the attitudes or knowledge of large numbers of people. You could carry out many face-to-face or phone interviews to get the same information, but questionnaires have the advantages of economy, efficiency, and anonymity. Some questionnaires, such as ones you filled out in applying to college, just collect demographic information: your name, age, sex, home town, religious preference, intended major. Others, such as the Gallup and Harris polls, collect opinions on a wide range of issues. Prior to elections we are bombarded with the results of these kinds of polls. Still other kinds of questionnaires, ones used in academic research, are designed to help answer important questions about personal and societal problems.

This section will briefly outline procedures you can follow to carry out an informal questionnaire survey of people's opinions or knowledge, and then to write up the results. (For formal studies using questionnaires, you would need considerable technical information about designing the study, sampling the population of interest, and analyzing the data. This information is available from many sources, some of which are listed at the end of this chapter.)

Focusing your study

A questionnaire study usually has a limited focus. You might need to interview a few people in order to find this focus.

Let us assume that you went to your campus Student Health Clinic (SHC) and had to wait over an hour to see a nurse. Sitting there with many other students, you decide this is a problem that needs to be studied. Furthermore, it seems an ideal topic for a proposal essay (Chapter 7: Proposing Solutions) you have been assigned in your writing class.

To study this problem, you do not have to explore the entire operation of SHC. You are not interested in how nurses and doctors are hired or how efficient their system of ordering supplies is. You have a particular concern: how successful is SHC in scheduling appointments and organizing its resources to meet student needs? More specifically: do students often have to wait too long to see a nurse or doctor? You might also want to know *why* this is the case, if it is; but you can only seek an answer to that question by interviewing SHC staff. Your primary interest is in how long students usually wait for appointments, what times are most convenient for students to schedule appointments, whether SHC resources are concentrated at those times, and so on. Now you have a limited focus, and you can collect valuable information with a fairly brief questionnaire.

To be certain about your focus, however, you should talk informally to several students to find out whether they think there is a problem. You might also want to talk to people at SHC, explaining your plans and asking for their views on the problem.

Whatever your interest, be sure to limit the scope of your study. Try to focus on one or two important questions. With a limited focus, your questionnaire can be brief, and people will be more willing to fill it out. In addition, a study based on a limited amount of information will be easier to organize and report.

Writing questions

Two basic forms of questions—closed and open—were introduced earlier in this chapter. In the following section are additional illustrations of how these types of questions may be used in the context of a questionnaire.

Closed questions. Following are examples of some forms of closed questions for a possible student questionnaire. You probably will use more than one form in a questionnaire, because you will have several kinds of information to collect.

Checklists

With your present work and class schedule, when are you able to visit the SHC? (Check as many boxes as necessary.)

☐ 8–10 A.M.
☐ 10–12 A.M.
☐ noon hour
☐ 1–3 P.M.
☐ 3–5 P.M.

Which services do you expect to use at the SHC this year?

☐ allergy desensitization
☐ immunization
☐ optometry
☐ dental care
☐ birth control
☐ illness or infection
☐ counseling
☐ health education

Two-way questions

Have you made an appointment this year at SHC?
____ yes
____ no

Have you ever had to wait more than 30 minutes at SHC for a scheduled appointment?
____ yes
____ no

If you could, would you schedule appointments at the SHC after 7:00 P.M.?
____ yes
____ no
____ uncertain

Multiple-choice questions

How frequently have you had to wait more than 10 minutes at the SHC for a scheduled appointment?

_____ always
_____ usually
_____ occasionally
_____ never

From your experience so far with SHC, how would you rate its services?
_____ inadequate
_____ barely adequate
_____ adequate
_____ better than adequate
_____ outstanding

Ranking scales

With your present work and class schedule, which times during the day (Monday through Friday) would be most convenient for you to schedule appointments at SHC? Put a 1 by the most convenient time, a 2 by the next most convenient time, until you have ranked all the choices.
_____ mornings
_____ afternoons before 5 P.M.
_____ 5–7 P.M.
_____ 7–10 P.M.

Open questions. Open questions ask the respondent to write a brief answer.

What services do you expect to need at SHC this year?

_____

_____

_____

From your experiences with appointments at SHC, what advice would you give students about making appointments?

_____

_____

_____

What do you believe would most improve services at SHC?

_____

_____

_____

You may want to use a combination of closed and open questions for your questionnaire. Both offer advantages: closed questions will give you definite answers, but open questions can give information you may not have expected as well as providing lively quotations for your report.

Trying out the questions. As soon as you have a collection of possible questions, try them out on a few typical readers. You need to know which questions are unclear, which seem to duplicate others, which seem most interesting. These tryouts will enable you to assess which questions will give you the information you need. Readers also can help you come up with additional questions.

Designing the questionnaire

Write a brief, clear introduction stating the purpose of the questionnaire and explaining how you intend to use the results. Give advice on answering the questions, and estimate the amount of time needed to complete the questionnaire. If you are going to give the questionnaire to groups of people in person, you can give this information orally.

Select your most promising questions, and decide on an order. Any logical order is appropriate. You might want to begin with the least complicated questions or the most general ones. You may find it necessary or helpful to group the questions by subject matter or form. Certain questions may lead to others. You might want to place open questions at the end.

Design the questionnaire so that it looks attractive and readable. Make it look easy to complete. Do not crowd questions together to save paper. Provide plenty of space for readers to answer open questions, and remind them to use the back of the page if they need more space.

Testing the questionnaire

Make a few copies of your first design, and ask at least two or three readers to complete the questionnaire. Find out how much time they needed to complete it. Talk to them about any confusions or problems they experienced. Review their responses with them to be certain each question is doing what you want it to do. From what you learn, reconsider your design, and revise particular questions.

Administering the questionnaire

Decide who will fill out your questionnaire and how you can arrange for them to do it. The more readers you have, the better; but constraints of time and expense almost certainly will limit the number. You can mail questionnaires or distribute them to dormitories or workplace mailboxes, but the return will be low. It is unusual for even half the people receiving mail questionnaires to return them. If you do mail the questionnaire, be sure to mention the deadline for returning it. Give directions for returning the questionnaire, and include a stamped, addressed envelope for off-campus respondents.

You might want to arrange to distribute the questionnaire yourself to some groups in class, at dormitory meetings, or at work.

Note that if you want to do a formal questionnaire, you will need a scientifically representative group of readers (a random or stratified random sample). Even for an informal study, you should try to get a reasonably representative group. For example, to study satisfaction with the appointments schedule at SHC, you would want to have readers who had been to SHC fairly often. You might even want to include a concentration of seniors rather than freshman readers because after four years seniors would have made more visits to SHC. If many students commute, you would want to be sure to have commuters among your readers.

Your report will be much more convincing if you can demonstrate that your readers represent the group whose opinions or knowledge you claim to be studying. As few as 25 or 30 readers could be adequate for an informal study.

Writing up the results   Now that you have the completed questionnaires, what do you do with them?

Summarizing the results. Begin by tallying the results from the closed questions. Take an unused questionnaire, and tally the responses next to each choice. Suppose you had 25 readers. Here is how the tally might look for the first checklist question.

> With your present work and class schedule, when are you able to visit the SHC? (Check as many boxes as necessary.)
> ☐ 8–10 A.M. 卌 卌 卌 ||| (18)
> ☐ 10–12 A.M. 卌 || (7)
> ☐ noon hour 卌 卌 ||| (13)
> ☐ 1–3 P.M. ||| (3)
> ☐ 3–5 P.M. 卌 |||| (9)

Each tally mark represents one response to that item. The totals add up to more than 25 because readers were asked to check *all* the times they could make appointments.

Next consider the open questions. Read all 25 answers to each question separately to see the kind and variety of response to each. Then decide whether you want to code any of the open questions so that you can summarize results from them quantitatively, as you would with closed questions. For example, you might want to classify the types of advice given as responses to an open question proposed earlier: "From your experiences with appointments at SHC, what advice would you give students about making appointments?" You could then report the numbers of readers (of your 25) who gave each type of advice. For an opinion question ("How would you evaluate the most recent appointment you had at SHC?"), you might simply code the answers as positive, neutral, and negative and then tally the results accordingly for each kind of response. However, responses to open questions are perhaps most often used as a source of quotations for your report.

You can report results from the closed questions as percentages, either within the text of your report or in tables. (See the Fuchs essay in Chapter 9 for one possible format for a table. You can find other formats in social science texts you may be using or even in magazines or newspapers. Conventional formats for tables in social science reports are illustrated in *Publication Manual of the American Psychological Association,* 3rd edition, Washington, D.C.: American Psychological Association, 1983.) You can make tables of results either for individual questions or for groups of questions with identical forms.

You can quote responses to the open questions within your text. You can weave them into your discussion like quoted material from books (see Chapter 22: The Research Paper for strategies for integrating quoted material). Or you can organize several responses into lists and then comment on them. Since readers' interests can be engaged more easily with quotations than with percentages, plan to use many open responses in your report.

There are computer programs that will provide quantitative results from closed questions and will even print out tables you can insert into your report. For a small informal study, however, such programs probably would not save you much time.

Organizing and writing the report. If you planned your questionnaire to collect information about a trend (Chapter 9: Speculating About Causes) or a problem needing a solution (Chapter 7: Proposing Solutions), then your results would be only a small part of a larger essay. If you are writing a proposal, the Guide to Writing in Chapter 7 will help you explore the results and present them effectively.

In organizing the report of your results, you might want to consider a plan that usually is followed for research reports in the social sciences:

Statement of the Problem
    Context for your study
    Your question
    Need for your study
    Brief preview of your study and forecast of the plan of your report
Review of Other Related Studies (if you know of any)
Procedures
    Designing the questionnaire
    Selecting the readers
    Administering the questionnaire
    Summarizing the results
Results: presentation of what you learned, with little if any commentary or interpretation
Summary and Discussion: brief summary of your results, and discussion of their significance (commenting, interpreting, exploring implications, and comparing to other related studies)

SOURCES OF FURTHER INFORMATION ON FIELD RESEARCH

Babbie, Earl. (1973). *Survey research methods*. Belmont, California: Wadsworth.

Banaka, William H. (1971). *Training in depth interviewing*. New York: Harper & Row.

Brady, James. (1977). *The craft of interviewing*. New York: Vintage.

Brandt, Richard M. (1972). *Studying behavior in natural settings*. New York: Holt, Rinehart and Winston. (Chapters 4, 5, 6)

Fowler, Floyd J. (1984). *Survey research methods*. Beverly Hills: Sage.

Oppenheim, A. N. (1966). *Questionnaire design and attitude measurement*. New York: Basic Books.

Williamson, John B., Karp, David A., and Dalphin, John R. (1977). *The research craft: An introduction to social science methods*. Boston: Little, Brown. (Chapters 6, 7, 8)

Library Research

For many students, doing research in a library involves a variety of diverse activities: checking the card catalog, browsing in the stacks, possibly consulting the *Readers' Guide to Periodical Literature,* and asking the reference librarian for help. Although librarians are there to help in time of need, all college students should nevertheless learn basic library research skills. This chapter presents the search strategy, a systematic and efficient way of doing library research.

The search strategy was developed by librarians to make library research manageable and productive. Although specific search strategies will vary to fit the needs of individual research problems, the general process will be demonstrated here: how to get started; where to find sources; what types of sources are available and what sorts of information they provide; how to evaluate these sources; and, most important, how to go about this process of finding and evaluating sources *systematically.*

Before you begin doing research for a paper, you should familiarize yourself with your college library. College libraries differ from public libraries and high school libraries in that they are oriented more toward research.

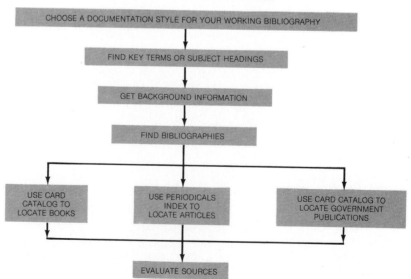

OVERVIEW OF A SEARCH STRATEGY

CHOOSE A DOCUMENTATION STYLE FOR YOUR WORKING BIBLIOGRAPHY

FIND KEY TERMS OR SUBJECT HEADINGS

GET BACKGROUND INFORMATION

FIND BIBLIOGRAPHIES

USE CARD CATALOG TO LOCATE BOOKS

USE PERIODICALS INDEX TO LOCATE ARTICLES

USE CARD CATALOG TO LOCATE GOVERNMENT PUBLICATIONS

EVALUATE SOURCES

21

Library research can be useful at various stages of the writing process. How you use the library depends on the kind of essay you are writing and the special needs of your subject, as the writing guides in Part I indicate. You may, for example, need to do research immediately to choose a subject. Or you may choose a topic without the benefit of research but then use the library to find specific information to support your thesis. But no matter when you use library research, you will need to have a search strategy. This search strategy will guide you in setting up a working bibliography and a documentation style, in searching for key words or subject headings, in seeking background information, in finding bibliographies, and in using the card catalog and specialty indexes. Finally, it will help you evaluate the sources that you will use in your writing.

A WORKING BIBLIOGRAPHY

A working bibliography is a preliminary, ongoing record of books, articles, pamphlets—all the sources of information you discover as you research your subject. (A final bibliography, on the other hand, lists only sources actually used in your paper. Some of the sources in your working bibliography may turn out to be irrelevant, while others simply will be unavailable.) In addition, you can use your working bibliography as a means of keeping track of any encyclopedias, bibliographies, and indexes you consult, even though you may not list these resources in your final bibliography.

Because you probably will have to cite many different sources, you must decide on a documentation style before you write. Chapter 22 presents the documentation styles sponsored by the Modern Language Association (MLA) and the American Psychological Association (APA). Other disciplines often have their own preferred styles of documentation, which your instructor may wish you to use. Determine a style to use at the beginning, when you are constructing a working bibliography, as well as later, when you compile a final bibliography.

Practiced researchers keep their working bibliography either in a notebook or on index cards. They make a point of keeping bibliographical information separate from notes they take on the sources listed in their bibliography. (At the end of this chapter is a brief discussion of taking notes from your reading.)

NOTEBOOK FORM

AUTHOR _____

CALL NUMBER _____

Anorexia Nervosa

RC 628
B72

Bruch, Hilde. Eating Disorders: Obesity, Anorexia Nervosa, and the Person Within.

FULL TITLE _____

PUBLISHING IMPRINT _____

BIBLIOGRAPHICAL SOURCE _____

Bibliographic Index

New York: Basic Books, 1973.

Sours, John A. Starving to Death in a Sea

AUTHOR _____

FULL TITLE BUT NO PUBLISHING IMPRINT _____

of Objects: The Anorexia Nervosa Syndrome.

BIBLIOGRAPHY IN BACK OF BOOK _____

Bibliography pp. 388-431.

INDEX CARD FORM

RC 628

B72

CALL NUMBER _____

AUTHOR _____

Bruch, Hilde. Eating Disorders: Obesity, Anorexia Nervosa, and the Person Within.

FULL TITLE _____

PUBLISHING IMPRINT _____

New York: Basic Books, 1973.

Many researchers find index cards more convenient because they are so easily alphabetized. Others find them too easy to lose and prefer, instead, to keep everything—working bibliography, notes, and drafts—in one notebook. Whether you use cards or a notebook, the important thing is to make your entries accurate and complete. If the call number is incomplete or inaccurate, you will not be able to find the book in the stacks. If the volume number for a periodical is incorrect, you may not be able to locate the article. If the author's name is misspelled, you may have trouble finding the book in the card catalog.

KEY SUBJECT HEADINGS

To research a subject, you need to know how it is classified, what key words are used as subject headings in encyclopedias, bibliographies, and the card catalog. As you learn more about your subject, you will discover how other writers refer to it, how it usually is subdivided, and also what subjects are related to it. To begin your search, you should consult the *Library of Congress Subject Headings*. This reference book lists the standard subject headings used in card catalogs and in many encyclopedias and bibliographies. It usually can be found near the card catalog.

Sometimes, the words you think would be used for subject headings are not the ones actually used. For example, if you look up "World War I," you will find a cross reference to "European War, 1914–1918." But, if you look up "bulimia," you will find neither a heading nor a cross reference. Since many people call bulimia an "eating disorder," you might try that heading. But again you would draw a blank. If you tried "appetite," however, you would be referred to "anorexia," a related disorder. Here is the entry for "appetite":

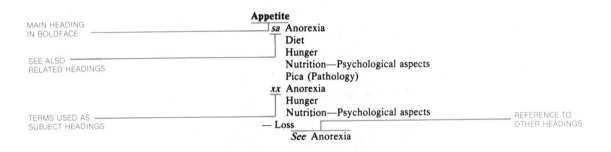

If you then look up "anorexia," you still will not find "bulimia," but you can expect some of the publications on anorexia to deal also with bulimia. In this process of trying possible headings and following up cross references, you also will find related headings such as "nutrition," "obesity," and "psychological."

BACKGROUND INFORMATION

Once you have decided on the form and style of a working bibliography and have found promising subject headings, your search strategy will lead you to the gathering of background sources of information. Such sources will give you a general understanding of the nature and scope of your research subject. They may also provide a historical perspective on the subject, helping you grasp its basic principles and ideas, suggesting what its major divisions or aspects might be, and identifying important people associated with it.

Encyclopedias are the best sources of background information. You have no doubt heard of the *Encyclopaedia Britannica,* probably the best-known general encyclopedia. But there are many specialized encyclopedias. To use encyclopedias effectively, you need to know what subject headings you are looking for. Check each encyclopedia's subject index to locate your subject.

General encyclopedias   General encyclopedias are usually multivolume works that contain articles on all areas of knowledge. Written by experts, the articles frequently conclude with a list of important works and bibliographies. Most encyclopedias arrange their subjects alphabetically. Following are the standard general encyclopedias:

Encyclopaedia Britannica

Encyclopedia Americana

Collier's Encyclopedia

World Book Encyclopedia

New Columbia Encyclopedia

Dictionary of the History of Ideas

Harper's Dictionary of Modern Thought

Here is the *Encyclopedia Americana* entry for "Anorexia Nervosa."

ANOREXIA NERVOSA, an-ə-rek′sē-ə nər-vō′sə, a psychosomatic illness in which self-inflicted starvation leads to a devastating loss of weight. It occurs chiefly among well-to-do high school and college girls, affecting about one out of every 200 girls in that group. Girls affected with this disorder have a pathological fear of being fat, which leads to a relentless pursuit of excessive slimness coupled with an intense interest in food. Severe personality problems are common. The typical patient is overcompliant in childhood, and thus inadequately prepared for adolescence and independence. Excessive control over weight —to the point of starvation—represents an effort to establish a sense of selfhood and autonomy. Starvation, in turn, creates its own physiological and psychological symptoms and complications.

Anorexics characteristically see themselves unrealistically and experience their bodies as something separate from, not part of, their true selves. Abstinence from food may alternate with eating binges, which are followed by efforts to remove the unwanted food through self-induced vomiting, laxatives, and diuretics. These practices may result in serious disturbances in the electrolyte balance, at times with a fatal outcome. Though anorexics give a first impression of being active and vigorous, they suffer from a paralyzing sense of ineffectiveness. They gain a sense of accomplishment from controlling their weight, and they experience deep feelings of depression and self-hatred when they regain any weight.

Anorexia nervosa has a tendency to be self-perpetuating, leading to chronic invalidism or even to death. These tragic outcomes are avoidable when proper treatment is started before the condition becomes firmly established. Early warning signs include fanaticism about losing weight, a frantic increase in activities, social isolation, and sleep deprivation. Treatment involves restitution of normal nutrition, resolution of the patient's overintense involvement with her family, and clarification of the underlying personality problems. Weight gain alone, without resolution of the psychological problems, is not sufficient.

HILDA BRUCH, M. D., *Author of "The Golden Cage: The Enigma of Anorexis Nervosa" and "Eating Disorders: Obesity, Anorexia Nervosa, and the Person Within"*

Specialized encyclopedias

Specialized encyclopedias focus on a single area of knowledge. To find specialized encyclopedias, look in the subject card catalog under the appropriate subject heading. Encyclopedias usually are catalogued under the subheading "Dictionaries" and are kept in the reference section of the library. Here is a partial list of specialized encyclopedias:

Encyclopedia of Education
Encyclopedia of Philosophy
Grove's Dictionary of Music and Musicians
International Encyclopedia of the Social Sciences
Harvard Encyclopedia of American Ethnic Groups
McGraw-Hill Dictionary of Art
McGraw-Hill Encyclopedia of Science and Technology
Oxford Classical Dictionary
Oxford Companion to American History

BIBLIOGRAPHIES

A bibliography is simply a list of publications on a given subject. Whereas an encyclopedia gives you background information on your subject, a bibliography gives you an overview of what has been published on the subject.

Its scope may be broad or narrow. Some bibliographers try to be exhaustive, including every title they can find, while most are selective. To discover how selections were made, check the bibliography's preface or introduction. Occasionally, bibliographies are annotated: that is, they provide brief summaries of the entries and, sometimes, also evaluate them. Bibliographies may be found in a variety of places: in encyclopedias, in the card catalog, and in secondary sources. To be efficient, however, the best way to locate a comprehensive, up-to-date bibliography on your subject is to use the *Bibliographic Index*.

The *Bibliographic Index* is a master list of bibliographies that contain fifty or more titles. It includes bibliographies from articles, books, and government publications. Here is a sample entry:

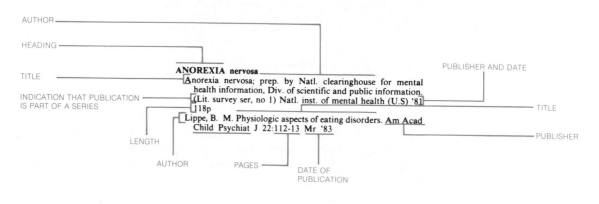

The first reference is to a bibliography put out by the National Institute of Mental Health—a government publication. The second is a bibliography included in a periodical article.

A new volume of *Bibliographic Index* is published every year. Because this index is not cumulative, you should check back over several years, beginning with the most current volume.

THE CARD CATALOG

The card catalog in your library contains cards with the names of authors, subjects, and titles. Author, subject, and title cards all give the same basic information.

1. The *call number*—always in the upper lefthand corner, indicates the numerical code under which the book is filed in the library. Books will be

filed in the library by their call numbers, which are assigned according to subject. Most college research libraries use the Library of Congress subject headings and numbering system. Call numbers have at least two rows of numbers. The top row indicates the general subject classification, whereas the second row places the book within this classification. Subsequent rows identify the copyright and publication date for multiple editions.

2. The *author*—appears last name first, followed by birth and death dates. If there are multiple authors, there is an author card under each author's name.

3. The *title*—appears exactly as it appears on the title page of the book, except here only the first word is capitalized.

4. The *imprint*—includes the place of publication (usually just the city), publisher, and year of publication. If the book was published simultaneously in the U.S. and abroad, both places of publication and both publishers are included.

5. *Collation*—offers descriptive information about the book's length and size. Roman numeral indicates the number of pages used for front matter (preface, contents, and acknowledgments).

6. *Notes*—indicate any special features (for example, a bibliography or an index).

7. *Subject headings*—indicate how the book is listed in the Subject Catalog. These suggest headings you can use to find other books related to your subject.

AUTHOR
CALL NUMBER

RC628
B72

Bruch, Hilde, 1904-
   Eating disorders; obesity, anorexia nervosa, and the person within. New York, Basic Books [1973]
   x, 396 p. 25 cm.
   Includes bibliographies.

TITLE
IMPRINT
COLLATION

NOTES

   1. Obesity--Psychological aspects.
2. Anorexia nervosa. I. Title

SUBJECT HEADINGS

The same basic card is used also for title and subject cards, but the latter have headings printed at the top. The title card has the title above the author's name:

TITLE

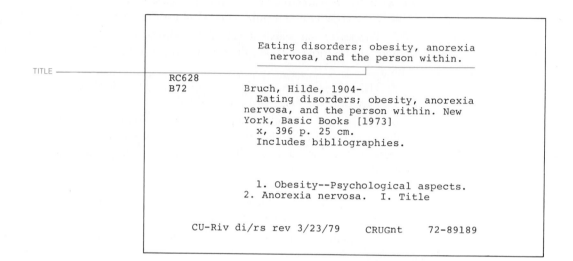

```
                        Eating disorders; obesity, anorexia
                          nervosa, and the person within.

         RC628
         B72           Bruch, Hilde, 1904-
                          Eating disorders; obesity, anorexia
                       nervosa, and the person within. New
                       York, Basic Books [1973]
                          x, 396 p. 25 cm.
                          Includes bibliographies.


                          1. Obesity--Psychological aspects.
                       2. Anorexia nervosa.  I. Title

             CU-Riv di/rs rev 3/23/79    CRUGnt    72-89189
```

The subject card has the subject above the author's name. Notice that the two subject cards that follow correspond to the subject headings at the bottom of the author and title cards.

PRIMARY
SUBJECT
HEADING

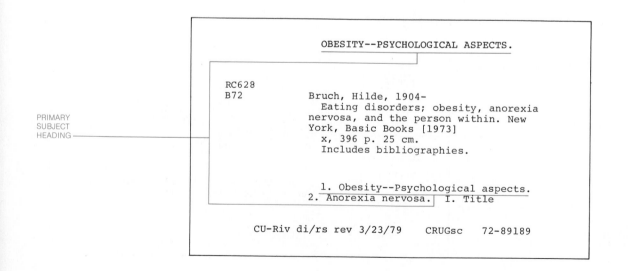

```
                      OBESITY--PSYCHOLOGICAL ASPECTS.


         RC628
         B72           Bruch, Hilde, 1904-
                          Eating disorders; obesity, anorexia
                       nervosa, and the person within. New
                       York, Basic Books [1973]
                          x, 396 p. 25 cm.
                          Includes bibliographies.


                          1. Obesity--Psychological aspects.
                       2. Anorexia nervosa.  I. Title

             CU-Riv di/rs rev 3/23/79    CRUGsc    72-89189
```

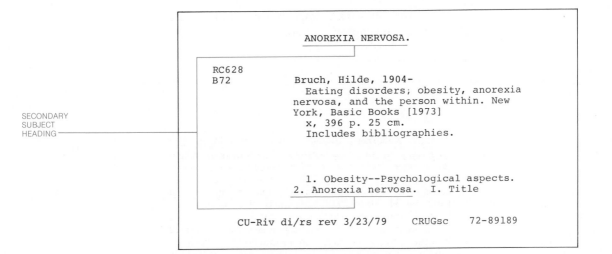

SECONDARY
SUBJECT
HEADING

ANOREXIA NERVOSA.

RC628
B72   Bruch, Hilde, 1904-
               Eating disorders; obesity, anorexia
           nervosa, and the person within. New
           York, Basic Books [1973]
               x, 396 p. 25 cm.
               Includes bibliographies.

               1. Obesity--Psychological aspects.
           2. Anorexia nervosa. I. Title

    CU-Riv di/rs rev 3/23/79   CRUGsc   72-89189

Remember: an "author" may be a person, a corporation, an association, a city, or a bureau. As such, author cards are filed alphabetically by an author's last name or by the first word in a group name (*International* for International Business Machines, for example). Title cards are filed alphabetically by the first word of the title, except if the first word is an article: a title beginning with *a, an,* or *the* is filed under its second word.

PERIODICALS INDEXES AND ABSTRACTS

The most up-to-date information on a subject usually is not found in books, but in recently published articles that appear in journals and serials, or periodicals, as they often are called. Periodicals appear daily, weekly, quarterly, or annually (hence the name *periodical*). Articles in such publications usually are not listed in the card catalog; to find them, you must instead use periodicals indexes and abstracts. Indexes will only list articles, whereas abstracts summarize as well as list them.

Following is an example from an index you may be familiar with already—the *Readers' Guide to Periodical Literature:*

SUBJECT HEADING ——— **Anorexia nervosa**
               Anorexia nervosa. D. K. Mano. *Natl Rev* 35:1626-8 D ——————— PERIODICAL
               23 '83
TITLE ——————— Anorexia nervosa: a hormonal link [abnormal levels of
               vasopressin] *Newsweek* 101:69 My 23 '83
               A brother remembers [K. Carpenter] R. Carpenter. il
VOLUME AND PAGE ——— pors *People Wkly* 20:152-3+ N 21 '83 ——————————— DATE
               Can an athlete take fitness too far? [M. Wazeter's suicide
               attempt linked to athletic competition] N. Amdur. il
               pors *Seventeen* 42:24+ Jl '83

The following example is from a less familiar, more specialized reference work: *Psychological Abstracts.*

AFFILIATION

AUTHOR

ITEM NUMBER

PERIODICAL

TITLE

DATE

VOLUME AND PAGE NUMBER

6565. **Kellerman, Jonathan.** (Children's Hosp, Los Angeles, CA) **Anorexia nervosa: The efficacy of behavior therapy.** *Journal of Behavior Therapy & Experimental Psychiatry,* 1977(Dec), Vol 8(4), 387–390. —Two criticisms of behavioral approaches to anorexia nervosa set forth by H. Bruch (1976), namely that weight gain brought about by behavioral approaches is subject to rapid attrition and that weight gain is not accompanied by other positive change, were examined by surveying a number of published articles utilizing behavior therapy with this disorder. Bruch's criticisms were not supported by the data. A critique of Bruch's critique is offered, and it is asserted that there is empirical support for the idea that behavior therapy is the treatment of choice for anorexia nervosa. (18 ref) —*Journal summary.*

SOURCE FOR ABSTRACT

Many periodicals indexes use the Library of Congress subject headings, but some have their own systems. *Psychological Abstracts,* for example, has a separate volume for subject headings. Following is an excerpt from that volume:

SUBJECT HEADING

VOLUME NUMBER

TITLE

ITEM NUMBER

Anorexia Nervosa
amenorrhea & variation of serum prolactin with changes in body weight & nutrition & gonadrotropin & thyroid hormone levels, females with anorexia nervosa, 64:10710
amitriptyline, treatment of bulimia & vomiting, 20 yr old female with anorexia nervosa, 60:7948
amitriptyline-induced obesity from state of anorexia nervosa, 20 yr old female, 62:4199
anorexia nervosa as psychosomatic disease, etiology & treatment in family context, book, 62:4094
anorexia nervosa, dizygotic female twins, case report, 61:6338
anorexia nervosa in children, 5–20 yr followup of patients, 60:5502
anorexia nervosa, predominating factors & personality profile, 16–25 yr old female anorexia nervosa patients vs patients with neurotic illness, 61:8763
anorexia nervosa, 2 adolescent males, 64:10669
anorexia nervosa, 55 yr old female with clivus tumor, 62:1353
anorexia nervosa, 7 yr old female, 63:3380

Check the opening pages of the index you are using to see how it classifies its subjects.

Like encyclopedias, periodicals indexes and abstracts exist in both general and specialized forms.

General indexes　　General indexes list articles in nontechnical, general interest publications. They cover a broad range of subjects. Most have separate author and subject listings as well as a list of book reviews. Following are some general indexes:

> *Readers' Guide to Periodical Literature* (1905–present) covers more than 180 popular periodicals.
>
> *Humanities Index* (1974–present) covers archaeology, history, classics, literature, performing arts, philosophy, and religion.
>
> *Social Sciences Index* (1974–present) covers economics, geography, law, political science, psychology, public administration, and sociology.
>
> *Public Affairs Information Service Bulletin* [PAIS] (1915–present) covers articles and other publications by public and private agencies on economic and social conditions, international relations, and public administration. Subject listing only.

Specialized indexes　　Specialized indexes list articles in periodicals devoted to technical or scholarly research reports. Following is a list of some specialized indexes:

> *Accountant's Index* (1944–present)
>
> *Almanac of American Politics* (1972–present)
>
> *American Statistics Index* (1973–present)
>
> *Applied Science and Technology Index* (1958–present)
>
> *Biological and Agricultural Index* (1964–present)
>
> *Congressional Digest* (1921–present)
>
> *Congressional Quarterly Weekly Reports* (1956–present)
>
> *Education Index* (1929–present)
>
> *Engineering Index* (1920–present)
>
> *Historical Abstracts* (1955–present)
>
> *Index Medicus* (1961–present)
>
> *MLA International Bibliography of Books and Articles in the Modern Languages and Literature* (1921–present)
>
> *Philosopher's Index* (1967–present)
>
> *Psychology Abstracts* (1927–present)
>
> *Statistical Abstracts of the United States* (annual)
>
> *Statistical Yearbook* (1949–present)

Newspaper indexes　　Newspapers often provide information unavailable elsewhere, especially accounts of current events, analyses of recent trends, texts of important speeches by public officials, obituaries, and film and book reviews. Libraries usually miniaturize newspapers and store them on microfilm (reels) or microfiche (cards), which must be placed in viewing machines in order to be read. Following are some general and specialized newspaper indexes:

General news indexes

Facts on File (1941–present)
Keesing's Contemporary Archives (1931–present)

Indexes to particular newspapers

Christian Science Monitor Index (1960–present)
(London) *Times Index* (1785–present)
New York Times Index (1851–present)
Wall Street Journal Index (1972–present)

Computerized newspaper and periodical indexes

The *National Newspaper Index*—lists items in the *New York Times, Wall Street Journal,* and *Christian Science Monitor.*
Magazine Index—lists articles in nearly 400 general periodicals.

GOVERNMENT PUBLICATIONS

The countless documents published by agencies of the United States government and by state governments and United Nations organizations may be an additional source of useful information. Most college research libraries have a government publications collection, usually catalogued and housed separately. The collection is likely to include agency publications, statistics, research reports, and public service pamphlets. Following are some indexes of government publications.

The *Monthly Index to the United States Government Publications* (1895–present)—separate cumulative index is published annually.
CIS Index and *CIS Abstracts* (1970–present)—Congressional Committee documents.
Public Affairs Information Service Bulletin [PAIS] (1915–present)—PAIS indexes government documents as well as books on political and social issues.
International Bibliography, Information, Documentation (1973–present)—indexes selected documents published by the United Nations and other international organizations.
United Nations Documents Index (1950–present)—comprehensive index to documents published by the United Nations.

EVALUATING SOURCES

The final phase of a search strategy involves evaluating the sources in your working bibliography to determine which to use in your essay. Obviously, you must decide which sources provide information relevant to the topic. But you also must decide how credible or trustworthy your sources are. Just because a book is published or an essay appears in print does not necessarily mean the information in it is reliable.

Begin the evaluation of your sources by narrowing your working bibliography to the most relevant sources. Then determine how reliable these sources are.

Scope. To decide how relevant a particular source is, you need to examine it in depth. Do not depend on title alone, for it may be misleading. If the source is a book, check its table of contents and index to see how many pages are devoted to the aspect of the subject you are exploring. You most likely will want an in-depth, not a superficial, treatment of the major aspects of your topic. Read the preface to discover the author's bias or special way of looking at the subject. The introduction to a book or opening paragraphs of an article should alert you to the author's basic approach to the subject. Abstracts, printed with many scholarly articles, give you a quick idea of the scope and approach of the selection.

Date of publication. The date of publication may be an important clue. If you are addressing a current trend or problem, then you want the most up-to-date sources available. Similarly, if you are writing about a scientific or technological subject that is undergoing rapid change, only the most recent information will be useful. However, older sources often establish the principles, theories, and data upon which later work rests. Since many older works are considered classics, you may want to become familiar with them. To determine which sources are classics, note the ones that are cited most often in encyclopedia articles, bibliographies, and recent works on the subject.

Variety. You will also want your sources to represent a variety of viewpoints on the subject. Just as you would not depend on a single author for all of your information, so you do not want to use authors who all belong to the same school of thought. To determine which school each author belongs to, look at the preface and introduction and the sources the author used.

Bibliographies. Selective bibliographies, particularly those with annotations, can also help you gauge the reliability of sources on your list. Check the bibliography's preface or introduction to discover the principle of selection. You may also want to check other bibliographies, particularly more recent ones and those included in respected books on the subject.

Book reviews. Book reviews can be very helpful in establishing the reliability of a source, but sometimes a reviewer's approach to the subject differs so radically from the author's that a *review* in and of itself is not a reliable gauge of a book's value. There are several indexes you can use to find book reviews, but you will need the book's author, title, and date of publication. If you are missing anything, you can consult the card catalog, the *National Union Catalog,* or *Books in Print.* Most book reviews appear within a year after a book's publication, but scholarly books tend to be reviewed later, if at all. Remember: not all books are reviewed.

Many indexes not only indicate where you can find reviews; they also summarize some of them. Here is an example from *Book Digest:*

TITLE

NUMBER OF PAGES

AUTHOR

PRICE

DATE AND PUBLISHER

LIBRARY OF CONGRESS NUMBER

DESCRIPTION OF BOOK

ABSTRACT

SOURCE FOR ABSTRACT

AUTHOR OF ABSTRACT

BRUCH, HILDE. Eating disorders; obesity, anorexia nervosa, and the person within. 396p $12.50 '73 Basic Bks.
616.3 Weight control—Psychological aspects
SBN 465-01784-3   LC 72-89189

The author presents a "summary of her personality theory and treatment techniques, how people who misuse the eating function, whether by overeating or self-starvation (anorexia nervosa), do so in an effort to solve or camouflage problems of living that to them appear otherwise insoluble." (Publisher's note) Index.

"Bruch, from a basis of 40 years' experience as a psychiatrist dealing with the emotional aspects of overeating or undereating, has written a masterpiece which should, but probably won't, put an end to some of the myths about diets and weight problems. Her discussion of the problems of the obese (and the overly thin, also, because, as she points out, they are essentially the same) is scientific and scholarly, but is written so clearly, and with such a lack of psychiatric jargon, that anyone should be able to read it. . . . While all ages are covered, Bruch emphasizes the problems of obese children and adolescents. The many case histories, presented with sensitivity and understanding, highlight the different manifestations of these disorders." E. A. Maass
Library J 98:3009 O 15 '73 140w

"Bruch says, in a book which beyond its thorough scientific treatment of eating disorders, is characterised by an enormous fund of good sense, [that] such disorders are merely the visible result of underlying physiological and psychological mechanisms. . . . The whole problem of body imagery is a fascinating one, and Dr Bruch has made an invaluable contribution to it. As a psychiatrist she has properly concentrated on the psychological aspects of her problem but throughout she has shown herself fully aware of the sociological factors, in particular the pressure of social ideals." Peter Riviére
New Statesman 87:296 Mr 1 '74 550w

"[It is because Bruch's book avoids the unjustified dogma of 'popular' dieting books] that it is outstanding. . . . On the other hand, two words of caution are necessary. The first is that Professor Bruch is a psychiatrist and . . . patients she sees tend to be either those who have gross psychological, or indeed psy-

chotic, features, or those who have failed to
respond to all other forms of therapy. . . .
Secondly [the] book is based entirely on experience in the United States. . . . Generally,
however, [she] presents a commendably balanced picture. She may overstress the psychiatric aspect, but not unduly; indeed, this may
almost be a commendation in view of the unbalanced stress laid on the physical aspect
by so many other writers on the subject."
TLS p296 Mr 22 '74 480w

Following is a list of some indexes of book reviews:

Book Review Digest (1905–present) covers about 70 British and American periodicals with a cumulative author and title index for 1905–1974.

Book Review Index (1965–present) covers 255 English language periodicals.

Current Retrospective Index to Book Reviews in Scholarly Journals (1886–1974) covers 500 social science periodicals. Volumes 1–11 list reviews and Volumes 12–15 list titles of books reviewed.

Index to Book Reviews in the Humanities (1960–present) covers many scholarly journals not covered elsewhere.

Richard A. Gray's *Guide to Book Review Citations: A Bibliography of Sources* lists specialized indexes.

TAKING NOTES

Having found your sources, you will need to take notes as you read. If you own the work or have a photocopy of the relevant parts, you may want to annotate to help you read analytically. You should also know how to para-phrase, summarize, and outline. All of these reading skills are discussed and illustrated in Chapter 11: Invention and Revision. In addition, you will want to write down quotations you might use in your essay. Conventions for quoting are covered in the next chapter, The Research Paper: Using and Acknowledging Sources.

You may already have a method of notetaking you prefer. Some people like to use index cards for notes as well as for their working bibliography. They use small 3 × 5 inch index cards for their bibliography and larger ones (4 × 6 or 5 × 7) for notes. Some even use a different color index card for each of their sources. Other people prefer to keep their notes in a notebook, and still others enter their notes into a computer. It really does not matter what method you use as long as you keep accurate notes.

Accuracy in notetaking is of paramount importance in order to minimize the risk of copying facts incorrectly or of misquoting. Another common error in notetaking is to use the author's words without enclosing them in quo-tation marks. This error could lead easily to plagiarism, the unacknowledged use of another's words or ideas. Double check all your notes and try to be as accurate as you can.

The Research Paper: Using and Acknowledging Sources

Much of the writing you will do in college requires you to use outside sources in combination with your own firsthand observation and reflection. Any time you get information and ideas from reading, lectures, and interviews, you are using sources.

Using sources is not only acceptable, it is expected in college. No matter how original their thinking, educated people nearly always base their original thought on the work of others. In fact, most of your college education is devoted to teaching you two things: (1) what Matthew Arnold called "the best that has been thought and said," and (2) ways to analyze the thoughts and words of others, integrate them into your own thinking, and effectively convey your thinking to others.

Writers—students and professionals alike—occasionally misuse sources by failing to acknowledge them properly. The word *plagiarism,* which derives from the Latin word for "kidnapping," refers to the unacknowledged use of another's words, ideas, or information. Students sometimes get into trouble because they mistakenly assume that plagiarizing occurs only when another writer's exact words are used without acknowledgment. Keep in mind, however, that depending on your topic and audience, you may need to indicate the source of any ideas or information you have taken note of in your research for a paper, even if you have paraphrased or summarized another's words rather than copied down direct quotations.

Some people plagiarize simply because they do not know the conventions for using and acknowledging sources. This chapter will make clear how to incorporate sources into your writing and how to acknowledge your use of those sources. Others plagiarize because they keep sloppy notes and thus fail to distinguish between what is their own and what is their source's. Either they neglect to enclose their source's words in quotation marks or do not indicate when they are paraphrasing or summarizing a source's ideas and information. If you keep a working bibliography and careful notes, as described in Chapter 21: Library Research, you will not make this mistake.

There is still another reason some people plagiarize: They feel unable to write the paper by themselves. They feel overwhelmed by the writing task or by the deadline or by their own and others' expectations of them. This sense of inadequacy is not experienced by students alone. In a *Los Angeles Times* article on the subject, a journalist whose plagiarizing was discovered explained why he had done it. He said that when he read a column by another journalist on a subject he was preparing to write about, he felt that the other writer "said what I wanted to say and he said it better." If you experience this same anxiety about your work, speak to your instructor. Don't run the risk of failing a course because of plagiarizing.

USING SOURCES

Writers commonly use sources by direct quotation as well as by paraphrase and summary. Be selective in using quotation. As a general rule, quote only when your source's language is particularly vivid, memorable, or well known, or when your source is so respected by your readers that quoting would lend authority to your writing. If the phrasing does not matter, it is preferable to paraphrase or summarize rather than quote.

Quoting   Quotations should duplicate the source exactly. If the source has an error, copy it and add the Latin word *sic* in brackets immediately after the error to indicate that it is not yours but your source's:

> According to a recent newspaper article, "Plagirism [*sic*] is a problem among journalists and scholars as well as students."

However, you can change quotations (1) to emphasize particular words by underlining or italicizing them, (2) to omit irrelevant information or to make the quotation conform grammatically to your sentence by using ellipses, and (3) to make the quotation conform grammatically or to insert information by using brackets.

Underlining or italicizing for emphasis. Underline or italicize the words you want to emphasize, and add the phrase *(emphasis added)* or *(italics added)* at the end of the sentence. In his essay on youth suicide in Chapter 9, Victor Fuchs emphasizes that part of the quotation that refers specifically to suicide:

> In a review of psychosocial literature on adolescence, Elder (1975) concludes: "Adolescents who fail to receive guidance, affection, and concern from parents—whether by parental inattention or absence—are likely to rely heavily on peers for emotional gratification, advice, and companionship, *to anticipate a relatively unrewarding future,* and to engage in antisocial activities" (italics added).

Using ellipses for omissions. Ellipsis marks of three periods with spaces before and after (. . .) should be used to indicate an omission. If the omission occurs at the end of a sentence, place a sentence period directly after the last word, followed by the three spaced periods. Here is an example from Sue Hubbard's piece on "Chiggers" in Chapter 5.

> Mulling over this curiosity, G. W. Krantz, an eminent acarologist, says, ". . . the intense itching reaction experienced by man . . . reflects a lack of host adaptation."

If the omission is followed by a parenthetical citation, use three spaced periods before the parentheses and a sentence period directly after them.

When you quote a small part of a sentence, you need not use ellipses; instead, you may integrate a single word or phrase into your sentence simply by enclosing it in quotation marks, as illustrated by this sentence from David Greene's essay on "The Digital Audiotape Controversy" in Chapter 5:

> Best of all, it offers studio-recording sound quality, "the best, most authentic sound to ever emerge from a speaker system" (McDougal 1).

Using brackets for insertions or changes. You may also use brackets to make a quotation conform grammatically to your sentence or to replace an unclear pronoun. In this example from an essay on James Joyce's "Araby," reprinted in Chapter 10, the writer adapts Joyce's phrases "we played till our bodies glowed" and "shook music from the buckled harness" to fit the tense of her sentences:

> In the dark, cold streets during the "short days of winter," the boys must generate their own heat by "[playing] till [their] bodies glowed." Music is "[shaken] from the buckled harness" as if it were unnatural, and the singers in the market chant nasally of "the troubles in our native land."

You may also use brackets to add or substitute explanatory material in a quotation. In her essay in Chapter 6, Sydney Young uses brackets to identify a reference politician Gary Hart makes to his wife:

Any unfaithfulness is, as the candidate phrased it, "between me and Lee [his wife] and me and God."

Several kinds of changes necessary to make a quotation conform grammatically to another sentence may be made without any signal to readers: (1) the first letter of the first word in a quotation may be changed from capital to lower case, (2) the punctuation mark at the end of a quotation may be changed, and (3) double quotation marks (enclosing the entire quotation) may be changed to single quotation marks (enclosing a quotation within the larger quotation).

Placing quotations   A quotation may either be incorporated into the text by enclosing it in quotation marks or set off from the text in a block without quotation marks.

In-text quotations. Incorporate brief quotations (no more than four typed lines of prose or three lines of poetry) into your text. When you quote poetry, use a slash with spaces before and after (/) to signal the end of each line of verse:

> Alluding to St. Augustine's distinction between City of God and Earthly City, Lowell writes that "much against my will / I left the City of God where it belongs."   Steven Gould Axelrod, *Robert Lowell: Life and Art*

You may identify the source at either the beginning or the end of a quotation, or you may interrupt the quotation to do so:

> Charles Ferris, a lawyer for the Home Recording Rights Coalition says, "Home taping has the documented effect of encouraging purchases of prerecorded music, either of entire albums that have only been partially taped, or of other albums by the artist or composer whose work was taped." (David Green, Chapter 5)

> "We're in *Ripley's Believe It or Not,* along with another funeral home whose owners' names are Baggit and Sackit," Howard told me, without cracking a smile. (Brian Cable, Chapter 4)

> "What counts with a candidate for President is his character," claims George Reedy, press secretary to former President Lyndon Johnson, "and nothing shows it like his relationship with women." (Sydney Young, Chapter 6)

Block quotations. Put in block form, *without quotation marks,* five or more typed lines of prose or four or more lines of poetry. This example comes from Sydney Young's position paper in Chapter 6:

> In the words of former vice presidential candidate Geraldine Ferraro:

> > The issue is not whether the press has the right to investigate. It's *what* they are investigating. The public is entitled to know if he is a person who has good judgment, the right to know if he is smart, the right to know if he understands what's going on. If the Miami *Herald* had reported that

Gary Hart had invited to his house a *contra* leader, then I'd be very angry because he has taken a strong stand against the *contras*. I don't find the Donna Rice story relevant to the campaign. ("Private" 33)

Punctuating introductory statements

Statements that introduce quotations take a range of punctuation marks and lead-in words. Here are several examples of ways writers in Part I introduce quotations:

Introducing a statement with a colon

Says Nan Hunter, an American Civil Liberties Union attorney: "You can't torture people for names." (Anastasia Toufexis, Chapter 5)

The President's State of the Union report included this statement: "We will seek a 'technological' solution to the potential problem of unauthorized copying of copyrighted material on digital audio tape recorders." (David Green, Chapter 5)

Introducing a statement with a comma

As Cheryl Hayes, director of the NAS study explains, "If teenagers have to wait in the rain for a bus to take them to a clinic, there is a good chance they will never make it to the clinic." (Adam Paul Weisman, Chapter 7)

Introducing a statement using *that*

Bennett concedes that "birth control clinics in schools may prevent some births." (Adam Paul Weisman, Chapter 7)

Introducing a statement using "what . . . as"

Young people may be succumbing to what Abraham Maslow (1959) forecast as the ultimate disease of our time—"valuelessness." (Victor Fuchs, Chapter 9)

Avoiding grammatical tangles

When you incorporate quotations into your writing and especially when you omit words, you run the risk of creating ungrammatical sentences. Here are three common errors you should make an effort to avoid: verb incompatibility, ungrammatical omissions, and sentence fragments.

Verb incompatibility. When this error occurs, the verb form in the introductory statement is grammatically incompatible with the verb form in the quotation. When your quotation has a verb form that does not fit in with your text, it is usually possible to use just part of the quotation, thus avoiding verb incompatibility. In the following example, *suggests* and *saw* do not fit together as the sentence is written; see how the sentence is revised for verb compatibility.

NOT The narrator suggests his bitter disappointment when "I saw myself as a creature driven and derided by vanity."

BUT The narrator suggests his bitter disappointment when <u>he describes seeing himself</u> "as a creature driven and derided by vanity."

An awkward omission. Sometimes the omission of text from the quotation results in an ungrammatical sentence. In the following example, the quotation was awkwardly and ungrammatically excerpted. The revised sentences show two ways of correcting the grammar: first, by adapting the quotation (with brackets) so that its two parts fit together grammatically; second, by using only one part of the quotation.

NOT From the moment of the boy's arrival in Araby, the bazaar is presented as a commercial enterprise: "I could not find any sixpenny entrance and . . . handing a shilling to a weary-looking man."

BUT From the moment of the boy's arrival at Araby, the bazaar is presented as a commercial enterprise: "I could not find any sixpenny entrance and . . . hand[ed] a shilling to a weary-looking man."

OR From the moment of the boy's arrival at Araby, the bazaar is presented as a commercial enterprise: he "could not find any sixpenny entrance" and <u>so paid "a shilling" to get in.</u>

An incomplete introductory sentence. Sometimes when a quotation is a complete sentence, writers will carelessly neglect the introductory sentence—often, for example, forgetting to include a verb. Even though the quotation is a complete sentence, the total statement is then a sentence fragment.

NOT The girl's interest in the bazaar leading the narrator to make what amounts to a sacred oath: "If I go . . . I will bring you something."

BUT The girl's interest in the bazaar <u>leads</u> the narrator to make what amounts to a sacred oath: "If I go . . . I will bring you something."

Paraphrasing and summarizing In addition to quoting their sources, writers have the option of paraphrasing or summarizing what others have written. This method allows writers to use the source's information, but to present it in their own words. Chapter 11: Invention and Revision offers a fuller discussion of paraphrasing and summarizing techniques.

The following examples show how writers summarize statistics and facts as well as thoughts and ideas:

A study at Bellevue Hospital in New York City of 102 teenagers who attempted suicide showed that only one third of them lived with both parents (*Newsweek*, August 28, 1978, p. 74). (Victor Fuchs, Chapter 9)

For an industry that says it already loses one and a half billion dollars annually to people who copy music from their friends, the record industry is fearful of that number growing astronomically (Buell 112). (David Green, Chapter 5)

William Faulkner, for example, had been working as a janitor and as a deckhand on a fishing boat in Mississippi while writing *The Sound and the Fury* and *As I Lay Dying*. When *Sanctuary* was published in 1931, he attended some New York literary parties, at one of which Tallulah Bankhead asked him to write a picture for her. The idea so appealed to him that he apparently began writing a screenplay immediately. Some months later, reporting to MGM for a six-week contract, he asked to write a picture script for Mickey Mouse but, no less absurdly, was assigned to a script for Wallace Beery. Despite the obvious need for trained screenwriters, no studio offered schooling. Faulkner was packed off to a small projection room to watch old movies. Bored after a few minutes, he wandered off for a week in Death Valley, then returned to write four treatments in five days, including one for Beery (Kawin 70–72). (Alice Marquis, *Hopes & Ashes: The Birth of Modern Times, 1929–1939*)

In the first example, Victor Fuchs paraphrases a *Newsweek* article in order to highlight the survey statistics pertinent to his own thesis, while in the second David Green paraphrases the ideas he introduces from another writer's research. The third example from an essay by Alice Marquis on Hollywood writers is a good instance of summary: Marquis has boiled down several pages of biographical data from her original source into a paragraph that focuses on the information of primary interest to her research.

Notice in the preceding examples that each writer acknowledges his or her source by name. Even when you use your own words to present someone else's information, you generally must acknowledge the fact that you borrowed the information. The only information that does not require acknowledgment is common knowledge (John F. Kennedy was assassinated in Dallas), familiar sayings ("haste makes waste"), and well-known quotations ("All's well that ends well").

ACKNOWLEDGING SOURCES

Although there is no universally agreed-upon system for acknowledging sources, there is agreement on both the need for documentation and the items that should be included. Writers should acknowledge sources for two reasons: to give credit to those sources, and to enable readers to consult the sources for further information. The following information should be included when documenting sources: (1) name of author, (2) title of publication, and (3) publication source, date, and page.

Most documentation styles combine some kind of citation in the text with a separate list of references keyed to the textual citations. There are basically two ways of acknowledging sources: (1) parenthetical citations keyed to a works-cited list, and (2) footnotes (or endnotes) plus a bibliography. The Modern Language Association (MLA), a professional organization of English instructors, for many years endorsed the footnote style of documentation. But, with the 1984 revision of the *MLA Handbook*, the MLA has gone over to the simpler parenthetical citation method. The new MLA style is similar to the style endorsed by the American Psychological Association (APA)—the style used by many social and natural science instructors.

In Part I of this book, you can find examples of current MLA style (David Green in Chapter 5, Sydney Young in Chapter 6) and APA style (Victor Fuchs and Kim Dartnell in Chapter 9). This chapter presents the basic features of both these styles.

If you have any questions, consult the *MLA Handbook for Writers of Research Papers*, Second Edition (1984), or the *Publication Manual of the American Psychological Association*, Third Edition (1983). The *MLA Handbook* includes both current MLA style and footnote style.

Parenthetical citation in text The MLA and APA styles both advocate parenthetical citations in the text keyed to a works-cited list at the end of the paper. However, they differ on what should be included in the parenthetical citation. The MLA uses an author-page citation, while the APA uses an author-year-page citation.

MLA Dr. James is described as a "not-too-skeletal Ichabod Crane" (Simon 68).

APA Dr. James is described as a "not-too-skeletal Ichabod Crane" (Simon, 1982, p. 68).

Notice that the APA style uses a comma between author, year, and page as well as "p." for page (Simon, 1982, p. 68), whereas the MLA puts nothing but space between author and page (Simon 68). Note also that the citations in both cases come before the final period. With block quotations, however, the citation comes after the final period preceded by two spaces.

If the author's name is used in the text, put the page reference in parentheses as close as possible to the quoted material, but without disrupting the flow of the sentence. For the APA style, cite the year in parentheses directly following the author's name, and place the page reference in parentheses before the final sentence period.

MLA Simon describes Dr. James as a "not-too-skeletal Ichabod Crane" (68).

APA Simon (1982) describes Dr. James as a "not-too-skeletal Ichabod Crane" (p. 68).

To cite a source by two or three authors, the MLA uses all the authors' last names; for works with more than three authors, the citation and the entry in the works-cited list give the first author's name followed by "et al." The APA uses all the authors' last names the first time the reference occurs and the last name of the first author followed by "et al., " subsequently.

MLA   Dyal, Corning, and Willows identify several types of students, including the "Authority-Rebel" (4).

APA   Dyal, Corning, and Willows (1975) identify several types of students, including the "Authority-Rebel" (p. 4).

MLA   The Authority-Rebel "tends to see himself as superior to other students in the class" (Dyal, Corning, and Willows 4).

APA   The Authority-Rebel "tends to see himself as superior to other students in the class" (Dyal et al., 1975, p. 4).

To cite one of two or more works by the same author(s), the MLA uses the author's last name, a shortened version of the title, and the page. The APA uses the author's last name plus the year and page. When more than one work being cited was published by an author in the same year, APA style uses letters with the date (1973a, 1973b).

MLA   When old paint becomes transparent, it sometimes shows the artist's original plans: "a tree will show through a woman's dress" (Hellman, *Pentimento* 1).

APA   When old paint becomes transparent, it sometimes shows the artist's original plans: "a tree will show through a woman's dress" (Hellman, 1973, p. 1).

To cite a work listed only by its title, both the MLA and the APA use a shortened version of the title.

MLA   An international pollution treaty still to be ratified would prohibit all plastic garbage from being dumped at sea ("Awash" 26).

APA   An international pollution treaty still to be ratified would prohibit all plastic garbage from being dumped at sea ("Awash," 1987, p. 26).

To quote material taken not from the original but from a secondary source that quotes the original, both the MLA and the APA give the secondary source in the works-cited list, and cite both the original and secondary sources in the text.

MLA   E. M. Forster says "the collapse of all civilization, so realistic for us, sounded in [Matthew Arnold's] ears like a distant and harmonious cataract" (qtd. in Trilling 11).

APA   E. M. Forster says "the collapse of all civilization, so realistic for us, sounded in [Matthew Arnold's] ears like a distant and harmonious cataract" (cited in Trilling, 1955, p. 11).

List of works cited Keyed to the parenthetical citations in the text, the list of works cited identifies all the sources the writer uses. Every source cited in the text must refer to an entry in the works-cited list. And, conversely, every entry in the works-cited list must correspond to at least one parenthetical citation in the text.

Whereas the MLA style manual uses the title "Works Cited," the APA prefers "References." Both alphabetize the entries according to the first author's last name. When several works by an author are listed, the APA recommends these rules for arranging the list:

☐ Same name single-author entries precede multiple-author entries:

Aaron, P. (1985).
Aaron, P., & Zorn, C. R. (1982).

☐ Entries with the same first author and different second author should be alphabetized according to the second author's last name:

Aaron, P., & Charleston, W. (1979).
Aaron, P., & Zorn, C. R. (1982).

☐ Entries by the same authors should be arranged by year of publication, in chronological order:

Aaron, P., & Charleston, W. (1979).
Aaron, P., & Charleston, W. (1984).

☐ Entries by the same author(s) with the same publication year should be arranged alphabetically by title (excluding *A, An, The*), and lowercase letters (*a, b, c,* and so on) should follow the year in parentheses:

Aaron, P. (1985a). Basic. . . .
Aaron, P. (1985b). Elements. . . .

For multiple works by the same author (or group of authors), MLA style recommends alphabetizing by title. The author's name is given for the first entry only; subsequent entries are preceded by three hyphens and a period.

Vidal, Gore. *Empire.* New York: Random House, 1987.
---. *Lincoln.* New York: Random House, 1984.

The essential difference between the MLA and APA styles of listing sources is the order in which the information is presented. The MLA follows this order: author's name; title; publication source, year, and page. The APA puts the year after the author's name. The examples that follow indicate other minor differences in capitalization and arrangement between the two documentation styles.

BOOKS

A book by a single author

MLA   Simon, Kate. Bronx Primitive. New York: Harper, 1982.

APA   Simon, Kate. (1982). Bronx primitive. New York: Harper and Row.

A book by an agency or corporation

MLA   Association for Research in Nervous and Mental Disease. The Circulation of the Brain and Spinal Cord: A Symposium on Blood Supply. New York: Hafner, 1966.

APA   Association for Research in Nervous and Mental Disease. (1966). The circulation of the brain and spinal cord: A symposium on blood supply. New York: Hafner Publishing Co.

A book by more than one author

MLA   Strunk, W., Jr., and E. B. White. The Elements of Style. 4th ed. New York: Macmillan, 1983.

APA   Strunk, W., Jr., & White, E. B. (1983). The elements of style (4th ed.). New York: Macmillan.

MLA   Dyal, James A., William C. Corning, and Dale M. Willows. Readings in Psychology: The Search for Alternatives. 3rd ed. New York: McGraw-Hill, 1975.

APA   Dyal, James A., Corning, William C., & Willows, Dale M. (1975). Readings in psychology: The search for alternatives (3rd ed.). New York: McGraw-Hill.

For works by more than three authors, MLA style lists the name of the first author followed by "et al."

MLA   Nielsen, Niels C., Jr., et al. Religions of the World. 2nd ed. New York: St. Martin's, 1988.

A book by an unknown author

Use title in place of author.

MLA   College Bound Seniors. Princeton, NJ: College Board Publications, 1979."

APA   College bound seniors. (1979). Princeton, NJ: College Board Publications.

An edition prepared by a named editor

APA   Arnold, Matthew. (1966). Culture and anarchy (J. Dover Wilson, Ed.). Cambridge: Cambridge University Press. (Originally published, 1869.)

If you refer to the text itself, begin with the author:

MLA   Arnold, Matthew. <u>Culture and Anarchy</u>. Ed. J. Dover Wilson. Cambridge: Cambridge UP, 1966.

If you cite the editor in your text, begin with the editor:

MLA   Wilson, J. Dover, ed. <u>Culture and Anarchy</u>. By Matthew Arnold. Cambridge: Cambridge UP, 1966.

An anthology

MLA   Dertouzos, Michael L., and Joel Moses, eds. <u>The Computer Age: A Twenty-Year View</u>. Cambridge, MA: MIT, 1979.

APA   Dertouzos, Michael L., & Moses, Joel. (Eds.). (1979). <u>The computer age: A twenty-year view</u>. Cambridge, MA: MIT Press.

A translation

APA   Tolstoy, Leo. (1972). <u>War and peace</u>. (Constance Garnett, Trans.). London: Pan Books. (Originally published, 1868–1869.)

If you are referring to the work itself, begin with the author:

MLA   Tolstoy, Leo. <u>War and Peace</u>. Trans. Constance Garnett. London: Pan, 1972.

If you cite the translator in your text, begin the entry with the translator's name:

MLA   Garnett, Constance, trans. <u>War and Peace</u>. By Leo Tolstoy. London: Pan, 1972.

A work in an anthology

MLA   Faulkner, William. ''Dry September.'' <u>Literature: The Human Experience</u>. Ed. Richard Abcarian and Marvin Klotz. 4th ed. New York: St. Martin's, 1986. 753–761.

OR   Bell, Daniel. ''The Social Framework of the Information Society.'' In <u>The Computer Age: A Twenty-Year View</u>. Ed. Michael L. Dertouzos and Joel Moses. Cambridge, MA: MIT, 1979. 163–211.

APA   Bell, Daniel. (1979). The social framework of the information society. In Michael L. Dertouzos and Joel Moses (Eds.), <u>The computer age: A twenty-year view</u> (pp. 163–211). Cambridge, MA: MIT.

An essay in an anthology by the same author

MLA   Weaver, Richard. ''The Rhetoric of Social Science.'' In his <u>Ethics of Rhetoric</u>. South Bend, Indiana: Gateway, 1953. 186–210.

APA   Weaver, Richard. (1953). The rhetoric of social science. In Weaver, Richard, Ethics of rhetoric (pp. 186–210). South Bend, Indiana: Gateway Editions.

ARTICLES

An article in a journal with continuous annual pagination

MLA   Dworkin, Ronald. "Law as Interpretation." Critical Inquiry 9 (1982): 179–200.

APA   Dworkin, Ronald. (1982). Law as interpretation. Critical Inquiry, 9, 179–200.

An article in a journal that paginates each issue separately

MLA   Festinger, Leon. "Cognitive Dissonance." Scientific American 2 (Oct. 1962): 93–102.

APA   Festinger, Leon. (1962, October). Cognitive dissonance. Scientific American, 2, 93–102.

An article from a daily newspaper

MLA   Lubin, J. S. "On Idle: The Unemployed Shun Much Mundane Work, at Least for a While." Wall Street Journal 5 December 1980: 1, 25.

APA   Lubin, J. S. (1980, December 5). On idle: The unemployed shun much mundane work, at least for a while. The Wall Street Journal, pp. 1, 25.

An anonymous article

MLA   "Awash in Garbage." New York Times 15 Aug. 1987, sec. 1: 26.

APA   Awash in garbage. The New York Times, section 1, August 15, 1987, p. 26.

OTHER SOURCES

Computer software

MLA   Hogue, Bill. Miner 2049er. Computer software. Big Five Software.

OR   Microsoft Word. Computer software. Microsoft, 1984.

APA   Hogue, Bill. (1982). Miner 2049er. [Computer program]. Van Nuys, CA: Big Five Software.

OR   Microsoft word. (1984). [Computer program]. Bellevue, WA: Microsoft.

Records and tapes

MLA   Beethoven, Ludwig van. Violin Concerto in D Major, op. 61. Cond. Alexander Gauk, U.S.S.R. State Orchestra. David Oistrakh, violinist. Allegro, ACS 8044, 1980.

OR   Springsteen, Bruce. "Dancing in the Dark." Born in the U.S.A. Columbia, QC 38653, 1984.

APA   Beethoven, Ludwig van. (Composer). (1980). Violin Concerto in D Major, op. 61. (Cassette Recording No. ACS 8044). New York: Allegro.

OR   Springsteen, Bruce. (Singer and Composer). (1984). "Dancing in the Dark." Born in the U. S. A. (Record No. QC 38653). New York: Columbia.

Interviews

MLA   Lowell, Robert. "Robert Lowell." With Frederick Seidel. Paris Review 25 (Winter–Spring): 56–95.

OR   Franklin, Anna. Personal interview. 3 September 1983.

APA   Lowell, Robert. [Interview with Frederick Seidel]. Paris Review, 25 (Winter–Spring), pp. 56–95.

OR   Franklin, Anna. [Personal Interview]. 3 September 1983.

A SAMPLE RESEARCH PAPER

Here is a student research paper on the effects of television viewing. To support the thesis that "television leaves the imprint of [its] distorted world on our consciousness, so much so that it becomes the world that we experience as real," the author cites seven different sources—books, articles, and a television program. He uses MLA documentation style and format.

AUTHOR IDENTIFICATION

Bruce Coughran

English 1

Ms. Brown

December 10, 19--

TITLE

Through the Eyes of Television:
A Look at Some Effects of Television Watching

2 DOUBLE SPACES

COMMON KNOWLEDGE

        Our modern society changes so rapidly that it is hard to imagine what life was like only a few generations ago. It is easy to forget that many of the things that we take so much for granted in our daily lives did not exist when some of our grandparents were born. Telephones, automobiles, airplanes, home electricity, radio and petroleum products all have come into popular use only in the last 75 years. These technological innovations have had a tremendous influence on our lives. In the last 25 years, scarcely one generation, a new technological marvel has grown into the very fabric of our society and has become its eyes, ears, heart, and voice.

5-SPACE INDENTATION

        That technology is television. It reaches throughout our society at almost every level and forms a shared experience that almost becomes a social conscience. Television has become our main storyteller. We learn from it about our history and our present. It forms the basis for social norms, what is accepted and what is not. It increas-

Coughran 2

ingly is our marketplace, our social meeting ground, and even the place where our political battles are won or lost. It has become our link with the "outside world." We can sometimes forget that it is not a true reflection of our world, but one that is distorted by the race for ratings and advertising dollars. And yet, television leaves the imprint of this distorted world on our consciousness, so much so that it becomes the world that we experience as real.

Television occupies a place in our society that could scarcely be imagined 35 years ago when the first sets began to trickle into American homes. Television sets are found in 98% of American households, and the amount of time involved in TV viewing eclipses that of all other leisure activities except sleeping (Swerdlow 86). The average American home has a television set turned on for six hours every day, and it has been reported that a child, by age 15, will have spent more hours watching television than he will spend in the classroom (Swerdlow 88).

What happens during all those hours in front of the set? We are bombarded with a constant stream of images, stories, characters, and situations that create, in effect, a self-contained world. Although there appears to be a wide variety of programs, this world varies little from a few broad, widely held stereotypes (Comstock et al. 19). The world of TV consists of similar stories, situations, and characters primarily because of the financial pressure on the modern television industry. Television's life blood is advertising revenue, and revenue is dependent on ratings.

SOURCE OF STATISTIC CITED

SOURCE OF IDEA CITED

Coughran 3

The television networks are increasingly unwilling to take any chances. They rely on proven formulas and material, and this leads to a total uniformity of the messages that television puts out.

Despite the fact that the bulk of research on television has focused on its effects on children (particularly with respect to the influence of televised violence on antisocial behavior), a much broader aspect is less studied. This is the effect of television on the broad social consciousness. This aspect of television's impact has been called the "most pervasive and least well documented" (Swerdlow 96). The creation of concepts of social reality, that is, the perception of "the way the world is," is heavily influenced by television. As an example, most of us have definite ideas about the process of law enforcement, what private detectives, doctors, and lawyers do in their day-to-day lives. This is true in spite of the fact that few of us have direct exposure to these situations. For many people, these conceptions come increasingly from the situations that we encounter through the television tube.

These images come across as a total impression, the trappings of an artificial environment where we live a portion of our daily lives. They are not "learned" per se, as one would learn from educational material (when one is consciously learning). These images and broad concepts about the world seep into our consciousness, unfiltered by our discrimination. Viewing, for almost all programs, is a passive activity, in which thought or judgement is rarely ex-

SOURCE OF QUOTATION CITED

Coughran 4

SOURCE OF INFORMATION
CITED

ercised. In addition, most television watching is habitual, and is done by the clock, not by the program (Hawkins and Pingree 292), so that the effect is one of a constantly reinforced image of society that trickles into our minds, hour after hour, year after year.

Not only is this image of society pervasive and easy to accept, it is also very different from reality. Television is dominated by white males in their "prime years," with the young and the old both underrepresented in proportion to their percentage in the population; the same is true for blacks and other ethnic minorities (Comstock et al. 3). In television's world, women tend to be under 35, and men tend to be over 35. As women get older on television, they become less successful, whereas men become more successful as they age ("Television" 7).

The distribution of occupations is also radically different in the world of television. Prime time TV shows contain about ten times as many doctors and lawyers, twenty five times as many judges and policemen, and fifty times as many private investigators as occur in the general population. Blue-collar workers are greatly underrepresented, making up 9.9% of the characters on prime time shows and 49.7% of the general population (Swerdlow 93).

Violence has been a hotbed of research and the evidence is irrefutable that television portrays a much more violent world than one would otherwise conclude from statistics or everyday experiences. Violence occupies a central place in many television shows, from crime dramas to

Coughran 5

children's Saturday morning cartoons. Violence is often committed by the "heroes" of television dramas. The use of violent, socially disapproved, or even illegal methods in order to achieve socially approved ends is a common theme (Comstock et al. 4). The average rate of violent acts is between six and ten per hour (Gerbner et al. 184). This creates an aggregate pattern of violence that is perceived as an integral part of society. Fully 64% of the main characters on prime time TV (and 30% of all characters) are involved in some type of violent act as either a perpetrator or a victim or both, in sharp contrast to the actual census data indicating a rate of violent crimes of .32 per 100 persons (a third of one percent) (Gerbner et al. 194).

It is easy to dismiss the wide discrepancies between television portrayals and real life as an inherent quality of fiction, which may make it more interesting. There is, however, at least some evidence that many of the aspects of the television world are accepted as accurate by a significant number of people. Studies have shown that children tend to believe that television is an accurate representation of reality, and many teenagers believe that television shows life "the way it really is" (Swerdlow 97). One study even indicated that real life experience failed to change the perceived reality of television; in other words, television seemed "truer" than personal experience (Swerdlow 97).

In addition, it has been suggested that TV trivializes

Coughran 6

violence, making it more likely that people will accept violence and violent behavior ("Television" 8). Television
shows frequently portray extremely violent situations:
fights, beatings, rape, and murder. These are situations
that arouse powerful emotions in us. Just when these emotions are starting to rise, it is time for a commercial. The
viewer's attention goes from the horror of rape or murder
in one moment to "BAN underarm deodorant" in the next.
This has the effect of defusing our most powerful emotional responses to these violent acts. Studies have shown
that although television can be a powerful teacher of how
activities are performed ("mechanics"), it is a very weak
teacher of the emotional responses that accompany those
actions (McGinley and Murray 257–58). We learn about
violence from the TV, but without the strong emotional
responses that accompany the actual experience of
violence.

There are even some indications that the role models
portrayed on television are emulated by society (Swerdlow
97). George Gerbner, who has studied the effects of television on society for more than fifteen years at the University of Pennsylvania, says: "Increasingly, media cultivated facts and values have become standards by which we
judge even personal experiences and family and community behavior" (193). Many people report that life is not
as exciting as it is "supposed to be" (Swerdlow 98). Phy-
sicians and medical schools speak about the "Marcus
Welby" syndrome. Many people have an idyllic view of doc-

tors. As patients, they expect quick, easy cures at little cost or inconvenience. As prospective medical students, they expect to find easy answers, never make mistakes, and have lower levels of stress than is possible in most medical careers. A recent study shows that many police detectives follow procedures similar to those shown on television, not in order to catch criminals, but to satisfy the public image of how they "should" behave (Swerdlow 97).

There has been relatively little attention paid to TV's "culturization" effects (i.e., how television is shaping the individual's self image, social image, and the culture in which he or she lives). This is partly due to the lack of recognition that such a process is taking place, but it is also due to the inherent experimental problems involved. Experiments are most easily performed on isolated subjects over short time scales to study easily measured effects. The types of effects we are talking about occur over years and are difficult to detect.

Perhaps the most serious problem is the lack of a scientific "control" group. Since virtually all members of society are exposed to at least some television on a regular basis, it is impossible to compare "nonviewers" with "viewers." Nonviewers are, almost by definition, abnormal. It is necessary to resort to comparing light viewers with heavy viewers (according to the number of hours per day of television exposure). This can present an inherent problem since heavy television viewing can be correlated with other factors such as race, education, age, and employ-

Coughran 8

ment status (Hughes 291). These factors must be taken into account, and it is difficult to know if there are others that have not been identified.

There is also the problem of eliminating the possibility of "reverse causation." For example, if heavy television viewers are more violent, is it because heavy TV viewing makes one more prone to violence, or that those who are more prone to violence tend to watch more television? Also, how can more subtle effects be detected?

There is a technique that was developed by Dr. Gerbner to try to measure the socialization effects. Gerbner formulated questions that dealt with aspects of society that are skewed on TV relative to the real world. He asked people questions about the world and about their television watching habits. His findings show that those who watch more television tend to adopt TV's warped picture of the world, i.e., they tend to give the "television answers" to questions about the real world.

Gerbner surveyed thousands of people over a period of fifteen years as to their viewing habits and asked them questions about their world. In apparent accord with the distortions of the world projected by television, heavy viewers were more prone to overestimate the number of people involved in law enforcement, and the number of times police use violence in their work (Gerbner et al. 195). They were also more prone to overestimate the number of people who are involved with crimes, and the proportion of crimes that are violent ("Television" 7).

Coughran 9

Coinciding with the underrepresentation of older people, heavy viewers were more likely to believe that the population of elderly persons is declining (Swerdlow 93), (it is not), and were more likely to view the elderly in an unfavorable light ("Television" 7).

Moreover, the surveys showed that the people who watched large amounts of television experienced more fear of victimization, and thought of the world as being a more violent place than those who watched less television. Heavy viewers tended to overestimate their chances of being involved in violence (Gerbner et al. 195). They were also more likely to say that they were afraid to walk alone at night, and were more likely to buy guns, locks, and dogs for protection (Gerbner et al. 196–99). In addition, heavy viewers were more likely to approve of violence as a means of solving problems than were light viewers (Gerbner et al. 196).

Heavy television watchers also tended to score higher on tests of suspicion and mistrust. They were more likely to say that most people only look out for themselves, take advantage of others, and cannot be trusted. More heavy viewers than light viewers tended to say that "you can't be too careful" when dealing with people (Gerbner et al. 195).

Gerbner presents strong evidence that people who watch large amounts of television do seem to live in a world that is more violent, where people are less trustworthy, and where crime is more to be feared, than their neighbors who watch less television. It seems reasonable,

Coughran 10

even probable, that other more subtle aspects of our perceived world are also heavily influenced by exposure to television's distorted images.

Television pervades our entire society. Our children will learn more about the way the world is from the television than they will from any other source, their parents included. We must increasingly become aware of the effects of this new guest in our homes, and seek to counteract some of its effects. We must strive to regain a sense of community and family, to regain that experience that we call reality.

Television will not go away. If anything, its influence will increase in the next decade as new technologies such as cable and satellite reception become commonplace. But what is needed is an understanding and an appreciation of the effects of television on one's experience of the wider world, and the knowledge that television is not always to be believed. We must retain our sense of reality apart from the world of TV, and this will only come with the recognition of the detrimental effects of habitual heavy TV viewing. Just as was the case with cigarette smoking, a widespread awareness of TV's detrimental effects will not eliminate this habitual (it has even been called addictive) behavior. However, without the widespread knowledge that television viewing in large amounts has harmful effects, its beneficial potentialities cannot begin to be exploited.

Coughran 11

Works Cited

Comstock, George, et al. Television and Human Behavior.
New York: Columbia UP, 1978.

Gerbner, George, et al. "Cultural Indicators: Violence Profile No. 9." Journal of Communication (Summer
1978): 176–207.

Hawkins, Robert, and Suzanne Pingree. "Uniform Messages and Habitual Viewing: Unnecessary Assumptions in Social Reality Effects." Human Communication Research 7 (1981): 291–301.

Hughes, Michael. "The Fruits of Cultivation Analysis: A
Reexamination of Some Effects of Television Watching." Public Opinion Quarterly 44 (1980): 287–302.

McGinley, Hugh, and Robert Murray. "Paired-Associate
and Emotional Learning Through Television Modeling." Journal of General Psychology 100 (1979):
251–58.

Swerdlow, Joel. "A Question of Impact." Wilson Quarterly
(Winter 1981): 86–99.

"The Television Explosion." Nova. Transcript. PBS. WGBH,
Boston. 14 Feb. 1982.

5-SPACE INDENTATION

2 SPACES

PART FOUR

Writing Under Pressure

Essay Examinations

Even though the machine-scorable multiple-choice test has sharply reduced the number of essay exams administered in schools and colleges,
you can be certain that essay exams will continue to play a significant role
in the education of liberal arts students. Many instructors—especially in the
humanities and social sciences—still believe an exam that requires you to
write is the best way to find out what you have learned and, more important,
how you can use what you have learned. Instructors who give essay exams
want to be sure you can sort through the large body of information covered
in a course, identify what is important or significant, and explain your decision. They want to see whether you understand the concepts that provide
the basis for a course and whether you can use those concepts to interpret
specific materials, to make connections on your own, to see relationships, to
draw comparisons and contrasts, to synthesize diverse information in support
of an original assertion. They may even be interested in your ability to justify
your own evaluations based on appropriate criteria and to argue your own
opinions with convincing evidence. Your instructors hope they are encouraging you to think more critically and analytically about a subject; they feel
a written exam best allows you to demonstrate that you are doing so.

As a college student, then, you will be faced with a variety of essay exams,
from short-answer identifications of a few sentences to take-home exams that
may require hours of planning and writing. You will find that the writing
activities and strategies discussed in Parts I and II of this book—particularly
reporting information, illustrating, defining, comparing and contrasting, and
arguing—as well as the mapping strategies in Chapter 11—clustering, listing,
and outlining—describe the skills that will help you do well on all sorts of
these exams. This chapter proposes some more specific guidelines for you to
follow in preparing for and writing essay exams, and analyzes a group of
typical exam questions to help you determine which strategies will be most
useful.

But you can also learn a great deal from your experiences with essay
exams in the past, the embarrassment and frustration of doing poorly on one
and the great pleasure and pride of doing well. Do you recall the very best
exam you ever wrote? Do you remember how you wrote it and why you
were able to do so well? How can you be certain to approach such writing
tasks confidently and to complete them successfully? Keep these questions
in mind as you consider the following guidelines.

23

First of all, essay exams require a comprehensive understanding of large amounts of information. Since exam questions can reach so widely into the course materials—and in such unpredictable ways—you cannot hope to do well on them if you do not keep up with readings and assignments from the beginning of the course. Do the reading, go to lectures, take careful notes, participate in discussion sections, organize small study groups with class-mates to explore and review course materials throughout the semester. Trying to cram weeks of information into a single night of study will never allow you to do your best.

Then, as an exam approaches, find out what you can about the form it will take. There is little that is more irritating to instructors than the pestering inquiry, "Do we need to know this for the exam?"; but it is generally legit-imate to ask whether the questions will require short or long answers, how many questions there will be, whether you may choose which questions to answer, and what kinds of thinking and writing will be required of you. Some instructors may hand out study guides for exams, or even lists of potential questions. However, beyond a sense of how the exam will be struc-tured, you will often be on your own in determining how best to go about studying.

Try to avoid simply memorizing information aimlessly. As you study, you should be clarifying the important issues of the course and using these issues to focus your understanding of specific facts and particular readings. If the course is a historical survey, distinguish the primary periods and try to see relations among the periods and the works or events that define them. If the course is thematically unified, determine how the particular materials you have been reading express those themes. If the course is a broad intro-duction to a general topic, concentrate on the central concerns of each study unit and see what connections you can discover among the various units. Try to place all you have learned into perspective, into a meaningful context. How do the pieces fit together? What fundamental ideas have the readings, the lectures, and the discussions seemed to emphasize? How can those ideas help you digest the information the course has covered?

One good way to prepare yourself for an exam is by making up questions you think the instructor might give and then planning answers to them with classmates. Returning to your notes and to assigned readings with specific questions in mind can help enormously in your process of understanding. The important thing to remember is that an essay exam tests more than your memory of specific information; it requires you to use specific information to demonstrate a comprehensive grasp of the topics covered in the course.

READING THE EXAM CAREFULLY

Before you answer a single question, read the entire exam and apportion your time realistically. Pay particular attention to how many points you may earn in different parts of the exam; notice any directions that suggest how long an answer should be or how much space it should take up. As you are doing so, you may wish to make tentative choices of the questions you will answer and decide on the order in which you will answer them. If you have immediate ideas about how you would organize any of your answers, you might also jot down partial scratch outlines. But before you start to complete any answers, write down the actual clock time you expect to be working on each question or set of questions. Careful time management is crucial to your success on essay exams; giving some time to each question is always better than using up your time on only a few and never getting to others.

You will next need to analyze each question carefully before beginning to write your answer. Decide what you are being asked to do. It can be easy at this point to become flustered, to lose concentration, even to go blank, if your immediate impulse is to cast about for ideas indiscriminately. But if you first look closely at what the question is directing you to do and try to understand the sort of writing that will be required, you can begin to recognize the structure your answer will need to take. This tentative structure will help focus your attention on the particular information that will be pertinent to your answer.

Consider this question from a sociology final:

> Drawing from lectures on the contradictory aspects of American values, discussions of the "bureaucratic personality" and the type of behavior associated with social mobility, discuss the problems of bettering oneself in a relatively "open," complex, industrial society such as the United States.

Such a question can cause momentary panic, but nearly always you can define the writing task you face. Look first at the words that give you directions: *draw from* and *discuss*. The term *discuss* is fairly vague, of course, but here it probably invites you to list and explain the problems of bettering oneself. The categories of these problems are already identified in the opening phrases: contradictory values, bureaucratic personality, certain behavior.

Therefore, you would plan to begin with an assertion (or thesis) that included the key words in the final clause (bettering oneself in an open, complex, industrial society) and then take up each category of problem—and maybe still other problems you can think of—in separate paragraphs.

This question essentially calls for recall, organization, and clear presentation of facts from lectures and readings. Though it looks confusing at first, once it is sorted out, it contains the key terms for the answer's thesis, as well as its main points of development. In the next section are some further examples of the kinds of questions often found on essay exams. Pay particular attention to how the directions and the key words in each case can help you define the writing task involved.

SOME TYPICAL ESSAY EXAM QUESTIONS

Following are nine categories of exam questions, divided according to the sort of writing task involved and illustrated by examples. You will notice that, although the wording of the examples in a category may differ, the essential directions are very much the same.

All of the examples are unedited and were written by instructors in six different departments in the humanities and social sciences at two different state universities. Drawn from short quizzes, mid-terms, and final exams for a variety of freshman and sophomore courses, these questions demonstrate the range of writing you may be expected to do on exams.

Define or identify   Some questions require you to write a few sentences defining or identifying material from readings or lectures. Almost always such questions allow you only a very few minutes to complete your answer.

You may be asked for a brief overview of a large topic, as in Question 23.1. This question, from a twenty-minute quiz in a literature course, could have earned as much as 15 of the 100 points possible on the quiz:

Question 23.1

Name and describe the three stages of African literature.

Answering this question would simply involve following the specific directions. A student would probably *name* the periods in historical order and then *describe* each period in a separate sentence or two.

Other questions, like 23.2, will supply a list of more specific items to identify. This example comes from a final exam in a communications course, and the answer to each part was worth as much as 4 points on a 120-point exam.

Question 23.2

Define and state some important facts concerning each of the following:
- A. Demographics
- B. Instrumental model
- C. RCA
- D. Telephone booth of the air
- E. Penny Press

With no more than three or four minutes for each part, students taking this exam would offer a concise definition (probably in a sentence). Then that definition would be briefly expanded with facts relevant to the main topics in the course.

Sometimes the list of items to be identified can be quite complicated, including quotes, concepts, and specialized terms; it may also be worth a significant number of points. The next example illustrates the first five items in a list of fifteen that opened a literature final. Each item was worth 3 points, for a total of 45 out of a possible 130 points.

Question 23.3

Identify each of the following items:
1. projection
2. "In this vast landscape he had loved so much, he was alone."
3. Balducci
4. *pied noir*
5. the Massif Central

Although the directions do not say so specifically, it is crucial here not only to identify each item but to explain its significance in terms of the overall subject, as well. In composing a definition or identification, always ask yourself a simple question: Why is this item important enough to appear on the exam?

Recall details of a specific source

Sometimes instructors will ask for a straightforward summary or paraphrase of a specific source—a report, for example, or a book or film. Such questions hold the student to recounting details directly from the source and do not encourage interpretation or evaluation. In the following example from a midterm exam in a sociology course, students were allowed about ten minutes and required to complete the answer on one lined page provided with the exam.

Question 23.4

In his article, "Is There a Culture of Poverty?", Oscar Lewis addresses a popular question in the social sciences. What is "the culture of poverty"?

How is it able to come into being, according to Lewis? That is, under what conditions does it exist? When does he say a person is no longer a part of the culture of poverty? What does Lewis say is the future of the culture of poverty?

The phrasing here invites a fairly clearcut structure. Each of the five specific questions can be turned into an assertion and illustrated with evidence from Lewis's book. For example, the first two questions could become assertions like these: "Lewis defines the culture of poverty as _____ ," and "According to Lewis the culture of poverty comes into being through _____ ." The important thing in this case is to stick closely to an accurate summary of what the writer said and not waste time evaluating or criticizing his ideas.

Explain the importance or significance   Another kind of essay exam question asks students to explain the importance or significance of something covered in the course. Such questions require you to use specific examples as the basis for a more general discussion of what has been studied. This will often involve interpreting a literary work by concentrating on a particular aspect of it, as in Question 23.5. This question was worth 10 out of 100 points and was to be answered in 75 to 100 words:

Question 23.5

In the last scene in *The Paths of Glory*, the owner of a cafe brings a young German girl onto a small stage in his cafe to sing for the French troops, while Colonel Dax looks on from outside the cafe. Briefly explain the significance of this scene in relation to the movie as a whole.

In answering this question, a student's first task would be to reconsider the whole movie, looking for ways this one small scene illuminates or explains larger issues or themes. Then, in a paragraph or two, the student would summarize these themes and point out how each element of the specific scene fits into the overall context.

You may also be asked to interpret specific information to show that you understand the fundamental concepts of a course. The following example from a communications mid-term was worth a possible 10 of 100 points and was allotted twenty minutes of exam time.

Question 23.6

Chukovsky gives many examples of cute expressions and statements uttered by small children. Give an example or two of the kind of statements that he finds interesting. Then state their implications for understanding the nature of language in particular and communications more generally.

Here, the student must start by choosing examples of children's utterances from Chukovsky's book. These examples would then provide the basis for demonstrating one's grasp of the larger subject.

Questions like these are usually more challenging than definition and summary questions because you must decide for yourself the significance or importance or implications of the information. You must also consider how best to organize your answer so that the general ideas you need to communicate are clearly developed.

Apply concepts to works Very often courses in the humanities and social sciences emphasize significant themes, ideologies, or concepts. A common essay exam question asks students to apply the concepts to works studied in the course. Rather than providing specific information to be interpreted more generally, such questions will present you with a general idea and require you to illustrate it with specific examples from your reading.

On a final exam in a literature course, an instructor posed this writing task. It was worth 50 points out of 100, and students had about an hour to complete it.

Question 23.7

Many American writers have portrayed their characters or their poetic speaker as being engaged in a quest. The quest may be explicit or implicit, external or psychological, and it may end in failure or success. Analyze the quest motif as it appears in the work of four of the following writers: Edwards, Franklin, Hawthorne, Thoreau, Douglass, Whitman, Dickinson, James, Twain.

On another literature final, the following question was worth 45 of 130 points. Students had about forty-five minutes to answer it.

Question 23.8

Several of the works studied in this course depict scapegoat figures. Select two written works and two films and discuss how their authors or directors present and analyze the social conflicts that lead to the creation of scapegoats.

Question 23.7 instructs students to *analyze*, Question 23.8 to *discuss;* yet the answers for each would be structured very similarly. An introductory paragraph would define the concept—the *quest* or a *scapegoat*—and refer to the works to be discussed. Then a paragraph or two would be devoted to each of the four separate works, developing specific evidence to illustrate the concept. A concluding paragraph would probably attempt to bring the concept into clearer focus, which is, after all, the point of answering these questions.

Comment on a quotation On essay exams, an instructor will often ask students to comment on quotations they are seeing for the first time. Usually such quotations will express some surprising or controversial opinion that complements or challenges basic principles or ideas in the course. Sometimes the writer being quoted is identified, sometimes not. In fact, it is not unusual for instructors to write the quotation themselves.

A student choosing to answer the following question from a literature final would have risked half the exam—in points and time—on the outcome.

Question 23.9

Argue for or against this thesis: "In *A Clockwork Orange*, both the heightened, poetic language and the almost academic concern with moral and political theories deprive the story of most of its relevance to real life."

The directions here clearly ask for an argument. A student would need to set up a thesis indicating that the novel either is or is not relevant to real life, and then point out how its language and its theoretical concerns can be viewed in light of this thesis.

The next example comes from a mid-term exam in a history course. Students had forty minutes to write their answers, which could earn as much as 70 points on a 100-point exam.

Question 23.10

"Some historians believe that economic hardship and oppression breed social revolt; but the experience of the United States and Mexico between 1900 and 1920 suggests that people may rebel also during times of prosperity."

Comment on this statement. Why did large numbers of Americans and Mexicans wish to change conditions in their countries during the years from 1900 to 1920? How successful were their efforts? Who benefited from the changes that took place?

Although here students are instructed to "comment," the three questions suggest evidence to be used in constructing an argument. Just as in Question 23.9, a successful answer will require a clear thesis stating a position on the views expressed in the quotation, specific reasons to support that thesis, and evidence from readings and lectures to argue for the reasons. In general, such questions don't require a "right" answer: whether you agree or disagree with the quotation is not as important as whether you can argue your case reasonably and convincingly, demonstrating a firm grasp of the subject matter.

Compare and contrast It could well be that instructors' most favored essay exam question is one that requires a comparison or contrast of two or three principles, ideas, works, activities, or phenomena. This kind of question requires you to explore fully the relations between things of importance in the course, to analyze each thing separately and then search out specific points of likeness or difference. Students must, thus, show a thorough knowledge of the things being compared, as well as a clear understanding of the basic issues on which comparisons and contrasts can be made.

Often, as in Question 23.11, the basis of comparison will be limited to a particular focus; here, for example, two works are to be compared in terms of their views of colonialism.

Question 23.11

Compare and analyze the views of colonialism presented in Memmi's *The Colonizer and the Colonized* and Pontecorvo's *The Battle of Algiers.* Are there significant differences between these two views?

Sometimes, however, instructors will simply identify what is to be compared, leaving students the task of choosing the basis of the comparison, as in the next three examples from a communications exam, a history exam, and a literature exam.

Question 23.12

In what way is the stage of electronic media fundamentally different from all the major stages that preceded it?

Question 23.13

What was the role of the United States in Cuban affairs from 1898 until 1959? How did our role there compare with our role in the rest of Spanish America during the same period?

Question 23.14

Write an essay on one of the following topics:
1. Squire Western and Mr. Knightley
2. Dr. Primrose and Mr. Elton

Whether the point of comparison is stated in the question or left for you to define for yourself, it is important that your answer be limited to those aspects of likeness or difference that are most relevant to the general concepts or themes covered in the course. (A thorough discussion of this writing strategy is in Chapter 18: Comparing and Contrasting.)

Synthesize information from various sources   In a course with several assigned readings, an instructor may give students an essay exam question that requires them to pull together (to synthesize) information from all the readings.

The following example was one of four required questions on a final exam in a course in Third World studies. Students had about thirty minutes to complete their answer.

Question 23.15

On the basis of the articles read on El Salvador, Nicaragua, Peru, Chile, Argentina, and Mexico, what would you say are the major problems confronting Latin America today? Discuss the major types of problems with references to particular countries as examples.

This question asks students to do a lot in thirty minutes. They must first decide which major problems to discuss, which countries to include in each discussion, and how to use evidence from many readings to develop their answers. A carefully developed forecasting statement, as discussed in Chapter 12: Cueing the Reader, will be essential to developing a coherent essay.

Summarize and explain causes or results In humanities and social science courses much of what students study concerns the causes or results of trends, actions, and events. Hence, it is not too surprising to find questions about causes and results on essay exams. Sometimes the instructor expects students to recall causes or results from readings and lectures. At other times, the instructor may not have in mind any particular causes or results and wants to find out what students are able to propose.

These examples come from mid-term and final exams in literature, communications, and sociology courses:

Question 23.16

Why do Maurice and Jean not succumb to the intolerable conditions of the prison camp (the Camp of Hell) as most of the others do?

Question 23.17

Given that we occupy several positions in the course of our lives and given that each position has a specific role attached to it, what kinds of problems or dilemmas arise from those multiple roles and how are they handled?

Question 23.18

Explain briefly the relationship between the institution of slavery and the emergence of the blues as a new Afro-American musical expression.

Question 23.19

Analyze the way in which an uncritical promotion of the new information technology (computers, satellites, etc.) may support, unintentionally, the maintenance of the status quo.

These questions are presented in several ways ("why," "what kind of problem," "explain the relationship," "analyze the way"), but they all require a list of causes or results in the answer. The causes or results would be organized under a thesis statement, and each cause or result would be argued and supported with evidence from lectures or readings.

If you write the essays assigned in Chapter 7: Proposing Solutions and Chapter 9: Speculating About Causes, you will be learning writing strategies for answering essay exam questions about causes or results.

Criticize or evaluate   Occasionally instructors will invite students to evaluate a concept or work. Nearly always they want more than opinion: they expect a reasoned, documented judgment based on appropriate criteria. Such questions not only test students' ability to recall and synthesize pertinent information; they also allow instructors to find out whether students can apply criteria taught in the course, whether they understand the standards of judgment that are basic to the subject matter.

On a final examination in a literature course a student might have chosen either one of the following questions about novels read in the course. Each would have been worth half the total points, with about an hour to answer it:

Question 23.20

Which has the more effective plot: *The Secret Agent* or *A Passage to India*?

Question 23.21

A Clockwork Orange and *The Comfort of Strangers* both attempt to examine the nature of modern decadence. Which does so more successfully?

To answer these questions successfully, students would obviously have to be very familiar with the novels under discussion. They would also have to establish criteria appropriate to evaluating an effective plot or a successful examination of modern decadence. Students would initially have to make a judgment favoring one novel over the other (although such a judgment need not cast one novel as a "terrible" and the other as a "perfect" illustration). The answer would then give reasons for this judgment, argue each reason with evidence from the novels, and probably use the writing strategies of comparison and contrast to develop the discussion.

This next question was worth 10 of 85 points in a communications course mid-term exam. Students were asked to answer the question "in two paragraphs."

Question 23.22

Eisenstein and Mukerji both argue that moveable print was important to the rise of Protestantism. Cole extends this argument to say that print set off a chain of events that was important to the history of the United States. Summarize this argument, and criticize any part of it if you choose.

Here students are asked to criticize or evaluate an argument in several course readings. The instructor wants to know what students think of this argument and also, even though this is not stated, why they judge it as they do. Answering this unwritten "why" part of the question is the challenge: students must come up with reasons appropriate to evaluating the arguments and with evidence to support their reasons.

Evaluative questions like these involve the same sorts of writing strategies as those discussed in Chapter 8: Making Evaluations.

PLANNING YOUR ANSWER

The amount of planning you do for a question will depend on how much time it is allotted and how many points it is worth. For short-answer definitions and identifications, a few seconds of thought will probably be sufficient. (Be careful not to puzzle too long over individual items like these. Skip over any you cannot recognize fairly quickly; often, answering other questions will help jog your memory.) For answers that require a paragraph or two, you may want to jot down several important ideas or specific examples to help focus your thoughts and give you a basis for organizing your information.

For longer answers, though, you will need to develop a much more definite strategy of organization. You have time for only one draft, so allow a reasonable period—as much as a quarter of the time allotted the question—for making notes, determining a thesis, and developing an outline. Jotting down pertinent ideas is a good way to begin; then you can plan your organization with a scratch outline (just a listing of points or facts) or a cluster (both illustrated in Chapter 11: Invention and Revision).

For questions with several parts (different requests or directions, a sequence of questions), make a list of the parts so that you do not miss or minimize one part. For questions presented as questions (rather than directives) you might want to rephrase each question as a writing topic. These topics will often suggest how you should outline the answer.

You may have to try two or three outlines or clusters before you hit on a workable plan. But be realistic as you outline—you want a plan you can develop within the limited time allotted for your answer. Hence, your outline will have to be selective—not everything you know on the topic, but what you know that can be developed clearly within the time available.

WRITING YOUR ANSWER

As with planning, your strategy for writing depends on the length of your answer. For short identifications and definitions, it is usually best to start with a general identifying statement and then move on to describe specific applications or explanations. Two sentences will almost always suffice, but make sure you write complete sentences.

For longer answers, begin by stating your forecasting statement or thesis clearly and explicitly. An essay exam is not an occasion for indirectness: you want to strive for focus, simplicity, and clarity. In stating your point and developing your answer use key terms from the question; it may look as though you are avoiding the question unless you use key terms (the same key terms) throughout your essay. If the question does not supply any key terms, you will find that you have provided your own by stating your main point. Use these key terms throughout the answer.

If you have devised a promising outline for your answer, then you will be able to forecast your overall plan and its subpoints in your opening sentences. Forecasting always impresses readers and has the very practical advantage of making your answer easier to read. You might also want to use briefer paragraphs than you ordinarily do and signal clear relations between paragraphs with transition phrases or sentences. Such strategies are illustrated fully in Chapter 5: Reporting Information and Chapter 12: Cueing the Reader.

As you begin writing your answer, freely strike out words or even sentences you want to change by drawing through them neatly with a single line. Do not stop to erase. Do not strike out with elaborate messy scratchings. Instructors do not expect flawless writing, but they are put off by unnecessary messiness.

As you move ahead with the writing, you will certainly think of new subpoints and new ideas or facts to include later in the paper. Stop briefly to make a note of these on your original outline. If you find that you want to add a sentence or two to sections you have already completed, write them sideways in the margin or at the top of the page, with a neat arrowed line to show where they fit in your answer.

Do not pad your answer with irrelevancies and repetitions just to fill up space. You may have had one instructor who did not seem to pay much attention to what you wrote, but most instructors read exams carefully and are not impressed by the length of an answer alone. Within the time available, write a comprehensive, specific answer without padding.

Watch the clock carefully to ensure that you do not spend too much time on one answer. You must be realistic about the time constraints of an essay exam, especially if you know the material well and are prepared to write a lot. If you write one dazzling answer on an exam with three required questions, you earn only 33 points, not enough to pass at most colleges. This may seem unfair, but keep in mind that instructors plan exams to be reasonably comprehensive. They want you to write about the course materials in two or three or more ways, not just one way.

If you run out of time when you are writing an answer, jot down the remaining main ideas from your outline, just to show that you know the material and with more time could have continued your exposition.

Write legibly and proofread. Remember that your instructor will likely be reading a large pile of exams. Careless scrawls, misspellings, omitted words, and missing punctuation (especially missing periods needed to mark the ends of sentences) will only make that reading difficult, even exasperating. A few seconds of careful proofreading can improve your grade.

MODEL ANSWERS TO SOME TYPICAL ESSAY EXAM QUESTIONS

Here we will analyze several successful answers and give you an opportunity to analyze one for yourself. These analyses, along with the information we have provided elsewhere in this chapter, should greatly improve your chances of writing successful answers.

Short answers   A literature mid-term exam opened with ten items to identify, each worth 3 points. Students had only about two minutes to identify each item. Here are three of freshman Brenda Gossett's identifications, each one earning her the full 3 points.

Rauffenstein: He was the German general who was in charge of the castle where Boeldieu, Marical, and Rosenthal were finally sent in *The Grand Illusion.* He along with Boeldieu represented the aristocracy, which was slowly fading out at that time.

Iges Peninsula: This peninsula is created by the Meuse River in France. It is there that the Camp of Hell was created in *The Debacle.* The Camp of Hell is where the French army was interned after the Germans defeated them in the Franco-Prussian War.

Pache: He was the "religious peasant" in the novel *The Debacle.* It was he who inevitably became a scapegoat when he was murdered by Loubet, LaPoulle, and Chouteau because he wouldn't share his bread with them.

The instructor said only "identify the following" but clearly wanted both identification and significance of the item to the work in which it appeared.

Gosset gives both and gets full credit. She mentions particular works, characters, and events. Though she is very rushed, she answers in complete sentences. She does not misspell any words or leave out any commas or periods. Her answers are complete and correct.

Paragraph-length
answers

One question on a weekly literature quiz was worth 20 points of the total of 100. With only a few minutes to answer the question, students were instructed to "answer in a few sentences." Here is the question and Camille Prestera's answer:

> In *Things Fall Apart,* how did Okonkwo's relationship with his father affect his attitude toward his son?

> Okonkwo despised his father, who was lazy, cowardly, and in debt. Okonkwo tried to be everything his father wasn't. He was hard-working, wealthy, and a great warrior and wrestler. Okonkwo treated his son harshly because he was afraid he saw the same weakness in Nwoye that he despised in his father. The result of this harsh treatment was that Nwoye left home.

Prestera begins by describing Okonkwo and his father, contrasting the two sharply. Then she explains Okonkwo's relationship with his son Nwoye. Her answer is coherent and straightforward.

Long answers

On final exams, at least one question requiring an essay-length answer is not uncommon. John Pixley had an hour to plan and write this essay for a final exam in a literature course.

Question

Many American writers have portrayed their characters or their poetic speaker as being engaged in a quest. The quest may be explicit or implicit, external or psychological, and it may end in failure or success. Analyze the quest motif as it appears in the work of four of the following writers: Edwards, Franklin, Hawthorne, Thoreau, Douglass, Whitman, Dickinson, James, Twain.

John Pixley's Answer

Americans pride themselves on being ambitious and on being able to strive for goals and to tap their potentials. Some say that this is what the "American Dream" is all about. It is important for one to do and be all that one is capable of. This entails a quest or search for identify, experience, and happiness. Hence, the idea of the quest is a vital one in America, and it can be seen as a theme throughout American literature.

1

In eighteenth-century Colonial America, Jonathan Edwards dealt with this theme in his autobiographical and personal writings. Unlike his

2

Key term *(quest)* is mentioned in introduction and thesis.

First writer is identified immediately.

fiery and hardnosed sermons, these autobiographical writings present a sensitive, vulnerable man trying to find himself and his proper, satisfying place in the world. He is concerned with his spiritual growth, in being free to find and explore religious experience and happiness. For example, in *Personal Narrative,* he very carefully traces the stages of religious beliefs. He tells about periods of abandoned ecstasy, doubts, and rational revelations. He also notes that his best insights and growth came at times when he was alone in the wilderness, in nature. Edwards's efforts to find himself in relation to the world can also be seen in his "Observations of the Natural World," in which he relates various meticulously observed and described natural phenomena to religious precepts and occurrences. Here, he is trying to give the world and life, in which he is a part, some sense of meaning and purpose.

Although he was a contemporary of Edwards, Benjamin Franklin, who was very involved in the founding of the U.S. as a nation, had a different conception of the quest in his writings. He sees the quest as being one for practical accomplishment, success, and wealth. In his *Autobiography,* he stresses that happiness involves working hard to accomplish things, getting along with others, and establishing a good reputation. Unlike Edwards's, his quest is external and bound up with society. He is concerned with his morals and behavior, but, as seen in Part 2 of the *Autobiography,* he deals with them in an objective, pragmatic, even statistical way, rather than in sensitive pondering. It is also evident in this work that Franklin, unlike Edwards, believes so much in himself and his quest that he is able to laugh at himself. His concern in this society can be seen in *Poor Richard's Almanac,* in which he gives practical advice on how to find success and happiness in the world, how to "be healthy, wealthy, and wise."

Still another version of the quest can be seen in the poetry of Walt Whitman in the mid-nineteenth century. The quest that he portrays blends elements of those of Edwards and Franklin. In "Song of Myself," which clearly is autobiographical, the speaker emphasizes the importance of finding, knowing, and enjoying oneself as part of nature and the human community. He says that one should come to realize that one is lovable, just as are all other people and all of nature and life. This is a quest for sensitivity and awareness, as Edwards advocates, and for great self-confidence, as Franklin advocates. Along with Edwards, Whitman sees that peaceful isolation in nature is important; but he also sees the importance of interacting with people, as Franklin does. Being optimistic and feeling good—both in the literal and figurative sense—is the object of this quest. Unfortunately, personal disappointment and national crisis (i.e., the Civil War) shattered Whitman's sense of confidence, and he lost the impetus of this quest in his own life.

Margin annotations:

Edwards's work and the details of his quest are presented.

Transition sentence identifies second writer. Key term is repeated.

Contrast with Edwards adds coherence to essay.

Another key term (external) from the question is included

Franklin's particular kind of quest is described

Transition sentence identifies third writer. Key term is repeated.

Comparison of Whitman to Edwards and Franklin sustains coherence of essay.

Whitman's quest is defined.

3

4

5

Transition: key term is repeated and fourth writer is identified.

This theme of the quest can be seen in prose fiction as well as in poetry and autobiography. One interesting example is "The Beast in the Jungle," a short story written by Henry James around 1903. It is interesting in that the principal character, John Marcher, not only fails in his life-long quest, but his failure comes about in a most subtle and frustrating way. Marcher believes that something momentous is going to happen in his future. He talks about his belief to only one person, a woman named May. May decides to befriend him for life and watch with him for the momentous occurrence to come about, for "the beast in the jungle" to "pounce." As time passes, May seems to know what this occurrence is and eventually even says that it has happened; but John is still in the dark. It is only long after May's death that the beast pounces on him in his recognition that the "beast" was his failure to truly love May, the one woman of his life, even though she gave him all the encouragement that she possibly, decently could. Marcher never defined the terms of his quest until it was too late. By just waiting and watching, he failed to find feeling and passion. This tragic realization, as someone like Whitman would view it, brings John Marcher's ruin.

Quest of James character is described.

As seen in these few examples, the theme of the quest is a significant one in American literature. Also obvious is the fact that there are a variety of approaches to, methods used in, and outcomes of the quest. This is an appropriate theme for American literature since Americans cherish the right to "the pursuit of happiness."

Conclusion repeats key term.

This is a strong answer for two reasons: (1) Pixley has the information he needs, and (2) he has organized it carefully and presented it coherently and correctly.

EXERCISE 23.1

The following essay was written by Don Hepler. He is answering the same essay exam question as his classmate John Pixley. Analyze Hepler's essay to discover whether it meets the criteria of a good essay exam answer. Review the criteria earlier in this chapter under "Writing Your Answer" and in the annotated commentary of John Pixley's answer.

Try to identify the features of Hepler's essay that contribute to its success.

Don Hepler's Answer

The quest motif is certainly important in American literature. By considering Franklin, Thoreau, Douglass, and Twain, we can see that the quest may be explicit or implicit, external or psychological, a failure or a success. Tracing the quest motif through these four authors seems to show a developing concern in American literature with transcending materialism to address deeper issues. It also reveals a drift toward ambiguity and pessimism.

Benjamin Franklin's quest, as revealed by his *Autobiography*, is for material comfort and outward success. His quest may be considered an explicit one, because he announces clearly what he is trying to do: perfect a systematic approach for living long and happily. The whole *Autobiography* is a road map intended for other people to use as a guide; Franklin apparently meant rather literally for people to imitate his methods. He wrote with the assumption that his success was reproducible. He is possibly the most optimistic author in American literature, because he enjoys life, knows exactly *why* he enjoys life, and believes that anyone else willing to follow his formula may enjoy life as well. 2

By Franklin's standards, his quest is clearly a success. But his *Autobiography* portrays only an external, not a psychological success. This is not to suggest that Franklin was a psychological failure. Indeed, we have every reason to believe the contrary. But the fact remains that Franklin *wrote* only about external success; he never indicated how he really felt, emotionally. Possibly it was part of Franklin's over-riding optimism to assume that material comfort leads naturally to emotional fulfillment. 3

Henry David Thoreau presents a more multi-faceted quest. His *Walden* is, on the simplest level, the chronicle of Thoreau's physical journey out of town and into the woods. But the moving itself is not the focus of *Walden*. It is really more of a metaphor for some kind of spiritual quest going on within Thoreau's mind. Most of the action in *Walden* is mental, as Thoreau contemplates and philosophizes, always using the lake, the woods, and his own daily actions as symbols of higher, more eternal truths. This spiritual quest is a success, in that Thoreau is able to appreciate the beauty of nature, and to see through much of the sham and false assumptions of town life and blind materialism. 4

Thoreau does not leave us with nearly as explicit a "blueprint" for success as does Franklin. Even Franklin's plan is limited to people of high intelligence, personal discipline, and sound character; Franklin sometimes seems to forget that many human beings are in fact weak and evil, and so would stand little chance of success similar to his own. But at least Franklin's quest could be duplicated by another Franklin. Thoreau's quest is more problematic, for even as great a mystic and naturalist as Thoreau himself could not remain in the woods indefinitely. This points toward the idea that the real quest is all internal and psychological; Thoreau seems to have gone to the woods to develop a spiritual strength that he could keep and take elsewhere on subsequent dealings with the "real world." 5

The quest of Frederick Douglass was explicit, in that he needed physically to get north and escape slavery, but it was also implicit because he 6 sought to discover and re-define himself through his quest, as did Thoreau. Douglass's motives were more sharply focused than either Franklin's or Thoreau's; his very humanness was at stake, as well as his physical well-being and possibly even his life. But Douglass also makes it clear that the most horrible part of slavery was the mental anguish of having no hope of freedom. His learning to read, and his maintenance of this skill, seems to have been as important as the maintenance of his material comforts, of which he had very few. In a sense, Douglass's quest is the most psychological and abstract so far, because it is for the very essence of freedom and humanity, both of which were mostly taken for granted by Franklin and Thoreau. Also, Douglass's quest is the most pessimistic of the three; Douglass concludes that physical violence is the only way out, as he finds with the Covey incident.

Finally, Mark Twain's *Huckleberry Finn* is an example of the full   7
range of meaning that the quest motif may assume. Geographically, Huck's quest is very large. But again, there is a quest defined implicitly as well as one defined explicitly, as Huck (without consciously realizing it) searches for morality, truth, and freedom. Twain's use of the quest is ambiguous, even more so than the previous writers, because while he suggests success superficially (i.e., the "happily-ever-after" scene in the last chapter), he really hints at some sort of ultimate hopelessness inherent in society. Not even Douglass questions the good or evil of American society as deeply as does Twain; for Douglass, everything will be fine when slavery is abolished; but for Twain, the only solution is to "light out for the territories" altogether—and when Twain wrote, he knew that the territories were no more.

Twain's implicit sense of spiritual failure stands in marked contrast   8
to Franklin's buoyant confidence in material success. The guiding image of the quest, however, is central to American values and, consequently, a theme that these writers and others have adapted to suit their own vision.

EXERCISE 23.2

Analyze the following essay exam questions in order to decide what kind of writing task they present. What is being asked of the student as a learner in the course and as a writer? Given the time constraints of the exam in which this question appeared, what plan would you propose for writing the answer?

Following each question is the number of points it is worth and the amount of time allotted to answer it.

1. Cortazar is a producer of fantastic literature. Discuss first what fantastic literature is. Then choose four stories by Cortazar (any four) as ex-

amples and discuss the fantastic elements in these stories. Refer to the structure, techniques, and narrative styles that he uses in these four stories. If you like, you may refer to more than four, of course. (Points: 30 of 100. Time: 40 of 150 minutes.)

2. During the course of the twentieth century, the United States has experienced three significant periods of social reform—the progressive era, the age of the Great Depression, and the decade of the 1960s. What were the sources of reform in each period? What were the most significant reform achievements of each period as well as the largest failings? (Points: 35 of 100. Time: 75 of 180 minutes.)

3. Since literature is both an artistic and ideological product, each writer comments on his material context through his writing.

   a. What is Rulto's perspective of his Mexican reality and how is it portrayed through his stories?

   b. What particular themes does he deal with, especially in these stories: "The Burning Plain," "Luvina," "They gave us the land," "Paso del Norte," and "Tell them not to kill me."

   c. What literary techniques and structures does he use to convey his perspective? Refer to a specific story as an example.
(Points: 30 of 100. Time: 20 of 50 minutes.)

4. Why is there a special reason to be concerned about the influence of TV watching on kids? In your answer include a statement of:

   a. Your own understanding of the *general communication principles* involved for any TV watcher.

   b. What's special about TV and kids?

   c. How advertisers and producers use this information. (You should draw from the relevant readings as well as lectures.)
(Points: 20 of 90. Time: 25 of 90 minutes.)

5. Analyze the autobiographical tradition in American literature, focusing on differences and similarities among authors and, if appropriate, changes over time. Discuss four authors in all. In addition to the conscious autobiographers—Edwards, Franklin, Thoreau, Douglass—you may choose one or two figures from among the following fictional or poetic quasi-autobiographers: Hawthorne, Whitman, Dickinson, Twain. (Points: 50 of 120. Time: 60 of 180 minutes.)

6. How does the system of (media) sponsorship work and what, if any, ideological control do sponsors exert? Be specific and illustrative! (Points: 33 of 100. Time: 60 of 180 minutes.)

7. Several of the works studied in this course analyze the tension between myth and reality. Select two written works and two films and analyze how their authors or directors present the conflict between myth and reality and how they resolve it—if they resolve it. (Points: 45 of 130. Time: 60 of 180 minutes.)

8. *Man's Hope* is a novel about the Spanish Civil War written while the war was still going on. *La Guerre est Finie* is a film about Spanish revolutionaries depicting their activities nearly thirty years after the Civil War. Discuss how the temporal relationship of each of these works to the Civil War is reflected in the character of the works themselves and in the differences between them. (Points: 58 of 100. Time: 30 of 50 minutes.)

9. Write an essay on one of these topics: The role of the narrator in the novels *Tom Jones* and *Pride and Prejudice,* or the characters of Uncle Toby and Miss Bates. (Points: 33 of 100. Time: 60 of 180 minutes.)

Acknowledgments (continued from page iv)

Hubbell, Sue. From A COUNTRY YEAR by Sue Hubbell. Copyright © 1983, 1984, 1985, 1986 by Sue Hubbell. Reprinted by permission of Random House, Inc.

Joyce, James. From DUBLINERS by James Joyce. Definitive text Copyright © 1967 by the Estate of James Joyce. Reprinted by permission of Viking Penguin Inc.

King, Stephen. Reprinted by permission of the author's agent Kirby McCauley Ltd. Originally appeared in *Playboy* Magazine: Copyright © 1982 by *Playboy*.

Keeton, William. Excerpts reprinted from BIOLOGICAL SCIENCE by William T. Keeton, by permission of W. W. Norton & Company, Inc. Copyright © 1980, 1979, 1978, 1972, 1967 by W. W. Norton & Company, Inc.

Mader, Sylvia. From Mader, Sylvia S., INQUIRY INTO LIFE 3d ed. © 1976, 1979, 1982 Wm. C. Brown Publishers, Dubuque, Iowa. All Rights Reserved. Reprinted by permission.

McPhee, John. Excerpts from "The Pinball Philosophy" from GIVING GOOD WEIGHT by John McPhee. Copyright © 1975, 1976, 1978, 1979 by John McPhee. Reprinted by permission of Farrar, Straus and Giroux, Inc.

Merriam-Webster definition of "brave." By permission. From Webster's New Dictionary of Synonyms © 1984 by Merriam-Webster Inc., publisher of the Merriam-Webster ® dictionaries.

Meyerowitz, Joshua. Joshua Meyerowitz is a professor of communication at the University of New Hampshire. He is the author of the award-winning NO SENSE OF PLACE: THE IMPACT OF ELECTRONIC MEDIA ON SOCIAL BEHAVIOR (Oxford University Press). This essay originally appeared in *Newsweek.*

Noonan, David. "Inside the Brain" from BRAIN SURGERY: THE HUMAN ADVENTURE by David Noonan. Copyright © 1985 by David Noonan. Reprinted by permission of Simon & Schuster, Inc.

Orwell, George. From SHOOTING AN ELEPHANT AND OTHER STORIES by George Orwell, copyright © 1950 by Sonia Brownell Orwell; renewed 1978 by Sonia Pitt-Rivers. Reprinted by permission of Harcourt Brace Jovanovich, Inc. and by permission of the estate of the late Sonia Brownell Orwell and Secker & Warburg Limited.

Owen, David. From NONE OF THE ABOVE by David Owen. Copyright © 1985 by David Owen. Reprinted by permission of Houghton Mifflin Company.

Rodriguez, Richard. From HUNGER OF MEMORY by Richard Rodriguez. Copyright © 1982 by Richard Rodriguez. Reprinted by permission of David R. Godine, Publisher.

Roget's Thesaurus definition of "brave." Copyright © 1980 by Houghton Mifflin Company. Reprinted by permission from ROGET'S II THE NEW THESAURUS.

Rosenfeld, Albert. Reprinted by permission from the June issue of *Science* '81. Copyright © 1981 by the American Association for the Advancement of Science.

Russell, Bertrand. Reprinted with permission of *The New Leader,* May 30, 1955. Copyright © the American Labor Conference on International Affairs, Inc.

Simon, Kate. Excerpt from A WIDER WORLD by Kate Simon. Copyright © 1986 by Kate Simon. Reprinted by permission of Harper & Row, Publishers, Inc.

Smith, Rachel Richardson. "Abortion, Right and Wrong," from *Newsweek,* March 25, 1985. Reprinted by permission.

Toufexis, Anastasia. Copyright 1987 Time Inc. All rights reserved. Reprinted by permission from *Time.*

Weisman, Adam Paul. Reprinted by permission of *The New Republic,* © 1987, The New Republic, Inc.

White, E. B. "Death of a Pig" from ESSAYS OF E. B. WHITE. Copyright 1947 by E. B. White. Reprinted by permission of Harper & Row, Publishers, Inc.

Wideman, John Edgar. From BROTHERS AND KEEPERS by John Edgar Wideman. Copyright © 1984 by John Edgar Wideman. Reprinted by permission of Henry Holt and Company, Inc.

Zukav, Gary. Excerpted from THE DANCING WU LI MASTERS by Gary Zukav. Copyright © 1979 by Gary Zukav. By permission of William Morrow & Company.

Author and Title Index

Subject Index

Questions, 379–81
  closed, 524, 527–28
  for interviews, 523
  open, 523–24, 528
  for questionnaires, 526–29
Quotation marks, 553
Quotations, 349, 385, 551–55
  block, 553–54, 557
  in causal analysis, 310
  dialogue and, 431
  emphasis in, 552
  errors in, 551
  essay examination questions
    and, 583
  in information writing,
    161–62, 170, 177–79
  insertions or changes in,
    552–53
  in-text, 553
  introducing, 554
  omissions in, 552, 555
  placement of, 553–54
  punctuation in, 553

Readability
  of autobiographical writing, 58
  of biographical essays, 97
  of causal analyses, 324
  of position pieces, 212
  of profiles, 140
  of proposals, 252–53
  revising for, 359
Readers. See Audience
Reading, invention strategies and,
    381–87
  annotations, 381–84
  inventorying, 384–85
  outlining, 385
  paraphrasing, 385–86
  summarizing, 386–87
Reasoning. See also Logic; Logi-
    cal fallacies
  in evaluations, 277, 281–82
  in position papers, 199–200,
    205–6
  in proposals, 222, 245
Records, citation of, 563
Red herring fallacy, 516

Re-envisioning, 388, 394–95,
    397–98
Repetition
  of sentence structure, 414
  of words and phrases, 413–14
Reportage, 67
Reports, 20
  features of, 115
  of information. See Information
    writing
  of interviews, 143–45
Rereading, 388, 390–94, 397
Research, 501, 517–74
  for causal analysis, 310, 317,
    324–26
  for evaluations, 278–82
  field. See Field research
  for information writing,
    168–69
  library, 169–70, 501, 534–49
  for literary interpretation,
    354–55
  for position papers, 204
  for profiles, 105, 114, 129–33
  for proposals, 246
  revision and, 394
Research paper, 161, 550–74
  sample, 564–74
  source acknowledgment in,
    556–63
    list of works cited, 559–63
    parenthetical citations,
      557–58
    sources used in, 551–56
    quotations, 551–54
Revising, 5–7, 9, 366, 387–98
  of autobiographical writing,
    57–59, 65
  of biographical essays, 96–102
  of causal analysis, 323–24
  of evaluations, 287–88
  of information writing,
    175–75
  of literary interpretation,
    359–60
  of position papers, 211–12
  of profiles, 139–40
  of proposals, 252–53

Revising (cont.)
  of questionnaire results, 531
  re-envisioning and, 388,
    394–95, 397–98
  rereading and, 388, 390–94,
    397
  rewriting and, 388, 395–98
  sentence-level, 396
  steps in, 12–13
  word processors and, 15–16
Rewriting, in revision, 388,
    395–98
Rhythm, sentence, 30, 46,
    431–32
Run together sentence. See End-
    stop error

Scenarios, 504–6
Scenes, in autobiographical
    writing, 86
Scratch outlines, 369–70, 391
Self-disclosure
  in autobiographical writing,
    25, 30–31, 47–48
  in biographical essays, 72
Self-discovery, autobiographical
    writing and, 45
Self-presentation
  in autobiographical writing,
    25, 30–31, 45, 47, 48
  in biographical essays, 84
  at interviews, 522
Sensory description, 444–49
Sensory imagery, 127–28
Sentence definitions, 464–69
  announcing and, 464–66
  appositive phrases and, 467–68
  comparative, 468
  subordinate clauses and,
    466–67
Sentence fragments, 81–82, 554
Sentence outlines, 369–71
Sentences, 275
  introductory quotations and,
    554, 555
  rhythm of, 30, 46, 431–32
Sequencing, 486, 488–90
  in narration, 420–26